# SUPERPLONK 2001

ABOUT THE AUTHOR

Malcolm Gluck is wine correspondent of the *Guardian*. His column, *Superplonk*, appears every Saturday in the newspaper's weekend supplement. In his capacity as consultant editor, he also writes monthly wine columns for Sainsbury's Magazine. He found the stamina to flirt briefly with BBC-TV, presenting his own wine series, *Gluck, Gluck, Gluck*, and time to put together a double-CD of classical wine music for Deutsche Grammophon. This year saw paperback publication of his guide to wine tasting, *The Sensational Liquid*, and the launch of a Superplonk website: Superplonk.com.

# SUPERPLONK 2001

## MALCOLM GLUCK

Hodder & Stoughton

British Library Cataloguing in Publication Data
Gluck, Malcolm
Superplonk 2001
1. Wine and wine making – Great Britain – Guidebooks
I. Title
642.1'2'0296'41

ISBN 0 340 71315 1

Book design by Georgina Widdrington
Author caricature by Gordon Thompson

Typeset by Rowland Phototypesetting Ltd,
Bury St Edmunds, Suffolk
Printed and bound in Great Britain by
Clays Ltd, St Ives plc

Hodder and Stoughton
A division of Hodder Headline
338 Euston Road
London NW1 3BH

In memory of Dawson Yeoman
and all the bottles we sank together in the 60s.

*As each sidereal spin*
  *impartially hustles us on*
*towards yet another birthday*
  *and extirpation at last,*
*three consolations at least:*
  *verse;  viticulture;  love*

51ST BY PETER READING

# CONTENTS

# INTRODUCTION

## THE NEW FACE

Welcome to the new face of *Superplonk*. It now includes all the retailers that previously appeared in my separate *Streetplonk* as well as being a bigger, richer, more comprehensive book than ever before. It contains far more wine entries, and it remains the most up-to-date wine guide in the UK, being a pertinent route map through the maze of the nation's wine shelves which is designed to stay fresh for many months.

Facing a new millennium, and after ten years of writing this wine guide, deep and meaningful changes seemed necessary. Out has gone my often rambling and discursive book signing/wine tasting diary which introduced previous editions but the retailer introductions are still animated and, I hope, pithy conveyances of the essential ethos of each one.

I have been persuaded that the book must change to meet the demands of an increasingly demanding readership. You can readily appreciate the changes just by feeling this book in your hands. It is plumper, more concise, and it concentrates to a far greater degree than ever before on the entries for the individual wines. It has been completely redesigned to make access more appropriate for whatever your wine interest happens to be.

## THE NEW LAYOUT

A glance at the index demonstrates the extent of the new layout. It is broken down into five broad areas.

**1.** An A to Z of all wines by country, with the usual rating system (explained a few pages further on) and, where I've felt inclined, a bristle of verbiage about a particular wine. Each country has a very short introduction. The roll call of the countries now supplying the ever-expanding thirst of us Britons, but not all represented in this book, is enough to astonish a wine merchant as recently as twenty years ago. The list covers Algeria, Argentina, Armenia, Australia, Austria, Brazil, Bulgaria, Chile, China, Czech Republic, Cyprus, England, France, Georgia, Germany, Greece, Hungary, India, Israel, Italy, Lebanon, Malta, Mexico, Moldova, Moravia, Montenegro,

Morocco, New Zealand, Portugal, Romania, Russia, Slovakia, Slovenia, South Africa, Spain, Switzerland, Turkey, Ukraine, Uruguay and the USA. Japan also makes wine, but I have yet to taste any.

**2.** Following this are the entries for all the fortified and sparkling wines.

**3.** Next comes the wine entries for individual retailers. The introduction to each is comprehensive and as informative as I can make it concomitant with reporting on the most amusing and/or crucial news concerning each plus any scandal (very little, alas). Retailer entries include dynamic Asda, bouncing Booths, bustling Budgens, concentrated Co-op, mouth-watering Marks & Spencer, marvellous Majestic, magnificent Morrisons, orgasmic Oddbins, sensational Safeway, superb Sainsbury's, stunning Somerfield (including Kwik Save), sedate Spar, terrific Tesco, unctuous Unwins, and vivacious Victoria Wine/Thresher (including Bottoms Up and Wine Rack), wonderful Waitrose, and wacky Wine Cellar/Parisa.

The wines are broken down within each retailer category by country in alphabetical order, red and white, and then sparkling and fortified.

**4.** This section is designed to be both highly informative, hugely selective and mildly entertaining. It is a breakdown of wines in 5 categories:

- My top ten pre-coital masterpieces (i.e. aperitifs, pre-prandial tipples, libations for the libido).
- My top ten reflective-pursuit bottles (i.e. wines as stimulating companions for the mind).
- My top ten *vins pour les grandes bouffes* (i.e. impressive bottles for festive meals and important dinners).
- My top ten super-model wines (i.e. exceptionally elegant white wines).
- My top ten tipples to enjoy before facing a firing squad (i.e. gorgeous reds to stiffen the sinews and summon up the blood).

These wines are among the highest scoring in the book, and readers are advised here and now that anyone who receives this book as a birthday present in late spring 2001 will probably encounter problems finding all these wines still on the shelf. I cannot for the life of me explain why this should be, but any reader who does have a plausible theory, or indeed an implausible one, then please write to me care of the publisher.

**5.** The STOP PRESS. This has been a tradition with this book for some years now and it includes all the wines, worthy bottles each, which I managed to taste in the fortnight before the book went to press. This is one reason why

I can truthfully say, hand on heart, that this is the most up-to-date wine guide you can lay your hands on.

## SOME THINGS WILL NEVER CHANGE

I hope the above makes everything clear. If it isn't, please contact me at the publisher's, or at the *Guardian*, or access the new Superplonk website (www.superplonk.com) for an e-mail address where you can get in touch with me direct. I am hugely interested in what readers make of this new layout and, for that matter, any views you may have of any aspect of this book, my work in general, and wine matters.

However much this book may change, I will not. I have said for many years that my readers give me my living and I give my readers my liver, and this will not alter as long as there is breath in my body, a taste bud left in my mouth, a drop of ink remaining in my pen, and volition in my limbs.

## HEALTH WARNING!

Health Warning is an arresting phrase and I have used it for some years now. I hope by employing it I may save you from working yourself up into a state. Let me explain.

I get a few letters a week from readers (both column and book) telling me that a wine which I have said is on sale in a certain supermarket is not there and that the wine has either sold out or the branch claims to have no knowledge of it; I get letters telling me that a wine is a bit dearer than I said it was; and I get the odd note revealing that the vintage of the 16-point wine I have enthused about and which my correspondent desperately wants to buy is different from the one listed.

First of all, let me say that no wine guide in the short and inglorious history of the genre is more exhaustively researched, checked and double-checked than this one. I do not list a wine if I do not have assurances from its retailer that it will be widely on sale when the guide is published. Where a wine is on restricted distribution, or stocks are short and vulnerable to the assault of determined readers (i.e. virtually all high-rating, very cheap bottles), I will always clearly say so. However, large retailers use computer systems which cannot anticipate uncommon demand and which often miss the odd branch off the anticipated stocking list. I cannot check every branch myself (though I do nose around them when I can) and so a wine in this book may well, infuriatingly, be missing at the odd branch of its retailer and may not even be heard of by the branch simply because of inhuman error. Conversely, the same technology often tells a retailer's head office that a wine is out of stock when it has merely been cleared out of the warehouse. It may still be on sale in certain branches. Then there is the fact that not every wine I write about is stocked by every single branch of its listed supermarket. Every store has what are called retail plans and there may be half a dozen of these, and every wine is subject to a different stocking policy according to the dictates of these cold-hearted plans.

I accept a wine as being in healthy distribution if several hundred branches, all over the country not just in selected parts of it, stock the wine. Do not assume, however, that this means every single branch has the wine.

I cannot, equally, guarantee that every wine in this book will still be in the same price bracket as printed. The vast majority will be. But there will always be the odd bottle from a country suddenly subject to a vicious swing in currency rates, or subject to an unprecedented rise in production costs which the supermarket cannot or is not prepared to swallow, and so a few pennies will get added to the price. If it is pounds, then you have cause for legitimate grievance. Please write to me. But don't lose a night's sleep if a wine is 20p more than I said it is. If you must, write to the appropriate supermarket. The department and the address to write to is provided with each supermarket's entry.

Now the puzzle of differing vintages. When I list and rate a wine, I do so only for the vintage stated. Any other vintage is a different wine requiring a new rating. Where vintages do have little difference in fruit quality, and more than a single vintage is on sale, then I say this clearly. If two vintages are on sale, and vary in quality and/or style, then they will be separately rated. However, be aware of one thing.

*Superplonk* is the biggest-selling wine guide in the Queendom. I say this not to brag but, more important, to acquaint you with a reality which may cause you some irritation. When *Superplonk* appears on sale there will be lots of eager drinkers aiming straight for the highest-rating wines as soon as possible after the book is published. Thus the supermarket wine buyer who assures me that she has masses of stock of Domaine Piddlewhatsit and the wine will withstand the most virulent of sieges may find her shelves emptying in a tenth of the time she banked on – not knowing, of course, how well I rate the wine until the book goes on sale. It is entirely possible, therefore, that the vintage of a highly rated wine may sell out so quickly that new stocks of the follow-on vintage may be urgently brought on to the shelf before I have tasted them. This can happen in some instances. I offer a bunch of perishable pansies, not a wreath of immortelles. I can do nothing about this fact of wine writing life, except to give up writing about wine.

Lastly, one thing more:

*'Wine is a hostage to several fortunes (weather being even more uncertain and unpredictable than exchange rates) but the wine writer is hostage to just one: he cannot pour for his readers precisely the same wine as he poured for himself.'*

This holds true for every wine in this book and every wine I will write about in the years to come (for as long as my liver holds out). I am sent wines to taste regularly and I attend wine tastings all the time. If a wine is corked on these occasions, that is to say in poor condition because it has been tainted by the tree bark which is its seal, then it is not a problem for a bottle in decent condition to be quickly supplied for me to taste. This is not, alas, a luxury which can be extended to my readers.

So if you find a wine not to your taste because it seems pretty foul or 'off' in some way, then do not assume that my rating system is up the creek; you may take it that the wine is faulty and must be returned as soon as possible to its retailer. Every retailer in this book is pledged to provide an instant refund for any faulty wine returned – no questions asked. I am not asking readers to share all my tastes in wine, or to agree completely with every rating for every wine. But where a wine I have rated well is obviously and patently foul then it is a duff bottle and you should be compensated by getting a fresh bottle free or by being given a refund.

# HOW I RATE A WINE

Value for money is my single unwavering focus. I drink with my readers'
pockets in my mouth. I do not see the necessity of paying a lot for a bottle
of everyday drinking wine and only rarely do I consider it worth paying a
high price for, say, a wine for a special occasion or because you want to
experience what a so-called 'grand' wine may be like. There is more
codswallop talked and written about wine, especially the so-called 'grand'
stuff, than any subject except sex. The stench of this gobbledygook regularly
perfumes wine merchants' catalogues, spices the backs of bottles, and
rancidises the writings of those infatuated by or in the pay of producers of
a particular wine region. I do taste expensive wines regularly. I do not,
regularly, find them worth the money. That said, there are some pricey
bottles in these pages. They are here either because I wish to provide an
accurate, but low, rating of their worth so that readers will be given pause
for thought or because the wine is genuinely worth every penny. A wine
of magnificent complexity, thrilling fruit, superb aroma, great depth and
finesse is worth drinking. I would not expect it to be an inexpensive bottle.
I will rate it highly. I wish all wines which commanded such high prices
were so well deserving of an equally high rating. The thing is, of course,
that many bottles of wine I taste do have finesse and depth but do not come
attached to an absurdly high price tag. These are the bottles I prize most.
As, I hope, you will.

20  Is outstanding and faultless in all departments: smell, taste and finish in
the throat. Worth the price, even if you have to take out a second
mortgage.

19  A superb wine. Almost perfect and well worth the expense (if it is an
expensive bottle).

18  An excellent wine but lacking that ineffable sublimity of richness and
complexity to achieve the very highest rating. But superb drinking and
thundering good value.

17 An exciting, well-made wine at an affordable price which offers real glimpses of multi-layered richness.

16 Very good wine indeed. Good enough for *any* dinner party. Not expensive but terrifically drinkable, satisfying and multi-dimensional – properly balanced.

15 For the money, a good mouthful with real style. Good flavour and fruit without costing a packet.

14 The top end of the everyday drinking wine. Well made and to be seriously recommended at the price.

13 Good wine, true to its grape(s). Not great, but very drinkable.

12 Everyday drinking wine at a sensible price. Not exciting, but worthy.

11 Drinkable, but not a wine to dwell on. You don't wed a wine like this, though you might take it behind the bike shed with a bag of fish and chips.

10 Average wine (at a low price), yet still just about a passable mouthful. Also, wines which are terribly expensive and, though drinkable, cannot justify their high price.

9 Cheap plonk. Just about fit for parties in dustbin-sized dispensers.

8 On the rough side here.

7 Good for pickling onions or cleaning false teeth.

6 Hardly drinkable except on an icy night by a raging bonfire.

5 Wine with more defects than delights.

4 Not good at any price.

3 Barely drinkable.

2 Seriously – did this wine come from grapes?

1 The utter pits. The producer should be slung in prison.

The rating system above can be broken down into six broad sections.

0 to 10 : Avoid – unless entertaining stuffy wine writer.

10 , 11 : Nothing poisonous but, though drinkable, rather dull.

12 , 13 : Above average, interestingly made. Solid rather then sensational.

14 , 15 , 16 : This is the exceptional, hugely drinkable stuff, from the very good to the brilliant.

17 , 18 : Really wonderful wine worth anyone's money: complex, rich, exciting.

19 , 20 : A toweringly brilliant world-class wine of self-evident style and individuality.

## PRICES

It is impossible to guarantee the price of any wine in this guide. This is why instead of printing the exact shop price, each wine is given a price bracket. This attempts to eliminate the problem of printing the wrong price for a wine. This can occur for all the usual boring but understandable reasons: inflation, economic conditions overseas, the narrow margins on some supermarket wines making it difficult to maintain consistent prices and, of course, the existence of those freebooters at the Exchequer who are liable to inflate taxes which the supermarkets cannot help but pass on. But even price bracketing is not foolproof. A wine listed in the book at, say, a lower price bracket might be on sale at a higher bracket. How? Because a wine close to but under, say, £3.50 in spring when I tasted it might sneak across the border in summer. It happens rarely enough not to concern me overmuch, but wine is an agricultural import, a sophisticated liquid food, and that makes it volatile where price is concerned. Frankly, I admire the way in which retailers have kept prices so stable for so many years. We drink cheaper (and healthier) wine now than we did thirty years ago.

## NOTE:

1) The prices of 3-litre wine boxes have been adjusted to their 75cl bottle equivalent.
2) Only in the Top Ten section are prices as they were given to me at time of going to press.

# ACKNOWLEDGEMENTS

I drink alone, rate alone, read alone, and often eat alone – and I write alone. However, Linda Peskin is my invaluable administrative right hand. Ben Cooper does crucial research into wine retailers on my behalf and various bodies at my publisher make the annual compilation of this guide less of a nightmare than it might otherwise be and they are Martin Neild, Kate Lyall Grant, Sheila Crowley, Karen Geary, Jamie Hodder-Williams, Ian Hughes, Stewart Larking, David Brimble, Elizabeth Hallett and the brilliant Georgina Moore. Felicity Rubinstein, my agent, and her partner-in-business, Sarah Lutyens, are thanked for their encouragement and will-power.

# PART 1

# A TO Z OF COUNTRIES

# ARGENTINA

Some grand wines emanate from here, with an individuality which sets them apart from those produced by the chic vineyards the other side of the Andes. By 2012, Argentina could overhaul Germany and reach top five status among UK wine imports. It has the capacity to do this, but only if it could produce wine as cheaply as Chile could it really take Germany's position. Labour costs in Argentina are higher than Chile's which is one reason the wines are generally higher in price, but who knows? We're only talking about a quid here. A terrific Chilean chardonnay can cost £3.99, an equivalent Argentinian £4.99. Time may, as time often does, erode this differential.

## ASDA RED

**Argentinian Bonarda 1999, Asda**  14.5  −£5.00
A rampagingly rich food wine. Loads of personality and bounce.

**Argentinian Pinot Noir Oak Aged 1997, Asda**  12  −£5.00

**Argentinian Red 1998, Asda**  15.5  −£3.50

**Argentinian Sangiovese 1999, Asda**  15.5  −£5.00
Stunningly well-textured and ripe. Unites warm tannins, deep fruit (hint of tobacco) and a firm, well-polished finish.

**Argentinian Syrah 1999, Asda**  16  −£5.00
Not remotely like Aussie Shiraz or Rhône Syrah, this spicy, rich, deeply textured, well-fruited wine is a revelation. Great concentration of elements.

**Far Flung Cabernet Merlot 1999**  13  −£5.00
So juicy and ripe.

**Far Flung Malbec 1999**  14  −£5.00
Food wine par excellence. Curry? Aren't you fed up with curry by now?

**Santa Julia Tempranillo Reserva 1999**  16.5  £5–7
Delicious! Delicious! Delicious! I'll say it again . . .

**Santa Julia Tempranillo Selection 1999**  16  £5–7
Very savoury and rich, almost like catering chocolate and game sauce. Wonderful with rich, spicy, robust food.

## BOOTHS RED

**El Montonero Bonarda Barbera 1999**  15.5  −£5.00
Joyously juicy and bouncing with

baked fruit flavours. A marvellous companion for Indian dishes.

**Finca el Retiro Malbec,** 15 £5–7
**Mendoza 1999**
Juicy with a hint of old boots in the background. Terrific with food.

**Libertad Malbec Bonarda** 15 −£5.00
**1999**
Rich and ready, great for gulping and greedy to be matched with modern ethnic cuisine.

**Libertad Sangiovese** 15 −£5.00
**Malbec 1998**
A superb food wine which makes many a Chianti (employing the same Sangiovese grape) seem jejune and unjoyous in comparison.

**Mission Peak Red NV** 15.5 −£3.50
Marvellous texture and rich fruit. Throbs with pleasure-giving generosity and depth.

**Terrazas Alto Cabernet** 14.5 £5–7
**Sauvignon 1999**
Cigars, jam, herbs, tannins and blackcurrants. A rich array here.

## BUDGENS RED

**Etchart Rio de Plata** 14 −£5.00
**Tempranillo/Malbec**
**1998**
Gentle yet insistent. Pacific yet ambitious. Needs spaghetti pomadoro.

## CWS RED

**Adiseno Cabernet** 16 −£5.00
**Sauvignon Shiraz 1999**
An affront to civilised values this rumbustiously rich, outspoken wine. It's hugely lovable, ripe, textured,

fleshy and deep and it never shuts up. Great stuff. Superstores only.

**Adiseno Tempranillo** 15 −£5.00
**1999**
Thick as a reduced wine sauce, just as meaty and rich, so pour it liberally over live tongue,

**Argentine Malbec 1999,** 15.5 −£5.00
**Co-op**
Throbs with exotic riches and softly engaging fruit. Really warmly textured and yielding. Great value for big supper parties.

**Argento Malbec 1999** 16.5 −£5.00
Double whammy of ripe plums and cherries with a layering of rich blackcurrants and then a hint of marzipan. A real thriller for under a fiver.

**Balbi Malbec 1999** 13.5 −£5.00
Very juicy and ripe. Best playground is spicy food.

**Bianchi Cabernet** 17 £7–10
**Sauvignon 1996**
A stunningly well-composed wine of restraint yet full-blooded richness. The acids and tannins supply the guile, the fruit the gentle spice and firm cassis and chocolate edging. A terrific wine for all sorts of roast bird. Superstores only.

**First Ever Shiraz 2000** 16 −£5.00
Aussies, watch your backs! The Argentinians are growing Shiraz fruit to die for.

**La Nature Organic** 14.5 −£5.00
**Barbera 2000**
Wonderful freshness and bitingly plummy fruit. A terrific glugging wine and for rich pasta concoctions.

Lost Pampas Cabernet `14` `–£5.00`
Malbec 1999, Co-op
Rich, dry, juicy.

Malbec/Bonarda `14` `–£3.50`
Mendoza Soft Red Wine
1998

Mission Peak Argentine `15.5` `–£3.50`
Red NV
Marvellous texture and rich fruit.
Throbs with pleasure-giving
generosity and depth.

Weinert Malbec 1994 `16` `£7–10`
Again, the superb creamy tannins of
Argentina give the wine distinctive
richness.

Y2K Shiraz 1999 `16` `£5–7`
Has more personality and certainly wit
(dry and wry) than many an Aussie of
the same savoury grape.

## KWIK SAVE RED

Maranon Malbec NV `13` `–£3.50`

## M&S RED

Rio Santos Bonarda `13.5` `–£5.00`
Barbera 1999

Rio Santos Cabernet `13.5` `–£5.00`
Syrah 1999
Juicy and dry – for large pasta parties.

Rio Santos Malbec 1999 `14` `–£5.00`
Some energy here – from the fruit and
the tannins.

## MAJESTIC RED

Carrascal Cavas de `14` `£5–7`
Weinert 1996
Jammy and ripe.

## MORRISONS RED

Balbi Barbaro 1997 `16` `£7–10`
A treat for rich game dishes. The fruit
is packed with flavour – from
raspberries to spiced prunes – and the
tannins are electric.

Balbi Malbec 1999 `13.5` `–£5.00`
Very juicy and ripe. Best playground is
spicy food.

Balbi Shiraz 1999 `13.5` `–£5.00`
Juicy and ripe with a hint of charcoal.
Great curry wine.

Santa Julia Sangiovese `15.5` `–£5.00`
Bonarda 1999
Packed with flavour and personality.
Terrific warmth of texture and
controlled, ripe blackcurrant/plum
fruit with a subtle hint of spice.

## ODDBINS RED

Alamos Ridge Bonarda, `16` `£5–7`
Mendoza 1998
Bounces with ripely generous fruit.

Alamos Ridge Merlot, `16` `£5–7`
Mendoza 1997
Ripe and ready, lovely tannins, soft
juiciness relieved by a dry undertone.

Bodegas Rosca Malbec, `15` `–£5.00`
Mendoza 1999
Ripe, savoury, meaty, mouth-filling.

Bodegas Rosca Shiraz, `16.5` `£5–7`
Mendoza 1999
McLaren Vale watch out! Here comes
bargain spicy Shiraz!

Bodegas Rosca Shiraz `16` `£5–7`
Reserve, Mendoza 1999
Goes down like the non-reserve,
except it's juicier.

**Famiglia Bianchi** 17 £13–20
Cabernet Sauvignon, San
Rafael 1996
Has such superb multi-layered, faintly
lush cassis and cheroot-tinged fruit
that it surprises the palate by its
developing richness on the tongue. A
very classy red.

**Las Lilas Malbec** 15.5 –£5.00
Sangiovese, Mendoza
1997

**Norton Reserve Syrah** 15.5 £5–7
Cabernet, Mendoza 1997

**Valentin Bianchi** 16.5 £7–10
Cabernet Sauvignon, San
Rafael 1996
A stunningly well-composed wine of
restraint yet full-blooded richness. The
acids and tannins supply the guile, the
fruit the gentle spice and firm
chocolate edging. A terrific wine for all
sorts of roast bird.

**Valentin Bianchi Malbec** 15 £7–10
Reserve, San Rafael 1996

**Valentin Bianchi Malbec,** 16 –£5.00
San Rafael 1997
Bargain savoury juiciness.

**Valentin Bianchi Merlot** 16.5 £7–10
Reserve, San Rafael 1997
One of the most elegant merlots out of
South America. Superb leather and
eager tannins.

## SAFEWAY RED

**Adiseno Bonarda 1999** 15.5 –£5.00
Warm, soft, spicy, and it finishes
confidently and richly.

**Adiseno Reserve Malbec** 15 £5–7
1999
Curious fruit yoghurt edge. Needs

curry. In fact, it's made for it. Selected
stores.

**Argentinian Bonarda** 14 –£5.00
1999, Safeway
The perfect curry red. Also good with
game dishes with sweet/savoury
sauces.

**Argentinian Cabernet** 14 –£5.00
Sauvignon 1999, Safeway
Juicy but this ripeness has warm
tannins. It's the Argentinian wine trick
– brilliant!

**Argentinian Red 1999,** 14 –£3.50
Safeway
Very simple and juicy but, hark, is that
not tannins arriving? Late? But
beautifully . . .

**Caballo de Plata** 13 –£3.50
Bonarda/Barbera 2000
Like a sauce for fruit salad.

**Diego Murillo Malbec,** 17 £5–7
Patagonia 1997
Fabulous roast fowl wine. Combines
rich baked spicy fruit and evolved
tannins. Incredible richness.

**Rafael Estate Malbec,** 16 £5–7
Mendoza 1997
Good heavens, what nerve! It's the
cheekiest amalgam of fruit and
tannin I've tasted for years. Top 212
stores.

**Simonassi Lyon Barbera** 14 £5–7
1998

**Weinert Malbec 1994** 16 £7–10
Again, the superb creamy tannins of
Argentina give the wine distinctive
richness. 79 stores.

## SAINSBURY'S RED

**Alamos Ridge Cabernet Sauvignon 1997**  16.5  £5–7
Compellingly soft yet thickly knitted fruit of huge style and precision. Incredibly well tailored yet has character and bite. Great class, terrific polish, loads of richness. Selected stores.

**Argento Malbec 1999**  16  –£5.00
Vivacious, vivid, voluptuous. Terrific!

**Bright Brothers Reserve Shiraz 1999**  15.5  –£5.00
A rather reserved wine at first sip and mouthing but then it shifts a bit and turns tense and tenacious. Very, very soft fruit. Not at all stores.

**Bright Brothers Vistalba Malbec 1999**  14.5  –£5.00
Extremely slip-downable. It slides past like plums on oiled rollers. Most stores.

**Catena Cabernet Sauvignon 1997**  16.5  £7–10
A serious claret-style wine of unclaret-like lushness and depth but in its dry tannins and arching finish of rich herbiness is like a marvellous Médoc in a freak year. 50 stores.

**First Ever Shiraz 2000**  16  –£5.00
Aussies, watch your backs! The Argentinians are growing Shiraz fruit to die for.

**Mendoza Cabernet Sauvignon/Malbec NV, Sainsbury's**  15.5  –£5.00

**Mendoza Country Red NV, Sainsbury's**  15  –£3.50

**Santa Julia Oak Aged Tempranillo 1999**  15.5  –£5.00

Remarkably rich and savoury, almost excessively so. Certainly not subtle, the depth of fruit is best balanced by casseroles.

**Trapiche Oak Cask Reserve Cabernet Sauvignon 1995**  17  £5–7
Superb class here: richness, savouriness, thickness and brilliant fruit. It is utterly lovely. 175 stores.

## SOMERFIELD RED

**Argentine Tempranillo 1999, Somerfield**  16  –£5.00
Outguns Rioja with the brilliance of its tannins and creamy richness. Great glugging, great with food.

**Bright Brothers San Juan Cabernet Sauvignon 1999**  16.5  –£5.00
Totally convincing performance, harmonious, collected, full of subtle twists and turns. Dry, delicious, very stylish finish.

**First Ever Shiraz 2000**  16  –£5.00
Aussies, watch your backs! The Argentinians are growing Shiraz fruit to die for.

**Santa Julia Sangiovese 1999, Somerfield**  15.5  –£5.00

**Trivento Syrah 1999**  15.5  –£5.00

## TESCO RED

**Anubis Tempranillo 1999**  16  £5–7
Most individual approach to the old Spanish grape: quirky soft/hard fruit edge, dry yet soft texture and a lilting finish. 100 selected stores.

**Argentinian Bonarda/** `13` `−£3.50`
**Barbera 1999, Tesco**
Most stores.

**Argento Malbec 1999** `16.5` `−£5.00`
Vivacious, vivid, voluptuous. Terrific!

**Bright Brothers Barrica** `15` `£5–7`
**Reserve Cabernet**
**Sauvignon/Syrah 1998**
Juicy but justly so. Not at all stores.

**Bright Brothers Barrica** `16` `£5–7`
**Reserve Syrah 1998**
Outguns many a fancy Aussie with the
same grape. Loads of jammy rich fruit
but it's the tannins which pull the
whole wagonload of flavours along.
Not at all stores.

**Bright Brothers San Juan** `14` `−£5.00`
**Reserve Cabernet/Shiraz**
**1998**

**Bright Brothers San Juan** `14.5` `−£5.00`
**Reserve Shiraz 1998**

**Catena Cabernet** `17` `£7–10`
**Sauvignon 1996**
A quite compellingly concentrated
amalgam of very comely Cabernet
vegetality and subtle spiciness and big
tannins. An excellent bottle for festive
lunch (or dinner) where its presence at
table will be more amusing, and more
explosive, than the funniest Christmas
cracker. Available at the 25 Wine
Adviser Stores only.

**Monster Spicy Red Syrah,** `16` `−£5.00`
**Tesco**
Fabulous! And it's spicy and deep and
intense. A lovely rip-roaring, juicy
wine with a dry underbelly of insistent
richness and classiness. Great stuff.

**Picajuan Peak Bonarda** `15.5` `−£5.00`
**NV**
Wonderful rich and invigorating
jammy richness which manages to stay
dry and characterful.

**Picajuan Peak Malbec** `14.5` `−£5.00`
**1999, Tesco**
Very good texture, warm and bright,
with a fine-flowing richness of
plummy fruit plus a hint of Marmite.

**Picajuan Peak Sangiovese** `16` `−£5.00`
**1998, Tesco**
Rich, ripe, riveting, well organised and
engaging. Lovely savoury touches to
the tannin, hint of plum and
blackcurrant to the dry fruit. Certainly
a contender for the £3.80 (and under)
wine of the year.

**'Q' Cabernet Sauvignon** `17` `£7–10`
**1998**
Exotically warm and gently spicy and
very stylishly tannic Cabernet. The
cliché, blackcurrant, is given a new
and exciting metaphoric definition
here. 100 selected stores.

**'Q' Tempranillo 1998** `16.5` `£7–10`
This is what more Riojas should be
like: energetic, rich, tobacco-tinged,
deep, jammy but dry, and full of
flavoursome layers of surprises.

**Santa Julia Oaked** `16` `−£5.00`
**Tempranillo 1997**
Rioja?! Look to your laurels . . .
Argentina's Tempranillo is
extraordinarily delicious and
beautifully textured.

## THRESHER RED

**Anubis Malbec 1999** `16` `£5–7`
Juicy but with a wonderfully polished
turn of speed. Tremendous texture to
the fruit.

**Argento Malbec 1999** `16.5` `−£5.00`

Vivacious, vivid, voluptuous. Terrific!

**Corazon Bonarda 1999**  16  −£5.00
Superb spicy food wine which makes
up for everything Beaujolais has lost:
juice, freshness, personality and
gushing fruit.

**Corazon Tempranillo**  16.5  −£5.00
**1999**
Stunning, vivacious, exotic, sexy,
concentrated and cheap – everything
you could ask for in a whore or a
wine.

**Libertad Malbec Bonarda**  15  −£5.00
**1999**
Rich and ready, great for gulping and
greedy to be matched with modern
ethnic cuisine.

**Libertad Malbec/**  15  −£5.00
**Sangiovese 1998**
A superb food wine which makes
many a Chianti (employing the same
Sangiovese grape) seem jejune and
unjoyous in comparison.

**Martins Andino Malbec**  14  −£5.00
**Bonarda 1998**
A fat, rich, uncompromisingly fruity
wine of no subtlety but great food
charms.

**Norton Privada 1998**  16.5  £7–10
Serious, dry, dusky, subtly spicy,
sustaining – excellent tannins are the
reason. And food its destiny. Wine
Rack and Bottoms Up only.

**'Q' Tempranillo 1998**  16.5  £7–10
This is what more Riojas should be
like: energetic, rich, tobacco-tinged,
deep, jammy but dry, and full of
flavoursome layers of surprises. Wine
Rack only.

**Santa Julia Pinot Noir**  15.5  −£5.00
**1999**

Delicious chewy fruit of wild cherry
and cassis with a hint of earthworm.
Ah! The metaphors of earthiness it
inspires! Wine Rack and Bottoms Up
only.

**Villa Atuel Syrah 1999**  15.5  −£5.00
Vivid richness, underpinned by soft,
dry tannins. Great for casseroles and
also vegetative pursuits (sofas,
Beethoven, Luis Borges, *The Times*
crossword).

## UNWINS RED

**J & F Lurton Bonarda/**  10  −£5.00
**Tempranillo 1998**
Anodyne.

**Magdalena River Malbec/**  13  −£5.00
**Cabernet Sauvignon,**
**Mendoza 1997**

**Magdalena River**  12  −£5.00
**Sangiovese/Bonarda,**
**Mendoza 1998**

**Norton Cabernet**  15  −£5.00
**Sauvignon 1999**
Great food wine with its extravagance
of fruit with perfectly matched
tannins.

**Santa Julia Malbec Oak**  16  £5–7
**Reserve 1998**
Quirky, ripe, rich, deep – jammy but
controlled – and supported by
wonderful tannins and acids.

**Santa Julia Tempranillo**  17  £5–7
**Oak Reserve 1998**
Incredibly well and warmly textured,
warm and gently spicy. Outstanding
tannins and complex fruit.

**Terrazas Malbec 1999**  15  £5–7
Nice ripe attack which doesn't go

gooey or flabby at the knees as the fruit softens.

## VICTORIA WINE RED

**Anubis Malbec 1999** | 16 | £5–7
Juicy but with a wonderfully polished turn of speed. Tremendous texture to the fruit.

**Argento Malbec 1999** | 16.5 | –£5.00
Vivacious, vivid, voluptuous. Terrific!

**Corazon Bonarda 1999** | 16 | –£5.00
Superb spicy food wine which makes up for everything Beaujolais has lost: juice, freshness, personality and gushing fruit.

**Corazon Tempranillo 1999** | 16.5 | –£5.00
Stunning, vivacious, exotic, sexy, concentrated and cheap – everything you could ask for in a whore or a wine.

**Libertad Malbec Bonarda 1999** | 15 | –£5.00
Rich and ready, great for gulping and greedy to be matched with modern ethnic cuisine.

**Libertad Malbec/Sangiovese 1998** | 15 | –£5.00
A superb food wine which makes many a Chianti (employing the same Sangiovese grape) seem jejune and unjoyous in comparison.

**Martins Andino Malbec Bonarda 1998** | 14 | –£5.00
A fat, rich, uncompromisingly fruity wine of no subtlety but great food charms.

**Villa Atuel Syrah 1999** | 15.5 | –£5.00
Vivid richness, underpinned by soft, dry tannins. Great for casseroles and also vegetative pursuits (sofas, Beethoven, Luis Borges, *The Times* crossword).

## WAITROSE RED

**Familia Zuccardi 'Q' Merlot 1998** | 16.5 | £7–10
Saucy, irreverent, ripe, dry-humoured, potent, completely delicious.

**Finca el Retiro Malbec, Mendoza 1999** | 15.5 | £5–7
Juicy with a hint of old boots in the background. Terrific with food.

**Finca el Retiro Tempranillo, Mendoza 1999** | 15 | £5–7
Very deep, almost mud-like in its adhesive texture and so savoury it must be drunk with food.

**Sierra Alta Cabernet Sauvignon/Malbec, Mendoza 1999** | 14 | –£5.00

**Sierra Alta Shiraz, Mendoza 1999** | 16.5 | –£5.00
Brilliant richness and smoothness and with plenty to occupy nose and throat. A gently throbbing undertone of excitement here.

**Trivento Sangiovese, Mendoza 1999** | 15 | –£5.00
The most brilliant pasta partner you can imagine. Terrific tannins here.

## ASDA WHITE

**Argentinian Chardonnay 1998, Asda** | 15.5 | –£5.00

**Argentinian White NV, Asda** | 14 | –£3.50

Far Flung Viognier 1999  16  −£5.00
Wonderfully soft, subtly spicy peach
and apricot fruit. Delicious.

## BOOTHS WHITE

El Montonero Torrontes  15  −£5.00
1999
Delicious floral-scented aperitif.

Libertad Chenin/  14.5  −£5.00
Sauvignon 1999
Lemon, melon and lettuce leaf acidity.
Great with food.

Terrazas Alto  15.5  £5–7
Chardonnay 1999
Very woody and creamy, a hint of
cauliflower, touch of raspberry,
suggestion of yoghurt on the lingering
finish.

## BUDGENS WHITE

Etchart Rio de Plata  13.5  −£3.50
Torrontes 1999
Plain on the finish.

Etchart Rio de Plata  13  −£5.00
Torrontes/Chardonnay
1998
I find, sometimes, the Torrontes grape
has an unattractive cosmetic edge.

## CWS WHITE

Argentine Sauvignon/  15  −£3.50
Chenin Blanc 1998

Balbi Shiraz Rosé 1999  14  −£5.00
Fruit lover's dream. Classic dry rosé
lover's nightmare. Superstores only.

Bright Brothers Viognier  15  £5–7
Reserve 1999
Hint of ripe peach and honey to the

dry fruit which finishes softly. Co-op
Superstores only.

Etchart Rio de Plata  13.5  −£5.00
Torrontes 1999
Mild and inoffensive. Churlish to say
more. Superstores only.

First Ever Chardonnay  13.5  −£5.00
2000
Most underwhelming – but drinkable.

La Nature Organic  15.5  −£5.00
Torrontes 2000
Compellingly crisp, compacted and
classy. Has a chewy edge of striking
originality.

Lost Pampas Oaked  16  −£5.00
Chardonnay 1999, Co-op
Lovely nutty fruit, chewy and fresh,
hint of lettuce crispness.

Mission Peak Argentine  15.5  −£3.50
White NV
Delicious rich fruit. An absolute
bargain.

Y2K Chardonnay, San  16  −£5.00
Juan 1999
Very fresh – saves its melon richness
for the back of the throat.

## M&S WHITE

Rio Santos Torrontes  13.5  −£5.00
1999
Another crisp clean wine from M&S.
Formula?

## MORRISONS WHITE

Etchart Rio de Plata  13  −£5.00
Torrontes/Chardonnay
1998
I find, sometimes, the Torrontes grape
has an unattractive cosmetic edge.

Rio de Plata Chardonnay `13.5` `−£5.00`
1997

Tupungato Chardonnay `13` `−£5.00`
NV, Sainsbury's

## ODDBINS WHITE

Alamos Ridge `16` `£5–7`
Chardonnay 1997
Superb chewy texture and ripe, woody
fruit.

Bodegas Rosca Dry `15` `−£3.50`
White, Mendoza 1999
Fantastic value: very subtle smoky/
creamy fruit which finishes with verve
and dash.

Catena Chardonnay 1997 `14` `£7–10`
Expensive compared with many other
compatriots.

## SAFEWAY WHITE

Argentinian Chardonnay `16` `−£5.00`
1999, Safeway
Delightful union of buttery ripeness,
and melon and pineapple acidity.

Caballo de Plata `13.5` `−£3.50`
Torrontes 2000
Very cosmetic and talcum-powdery, as
the Torrontes often is, I find.

## SAINSBURY'S WHITE

Bright Brothers San Juan `15.5` `−£5.00`
Chardonnay Reserve
1999
Terrific freshness of fruit and great
with food. Not at all stores.

First Ever Chardonnay `13.5` `−£5.00`
2000
Most underwhelming – but drinkable.

Mendoza Country White `14.5` `−£3.50`
NV, Sainsbury's

## SOMERFIELD WHITE

Argentine Chardonnay `16` `−£5.00`
1999, Somerfield
Wonderfully rich, buttery fruit –
almost savoury in its depth.

Bright Brothers `16` `−£5.00`
Argentine Chardonnay
1999, Somerfield
Superb richness and nuttiness here.
Has a gentility to its lushness so it's
not OTT, and the texture is
outstanding.

Bright Brothers San Juan `15.5` `−£5.00`
Chardonnay Reserve
1999

First Ever Chardonnay `13.5` `−£5.00`
2000
Most underwhelming – but drinkable.

Santa Julia Syrah Rosé `15.5` `−£5.00`
2000
Great cherry fruit with a hint of plum
jam. Great with food. Don't let the
colour put you off – it reminds me of
adolescent medicines I was forced to
endure.

## TESCO WHITE

Argentinian Torrontes `13` `−£3.50`
1999, Tesco

Argento Chardonnay `17` `−£5.00`
1999
What class for the money here.
Combines melons, ripe pineapples,
pears, raisins and delicate acids to great
effect. Fine, frolicsome, cheap, and so
cheerfully complex that you smile as

you sip – as this is a sipping wine, such is its provocative approach (soft). Not at all stores.

**Picajuan Peak Viognier 1999** 15 –£5.00

Rich and deep to begin then peachy and lemonic as it descends the gullet. Delicious tippling here.

## THRESHER WHITE

**Corazon Pinot Gris 1999** 15 –£5.00

Remarkable apricot fruit. Dry, dainty, delicious derring-do.

**Correas Torrontes Chardonnay 1999** 14 –£5.00

A good, solid, no-frills food wine.

**Norton Semillon/ Chardonnay 1999** 16 –£5.00

Fantastic plumpness and richness of purpose. Wonderful baked melon vinosity, soft textured acids and a gorgeous finish.

**Norton Torrontes, Mendoza 1999** 15.5 –£5.00

Delightfully elegant and gentle, pastry-edged fruit. Marvellously generous tippling.

**Santa Julia Viognier 1999** 17 –£5.00

A remarkably well-textured, subtly smoky, apricot/peach and cherry-rich wine which is never less than stylish and insistent. It's remarkably lovely for a fiver. Wine Rack and Bottoms Up only.

## UNWINS WHITE

**Alamos Ridge Chardonnay 1997** 16 £5–7

Superb chewy texture and ripe, woody fruit.

**Catena Agrelo Vineyards Chardonnay 1997** 14 £7–10

Expensive compared with many other compatriots.

**J & F Lurton Pinot Gris 1998** 13 –£5.00

**Magdalena River Chardonnay, Mendoza 1997** 15 –£5.00

**Santa Julia Oak Reserve Chardonnay 1997** 16.5 £5–7

Sheer unadulterated luxury of fruit: rich, thick, aromatic, impactful, massively elegant.

## VICTORIA WINE WHITE

**Corazon Pinot Gris 1999** 15 –£5.00

Remarkable apricot fruit. Dry, dainty, delicious derring-do.

**Correas Torrontes Chardonnay 1999** 14 –£5.00

A good, solid, no-frills food wine.

**Norton Semillon/ Chardonnay 1999** 16 –£5.00

Fantastic plumpness and richness of purpose. Wonderful baked melon vinosity, soft textured acids and a gorgeous finish.

**Norton Torrontes, Mendoza 1999** 15.5 –£5.00

Delightfully elegant and gentle, pastry-edged fruit. Marvellously generous tippling.

## WAITROSE WHITE

**Bodega Lurton Pinot Gris, Mendoza 1999** 14.5 –£5.00

Handsome, correct, well-cut, gently warm on the finish.

## ARGENTINIAN WHITE

**Santa Julia Viognier**  16.5  £5–7
**Reserve 1999**
So elegant! Yet plump and smooth and
subtly apricotty.

# AUSTRALIA

The revelations concerning just one producer, Kingston Estate (who were caught using banned substances to remove the smell of rotten eggs from wine and employing red grape skins to turn white wine into something less flabby), are minor blemishes in the Aussie wine miracle. New vineyards are being planted, and the creation of more expensive, status-seeking reds continues. Between £6 and £10, this is the country whose red and white bottles most unnerve the French.

## ASDA RED

**Andrew Peace Cabernet/ Merlot 1999**   `15`  `£5–7`
If this is Cabernet as grown in Bordeaux I'm a monkey's uncle. (I have the hairy armpits to prove it.)

**Andrew Peace Mighty Murray 1999**   `13`  `–£5.00`

**Andrew Peace Shiraz 1999**   `13`  `£5–7`
So jammy and fleshy and ripe.

**Fox River Pinot Noir 1998**   `13`  `£5–7`

**Hardys Nottage Hill Cabernet Sauvignon/ Shiraz 1997**   `14`  `£5–7`

**Hardys Stamp Cabernet Shiraz Merlot 1997**   `15`  `£5–7`
Hints of developed tannin to the jammy ripeness. Good with roast meats and cheese dishes.

**Houghtons Shiraz 1998**   `15`  `£5–7`
Sweet, dry to finish. Brilliant with food.

**Karalta Cabernet 1999, Asda**   `12`  `–£5.00`
Even sweeter!!!

**Karalta Red 1999, Asda**   `13.5`  `–£3.50`
Intensely juicy and sunny. Very ripe.

**Karalta Shiraz/Cabernet 1999, Asda**   `13`  `–£3.50`
Even sweeter!!

**Lindemans Bin 50 Shiraz 1998**   `14.5`  `–£5.00`
Simply delicious!

**Maglieri Shiraz 1998**   `15.5`  `£7–10`
The immense charm of the rich sweet wine is irresistible.

**Mount Hurtle Grenache 1997**   `16`  `£5–7`
Rated eaten with Indian food. It is the greatest curry wine in the world and indeed the food will struggle to keep up with it. Chillies will only enhance the awesome solidity of the rich, dark fruit which is like a melted chocolate in texture. Very alcoholic (14.5%) and this gives it aromatic wallop and sweetness.

**Peter Lehmann Seven** `16` `£5–7`
**Surveys Mourvedre/**
**Shiraz/Grenache 1997**
Intense, invincible, insidiously
drinkable, impish, insistent, inevitable
– aye, aye, aye.

**Rochcombe Pinot Noir** `12` `£5–7`
**1998**
Very juicy Pinot. No backbone.

**Rosemount Estate Shiraz** `15` `£7–10`
**1997**

**Rosemount Estate Shiraz** `15.5` `£5–7`
**Cabernet 1998**

**Rymill Merlot/Cabernet** `15.5` `£7–10`
**Sauvignon/Cabernet**
**Franc 1996**
Very sveltely ripe and at the peak of
drinkability.

**Secession Xanadu Shiraz/** `14.5` `£5–7`
**Cabernet 1999**
Very warm and soft.

**South Australia Cabernet** `14` `–£5.00`
**Sauvignon 1996, Asda**

**Vine Vale Grenache 1998** `15` `£5–7`
**(Peter Lehmann)**
Another Asda Aussie Grenache which
defies gravity and goes up the throat
rather than down.

## BOOTHS RED

**Australian Red Shiraz** `14` `–£5.00`
**Cabernet Sauvignon NV,**
**Booths**
Typical, hot-blooded fruit – hints of
plums, figs and raisins.

**Australian Red, South** `11` `–£3.50`
**Eastern Australia NV,**
**Booths**

**Brown Brothers** `13` `–£5.00`
**Tarrango 1998**

**CV Capel Vale Shiraz** `14.5` `£7–10`
**1997**
Juicy – sorry, but there it is, it's juicy –
and very immediately all-embracing.

**d'Arenberg d'Arrys** `15` `£5–7`
**Original Shiraz/Grenache**
**1998**

**Ironstone Shiraz** `16.5` `£5–7`
**Grenache 1998**
Deliciously concentrated and incisive.
Rich, deep, ready, ripe (but not OTT),
full of interesting fruits (including a
hint of liquorice) and it finishes fully
and profoundly.

**Knappstein Cabernet** `15` `£7–10`
**Franc 1998**
Tang of raspberry to the rich plums.
Very satisfying quaffing bottle.

**Marktree Premium Red** `11` `–£5.00`
**1998**
My God – if this is the premium,
what's that basic stuff like? Sally,
what's going on here?

**Penfolds Bin 407** `15` `£10–13`
**Cabernet Sauvignon 1996**
Pricey and a touch po-faced. But the
tannins are good, even if they might
have been added to the wine, and the
subtle eucalyptus richness is
impressive.

**Rosemount Estate** `15.5` `£5–7`
**Shiraz/Cabernet**
**Sauvignon 1998**

**Wakefield Estate** `16` `£5–7`
**Cabernet Sauvignon 1998**
Subtle spicy hints here to some gentle
rugged, dry, superbly tannic fruit. Very
elegant and so easy to glug.

Yaldara Grenache 1998　13.5　£5–7

## BUDGENS RED

Oxford Landing Cabernet　14　£5–7
Sauvignon Shiraz 1999
Terrific! One of Australia's top-notch brands on the basis of its rich texture, good layers of fruit, warm, friendly tannins, and overall lushly impactful structure. An adults Shiraz of great charm and persistence.

Wolf Blass Yellow Label　15　£7–10
Cabernet Sauvignon 1998
The essence of the Oz success story. Rip-roaringly rich, soft, jammy fruit with just enough tannins to remind you it's wine.

Wynns Coonawarra　16.5　£5–7
Shiraz 1997
A most invigorating mouthful of very high class fruit. The mineral tanginess is delicious but what really impresses is the way the fruit spreads itself over the tongue revealing dry, rich nuances. Has superb tannins.

## CWS RED

Australian Cabernet　14　–£5.00
Sauvignon 1998, Co-op
Super juice with a savoury finish.

Australian Grenache　14　–£5.00
1999, Co-op
Bit tardy on the fruit, the acids get in first, and the manner is jumpy and nervous. But with food, it would settle down and even have children.

Australian Merlot 1999,　13.5　–£5.00
Co-op
Very juicy and ripe.

Brown Brothers　13.5　£5–7
Tarrango 1999
Juicy! Needs spicy food. Superstores only.

Chateau Reynella Basket　16.5　£10–13
Press Cabernet Merlot
1996
Interestingly, I saw the grapes for this wine go into the old-fashioned basket press – the device which permits such a sympathetic crush and beautifully evolved tannins to emerge. One of Australia's most civilised Cabernet Merlots.

E & E Black Pepper　16　£20+
Shiraz 1996
Complex perfume of tea, chocolate and very subtle cinnamon. The fruit is very tufted and textured but ultimately polished and unturbulent, but £27? It's a lot of money. But this is a lot of wine. It is rugged yet refined. Superstores only.

Hardys Coonawarra　16　£10–13
Cabernet Sauvignon 1996
Soupy yet with savoury tannins which keep it adult and x-rated. The seductiveness of the perfume is only the beginning.

Hardys Stamp Cabernet　15　£5–7
Shiraz Merlot 1997
Hints of developed tannin to the jammy ripeness. Good with roast meats and cheese dishes.

Leasingham Cabernet　16.5　£7–10
Sauvignon/Malbec 1996
The marriage of the wood, fruit and tannins is a sensual ménage à trois of guile and gutsiness. Superstores only.

Rosemount Estate　15　£5–7
Grenache/Shiraz 1998

## KWIK SAVE RED

**Australian Dry Red 1999,** `14.5` `−£5.00`
**Somerfield**
Jammy yet not OTT. Great with spicy
food.

**Australian Shiraz** `15` `−£5.00`
**Cabernet 1999,**
**Somerfield**
Delicious, quite quite delicious. Thick
as a woolly sweater, just as warming.

**Banrock Station Shiraz** `15` `−£5.00`
**Mataro 1999**
Jammy, thick and hugely food friendly.

**Hardys Stamp Shiraz** `14` `−£5.00`
**Cabernet 1999**
Sweet and rich? Curry? Sorry to go on
about curries, but what else is one to
do with a wine like this?

## M&S RED

**Australian Shiraz 1999** `15` `£5–7`
The chewy touch of the tannins gives
the jam some backbone of resistant
spreadability.

**Fusion Shiraz 1998** `16` `£5–7`
Heavens to Murgatroyd! An under-six
quid Aussie Shiraz with exciting
tannins. Has spice and hedgerow fruit
too.

**HoneyTree Grenache** `13` `£5–7`
**Shiraz 1999**
Juice.

**HoneyTree Reserve** `13` `£7–10`
**Pinot Noir 1998**
I've never tasted a Pinot so untypical.
Listen to me!! You old fart! What's
wrong with a break from the
straitjacket of convention? Nothing.
You just have to *like* them, that's all.

**HoneyTree Shiraz** `15.5` `£5–7`
**Cabernet 1999**

**HoneyTree Shiraz** `14` `£7–10`
**Reserve 1998**

**Shiraz Ruby Cabernet** `12.5` `−£5.00`
**Merlot Bin 312 1999**
Very juicy.

**South East Australian** `14` `−£5.00`
**Cabernet 1999**
Very available and free with its charm.
All juice. Not a subtle bone in its body.

**South East Australian** `13.5` `−£5.00`
**Merlot 1999**

## MAJESTIC RED

**Bethany Cabernet Merlot** `14` `£7–10`
**1998**
One in the sweet line. Has even a
toasted marshmallow subtlety to it –
but it's easy to miss.

**Bethany Grenache 1998** `13` `£5–7`
So terribly sweet.

**Capel Vale 'CV' Pinot** `13` `£7–10`
**Noir 1998**

**Capel Vale 'CV' Shiraz** `14.5` `£7–10`
**1998**
Curious, nervous, stringy edge.

**Capel Vale Howecroft** `15.5` `£13–20`
**Cabernet 1996**
Curiously bruised fruit ripeness on the
finish somehow mars any claim to
elegance but it does have presence –
and with food it would spring several
delicious surprises.

**Ironstone Shiraz** `16.5` `£5–7`
**Grenache, Margaret**
**River and Swan Valley**
**1996**
Takes Shiraz into a new dimension of

such balance of fruit, acid and tannin, all so deftly interwoven and gorgeously textured, that it makes offerings from other Oz regions seem either mean or too expensive. It's a terrific wine with a hint of wildness.

**Kangarilla Road Cabernet, Cabernet Franc, Malbec 1998** 14 £7–10
Very sweet and cosily modulated.

**Kangarilla Road Shiraz 1998** 15.5 £7–10
Immensely elegant and richly polished – indeed so polished is it that it reflects every facet of its maker's personality.

**Mamre Brook Cabernet Shiraz 1996** 16 £5–7
At its peak of savoury smoothness and richness. Lovely texture and temperature: warm but not steamy.

**Mirrabrook Shiraz Cabernet 1999** 14 –£3.50
Good value happy juice.

**Mount Langi Ghiran Shiraz Grenache 1997** 13 £7–10
Juice.

**Oxford Landing Cabernet Sauvignon Shiraz 1999** 15.5 £5–7
Terrific! One of Australia's top-notch brands on the basis of its rich texture, good layers of fruit, warm, friendly tannins, and overall lushly impactful structure. An adults Shiraz of great charm and persistence.

**Penfolds Bin 128 Coonawarra Shiraz 1996** 15.5 £7–10
Lush, rich, usual Penfolds recipe for this sort of turn out. Correct and controlled. Makes for a delicious companion to casseroles.

**Penfolds Bin 28 Kalimna Shiraz 1996** 15.5 £7–10
Minty and rich. Good tight finish with some spice and controlled, dry richness up front.

**Penfolds Bin 389 Coonawarra Cabernet Shiraz 1996** 16 £10–13
Lovely blend of vegetal, tannic cabernet with the spicy shiraz. It has a terrific texture and a warm, coaxing finish.

**Penfolds Bin 407 Coonawarra Cabernet 1996** 15 £10–13
Pricey and a touch po-faced. But the tannins are good, even if they might have been added to the wine, and the subtle eucalyptus richness is impressive.

**Penfolds Old Vine Syrah Grenache Mourvedre, Barossa 1996** 13.5 £7–10
Too expensive for juice, even high class juice.

**Penfolds Rawsons Retreat Bin 35 Cabernet Sauvignon/Shiraz/Ruby Cabernet 1998** 14 £5–7
Soft and curry-friendly.

**Pirramimma Cabernet Sauvignon 1998** 17 £7–10
Intensely concentrated and deep, it has a lovely textured tightness which opens up deliberately and deliciously with stunning tannins.

**Pirramimma Petit Verdot 1997** 17 £7–10
Tremendous stuff. Really races over the taste buds sweeping all before it. It has a sullen spiciness of the Greta Garbo sort, at first, then the huge

tannins arrive and it's one long torrent of riches.

**Pirramimma Premium** 15.5 £7–10
**Shiraz 1997**
Cough mixture tang and linctus-thick richness. Marvellous chutzpah to it. Quite iconoclastic and individual. Needs very robust spicy food. A curry?

**Pirramimma Stocks Hill** 16 £5–7
**Shiraz 1998**
More character than most inexpensive Aussie shirazes: richness and depth with real, elongated hedgerow sweetness. Good balance.

**Rymill Coonawarra** 12.5 £7–10
**Cabernet 1996**
Too creamy and thick.

**Rymill Coonawarra** 12 £7–10
**Shiraz 1996**
Stale Bovril.

**Tatachilla Breakneck** 14 £5–7
**Creek Cabernet**
**Sauvignon 1999**
A cab to take to oriental food. It has a quirky spiciness of its own.

**Tatachilla Breakneck** 15 £5–7
**Creek Merlot 1999**
A deeply sunburnt, soft and savourily leather skinned Merlot – very Aussie, very accommodating with food.

**Woodstock McLaren** 13 £7–10
**Vale Grenache 1997**

**Woodstock 'The Stocks'** 10 £10–13
**McLaren Shiraz 1996**
Just juice with attitude.

## MORRISONS RED

**Barramundi Shiraz/** 15.5 –£5.00
**Merlot NV**

**Cranswick Kidman Way** 14 –£5.00
**Cabernet Sauvignon 1998**
Touch sweet but good with food.

**Cranswick Nine Pines** 14 –£5.00
**Cabernet Sauvignon 1998**
A bit resinated, very dry and tannic, but with an ostrich casserole it might be a marvel.

**Deakin Estate Merlot** 15 £5–7
**1998**
Getting juicy as it matures and the leather is softening to jam – congealing you might say.

**Hardys Cabernet Shiraz** 15 £5–7
**Merlot 1998**
Big and jammy but has civilised tannins to give it backbone and bite.

**Jindalee Shiraz 1998** 13 –£5.00
Very sweet and sticky.

**Lindemans Bin 45** 15 £5–7
**Cabernet Sauvignon 1999**
Jammy yet not OTT, fruity yet not overly adolescent, this is a reasonably entertaining adult beverage – for blackcurrant lovers.

**'M' Australian Shiraz** 10 –£5.00
**Cabernet NV**
Not good enough, not typical, too rushed, too clumsy on the finish.

**Nottage Hill Cabernet** 14 £5–7
**Sauvignon Shiraz 1998**
Very sweet vintage, '98, and it's getting sweeter.

**Rosemount Estate Shiraz** 15.5 £7–10
**1998**
Hints of savouriness impinge on the great juicy depths.

**Thomas Mitchell Shiraz** 13 £5–7
**1998**

Dry, bit flat as it hits the taste buds, tannins ho-hum.

## ODDBINS RED

**Annie's Lane Shiraz,** `13` `£7–10`
**Clare Valley 1997**

**Baileys Shiraz 1997** `14` `£5–7`
Baileys has stopped being a tannic tyrant and become a simpering fat-boy idiot – trying to be sweet and entertaining. It's not good news.

**Brokenwood Shiraz 1998** `15` `£7–10`
Odd dry savoury frontal attack which turns very jammy on the finish.

**Cape Jaffa Mount Benson** `13` `£7–10`
**Shiraz 1998**
Too juicy and raisiny ripe for me.

**Church Block Cabernet** `17` `£7–10`
**Shiraz Merlot, Wirra**
**Wirra Vineyards 1998**
Wonderful brisk tannins coat the chocolate and cassis fruit. Marvellous stuff. Benchmark blend.

**d'Arenberg The Footbolt** `15.5` `£5–7`
**Old Vine Shiraz,**
**McLaren Vale 1998**

**d'Arry's Original Shiraz** `16` `£5–7`
**Grenache, McLaren Vale**
**1997**
Rampant fruit which takes no prisoners. Lovely stuff to match against an old style coq au vin.

**Deakin Estate Cabernet** `15.5` `£5–7`
**Sauvignon, Victoria 1999**
Juicy, baked-fruit edge. Delicious with rich food.

**Deakin Estate Shiraz** `15` `–£5.00`
**Cabernet Sauvignon,**
**Victoria 1999**

Blackcurrant and plum jam meets ripe tannins. The aroma is salivatory.

**Deakin Estate Shiraz,** `15` `£5–7`
**Victoria 1999**
Free-flowing and energetic. Very soft and ripe but not over-cooked.

**E & C Cabernet** `16` `£5–7`
**Sauvignon, McLaren Vale**
**1998**
Sheer heaven-juice. Touch of spice, hint of liquorice. Very lush, intensely lovable.

**E & C Shiraz, McLaren** `15.5` `£5–7`
**Vale 1998**
Touch of menthol to the beautifully soft, rich fruit which smacks of plums / blackberries and dates.

**Elderton Cabernet** `16` `£10–13`
**Sauvignon, Barossa 1996**
Has a handsome gamut of flavours running from dry and savoury to rich and sweet. Fine Wine Stores.

**Elderton Merlot, Barossa** `14` `£13–20`
**1996**
Fine Wine Stores only.

**Elderton Shiraz, Barossa** `17` `£10–13`
**1996**
Hums and literally vibrates with spicy, savoury fruit of massive depth. Fine Wine Stores.

**Elderton Tantalus** `16` `£5–7`
**Shiraz / Cabernet**
**Sauvignon 1998**
The very essence of what so many palates exult in with soft, ripe Aussie Shiraz and Cab.

**Hillstowe 'Buxton'** `15` `£7–10`
**Cabernet Merlot,**
**McLaren Vale 1998**
Very juicy, though the aroma is unusually savoury and enticing.

Hillstowe Udy's Mill Pinot Noir, Lenswood 1997 | 14 | £7–10

Mamre Brook Cabernet Shiraz 1996 | 16 | £5–7
At its peak of savoury smoothness and richness. Lovely texture and temperature: warm but not steamy.

Merrill's Mount Hurtle Bush Vine Grenache, McLaren Vale 1996 | 13.5 | £5–7

Normans White Label Cabernet Sauvignon, South Eastern Australia 1998 | 13 | £5–7

Normans White Label Merlot, South Australia 1998 | 13 | £5–7

Oxford Landing Cabernet Sauvignon Shiraz 1999 | 15.5 | £5–7
Terrific! One of Australia's top-notch brands on the basis of its rich texture, good layers of fruit, warm, friendly tannins, and overall lushly impactful structure. An adults' Shiraz of great charm and persistence.

Penny's Hill Shiraz, McLaren Vale 1998 | 16 | £7–10
Quintessential, quantastic, quashy, quaint, quagmirish fruit. A long queue of attributes.

Peter Lehmann The Barossa Shiraz 1998 | 17 | £5–7
Quite the best value Shiraz from Australia I can think of: dry, elegant, deep, beautifully textured.

Preece Shiraz 1997 | 15.5 | £5–7
Curious, very subtle tang, almost malt whisky-like, but though an eccentric wine it'll be marvellous with staid food – like tofu hamburger with chillies.

Rufus Stone Heathcote Shiraz, Victoria 1998 | 14.5 | £10–13
Very juicy and ripe for twelve quid.

Rufus Stone Shiraz, McLaren Vale 1998 | 16.5 | £7–10
Gorgeous sticky tannins and tenacious fruit. So everything not only works together but stays together.

Tatachilla Shiraz, South Australia 1998 | 15.5 | £5–7

Wirra Wirra Original Blend Grenache Shiraz, McLaren Vale 1997 | 16.5 | £7–10
Lovely lingering depths of cigar-tinged fruit. Also has some catering chocolate and some superb layers of berries and solid tannins. Exceptional wine.

Wirra Wirra Vineyards The Angelus Cabernet Sauvignon 1996 | 13 | £10–13
Fine Wine Stores only.

Wirra Wirra W2 Grenache Shiraz Cabernet 1999 | 15 | £5–7
Juicy but not injudicious.

Yarra Valley Hills Cabernet Sauvignon 1996 | 15 | £10–13

Yarra Valley Hills Warranwood Pinot Noir 1998 | 14 | £7–10

## SAFEWAY RED

Australian Oaked Cabernet Sauvignon 1999, Safeway | 14.5 | –£5.00
Oak? Can't spot it myself. Mostly I was rushed off my taste buds by the lushness of the blackberries.

Australian Oaked Shiraz 14 −£5.00
1999, Safeway
The usual Aussie fruit juice – with attitude.

Australian Shiraz 1999, 15 −£5.00
Safeway
The juicy version of Syrah. Very warm and virile.

Australian Shiraz/Ruby 14 −£5.00
Cabernet 1999, Safeway
Very jammy but the texture is so thick it contains this rich onslaught very well. Great with rich spicy foods.

Basedow Bush Vine 15 £5–7
Grenache 1998
Serenely well fruited and calmly charming. Selected stores.

Capel Vale Shiraz 1998 14 £7–10
Curious, nervous, stringy edge.

Clancy's Shiraz/Cabernet 17 £7–10
Sauvignon/Merlot/
Cabernet Franc 1998
Perfection at its peak – almost. Will it rate higher? How can it? It has wonderfully integrated generous tannins and plum/cherry/blackberry fruit.

Dawn Ridge Australian 15 −£3.50
Red (3 litre box)
Price band reflects the 75cl equivalent.

Endeavour Cabernet 13 £7–10
Sauvignon 1998
Very juicy.

Evans & Tate Shiraz 1999 16.5 £7–10
Concentrated, nutty, figgy richness of delicacy yet considerable weight of purpose.

Geoff Merrill Reserve 15 £10–13
Cabernet Sauvignon 1995
An expensive Christmas treat. Very

dry, classy, haughty stuff. Selected stores.

Hardys Stamp of 14 −£5.00
Australia Shiraz Cabernet
1999
Very ripe and all-embracing, hardly subtle (maybe they should change the name of the company).

Haselgrove 'Bentwing' 14 £7–10
Shiraz, Wrattonbully
1998
Extremely ripe and soft and with a very faint mineral undertone. Very textured and thick. Selected stores.

Haselgrove Shiraz, 14 £7–10
McLaren Vale 1998
Thick knitted plummy fruit with a hint of spice. Selected stores.

Jindalee Shiraz, Murray- 13 −£5.00
Darling Region 1998

Knappstein Cabernet/ 16.5 £7–10
Merlot 1998
Runs away with itself but stays in control of one's taste buds. Bright, bonny, textured, serious mid-palate polish and plummy flavours, and an elegant finish. Lovely wine here.

Koltz LFD Shiraz 1998 16 £7–10
Savoury bite to the tannins is superb and gives the rampant fruit a run for its money. An outstanding Aussie Shiraz. 70 stores.

Lindemans Pyrus 16.5 £13–20
Cabernet Sauvignon/
Merlot/Cabernet France
1997
One of Coonawarra's most elegant reds. Marvellous soft tannins to the cassis and thyme fruit.

Mamre Brook Cabernet 15 £7–10
Sauvignon 1997

23

Oh God! How much more Aussie juicy-fruit can a mortal stand!? (But I love it really.) Top 70 stores.

**Mamre Brook Cabernet Shiraz 1996**   16   £5–7
At its peak of savoury smoothness and richness. Lovely texture and temperature: warm but not steamy.

**Masterpeace Shiraz Malbec 2000**   14   £5–7
Curiously medicinal tang to the soft, ripe fruit. An odd blend of Bordeaux and Rhone grapes which would turn a Frenchman's hair white with incomprehension (it made my hair curl, too).

**Metala Shiraz/Cabernet Sauvignon 1997**   14   £5–7
An expensive tandoori chicken red.

**Oxford Landing Limited Release Shiraz 1998**   13.5   £5–7
A very juicy Shiraz. But that's Oxford Landing all over.

**Penfolds Bin 128 Coonawarra Shiraz 1996**   15.5   £7–10
Lush, rich, usual Penfolds recipe for this sort of turn out. Correct and controlled. Makes for a delicious companion to casseroles. 70 stores.

**Penfolds Bin 389 Cabernet Shiraz 1996**   16   £10–13
Lovely blend of vegetal, tannic Cabernet with the spicy Shiraz. It has a terrific texture and a warm, coaxing finish. Top 36 stores.

**Penfolds Organic Merlot Shiraz Cabernet 1998**   15.5   £7–10
Rather detached tannins as if stuck on later, but there's no gainsaying the delicious ripe plumptitude of the rousing plummy fruit.

**Peter Lehmann The Barossa Shiraz 1998**   17   £5–7
Oh, it's so savoury and ripe yet so elegantly purposeful. A quite gorgeous artefact providing rivulets of rich flavours.

**Riddoch Cabernet Shiraz 1998**   16   £7–10
It's the mineral limey edge which sets it apart. Distinctive and very delicious. Selected stores.

**Rosemount Estate Grenache Shiraz 1998**   15   £5–7

**Rosemount Estate Merlot 1998**   13   £7–10

**Rosemount Estate Shiraz 1998**   15.5   £7–10
Hints of savouriness impinge on the great juicy depths.

**Rosemount Estate Show Reserve Cabernet Sauvignon 1996**   13   £13–20

**Rosemount 'Hill of Gold' Shiraz, Mudgee 1998**   17.5   £7–10
At last! A Rosemount red with world-class tannins. And it's under a tenner. Beautifully well knit fruit here, totally captivating, and the texture is gripping, grand, and you feel greedy for more.

**Tatachilla Breakneck Creek Cabernet Sauvignon 1999**   14   £5–7
A Cab to take to oriental food. It has a quirky spiciness of its own.

**Tatachilla Breakneck Creek Merlot 1999**   15   £5–7
A deeply sunburnt, soft and savourily leather skinned Merlot – very Aussie, very accommodating with food.

**Tatachilla 'Foundation'** 16 £13–20
**Shiraz 1998**
Very tangy and ripe, hint of almond
and raisin, but overall it's the
impressive build of the tannins which
gives it its evident class.

**Tatachilla Padthaway** 16.5 £7–10
**Cabernet Sauvignon 1998**
The essence of ripe, dry, richly flowing
Aussie Cab. Sheer hedonism liquefied.
Selected stores.

**Wirrega Vineyards** 16 £5–7
**Cabernet Sauvignon/**
**Petit Verdot 1999**
Terrific mineral aroma, jammy fruit,
nice simple tannins. An
unpretentiously delicious specimen.

**Wirrega Vineyards Shiraz** 16.5 £5–7
**1999**
Stunning impact with its compelling
layers of generous fruit of great style
and warmly textured richness.
Absolutely terrific finish.

**Woolshed Cabernet/** 17 £5–7
**Shiraz/Merlot,**
**Coonawarra 1998**
Stunning richness and textured, tangy
fruit of huge depth and charm. Multi-
layered and magnificently mouth-
watering. Top 220 stores.

## SAINSBURY'S RED

**Australian Shiraz 1999,** 15.5 −£5.00
**Sainsbury's**
Totally gluggable and generously
fruity. Extremely well balanced and
very well finished off. An excellent
example of what Oz can still do for
under a fiver. Most stores.

**Banrock Station Mataro** 14.5 −£5.00
**Shiraz NV, (3 litre box)**

Preferable to the bottled product, it
seems freer here, more flowing and
not so tarrily rich and cloying. A very
thick wine which loves food. The price
band reflects the equivalent price for a
75cl bottle.

**Banrock Station Shiraz** 15 £5–7
**Mataro 1999**
Well, it's a lot better built than the '98
which was like chewing toffee. This is
thick but has some energy to it. Very
soft and ripe, though. (Just like toffee.)
Most stores.

**Brown Brothers** 13.5 £5–7
**Tarrango 1999**
Juicy! Needs spicy food.

**Hardys Cabernet Shiraz** 15 £5–7
**Merlot 1998**
Big and jammy but has civilised
tannins to give it backbone and bite.
Most stores.

**Hardys Coonawarra** 16 £10–13
**Cabernet Sauvignon 1996**
Soupy yet with savoury tannins which
keep it adult and x-rated. The
seductiveness of the perfume is only
the beginning.

**Hardys Stamp of** 14 −£5.00
**Australia Shiraz Cabernet**
**1999**
Very ripe and all-embracing, hardly
subtle (maybe they should change the
name of the company). Selected stores.

**Leasingham Domaine** 15 £7–10
**Shiraz 1996**

**Lindemans Bin 45** 15 £5–7
**Cabernet Sauvignon 1999**
Jammy yet not OTT, fruity yet not
overly adolescent, this is a reasonably
entertaining adult beverage – for
blackcurrant lovers. Selected stores.

**Lindemans Cawarra** `12` `−£5.00`
**Merlot 1999**
So sweet! Needs . . . yes, you guessed
it, a big fat curry.

**Lindemans Cawarra** `12` `−£5.00`
**Merlot Shiraz Ruby**
**Cabernet 1999**
Junior league stuff. Most stores.

**Lindemans Limestone** `15.5` `£5–7`
**Coast Shiraz 1998**
Lovely tang of limestone to it. Rich,
blackberryish, ripe – yet very elegant.
Selected stores.

**Oxford Landing Cabernet** `15.5` `£5–7`
**Sauvignon Shiraz 1999**
Terrific! One of Australia's top-notch
brands on the basis of its rich texture,
good layers of fruit, warm, friendly
tannins, and overall lushly impactful
structure. An adults' Shiraz of great
charm and persistence.

**Penfolds Bin 389** `16.5` `£10–13`
**Cabernet Shiraz 1997**
Very forward and full, big and deep,
and with soft, accelerated tannins
which evolve by delicious degrees on
the taste buds. Selected stores.

**Petaluma Bridgewater** `15` `£7–10`
**Mill Shiraz 1997**
Full of juicy riches which stay the
plummy side of baked pie-ness. Not at
all stores.

**Petaluma Coonawarra** `16.5` `£13–20`
**Cabernet Merlot 1997**
Stunning whirl of complex tannins and
warm, rich fruit. Deliciously intrusive
on the palate – excitingly so – it
trumpets its way so happily to the
throat – and beyond. 10 stores.

**Rosemount Estate** `15` `£5–7`
**Cabernet Merlot 1999**

Has some plump ripe plums, very soft
and delicious, intermingled with which
are some handsomely intrusive
tannins. 50 stores.

**Rosemount Estate** `15` `£5–7`
**Grenache/Shiraz 1999**
Intense hedgerow sweetness. Very
juicy. Most stores.

**Rosemount Estate Shiraz** `15.5` `£7–10`
**1998**
Hints of savouriness impinge on the
great juicy depths. Most stores.

**Rosemount Estate Shiraz** `15.5` `£5–7`
**Cabernet 1999**
Hugely friendly, it's archetypical
Aussie Shiraz and really defines what
this grape means at this price from this
region. Most stores.

**Tatachilla Breakneck** `14` `£5–7`
**Creek Cabernet**
**Sauvignon 1999**
A Cab to take to oriental food. It has a
quirky spiciness of its own.

**Tatachilla Breakneck** `15` `£5–7`
**Creek Merlot 1999**
A deeply sunburnt, soft and savourily
leather skinned Merlot – very Aussie,
very accommodating with food.

**Tyrrells Old Winery** `13.5` `£5–7`
**Cabernet Merlot 1998**
Juicy, so juicy. Not at all stores.

**Wynns Coonawarra** `16.5` `£5–7`
**Shiraz 1997**
Gripping elegance and polished fruit
here. Has a mineral edge, great
plummy richness and lovely soft
tannins. Selected stores.

## SOMERFIELD RED

**Australian Cabernet** 15.5 −£5.00
**Sauvignon 1999,**
**Somerfield**
Has everything that claret would give
its eye teeth for. (Including the tannins
which cling to the same teeth.)

**Australian Dry Red 1999,** 14.5 −£5.00
**Somerfield**
Jammy yet not OTT. Great with spicy
food.

**Australian Shiraz** 15 −£5.00
**Cabernet 1999,**
**Somerfield**
Delicious, quite quite delicious. Thick
as a woolly sweater, just as warming.

**Banrock Station Shiraz** 15 −£5.00
**Mataro 1999**
Jammy, thick and hugely food friendly.

**Hardys Cabernet Shiraz** 15 £5–7
**Merlot 1998**
Big and jammy but has civilised
tannins to give it backbone and bite.

**Hardys Nottage Hill** 16.5 £5–7
**Cabernet Sauvignon/**
**Shiraz 1999**
Under six quid, one of Aussie's best big
red wine bargains. Thrilling tannins
and subtle spiciness.

**Hardys Stamp Shiraz** 14 −£5.00
**Cabernet 1999**
Sweet and rich? Curry? Sorry to go on
about curries, but what else is one to
do with a wine like this?

**Penfolds Bin 28 Kalimna** 17 £7–10
**Shiraz 1997**
Quite gorgeous and uplifting. It
smothers the palate with prunes,
blackberries and liquorice, and then
lifts the heart.

**Penfolds Coonawarra Bin** 15.5 £7–10
**128 Shiraz 1996**
Lush, rich, usual Penfolds recipe for
this sort of turn out. Correct and
controlled. Makes for a delicious
companion to casseroles.

**Penfolds Koonunga Hill** 16.5 £5–7
**Shiraz Cabernet**
**Sauvignon 1998**
Superb quality and this is the best
vintage yet of this well-established
brand. Superb fruit, great texture.

**Rosemount Estate Shiraz** 15.5 £7–10
**1998**
Hints of savouriness impinge on the
great juicy depths.

**Rosemount Estate Shiraz** 15.5 £5–7
**Cabernet 1998**

## SPAR RED

**Australian Shiraz** 13.5 −£5.00
**Cabernet 1998, Spar**
An excellent pasta wine. Unusually dry
for an Aussie at this price.

**Hardys Bankside Shiraz** 16.5 £7–10
**1997**
By far the best red I've tasted at Spar.
Good age, lovely rich fruit (savoury
and spicy) and lovely tannins.

## TESCO RED

**Australian Cabernet/** 14 −£5.00
**Merlot NV, Tesco**

**Australian Red, Tesco** 14 −£3.50
The cheapest Aussie red in the world?
Just possibly. Yet it is far from being
the worst.

**Australian Ruby** 14 −£5.00
**Cabernet, Tesco**

Australian Shiraz NV,    `13`  −£5.00
Tesco

Australian Shiraz/    `14`  −£5.00
Cabernet NV, Tesco

Banrock Station Shiraz    `13`  £5–7
1999
Six quid seems a bit steep when the
fruit is stretched to climb the taste
buds and finish with any firmness.

Banrock Station Shiraz/    `15`  −£5.00
Mataro 1999
What a Lebanese food performer we
have here! Even has a touch of
coriander to it already. Juicy and ripe
and richly textured.

Barramundi Shiraz/    `15.5`  −£5.00
Merlot NV

Best's Great Western    `15.5`  £5–7
Dolcetto 1998
Interesting curiosity of substance and
wit. Takes a few seconds, from the
juicy start, to get going, but it's soft,
pliant and very pleasing. Wine Advisor
stores.

Blue Pyrenees Estate Red    `14`  £10–13
1996
The big, blustering, love-me-or-leave-
me style of Aussie fruit. Wine Advisor
stores.

Brown Brothers    `13.5`  £5–7
Tarrango 1999
Juicy! Needs spicy food.

Buckleys Grenache/    `14`  £7–10
Shiraz/Mourvedre 1998
Rather expensive for the style but it
does possess some solid fruit and good
tannins – and the finish is excellent.
Top 200 stores.

Chapel Hill Cabernet    `14`  £7–10
Sauvignon 1997

Touch expensive for the juicy style –
the tannins are very subdued.

Coonawarra Cabernet    `16`  £5–7
Sauvignon 1998, Tesco
Very elegant and chic. Exceptional
concentration of fruit, balance and
polish. The tannins are refined yet
crunchy.

Hardys Nottage Hill    `16.5`  £5–7
Cabernet Sauvignon/
Shiraz 1999
Under six quid, one of Aussie's best big
red wine bargains. Thrilling tannins
and subtle spiciness.

Lindemans Bin 50 Shiraz    `14.5`  £5–7
1998
Simply delicious!

Lindemans Cawarra    `14`  −£5.00
Shiraz/Cabernet 1999
Juicy, very very juicy and curry-
friendly.

McLaren Vale Grenache    `13.5`  £5–7
1998, Tesco
At most stores.

McLaren Vale Shiraz    `14`  £5–7
1997, Tesco
At most stores.

Miranda 'Left Field' Tinta    `13`  −£5.00
Cao 1998
A most curiously resinous and bitter
wine.

Oxford Landing Cabernet    `15.5`  £5–7
Sauvignon Shiraz 1999
Terrific! One of Australia's top-notch
brands on the basis of its rich texture,
good layers of fruit, warm, friendly
tannins, and overall lushly impactful
structure. An adults' Shiraz of great
charm and persistence.

Penfold Koonunga Hill    `16.5`  £5–7

Shiraz/Cabernet
Sauvignon 1998
Superb quality and this is the best
vintage yet of this well-established
brand. Superb fruit, great texture.

**Rosemount Estate**   15   £5–7
**Grenache/Shiraz 1999**
So juicy it screams for chillies,
cardamoms and stewed garlic.

**Rosemount Estate Shiraz**   15.5   £5–7
**Cabernet 1999**
Hugely friendly, it's archetypical
Aussie Shiraz and really defines what
this grape means at this price from this
region.

**Rosemount Shiraz 1998**   15.5   £7–10
Hints of savouriness impinge on the
great juicy depths.

**Sunstone Fresh Spicy Red**   12   –£5.00
**NV**

**Temple Bruer**   14   £5–7
**Cornucopia Grenache
1997**

**Tim Adams Shiraz 1997**   14.5   £7–10

**Woolpunda Cabernet**   15   –£5.00
**Sauvignon 1998**
Hint of dryness to the juicy fruit gives
it some seriousness.

**Woolpunda Shiraz 1998**   16   –£5.00
Soft, very cushy fruit of great style and
mannered richness. It is wholly
without pretension but it does have
poise and plummy depths. Most
stores.

## THRESHER RED

**Hardys Nottage Hill**   15.5   £5–7
**Cabernet Sauvignon
Shiraz 1998**

Juicy and ripe but maturing
handsomely and reaching its peak of
textured concentration and tannic
tightness. After a while, this will
loosen as it does with many Aussie-
like blends. So drink it soon. It won't
keep.

**Leasingham Domaine**   17   £7–10
**Cabernet/Malbec 1997**
Piles it on from every direction
including the price tag. At £9.99 it
must be compared to great Bordeaux
and it simply knocks them into a
cocked chapeau. It is beautifully
rounded yet firmly dry, complex and
very very bold to finish.

**Lindemans Padthaway**   15.5   £7–10
**Shiraz 1997**
Possibly fades too quickly on the finish
to rate higher but on the palate it has
some classic Shiraz warmth with a
very subtle eucalyptus edging.
Charming companion if you don't like
gob-smacking endings.

**Nanya Estate Malbec/**   10   –£5.00
**Ruby Cabernet 1998**
This as a skimpy g-string but not so
teasing.

**Oxford Landing Cabernet**   15.5   £5–7
**Sauvignon Shiraz 1999**
Terrific! One of Australia's top-notch
brands on the basis of its rich texture,
good layers of fruit, warm, friendly
tannins, and overall lushly impactful
structure. An adults' Shiraz of great
charm and persistence.

**Oxford Landing Merlot**   14   £5–7
**1999**
Juicy yet finishes dry. Only at Wine
Rack and Bottoms Up.

**St Hallett Barossa Shiraz**   13   £7–10
**1997**

**Tatachilla Grenache** `16` `£5–7`
**Shiraz 1998**
This estate has come on so much since
it changed ownership. A decade ago I
saw grapes destined for Tatachilla
swollen with irrigated water but not
the beauties which went into this
bargain blend. The wine has style,
bravura, loads of fruit but is never silly
or too juicy. The tannins are
temperate and tasty. With increasing
Oz prices, this is a sane specimen in a
mad world.

**Tollana Red, S E** `13.5` `–£5.00`
**Australia NV**

**Yalumba Bush Vine** `14` `£7–10`
**Grenache 1997**
Very chewy and ripe with an
overbaked edge to it. Can only be
enjoyed with food.

## UNWINS RED

**Baileys 1904 Block Shiraz** `14` `£10–13`
**1994**
Juicy and savoury and rather pricey
now the fruit's turning so sweet. The
tannins are the thing and they're
becoming a touch wimpish now after
six years.

**Banrock Station Shiraz** `11` `–£5.00`
**1997**
Too old, too juicy, too cosmetic, too
sticky, too everything.

**Clancy's Shiraz/Cabernet** `17` `£7–10`
**Sauvignon/Merlot/**
**Cabernet Franc 1998**
Perfection at its peak – almost. Will it
rate higher? How can it? It has
wonderfully integrated generous
tannins and plum/cherry/blackberry
fruit.

**Hill of Hope Shiraz 1997** `14` `£5–7`
Not much life left in it – or rather the
fruit has plenty of years but the
tannins are at their last gasp.

**Ironstone Shiraz** `16.5` `£5–7`
**Grenache 1998**
Deliciously concentrated and incisive.
Rich, deep, ready, ripe (but not OTT),
full of interesting fruits (including a
hint of liquorice) and it finishes fully
and profoundly.

**J J McWilliam Merlot** `13` `£5–7`
**1997**

**Leasingham Clare Valley** `14.5` `£7–10`
**Grenache 1996**
Getting on a bit. The tannins are
losing grip but it is still a contender for
the Christmas bird.

**Oxford Landing Cabernet** `15.5` `£5–7`
**Sauvignon Shiraz 1999**
Terrific! One of Australia's top-notch
brands on the basis of its rich texture,
good layers of fruit, warm, friendly
tannins, and overall lushly impactful
structure. An adults' Shiraz of great
charm and persistence.

**Penfolds Koonunga Hill** `15` `£5–7`
**Shiraz/Cabernet**
**Sauvignon 1999**
Lovely spicy richness. A great branded
red.

**Rosemount Estate Shiraz** `15.5` `£5–7`
**Cabernet 1999**
Hugely friendly, it's archetypical
Aussie Shiraz and really defines what
this grape means at this price from this
region.

**Vine Vale Grenache 1998** `14.5` `–£5.00`
An almost toffee-apple texture to it.
Great chilled.

**Wakefield Cabernet** `16` `£5–7`

Sauvignon, Clare Valley
1998
Handsome chocolate fruit.

Woodvale Shiraz 1998   13   −£5.00

## VICTORIA WINE RED

**Hardys Nottage Hill**   15.5   £5–7
**Cabernet Sauvignon**
**Shiraz 1998**
Juicy and ripe but maturing
handsomely and reaching its peak of
textured concentration and tannic
tightness. After a while, this will
loosen as it does with many Aussie-like
blends. So drink it soon. It won't keep.

**Leasingham Domaine**   17   £7–10
**Cabernet/Malbec 1997**
Piles it on from every direction
including the price tag. At £9.99 it
must be compared to great Bordeaux
and it simply knocks them into a
cocked chapeau. It is beautifully
rounded yet firmly dry, complex and
very very bold to finish.

**Leasingham Grenache**   14.5   £7–10
**1996**
Getting on a bit. The tannins are
losing grip but it is still a contender for
the Christmas bird.

**Lindemans Padthaway**   15.5   £7–10
**Shiraz 1997**
Possibly fades too quickly on the finish
to rate higher but on the palate it has
some classic Shiraz warmth with a
very subtle eucalyptus edging.
Charming companion if you don't like
gob-smacking endings.

**Nanya Estate Malbec/**   10   −£5.00
**Ruby Cabernet 1998**
This as a skimpy g-string but not so
teasing.

**Tatachilla Grenache**   16   £5–7
**Shiraz 1998**
This estate has come on so much since
it changed ownership. A decade ago I
saw grapes destined for Tatachilla
swollen with irrigated water but not
the beauties which went into this
bargain blend. The wine has style,
bravura, loads of fruit but is never silly
or too juicy. The tannins are
temperate and tasty. With increasing
Oz prices, this is a sane specimen in a
mad world.

**Wynn's Coonawarra**   16.5   £5–7
**Shiraz 1996**
Superbly classy and rich. Hints of mint
cling to the deeply textured (denim
and corduroy) fruit (plums, cherries
and blackcurrants) and the sheer cheek
of the fruit, its bounce yet gravitas, is
terrific – the finish is syrup of figs.
Martha's Vineyard only.

**Yalumba Bush Vine**   14   £7–10
**Grenache 1997**
Very chewy and ripe with an
overbaked edge to it. Can only be
enjoyed with food.

## WAITROSE RED

**Brown Brothers Barbera**   14   £5–7
**1996**
Juicy and ripe but great with food. Has
some character on the finish.

**Brown Brothers Nebbiolo**   13.5   £7–10
**1996**
Old, raisiny, very juicy. Not at all
stores.

**Brown Brothers**   13   £5–7
**Tarrango 1999**

**Bushmans Crossing**   14   −£5.00
**Cabernet/Merlot 1999**

Ripe, raunchy, ready.

**Chateau Reynella Basket-** `17` `£10–13`
**Pressed Shiraz 1997**
Lovely minty edge (subtle eucalyptus),
beautifully smooth, wonderfully
balanced and witty to finish.

**Church Block Cabernet** `17` `£7–10`
**Shiraz Merlot, Wirra**
**Wirra Vineyards 1998**
Wonderful brisk tannins coat the
chocolate and cassis fruit. Marvellous
stuff. Benchmark blend. Not at all
stores.

**Clancy's Red 1998** `15` `£7–10`
Coffee edge to a chocolate-rich centre.
Very palate-embracing and ripe.

**Deakin Estate Merlot** `15.5` `£5–7`
**1999**
Lovely plump richness, really big and
mouthfilling, allied to pert tannins. A
terrific Merlot for the money.

**Eileen Hardy Shiraz 1996** `14.5` `£20+`
Huge and motherly. Crushes the
palate with fruit.

**Fishermans Bend** `12` `–£5.00`
**Cabernet Sauvignon 1998**
Simple fruit juice with alcohol.

**Garry Crittenden** `13.5` `£10–13`
**Sangiovese 1998**

**Henschke Keyneton** `12` `£13–20`
**Shiraz/Cabernet**
**Sauvignon/Merlot 1996**
Poor value. Great juice at six quid.
Only from Waitrose Direct.

**Jindalee Shiraz 1999** `14` `–£5.00`
Very ripe and forward.

**Kingston Reserve Petit** `12` `£13–20`
**Verdot 1997**
Too pricey by half. Not at all stores.

**Nanya Vineyard Malbec/** `12` `–£5.00`
**Ruby Cabernet 1999**
Too juicy and super-ripe.

**Penfolds Organic Merlot/** `15.5` `£7–10`
**Shiraz/Cabernet 1998**
Immensely smooth (almost smug with
it). Good rich texture and wrap-it-up-
slow finish.

**Peter Lehmann The** `17` `£5–7`
**Barossa Shiraz 1998**
A broad-shouldered wine of some
muscularity and yet fleet-of-foot
deftness. Very textured, deep and
flavoursome.

**Rosemount GSM,** `15` `£13–20`
**McLaren Vale 1996**
Very juicy, raunchy and flinty with
great warm tannins. Only from
Waitrose Direct.

**Rosemount 'Hill of Gold'** `17.5` `£7–10`
**Shiraz, Mudgee 1998**
At last! A Rosemount red with world-
class tannins. And it's under a tenner.
Beautifully well knit fruit here, totally
captivating, and the texture is gripping,
grand, and you feel greedy for more.

**Settler's Station** `13` `£5–7`
**Tempranillo 1999**
Very very juicy.

**Stonewell Shiraz, Barossa** `14` `£13–20`
**Valley 1994**
Very very expensive; very very
elongated and palate-gripping.

**Tatachilla Cabernet** `14.5` `£7–10`
**Sauvignon/Merlot,**
**McLaren Vale 1998**
Not as gripping as the '97 vintage. It's
very ripe and jammy.

**Tatachilla Foundation** `14` `£13–20`
**Shiraz 1997**

Ripe and juicy. Why do I imagine communion wine is like this?

**Tatachilla Growers Grenache Mataro 1999** | 10 | −£5.00
So juicy and ripe I couldn't spit it out fast enough. Makes a good sauce for a game bird (and a game clot).

**The Angelus Cabernet Sauvignon, Wirra Wirra 1997** | 14 | £13–20
Very rich, bit cloying and unsubtle on the finish. Only from Waitrose Direct.

**Wrattonbully Cabernet Sauvignon, Limestone Coast 1998** | 16 | £5–7
Great fat fruit with incisive acids and soft, subtle tannins.

## WINE CELLAR RED

**Cleveland Brien Shiraz/ Cabernet 1994** | 11 | £7–10
Very stalky, grudging opening and the fruit is too sweet and tanninless.

**Cleveland Macedon Pinot Noir 1996** | 10 | £10–13
Fruit juice pretending to be Pinot. Actually, there is a faint echo of Pinot as the wine has long quit the throat and you feel a sense of wild raspberry but you more feel a sense of loss.

**Jim Barrie McCrae Wood Shiraz 1996** | 14.5 | £13–20
Very minty and ripe with huge waves of sweet, almondy fruit at its peak. A lot of money, though, for those waves. If only they'd not used egg whites to take out the tannins, there might have been a great wine here.

**Penfolds Rawsons Retreat Bin 35 Cabernet** | 14 | £5–7

**Sauvignon/Shiraz/Ruby Cabernet 1998**
Soft and curry-friendly.

**Rosemount Estate Grenache/Shiraz 1999** | 15 | £5–7
Intense hedgerow sweetness. Very juicy.

**Three Steps Cabernet Sauvignon 1998** | 13.5 | £5–7
Odd, gets odder, finishes oddly. Now, I am an admirer of oddness and oddities. But here Pelion piles on Ossa and, at seven quid, I would prefer more elegance.

**Vasse Felix Cabernet Sauvignon 1997** | 16 | £13–20
One of Western Australia's smoothest customers. Lovely texture of such softness it's like velvet plus silk.

## ASDA WHITE

**Andrew Peace Chardonnay 1999** | 15.5 | −£5.00

**Cranswick Nine Pines Vineyard Marsanne 1998** | 16.5 | −£5.00
Astonishing value here and surprising level of mature layers of rich, ripe fruit. Textured and taut.

**Hardys Chardonnay Semillon 1999** | 16 | £5–7
Throbs with richness! Just wallow in it.

**Hardys Nottage Hill Chardonnay 1997** | 16.5 | −£5.00
Ooh..! It oozes with controlled richness yet calm, insouciant, relaxed fruitiness of inexpressibly delicious firmness and flavour.

**Hardys Stamp Riesling Traminer 1997** | 15 | −£5.00

**Houghton HWB 1998**  `16`  `£5–7`
HWB stands for Houghton White Burgundy even though the grapes are not Burgundian. It is no compliment to compare it with inexpensive Burgundy, though. It's better.

**Karalta Chardonnay 1998,**  `15.5`  `–£5.00`
**Asda**
Exuberance and vivacity here. Brilliant toffeed edge to it (never OTT) and the ripeness makes it great with modern foods.

**Karalta Chardonnay/**  `13.5`  `–£3.50`
**Semillon 1999, Asda**
Very soft and ripe.

**Karalta Semillon 1999,**  `14`  `–£5.00`
**Asda**
Thai food white.

**Karalta White 1999, Asda**  `14`  `–£3.50`
A brilliant value party wine.

**Maglieri Semillon 1999**  `16.5`  `£5–7`
Very elegant and subtly ripe. Brilliant wood and fruit integration and a clear, purposeful fruitiness.

**Mount Hurtle Chenin**  `15.5`  `–£5.00`
**Blanc 1999**
Controlled lushness here. A big mouthful of warm fruit.

**Penfolds Rawson's**  `15`  `–£5.00`
**Retreat Bin 21 Semillon**
**Chardonnay Colombard**
**1997**

**Peter Lehmann Eden**  `15.5`  `£5–7`
**Valley Riesling 1999**
A warm, richly textured wine which will get oilier and more stickily exciting as it ages.

**Peter Lehmann The**  `16`  `£5–7`
**Barossa Semillon, 1998**
Superb texture here. Lordly richness.

**Rosemount Estate**  `15`  `£5–7`
**Semillon/Chardonnay**
**1997**

**Rymill Sauvignon Blanc**  `15.5`  `£5–7`
**1999**
Elegant and easy-going.

**Temple Bruer Chenin**  `15.5`  `£5–7`
**Blanc 1999**
Baked fruit salad with even a hint of cream. Wine from another planet. Delicious!

## BOOTHS WHITE

**Chateau Tahbilk**  `15.5`  `£5–7`
**Marsanne 1998**
Delicious texture, hint of sesame oil, touches of raspberry, lime and butter. All subtle but unmistakable.

**Cranswick Botrytis**  `15`  `£10–13`
**Semillon 1996 (half-**
**bottle)**
Terrific acids here, they give the honeyed fruit superb freshness. A great wine for fresh fruit.

**CV Capel Vale**  `16`  `£7–10`
**Unwooded Chardonnay**
**1998**
Better, in its steely yet rich fruit, than so many vaunted Chablis.

**CV Capel Vale Verdelho**  `16.5`  `£7–10`
**1998**
This is a lovely, softly textured, gently spicy artefact of immense charm.

**d'Arenberg The Olive**  `16`  `£5–7`
**Grove Chardonnay 1998**
Does it have a kind of green olive to the lime and melon fruit? Sheer fantasy I think.

d'Arenberg White Ochre `13` `£5–7`
1999
Bit simplistic for a fiver.

Deakin Estate `15.5` `–£5.00`
Chardonnay 1999
One of Australia's bargain Chardies.
Lovely hints of butter, lime, melon
and strawberry.

Hardys Stamp Riesling `15.5` `–£5.00`
Gewurztraminer 1999
Super Chinese food wine. Has a rich
spice undertone coupled with teasing
acids.

Ironstone Semillon `17` `£5–7`
Chardonnay 1999
Juicy rich pineapples and pears, plus
lime and gooseberries – they're all
there. Superb texture.

Marktree White SE `13.5` `–£5.00`
Australia 1999

Ninth Island Chardonnay `13` `£7–10`
1999
Very sullen on the finish and doesn't
quite ignite under the tongue. Far too
expensive.

Oxford Landing Viognier `16` `£5–7`
1998
Compelling argument for the grape
(Viognier) and the region (south Oz).
Gorgeously subtle yet rich apricot
fruit.

Penfolds Bin 21 Rawson's `14` `–£5.00`
Retreat Semillon/
Colombard/Chardonnay
1999
A real mouthful of fruity grapes – in
name and nature.

Penfolds Clare Valley `15.5` `£7–10`
Organic Chardonnay/
Sauvignon Blanc 1998
Very smooth, elegant and polished.

However, do remember, as Philip
Larkin pointed out, that only surface
can be polished.

Riddoch Coonawarra `15` `£5–7`
Chardonnay 1998
Very warmly textured and rich, hot
and buttery on the tongue, and needs
food to temper this enthusiasm for all-
embracing flavoursomeness.

Shaw & Smith Sauvignon `15` `£7–10`
Blanc 1998
Wonderful fish wine. Better than
many a so-called great Sancerre.

## BUDGENS WHITE

Hardys Stamp Grenache `13.5` `–£5.00`
Shiraz Rosé 1999
Sweet, and a touch cosmetic.

Oxford Landing `15.5` `£5–7`
Chardonnay 1999
Most accomplished warmth and
elegance here.

Rawsons Retreat Bin 202 `15` `–£5.00`
Riesling 1999
Delicious ripe fruit with gentle
pineapple and lemon acids.

Rosemount Estate `16` `£5–7`
Chardonnay 1999
One of the most stylish whites on
Budgens' shelves.

Rosemount Estate `15` `£5–7`
Semillon/Chardonnay
1997

Rosemount GTR 2000 `14` `£5–7`
Almost sweet, so rich is it. A white for
oriental food.

White Pointer 2000 `13` `–£5.00`
Fresh and ripe. Like many an Aussie,
indeed.

## CWS WHITE

**Australian Chardonnay 1999, Co-op** `15.5` `–£5.00`
Restrained richness and dry fruit – rather refined for the price.

**Bethnay Chardonnay 1998** `16` `£5–7`
The extra year of maturity has added layers of interest. It has a gorgeous aroma of cooking butter, the fruit is ripe and nutty, the finish brings in lime, butter and almonds. Nice lingering vegetality. Superstores only.

**Hardys Chardonnay Sauvignon Blanc 1998** `15` `£5–7`
A solid blend of each grape's more distinguished virtues.

**Jacaranda Hill Semillon 1999, Co-op** `14` `–£5.00`
Fresh, good layer of lemon tanginess. Great with fish.

**Lindemans Bin 65 Chardonnay 1999** `16.5` `–£5.00`
One of Oz's best under-a-fiver Chardonnays.

**Lindemans Cawarra Chardonnay 1999** `15.5` `–£5.00`
Nice turn of richness on the back of the palate and it goes from ripe melon to dusky pear and lemon.

**Rosemount GTR 2000** `14` `£5–7`
Almost sweet, so rich is it. A white for oriental food. Superstores only.

## KWIK SAVE WHITE

**Banrock Station Chardonnay 1999** `14` `–£5.00`
Hints of spiced pear to the rich, ripe ogen melon fruit. Great with scallops and seaweed.

**Banrock Station Colombard Chardonnay 1999** `15` `–£5.00`
Much better vintage! The '99 is rich yet balanced, ripe and melony with good pineapple acidity.

**Lindemans Bin 65 Chardonnay 1999** `16.5` `–£5.00`
Simply one of the tastiest, classiest examples of grape under-a-fiver in the world.

**Pelican Bay Medium Dry White** `14` `–£3.50`

**Penfolds Rawsons Retreat Semillon/ Chardonnay/Colombard 1999** `15` `–£5.00`
One of Australia's great blends, Sem and Chard, and this example, whilst hardly subtle, has some attractive elements.

## M&S WHITE

**Fusion Riesling 1999** `15` `–£5.00`
Lovely collation of mineral dryness and lemony richness. A direct statement of Riesling's myriad virtues when young plus the potential to age with grace for decades.

**HoneyTree Gewürztraminer Riesling 1999** `12` `£5–7`
Too sweet for me.

**HoneyTree Semillon Chardonnay 1999** `15` `£5–7`

**Hunter Valley Chardonnay Bin 109 1999** `14.5` `–£5.00`
Lean and dry, oddly untypical but

deliciously mineral-tinged and subtly citric.

**Lindemans Bin 65** 16.5 —£5.00
**Chardonnay 1999**
Simply one of the tastiest, classiest examples of grape under-a-fiver in the world.

**Semillon Bin 381 1999** 13 —£5.00
Pear-drop edge, powdery edge to the fruit. Odd stuff altogether.

**South East Australian** 13 —£5.00
**Medium Dry 1999**
Very soft and yet curiously under-ripe.

**South Eastern Australian** 15 —£5.00
**Chardonnay 1999**
Elegant and rewarding. A very accomplished silkiness of texture and elegance of finish.

**South Eastern Australian** 12 —£5.00
**Riesling 1999**
Bit muted and not varietally compelling.

**Verdelho 1999** 12 —£5.00
Very mild and meek.

## MAJESTIC WHITE

**Bethany Riesling 1998** 16.5 £5–7
Riesling from an alien life form. Compelling richness and crisp mineral tanginess combine to classic effect. It will age and become a twenty-point wine over the next five to seven years.

**Bethany Semillon** 16 £5–7
**Riesling Chardonnay**
**1998**
Brilliant blend of unlikely grapes (in marriage). Really fantastic fruit value.

**Capel Vale Riesling 1999** 15 £7–10
Needs two or three years to be at its best – will be seventeen points at least, I would hazard.

**Capel Vale Verdelho 1999** 16 £7–10
Wonderful concentrated vintage for this warmly coated, subtly spicy wine.

**Lindemans Bin 65** 16 —£5.00
**Chardonnay 1998**
A hugely elegant vintage, this, for a classic Aussie Chardonnay. It has purpose, stealth, wit and warmth, and invites comparison with Chardonnays daring to cost a lot more.

**Mamre Brook** 14 £5–7
**Chardonnay 1997**

**Mirrabrook Chardonnay** 15 —£3.50
**1999**
Remarkable value. True, it's subtle and doesn't become very rich and the finish is demure but it has simple, delicious, well-wrought fruit of unpretentious demeanour.

**Noble Road Verdelho** 14.5 £5–7
**1998**
Sticky fruit and Chinese food friendly.

**Oxford Landing Limited** 17 £5–7
**Release Viognier 1999**
One of the greatest Viogniers in the world in this vintage. The lingering apricots and gentle spice are remarkable.

**Oxford Landing** 15 —£5.00
**Sauvignon Blanc 1999**
Keen and fresh with more than a hint of gooseberry.

**Penfolds Koonunga Hill** 16 £5–7
**Chardonnay 1999**
Crisp, clean, classy.

**Pirramimma Chardonnay** 17 £5–7
**1997**
Surprisingly complex and complete, it

develops delicious toasty nuances on the taste buds and encompasses many fruits I cannot put a name to. The balance, the texture, the excitement on the finish, though, are deliciously effable.

**Pirramimma Late** `15` `£5–7`
**Harvest Riesling 1998**
**(half-bottle)**
Delicious ice cream wine. Can the Pirramimma range at Majestic do no wrong? Apparently not.

**Rosemount Estate** `16` `£5–7`
**Diamond Semillon 1997**
Unconscionably yummy and compellingly priced.

**Rosemount GTR 1998** `16` `£5–7`
What a whizzbang of a wine! Rich, spicy – but not aggressive – it offers the perfect credentials to go with oriental food.

**Tatachilla Breakneck** `16` `−£5.00`
**Creek Chardonnay 1999**
Almost a yoghurt ripeness here. Great with mood and/or food, it's an assertive wine of some style.

**Wynns Coonawarra** `16` `−£5.00`
**Riesling 1998**
Thrilling bargain and a great competition to Chardonnay. Lush yet has beautiful mineral and lime undertones.

**Yalumba Griffith-Barossa** `16` `£7–10`
**Botrytis Semillon**
**Sauvignon Blanc 1997**
**(half-bottle)**
Lovely complexity and toffeed edge.

**Yalumba Growers** `17` `£5–7`
**Chardonnay 1999**
Why bother with Montrachet at £75???

## MORRISONS WHITE

**Barramundi Semillon/** `16` `−£5.00`
**Chardonnay NV**
Lovely oily fruit, hint of bellpepper and mango, and the whole thing is altogether more serious than the playful label suggests. A great wine to quaff or to match with oriental, European or South American meat and fish dishes.

**Brown Brothers Chenin** `14` `−£5.00`
**Blanc 1998**
Great with Chinese food. Pure apricot and lemon fruit here.

**Cranswick Kidman Way** `15.5` `−£5.00`
**Chardonnay 1998**
Robust, spicy food – meet your match! No, it's not a sweet wine but it's so rich and thickly knit that it'll work like a butter sauce.

**Deakin Estate** `15.5` `−£5.00`
**Chardonnay 1999**
One of Australia's bargain Chardies. Lovely hints of butter, lime, melon and strawberry.

**Jindalee Chardonnay** `16` `−£5.00`
**1998**
Compelling richness and lemony elegant buttery fruit. Beautiful balance and precision.

**Lindemans Bin 65** `16.5` `−£5.00`
**Chardonnay 1999**
One of Oz's best under-a-fiver Chardonnays.

**Nottage Hill Chardonnay** `15.5` `−£5.00`
**1999**
Almost in the same league as Lindeman's. Perhaps its true score should be sixteen and three quarters.

**Penfolds Koonunga Hill** `16.5` `£5–7`
**Chardonnay 1998**
What a great brand! Stunning richness
and balanced, classy finish. If only
white Burgundians at three times the
price could be this good.

**Rosemount Estate** `16.5` `£5–7`
**Chardonnay 1998**
Very elegant in spite of being richly
cut and extravagant on the finish. A
gorgeous wine.

**Rosemount Estate GTR** `15` `£5–7`
**1999**
Curiously lime-laden and demi-sec.
Good for tandoori fish etc.

## ODDBINS WHITE

**Annie's Lane Riesling,** `15` `£5–7`
**Clare Valley 1999**
Lovely mineral hints as the lemon fruit
surges down the throat.

**Antipodean Unwooded** `15` `£5–7`
**Chardonnay 1999**
Knocks Chablis into a cocked chapeau.
Wonderful pastry-rich fruit.

**Bleasdale 'Sandhill** `13` `£5–7`
**Vineyard' Verdelho,**
**Langhorne Creek 1999**
I'd lay it down for ten or twelve years
and watch it put on five points more.

**Brokenwood Cricket** `16` `£7–10`
**Pitch Sauvignon/**
**Semillon 1999**
Has a gently waxy finish to the richly
chiming elements of fruit (melon) and
acid (lemon) and this is its original
touch.

**Campbells Liqueur** `16.5` `£5–7`
**Muscat, Rutherglen NV**
**(half-bottle)**

A magnificent Christmas pudding wine
of great depth. Has baked fruit and
molasses, toffees and toasted nuts.
Incredibly good value for money. A
real ambrosia of a wine.

**Cranswick Estate Zirilli** `16.5` `£7–10`
**Vineyard Botrytis**
**Semillon, Riverina 1996**
Medicinal, thick, rich, very sweet but
with the textured fruit so well served
by the brilliant tannins.

**d'Arenberg The Olive** `16` `£5–7`
**Grove Chardonnay,**
**McLaren Vale 1998**
Does it have a kind of green olive to
the lime and melon fruit? Sheer fantasy
I think.

**d'Arenberg White Ochre,** `13` `–£5.00`
**McLaren Vale 1999**

**Deakin Estate** `15.5` `–£5.00`
**Chardonnay 1999**
One of Australia's bargain chardies.
Lovely hints of butter, lime, melon
and strawberry.

**E & C Chardonnay,** `13.5` `£5–7`
**McLaren Vale 1999**

**Hillstowe Sauvignon** `13.5` `£5–7`
**Blanc, Adelaide Hill 1999**
Sharpish.

**Killawarra Chardonnay** `15.5` `–£5.00`
**1999**
Bargain! Bounteous butter and rich
acids. Terrific balance of style for the
money.

**Knappstein Riesling,** `16` `£5–7`
**Clare Valley 1998**
Wonderful seafood compatibility
here: almost has the mineral tang of
ozone.

**Lindemans Bin 65** `16.5` `−£5.00`
Chardonnay 1999
One of Oz's best under-a-fiver
Chardonnays.

**Nepenthe Vineyards** `15.5` `£7–10`
Lenswood Unwooded
Chardonnay 1999
How do they achieve such depth,
texture and richness? A debating point.
Not so the absence of wood, which is
a great virtue.

**Oxford Landing** `15` `−£5.00`
Sauvignon Blanc 1999
Keen and fresh with more than a hint
of gooseberry.

**Penny's Hill Chardonnay,** `16` `£7–10`
McLaren Vale 1999
Wonderful present for someone this
Christmas: this wine and anything by
Jim Crace. Perfect partners.

**Peter Lehmann Semillon,** `16` `£5–7`
Barossa 1999
Very faintly exotic, lime-tinged
richness to the fresh, lemon fruit.
Delicious charms here.

**Rothbury Estate Hunter** `16` `£5–7`
Valley Verdelho 1998
Class verdelho apricot/peach richness
– which will develop well in bottle for
a couple of years – gives this wine real
charm. It's dry, tangy, ripe, and great
with mild oriental food.

**Rufus Stone Sauvignon** `13.5` `£5–7`
Blanc 1999
Sharp.

**Seaview Chardonnay,** `14` `−£5.00`
McLaren Vale 1998
Very fresh and tangy and great with
food.

**Tatachilla Sauvignon** `15.5` `£5–7`
Semillon, McLaren Vale
& Adelaide Hills 1998

**Wirra Wirra 'Sexton's** `15` `£5–7`
Acre' Unwooded
Chardonnay, McLaren
Vale 1999
Still young – and maybe needs a year
to concentrate itself – but delicious
under-ripe melon and lime fruit here.

**Wirra Wirra W2 Riesling** `14` `−£5.00`
1998
Curious tang to it, but wonderful with
oriental fish dishes.

**Wolf Blass South** `16` `£7–10`
Australia Barrel
Fermented Chardonnay
1999
Nutty, rich, unrestrainedly youthful
and zippy, and utterly tongue-
tinglingly slurpable. It has, withal,
curiously Burgundian undertones.

**Wolf Blass South** `16` `£7–10`
Australia Chardonnay
1999
Has a restrained buttery bravado.

**Yarra Valley Hills Kiah** `12.5` `£7–10`
Yallambee Chardonnay
1998

## SAFEWAY WHITE

**Annie's Lane Semillon,** `15.5` `£5–7`
Clare Valley 1999
Strides across the taste buds freshly,
nuttily, fruitily and very satisfyingly.
77 stores.

**Australian Chardonnay/** `12` `−£5.00`
Colombard 1999, Safeway

**Australian Oaked**   15   −£5.00
**Chardonnay 1999,**
**Safeway**
Full of all-embracing, fruity charms.
Quite delicious.

**Basedow Semillon,**   16.5   £5–7
**Barossa Valley 1998**
A real mouthful of stylish, gung-ho
fruit which, magically, never becomes
boringly OTT.

**Capel Vale Unwooded**   15   £7–10
**Chardonnay 1999**
Very elegant and easy going. Top 145
stores.

**Capel Vale Verdelho 1999**   16   £7–10
Wonderful concentrated vintage for
this warmly coated, subtly spicy wine.
Top 28 stores.

**CV Chenin Blanc 2000**   16   £5–7
Deliciously richly textured and gently
smoky. Perfect for garlic scallops and
clams.

**Endeavour Barrel-**   14.5   £7–10
**fermented Chardonnay**
**1998**
Creamy ripeness here. Good with
Chinese food. Selected stores.

**Goundrey Reserve**   16.5   £10–13
**Selection Chardonnay**
**1998**
Expensive but very purposeful and
complex. The wood is urgent but
submits to the rich fruit. So the finish
is striking. Selected stores.

**Hardys Nottage Hill**   15   −£5.00
**Chardonnay 1999**
Brighter and fresher than previous
vintages. Superb purity of fruit!

**Jindalee Chardonnay,**   16   −£5.00
**Murray-Darling Region**
**1998**

Huge fun: spicy, cultured, beautifully
plump and textured yet not over-ripe
and the finish is lingering and
evocative.

**Lindemans Bin 65**   16.5   −£5.00
**Chardonnay 1999**
Simply one of the tastiest, classiest
examples of grape under-a-fiver in the
world.

**Loxton Low Alcohol**   11   −£3.50
**Chardonnay (1.2% vol)**

**Mamre Brook**   16   £5–7
**Chardonnay 1999**
Terrific pulsating melon richness. Yet
it's balanced and sane.

**Ninth Island Sauvignon**   14   £7–10
**Blanc, Tasmania 1999**
Expensive treat – though it does finish
oddly.

**Penfolds Bin 21 Rawson's**   14   −£5.00
**Retreat Semillon/**
**Colombard/Chardonnay**
**1999**
A real mouthful of fruity grapes – in
name and nature.

**Penfolds Eden Valley**   13.5   £7–10
**Reserve Riesling 1999**
Bit numb, as yet. Cellar it for two
years. It'll come round and score much
higher. 28 stores.

**Peter Lehmann 'The**   16   £5–7
**Barossa' Semillon 1999**
What a marvellous mouthful. Has a
very subtle smoke and mineral edge
with a faraway hint of pineapple. It'll
age for years too. So put some down
for 2008.

**Peter Lehmann Vine Vale**   13   −£5.00
**Riesling, Barossa Valley**
**2000**

Oddly uncouth on the finish for Mr Lehmann.

**Riddoch Coonawarra** `15` `£5-7`
**Chardonnay 1998**
Very warmly textured and rich, hot and buttery on the tongue, and needs food to temper this enthusiasm for all-embracing flavoursomeness.

**Robertson Barrel** `13` `-£5.00`
**Fermented Colombard 1999**

**Rosemount Show** `15` `£7-10`
**Reserve Chardonnay 1998**
Expensive creamy treat. At most stores.

**Rothbury Estate Hunter** `16` `£5-7`
**Valley Verdelho 1999**
Class Verdelho apricot/peach richness – which will develop well in bottle for a couple of years – gives this wine real charm. It's dry, tangy, ripe, and great with mild oriental food.

**Taltarni Sauvignon** `15.5` `£5-7`
**Blanc, Victoria 1999**
A moody Sauvignon combining baked melon richness with fine mineral-edged dryness.

**Tatachilla Breakneck** `16` `-£5.00`
**Creek Chardonnay 1999**
Almost a yoghurt ripeness here. Great with mood and/or food, it's an assertive wine of some style.

**Tatachilla Chardonnay** `16` `£7-10`
**1998**
Good woody creamy richness here, and it lingers lushly and delightfully. 77 stores.

**Tatachilla Padthaway** `16` `£5-7`
**Chardonnay 1999**

The rampancy is controlled on the finish. Marvellous! Selected stores.

**Woolshed Chardonnay,** `16` `£5-7`
**Coonawarra 1998**
The tang of minerals is very subtle. Mostly it's the gorgeous texture which impacts greatest – and the gently lush fruit.

## SAINSBURY'S WHITE

**Australian Chardonnay** `16` `-£5.00`
**NV, Sainsbury's**
Superb value for money. Great richness and acidic balance here. Remarkable value.

**Brown Brothers Late** `16.5` `£5-7`
**Harvested Orange**
**Muscat & Flora 1999**
**(half-bottle)**
It's the gorgeous honeyed hard-fruit acids which make it so exceptional as a pudding wine. Great with ice cream. Selected stores.

**Hardys Chardonnay** `15.5` `£5-7`
**Sauvignon Blanc 1999**
Lush yet light, potent yet delicate, focused yet multifaceted. A delightful conundrum. Selected stores.

**Hardys Stamp of** `15.5` `-£5.00`
**Australia Chardonnay**
**Semillon (3 litre box)**
Delicious fruit, ripe yet not overflowing, dry yet quietly and unambitiously rich and relaxed. A first class welcome-home-from-the-coalface thirst quencher and mood enhancer. Not at all stores. The price band reflects the equivalent price for a 75cl bottle.

Hardys Stamp of `15.5` `–£5.00`
Australia Riesling
Gewurztraminer 1999
Off-dry style which admirably suits
Peking duck.

Lindemans Limestone `16.5` `£5–7`
Coast Chardonnay 1999
Wonderful surge of lemon, lime,
raspberries, spice and rich melon, plus
a very subtle echo of greengage. A
fantastic Chardonnay for the money.
Selected stores.

Penfolds Botrytis `15` `£5–7`
Semillon 1998 (half-
bottle)
Gorgeous honeyed, almost sweet-
marmalade richness. Great with blue
cheese and foie gras. 50 stores.

Penfolds Koonunga Hill `16` `£5–7`
Chardonnay 1999
One of the best vintages of this brand
for some years. Has a gripping
elegance to it of demure ripeness and
class. Selected stores.

Penfolds Organic `15.5` `£7–10`
Chardonnay Sauvignon
Blanc 1999
A stylish construct of lemon/melon
fruit and handsome texture. 70 stores.

Penfolds Rawsons `15` `–£5.00`
Retreat Bin 202 Riesling
1999
Delicious ripe fruit with gentle pineapple and lemon acids. Not at all stores.

Penfolds Rawsons `15` `–£5.00`
Retreat Semillon/
Chardonnay/ Colombard
1999
One of Australia's great blends, sem
and chard, and this example, whilst
hardly subtle, has some attractive
elements. Most stores.

Petaluma Bridgewater `16` `£7–10`
Mill Chardonnay 1998
Turns and twists in its fruity layered
richness and thus provides a helter-
skelter of sensations for the palate –
going from gooseberry tanginess to
ripe melon moodiness. 75 stores.

Petaluma Chardonnay `13` `£13–20`
1998
Not fifteen quid. No, never. 30 stores.

Peter Lehmann The `16.5` `£5–7`
Barossa Semillon 1999
What a marvellous mouthful. Has a
very subtle smoke and mineral edge
with a faraway hint of pineapple. It'll
age for years too. So put some down
for 2008. Selected stores.

Rosemount Estate `16` `£5–7`
Diamond Label
Chardonnay 1999
Ripe and rich, but not over-rampant.
Intensely pleasing fruitiness on the
finish. At most stores.

Rosemount Estate Show `14` `£7–10`
Reserve Chardonnay
1999
Lot of money but it tries to be a lot of
wine. It's not OTT and the melonosity
of the fruit is elegant, but a tenner is
serious money. Selected stores.

Stowells of Chelsea `15.5` `–£5.00`
Australian Chardonnay
NV (3 litre box)
Excellent buttery richness allied to dry
yet soft acids and the finish is lingering
and never too lush. A balanced serious
specimen. The price band reflects the
equivalent price for a 75cl bottle.

Tatachilla Breakneck `16` `–£5.00`
Creek Chardonnay 1999
Almost a yoghurt ripeness here. Great

with mood and/or food, it's an assertive wine of some style.

**Tyrrells Old Winery Chardonnay 1999**   `14`  `£5–7`
Pleasant, cool, collected, not remotely Aussie in finish. It trembles rather than pulsates with fruit. 100 stores.

## SOMERFIELD WHITE

**Australian Chardonnay 1999, Somerfield**   `15.5`  `–£5.00`

**Australian Semillon/ Chardonnay 1999, Somerfield**   `14.5`  `–£5.00`
A richly engaging pasta plonk, especially those with tomato sauces.

**Banrock Station Chardonnay 1999**   `14`  `–£5.00`
Hints of spiced pear to the rich, ripe ogen melon fruit. Great with scallops and seaweed.

**Banrock Station Colombard Chardonnay 1999**   `15`  `–£5.00`
Much better vintage! The '99 is rich yet balanced, ripe and melony with good pineapple acidity.

**Hardys Chardonnay Sauvignon Blanc 1998**   `15`  `£5–7`
A solid blend of each grape's more distinguished virtues. Limited distribution.

**Hardys Padthaway Chardonnay 1996**   `16`  `£7–10`
Do you like Meursault? You'll like this, then. This kind of woody, hay-rich, vegetal fruitiness is a miracle under eight quid. Top 200 stores.

**Hardys Stamp of**   `15`  `–£5.00`
**Australia Chardonnay Semillon 1999**
Very gentle toffeed edge, almost like butterscotch. But the lemon acids compete.

**Hardys Stamp of Australia Riesling Gewürztraminer 1999**   `15.5`  `–£5.00`
Off-dry style which admirably suits Peking duck.

**Hardys Stamp Semillon/ Chardonnay 1999**   `15`  `–£5.00`
The usual buttery richness which stays the sane side of OTT. Delicious with food.

**Jacobs Creek Semillon/ Chardonnay 1999**   `15.5`  `–£5.00`
One of the best of this blend of grapes, under a fiver. Purposeful and nicely plump on the finish.

**Jindalee Chardonnay 1999**   `16`  `–£5.00`
Lovely gripping texture and warmly woven melon, cherry, peach and pineapple fruit. Touch of exotic spice on the finish, too.

**Lindemans Bin 65 Chardonnay 1999**   `16.5`  `–£5.00`
Simply one of the tastiest, classiest examples of grape under-a-fiver in the world.

**Lindemans Padthaway Chardonnay 1999**   `16.5`  `£7–10`
When they write the book on great Oz Chardonnays under a tenner, this specimen will be near the top.

**Loxton Lunchtime Light Chardonnay (4% vol)**   `12`  `–£3.50`

**Penfolds Koonunga Hill Chardonnay 1999**   `16`  `£5–7`
Crisp, clean, classy.

Penfolds Rawsons    15   −£5.00
Retreat Semillon/
Chardonnay/Colombard
1999
One of Australia's great blends, Sem
and Chard, and this example, whilst
hardly subtle, has some attractive
elements.

## SPAR WHITE

Australian Semillon    16   −£5.00
Chardonnay 1999, Spar
Terrific oily fruit: bold, thick, rich and
purposeful. A positive pleasure-
providing mouthful.

Burraburra Hill    15.5   −£5.00
Chardonnay 1999, Spar
Big, fat and wide. Like a juicy slab of
melted butter. Great to spread on
food, like rich fish dishes.

Lindemans Bin 65    16.5   −£5.00
Chardonnay 1999
Simply one of the tastiest, classiest
examples of grape under-a-fiver in the
world.

## TESCO WHITE

Australian Chardonnay,    16   −£3.50
Tesco
Terrific value here, fully represented
by the exuberance of the blue rollers
on the label as much as by the tidal
wave of flavour in the fruit. Lush,
loving, warm, delicious.

Banrock Station    14   −£5.00
Chardonnay 1999
Better than the '98, that's for sure. The
toffeed richness is more controlled
thanks to some acidic presence.

Barramundi Semillon/    16   −£5.00
Chardonnay NV
Lovely oily fruit, hint of bellpepper
and mango, and the whole thing is
altogether more serious than the
playful label suggests. A great wine to
quaff or to match with oriental,
European or South American meat
and fish dishes. At most stores.

Blue Pyrenees Estate    16.5   £10–13
Chardonnay 1997
A big sticky wine where sticky
butterscotch fruit offers a fruit custard
finish of striking texture and tenacity.
Not subtle but not OTT either. It's
deeply meaningful and looking for a
relationship. Wine Advisor stores only.

Blues Point Semillon/    12.5   £5–7
Chardonnay 1998

Brown Brothers Dry    15   £5–7
Muscat 1999
Individual in character, remarkable in
its make-up: lemon sherbety, rich, dry,
hint of ripe Muscat grapes on the finish
slightly exotic and spicy. A delicious
aperitif.

Chapel Hill Unwooded    15.5   £5–7
Chardonnay 1998
Delicious buttery richness, plus a
subtle pastry-like edge to the fruit. An
immense slurper.

Clare Valley Riesling    15.5   −£5.00
1999, Tesco
Superb mineralised fruit, slightly
nervous edge (typical of the grape in
its new world manifestation) but
wholly convincing. It will age well,
developing a more intense expression,
over the next five to ten years, but you
may feel disinclined to wait.

Geoff Merrill Chardonnay    17   £7–10
Reserve 1995

Delicious Le Montrachet style Aussie with all the thrilling vegetality that implies but no sullenness on the finish. A brilliant wine of great class and world-class winemaking. Top 80 stores.

**Hardys Grenache/Shiraz Rosé 1999** `14` `–£5.00`

**Hardys Stamp of Australia Chardonnay Semillon 1999** `15` `–£5.00`
Very gentle toffeed edge, almost like butterscotch. But the lemon acids compete.

**Hunter Valley Semillon 1999, Tesco** `13.5` `£5–7`
Expensive, at six quid, when it's a £3.99 fruit style.

**Jacobs Creek Dry Riesling 2000** `14` `–£5.00`
It is very dry, too dry for oriental food, so it's a riesling for fish cakes, etc.

**Langhorne Creek Verdelho 1998, Tesco** `15.5` `–£5.00`

**Limited Release Barramundi Marsanne 1998** `16.5` `£5–7`
I love the big oily richness of this thickly textured, tautly designed wine. The fruit is dry peach with a hint of waxy pineapple.

**Lindemans Bin 65 Chardonnay 1999** `16.5` `–£5.00`
Simply one of the tastiest, classiest examples of grape under-a-fiver in the world.

**Lindemans Cawarra Chardonnay 1999** `15.5` `–£5.00`
Nice turn of richness on the back of the palate and it goes from ripe melon

to dusky pear and lemon. Not at all stores.

**McLaren Vale Chardonnay 1999, Tesco** `15` `£5–7`
Very rich and full – marvellous for food. Has melons, pineapples, lemons.

**Miranda White Pointer 1999** `15` `–£5.00`
Crisp, dry, flavoursome.

**Mount Pleasant Elizabeth Semillon 1994** `15.5` `£7–10`

**Ninth Island Chardonnay 1998** `14` `£7–10`
Ripe, nervous, expensive, drinkable, fish friendly.

**Normans Unwooded Chardonnay 1999** `16.5` `–£5.00`
Utterly gorgeous buttery, slightly baked richness and depth of fruit here. Awesomely Aussie – in the most discreet way.

**Oxford Landing Sauvignon Blanc 1999** `15` `–£5.00`
Keen and fresh with more than a hint of gooseberry.

**Pendulum Chardonnay 1999** `15` `–£5.00`
Made in stainless steel tanks (with chips of oak added) and bottled in what looks like steel (no added wood noticeable). The fruit is forward, creamy, ripe and very ready. Great with Thai food. Most stores.

**Penfolds Koonunga Hill Chardonnay 1999** `16` `£5–7`
Oh, I didn't like it when it went over a fiver but there's no gainsaying the general excellence of the wine's firm, fruit flow. It has two levels of flavour, and a good texture.

**Pewsey Vale Eden Valley** 15.5 £5–7
**Riesling 1999**
Delicious Aussie-style of the ancient
teutonic grape. Still minerally and
citric but has terrific warmth yet
freshness to it.

**Provenance Chardonnay** 13.5 £10–13
**1997**
Very rich and cloying and it fails to
finish with a balanced sense of poise or
passion. Wine Advisor stores only.

**Rosemount Chardonnay** 16 £5–7
**1999**
One of the most stylish Australian
whites in the country.

**Rosemount Sauvignon** 15 £5–7
**Blanc 2000**
Deliciously ripe yet fresh with that
tart, tight, terrific Sauvignon tang of
minerals and gooseberries. Echo of
lime in there, too.

**Rosemount Semillon/** 14 £5–7
**Sauvignon 1999**
A good fish wine with its fresh, tangy
fruit.

**Smithbrook Chardonnay** 15 £7–10
**1998**
Very soft and almost succulent, but
saved from this puppyish fate by the
gentle yet firm acids. Selected stores.

**Smooth Voluptuous** 15 –£5.00
**White NV, Tesco**

**St Hallett Poachers Blend** 16 –£5.00
**1998**
A thundering bargain here: dry (yet
rich), full (yet subtle and with some
complexity), cheap (yet expensive in
feel), classy (yet with a down-to-earth
unpretentious personality).

**Tasmanian Chardonnay** 13 £5–7
**1999, Tesco**

Curious schizophrenic fruit – can't
make up its mind whether it's an
overripe melon or an under-ripe
lemon.

**Tim Adams Riesling 1998** 16 £7–10
Very classy and very advanced
acidically (limey and mineral-tinged)
and it has years of development ahead
of it. But it is striking now – and
superb with smoked fish. 200 stores.

**Woolpunda Blue Rock** 15.5 –£5.00
**Chardonnay 1998**
Brilliant starter off the blocks, aroma
and rich fruit hit the front of the palate
biggishly, then a demure side is
apparent. Not at all stores.

**Yendah Vale** 12 –£5.00
**Chardonnay/Merlot Rosé**
**1999**
Curious fruit-juicy richness.

**David Traeger Verdelho,** 16 £7–10
**Victoria 1998**
A real spicy treat! Lovely pineapple/
citrus edging to ripe peach and pear
fruit. Great quaffing and oriental food
wine.

**Hardys Nottage Hill** 15.5 –£5.00
**Riesling 1998**
Lovely mineral acids and subtle hard
fruit flavours. Will age well (possibly
spectacularly – seven to eight years)
but it shows finesse and style now.
Only at Wine Rack.

**Oxford Landing** 15 –£5.00
**Sauvignon Blanc 1999**
Keen and fresh with more than a hint
of gooseberry.

**Penfolds Rawsons** 15 –£5.00

**Retreat Bin 202 Riesling
1999**
Delicious ripe fruit with gentle
pineapple and lemon acids.

**Pewsey Vale Riesling** 16 £5–7
**1997**
The satin texture is one thing, the
nigh-classic aroma is another
(something no European Riesling
acquires so young), and the finish is
yet another. Even so, you can cellar it
for five more years and who knows if
perfection won't emerge?

**Riddoch Coonawarra** 15 £5–7
**Chardonnay 1998**
Very warmly textured and rich, hot
and buttery on the tongue, and needs
food to temper this enthusiasm for all-
embracing flavoursomeness.

**Samuels Bay Riesling,** 16 £5–7
**Eden Valley 1997**
Very rich, thick fruit with a touch of
exoticism which will be brilliant with
oriental food.

**Tollana Unoaked** 15.5 –£5.00
**Chardonnay 1999**

## UNWINS WHITE

**Capel Vale C V** 15 £7–10
**Unwooded Chardonnay
1999**
Very elegant and easy going.

**David Wynn** 16 £5–7
**Chardonnay, S. Australia
1998**
Terrific acids and warm fruit. Quite
delicious.

**Grant Burge Late Harvest** 16 –£5.00
**Muscat 1997**
Menthol-laden, pineappley, very rich

and half-sweet. A wonderfully different
aperitif and Chinese food wine, with
sweet plum sauce.

**Grant Burge Old Vine** 14 £7–10
**Semillon, Barossa Valley
1997**

**Howcroft Bin 6000** 15.5 £5–7
**Verdelho 1998**
Gorgeous lushness without being
OTT. Great with Thai food.

**Ironstone Semillon** 17 £5–7
**Chardonnay 1999**
Superb minerals here. Quite
remarkably stylish and classy for the
money.

**Lindemans Botrytis** 16 £5–7
**Riesling 1997 (half-bottle)**
Lovely sweet honeyed fruit with an
undertone of ripe pineapple and juicy
raisins. A superb pudding wine in the
perfect half-bottle size for the lonely
hedonist sitting in front of blue cheese
and a big bunch of grapes.

**Oxford Landing** 15 –£5.00
**Sauvignon Blanc 1999**
Keen and fresh with more than a hint
of gooseberry.

**Oxford Landing Viognier** 16 £5–7
**1998**
Compelling argument for the grape
(Viognier) and the region (south Oz).
Gorgeously subtle yet rich apricot
fruit.

**Peter Lehmann The** 16.5 £5–7
**Barossa Semillon 1998**
Superbly elegant richness and ripeness
of expression without heaviness or
blatant fruitiness. Fine, elegant,
individual.

**Peter Lehmannn Vine** 15.5 –£5.00
**Vale Chenin Blanc 1998**

Very rich and vivacious. Marvellous oriental food wine.

**Rosemount Estate Diamond Label Chardonnay 1999** 16 £5–7
Ripe and rich, but not over-rampant. Intensely pleasing fruitiness on the finish.

**Stanton & Killeen Rutherglen Muscat NV (half-bottle)** 16 £5–7
Wonderful with ice cream.

**Stockman's Bridge White NV** 14 –£5.00
Crisp pineapple and melon fruit.

**Tim Gramp Watervale Riesling 1997** 16.5 £7–10
Riesling as striking as can be with its chewy minerals and rich, textured fruit.

**Tyrrells Long Flat Chardonnay 1999** 14 £5–7
Hint of sweetness on the finish.

**Wakefield Chardonnay, Clare Valley 1997** 13 £5–7

**Wakefield White Clare Crouchen/Chardonnay 1997** 14 £5–7
Ripe, clashing elements.

**Woodvale Chardonnay 1999** 15 –£5.00
Bargain richness here. Very calm and cool.

**Woodvale Semillon/Chardonnay 1999** 15.5 –£5.00
Utterly delicious. Superb texture and plump-edged fruit with lovely incisive acids. A vibrant wine of great style.

## VICTORIA WINE WHITE

**David Traeger Verdelho, Victoria 1998** 16 £7–10
A real spicy treat! Lovely pineapple/citrus edging to ripe peach and pear fruit. Great quaffing and oriental food wine. Selected stores.

**Hardys Nottage Hill Riesling 1998** 15.5 –£5.00
Lovely mineral acids and subtle hard fruit flavours. Will age well (possibly spectacularly – seven to eight years) but it shows finesse and style now.

**Lindemans Botrytis Riesling 1996 (half-bottle)** 17 £5–7
Magnificently alluring bouquet suggestive of spiced soft fruit. Thereafter it's like an eccentric Trockenbeerenauslese of unusual ripeness and limpidity.

**Mitchelton Chardonnay 1996** 15 £7–10

**Oxford Landing Sauvignon Blanc 1999** 15 –£5.00
Keen and fresh with more than a hint of gooseberry.

**Pewsey Vale Riesling 1997** 16 £5–7
The satin texture is one thing, the nigh-classic aroma is another (something no European riesling acquires so young), and the finish is yet another. Even so, you can cellar it for five more years and who knows if perfection won't emerge?

**Tollana Unoaked Chardonnay 1999** 15.5 –£5.00

**Wolf Blass South Australia Barrel** 16 £7–10

Fermented Chardonnay
1999
Nutty, rich, unrestrainedly youthful
and zippy, and utterly tongue-
tinglingly slurpable. It has, withal,
curiously Burgundian undertones.

**Wolf Blass South**    16    £7–10
**Australia Chardonnay**
**1999**
Has a restrained buttery bravado.

## WAITROSE WHITE

**Broken Bridge**    13    −£3.50
**Chardonnay/Colombard**
**1999**
Tries hard but how can you produce
an interesting Aussie white under
three quid? T'aint possible, mate.

**Broken Bridge**    14.5    −£3.50
**Colombard Chardonnay**
**1999**
Brilliant value fish-'n'-chip party
wine.

**Brown Brothers Late**    16.5    £5–7
**Harvested Orange**
**Muscat & Flora 1999**
**(half-bottle)**
It's the gorgeous honeyed hard-fruit
acids which make it so exceptional as a
pudding wine. Great with ice cream.

**Bushmans Crossing**    13.5    −£5.00
**Semillon/Chardonnay**
**1999**
Oddly uncertain on the finish.

**Chateau Tahbilk**    16    £5–7
**Unwooded Marsanne,**
**Victoria 1998**
Love its unashamed purity of full-fruit
freshness. Grapes all the way through
– no other influences are apparent.

Lovely richness and texture and a
lilting finish.

**Hardys Stamp of**    13.5    −£5.00
**Australia Grenache**
**Shiraz Rosé 1999**

**Houghton Classic Dry**    15.5    £5–7
**White 1998**

**Leasingham Domaine**    16    £5–7
**Chardonnay 1997**
Gorgeous gooseberry/melon/lemon
fruit.

**Nepenthe Vineyards**    14    £7–10
**Sauvignon Blanc 1999**
Lot of money. Limited branches.

**Oxford Landing**    14    −£5.00
**Sauvignon Blanc 2000**
Typical Sauvignon dryness and fish
friendliness.

**Pendulum Chardonnay**    15    −£5.00
**1999**
Made in stainless steel tanks (with
chips of oak added) and bottled in
what looks like steel (no added wood
noticeable). The fruit is forward,
creamy, ripe and very ready. Great
with Thai food.

**Penfolds Bin 95a**    13.5    £13–20
**Chardonnay**

**Penfolds Clare Valley**    15.5    £7–10
**Organic Chardonnay/**
**Sauvignon Blanc, 1998**
**(organic)**
Appealing blend of rich melonic
ripeness and cool citric crispness.

**Penfolds Old Vine**    16    £5–7
**Semillon, Barossa 1998**
I love the strident buttery richness as it
impacts on the buds and then the
stream of lush acidity which strikes the
throat.

Penfolds Rawson's 15 −£5.00
retreat Bin 202 Riesling
1999
Tangy and rich, will age interestingly
for a couple of years (screw-capped,
it'd be interesting for twenty years).

Petaluma Piccadilly 16.5 £13–20
Chardonnay 1998
Superb balance of elements with this
wine: one of Oz's classiest
Chardonnays.

Tatachilla Sauvignon/ 15 −£5.00
Semillon, McLaren Vale
1999
Very cool and collected and not your
usual buttery Aussie display.

Voyager Estate 17.5 £10–13
Chardonnay 1997
Remarkably chewy, ripe, creamy,
vegetal, outstandingly elegant and
hugely classy.

Wirra Wirra Oaked 17 £7–10
Chardonnay 1998
Superb class here really stretches what
Chardonnay can do without coming
apart. Lovely ripeness yet delicacy and
huge immediacy of impact. Drink it
young. It's wonderful young. Limited
branches.

## WINE CELLAR WHITE

Capel Vale Verdelho 1999 16 £7–10
Wonderful concentrated vintage for
this warmly coated, subtly spicy wine.

Hardys Stamp of 15 −£5.00
Australia Chardonnay
Semillon 1999
Very gentle toffeed edge, almost like
butterscotch. But the lemon acids
compete.

Heggies Chardonnay 16 £7–10
1997
Richness and depth and a lovely
creamy, woody feel. Subtle, single-
minded, substantial – a ravishing wine.

Three Steps Chardonnay 13.5 £5–7
1998
A most unusually thickly-fruited
Chardonnay (I nearly wrote cardie)
and the fruit is bruised and ripe. Needs
food, though the lack of acidity is a
problem . . . What food?

Wolf Blass President's 17 £7–10
Selection McLaren Vale
Chardonnay 1997
Big, smoky fruit of unabashed lushness
and woody richness. Marvellous with
rich fish dishes, salamis, poultry, and
torrid conversation.

# AUSTRIA

A boutique wine producer with an incorrigibly quaint streak up its backside. Produces some amusingly voluptuous sweet whites and one eminently quaffable red, Blauer Zweigelt, which has more guts and personality than the Beaujolais it resembles.

## TESCO RED

**Blauer Zweigelt Lenz Moser 1997**  `14.5`  `−£5.00`
Like a Beaujolais, only rawer and more naturally fruity (i.e. no sugar added to boost the alcohol). It's juicy and cherry and plum laden. Very refreshing. Very charming.

Disastrous name, gawky packaging, uncertain fruit – its rating is charity.

## TESCO WHITE

**Lenz Moser's Prestige Beerenauslese 1995 (half-bottle)**  `15`  `£5–7`

## ODDBINS WHITE

**Polz Grassnitzberg Grauburgunder 1998**  `11`  `£7–10`
Immensely unexciting for eight pounds.

## WAITROSE WHITE

**Bouvier Beerenauslese Munzenrieder 1996**  `12`  `£5–7`
The butterscotch sweetness fades into jejune acidity on the finish which mars the effect.

## SAFEWAY WHITE

**Cat's Leap Grüner Veltliner 1999**  `12`  `−£5.00`

# BULGARIA

The land which, as Thrace, supplied the Greek troops of the Trojan War with booze is emerging slowly from the dead hand and crippling mind-set of Communism. New ventures, new initiatives with wine co-operatives (with genuine worker and grape-grower shareholdings), and new investment in state-of-the-art equipment, all promise to create a new dynamic in this favourite source of some of the UK's most remarkable red wine bargains. I expect to see more and more branded wine ranges coming out of Bulgaria, and many of them will be outstanding.

## ASDA RED

Bulgarian Cabernet Sauvignon, Svichtov 1995, Asda   14   –£5.00

Bulgarian Country Red, Asda   14   –£3.50

Bulgarian Oak Aged Cabernet Sauvignon, Svichtov 1993, Asda   15   –£5.00

## BOOTHS RED

Boyar Cabernet Merlot 1998   12.5   –£3.50
Very juicy and dries out, and dies out, on the finish.

## CWS RED

Plovdiv Cabernet Sauvignon Rubin 1996   15.5   –£3.50

Pomorie Country Cabernet/Merlot 1998   15.5   –£3.50

Simply a masterpiece of deft gluggability. Yet, it has dry tannins to go with food.

Sliven Merlot/Pinot Noir NV   13.5   –£3.50

## KWIK SAVE RED

Boyar Merlot 1999   15   –£3.50
Immensely charming. Great tannins and warmth of fruit.

Bulgarian Cabernet Sauvignon 1999. Somerfield   13.5   –£3.50
Juicy yet dry.

Bulgarian Country Red NV, Somerfield   14   –£3.50
Dry, earthy cherries. Great chilled.

## MORRISONS RED

Boyar Bulgarian Gamza 1998   14   –£3.50

Boyar Iambol Cabernet `14.5` `-£3.50`
Sauvignon 1999
Bargain basement dry blackcurrants.

Boyar Premium Oak `13.5` `-£5.00`
Merlot 1997

Danube Red 1999 `13.5` `-£3.50`
Dry but rich and jammily textured.

## SAFEWAY RED

Azbuka Merlot 1996 `15` `£5-7`
Savoury, intensely so, and it packs a
wallop on the finish. Selected stores.

Bulgarian Country Red, `15.5` `-£3.50`
Merlot/Gamza 1999,
Safeway
Oh! What joyous fruit! It veritably
melts in the mouth.

Nazdrave Cabernet `15.5` `-£5.00`
Sauvignon 1999
Terrific! The new wave of Bulgars and
they're right up my street. This one is
dry yet blackcurranty, deftly tannic
without being Bordeaux about it and
deliciously well-textured.

Sapphire Cove NV `14.5` `-£3.50`
Marvellous dry richness and textured
fruit.

Suhindol Merlot Reserve `14` `-£5.00`
1996
Juicy, yes, touch obvious, yes,
unsubtle, yes – but . . . great with rich
food.

Young Vatted Cabernet `14` `-£3.50`
Sauvignon 1999, Safeway
Very juicy and jammy. Delicious with
Indian food.

Young Vatted Merlot `14.5` `-£3.50`
1999, Safeway
Merlot as all-embracingly fruity.

## SAINSBURY'S RED

Bulgarian Cabernet `15.5` `-£3.50`
Sauvignon, Sainsbury's
(3 litre box)
Terrific richness and typical cabernet
bell pepper dryness. An excellent study
in bargain fruit sufficiently meaty and
well formed to please any wine
drinker (at fifty pence a glass). The
price band reflects the equivalent price
for a 75cl bottle.

Bulgarian Country Dry `14.5` `-£3.50`
Red, Russe, Sainsbury's
(1.5 litre)
The price band reflects the equivalent
price for a 75cl bottle.

Bulgarian Merlot NV, `15.5` `-£3.50`
Sainsbury's
World's dullest wine label. Hiding
behind which is some delicious purple
fruit of style and wit. Most stores.

Domaine Boyar Premium `14` `-£5.00`
Oak Barrel Aged Merlot
1997

Domaine Boyar Premium `14.5` `-£5.00`
Reserve Cabernet
Sauvignon 1997
Cabernet as jammy yet dry, rich yet
fresh. Great glugging for stand-up
drinks parties. Most stores.

Domaine Boyar Premium `15` `-£5.00`
Reserve Merlot 1997
It's more Aussie in its soft ripeness
than many an Aussie. Remarkable
juice. Selected stores.

## SOMERFIELD RED

Boyar Merlot 1999 `15` `-£3.50`
Immensely charming. Great tannins
and warmth of fruit.

Bulgarian Cabernet `13.5` `−£3.50`
Sauvignon 1999,
Somerfield
Juicy yet dry.

Bulgarian Country Red `14` `−£3.50`
NV, Somerfield
Dry, earthy cherries. Great chilled.

Reserve Cabernet
Sauvignon 1996
Sweet with a bitter undertone.

Domaine Boyar Premium `14.5` `−£5.00`
Reserve Merlot 1996
Very ripe, rich and full. Not typically
merlot. Very quaffable and polished.

## SPAR RED

Bulgarian Country Wine `13` `−£3.50`
Cabernet Sauvignon &
Merlot NV, Spar
Good pasta plonk. Has some assertive
tannins.

## UNWINS RED

Country Wine Merlot/ `14` `−£3.50`
Pinot Noir NV, Sliven

## VICTORIA WINE RED

Domaine Boyar Premium `13.5` `−£5.00`
Oaked Cabernet Shumen
1997

## TESCO RED

Azbuka Cabernet `14` `£5–7`
Sauvignon 1994
Juicy, teeth-wrenching style. Jammy
and super-ripe. 100 selected stores.

Bulgarian Cabernet `14` `−£5.00`
Sauvignon Reserve 1995,
Tesco
Again, I'm not keen on the aroma but
I do like the vivid tannins and fruit.

Reka Valley Bulgarian `14.5` `−£3.50`
Cabernet Sauvignon NV,
Tesco
A really solid Cabernet with firm, rich
tannins. Absurdly impressive for the
risible price-tag.

Domaine Boyar Premium `14` `−£5.00`
Reserve Cabernet
Sauvignon 1996
Sweet with a bitter undertone.

Domaine Boyar Premium `14.5` `−£5.00`
Reserve Merlot 1996
Very ripe, rich and full. Not typically
merlot. Very quaffable and polished.

## WAITROSE RED

Domaine Boyar Merlot/ `15` `−£3.50`
Gamza, Iambol 1999
Brisk, touch brusque, brilliant value.

## THRESHER RED

Copper Crossing Red NV `14` `−£3.50`

Domaine Boyar Premium `13.5` `−£5.00`
Oaked Cabernet Shumen
1997

Domaine Boyar Premium `14` `−£5.00`

## WINE CELLAR RED

Domaine Boyar Cabernet `15.5` `−£3.50`
Sauvignon NV
Hints of marzipan to the deliciously
ripe fruit (plums and blackcurrants)
and the tannins are impressively
congealed.

**Domaine Boyar** `14` −£3.50
**Cabernet/Merlot 1998**
Bargain quaffing. Has a dry underbelly
but it's mostly hedgerows and happy-
juice.

**Domaine Boyar Reserve** `14.5` −£5.00
**Merlot/Gamza 1996**
Lovely texture and very lingering
tannins which hold the fruit on the
taste buds for some time after the
liquid has quit the throat.

## KWIK SAVE WHITE

**Bulgarian Country White** `14.5` −£3.50
**1999, Somerfield**
An excellent blend of crispness and
soft melonicity.

## MORRISONS WHITE

**Boyar Pomorie** `10` −£3.50
**Chardonnay 1998**
Pretty ugly (as the French say).

## SAFEWAY WHITE

**Bulgarian Chardonnay,** `13` −£3.50
**Rousse 1999, Safeway**

**Bulgarian Country Wine,** `12.5` −£3.50
**Welschrizling/Rikat**
**1999, Safeway**

**Bulgarian Oaked** `10` −£5.00
**Chardonnay Reserve**
**1998, Safeway**
Do you like chewing planks?

**Preslav, Barrel** `16` −£5.00
**Fermented Chardonnay**
**1997**
Terrific spicy melon and lemon fruit.

Brilliantly textured and plump without
being obese.

**Valley of the Roses** `13` −£3.50
**Cabernet Sauvignon Rosé**
**1999**

## SOMERFIELD WHITE

**Bulgarian Chardonnay** `14` −£3.50
**1998, Somerfield**

**Bulgarian Country White** `14.5` −£3.50
**1999, Somerfield**
An excellent blend of crispness and
soft melonicity.

## SPAR WHITE

**Bulgarian Country White** `11` −£3.50
**NV, Spar**
Very cosmetic finish, powdery and a
little uncongenial.

## THRESHER WHITE

**Boyar Muskat & Ugni** `11` −£3.50
**Blanc NV**

**Copper Crossing Dry** `10` −£3.50
**White NV**
Rather like a cordial. Thresher Wine
Stores only.

**Copper Crossing Medium** `12` −£3.50
**White NV**
A medium rating, then. And no dry
remarks. Thresher Wine Stores only.

## UNWINS WHITE

**Country Wine Muskat &** `14` −£3.50
**Ugni Blanc, Shumen NV**

## VICTORIA WINE WHITE

Boyar Muskat & Ugni
Blanc NV    11  −£3.50

Copper Crossing Dry
White NV    10  −£3.50
Rather like a cordial.

Copper Crossing Medium    12  −£3.50
White NV
A medium rating, then. And no dry
remarks.

Domaine de Boyar    12  −£3.50
Targovischte
Chardonnay 1997

# CHILE

This paradise for grapes continues to keep the baton in its grasp and does not seem inclined to pass it on to anyone. I don't think it will relinquish its grip. The wines, for the greater part, are simply sublime, great value, complex without contortion, elegant without being prissy. That said, however, I am tasting an increasing number of routinely made red and white Chilean wines which smack horribly of mass production and overyields of grapes. These are invariably found at unfashionable retailers rushing, witlessly, to buy anything with Chile on the label.

## ASDA RED

**35 Sur Cabernet Sauvignon 1999**   17   −£5.00
Utter magic. Dark, rich, firm yet supple, wonderfully seriously fruity (leather, spice, blackcurrants) and hugely lingering. Brilliant for the money, quite brilliant. Selected stores.

**Casas del Bosque Merlot 1999**   14   £5–7
Juicy ripeness.

**Castillo de Molina Cabernet Sauvignon 1998**   15.5   £5–7
Immensely friendly and soft. It really charms the taste buds, almost sweet-talks them.

**Chilean Cabernet Sauvignon 1999, Asda**   16.5   −£5.00
So drinkable and well-knit it performs like a wine costing a good deal more. Great texture, richness and warm, aromatic fruit.

**Chilean Red 1997, Asda**   14.5   −£3.50

**Cono Sur Merlot 1999**   16   −£5.00
It's the rich, soft texture which carries the points. The fruit is in decent plummy shape, too, but the sheer velvet of the delivery is superlative.

**Cono Sur Merlot Reserve 1999**   16.5   £5–7
Not chilly or austere like cabernet from Bordeaux but warm, friendly, full, and huge fun. Wonderful quaffing here.

**Cono Sur Pinot Noir 1999**   16   −£5.00
Fantastic Pinot profile: rich, elegant, thorny, classic . . . and with typical Chilean extra richness and texture.

## BOOTHS RED

**Carmen Grande Vidure Cabernet Sauvignon 1998**   16.5   £7–10
Rousingly perfumed, nobly leathery and cassis fruit, with piles of fruity texture. A lovely wine.

**Cono Sur Pinot Noir 1998**   16.5   −£5.00

Very rich and ripe, not classic, but feral raspberries and truffles are detectable and the texture is super-deep. But it elevates itself over ten thousand red Burgundies asking five times more.

**Vistasur Cabernet Malbec** 14 −£5.00
**1998**
Very jammy and taste-bud-spreadable. Needs robust, spicy food.

## BUDGENS RED

**Antu Mapu Merlot 1998** 15 −£5.00
Stalky, ripe, touch of elegance on the finish but it's mostly controlled fruit of some style.

**Antu Mapu Merlot** 14 £5–7
**Reserva 1998**

**Millaman Cabernet** 13 £5–7
**Malbec 1998**
Touch expensive for the style.

**Millaman Merlot 1999** 14 £5–7
Ripe but friendly.

**Stowells of Chelsea** 14.5 −£5.00
**Cabernet Merlot NV**
Very thick and creamily clotted with prunes and blackberries. Great for robust meat dishes. South America chillied chicken would be perfect.

**Terra Andina Cabernet** 14 −£5.00
**Merlot 1999**
Hint of pepper, touch of the sun, suggestion of leather and plums.

**Terra Andina Cabernet** 14 −£5.00
**Sauvignon 1998**
Very big and fruity. Good spicy sausage wine.

**Vina Gracia Cabernet** 15 −£5.00
**Sauvignon 1998**

Soupy and warm, thickly textured, full of richness.

## CWS RED

**Antares Merlot 1998** 16 −£5.00
Touch of spice to the leather but it's the grip of the wine, the sheer effrontery of the texture, which wins it. Not at Convenience Stores.

**Casa Lapostolle Merlot** 17.5 £10–13
**Cuvee Alexandre 1997**
One of the world's most delicious Merlots, it is also stonking good value and unusually health-giving. A remarkable performer (for heart and soul).

**Chilean Cabernet** 15 −£5.00
**Sauvignon, Co-op**
So unusually well polished and proper, it's like a schoolchild with a perfectly knotted tie. Yet it reveals, at the death, some rich character.

**Chilean Fair Trade** 15.5 −£5.00
**Carmenere 2000, Co-op**
Touch of spicy yoghurt to the fruit as it descends is only the last act of a drama which is fruity, entertainingly layered and ripe, and very involving.

**La Palmeria Cabernet** 16 −£5.00
**Sauvignon 1998**
More like a Merlot in its leathery odiferousness and softness. Utterly delicious, civilised tannins.

**La Palmeria Merlot Gran** 17 £7–10
**Reserva 1998**
Such lush class! Beautiful texture, like crumpled velvet, lovely leather aroma and rich fruit.

**Las Lomas Cot Rouge** 15 £5–7
**Reserva 1998**

Superbly juicy and rich. Why it's called Cot rather than Malbec (same grape) I know not unless it's supposed to resemble Cahors (which it doesn't). Superstores only.

**Las Lomas Organic** 16 £5–7
**Chilean Red, Vinas Viejas**
**1998**
Spicy, nutty, tannic, ripe, individual, generous, warmly textured: an audacious performance. Superstores only.

**Long Slim Cabernet** 16 −£5.00
**Merlot 1999**
Bargain claret-style undertone but it's the Chilean warmth and wit (in the merlot component especially) which hogs the limelight as the delicious fruit quits the throat.

**Old Vines Carignan 1999,** 14 −£5.00
**Co-op**
Hugely gluggable (and chillable for fish dishes). Not at Co-op Convenience stores.

**Terramater Malbec 1999** 15.5 −£5.00
Hint of spice to the cherries and blackberries, touch of herb, suggestion of earth – plus tannins. Superstores only.

**Vina Gracia Cabernet** 15.5 £5–7
**Sauvignon Reserve 1999**
Bitter chocolate and dark cherries is the theme played on deep pile carpet fruit of substance and longevity. Superstores only.

**Vina Gracia Carmenere** 16 −£5.00
**Reserve Especial 1999**
Vibrant, sexy, textured, beautifully harmonised elements (fruit, tannins, acids) and a real flurry of delicious acidity on the finish.

**Vina Gracia Merlot 1998** 16 −£5.00
Open, hearty, welcoming, rich, soft and leathery, this is an utterly luscious merlot of consummate quaffability.

## KWIK SAVE RED

**Chilean Cabernet** 16.5 −£5.00
**Sauvignon Vina La Rosa**
**1999, Somerfield**
The warmth and generosity of the fruit and the tannins are meaningful enough, but there is also the beauty of the subtle wood touches to consider. Very classy wine.

## M&S RED

**Casa Leona Cabernet** 16.5 −£5.00
**Sauvignon 1999**
Real posh fruit here with only the generosity of the cocoa and cassis undertone giving us the clue it's Chile and not Château Lafite.

**Casa Leona Merlot 1999** 16 £5–7
One of the most delightfully quaffable Merlots it is possible to conceive.

**Sierra Los Andes Merlot** 16 £5–7
**Cabernet 1999**
The strawberry food aroma only kids you: it's serious stuff here with piles of flavour, true, but under it some gorgeous rich fruit of vivacity and vim.

**Sierra Los Andes Merlot** 15 £5–7
**Cabernet Reserve 1998**
Sweeter, oddly, than the non-reserve wines but still a high-ranking specimen of elegance and length. It has a languorous, almost casual, fruitiness and demeanour.

## MAJESTIC RED

**Luis Felipe Edwards
Pupilla Cabernet
Sauvignon 1999**   `14`  `−£5.00`
The Aussie now making these wines
for Senor Edwards has made changes
to the style. It's lusher and less well
disciplined. I rate it lower.

**Montes Alpha Merlot
1997**   `14`  `£7–10`

**Santa Rita Reserva
Cabernet Sauvignon,
Maipo 1997**   `16`  `£5–7`
Classy, correct, cosy, composed,
concentrated – it hits all the right high
Cs.

**Santa Rita Triple C 1997**   `17`  `£10–13`
Full of densely-packed, gently savoury
plums and pear and apricots and
leather – and earthy tannins. Like a
crazy claret.

**Valdivieso Barrel
Selection Malbec 1999**   `16`  `£5–7`
So soft and stealthy it slips down
remarkably swiftly but then the
residue of the fruit strikes home.

**Valdivieso Barrel
Selection Merlot 1998**   `17`  `£5–7`
Wonderful happy juice here: leather,
spice, tannins, blackberries and plums
and a hint of cinnamon and a lingering
finish. Very new world. Very delicious.

**Vistasur Cabernet
Sauvignon 1998**   `15.5`  `−£5.00`

## MORRISONS RED

**35 Sur Cabernet
Sauvignon 1998**   `15`  `−£5.00`
The most vegetally interesting Chilean
Cabernet I've tasted all year. Excellent
food wine.

**Antares Merlot 1999**   `13.5`  `−£5.00`
Again, a lot of juicy fruit.

**Castillo de Molina
Reserve Cabernet
Sauvignon 1998**   `16`  `£5–7`
Delicious layers of ripely textured,
cassis-edged fruit which expand and
contract on the taste buds with great
effect. Rousing, complex finish.

**Curioso Gracia de Chile
Merlot 1998**   `16`  `−£5.00`
Very stalky, atypical Merlot, with an
almost pea-pod peppery edge to the
fruit. The tannins are intense and
interesting. The finish is dramatic, dry.
A very food friendly wine.

**'M' Chilean Cabernet
Sauvignon 1999**   `15`  `−£5.00`
Dry yet rich and rolling. Not elegant
but drinkable enough.

**Undurraga Merlot 1999**   `13`  `−£5.00`
Has some opening interest but the
fruit flags at the end.

**Villa Montes Cabernet
Sauvignon 1999**   `15.5`  `−£5.00`
Very ripe, severely pricey but very
entertaining. Lovely tannins.

**Vina Gracia Cabernet
Sauvignon 1998**   `15`  `−£5.00`
Soupy and warm, thickly textured, full
of richness.

**Vina Gracia Merlot 1998**   `16`  `−£5.00`
Open, hearty, welcoming, rich, soft
and leathery, this is an utterly
luscious merlot of consummate
quaffability.

## ODDBINS RED

**Carmen Reserve Grande** `16` `£5–7`
**Vidure Cabernet, Maipo**
**1997**
Very Bordeaux-like in its dry tannins.
But the blackcurrant fruit comes
zinging through.

**Carmen Reserve Merlot,** `16.5` `£7–10`
**Rapel 1998**
Such meat on the fruit! It's
breathtakingly delicious.

**Carmen Reserve Pinot** `16` `£7–10`
**Noir 1998**
Even Domaine de la Romanee Conti
would be impressed with this aromatic
aplomb.

**Casa Lapostolle Cabernet** `17` `£5–7`
**Sauvignon 1997**
Wonderful texture. Very exciting
experience.

**Casa Lapostolle Cuvee** `16.5` `£7–10`
**Alexandre Cabernet**
**Sauvignon 1997**
Superb chewy fruit.

**Casa Lapostolle Cuvee** `17.5` `£13–20`
**Alexandre Merlot, Rapel**
**1998**
An immense construct which as the
thoughtful taster gargles with it
around the molars is like some game
sauce of quite unusual savoury, ripe,
then sweet, then dry complexity. A
truly marvellous wine.

**Casa Lapostolle Merlot** `16.5` `£5–7`
**1998**
Gorgeous tannins.

**Cono Sur Reserve** `16` `£5–7`
**Cabernet Sauvignon 1999**
The final touch of arrogance is the
cassis and coffee as it descends.

**Errazuriz Merlot, Curico** `16.5` `£5–7`
**Valley 1999**
So textured, like ruffled velvet, that
you can't figure out how it grips so
lushly.

**Isla Negra Cabernet** `15.5` `–£5.00`
**Sauvignon, Rapel 1998**
Very catering chocolate coloured and
fruited – it'll give the claret lover
apoplexy.

**La Palmeria Merlot** `16.5` `£7–10`
**Cabernet Gran Reserva**
**1998**

**La Palmeria Reserve** `16.5` `£5–7`
**Cabernet Sauvignon/**
**Merlot 1998**
Juicy and dry to finish and between
these two contrasting features is a
rippling river of flavour.

**Santa Rita Medalla Real** `16` `£7–10`
**Cabernet Sauvignon 1998**
Dry, coffee-edged, rich fruit with
chewy tannins.

**Santa Rita Reserva** `16.5` `£5–7`
**Cabernet 1998**
Tongue-tinglingly tenacious and
tellingly complex. Remarkably lovely
texture.

**Santa Rita Reserva** `16.5` `£5–7`
**Merlot Unfiltered, 1999**
Mingles blackberries, raspberries and
strawberries – in with the dusky
tannins.

**Veramonte Cabernet** `16` `£5–7`
**Sauvignon, Alto de**
**Casablanca 1997**
Consummately concentrated, juicy,
fresh, fruity, characterladen, deep,
shallow, subtle, extravagant – how
many contradictions can a mouthful of
alcoholic grape juice contain?

Veramonte Merlot 1998 · 14 · £5–7
The juicy end of the Merlot spectrum.

Vina Porta Cabernet · 16.5 · –£5.00
Sauvignon, Maipo 1999
Superbly savoury and thickly textured
with chocolate and cigar-fume laden
fruit with a touch of leather and old
saddlebags. Wonderful!

Vina Porta Reserva · 17 · £7–10
Unfiltered Cabernet
Sauvignon 1995
Utterly stunningly savoury cabernet
with tannins, tenacity and sublime
typicity.

## SAFEWAY RED

35 Sur Cabernet · 15 · –£5.00
Sauvignon 1998
The most vegetally interesting Chilean
Cabernet I've tasted all year. Excellent
food wine.

Acacias Estate Merlot, · 14 · –£5.00
Maipo Valley 1998,
Safeway
Very stalky and dry but it gets really
rampant on the finish.

Carta Vieja Merlot 1999 · 14 · –£5.00
Unusually juicy and ripe Chilean. Very
forward. Most stores.

Castillo de Molina · 16 · £5–7
Cabernet Sauvignon
Reserva, Lontue 1998
So friendly and full of charm you
wonder how it can be the same
Cabernet Sauvignon which grows
elsewhere in the world. Top 157
stores.

Chilean Cabernet · 16.5 · –£5.00
Sauvignon 1999, Safeway
Quite superbly meaty fruit. Soft, ripe,

perfumed, very deep and warmly
textured.

Chilean Red 1999, · 15 · –£5.00
Safeway
Warm rubbery supple fruit of plummy
richness.

Concha y Toro Casillero · 16.5 · –£5.00
del Diablo Cabernet
Sauvignon, Maipo 1998

Cono Sur Cabernet · 14 · –£5.00
Sauvignon, Rapel Valley
1999
Very jammy and immediate.
Untypically Chilean.

Cono Sur Reserva Merlot · 16.5 · £5–7
1999
Not chilly or austere like cabernet
from Bordeaux but warm, friendly,
full, and huge fun. Wonderful quaffing
here. Most stores.

Errazuriz Cabernet · 17.5 · £5–7
Sauvignon, El Ceibo
Estate, Aconcagua 1998
Wonderful baked, brown fruit here,
full of fleshiness contained by a
delicious shellac of prime tannins.
Immense drinkability combined with
sublime, provocative richness. A
stunning wine.

Errazuriz Merlot Reserva, · 16 · £7–10
Don Maximiano Estate
Aconcagua, 1997
Beautifully tanned, high class leather
too soft for belief. Top 129 stores.

Errazuriz Syrah Reserva · 16 · £7–10
1998
In its rich purity of fruit it combines
the juiciness of Aussie shiraz with the
smoky tannins and deep dryness of the
northern Rhone. The result, I guess, is
uniquely Chilean. Selected stores.

CHILEAN RED

**Isla Negra Merlot 1998** `16.5` `£5-7`
What superb dryness yet riveting rich leathery fruit! It's marvellous drinking. Top 219 stores.

**Santa Rita Reserva** `16` `£5-7`
**Cabernet Sauvignon, Alto Jahull Vineyards Maipo 1997**
Rampant flavoursomeness and fullness. At most stores.

**TerraMater Zinfandel/** `16.5` `-£5.00`
**Syrah, Maipo 1998**
Gallops juicily over the taste buds in fairly rumbustious fashion, then it cools its heels, then it courses softly down the throat, and then, yes there is a further dimension, it leaves a lush, savoury afterglow. Top 157 stores.

**Valdivieso Cabernet** `17.5` `£7-10`
**Franc Reserve 1997**
It's wonderfully expressive of herbs, spice, vegetal fruit and ripe tannins.

**Valdivieso Malbec** `15.5` `£7-10`
**Reserve, Lontue 1996**

**Valdivieso Single** `16.5` `£7-10`
**Vineyard Merlot Reserve, Lontue 1998**
Heaven has arrived!

**Villard Estate Cabernet** `16` `£5-7`
**Sauvignon, Central Valley 1997**
Classic dryness, hint of vegetality, very long, richly tannic finish. Top 121 stores.

**Vina Morande Merlot** `15.5` `-£5.00`
**1999**

**Vina Morande Pinot Noir** `14` `-£5.00`
**1998**
Only the juiciness spoils the effect of the feral aroma and wild raspberry

flavour. For the price, though, more exciting than Nuits St Georges.

**Vina Morande Syrah 1998** `10` `-£5.00`
Too much sulphur in the bottle I tasted.

## SAINSBURY'S RED

**35 Sur Cabernet** `17` `-£5.00`
**Sauvignon 1999**
Utter magic. Dark, rich, firm yet supple, wonderfully seriously fruity (leather, spice, blackcurrants) and hugely lingering. Brilliant for the money, quite brilliant. Selected stores.

**Chilean Cabernet Merlot** `16` `-£5.00`
**NV, Sainsbury's (3 litre box)**
It's the best red in a box. It has oodles of flavour, toffeed and blackcurranty, with good acids and fine tannins. It is both a great food wine and a great quaffer. The price band reflects the equivalent price for a 75cl bottle.

**Chilean Merlot,** `16.5` `-£5.00`
**Sainsbury's**
Wonderful richness of tone, texture, and even a touch of soulfulness. A gorgeous, savoury, smooth wine of lingering depth.

**Chilean Red, Sainsbury's** `13` `-£5.00`

**La Palma Merlot Gran** `17` `£7-10`
**Reserva 1998**
Such lush class! Beautiful texture, like crumpled velvet, lovely leather aroma and rich fruit. 60 stores.

**Los Robles Carmenere** `16.5` `-£5.00`
**1999**
Staggeringly toothsome, meaty fruit with wonderful lingering richness of

roast partridge, truffle sauce and game-chips – plus a thick gravy. Not at all stores.

**MontGras Cabernet Sauvignon Reserva 1998**   `15.5`   `£5–7`
Always serious contenders, MontGras wines, this example no exception. It has heavy fruit, dry yet warm and rich, and the texture, though free-flowing, is full of interest and eddies of flavour. Selected stores.

**MontGras Carmenere Reserva 1998**   `14`   `£5–7`
A big food wine. Roast vegetables and melted cheese dishes and pungent risottos. 120 stores.

**MontGras Single Vineyard Syrah 1999**   `16`   `£5–7`
Outfruits many an Aussie Shiraz (certainly for the same money) and outlingers many a northern Rhone with the same grape. A soft, aromatic, very supple wine. 100 stores.

**MontGras Single Vineyard Zinfandel 1999**   `15`   `£5–7`
Has an unusual cherry spiciness and nutty edge on the finish. Not a typical zin – hugely quaffable, though. 100 stores.

**Terra Mater Zinfandel Shiraz 1999**   `16.5`   `–£5.00`
Gallops juicily over the taste buds in fairly rumbustious fashion, then it cools its heels, then it courses softly down the throat, and then, yes there is a further dimension, it leaves a lush, savoury afterglow. Most stores.

**Valdivieso Malbec 1998**   `16`   `–£5.00`
Deliciously simple and almost casually brilliant. The fruit is effortless, polished, unpretentious, gifted and downright delicious.

**Valdivieso Malbec Reserve 1998**   `16.5`   `£7–10`
Quite superbly lithe and tautly muscled. Warm and satisfying fruit, hint of spice to it, and a rolling finish of multi-layered depth. 135 stores.

**Valdivieso Merlot 1999**   `15.5`   `–£5.00`
Classic Chilean double act: richness and dryness in league with hedgerow fruits. Not classic Merlot, perhaps, but classic quaffing.

## SOMERFIELD RED

**Chilean Cabernet Sauvignon Vina La Rosa 1999, Somerfield**   `16.5`   `–£5.00`
The warmth and generosity of the fruit and the tannins are meaningful enough, but there is also the beauty of the subtle wood touches to consider. Very classy wine.

**Chilean Cabernet Sauvignon/Merlot Vina La Rosa 1999, Somerfield**   `16.5`   `–£5.00`
What a marvel of a marriage between Merlot and Cabernet. Spice, blackcurrants, leather, plums, and they're rolled up into a powerful knot of intense flavour.

**Chilean Merlot 1999, Somerfield**   `17`   `–£5.00`
It ignites in the mouth like a leather and spicy cherry/blackcurrant grenade. Hugely impressive depth and richness here.

**Cono Sur Cabernet Sauvignon Reserve 1998**   `17`   `£5–7`
Nothing reserved about the fruit. It pulsates with generosity and tongue-lashing tannic tenacity.

Cono Sur Pinot Noir 1999  `16`  `−£5.00`
Fantastic Pinot profile: rich, elegant, thorny, classic . . . and with typical Chilean extra richness and texture.

Isla Negra Merlot 1999  `16.5`  `£5–7`
Deeply delicious and warm-hearted fruit of gallant texture and great depth. Has a beautiful warmth to it.

## SPAR RED

Canepa Cabernet  `10`  `−£5.00`
Sauvignon 1998, Spar
The least arousing Chilean Cabernet I've tasted.

Canepa Merlot 1998, Spar  `15`  `−£5.00`
Hints of old leather to the lush fruit where tannins, like a dam, prevent the fruit bursting out. An interesting mouthful.

## TESCO RED

Altum Cabernet  `14`  `£7–10`
Sauvignon Reserve 1997

Altum Merlot Reserve  `14`  `£7–10`
1997

Canepa Zinfandel 1998  `14`  `−£5.00`

Chilean Cabernet  `16`  `−£5.00`
Sauvignon NV, Tesco
Chocolate with raspberry with a hint of earth and blackcurrant on the finish. And that's just the finish.

Chilean Cabernet  `16`  `−£5.00`
Sauvignon Reserve 1999, Tesco
Compellingly fruity – has a hint of coffee and cream to the blackcurrant as it quits the throat.

Chilean Merlot Reserve  `16`  `−£5.00`
1999, Tesco
Does the 16 say it all? Well, I might usefully add that this score takes into account the wine's superb balance and lingering, leathery fruit.

Chilean Red NV, Tesco  `15`  `−£3.50`

Cono Sur Pinot Noir 1999  `16`  `−£5.00`
Fantastic Pinot profile: rich, elegant, thorny, classic . . . and with typical Chilean extra richness and texture.

Cono Sur Pinot Noir  `14`  `£5–7`
Reserve 1996
Extraordinarily thick and balsamic-rich Pinot. Sticks to the palate very warmly.

Errazuriz Cabernet  `16.5`  `£7–10`
Sauvignon Reserva 1998
Hints of cigar box, spice, blackcurrants, raisins, liquorice and a very subtle lingering after-tang of coriander. Utterly delicious. Serious yet totally, captivatingly entertaining.

Errazuriz Merlot 1999  `16.5`  `£5–7`
Delicious quaffing and food-friendly merlot with piles of flavour and leathery undertones, touch of coffee and tobacco, and a lovely warm texture. Brilliant finish, lingering and thought-provoking.

Errazuriz Syrah Reserva  `16`  `£7–10`
1998
Beautifully aromatic, smooth, fruity and completely kitted out. Has hints of tobacco and cocoa to the voluptuous texture and the finish is highly cultured.

Isla Negra Cabernet  `16`  `−£5.00`
Sauvignon 1998
The jammy side of serious with its rich plums and ripe blackberries. Very

supple tannins. Delicious book-worm's bottle.

**Isla Negra Merlot 1999**  16.5  £5–7
Deeply delicious and warm-hearted fruit of gallant texture and great depth. Has a beautiful warmth to it. Top 220 stores.

**Mont Gras Quatro 1998**  15  £5–7
Very aggressive at first, then it softens, then it goes tannic and dry on the finish and then it turns almost sweet and rich. Terrific wine for dinner parties (vegetarian ones especially since the wine provides a sauce of its own).

**Montgras Merlot 1998**  16  –£5.00
Staggering good value here. The fruit is bold, leathery, hint of spice, firm and all in order from nose to throat. It energises the corpuscles and caresses the palate. At most stores.

**Salsa Cabernet Sauvignon 1999**  14  –£5.00
Cheap enough and reasonably cheerful. Good rich tannins which tighten on the fruit at the finish.

**Santa Catalina Cabernet Sauvignon 1999**  15.5  –£5.00
Takes its time. It flexes its fruit muscles slowly and richly, then the tannins clock in and start to work, then more layers of blackcurrant are revealed. An interesting experience.

**Santa Catalina Merlot 1999**  16  –£5.00
Very cigar-fumaceous riches here and the fruit, harnessing this aromatic intensity, is deep, rich, savoury and broad-shouldered. It is hardly a quaffing wine, it's far too concentrated

for that, but with roast meat and vegetable dishes it would be superb.

**Santa Ines Cabernet/ Carmenere Reserva, Legado de Armida 1999**  17.5  £5–7
Has a level richness and balanced tannicity which defies belief at this price level. The ruffled velvet texture is very classy, so are the finely meshed acids. A triumph of a wine. Totally convincing at three times the price.

**Santa Ines Cabernet/ Merlot 1998**  16  –£5.00
Unfair isn't it? A Cab/Merl this good at this price? So it's full and deep and rich and uncompromisingly fruity but it's classy with it. That's the decisive dimension.

**Stowells Chilean Cabernet/Merlot NV**  14.5  –£5.00
This production appears to have been produced by a committee but the fruit in the bottle is solid, meaty and full of typical Chilean nuances of fruit. Excellent texture.

**TerraMater Cabernet Sauvignon 1998**  16  –£5.00
Develops in graduated rivulets of flavour which linger and refresh, enliven and delight. A really gluggable Cabernet.

**Undurraga Familia Cabernet Sauvignon 1995**  14  £7–10

**Undurraga Pinot Noir 1999**  14  –£5.00
Not typical Pinot but a good rich mouthful of tannic tenacity.

**Valdivieso Cabernet Franc Reserve 1997**  17.5  £7–10
It's wonderfully expressive of herbs,

spice, vegetal fruit and ripe tannins.
Top 85 stores.

**Valdivieso Carignan 1999** 16 −£5.00
Lovely earthy fruit, herby and warm,
with a resounding sense of pleasure-
seeking demeanour. A terrific quaffing
wine – as well as going robustly with
food. Selected stores.

**Valdivieso Malbec** 16.5 £7–10
**Reserve 1997**
Gorgeous baked fruit texture which
hardens – encrusted with superb
tannins. Very rich and deep, full of
stylish edges, and hugely elegant
overall. Selected stores only.

## THRESHER RED

**Caliterra Cabernet** 15.5 −£5.00
**Sauvignon 1998**
Delicious amalgam of dark cherries,
blackcurrants, prunes and tannins.
Serious glugging, serious food wine.

**Casa Lapostolle Cuvee** 16.5 £7–10
**Alexandre Cabernet**
**Sauvignon 1997**
Superb chewy fruit.

**Casa Lapostolle Cuvee** 17.5 £10–13
**Alexandre Merlot 1997**

**Casa Lapostolle Merlot** 16.5 £5–7
**1998**
Gorgeous tannins.

**Concha y Toro Casillero** 16.5 −£5.00
**del Diablo Cabernet**
**Sauvignon 1998**
Consummately concentrated, juicy,
fresh, fruity, characterladen, deep,
shallow, subtle, extravagant – how
many contradictions can a mouthful of
alcoholic grape juice contain?

**Cono Sur Cabernet** 16.5 −£5.00
**Sauvignon, Rapel 1998**
Terrific tannins, evolved and vibrant,
combined with cassis and tobacco
fruitiness.

**Errazuriz Cabernet** 17.5 £5–7
**Sauvignon 1998**
Wonderful baked, brown fruit here,
full of fleshiness contained by a
delicious shellac of prime tannins.
Immense drinkability combined with
sublime, provocative richness. A
stunning wine.

**Errazuriz Reserva** 16 £7–10
**Cabernet Sauvignon 1997**
It is not as gripping yet it's more
expensive than the '98 non-reserve
Cabernet. Of course, it's still a fine,
elegant construct, rewarding to taste
and to enjoy with food. Wine Rack
only.

**Isla Negra Cabernet** 15.5 £5–7
**Sauvignon 1998**
Very catering chocolate coloured and
fruited – it'll give the claret lover
apoplexy.

**La Palmeria Cabernet/** 16 −£5.00
**Merlot 1998**
Very dark and savoury. A big-
shouldered wine which pulls its weight
with food.

**Las Colinas Cabernet** 15 −£5.00
**Merlot 1999**
Engagingly warm and ripe and really
packed with firm fruit.

**Las Colinas Chilean Red** 13.5 −£3.50
**NV**
Dry, mild, will be swamped by most
foods. Not at Wine Rack.

**Las Colinas Merlot 1999** 15 −£5.00

Lovely texture and sunniness of disposition. Good tannins help the fruit to a solid climax.

**Martins Don Rui** 13.5 £5–7
**Cabernet Sauvignon 1997**
Dries out on the palate a mite quickish from an excellent start.

**Santa Ines Legado de** 16.5 £5–7
**Armida Cabernet**
**Sauvignon Reserve 1997**
Almost dainty, at first sip, then it turns ferociously eloquent and rich in the back of the gullet and shows great dry character and teeth-clenchingly classy tannins.

**Santa Ines Legardo de** 16 £5–7
**Armida Reserve Malbec**
**1997**
Rich, gentle and powerful, very dry and lingering. Wine Rack and Bottoms Up only.

**Valdivieso Malbec 1998** 16 –£5.00
Deliciously simple and almost casually brilliant. The fruit is effortless, polished, unpretentious, gifted and downright delicious.

**Valdivieso Merlot 1999** 15.5 –£5.00
Classic Chilean double act: richness and dryness in league with hedgerow fruits. Not classic Merlot, perhaps, but classic quaffing.

**Valdivieso Reserve Pinot** 14.5 £7–10
**Noir 1996**
Good bright cherry-ripe fruit with some weight of texture. Not typical of the grape or Chile. Wine Rack and Bottoms Up only.

**Veramonte Cabernet** 16 £5–7
**Sauvignon 1997**
By far the most concentrated and convincing of the Veramonte wines:

rich dark chocolate fruit with humour and weight.

**Veramonte Merlot 1997** 14 £5–7
The juicy end of the Merlot spectrum.

## UNWINS RED

**Canepa Cabernet** 16 –£5.00
**Sauvignon/Malbec 1999**
Juicier than many a Chilean Cab/Mal but no bad thing to be different.

**Canepa Zinfandel 1999** 14 –£5.00
Savoury jam – with tannins.

**Carmen Cabernet** 16 –£5.00
**Sauvignon 1996**
Delicious, savoury, ripe plums, herbs, tannins and rich acids. Great texture and tearing fruit here.

**Casa Donoso Cabernet** 12.5 –£5.00
**Sauvignon Domaine**
**Oriental 1998**
Juicy and loose on the finish. Not typical, not elegant. I cannot see what appeals to Unwins in the Donoso wines, they are patently ill-equipped.

**Casa Donoso Reservado** 12 £5–7
**Cabernet Sauvignon 1998**
Juicy and jammy.

**Cono Sur Reserve Pinot** 16 £5–7
**Noir 1998**
Not classic Pinot but a terrific quaffing pinot – it even has delicious earthy tannins.

**Donoso Limited Edition** 13.5 £13–20
**1997**
At last! A thoroughbred tasting Donoso wine. But at seven pounds, not seventeen.

**Errazuriz Cabernet** 17.5 £5–7
**Sauvignon 1998**

CHILEAN RED

Stunning lushness yet extruded
elegance – superb texture and heart-
stoppingly delicious blackcurrant
richness.

**Errazuriz Merlot 1999**  16.5  £5–7
Vivacious and full of delicious twists
and turns – of raspberry, leather,
cherry, subtle spices, and warm
tannins. A superb Merlot.

**Errazuriz Syrah Reserva**  16  £7–10
**1998**
Big, berried fruit, rugged yet
immensely soft, huge depth, flavour
and commanding richness. This is
even better than it was in the summer
of '98 when I first tasted it.

**Gracia Merlot Reserve,**  16.5  £7–10
**Aconcagua 1997**
Huge depth of flavour here, leather/
blackcurrant/plum, and great
developed tannins. Brilliant tone,
polish, character and style.

**La Palmeria Merlot 1999**  17  –£5.00
Fantastic savoury fruit of dryly
textured tenacity and great aplomb. A
lovely tobacco-edge to the fruit gives it
complexity, class and cohesion with
the warmth of the tannins.

**Penta Morande Cabernet**  16.5  –£5.00
**Sauvignon/Malbec 1999**
What a bargain! Lush tannins, pacy
blackcurrants, incisive acids – all
wrapped in a thick textured coat.

**Valdivieso Cabernet**  17.5  £7–10
**Franc Reserve 1997**
Wonderfully expressive of herbs, spice,
vegetal fruit and ripe tannins.

**Vina Porta Cabernet**  16.5  –£5.00
**Sauvignon, Maipo 1999**
Superbly savoury and thickly textured
with chocolate and cigar-fume laden

fruit with a touch of leather and old
saddlebags. Wonderful!

**Vina Porta Limited**  15  –£5.00
**Edition Merlot 1998**
Galloping fruit, frisky and energetic.
Perfectly rich and ripe and drinkable.

**Vina Porta Reserve**  16  –£5.00
**Cabernet Sauvignon 1998**
Terrific tannic richness and solid,
meaty fruit. Utterly convincing.

## VICTORIA WINE RED

**Casa Lapostolle Cuvee**  16.5  £7–10
**Alexandre Cabernet**
**Sauvignon 1997**
Superb chewy fruit.

**Casa Lapostolle Cuvee**  17.5  £10–13
**Alexandre Merlot 1997**

**Casa Lapostolle Merlot**  16.5  £5–7
**1998**
Gorgeous tannins.

**Cono Sur Cabernet**  16.5  –£5.00
**Sauvignon, Rapel 1998**
Terrific tannins, evolved and vibrant,
combined with cassis and tobacco
fruitiness.

**Cono Sur Pinot Noir 1998**  14.5  –£5.00

**Errazuriz Cabernet**  17.5  £5–7
**Sauvignon 1998**
Wonderful baked, brown fruit here,
full of fleshiness contained by a
delicious shellac of prime tannins.
Immense drinkability combined with
sublime, provocative richness. A
stunning wine.

**Errazuriz Reserva**  16  £7–10
**Cabernet Sauvignon 1997**
It is not as gripping yet it's more
expensive than the '98 non-reserve

70

cabernet. Of course, it's still a fine, elegant construct, rewarding to taste and to enjoy with food.

**Isla Negra Cabernet Sauvignon 1998** `15.5` `£5–7`
Very catering chocolate coloured and fruited – it'll give the claret lover apoplexy.

**La Palmeria Cabernet/ Merlot 1998** `16` `£5–7`
Very dark and savoury. A big-shouldered wine which pulls its weight with food.

**Las Colinas Cabernet Merlot 1999** `15` `–£5.00`
Engagingly warm and ripe and really packed with firm fruit.

**Las Colinas Chilean Red NV** `13.5` `–£3.50`
Dry, mild, will be swamped by most foods.

**Las Colinas Merlot 1999** `15` `–£5.00`
Lovely texture and sunniness of disposition. Good tannins help the fruit to a solid climax.

**Martins Don Rui Cabernet Sauvignon 1997** `13.5` `£5–7`
Dries out on the palate a mite quickish from an excellent start.

**Valdivieso Malbec 1998** `16` `–£5.00`
Deliciously simple and almost casually brilliant. The fruit is effortless, polished, unpretentious, gifted and downright delicious.

**Valdivieso Merlot 1999** `15.5` `–£5.00`
Classic Chilean double act: richness and dryness in league with hedgerow fruits. Not classic Merlot, perhaps, but classic quaffing.

**Valdivieso Reserve Pinot Noir 1996** `14.5` `£7–10`
Good bright cherry-ripe fruit with some weight of texture. Not typical of the grape or Chile.

**Veramonte Cabernet Sauvignon 1997** `16` `£5–7`
By far the most concentrated and convincing of the Veramonte wines: rich dark chocolate fruit with humour and weight.

**Veramonte Merlot 1997** `14` `£5–7`
The juicy end of the Merlot spectrum.

## WAITROSE RED

**Carmen Nativa Cabernet Sauvignon 1998 (organic)** `15` `£7–10`
Very jammy but the resilience of the earthy tannins gives it brilliance and backbone. Not at all stores.

**Errazuriz Merlot 1999** `16` `£5–7`
Controlled yet rampant. Delightful attack of soft leathery fruit.

**Gracia Estate Vineyards Cabernet Sauvignon Reserva 1997** `15` `£5–7`
Jaunty, juicy, yet finishing serious and dry.

**Mont Gras Carmenere Reserva 1998** `14` `£5–7`
A big food wine. Roast vegetables and melted cheese dishes and pungent risottos.

**Valdivieso Barrel Selection Cabernet/ Merlot 1997** `16.5` `£5–7`
Marvellous evolving fruit which takes delicious seconds to go from ripe blackcurrant to spicy plum. Gorgeous texture and lingering finish.

**Valdivieso Pinot Noir** `16` `£5-7`
**Reserve 1997**
Lovely chewy, gently exotic edge to
the pinot riches which include
chocolate and spicy cherries.

## WINE CELLAR

**Casa del Bosque Merlot** `12` `£5-7`
**1998**
Not very elegant or subtle. Goes with
Bangladeshi fish Madras.

**Cono Sur Merlot 1999** `15.5` `£5-7`
It's the rich, soft texture which carries
the points. The fruit is in decent
plummy shape, too, but the sheer
velvet of the delivery is superlative.

**Mapocho Cabernet** `13` `−£5.00`
**Sauvignon 1998**
Not the most impressive of Chilean
Cabs: bland on the finish.

**Mont Gras Cabernet** `14.5` `£5-7`
**Sauvignon 1998**
Chunky and hairy-chested but not
uncivilised. Lovely texture and very
warm tannins.

**Mont Gras Quatro 1998** `15` `£5-7`
Juicy with a hint of old tree and leaves.
The Cabernet pepperiness is mildly
counterpointed by the malbec's
moody richness.

**Valdivieso Barrel Select** `15.5` `£5-7`
**Merlot 1999**
Oddly sweetly-undertoned for a
Chilean Merlot, but it spreads itself
generously over the taste buds with
plum and blackcurrant effortlessness.

**Valdivieso Pinot Noir** `16` `£5-7`
**Reserve 1997**
Lovely chewy, gently exotic edge to

the Pinot riches which include
chocolate and spicy cherries.

## ASDA WHITE

**35 Sur Sauvignon Blanc** `15.5` `−£5.00`
**1999**
Rather like Asda's own label wine.

**Casas del Bosque** `15` `£5-7`
**Sauvignon Blanc 1999**
Sauvignon as sassy and rich. Great
with food.

**Chilean Sauvignon Blanc** `15.5` `−£5.00`
**1999, Asda**
The warm style of Sauvignon, well-
tailored and subtly rich. Delicious
nutty edge to the finish.

**Chilean White 1999, Asda** `16` `−£3.50`
One of the country's great white wines
– under three quid. It's terrifically
fruity, bold and brave.

**Cono Sur Chardonnay** `14` `−£5.00`
**1999**
Not as concentrated as previous
vintages.

## BOOTHS WHITE

**Isla Negra Chardonnay** `16` `£5-7`
**1998**
Gorgeous, rich, almost smoky and
gently herby, nicely textured, ripe but
not overbaked.

**Tocornal White NV** `13.5` `−£3.50`

**Via Vina Chardonnay** `14` `−£5.00`
**1999**
Not as typically smooth as most
Chilean Chardonnays, and it hides its
fruit somewhat, but this elemental
personality makes for a great aperitif.

Vistasur Chardonnay `13` `–£5.00`
Sauvignon Vistamar 1999
Odd dry edge to an eccentric fruity
onslaught. Good with Chinese food.

Vina Morande Chilean `15.5` `–£5.00`
Chardonnay 1999,
Somerfield
Superb! Superbness, indeed, bottled.

## BUDGENS WHITE

Antu Mapu Sauvignon `12.5` `–£5.00`
Blanc 1999
Very sticky rich.

Terra Andina `14` `–£5.00`
Chardonnay 1998
Ripe and melony.

Terra Andina Semillon `14` `–£5.00`
Chardonnay 1999
Very pert and bright with a good nutty
fresh finish.

## M&S WHITE

Alta Mira Chilean White `15` `–£5.00`
1999
Yes it's dry but it has compelling
echoes of melon and strawberry. A
most elegant performer.

Casa Leona Chardonnay `16.5` `–£5.00`
1999
Superb finesse here combined with
personality and subtle strength. It has
a lovely texture, gently plump, and a
whistle-clean, lemony finish.

Casa Leona Merlot/ `14` `–£5.00`
Cabernet Sauvignon Rosé
2000
Dry, elegant, cherry-rich fruit of no
uncertain style. An excellent food rosé.

Sierra Los Andes `16` `–£5.00`
Chardonnay 1999
Baked melon richness is not OTT but
fresh and fine and the finish is very
elegant.

Sierra Los Andes `16` `£5–7`
Chardonnay Reserve
1999
It has some woody chewiness to add
to the smooth fruit and thus the
vegetality of Burgundy is an
undertone. However, the richness of
the fruit is pure Chilean on the finish
which develops as it fades.

Sierra Los Andes `16` `–£5.00`
Gewurztraminer 1999
Stunning! Absolutely delicious!
Controlled spice, good acids, great

## CWS WHITE

Four Rivers Chardonnay `14` `–£5.00`
1998

Long Slim Chardonnay `14.5` `–£5.00`
Semillon 1999
Lip smacking richness of fruit allied to
pineapple acids. Good texture, if
somewhat loosely assembled.

Santa Carolina `16.5` `–£5.00`
Chardonnay 1999
Concentrated elegance here, but not a
hair is out of place; nothing overdone.
Understated? Maybe, but very classy.

## KWIK SAVE WHITE

Chilean White 1999, `15.5` `–£3.50`
Somerfield
Delicious, classy, rich, firm, structured,
ludicrously inexpensive.

balance. A wonderful dry style
Gewürz.

## MAJESTIC WHITE

**Chardonnay Reserve** 16.5 £5–7
**Cono Sur 1998**
Terrific texture here, so warm and
fulsome and rich yet it does not finish
with OTTness – on the contrary, it
shows deftness and wit.

**Luis Felipe Edwards** 14 –£5.00
**Chardonnay 1998**

**Santa Rita Cabernet** 16 –£5.00
**Sauvignon Rosé 1999**
The best rosé under a fiver on the
planet? Likely as not.

**Santa Rita Dona Paula** 14 –£5.00
**Cabernet Sauvignon Rosé**
**1998**

**Vistasur Sauvignon Blanc** 15.5 –£5.00
**1999**
Fatter style of Sauvignon, more
gooseberry richness. Lovely to glug
and to drink with robust fish and
smoked fish dishes.

## MORRISONS WHITE

**35 Sur Chardonnay 1999** 14.5 –£5.00
Cheerful enough, if hardly classic, but
the ripe melon fruit is refreshingly
balanced by good acids.

**35 Sur Sauvignon Blanc** 15 –£5.00
**1999**
Dry, wry and delicate on the finish. A
very charming quaffing wine.

**Antares Santa Carolina** 16 –£5.00
**Chardonnay 1999**
Bargain: dry melony fruit, a hint of
lemon, a touch of oil, a suggestion of
spice.

**Antu Mapu Reserva Rosé** 13 –£5.00
**1999**
Very cosmetic.

**Antu Mapu Sauvignon** 13 –£3.50
**Blanc 1999**
Muddy on the finish. Not well-defined
enough.

**Castillo de Molina** 16 £5–7
**Reserve Chardonnay**
**1998**
Superb butter and strawberry/melon/
lemon construct. Utterly delicious.

**Montes Alpha** 17.5 £7–10
**Chardonnay 1998**
Chile's Montrachet – if that isn't to
insult it. It has a creamy vegetality,
beautiful smooth texture, subtle
complex charms on the tongue, and a
lingering smokiness as it descends –
and hits the soul.

**Stowells Chilean** 13 –£3.50
**Sauvignon Blanc NV**
**(3 litre box)**
Price bracket reflects 75cl equivalent.

**Villa Montes Sauvignon** 14 –£5.00
**Blanc 1999**
Oddly over-ripe Sauvignon, but good
news for lovers of rich fish dishes.

## ODDBINS WHITE

**Carmen Chardonnay,** 16.5 –£5.00
**Central Valley 1998**
Lovely plump, rich, smoky fruit of
high class texture. Hint of ripe hay,
soft yet dry.

**Casa Lapostolle** 17 £5–7
**Chardonnay 1998**
Breathtakingly elegant, subtle,
complex, rich and so quaffable it has

undertones of ambrosia and choirs of angels.

**Casa Lapostolle Cuvee Alexandre Chardonnay 1997**    18.5   £7–10

Utterly magical oily texture, huge depth of woodily creamy fruit and a magnificent finish. It is a great wine at any price and hugely drinkable and food friendly. It has everything great Meursault has and doubles it. Classicists (aka snobs) will say it's OTT and the malolactic influence and the wood are too oppressive. But I think the fruit triumphs.

**Casa Lapostolle Sauvignon Blanc 1999**    16   £5–7

Delicious surging fruit, on the rich side of the minerally Sauvignon spectrum, but it has excitement.

**Casa Lapostolle Sauvignon Blanc 1999**    17   £5–7

Even more complex than the '98, more svelte.

**Casablanca Neblus Botrytis Chardonnay 1997 (half-bottle)**    16   –£5.00

Odd, very odd, a dry honey wine of nuttiness and waxy texture but not a hint of sweetness. Fine Wine Stores.

**Casablanca Santa Isabel Chardonnay 1998**    16.5   £5–7

Superb woody polish to the rich fruit which maintains an even flow of substance and style, lingering and subtly lush, for its whole performance.

**Casablanca Santa Isabel Gewurztraminer 1999**    14   £5–7

A very dry, subtly spicy wine for moules.

**Cono Sur Gewurztraminer 1999**    16   –£5.00

Delightfully dry Gewürz! The spiciness is controlled and clean, the medley of roseate fruit and flavours trim and well-honed, the finish lingering and subtly lavish.

**Errazuriz La Escultura Estate Chardonnay, Casablanca 1998**    17.5   £5–7

Nuts, touch of smoke, hint of spice, complex soft and hard fruits, lingering finish of polish and satin-textured excitement. A lovely wine.

**Errazuriz Wild Ferment Chardonnay, Casablanca 1998**    17   £7–10

A beautiful flaxen plastic cork; gorgeous golden wine. Like a throbbing Meursault made in Alsace in conditions they only get in Provence. Wine with soul.

**Isla Negra Chardonnay 1998**    16   £5–7

Lovely smoky melon fruit.

**La Palmeria Chardonnay Gran Reserva 1998**    15.5   £7–10

Has Burgundian pretensions, which isn't to insult it, so much as to convey the nature of its creamy vegetality. It's all-Chilean though on the finish, where there's a soft nuttiness. Overall, an elegant wine of substance, subtlety and class.

**Veramonte Chardonnay, Alto de Casablanca 1998**    14   £5–7

**Villard Chardonnay, Casablanca Valley 1998**    16   £7–10

Delicious ripeness and plumpness here. Real big, mouthfilling richness.

**Villard Reserve**    15.5   £7–10

Chardonnay, Casablanca
Valley 1998
More lemon than the non-reserve and
arguably more complex but I'm not
persuaded it's better value.

Vina Porta Chardonnay,  14  −£5.00
Cachapoal 1998

## SAFEWAY WHITE

35 Sur Sauvignon Blanc  15.5  −£5.00
1999
Rich and ready. Excellent food wine.

Chilean Dry White 2000,  16  −£3.50
Safeway
Quite superb subtly grassy yet rich-to-
finish fruit. Much better than a
hundred Sancerres.

Chilean Sauvignon Blanc  16  −£5.00
Lontue 1999, Safeway
Superb freshness and compelling
cleanness if subtle richness. Lovely fish
wine.

Chilean Sauvignon  15.5  −£5.00
Blanc/Chardonnay 1999,
Safeway
Delightful combo of melon and
lemon. A very bonny blend of grapes.

Cono Sur Chardonnay  14  −£5.00
1999
Very rich and ripe.

Cordillera Estate Oak  15.5  −£5.00
Aged Chardonnay
Reserva 1997, Safeway

Errazuriz La Escultura  17.5  £5−7
Estate Chardonnay,
Casablanca 1998
Nuts, touch of smoke, hint of spice,
complex soft and hard fruits, lingering
finish of polish and satin-textured
excitement. A lovely wine.

TerraMater Estates  15.5  £5−7
Sauvignon Blanc, Select
Cuvee, 1999
Unusually assertive asparagus and
tight gooseberry fruit. Remarkably
efficient food wine.

## SAINSBURY'S WHITE

35 Sur Sauvignon Blanc  15.5  −£5.00
1999
Very grassy and fresh. Selected
stores.

Canepa Winemaker's  16.5  −£5.00
Selection
Gewürztraminer 1999
Gewürz as spice, sure, but also as a
playful (if gently crisp) construct of
massive quaffability. Soft, roseate,
subtle yet insistent.

Casablanca Sauvignon  14.5  −£5.00
Blanc 1998

Chilean Cabernet  15.5  −£5.00
Sauvignon Rosé NV,
Sainsbury's

Chilean Chardonnay NV,  15  −£5.00
Sainsbury's

Chilean Sauvignon Blanc  15.5  −£5.00
NV, Sainsbury's

Chilean Semillon  13.5  −£3.50
Sauvignon NV,
Sainsbury's (3 litre box)
The price band reflects the equivalent
price for a 75cl bottle.

La Palmeria Chardonnay  15.5  £7−10
Gran Reserva 1998
Has Burgundian pretensions, which
isn't to insult it, so much as to convey
the nature of its creamy vegetality. It's
all-Chilean though on the finish,
where there's a soft nuttiness. Overall,

an elegant wine of substance, subtlety and class.

**MontGras Reserve Chardonnay 1998** `15` `£5–7`
A big, chewy, very musky and woody food wine. Terrific with fish dishes with complex sauces. Not at all stores.

**Santa Carolina Chardonnay 1999** `16.5` `–£5.00`
Concentrated elegance here, but not a hair is out of place; nothing overdone. Understated? Maybe, but very classy. Most stores.

**Stowells Chilean Sauvignon Blanc NV (3 litre box)** `15.5` `–£3.50`
Dry, dainty, deliciously controlled and gooseberryish. The price band reflects the equivalent price for a 75cl bottle.

## SOMERFIELD WHITE

**Chilean Sauvignon Blanc, Canepa 1999, Somerfield** `16` `–£5.00`
Simply superb balance and charm here.

**Chilean Semillon Chardonnay 1999, Somerfield** `16` `–£5.00`
Compelling blend offering a sushi-knife-edged keenness allied to gooseberries and a hint of ripe melon. Lovely wine.

**Chilean White 1999, Somerfield** `15.5` `–£3.50`
Delicious, classy, rich, firm, structured, ludicrously inexpensive.

**Cono Sur Viognier 1999** `16` `–£5.00`
Delicious apricot fruit with a touch of apple and pineapple and a vigorous finish. Limited distribution.

**Isla Negra Chardonnay 1999** `16.5` `–£5.00`
Even more energy and richness to the new vintage.

**Vina Morande Chilean Chardonnay 1999, Somerfield** `15.5` `–£5.00`
Superb! Superbness, indeed, bottled.

## SPAR WHITE

**Canepa Chilean Chardonnay 1999, Spar** `14.5` `–£5.00`
Anxious moments as you wonder if the rich fruit will last to the throat, but it does.

**Canepa Chilean Sauvignon Blanc 1998, Spar** `14` `–£5.00`
Touch sullen, but picks up some warmth on the finish.

**Chilean Sauvignon Blanc 1998** `15.5` `–£5.00`

## TESCO WHITE

**Chilean Chardonnay Reserve 1998, Tesco** `15.5` `–£5.00`
Gallops along nicely over the taste buds with perhaps more soft-hooved richness than most Chilean Chardonnays. Touch more exoticism on the finish, though it's subtle.

**Chilean Chardonnay, Tesco** `14` `–£5.00`

**Chilean Sauvignon Blanc NV, Tesco** `14.5` `–£5.00`

**Chilean White NV, Tesco** `14.5` `–£5.00`

**Cono Sur Gewürztraminer 1999** `16` `–£5.00`

Delightfully dry Gewürz! The spiciness is controlled and clean, the medley of roseate fruit and flavours trim and well-honed, the finish lingering and subtly lavish. 100 selected stores.

**Errazuriz Chardonnay 1999**  16  £5–7
Very distinguished in feel as it slithers over the taste buds, proving, if any further proof were necessary, that Chile makes abundantly toothsome Chardonnays at a remarkable price.

**Errazuriz Chardonnay Reserva 1997**  16  £7–10
Deep and richly resounding, it has hauteur and highly developed manners. Very classy and cool. Not at all stores.

**Santa Ines Sauvignon Blanc 1999**  16  –£5.00
Remarkable able-bodied wine for the money, offering as it does such precision of purpose and poise in effect.

**Stowells Chilean Sauvignon Blanc NV**  12  –£5.00
Untypically blowsy for a Chilean wine. Where, Stowells, did you lose the elegance we take for granted with Chilean Sauvignons?

**TerraMater Chardonnay 1999**  15.5  –£5.00
Deliciously textured and plump, lingering fruit of subtle dexterity and a calm, cool finish of class and precision.

**Undurraga Chardonnay/ Sauvignon Blanc 1999**  15  –£5.00
Odd effect but it's an odd blend (Loire with Burgundy, as the French would grouch) but it's an excellent rich fish wine.

**Undurraga Gewürztraminer 1998**  13.5  –£5.00

**Vina Casablanca Santa Isabel Sauvignon Blanc 1998**  16  £5–7
Very clotted and rich but this relents on the finish. A food wine paramountly – rich scallop and sole and monkfish dishes. 100 selected stores.

## THRESHER WHITE

**Casa Lapostolle Sauvignon Blanc 1999**  17  £5–7
Even more complex than the '98, more svelte.

**Concha y Toro Casillero del Diablo Chardonnay 1997**  17  –£5.00
Beautifully ornate fruit, oily and rippling with multi-flavoured riches, and the acidity gives the whole structure backbone and precision.

**La Palmeria Chardonnay 1998**  16  –£5.00
Amazing price for such a surge of poised, precise, purposeful fruit. Not at Wine Rack or Bottoms Up.

**Las Colinas Chardonnay 1999**  15  –£5.00
Curious bruised apple and baked pear fruit. Delicious!? In its own way.

**Las Colinas Riesling 1997**  15.5  –£5.00
Riesling as dry-edged, sullenly rich, demure and subtle. Needs food. Not at Wine Rack.

**Santa Ines Legardo de Armida Reserve Chardonnay 1998**  16.5  £5–7
Wonderful! Has overtones of the New World, creamy and rich, and

undertones of the Burgundian old: vegetal and aristocratic. Wine Rack and Bottoms Up only.

**Veramonte Chardonnay** 13.5 £5–7
**1998**
A very manufactured and constructed Veramonte. Everything about it reeks 'Look at me! Aren't I cute!?' No, baby, no. Wine Rack only.

**Canepa Semillon,** 16.5 –£5.00
**Colchagua Valley 1999**
Great value here for a wonderfully rich, textured wine of fruity butter oiliness and fine interwoven acids. Terrific style and oomph to it yet it isn't OTT or too obvious.

**Casa Donoso** 13 –£5.00
**Chardonnay Domaine Oriental 1999**
Very untypical and inelegant.

**Casa Donoso Reservado** 12 £5–7
**Chardonnay Domaine Oriental 1999**
Odd, not good.

**Casa Lapostolle** 17 £5–7
**Chardonnay 1998**
Breathtakingly elegant, subtle, complex, rich and so quaffable it has undertones of ambrosia and choirs of angels.

**Casa Lapostolle Cuvee** 17.5 £7–10
**Alexandre Chardonnay, Casablanca 1996**
One of the best Chardonnays in the world. Simply gorgeous texture, complex fruit and sheer charm.

**Casablanca Chardonnay** 15.5 £5–7
**1998**

**Concha y Toro** 16 –£5.00
**Gewürztraminer 1999**
Wonderful spicy richness and rosy-edged fruit. Marvellous smell, tang and finish. Great spicy fish wine.

**Errazuriz Wild Ferment** 17 £7–10
**Chardonnay, Casablanca 1998**
A beautiful flaxen plastic cork; gorgeous golden wine. Like a throbbing Meursault made in Alsace in conditions they only get in Provence. Wine with soul.

**Isla Negra Chardonnay** 16 £7–10
**1997**
Plump and delicious.

**La Palmeria Chardonnay** 15.5 –£5.00
**2000**
Subtle yet substantial, deep yet delicate, energetic yet easy-going.

**Valdivieso Chardonnay** 16.5 –£5.00
**1999**
Gorgeous chewy fruit, vegetal and ripe but classy, bold and absurdly cheap.

**Valdivieso Reserve** 15.5 £5–7
**Chardonnay 1997**
Delicious but unreserved.

**Casa Lapostolle** 17 £5–7
**Sauvignon Blanc 1999**
Even more complex than the '98, more svelte.

**Concha y Toro Casillero** 17 –£5.00
**del Diablo Chardonnay 1997**
Beautifully ornate fruit, oily and rippling with multi-flavoured riches, and the acidity gives the whole structure backbone and precision.

**Cono Sur** `15.5` `−£5.00`
**Gewürztraminer 1998**
A dry example of the grape, and very
fresh, but great with oriental food.

**La Palmeria Chardonnay** `16` `−£5.00`
**1998**
Amazing price for such a surge of
poised, precise, purposeful fruit.

**Las Colinas Chardonnay** `15` `−£5.00`
**1999**
Curious bruised apple and baked pear
fruit. Delicious!? In its own way.

**Las Colinas Riesling 1997** `15.5` `−£5.00`
Riesling as dry-edged, sullenly rich,
demure and subtle. Needs food. Not at
Wine Rack.

**Santa Ines Legardo de** `16.5` `£5−7`
**Armida Reserve**
**Chardonnay 1998**
Wonderful! Has overtones of the New
World, creamy and rich, and
undertones of the Burgundian old:
vegetal and aristocratic.

**Veramonte Chardonnay** `13.5` `£5−7`
**1998**
A very manufactured and constructed
Veramonte. Everything about it reeks
'Look at me! Aren't I cute!?' No, baby,
no.

## WAITROSE WHITE

**Canepa Semillon,** `16.5` `−£5.00`
**Colchagua Valley 1999**
Great value here for a wonderfully
rich, textured wine of fruity butter
oiliness and fine interwoven acids.
Terrific style and oomph to it yet it
isn't OTT or too obvious.

**Carmen Vineyards** `16` `£5−7`
**Insigne Gewürztraminer**
**1999**
Warm, spicy, sticky, rich and very
jaunty and easy-going. It has a real
joyous strain running through it.

## WINE CELLAR WHITE

**Casa del Bosque** `10` `£5−7`
**Sauvignon Blanc 1998**
The feeblest Chilean Sauvignon Blanc
I ever wet my whistle with.

**La Palmeria Chardonnay** `16` `−£5.00`
**1999**
Gorgeous buttery richness, hint of
lemon, touch of ogen melon.

# CYPRUS

The days of Cyprus sherry are dead. The vineyards that grew the grapes, however, are capable of much greater things. I have, though, yet to taste more than the odd one, but the potential is patently there.

## ASDA RED

Ancient Isle Red 1998    15.5  −£3.50

## CWS RED

Mountain Vines Reserve    16  −£5.00
Cabernet/Maratheftiko
1999, Co-op
One of the odder wines I tasted this year in that the Maratheftiko adds a curious nutty, cooked, almost herby/ spicy element to the dry, peppery Cabernet and the result is some

extremely engaging fruit of lingering lushness. Superstores only.

## CWS WHITE

Island Vines White Wine    15.5  −£3.50
1998, Co-op

Mountain Vines Sémillon    13  −£5.00
1999, Co-op
Nice to sip in its country of origin, under a rich blue sky. Superstores only.

# ENGLAND

This pitifully wet and windy wine producer struggles to create drinkable white wines from scrawny grapes, jejune reds from the wrong varieties, and sullen bubblies from anything. There are, it is true, half a dozen accomplished English wine producers but most are in it for much the same reason that a man creates Canterbury Cathedral out of ten million matchsticks – or rather a combustible miniature facsimile of that marvellous temple.

## WAITROSE RED

**Chapel Down Epoch I 1998** | 10 | £5–7
Has some intriguing aromatic qualities but the finish? Like a British heavyweight boxer . . . splat! Out for the count.

## ASDA WHITE

**Three Choirs Coleridge Hill English White 1998** | 12 | −£5.00

## SAINSBURY'S WHITE

**Denbies Estate English table Wine NV** | 10 | −£5.00

## TESCO WHITE

**Chapel Down Bacchus 1997** | 12 | −£5.00

**Chapel Down Summerhill Oaked NV** | 12 | −£5.00

## WAITROSE WHITE

**Chapel Down Flint Dry 1998** | 13.5 | −£5.00
Yes, well, it is flinty and it is dry. Time to swallow my words where English wine is concerned? Almost. Almost.

**Summerhill Oaked Dry White NV** | 12 | −£5.00
Bit gooey with a touch of plank.

# FRANCE

France was once the wine producer that everyone copied (and certain Aussies still do, not having entirely given up their European wet dreams). Its share of the UK wine market has dropped dramatically over the past decade. Bordeaux, Burgundy and Champagne still remain areas where no one should buy without in-depth knowledge of specific individual producers. It is Languedoc and Roussillon, and the southern Rhône, where the rich, complex, generous wines are born and raised and being so in increasing numbers.

## ASDA RED

Beaujolais Villages 1998, Asda — 14 — −£5.00

Bourgeuil Domaine de l'Ereau 1999 — 13.5 — £5–7
Needs time to come around. Very very dry.

Buzet Cuvée 44 1997 — 15 — −£5.00
Good stuff! And stuffed with generous tannins and savoury fruit.

Château de Parenchere Bordeaux Supérieur 1997 — 16.5 — £5–7
A superb young claret. Textures, classy, rich, handsomely tannic and well concentrated.

Château Guerin Bellevue Saint-Emilion 1997 — 16 — £5–7
Simply one of the best clarets around for the money. Superb texture and concentration.

Château Haut Canteloupe Médoc 1998 — 16.5 — £7–10

Lovely sweet/tannin finish on it gives it great lingering classiness. It is a complex claret, possessing remarkable quaffability.

Château Lahore Bergez, Fitou 1998 — 16.5 — −£5.00
Superb richness, character, weight and finesse. Yes, it has some mild rusticity but this is its charm. It's a great food wine.

Château Vieux Gabiran 1999 (organic) — 14 — −£5.00
Mild fruit, not too dry; subtle modern hints.

Chénas 1997, Asda — 14 — −£5.00

Claret NV, Asda — 14.5 — −£3.50

Comte de Gasparin, Côtes du Rhône 1997 — 16 — £5–7
Curiously cheeky Rhône red. It carries its herby tannins with vigour, youth and ripe intent.

Domaine de Picheral VdP d'Oc 1999 (organic) — 15 — −£5.00

Delicious softness and ripeness with a nice lining (warm) of Midi herbs and a touch of earth.

**Domaine des Hardiers** | 16.5 | −£5.00
**Anjou-Villages 1999**
The essence of what fine Cabernet Franc from the Loire is. And at £4.29! It beggars belief (or will, if you let this wine age for up to seven more years). It's dry, raspberry/strawberry/leather/pepper and plum fruited, and it finishes lingeringly and with a certain plumpness.

**Domaine Pont Pinot Noir** | 13 | £5–7
**1996**

**La Domeque 'Vieilles** | 16 | £5–7
**Vignes' Syrah 1997**
Jammy hints to a dry wine of great style. Superb acids balance the warm fruit.

**Merlot, Vin de Pays d'Oc** | 15 | −£3.50
**1998, Asda**
Terrific earthy bite and dark cherry fruit.

**Moulin-à-Vent Oak Aged** | 13.5 | £5–7
**1997, Asda**

**Oak Aged Côtes du** | 15 | −£5.00
**Rhône 1999, Asda**
Juicy, dark cherries, jam and good clods of earth and Rhône warmth.

**Organic Claret Château** | 15.5 | £5–7
**Vieux Georget, Bordeaux**
**1998**
If this is what happens when Bordeaux goes organic, then maybe they should try it. Brilliant quaffability here.

**Réserve du Mouton 1997** | 13.5 | £5–7

**Tramontane Grenache** | 16 | −£5.00
**VdP d'Oc 1998, Asda**

Juicy with hints of herbs. Great rollicking style.

**Tramontane Merlot VdP** | 16 | −£5.00
**d'Oc 1999, Asda**
Again that delicious characterful earthiness.

**Tramontane Red VdP de** | 16 | −£3.50
**l'Aude 1999, Asda**
Brilliant earthy richness and ripeness. Real bargain here.

**Tramontane Réserve Oak** | 14.5 | −£5.00
**Aged Cabernet**
**Sauvignon VdP d'Oc**
**1998, Asda**

**Tramontane Réserve** | 16.5 | £5–7
**Syrah VdP d'Oc 1996,**
**Asda**
Superb Aussie confidence-shaker. From Aussies in the Languedoc this lovely rich, deep, aromatic, textured wine knocks many a homespun Aussie wine into a cocked hat.

**Tramontane Syrah VdP** | 13.5 | −£5.00
**d'Oc 1997, Asda**

**Tramontane Syrah/** | 14.5 | −£3.50
**Merlot VdP d'Oc 1997,**
**Asda**

**Vacqueyras Domaine de** | 16.5 | £5–7
**l'Oiselet 1999**
Superbly herby and ripe, rivulets of leather/plump blackcurrant fruit and marvellous alert tannins. Gorgeous fruit of great style here.

## BOOTHS RED

**Bergerac Organic Red** | 14 | −£5.00
**1998**
Gently earthy fruit and juicy tannins.

**Bergerac Rouge NV,** `13` `−£3.50`
**Booths**
So rustic in demeanour and earthiness
that the assiduous drinker might
examine his glass for evidence of
toenail clippings from the peasants
who pressed the grapes.

**Bourgogne Rouge Jean-** `12.5` `£5–7`
**Luc Joillet 1998**
Oh my! All those grapes! What a dull
end to so much growth.

**Bourgueil Domaine** `15` `−£5.00`
**Pierre Gautier 1995**

**Cahors 1998** `14` `−£5.00`
Rustic chewiness and very warmly
textured fruit.

**Chapoutier La Ciboise** `15.5` `−£5.00`
**Coteaux du Tricastin**
**1998**
An impressively rich organic red with
a lovely herby undertone. Unique
Rhône personality to it.

**Château Ducla, Bordeaux** `15` `£5–7`
**1997**

**Château l'Euziere Pic St-** `14.5` `£5–7`
**Loup 1997**

**Château Mayne-Vieil,** `16.5` `−£5.00`
**Fronsac 1996**
What wonderful claret! Lovely
cheroot undertoned richness, great
dryness, yet a compelling fruity finish.
Sophisticated and svelte.

**Château Pierrail** `15` `£5–7`
**Bordeaux Supérieur 1996**

**Château Pouchaud-** `15.5` `£5–7`
**Larquey, Bordeaux 1996**

**Chaume Arnaud** `17` `£7–10`
**Domaine Côtes du**
**Rhône-Villages 1998**
**(organic)**

It develops on the palate with
insidious deliciousness providing
herbs, savoury tannins, a hint of rustic
orchards, and a deal of characterful
texture. Marvellous stuff.

**Côtes du Rhône-Villages** `13.5` `£5–7`
**Georges Darriaud 1998**
Odd juicy edge as it finishes.

**Domaine du Trillol** `15.5` `−£5.00`
**Corbières 1996**

**Faugères Gilbert Alquier** `15` `£7–10`
**1997**

**Fitou Madame** `13.5` `−£5.00`
**Parmentier 1998**
Very juicy edge, touch loose here (as it
finishes).

**Gigondas Domaine** `16` `£7–10`
**Paillere et Pied 1998**
Superb lesson in integrated rich, soft
tannicity and herb-drenched plums,
blackberries and baked earth. Hugely
civilised tippling.

**Julienas Paul Boutinot** `11` `£5–7`
**1997**
Uninspiring, largely.

**La Passion Rouge VdP de** `14` `−£3.50`
**Vaucluse 1999**
A charming, dry party wine. Works
well chilled with fish, too.

**La Réserve du Reverend** `13.5` `−£5.00`
**Corbières 1999**
Becomes very juicy in this vintage.
Not as gripping as previously.

**Marcillac 1997** `15` `£5–7`

**Oak Aged Claret** `14` `−£5.00`
**Bordeaux Supérieur NV,**
**Booths**
Genuine claret of tannic tenacity yet
soft natural finishing charms.

**Old Git Grenache Syrah** `15.5` `−£5.00`
**1999**
Great fun. I'm bound to love the name
and the dry, Midi fruit.

**Pernands Vergelesses,** `10` `£7–10`
**Cornu 1997**

**Rasteau Domaine des** `16.5` `£5–7`
**Coteaux des Travers 1998**
Thrilling tannins to marvellously
complex, dry and earthy fruit which
melts in the mouth to reveal
hedgerow juice as it finishes.

**Vin Rouge NV, Booths** `11` `−£3.50`
Well, the label's on straight. And the
fruit's honest – honestly boring.

## BUDGENS RED

**Bourgogne Rouge Vienot** `12` `£5–7`
**1996**

**Château de Malijay Côtes** `13.5` `−£5.00`
**du Rhône 1996**

**Corbières Château Saint-** `13` `−£5.00`
**Louis 1997**
Raisiny and maturing fast. Good for
robust casseroles.

**Côtes du Rhône-Villages** `14` `−£5.00`
**Cuvée Réserve 1997**

**Côtes Marmandais,** `13.5` `−£5.00`
**Beaupuy 1996**

**Domaine St-Roche VdP** `12` `−£3.50`
**de l'Aude NV**
Rustic bargain: socks, planks, earth . . .
oh . . . yes, grapes.

**Gargantua Côtes du** `14` `−£5.00`
**Rhône 1997**

**Organic Red VdP du Pays** `13` `−£3.50`
**du Gard NV**
Soft and plummy and very direct.

**Premium Oaked** `15.5` `−£3.50`
**Cabernet Franc/Syrah**
**VdP d'Oc, Devereux NV**
The best red wine bargain on
Budgens' shelves: rich, dry,
characterful, blackcurranty and
plummy, good thwack of Midi sun.

## CWS RED

**Beloup St-Chinian 1998** `14.5` `−£5.00`
Grand little juicy glugger.

**Château Laurençon** `14` `−£5.00`
**Bordeaux Supérieur 1998**
Smoky-charcoal edge to the fruit.
Great wine for meat dishes.
Superstores only.

**Château Pierrousselle** `14` `−£5.00`
**Bordeaux 1999**
A pleasant little claret of admirable
tannins.

**Chevaliere Réserve** `14` `−£5.00`
**Grenache Vieilles Vignes**
**1998**
Soft and ripe, full of fruit. Not subtle,
this wine.

**Claret NV** `15` `−£3.50`
Possibly – no, is – the cheapest
drinkable, well-ordained claret in the
UK for the money. Decant it into big
jugs when wine buffs come to dinner
and watch them dispute which
château it is.

**Corbières Rouge NV,** `15` `−£3.50`
**Co-op**

**Corso Merlot 1999** `15.5` `−£5.00`
A Corsican red of compelling warmth
and spicy richness. Lovely texture and
balance and stylish finish of some
weight. Superstores only.

Domaine les Combelles `13.5` `−£5.00`
Minervois 1998
Not the bustling busybody of the '96.
Superstores only.

Fleurie Pierre Leduc 1998 `13.5` `£7–10`

La Baume Syrah 1997 `15.5` `−£5.00`

Louis Mousset Crozes- `15` `£5–7`
Hermitage 1997

Oak Aged Claret NV, `13` `−£5.00`
Co-op
Touch crusty and old hat.

Rhône Valley Red 1999 `14.5` `−£3.50`
Very juicy and jammy but the tannins
tighten and heighten the final effect.

Valreas Domaine de la `16.5` `£5–7`
Grande Bellane 1998
(organic)
Wonderful energy and strikingly
stylish tannins here. Offers hedgerow
fruit, herbs, a soft earthiness, and
brilliant tannins as it glides effortlessly
home. Superstores only.

Vin de Pays d'Oc `15` `−£5.00`
Cabernet Merlot NV,
Co-op

Vin de Pays d'Oc `14` `−£3.50`
Cabernet Sauvignon,
Co-op
Cabernet as charming as they come:
soft, ripe, blackcurranty.

Vin de Pays d'Oc Merlot `14.5` `−£3.50`
NV, Co-op

Vin de Pays d'Oc Syrah, `14` `−£3.50`
Co-op
Sheer happiness bottled. Jammy and
delicious.

Vin de Pays d'Oc Syrah/ `14` `−£5.00`
Malbec, Co-op
(vegetarian)

## KWIK SAVE RED

Brouilly Les Celliers de `12` `£5–7`
Bellevue 1998
Too pricey.

Cabernet Malbec VdP `15.5` `−£3.50`
d'Oc 1997

Cabernet Sauvignon d'Oc `14` `−£3.50`
Val d'Orbieu 1998,
Somerfield
Real blackcurrant and pepper – but
very soft and thick.

Claret NV, Somerfield `13.5` `−£3.50`
Claret as real juice of the vine: no
earth, no stalks, no green leaves.

Corbières Rouge Val `15` `−£3.50`
d'Orbieu 1998,
Somerfield
Superb texture and tension between
spicy plums, tannins (savoury) and
subtle acids. What a bargain!

Fitou Rocher d'Ambrée `14.5` `−£5.00`
1998, Somerfield
Sticky tar tannins make it a real
mouthful.

Les Oliviers VdT Francais `12` `−£2.50`
Red NV

March Hare VdP d'Oc `15.5` `−£5.00`
1997

Minervois Château la `16` `−£3.50`
Reze 1996
Wonderful teeth-embracing, tongue-
curling, throat-charming, fruit of style
and wit. Fantastic value.

Morgon 1998 `12.5` `−£5.00`

Rivers Meet Merlot/ `14` `−£5.00`
Cabernet, Bordeaux 1997

Skylark Hill Merlot VdP `15.5` `−£3.50`
d'Oc 1997

Skylark Hill Syrah VdP 15.5 −£3.50
d'Oc 1997

Skylark Hill Very Special 14 −£3.50
Red VdP d'Oc 1997

St-Didier VdP du Tarn 15.5 −£3.50
1997

VdP des Coteaux de 14 −£3.50
l'Ardèche Rouge 1999,
Somerfield
Dry, hint of rustic sod, barbecue wine.

## M&S RED

Abbaye de Tholomies 16.5 £5–7
Minervois 1996
Superb texture, ruffled velvet with
touches of raw denim. Perfect balance
of alcohol and tannins, fruit and
acidity, herbs and meat. A masterpiece
of rustic richness and unpretentious
gluggability.

Burgundy Pinot Noir 12 £7–10
1998
Always something rum when a wine
says it's Burgundy *and* Pinot Noir. I'm
surprised it's allowed. But then that's
true of so much modern Burgundy.

Château de Sauvanes 15.5 £5–7
Faugères 1997
Marvellous casserole mouthful. A
savoury, dry wine of tannins and
tenacity.

Château de Surville 16 £5–7
Costières de Nîmes 1998
Gripping tannins here of great style,
and they give the fruit succulence and
a terrific texture and dry food-
friendliness.

Château des Lanes, 16 £5–7
Corbières 1998
Gorgeous medley of herbs and

hedgerow fruits here plus strong
tannins holding the whole structure
tightly together. A deliciously
compact, seriously fruity specimen.

Château Planezes, Côtes 16.5 £5–7
du Roussillon-Villages
1998
What warmth and savoury stealth
here! It oozes class like an exceptional
claret (curiously, given its grapes, not
like a northern Rhône). Super all-
action red with depth and daring. The
spicy plum and peppery richness of the
fruit is jammy but never OTT. The
finish is complex, concentrated, classy.

Côtes du Parc, Coteaux 15.5 −£5.00
du Languedoc 1999
(organic)
A wonderful dry organic red. Lovely
character and bite to it. The Midi earth
is very active in the wine.

Devois des Agneaux 15.5 £7–10
Coteaux du Languedoc
1998
Juicy but deliciously dry and food-
friendly. Has lovely herbs and hints of
tobacco.

Domaine St-Pierre VdP 11 −£3.50
de l'Herault 1999

Gold Label Cabernet 15 −£5.00
Sauvignon VdP d'Oc
1998
Juicy yet authentically blackcurrant
rich – not an obvious wine. It has
some hidden passages to explore.

Gold Label Reserve 16.5 £5–7
Barrel Aged Syrah VdP
d'Oc 1998
Superb meaty fruit, touch of old
cheroot to the spicy plums and
blackberries, and a great rousing finish

of oregano and coriander. Brilliant dinner party companion.

**Gold Label Syrah VdP** `16` `−£5.00`
**d'Oc 1999**
Delicious – one of the most convincing reds at this price here. Rich ripe fruit, deftly herby and warm, dry to finish, not overly tannic, good texture.

**House Red Wine, VdP du** `12` `−£3.50`
**Comte Tolosan 1999**
Basic, touch brutal.

**La Tour du Prevot Côtes** `16` `−£5.00`
**du Ventoux 1999**
This is what terrific under-a-fiver French country reds are all about: deep, herby, rich, warm, drinkable, unpretentious, food-friendly, full of character. I like this wine a lot.

**Margaux 1997** `13.5` `£10–13`
Very drinkable. But £13?

**Merlot Cave de Rauzan** `13.5` `−£5.00`
**1998**
Juicy and soft.

**Oak Aged Bordeaux 1997** `13` `£5–7`
Good perfume but gets confused on the finish as juicy fruit and wood tannins clash.

## MAJESTIC RED

**Beaune 1er Cru Les** `12` `£13–20`
**Chauacheaux 1997**

**Beaune Louis Latour** `11` `£7–10`
**1997**
Dull.

**Beaune-Epenotes 1979** `10` `£20+`

**Bois de Lamothe** `16` `−£3.50`
**Cabernet Franc, Côtes de Duras 1997**
Fantastic value: black, sticky-cherry

fruit with good, volcanic tannins alongside and a finish of textured richness. Great glugging and food wine.

**Bott-Geyl Pinot Noir** `15.5` `£7–10`
**Beblenheim 1997**
A real aficionado's, of which I am one, delight: bitter and twisted fruit, real farmyard pong, great nutty richness on the finish.

**Bourgeuil La Vernelle** `16` `−£5.00`
**1997**
The essence of young great Cab Franc: cherry and raspberry, slate tiles, rich and ready. Very dry.

**Bouton d'Or Cairanne,** `14` `−£5.00`
**Côtes du Rhône-Villages 1998**
Unusually ripe and fresh.

**Calvet Reserve Claret** `14.5` `£5–7`
**1998**
Best vintage yet of this wine. Most charming and good value. A real dry yet fruity claret.

**Cave de Ribeauville Pinot** `14` `£5–7`
**Noir 1998**
Try it chilled with fish. It's magic: truffley and cherried.

**Chambolle-Musigny** `10` `£10–13`
**Jaffelin 1996**
Just so dull and unexceptional.

**Château de Bosc Côtes** `11` `£5–7`
**du Rhône 1997**

**Château de Candale,** `14` `£10–13`
**Haut-Médoc 1996**

**Château de Gaudou** `15.5` `−£5.00`
**Cuvée Tradition Cahors 1998**
Superb earthy richness here, a woody, chewy edge to it is very stern and

takes no prisoners, but the final flow of blackcurrant depth is compelling.

**Château de Haute Serre** `13` `£7–10`
**Cahors 1989**
Too juicy, too old.

**Château de Nardon 1998** `14` `£5–7`
Very stalky and dry – hint of juiciness on the finish.

**Château de Sales,** `13.5` `£20+`
**Pomerol 1996**

**Château Flauguergues** `17.5` `£5–7`
**Coteaux du Languedoc 1998**
Very elegant. The tannins and the fruit are deliciously melded and softened one into the other and the finish is excellent. A very serious yet fun-to-drink wine.

**Château Guiot Costières** `15.5` `–£5.00`
**de Nîmes 1999**
Delicious richness and textured ripeness. Charming rusticity, controlled and concentrated.

**Château Haut Mazières,** `14` `£5–7`
**Bordeaux 1997**
Dry with a struggling border of richness.

**Château l'Abbaye de St-** `15.5` `£5–7`
**Ferme Bordeaux Supérieur 1998**
Superb value for a dry, classy claret. Brilliant with roast meats.

**Château Lamartine,** `15` `£5–7`
**Côtes de Castillon 1997**
Splendid stalky richness. Very gruff-voiced and vigorous.

**Château Ludon Pomies** `12` `£10–13`
**Agassac, Bordeaux 1997**
Very sweet to finish.

**Château Méaume** `16` `£5–7`
**Bordeaux Supérieur 1997**
Lovely lively-tannined claret. It's the way to go, messiuers!!!

**Château Morin, St-** `16.5` `£7–10`
**Estephe 1997**
Old-fashioned but awesomely French and historically correct. Unbendingly dry and tannic, it has lovely blackcurrant (almost cassis) richness – but the dryness! It crunches the back teeth.

**Château Tour Saint-Paul,** `13` `£5–7`
**Bordeaux Supérieur 1997**

**Châteauneuf-du-Pape** `13` `£10–13`
**Domaine Cailloux 1997**

**Châteauneuf-du-Pape** `14.5` `£13–20`
**Domaine Pegau 1997**
Lovely tannins and sweet-to-finish fruit. But £20? Well, the wine, if impressive, is not grand value. At £20 you want magic in a wine and this is merely delicious.

**Chinon les Garous,** `16` `£5–7`
**Couly-Dutheil 1997**
Classic Cab Franc with hints of wild raspberry insinuated into the dry-yet-rich coal-edged fruit. Delicious chilled with fish.

**Claret Cuvée 090 1998** `14` `–£5.00`

**Claret Lot 278 1998** `14` `–£5.00`
A thoroughly claret-like claret. Preposterous? It happens – sometimes. These remarkable coincidences of intention with effect are romantic and easy to swallow.

**Corbières Domaine** `14` `–£5.00`
**Madelon 1999**
Very sweet finishing.

Corton Grancey Grand 12.5 £20+
Cru 1995

Coteaux du Tricastin 15 −£5.00
Domaine Saint-Remy
1997

Côte de Nuits-Villages 10 £7–10
Louis Latour 1996
Dull.

Côtes du Rhône Guigal 14 £5–7
1997
Good basic CdR at, sadly, an above-
average CdR price.

Côtes du Rhône Guigal 16 £7–10
1998
Always, incredibly, a consistently rich
and svelte performer on the taste
buds.

Côtes du Rhône Les 13 −£3.50
Chevaliers aux Lys d'Or
1998
Thin, anodyne – like a supermodel on
Sundays.

Côtes du Ventoux Vidal- 14 −£5.00
Fleury 1998
Falls away a bit on the finish but very
drinkable and fruity upfront.

Crozes-Hermitage Cave 14 £5–7
Tain l'Hermitage 1998
Bacon bits and fresh liquefied coal.

Domaine de l'Ile St-Pierre 16.5 −£5.00
Cabernet Franc 1998
More tannins here than your average
racing saddle. As such it might seem
fearsome, but the fruit is also racy and
urgent and the overall effect is of a
quirky claret from a brilliant,
undiscovered château. A great grilled
food wine: savoury and cheroot-
tinged.

Domaine de la Closerie 13 £5–7
St-Nicolas-de-Bourgueil
1997

Domaine de Rodes 15 −£5.00
Grenache VdP d'Oc 1998
Sweet, delicious, modern. Hasn't the
tannin or depth of its Syrah brother.

Domaine de Rodes Syrah 16.5 −£5.00
VdP d'Oc 1998
Quite superb richness and complex,
earthy fruit here. Amazing value at the
two-bottle price (£3.49)

Domaine des Bois du 16 −£5.00
Garn Côtes du Vivarais
1998
Lovely herby, rustic richness here. Has
terrific tannins.

Fixin Jaffelin 1996 12 £7–10

Gigondas Guigal 1997 16.5 £10–13
Sweet, dark, herby, subtle mineral
edge – a classic Gigondas.

Givry 1er Cru Steinmaier 15 £7–10
1998
Love the slaty dryness. Odd Burgundy
but the oddness is not egregious so
much as quirkily unfashionable.

Givry Louis Latour 1997 11 £7–10

Grenache/Cabernet VdP 16 −£3.50
de l'Ardèche 1998
A superb bargain. One of the most
satisfying under-£3 reds, dry and rich,
I've tasted. Snap it up for parties!

Hautes-Côtes de Beaune 13.5 £5–7
Cave Co-op 1997
Not revolting but not hugely palate-
engaging either. A modern Burgundy,
high priced for the meat on offer,
which is too bony for this drinker.

La Fauve Merlot VdP `15` `−£5.00`
d'Oc 1998

La Fauve Syrah VdP d'Oc `15.5` `−£5.00`
1998

La Ramillade Gigondas `15` `£7–10`
1998
Very warm and sweetly dispositioned.

Lirac Domaine de la `16` `£5–7`
Rocalière 1997
Excellent array of Rhône values:
dryness, richness, tannicity, earthiness,
textured plumpness and a bravura
finish.

Mâcon St-Gengoux 1998 `14` `−£5.00`
Just about makes its rating though it'll
curdle New World wine-fruit lovers'
toenails. It's dry, a touch earthy and
mildly gravelly. Good with food,
though.

Madiran Meinjarre Alain `15` `£5–7`
Brumont 1997
Has the typical Madiran hard edge
which is superb with food. It has loads
of personality and richness and finishes
very fresh and firm. Loads of great
acids temper the fruit and tannin.

Mas de Bressades `17` `£5–7`
Cabernet Syrah VdP du
Gard 1998
Splendid, irreproachable tannins linked
to thrusting hedgerow ripeness and
characterfulness. Marvellous stuff!

Mas de Guiot Cabernet `17.5` `£5–7`
Syrah VdP du Gard 1998
Utterly superb blend of grapes
providing vegetality, texture, richness
and hugely well-tempered tannins of
great style. A superb wine to surprise
even the most buffed-up of wine
buffs.

Merlot VdP de la Haute `14` `−£3.50`
Vallée de l'Aude 1998
Cheap and very cheerful.

Morgon Jean Descombes `13` `£7–10`
1998

Pernand-Vergelesses `12.5` `£7–10`
Jaffelin 1996

Régnié Vallières 1998 `14` `−£5.00`
One of the more appealing Beaujolais
with its pert dry edge. Not typically
firmly fruity Beaujolly at all here.
Well, well.

Sancerre Rouge Les `14.5` `£13–20`
Belles Dames Vacheron
1997
Can only be compared with Volnay
and the Yarra Valley. It has the
former's dry vegetality, the latter's
Pinot sweetness and cherry brightness.
Lot of money for an unlikely marriage.

Sancerre Rouge `15.5` `£7–10`
Vacheron 1998
Uncompromisingly French and take-
me-as-I-am attitude here. And many
drinkers, New World softies, will find
this wine, at ten quid my life, absurdly
dry and rocky. But, for some of us
sentimentalists, it has distinct charms.

Syrah Collines `13.5` `−£5.00`
Rhodaniennes, Co-op de
Tain Hermitage 1998

Syrah VdP du Cave Tain `13` `−£5.00`
l'Hermitage 1998

Vacqueyras Beaumes-de- `16.5` `£5–7`
Venise 1999
Immensely mouth-filling and
chocolate-rich fruit here, of great
thickly textured ripeness yet
beautifully soft and deftly interwoven
tannic tightness. Class act.

## MORRISONS RED

Beaujolais NV    13   −£5.00

Bouches-du-Rhône    15   −£3.50
Merlot NV

Château Cadillac    15   £5–7
Legourgues Bordeaux
1997
A dryly classic claret of perfect
proportions to go with loads of meat
dishes.

Château de Candale    15   £7–10
Haut-Médoc 1996

Château La Fage Côtes    13.5   −£5.00
de Bergerac 1997
Very dry and earthy and best suited to
rich food.

Château Saint-Galier    14.5   −£5.00
Graves 1997
Very dry and food-friendly.

Chinon Domaine de    16   −£5.00
Briançon 1997
What a bargain! Tobacco and wild
raspberries with gorgeous tannins, this
is a classic Chinon of great wit and
warmth, at a terrific price.

Claret Bordeaux NV,    13.5   −£3.50
Morrisons
Juicy yet dry and smooth. Must be the
cheapest drinkable 'claret' on the
market.

Falcon Ridge Cabernet    16   −£3.50
Sauvignon, VdP d'Oc
1999
Brilliant dryness and hugely arresting
blackcurrant richness. Fantastic
value.

Falcon Ridge Merlot VdP    15   −£3.50
d'Oc 1999
What a drop of stuff this is: ripe, rich,
a touch raucous but £3.50! It's a
miracle.

Falcon Ridge Syrah VdP    15.5   −£3.50
d'Oc 1999
Joyous fruit here. Lovely tangy
richness and plump ripeness.

Fitou NV    13   −£5.00

Heritage des Caves des    15.5   −£5.00
Papes Côtes du Rhône
1998
Plumpish, dry, gently herby, and on
the classy side of rustic. Terrific food
wine.

La Chasse du Pape    16   −£5.00
Reserve Côtes du Rhône
1998
It has a country bumpkin
temperament allied to a city slicker's
intellect. Thus we get great dry rip-
roaring herby fruit.

Les Planels Minervois    14   −£5.00
1997
Dry but rollingly rich.

'M' Côtes du Rhône NV    13   −£3.50
Rustic charm.

'M' Côtes du Roussillon    13   −£3.50
Red NV
Very sticky and rich.

Minervois Cellier la    13   −£3.50
Chouf NV

Oak Matured Bordeaux    13   −£5.00
1997
Touch dull.

Rhône Valley Red 1998    14   −£3.50

Saint-Emilion NV,    14   £5–7
Morrisons
Authentic, dry, warm, fruity, very
quaffable and hugely casserole-
friendly.

Sichel Médoc NV ` 13 ` ` £5–7 `

Vacqueyras Domaine de ` 14.5 ` ` £5–7 `
Ameleraies 1998

Vin de Pays de ` 12 ` ` –£3.50 `
l'Hauterive NV

Winter Hill Red VdP ` 14 ` ` –£3.50 `
d'Oc 1999
Bargain bonny fruit.

## ODDBINS RED

Abbotts Ammonite Côtes ` 15 ` ` –£5.00 `
du Roussillon 1999
A juicy glugging red with a hint of the
hot, sweaty Midi sun.

Baron Saint-Pierre, ` 14.5 ` ` –£3.50 `
Coteaux du Languedoc
1998

Château de Combebelle ` 15.5 ` ` £5–7 `
Saint-Chinian 1998
(biodynamic)
Rich, juicy undertone to superb herby
fruit and tannins.

Château de Valcombe, ` 17 ` ` £5–7 `
Costières de Nîmes 1998
Cheroots, hedgerows, garigues,
leather, smoke, tannins, hint of old
wood – enough for you?

Château de Valcombe ` 16 ` ` £5–7 `
Prestige, Costières de
Nîmes 1998
A touch less grip than the cheaper
wine from this property.

Château Depaule, ` 16.5 ` ` –£5.00 `
Cabardes 1998
Tobacco, coffee, plums – plus texture
and tension between fruit and acidity.
Complex and bold.

Château Grand Escalion, ` 17 ` ` £5–7 `
Costières de Nîmes 1998

A lot like Ch de Valcombe except it's
more difficult to get your tongue
round the name.

Château Lamarche ` 15 ` ` £7–10 `
Canon 'Candelaire',
Canon-Fronsac 1998
An accomplished claret with genuine
claims to be ranked alongside grands
crus – the tannins are certainly in this
class.

Château Maris Minervois ` 16 ` ` £5–7 `
1998 (biodynamic)
So deep and gravely, gravelly savoury
it must have rich cheese to go with it.
Great tannins here.

Château Ollieux ` 17 ` ` £5–7 `
Romanis, Corbières 1998
Quite delicious in a way a great Médoc
can sometimes be: tobaccoey, coffee-
edged, beautifully smooth tannins,
elongated fruit. Outstanding fruit here.

Château St-Jean de ` 13 ` ` –£5.00 `
Conques, Saint-Chinian
1998

Château Vaugelas Cuvée ` 15.5 ` ` –£5.00 `
Prestige Corbières 1998
Cherries and plums, ripe and ready,
with a smoothly delivered, stylish
finish.

Comte Cathare Fitou ` 16 ` ` £5–7 `
1998
The tannins lurk under the surface of
the ripe fruit and so we get great
smooth texture.

Comte Cathare Le Clot ` 16.5 ` ` £5–7 `
La Clap Coteaux du
Languedoc 1999
Very elegant in spite of its insistent
tannins and all-embracing fruit.

Côte-Rôtie Guigal 1996 ` 17 ` ` £20+ `
The wine rates twelve points –

twenty-four hours after being opened. But if poured into a large jug and allowed to breathe for forty-eight hours a vigorous, beautiful Côte-Rôtie emerges. Odd world, isn't it, that an artefact should require such handling?

**Côtes du Rhône, Clos** 16 £5–7
**Petite Bellane 1999**
The surge of herby tannins is checked on the finish by lovely rich fruit.

**Côtes du Rhône,** 15 £5–7
**Domaine d'Andezon 1999**
Terrific tannins and deep warm fruit.

**Côtes du Rhône Guigal** 16 £7–10
**1998**
Always, incredibly, a consistently rich and svelte performer on the taste buds.

**Côtes du Rhône Les** 14 £5–7
**Arbousiers, Remejeanne**
**1997**

**Crozes-Hermitage** 15 £7–10
**Domaine du Pavillion-**
**Mercurol 1998**
Coal-edged chewy fruit.

**Crozes-Hermitage Les** 13 £7–10
**Pierrelles, Belle 1996**

**Crozes-Hermitage** 15.5 £7–10
**Meysonniers, Chapoutier**
**1998**
Typical Crozes: you either love the charcoal or you loathe it. I'm in the middle somewhere.

**Domaine Borie de Maurel** 17.5 £7–10
**Belle de Nuit, Minervois**
**1999**
Spreads itself lavishly on the taste buds and refuses to budge. A bottle might last a week, so lingering is the richly complex, stunningly tannic fruit.

**Domaine Borie de Maurel** 17 £5–7

**Esprit d'Automne,**
**Minervois 1999**
Lush edge to the cigar-tangy fruit. Very ripe and ready.

**Domaine Borie de Maurel** 14 £5–7
**Rêve de Carignan,**
**Minervois 1999**
Immensely juicy and ripe.

**Domaine de la Vistoule** 16 £5–7
**Cabernet Sauvignon, VdP**
**d'Oc 1998**
Gracious! The energy of the wine is superb. And the warmth!

**Domaine de la Vistoule** 15.5 £5–7
**Merlot, VdP d'Oc 1998**
Juicy, herby, dry and food-friendly.

**Domaine de Montine** 16 £5–7
**Coteaux du Tricastin**
**1998**
Terrifically tasty tannins!

**Domaine de Saint-** 15 £5–7
**Antoine Syrah, Costières**
**de Nîmes 1999**
Chewy, ripe, herby and deliciously dry.

**Domaine l'Aigueliere** 16.5 £7–10
**Grenat, VdP du Mont**
**Baudile 1998**
Spicy, creamy, a touch tobaccoey, and deliciously soft and fruit-crumbly on the finish.

**Domaine Lafage Cuvée** 15 £5–7
**Les Côtes du Roussillon**
**1998**
A very bright, almost juicy, plummy wine.

**Domaine Remaury** 17 –£5.00
**Cabernet Sauvignon VdP**
**d'Oc 1998**
Wonderfully invigorated, soulful, charcoal-chewy fruit of immense

depth and richness. The price is absurd given the potency and flavour on offer here.

**Domaine Saint-Jullien** `15.5` `–£5.00`
Coteaux du Languedoc
1998

**Dourthe No 1 Bordeaux** `13` `£5–7`
1998
Green tannins on the finish. Eaten with raw horse steak, this wine rates 16.

**Enclave des Papes Cuvée** `16` `–£5.00`
Spéciale, Côtes du Rhône
1999
Wonderfully smooth and unruffled fruit with a hint of spiced plum and tobacco. Fantastic value for money.

**Grangeneuve Vieilles** `17` `£5–7`
Vignes Coteaux du
Tricastin 1998
The chewy texture is fraught with deliciousness: tobacco, tea, chocolate, herbs and relaxed tannins.

**James Herrick Millia** `16.5` `£5–7`
Passum Syrah, VdP d'Oc
1998
Brilliant dark, dusky fruit of concentrated cassis and crunchy tannins.

**La Maquis Coteaux du** `16` `–£5.00`
Languedoc 1998
Stunning concentration of rich fruit and rich savoury tannins. Huge personality and poise.

**Le Grand Verdier,** `17` `£5–7`
Minervois 1998
Has tannins which grip, fruit which thrills, texture which excites – even the price is delicious.

**Les Bories Blanques,** `15` `–£5.00`
Minervois 1998
Rampant tannicity here.

**Les Grandes Vignes,** `16` `£5–7`
Côtes du Rhône 1999
Has delicious hedgerow ripeness and a warm, immensely soft texture.

**Mas Saint-Vincent** `16.5` `–£5.00`
Coteaux du Languedoc
1998
A stunningly complete and captivatingly rich masterwork of herbs, earth, hedgerows and passion.

**Mosaique Grenache** `14` `–£5.00`
Syrah VdP d'Oc 1999
Polished rusticity. Charmingly fruity price.

**Mosaique Syrah, VdP** `14` `–£5.00`
d'Oc 1999
Juicy fun drinking.

**Pavillion de l'Escalion,** `16.5` `–£5.00`
Costières de Nîmes 1998
Such warmth and herby richness, allied to sensational tannins, that you can't believe the price tag.

**Plan Macassan, Costières** `16.5` `–£5.00`
de Nîmes 1998
Brilliant wine to take to the restaurant – it can't be affected by cork taint. And the fruit, all-action and feisty, deserves preserving – it's terrific!

**Ptomaine de Blageurs** `14` `–£5.00`
Syrah, VdP de l'Ardèche
1997
Amusing pretension to the label, none to the fruit – except for the waggish tannins.

**Santenay 1er Cru Les** `13` `£10–13`
Gravières, Domaine
Bourgeot 1998
I love the tannins but I don't go a bundle on the bitterness of the fruit – not at £13.

## SAFEWAY RED

**Anciennes Vignes** `15.5` `−£5.00`
**Carignan, VdP de l'Aude**
**1998**
What great tannins here! The perfect
steak frites bistro wine.

**Baron de Lestac,** `15` `−£5.00`
**Bordeaux 1998**
Excellent class here. A real claret. Has
depth and decisiveness. No mucking
about. It gets straight on with it.

**Beaujolais Villages** `12` `£5–7`
**'Combes aux Jacques'**
**1998**
Selected stores.

**Bourgogne Pinot Noir** `12` `£5–7`
**'Réserve de la Famille'**
**1996**

**Cabernet Sauvignon VdP** `16` `−£5.00`
**d'Oc 1998, Safeway**
Great bargain. Claret-like tannins meet
Italian-style fruit in an earthy clash of
pleasure-giving, ripe, fat fruit.

**Calvet St-Emilion 1997** `13` `£5–7`

**Château Clos de la** `14` `£7–10`
**Chesnaie, Lalande de**
**Pomerol 1998**
Elegant and classy but its tannins make
it suitable for serious claret buffs only.
Selected stores.

**Château de Coulaine,** `16` `£5–7`
**Chinon 1998 (organic)**
Imagine earth cherries and pencil
shavings, herbs and good firm tannins.
Brilliant, serious, food-friendly. 67
stores.

**Château de Lausières,** `15.5` `−£5.00`
**Coteaux du Languedoc**
**1998**

**Château de** `16` `£7–10`
**Villenouvette, Cuvée**
**Marcel Barsalou**
**Corbières 1998**
So smooth you wonder how the
grapes are contained in it – let alone
the Midi sun, herbs and deep soil. Very
elegant. 70 stores.

**Château Grand Champs** `13.5` `£5–7`
**Bordeaux 1998**
Chewy and rich, very unclaret-like
(which is in its favour, in several
senses).

**Château Jouanin Cuvée** `15` `£5–7`
**Prestige, Côtes de**
**Castillon 1998**
Juicy and ripe but with richly
engaging, savoury tannins.

**Château La Rose Brisson** `16` `£10–13`
**St-Emilion Grand Cru**
**1998**
Deliciously woody and dry, but this
sensation is dispersed by the cassis-
edged finish. An impressively cultured
and perfectly mature claret.

**Château Limonier,** `15.5` `−£5.00`
**Bordeaux 1998**
Amazing! True concentrated claret at a
knock-down price.

**Château Liversan, Cru** `12` `£7–10`
**Bourgeois, Haut-Médoc**
**1997**
Selected stores.

**Château Maison Neuve** `15.5` `£7–10`
**Montagne St-Emilion**
**1998**
Very proper and claret-like in its
richest and most attractive way.
Gorgeous tannins here, soft and a
touch soupy.

FRENCH RED

**Château Montbrun** `16.5` `−£5.00`
**Corbières 1999**
Oh yes! The real thing. France uniquely produces great country wines, and this one is a fine, rich, deep, dry, earthy yet full rounded specimen. Fantastic value.

**Château Montbrun de** `15` `−£5.00`
**Gautherius Corbières 1999**
Spreads swiftly, like a forest fire, and engages the taste buds in a fight to sort out the soft, ripe plums from the earthy tannins.

**Château Philippe de** `15.5` `−£5.00`
**Vessière, Costières de Nîmes 1997**

**Château Pourchaud-** `15.5` `£5–7`
**Larquey, Bordeaux 1998 (organic)**
Terrific tannins here. Really biteable and expressive. Selected stores.

**Château Rozier, St-** `13` `£10–13`
**Emilion Grand Cru 1996**
I find it too expensive for the fruit on offer. I prefer Safeway's under-a-fiver clarets.

**Château Tour du Mont,** `13.5` `£5–7`
**Haut-Médoc 1998**
Has that underlying charcoal tannicity which puts so many Aussie fruit lovers off.

**Chevalier de Malle,** `14` `£7–10`
**Graves 1998**
Give it five years. Selected stores.

**Claret NV, Safeway** `13` `−£5.00`

**Corbières 1999, Safeway** `14` `−£3.50`
Juicy and very immediate. A great party wine.

**Côtes du Rhône 1999,** `14` `−£3.50`
**Safeway**
Great-value tippling. Characterful and correct.

**Crozes-Hermitage** `14.5` `£5–7`
**Etienne Barret 1999**
Ripe, soft and yielding. Unusually forward for so young a Crozes.

**Domaine Chris Limouzi,** `16.5` `£5–7`
**Corbières 1998**
Stunning softness and beautifully textured tobacco and blackberry fruit. Gorgeous wine. France fights back! Selected stores.

**Domaine de Contenson** `16` `−£5.00`
**Merlot, VdP d'Oc 1998**
Simply hugely quaffable and then some. The fruit is generous and warm.

**Domaine des Bruyeres,** `16.5` `−£5.00`
**Côtes de Malepere 1998**
What effrontery to be so rich and complex, dry and decisive, for such a small sum of money. It's a lovely wine.

**Domaine des Lauriers,** `16.5` `£5–7`
**Faugères 1997**
Thundering fruit collects the tannins as it gallops across the taste buds scattering everything in its path. Marvellous quaffing! Quite exceptional. Top 157 stores.

**Domaine Montmija,** `15.5` `−£5.00`
**Corbières 1999 (organic)**
Brilliant cheery cherry dryness and richness. Has herbs and earth and great food compatibility. Selected stores.

**Domaine Vieux Manoir** `15.5` `−£5.00`
**de Maransan Cuvée Spéciale 1998, Safeway**

**Enclos des Cigales** `14` `—£5.00`
**Merlot, VdP d'Oc 1999**
Nice touches of herbs and earth.
Selected stores.

**Enclos des Cigales Syrah,** `15.5` `—£5.00`
**VdP d'Oc 1999**
The label is so elegant you wonder at
the price ticket. The fruit? Equal to the
label. What a steal for under four quid.
Selected stores.

**Fleurie Domaine des** `13` `£7—10`
**Raclets 1998**

**French Révolution Le** `16` `—£5.00`
**Rouge 1999**
Hugely different from its white cousin,
in that there is real character and
effortless fruit here. Great depth,
marvellous tannins, firm, rich texture.

**Hautes-Côtes de Nuits** `10` `£7—10`
**Cuvée Spéciale 1996**

**James Herrick Millia** `16.5` `£5—7`
**Passum Syrah, VdP d'Oc**
**1998**
Brilliant dark, dusky fruit of
concentrated Cassis and crunchy
tannins. 70 stores.

**Jean Louis Denois** `17` `£5—7`
**Mourvèdre/Grenache,**
**VdP d'Oc 1998**
Stunningly well textured and cultured.
Potent fruit of complexity and minor
grandeur combined with rich herbs
and lovely warm tannins.

**L'If Merlot/Carignan,** `14.5` `—£5.00`
**VdP d'Oc 1999**
Handsome tannic structure. The fruit
is deep and rich.

**La Chasse du Pape** `16.5` `—£5.00`
**'Réserve Barrique' Côtes**
**du Rhône 1999**

Lovely warmth and ripeness here.
Torrents of flavour. Yet it's stylish and
controlled. Terrific value.

**La Cuvée Mythique VdP** `16` `£5—7`
**d'Oc 1998**
One of the most elegantly robust Oc
reds for a couple of years now. This
vintage is urgent and very severely
impressive. Selected stores.

**La Provincia Cabernet** `15.5` `£5—7`
**Sauvignon/Syrah, VdP**
**d'Oc 1998**
Happy juice from nose to throat. Keen
tannins well held by the blackcurrant
fruit. 70 stores.

**La Source Merlot/Syrah** `15` `—£5.00`
**VdP d'Oc 1999**
Now here the hedgerow sweetness of
the fruit is offset by some Midi-warm
tannins and a dry, earthy finish.

**'Les Tourelles' Cahors** `15.5` `—£5.00`
**1999**
Lush, warm, herby, dry-edged,
gorgeously charged with savoury
tannins, and a striking finish.

**Mercurey Raoul Clerget** `12` `£7—10`
**1996**

**Merlot Vin de Pays d'Oc** `14` `—£3.50`
**1999, Safeway**
A very jammy Merlot.

**Minervois 1999, Safeway** `14` `—£3.50`
Sheer love juice.

**Mont Tauch Merlot,** `17` `£7—10`
**Barrel Matured, VdP du**
**Torgan 1998**
Superb tobacco undertones to the
leather and plummy spiciness. The
Pétrus of the Midi? Extraordinarily
complex and beautifully textured
richness. Selected stores.

**Moulin de Ciffre** `16.5` `£5–7`
**Faugères 1998**
Gorgeous dusky, chewy fruit of
flavour, depth and stature. Power,
elegance, personality – it's impressive
stuff.

**No 2 Château Lafon-** `13.5` `£13–20`
**Rochet, St-Estephe 1996**
Selected stores.

**Oak-aged Côtes du** `13.5` `–£5.00`
**Rhône 1999, Safeway**
Very dry.

**Organic French Red VdP** `13` `–£5.00`
**du Gard 1999, Safeway**
Chewy plums and raspberries. Don't
like the aroma much but the fruit is
respectably clothed.

**Pinot Noir d'Autrefois** `13` `–£5.00`
**VdP d'Oc 1999**
Quite what these other times, or olden
times, were like it is difficult to say,
but Burgundians won't quake in their
nostalgic clogs.

**Pommard Premier Cru** `11` `£13–20`
**Le Clos Blanc 1997**
Simply appalling price for such
simpering simplicity.

**Pommard Premier Cru** `12` `£13–20`
**Les Arvelets 1996**
Good pong, lousy juicy finish. Yields
of grapes far too high.

**Réserve Valseque VdP de** `14` `–£3.50`
**l'Aude 1999**
Thin, touch ascetic, but firmly stoic in
the face of this deprivation to become
wirily fruity on the finish. Very
pleasant chilled.

**Savigny du Domaine du** `11` `£7–10`
**Château de Meursault**
**1996**

**Syrah VdP d'Oc 1999,** `15` `–£3.50`
**Safeway**
Fantastic value for such deliciously
juicy richness and tannic balance.
Forward and very modern.

**Valreas Cuvée Prestige,** `16` `–£5.00`
**Côtes du Rhône-Villages**
**1999**
Very thick and blackcurranty with
hints of plum and raspberry and a
touch of fig. A terrifically rich texture
and ripe, savoury tannins.

**Young Vatted Grenache** `15` `–£3.50`
**VdP de l'Ardèche 1999**
Superbly active plum and strawberry
fruit, fine-grained tannins and a
flourish on the finish. Great chilled
with fish.

**Young Vatted Syrah VdP** `15` `–£5.00`
**de Vaucluse 1999,**
**Safeway**
A very plump rich red with depths
which few wines at this price plumb.

## SAINSBURY'S RED

**Beaujolais NV,** `13.5` `–£5.00`
**Sainsbury's**

**Beaujolais Villages Les** `12` `£5–7`
**Roches Grillées 1999**
Falls a bit short of what I look for in a
£5.50 wine. Most stores.

**Bordeaux Rouge,** `13` `–£3.50`
**Sainsbury's**

**Cabernet Sauvignon d'Oc** `15.5` `–£3.50`
**NV, Sainsbury's**
Meaty with warm tannins, a vegetal
undertone and very smooth exterior.
The wine's interior, and it isn't
shallow, is soft blackcurrant fruit.

Cabernet Sauvignon d'Oc `14.5` `-£3.50`
NV, Sainsbury's (3-litre
box)
Like a claret (old-style) in its very dry
peppery grouchiness. Needs food. The
price band reflects the equivalent price
for a 75cl bottle.

Château Beaumont Cru `15` `£13-20`
Bourgeois, Haut-Médoc
1995

Château Clement-Pichon, `13` `£10-13`
Haut-Médoc 1995

Château Coufran Cru `13` `£10-13`
Bourgeois, Haut Medoc
1996

Château de la Grande `16.5` `£10-13`
Gandiole Châteauneuf-
du-Pape 1997
Rolling fruit which unfurls like a
complex carpet of tufted fruits and dry,
woody richness. Lovely toe-tingling
finish. 100 selected stores.

Château de la Tour `14` `£5-7`
Bordeaux Rouge 1998
Quite a bouncy claret as these things
go. And down the throat it goes very
prettily. Selected stores.

Château Haut Bergey, `14` `£10-13`
Pessac-Léognan 1995

Château Haut de la `16` `£5-7`
Pierriere Côtes de
Castillon 1998
Marvellous little claret of substance
and warmth. Lovely gripping tannins
and chocolate and Cassis fruit. Most
stores.

Château Memoires, `14` `£5-7`
Bordeaux Rouge 1996

Château Semeillan `14` `£13-20`

Mazeau Cru Bourgeois,
Listrac 1996

Château Tassin `15` `-£5.00`
Premières Côtes de
Bordeaux 1999
A very dry but very convincing claret
of lingering tannicity and subtle
lushness. At most stores.

Châteauneuf-du-Pape `17` `£10-13`
Château de la Grande
Gardiole 1998
Expensive but mountainous. Intense
richness and herby hauteur. Selected
stores.

Châteauneuf-du-Pape, `15.5` `£10-13`
Domaine Michel Bernard
1997
A massively dry, tannic Rhône red
which grips the molars in a very
austere vice. A brilliant food wine –
rare meat is bred for it. Selected stores.

Chinon Domaine de `16.5` `-£5.00`
Colombier 1999
Best vintage for some years of this
terrific Cabernet Franc. Has ripe
cherries, slatey tannins and a lovely
bitter cherry/cobnut finish. Utterly
delicious. Selected stores.

Claret Cuvée Prestige `14` `-£5.00`
NV, Sainsbury's
Oddly rich and firm but the typical
claret tannins get going after a few
seconds to prove themselves savoury
and tasty. Most stores.

Claret, Sainsbury's `14.5` `-£5.00`

Classic Selection Brouilly `14` `£5-7`
1997, Sainsbury's

Classic Selection `15` `£7-10`
Châteauneuf-du-Pape
1998, Sainsbury's
Most individual and walnutty rich and

softly savoury. Has a modern feel to it. Finishes like an exotic gravy. Most stores.

**Classic Selection St-** `14` `£7–10`
**Emilion 1996, Sainsbury's**
A gutsy St-Em which really suits meat dishes – it isn't for quaffing.

**Clos Magne Figeac, St-** `16` `£7–10`
**Emilion 1997**
Class act. Real Merlot magic here along with deep, savoury tannins. A terrific claret of style and substance. 195 stores.

**Clos René, Pomerol 1994** `16.5` `£20+`
If one must spend £25 on a claret, this is worth every penny. It drips with developed tannins, has huge complexity of fruit, will age for seven or eight years and it's all roaring now. 18 selected stores.

**Côtes du Rhône NV,** `13.5` `–£3.50`
**Sainsbury's**
Very dry and party spirited. Good chilled with grilled fish.

**Crozes-Hermitage Petite** `15.5` `£7–10`
**Ruche 1997**
Classic Crozes – has that extraordinary coal/charcoal edge to the rich fruit. Dry yet beautifully fruity. Selected stores.

**Cuvée Prestige Côtes du** `15` `–£5.00`
**Rhône 1998, Sainsbury's**
Full, dry, rich and handsomely textured and concentrated.

**French Révolution Le** `16` `–£5.00`
**Rouge 1999**
Hugely different from its white cousin, in that there is real character and effortless fruit here. Great depth, marvellous tannins, firm, rich texture.

**Hautes-Côtes de Nuits** `12` `£7–10`
**1998**
Selected stores.

**Hautes-Côtes de Nuits** `13.5` `£7–10`
**Dames Huguettes 1998**
Has some very good points. All thirteen and a half of them. 195 stores.

**Jacques Frelin Organic** `13` `£7–10`
**Crozes-Hermitage 1998**
Has the aroma of stale sausages. 50 stores.

**La Chasse du Pape Côtes** `16.5` `–£5.00`
**du Rhône 1998**
Stunning ripeness and big earthy, rich plum/blackcurrant dryness and urgency. Lovely tannins. Great texture. Selected stores.

**La Demoiselle de** `10` `£13–20`
**Sociando Mallet, Haut-**
**Médoc 1996**

**LPA Côtes de St-Mont** `14.5` `–£5.00`
**1997**
Like a minor juicy-but-dry claret. Terrific with undercooked meats. Selected stores.

**Marsannay Domaine** `15` `£7–10`
**Bertagna 1998**
Delicious: dry, cherry-edged, good tannins, warm fruit with a hint of truffle (subtle hint it's true, but at least it's a real Pinot phenomenon). 130 stores.

**Mercurey Clos la Marche** `13` `£13–20`
**1997**
100 stores.

**Merlot VdP d'Oc NV,** `15.5` `£5–7`
**Sainsbury's (1.5 litre)**
The price band reflects the equivalent price for a 75cl bottle.

Merlot VdP de la Cité de `16.5` `−£5.00`
Carcassonne, Caroline de
Beaulieu 1999
Spicy baked fruit aroma leads to some
stunning herby hedgerow-fruited
richness. Has a refined rusticity of
great, dry charm. Most stores.

Minervois, Sainsbury's `15` `−£3.50`

Old Git Grenache Syrah `15.5` `−£5.00`
1999
Great fun. I'm bound to love the name
and the dry, Midi fruit. Most stores.

Red Burgundy NV, `12` `£5−7`
Sainsbury's

Santenay, Château de `12` `£10−13`
Mercey 1996
Selected stores.

Stowells Claret NV `10` `−£5.00`
(3-litre box)
The price band reflects the equivalent
price for a 75cl bottle.

Stowells of Chelsea `15` `−£3.50`
Merlot VdP d'Oc (3-litre
box)
A dry, subtly leathery wine with a hint
of earthiness and herbs on the finish.
The price band reflects the equivalent
price for a 75cl bottle.

Syrah VdP d'Oc NV, `15` `−£3.50`
Sainsbury's
Soft, hugely gluggable, very light,
gentle tannins and subtle spicing.

Valreas Domaine de la `16.5` `£5−7`
Grande Bellane 1998
(organic)
Wonderful energy and strikingly
stylish tannins here. Offers hedgerow
fruit, herbs, a soft earthiness, and
brilliant tannins as it glides effortlessly
home. Most stores.

Vieux Château Landon, `13` `£7−10`
Médoc 1996

Vin de Pays de l'Aude `16` `−£3.50`
Rouge, Sainsbury's
Tremendous richness and savoury
depth here. Hint of leather, hedgerow
fruit, tannin. Fantastic. Selected stores.

Vin de Pays des Bouches- `14.5` `−£3.50`
du-Rhône NV,
Sainsbury's

Vin Rouge de France NV, `13` `−£3.50`
Sainsbury's (3-litre box)
Rough a touch, but it's only a touch
and it does offer some character.
Needs food to spark into life. The
price band reflects the equivalent price
for a 75cl bottle.

Vougeot Domaine `13` `£13−20`
Bertagna 1995

## SOMERFIELD RED

Buzet Cuvée 44 1997 `15` `−£5.00`
Good stuff! And stuffed with generous
tannins and savoury fruit.

Cabernet Sauvignon d'Oc `14` `−£3.50`
Val d'Orbieu 1998,
Somerfield
Real blackcurrant and pepper – but
very soft and thick.

Château Blanca, `15.5` `−£5.00`
Bordeaux 1999
A stunning claret for the money. Thick
as an Aussie, spicy as a Spaniard. The
future of Bordeaux?

Château Cazal Cuvée des `16` `£5−7`
Fées Vieilles Vignes, St-
Chinian 1998
A 100% Syrah of hugely rich and
hedgerow-fruited opulence. It spreads

itself slowly and lovingly over the taste buds. Selected stores.

**Château Plaisance,** `15.5` `£5–7`
**Montagne St-Emilion**
**1996**

**Château Valoussière** `16.5` `−£5.00`
**Coteaux du Languedoc**
**1997**

Gorgeous spices and tannins, fruit and acids. A really stylish character here of depth and deliciousness. Beautifully ruffled texture.

**Château Verdignan Haut-** `13.5` `£10–13`
**Médoc 1996**

Far too expensive for the level of excitement. It's fruity and sveltely tannic but so are several Somerfield wines at a third of the price. Selected stores.

**Claret NV, Somerfield** `13.5` `−£3.50`

Claret as real juice of the vine: no earth, no stalks, no green leaves.

**Corbières Rouge Val** `15` `−£3.50`
**d'Orbieu 1998,**
**Somerfield**

Superb texture and tension between spicy plums, tannins (savoury) and subtle acids. What a bargain!

**Côtes du Rhône-Villages** `14` `−£5.00`
**1999, Somerfield**

Lovely hedgerow sweetness offset by earthy tannins.

**Côtes du Roussillon** `15` `−£3.50`
**Rouge 1998, Somerfield**

A bountiful bargain. Not a barrel of laughs, but a stainless-steel tankful of ripe rich smiles.

**Crozes-Hermitage 1998** `14.5` `−£5.00`

It's the lovely touch of charcoal to the dark cherries I like so much.

**Domaine de Bisconte** `15` `−£5.00`
**Côtes du Roussillon 1998**

A blend of Grenache Noir, Carignan, Syrah and Mourvèdre which is ripe, forward and hugely food-friendly.

**Domaine de Courtilles** `15.5` `£5–7`
**Côte 125 Corbières 1998**

**Domaine Haut-St-** `16` `−£5.00`
**Georges Corbières 1998**

Almost sweet but the oak holds it back and the blackberries hold the fruit and the fruit is held by the tannins. An all-embracing wine.

**Domaine la Tuque Bel** `14` `£5–7`
**Air, Côtes de Castillon**
**1997**

**Fitou Rocher d'Ambrée** `14.5` `−£5.00`
**1998, Somerfield**

Sticky tar tannins make it a real mouthful.

**Goûts et Couleurs** `16` `−£5.00`
**Cabernet Sauvignon VdP**
**d'Oc 1998**

Delicious Cabernet of great style and purposeful fruitiness. It's lavish on the finish.

**Goûts et Couleurs Syrah** `16` `−£5.00`
**Mourvèdre VdP d'Oc**
**1999**

Real class here: personality, wit, warmth, depth, texture, balanced elements and complexity.

**Hautes-Côtes de Beaune** `12` `£5–7`
**Rouge, G. Desiré 1999**

Simplistic.

**James Herrick Cuvée** `16.5` `−£5.00`
**Simone VdP d'Oc 1998**

An intensely sophisticated and chic bottle of fruit which accompanies a good book or a complex CD like a dream. Subtle yet tenacious.

Médoc NV, Somerfield `13` `~£5.00`
Bit too juicy to rate higher. Selected stores.

Oak Aged Claret NV, `15` `~£5.00`
Somerfield
Great style and texture. A really charming claret.

Red Burgundy 1997, `12` `£5–7`
Somerfield
Too sweet.

Vacqueyras Côtes du `15.5` `~£5.00`
Rhône 1999
Warm, soupy, rich, clinging and urgent-to-please.

Vacqueyras Domaine de `15` `~£5.00`
la Soleiade 1998
Unusually forward for a Vacqueyras so young. Hugely drinkable and open-hearted.

VdP des Coteaux de `14` `~£3.50`
l'Ardèche Rouge 1999,
Somerfield
Dry, hint of rustic sod, barbecue wine.

VdP des Côtes de `15` `~£3.50`
Gascogne Rouge 1998,
Somerfield
A great little warm-hearted party wine.

Winter Hill Rouge, VdP `14` `~£3.50`
de l'Aude 1999
Very correct and stiff-upper-lippish. Dry, civilised, accomplished.

## SPAR RED

Brouilly Les Celliers de `12` `£5–7`
Bellevue 1998
Too pricey.

Claret NV, Spar `15` `~£5.00`
Terrific stuff. Really deliciously firm, savoury tannins and integrated

blackcurrant fruit. A bargain claret, authentic and food friendly.

Cordier Château Le `15.5` `£7–10`
Cadet de Martinens,
Margaux 1995
A solid claret, perhaps the woodiness showing over the fruit, but the texture is excellent and the typical blackcurrant fruit is elegant and free-flowing. Outstanding tannins make an impact on the finish. Overall, a festive food wine – especially meat dishes.

Coteaux du Languedoc `13` `~£3.50`
NV

Côtes du Ventoux Le `15.5` `~£5.00`
Rossignol, Spar 1998
The best cheap red at Spar: rich, balanced, characterful, good balance of fruit, alcohol and tannins. A terrific, genuine, highly quaffable, very dry country wine.

Fitou NV, Spar `16` `~£5.00`
Touch of tar, tobacco, coffee, then blackcurrants, herbs and earth. A wonderful rustic mouthful.

French Country VdP de `13` `~£3.50`
l'Herault NV, Spar (1 litre)
Has some interesting earthy presence but doesn't finish tellingly. Price band reflects the 75cl equivalent.

Gevrey-Chambertin Les `12` `£13–20`
Caves des Hautes-Côtes
1994

Hautes-Côtes de Beaune `10` `£5–7`
1995, Spar
All that's left on the bones is a shred of tannin.

La Côte Syrah Merlot `15.5` `~£5.00`
VdP d'Oc 1998, Spar
Lovely smooth ripe fruit, handsomely

textured and warm and with a delicious thwack of intense richness on the finish.

Lussac St-Emilion 1997 | 11 | £5-7

Merlot VdP d'Oc 1998, | 15.5 | -£5.00
Spar
Aromatic, feisty, very dry, terrific herbs and Midi sunshine – they all impact very agreeably. Terrific price for such a performance.

Salaison Shiraz/Cabernet | 15.5 | -£5.00
VdP d'Oc 1998, Spar
Gripping tannins to some smoky, rich, savoury fruit. Very dry to finish, but this is an attribute – it means food will be enhanced in flavour and pleasure.

Vin de Pays de l'Aude | 12 | -£3.50
NV, Spar
Real rusticity playacting at being smooth and plump.

## TESCO RED

Beaujolais NV, Tesco | 11 | -£3.50

Beaujolais-Villages 1999, | 12 | -£5.00
Tesco
Dullsville personified. Not at all stores.

Burgundy Pinot Noir | 13.5 | £5-7
1998, Tesco
Almost, almost . . .

Buzet Cuvée 44 1997 | 15 | -£5.00
Good stuff! And stuffed with generous tannins and savoury fruit.

Cabernet Sauvignon VdP | 14 | -£3.50
d'Oc NV, Tesco
Lovely dry touches of hedgerow fruitiness which is not remotely rough though it is charmingly rustic.

Chartron la Fleur | 13 | -£5.00
Château La Grave
Bordeaux 1997

Château Clement Pichon, | 13 | £13-20
Cru Bourgeois Haut-
Médoc 1996

Château de Côte de | 15.5 | £5-7
Montpezat, Côtes de
Castillon 1997
One of my favourite Tesco clarets because it has efficient fruit, sufficient tannins, and a great warmth of texture holding it all together. An excellent claret for not a lot of money.

Château de Goelane | 13 | £5-7
Bordeaux Supérieur 1997
Soft and lissom, lacks a punchy finish.

Château Ginestière | 15.5 | -£5.00
Côteaux du Languedoc
1997

Château Haut-Chaigneau | 14 | £13-20
Lalande de Pomerol 1996

Château la Fleur Bellevue | 14 | £5-7
Premières Côtes de Blaye
1998
Softly spoken, politely tannic, firmly fruity. Charming friend to roast lamb with garlic and herbs.

Château La Raze | 14 | £5-7
Beauvalet Haut-Médoc
1997

Château la Tour de Mons | 13.5 | £13-20
Bordeaux 1996

Château Lafarque Pessac- | 12 | £13-20
Léognan 1996

Château Liliane-Ladouys | 12 | £13-20
Cru Bourgeois Supérieur
Saint-Estephe 1996

Château Maucaillou, Cru `12` `£20+`
Bourgeois Moulis en
Médoc 1996

Château Maurel `14.5` `−£5.00`
Fonsalade, St-Chinian
1997

Château Tour de `16` `−£5.00`
l'Espérance Bordeaux
Supérieur 1997
Classic claret at an astonishing price.
Has smoky richness, developed
charcoal tannin, and the fruit, brave
and battling, shines through. Top 200
stores.

Claret, Tesco `12.5` `−£3.50`

Clarity Bordeaux Rouge `14` `−£5.00`
1998
Has some bite to it. Great meat dish
companion.

Corbières NV, Tesco `13.5` `−£3.50`
Dry with a paradoxical juicy mesh of
fruit on the finish.

Corbiéres Réserve La `15` `−£5.00`
Sansoure 1999, Tesco
Soft, very ripe fruit. Very drinkable
and very good value.

Côte-Rôtie Guigal 1996 `17` `£20+`
The wine rates twelve points –
twenty-four hours after being opened.
But if poured into a large jug and
allowed to breathe for forty-eight
hours a vigorous, beautiful Côte-Rôtie
emerges. Odd world, isn't it, that an
artefact should require such handling?

Côtes du Rhône NV, `13.5` `−£3.50`
Tesco

Côtes du Rhône-Villages `14` `−£5.00`
Domaine de la Grande
Retour 1999, Tesco

I go for the herbs mostly. And the hint
of soil.

Dark Horse Barrique `14` `−£5.00`
Aged Cahors 1998

Domaine du Soleil `14.5` `−£5.00`
Syrah/Malbec VdP d'Oc
NV

Fitou NV, Tesco `14.5` `−£3.50`
Has charm and character and the
cherry-rich fruit controls its jammy
side as well as subsuming the earthy
tannins.

Fitou Réserve Baron de la `15.5` `−£5.00`
Tour NV, Tesco
A lovely rusticity controlled by its
smooth, urbane manners.

French Grenache `14.5` `−£5.00`
Prestige, Tesco

French Grenache, Tesco `14` `−£3.50`

French Merlot VdP d'Oc `14.5` `−£3.50`
NV, Tesco
A deliciously meaty party wine. Has
loads of flavour and finishes with some
gutsy fruit.

Gamay, Tesco `10` `−£3.50`

Gevrey-Chambertin 1997 `12` `£13–20`
Top 85 stores. Also available in 1.5-
litre bottle.

Goûts et Couleurs `16` `−£5.00`
Premium Cuvée
Cabernet Sauvignon VdP
d'Oc 1998
Hums with dry, impressively
compacted blackcurrant fruit. Very
elegant tannins here. Very deeply laid
fruit of textured class. Most stores.

Graves 1996, Tesco `14` `£7–10`
Very correct and subtly posh. Real

claret, so it costs, but it isn't too austere or ill-mannered.

**Les Etoiles French** `13` `−£5.00`
**Organic Red Wine NV**

**Louis Jadot Combe aux** `13` `£5–7`
**Jacques Beaujolais**
**Villages 1998**
Grrr . . .

**Margaux 1997, Tesco** `12` `£7–10`
I can't see, clearly, why £10 is a sane price for this wine unless one makes the excuse that the makers insist on a luxurious lifestyle (where they drink Californian Cabernets). Perhaps on these grounds Tesco found this a candidate for its 'Tesco Finest' range.

**Médoc 1997, Tesco** `13` `−£5.00`
Odd ripeness which lingers ahead of the tannins.

**Minervois NV, Tesco** `14` `−£3.50`
Very blackcurrant-jammy with a hint of herbs and earth. Great food/party wine.

**Nuits-St-Georges, Les** `13` `£13–20`
**Chezeaux 1996**

**Oak Aged Red Burgundy** `13.5` `£5–7`
**1998, Tesco**
Amazing presumption and close to being very likeable.

**Oaked Côtes du Rhône** `13.5` `−£5.00`
**NV**

**Pommard 1er Cru, Clos** `13.5` `£13–20`
**des Verger 1996**

**Rasteau Côtes du Rhône-** `16.5` `−£5.00`
**Villages 1998**
One of my favourite villages in the Rhône (anywhere in the world, I daresay) so can I be objective? Hopefully. The wine is drenched in herbs of subtlety yet rich incisiveness,

and the fruit is bold, textured and fully charged from nose to throat. Not at all stores.

**St-Emilion 1997, Tesco** `12.5` `£7–10`
Most stores.

**Syrah VdP d'Oc, Tesco** `13.5` `−£3.50`

**Valreas Domaine de la** `16.5` `£5–7`
**Grande Bellane 1998**
**(organic)**
Wonderful energy and strikingly stylish tannins here. Offers hedgerow fruit, herbs, a soft earthiness, and brilliant tannins as it glides effortlessly home.

**Yvecourt Claret Bordeaux** `12` `−£5.00`
**1998**
Claret? Bordeaux? On the same label? The fruit, alack, has no such double emphasis.

## THRESHER RED

**Abbotts Cumulus** `16.5` `£5–7`
**Minervois 1998**
The tannins are hugely gripping and classy but what leaves the most delicious sensory impression are the cheroot-edged blackberries.

**Beaujolais AC Regional** `13.5` `−£5.00`
**Classics 1997**

**Beaujolais-Villages** `13` `£5–7`
**Duboeuf 1997**

**Château Sauvage Premier** `13` `£5–7`
**Côtes de Bordeaux 1997**
Bit on the costive side.

**Château Suau, 1er Côtes** `13.5` `£5–7`
**de Bordeaux 1997**
**(unoaked)**

**Claret Regional Classic,** `14` `−£5.00`
**Sichel NV**

Côtes de Beaune-Villages 12 £7–10
1996

Côtes du Rhône-Villages 14 –£5.00
Les Faisans 1998

Dark Horse Cahors 1998 14 –£5.00
Hints of rusticity well controlled –
perhaps too well – but the tannins go
down fighting.

Domaine Peyrat 15 £5–7
Cabernet Sauvignon 1997
An outstandingly jammy and fresh
d'Oc Cab with the earthiness
subsumed under the sweetness. The
tannins arrive late, and welcomingly.

Fitou Terroir de Tuchan 17 £7–10
1998
Nine quid for a Fitou? When it's as
rich, thick, beautifully balanced as this,
yes. Yes a thousand times. It compares
with northern Rhône and Aussie
Shirazes costing a great deal more. It
has great style and riveting fruitiness.

Fleurie Georges Duboeuf 11 £7–10
1998

Fleurie Regional Classics 13.5 £5–7
1998

French Révolution Le 16 –£5.00
Rouge 1999
Hugely different from its white cousin,
in that there is real character and
effortless fruit here. Great depth,
marvellous tannins, firm, rich texture.

La Ramillade Côtes du 16 £7–10
Rhône Rasteau 1997
Gorgeous tobacco-scented, savoury-
rich fruit with lovely curves to the
tannins. Wine Rack and Bottoms Up
only.

Morgon Domaine des 13.5 £5–7
Côtes de Douby 1998

Good tannins here. Must be the
vintage of the millennium. Not at
Wine Rack.

Old Bush Vines Carignan 13.5 –£5.00
1998
Juicy and ripe.

Pinot Noir, Louis Jadot 12.5 £7–10
1998
Dull for the money. Not responsive to
the palate's needs.

Sirius Red 1997 13.5 £5–7
Tannic. Needs a casserole of dead
things.

## UNWINS RED

Ash Ridge Grenache/ 12 –£5.00
Merlot 1998

Ash Ridge Syrah d'Oc 13 –£5.00
1998

Chapelle St-Marie Syrah 16.5 –£5.00
1998
Superb savoury tannins allied to
marvellous earthy fruit, a thin price
tag and thick tannins.

Chassagne-Montrachet 11 £13–20
Louis Jadot 1994

Château Astruc 14.5 –£5.00
Minervois 1998

Château Beychevelle St- 12 £20+
Julien 4eme Cru 1995

Château de Cazeneuve 15 £7–10
Le Roc de Mates Pic St-
Loup 1997
Drier than its cheaper cousin and with
a raspberry edge.

Château de Cazeneuve 15.5 £5–7
Les Terres Rouges Pic St-
Loup 1997

Delicious tobacco-edged fruit and jammy tannins.

**Château Giscours** 11 £20+
**Margaux 3eme Cru 1995**

**Château Trignon Côtes** 17.5 £5–7
**du Rhône-Villages Sablet**
**Ramillades 1998**
Absolutely compelling richness and beautifully earthy tannins. The quintessence of elegant rusticity. Marvellous stuff! From nose to throat it's terrific, taut, tenacious.

**Châteauneuf-du-Pape** 13.5 £10–13
**Louis Mousset 1998**
The fruit struggles to keep pace with the tannins.

**Côte-Rôtie Guigal 1996** 17 £20+
The wine rates twelve points – twenty-four hours after being opened. But if poured into a large jug and allowed to breathe for forty-eight hours a vigorous, beautiful Côte-Rôtie emerges. Odd world, isn't it, that an artefact should require such handling?

**Côtes du Rhône Guigal** 16 £7–10
**1998**
Always, incredibly, a consistently rich and svelte performer on the taste buds.

**Domaine de l'Arneillaud** 18 £5–7
**Cairanne Côtes du**
**Rhône-Villages 1999**
Magnificent herby potency and extremely deep elegance here. Has world-class tannins and intense richness.

**Domaine de la Grand** 16 £5–7
**Bellane, Valreas 1997**
Ragged yet dainty on its feet, this richly finishing, very dry wine combines a fair spread of hedgerow fruit and delicious tannin. It is classic

Rhône-Villages red. Great drunk out of a Viking horn or sipped with *lièvre à la royale*.

**Domaine de la Soleiade,** 15 £5–7
**Vacqueyras 1998**
Unusually forward for a Vacqueyras so young. Hugely drinkable and open-hearted.

**Fitou Château de Segure** 15.5 £5–7
**1998**
Lovely, Midi-made fruit: herby, earthy, tannic, terrific.

**Gigondas Domaine des** 14 £7–10
**Amandiers 1998**
Uncommonly juicy. The tannins arrive late.

**Hautes-Côtes de Beaune** 10 £7–10
**1997**
Sweet nothing.

**James Herrick Cuvée** 16.5 –£5.00
**Simone VdP d'Oc 1998**
An intensely sophisticated and chic bottle of fruit which accompanies a good book or a complex CD like a dream. Subtle yet tenacious.

**La Cigalière Côtes du** 15 –£5.00
**Rhône 1998**

**Les Beaux Sites Domaine** 15.5 –£5.00
**de Castan Cabernet**
**Sauvignon 1997**

**Madiran Château de** 14 £7–10
**Crouseilles 1993**

**Mauregard Château La** 13.5 –£5.00
**Grave Bordeaux 1999**
Bit austere. But I love the tannins. The best use of these lovely tannins would be to use them to blend with a juicy Rosemount Aussie red. You might get a 16.5-point wine then.

Saumur Domaine de la    15.5   −£5.00
Sicardière 1997
Superb dry cherry / raspberry fruit,
clean and fresh with a hint of earth,
plus great texture, soft and delicious.
Hugely friendly, subtle tannins.

St-Emilion 1998    13    £5–7
Good tannins though the fruit gets lost
as it opens up.

Valreas Domaine de la    16.5    £5–7
Grande Bellane 1998
(organic)
Wonderful energy and strikingly
stylish tannins here. Offers hedgerow
fruit, herbs, a soft earthiness, and
brilliant tannins as it glides effortlessly
home.

Wild Pig Barrel Reserve    14    −£5.00
Shiraz 1998
Juice and tannins. Not a traditional
recipe.

## VICTORIA WINE RED

Abbotts Cumulus    16.5    £5–7
Minervois 1998
The tannins are hugely gripping and
classy but what leaves the most
delicious sensory impression are the
cheroot-edged blackberries.

Château Sauvage Premier    13    £5–7
Côtes de Bordeaux 1997
Bit on the costive side.

Château Suau, 1er Côtes    13.5    £5–7
de Bordeaux 1997
(unoaked)

Cornas Les Nobles Rives,    14    £10–13
Côtes de Tain 1994

Côte-Rôtie, Domaine de    10    £20+
Bonserine 1996

Côtes de Beaune-Villages    12    £7–10
1996

Côtes du Rhône-Villages    14    −£5.00
Les Faisans 1998

Dark Horse Cahors 1998    14    −£5.00
Hints of rusticity well controlled –
perhaps too well – but the tannins go
down fighting.

Domaine Peyrat    15    £5–7
Cabernet Sauvignon 1997
An outstandingly jammy and fresh
d'Oc Cab with the earthiness
subsumed under the sweetness. The
tannins arrive late, and welcomingly.

Fitou Special Reserve    14.5    −£5.00
1997

Fitou Terroir de Tuchan    17    £7–10
1998
Nine quid for a Fitou? When it's as
rich, thick, beautifully balanced as this,
yes. Yes a thousand times. It compares
with northern Rhône and Aussie
Shirazes costing a great deal more. It
has great style and riveting fruitiness.

Fleurie Georges Duboeuf    11    £7–10
1998

Fleurie Regional Classics    13.5    £5–7
1998

French Révolution Le    16    −£5.00
Rouge 1999
Hugely different from its white cousin,
in that there is real character and
effortless fruit here. Great depth,
marvellous tannins, firm, rich texture.

Grenache VdP des    14.5    −£3.50
Coteaux de l'Ardèche
1997

Mont Tauch Old Bush    13    −£5.00
Vines Carignan 1998

Morgon Domaine des | 13.5 | £5–7
Côtes de Douby 1998
Good tannins here. Must be the vintage of the millennium.

Old Bush Vines Carignan | 13.5 | –£5.00
1998
Juicy and ripe.

Pinot Noir, Louis Jadot | 12.5 | £7–10
1998
Dull for the money. Not responsive to the palate's needs.

Red Burgundy Vergy | 12 | –£5.00
1997

Sirius Red 1997 | 13.5 | £5–7
Tannic. Needs a casserole of dead things.

## WAITROSE RED

Abbotts Ammonite Côtes | 15 | –£5.00
du Roussillon 1999
A juicy glugging red with a hint of the hot, sweaty Midi sun.

Beaujolais Villages 1998 | 12 | £5–7

Bistro Rouge VdP d'Oc | 13.5 | –£5.00
1999

Boulder Creek Red VdP | 15 | –£3.50
du Vaucluse 1999
A superb party wine, pasta plonk, posh nosh bottle and altogether properly fruited glugging specimen.

Cabernet Sauvignon La | 15.5 | –£5.00
Cité VdP d'Oc 1998
Delicious plum/blackcurrant fruit, hint of spice, controlled tannins. Bargain price.

Cahors Côtes d'Olt 1999 | 14 | –£5.00

Château Cazal-Viel, | 16 | £5–7

Cuvée des Fées St-Chinian 1998
Terrific character and class here. Lingering finish of oomph and aplomb.

Château de Caraguilhes | 16 | –£5.00
Corbières 1998 (half-bottle) (organic)
Brigitte's wine is organic, vegan-friendly, rich, earthy, characterful, subtly spicy, very mellow, deep and delicious. It has, furthermore, more delicacy than its tannins suggest – so don't pair it with overly spicy food.

Château de Targe 'Les | 15.5 | £5–7
Tuffes' Saumur-Champigny 1997
Delicious spicy cherries here, quite remarkably calm and cool in the face of the tannins.

Château Falfas Côtes de | 14 | £7–10
Bourg 1997
Oddly juicy.

Château Haut d'Allard | 15 | £5–7
Côtes de Bourg 1997
Character and bite. Satisfying claret of some class here.

Château Haut Nouchet | 13 | £10–13
Pessac-Léognan 1996
(organic)

Château Léoville-Las-Cases 2eme Cru Classé, | 16 | £20+
St-Julien 1994
Superb tannins and ripe, soft structured texture. Only from Waitrose Direct.

Château Les Tuileries | 13.5 | –£5.00
Bordeaux Superieur 1998

Château Meynard | 14.5 | –£5.00
Bordeaux 1998

Lovely dry tannic tension. Great value claret.

**Château Palmer 3eme** `12` `£20+`
**Cru Classé Margaux 1990**
Absurd price even if the tannins are great. The fruit is soapy. Only from Waitrose Direct.

**Château Pech-Latt,** `15` `−£5.00`
**Corbières 1998**
Very dry and food-friendly organic fruit. A great casserole bottle.

**Château Saint-Maurice** `15` `−£5.00`
**Côtes du Rhône 1998**
Old-fashioned hints yet finally smooth and charming.

**Château Tayac Cru** `13` `£13–20`
**Bourgeois, Margaux 1995**
Waitrose's Special Reserve Claret is miles sprauncier.

**Clos de Tart Grand Cru** `15` `£20+`
**Mommessin 1993**
Delicious truffley richness and dry finishing aplomb. Only from Waitrose Direct.

**Cornas Chapoutier 1997** `13` `£13–20`

**Côte-Rôtie Les Jumelles** `13` `£20+`
**1997**
Only from Waitrose Direct.

**Côtes du Rhône 1999,** `13` `−£5.00`
**Waitrose**

**Côtes du Rhône-Villages,** `14` `−£5.00`
**Domaine de Cantemerle**
**1998**

**Côtes du Ventoux 1998** `14` `−£5.00`
Nice tight tannins.

**Crozes-Hermitage Cave** `14` `£5–7`
**des Clairmonts 1998**

**Crozes-Hermitage** `13` `£10–13`
**Domaine de Thalabert**
**1997**
Only from Waitrose Direct.

**Cuvée André St-Estephe** `14.5` `£13–20`
**1996**
Delicious, if rather pricey. Not at all stores.

**Cuvée Eugenie Château** `15` `£7–10`
**Capendu, Corbières 1998**
Very accomplished yet very pricey.

**Domaine de Courtille** `16` `£7–10`
**Corbières 1998**
Nine quid for a Corbières? Why not? Especially when it's raunchier than many a £20 claret or £15 Rhône red.

**Domaine de Rose Syrah/** `16` `−£3.50`
**Merlot, VdP d'Oc 1998**
Fantastic bargain. Full of hints of the Midi sun, herbs and landscape. A colourful, rich yet far from rustic wine.

**Domaine du Moulin 'The** `13` `−£5.00`
**Cabernets', VdP d'Oc**
**1998**

**Fleurie Montreynaud** `12` `£7–10`
**1999**
Falls a bit flat.

**Gallerie Tempranillo/** `15.5` `−£5.00`
**Syrah VdP d'Oc 1998**

**Good Ordinary Claret** `14` `−£5.00`
**Bordeaux, Waitrose**

**Hautes-Côtes de Nuits** `11` `£5–7`
**1998**

**L'Enclos Domecque** `14` `−£5.00`
**Mourvèdre/Syrah VdP**
**d'Oc 1998**
Rustic and unrefined. Great with goulash.

La Bernardine
Châteauneuf-du-Pape,
Chapoutier 1997 `14` `£13–20`

La Colombe Côtes du
Rhône 1999 (organic) `14` `–£5.00`
Juicy with a very savoury undertone.

Les Fontanelles Merlot/
Syrah VdP d'Oc 1998 `15.5` `–£5.00`

Maury, Les Vignerons du
Val d'Orbieu NV `16` `–£5.00`
A sweet red wine for chocolate-based
puddings. Did I say sweet? It hardly
does this complex wine justice.

Merchants Bay Merlot/
Cabernet Sauvignon 1997 `13.5` `–£5.00`

Mercurey Rouge 1er Cru
'Les Puillets', Château Le
Hardi 1998 `13` `£10–13`
Interesting ragged tannins – most
untypical in a Mercurey.

Oaked Merlot VdP d'Oc
1999 `14` `–£5.00`
Good sold organic fruit well organised
around tight, herby tannins.

Organic Merlot VdP d'Oc
1999 `13` `–£5.00`

Prieurs de Foncaire,
Buzet Grande Réserve
1998 `15.5` `–£5.00`
Very smooth and ripe. Better than
many a claret at three times the price.

Saint-Roche VdP du Gard
1999 (organic) `13.5` `–£5.00`
Juicy – hint of character on the finish.

Saint-Joseph, Cave de
Saint-Desiderat, Cuvée
Medaille d'Or 1997 `15.5` `£7–10`
Terrific dryness and stalky, almost
vegetal richness. A better vintage than

previous ones, this. More engaging,
quirkier, more wallop with the
tannins.

Santenay Bouchard Père
1997 `10` `£10–13`

Saumur Rouge Les
Nivières 1998 `14` `–£5.00`
Light, dry, cherry-bright.

Savigny-lès-Beaune
Bouchard Père 1998 `11` `£10–13`

Special Reserve Claret,
Côtes de Castillon
Limited Edition
Millennium Magnum
1996 (magnum) `16` `–£5.00`
Bargain claret in a big sexy bottle – the
fruit is subtly sensual too and wears a
thick, winter coat of nicely knitted
tannins. Price bracket shows the 75cl
equivalent.

St-Emilion Yvon Mau NV `13` `£5–7`
Jolie laide.

Valreas Côtes du Rhône
Chapoutier (half-bottle) `16.5` `–£3.50`
Superbly well-textured wine of
gentility yet passion. It is immensely
smooth, richly aromatic (violets and
liquorice) and the class is manifest. A
lovely half-bottle treat.

Volnay 1er Cru Les
Chevret 1996 `13` `£20+`
Only from Waitrose Direct.

Volnay 1er Cru les
Caillerets, Clos des 60
Ouvrées, Domaine de la
Passe d'Or 1996 `14` `£20+`
Classic? Almost. Only from Waitrose
Direct.

## WINE CELLAR RED

**Abbotts Cumulus Shiraz** 16.5 £5-7
**Minervois 1998**
The tannins are hugely gripping and
classy but what leaves the most
delicious sensory impression are the
cheroot-edged blackberries.

**Big Frank's Cabernet** 14 £5-7
**Frank 1998**
Very warm and accommodating.
Thickly knitted, soft, very gently spicy
and deeply approachable – like Frank
the man.

**Château Agnel Minervois** 16 –£5.00
**1998**
Very jammy but it isn't soppy with it.
It has very soft yet alert tannins allied
to delicious sweet hedgerow fruit.

**Château Bonhomme** 13 £5-7
**Minervois 1997**
Nice tobacco bouquet but goes all
simple and simpering as the fruit
surfaces.

**Château Côtes de** 13.5 £5-7
**Bellevue, Côtes de Bourg**
**1996**

**Château Grand Berthaud,** 16 £5-7
**Premières Côtes de Blaye**
**1997**
Dry yet full of good fruit. Has a tang
of the cigar box to it as it finishes,
romping home with aplomb. Sheer
aplomb in your mouth indeed.

**Château La Chapelle, St-** 14 –£5.00
**Chinian 1998**
Juicy with hints of pine and earth.

**Château Lamargue** 16 –£5.00
**Costières de Nîmes**
**Grand Réserve 1998**
Zips along, dripping with tobacco and
assorted herbs and rich blackcurrant
fruit, touch of earth, and excellent
tannins.

**Château Quinsac** 16 –£5.00
**Bellevue, Bordeaux 1998**
A superbly jammy claret which is
combative yet not overly austere or
too dry. Lovely charcoal edge to the
tannins.

**Château Saint-Germain** 13.5 £5-7
**Bordeaux Supérieur 1997**
Calvet take too many tannins out.
Please return them to the rightful
owner.

**Château Saint-Gilles, 1er** 14.5 –£5.00
**Côte de Bordeaux 1998**
Bargain quaffing, not necessarily for
claret lovers who may find the wine's
immediacy and unable-to-age tannins
insufficient. Highly drinkable.

**Domaine Coste Blanque,** 17 £5-7
**Montpeyroux, Coteaux**
**du Languedoc 1998**
Massively mouth-filling initial attack of
fruit, tannins and gentle acids in
perfect, overwhelming harmony. Then
it settles down to show its subtle side.
A terrific, energetic wine of weight
and wit.

**Domaine de Villemajou,** 16 £5-7
**Corbières 1998**
Wild cherries and strawberries,
blackcurrants, herbs and a hint of old
stable door – a terrifically generous
mouthful.

**Domaine des Amandiers,** 15 –£5.00
**Côtes du Roussillon-**
**Villages 1998**
Sweet-natured rusticity with fine-
grained tannins. Even has a hint of
almond on the finish.

**Domaine du Bosquet** `16` `£5–7`
**Merlot VdP d'Oc 1998**
Superb dry fruit which coats the taste
buds with Cassis, leather, earthy herbs
and great tannins.

**Domaine du Grand Bosc,** `15.5` `–£5.00`
**Fitou 1998**
Sweet/sour edge to the fruit which has
a wallop of tannicity as it coats the
tongue. It finishes with style.

**James Herrick Cuvée** `16.5` `–£5.00`
**Simone VdP d'Oc 1998**
An intensely sophisticated and chic
bottle of fruit which accompanies a
good book or a complex CD like a
dream. Subtle yet tenacious.

**La Chasse du Pape Côtes** `16.5` `–£5.00`
**du Rhône 1998**
Stunning ripeness and big earthy, rich
plum/blackcurrant dryness and
urgency. Lovely tannins. Great
texture.

**Old Git Grenache Syrah** `15.5` `–£5.00`
**1999**
Great fun. I'm bound to love the name
and the dry, Midi fruit.

**Rhône Valley Red VdP** `13` `–£5.00`
**de Vaucluse NV**

**Shiraz Foncalieu 1998** `16` `–£5.00`
Simply terrific value: dry yet rich,
fruity yet not juicy and puerile,
striking yet elegant, ripe yet not OTT.
A good glugging wine and casserole
candidate.

**Tastevinage Bourgogne** `10` `£7–10`
**Hautes-Côtes de Nuits**
**Yves Chaley 1997**
So spineless it will never walk off the
shelf – let alone trip down the throat
with any aplomb.

**Thierry & Guy Utter** `14.5` `£5–7`
**Bastard Syrah 1998**

**Vacqueyras Les Agapes** `16.5` `£5–7`
**1998**
Sweet fruit on top of soft ripe tannins.
There is a touch of liquorice to the
dark cherries and superb tannins. A
little marzipan shows up, too. Great
stuff.

**Wild Pig Barrel Reserve** `14` `–£5.00`
**Shiraz 1998**
Juice and tannins. Not a traditional
recipe.

## ASDA WHITE

**Baron de Turckheim** `16` `£7–10`
**Gewürztraminer 1998**
Deliciously subtly spicy and thickly
textured. Great with robust Chinese
food.

**Chablis Grand Cru** `13` `£13–20`
**Bougros 1996**

**Chardonnay, Jardin de la** `14` `–£3.50`
**France 1999**
Light, gently fruity, crisp and simply
fruity.

**Châteauneuf-du-Pape** `13` `£13–20`
**Blanc 1997**

**Chenin Blanc Loire 1999,** `14` `–£3.50`
**Asda**
Very simple and charming.

**La Domeque 'Tête de** `16.5` `–£5.00`
**Cuvée' Vieilles Vignes**
**VdP d'Oc 1998**
A superb blend of Roussanne,
Marsanne and Muscat grapes resulting
in a surprisingly dry, very elegant,
subtle rich wine of character, charm,
huge sippability and food versatility. It
possesses great class and texture.

Muscadet 1999, Asda `13` `–£3.50`
A deep and cheerful glug.

Oak Aged Côtes du `12` `–£3.50`
Rhône Blanc 1998, Asda

Rosé d'Anjou 1998, Asda `12.5` `–£3.50`

Sancerre 1999 `12` `£5–7`
Lot of loot for an average bucket of fruit.

St-Veran Domaine des `15` `£5–7`
Deux Roches 1998
Lovely plump fruit which has something in common with its Mâcon Davaye cousin.

Tramontane Chardonnay `16` `–£5.00`
VdP d'Oc 1999, Asda
Delicate, delicious, decisive.

Tramontane `13.5` `–£5.00`
Chardonnay/
Vermentino 1999, Asda
Very full and rich.

Tramontane Reserve Oak `14` `–£5.00`
Aged Chardonnay 1997,
Asda

Tramontane Sauvignon `15` `–£5.00`
Blanc 1999, Asda
Deliciously compressed and crisp.

Tramontane Viognier `15.5` `–£5.00`
1999, Asda
Lovely apricot fruit with a hint of lemon and pineapple.

Vouvray Denis Marchais `10` `–£5.00`
1999

## BOOTHS WHITE

Bergerac Blanc NV, `14` `–£3.50`
Booths
A clean, fresh fish wine.

Bordeaux Blanc Sec NV, `13.5` `–£3.50`
Booths

Bourgogne Chardonnay `12` `£5–7`
Domaine Joseph Matrot
NV
Bit boorish for seven quid.

Chablis Domaine de `10` `£7–10`
l'Eglantière 1998
Eight quid? I'd rather put it on a three-legged horse. At least its presumption would be entertaining.

Château d'Angludet Rosé `13` `£5–7`
1997

Château Lamothe `14` `–£5.00`
Vincent, Bordeaux 1999
A dry oyster catcher.

Château Petit Roubie, `13` `–£5.00`
Coteaux du Pinet 1999
(organic)
Organic Midi grapes, somewhat baked.

Château Pierrail Blanc `15.5` `£5–7`
Prestige 1996

Château Pique-Segue, `15` `–£5.00`
Montravel 1999
Classy, delicate ( yet rich), harmoniously organised and with a crisp, gooseberry undertone.

Clos de Monestier `13.5` `–£5.00`
Bergerac Blanc 1999

Clos de Monestier `14.5` `–£5.00`
Bergerac Rosé 1999
Delicious.

Côtes du Rhône Chaume `16` `£7–10`
Arnaud 1998
Why bother with white burgundy when you have real character here? Deliciously individual, dry, stony, complex pastry-edged fruit.

**Domaine de Pellehaut** `15` `–£5.00`
Côtes de Gascogne 1999
Pineapple scented and fruited, a vague
touch of mango, and strong hint of
lime.

**Domaine de Petit Roubie,** `15` `–£5.00`
Marsanne 1999 (organic)
Curiously rich and ready. Has a very
subtle toffeed tang.

**Edelzwicker Aimé Stentz** `14.5` `–£5.00`
1998

**Gewürztraminer d'Alsace** `15.5` `£5–7`
Turckheim 1999
Complex layers of gooseberry, lychee,
lemon and some unidentifiable,
possibly exotic, fruit all integrated and
charming.

**James Herrick** `16` `–£5.00`
Chardonnay VdP d'Oc
1999
Very elegant, subtle, gently fruity,
stylish and well-priced. Lovely lemon
edge as it finishes.

**La Passion Blanc VdP de** `15` `–£3.50`
Vaucluse 1999
Has some warm fruity touches, ripe
melon in style, but the overall theme
is simple refreshment.

**Louis Chatel Sur Lie VdP** `14` `–£3.50`
d'Oc 1999
Rich, plump and ready for food.

**Muscadet Sur Lie La** `13.5` `–£5.00`
Roche Renard 1998

**Pouilly-Fumé les Cornets,** `10` `£7–10`
Cailbourdin 1997

**Riesling d'Alsace Amie** `13` `£5–7`
Stentz 1997

**Sancerre Domaine du** `14.5` `£7–10`
Petit Roy, Dezat 1998

**Vermentino Les Yeuses** `15.5` `–£3.50`
VdP d'Oc 1999
Hints of gooseberry and a very subtle
touch of strawberry lurk amid the
clinging acids.

**Vin Blanc NV, Booths** `12` `–£3.50`
Rusticity is its middle name.

## BUDGENS WHITE

**Bordeaux Blanc Sec 1998** `15` `–£3.50`

**Bordeaux Sauvignon NV,** `13.5` `–£5.00`
Budgens
Most drinkable. Agreeably fruity and
firm.

**Chablis Delaroche 1999** `11` `£7–10`
Not hugely impressive for the money.

**Domaine Villeroy-** `14` `–£5.00`
Castellas Sauvignon 1998

**French Organic White** `13` `–£5.00`
NV
Fruity and earthy. Needs strong food.

**James Herrick** `16` `–£5.00`
Chardonnay 1999
Very elegant and controlled. A class
act. One of the Languedoc's top
Chardonnays.

**'L' Grande Cuvée VdP** `15.5` `£5–7`
d'Oc 1999
Very rich and warm with ripe ogen
melon fruit, slightly creamy and
vaguely smoky, with a hint of ripe
pineapple. A very classy, deep wine.

**Premium Oaked** `14` `–£5.00`
Chardonnay VdP d'Oc,
Devereux NV
Touch of class here.

**Alsace Gewürztraminer** `16.5` `£5–7`
Producteurs A.
Eguisheim 1997

What a delicious, rich, unpretentious, calm and collected Gewürz we have here! Wonderful fruit (hints of lime, mango, lychees, rowanberry, papaya, guava – okay, only kidding) but it is faintly spicy and rosy rich. Superstores only.

**Chablis, Les Vignerons de Chablis 1998**  `13.5`  `£7–10`
Yes, it's drinkable but eight quid makes you think (about things other than wine).

**Chardonnay VdP du Jardin Pierre Guery 1998**  `15`  `–£5.00`

**Chardonnay-Chenin Vegetarian NV, Co-op**  `12.5`  `–£5.00`

**Château Pierrousselle Blanc, Entre-Deux-Mers 1998**  `13`  `–£5.00`

**Domaine des Perruches Vouvray 1998**  `15.5`  `£5–7`
Superb clash of dry, dry honey and crisp, assertive acids. The result is a terrific aperitif. Superstores only.

**Fortant VdP d'Oc Sauvignon Blanc 1999**  `13`  `–£5.00`
Bit stand-offish.

**James Herrick Chardonnay 1999**  `16`  `–£5.00`
Very elegant, subtle, gently fruity, stylish and well-priced. Lovely lemon edge as it finishes.

**Monbazillac Domaine du Haut-Rauly 1995 (half-bottle)**  `14.5`  `–£5.00`

**Montagny 1er Cru 1998**  `13`  `£7–10`

**Orchid Vale Chardonnay Grenache Blanc 1999**  `13.5`  `–£5.00`
From a bottle which looks as if it might administer strychnine comes

curiously waspish fruit. Superstores only.

**Rhône Valley White 1999**  `14`  `–£3.50`
Handsome texture, good underripe fruit, touch of earth – a solid Rhône blanc, great with food.

**Sancerre Domaine Raimbault 1998**  `13`  `£7–10`

**VdP d'Oc Sauvignon Blanc NV, Co-op**  `14`  `–£5.00`

**Vin de Pays d'Oc Chardonnay 1999, Co-op**  `13`  `–£5.00`
Bruised fruit edge.

**Vin de Pays d'Oc Chardonnay Chenin Blanc NV, Co-op**  `14.5`  `–£5.00`

**Vin de Pays des Côtes de Gascogne, Co-op**  `14.5`  `–£3.50`

## KWIK SAVE WHITE

**Blanc de France Vin de Table NV**  `15.5`  `–£3.50`

**Chablis Domaine de Bouchots Cuvée Boissonneuse 1998**  `12.5`  `£5–7`

**Chardonnay en Sol Oxfordien, Bourgogne 1998**  `14`  `£5–7`

**Chardonnay VdP du Jardin de la France 1999**  `13`  `–£5.00`
Rather flat as it surges to the throat.

**Chenin Blanc VdP du Jardin de la France 1997**  `15.5`  `–£2.50`

**James Herrick Chardonnay VdP d'Oc 1999**  `16`  `–£5.00`
Very elegant, subtle, gently fruity,

119

stylish and well-priced. Lovely lemon
edge as it finishes.

**Les Marionettes** `15.5` `−£5.00`
**Marsanne VdP d'Oc 1999**
Deliciously rich and generous: creamy,
smoky, textured, good finish.

**Les Oliviers du Jardin Vin** `15.5` `−£2.50`
**de Table NV**

**VdP des Coteaux de** `14.5` `−£3.50`
**l'Ardèche Blanc 1999,**
**Somerfield**
Lemon and melon. Thoroughly
different and drinkable.

**VdP du Comte du** `14` `−£3.50`
**Tolosan, Les Chais**
**Beaucarois 1998**
Great with moules marinières – it
really hits those molluscs.

**Wild Trout VdP d'Oc** `15.5` `−£5.00`
**1997**

## M&S WHITE

**Bordeaux Sauvignon 1999** `13.5` `−£5.00`
Sour/dry edge to the finish inspires
the idea that shellfish will radically
change this wine's sullen disposition.

**Chablis 1997** `13.5` `£7–10`

**Chablis Grand Cru** `12` `£13–20`
**Grenouille 1994**

**Chablis Premier Cru 1996** `13` `£10–13`

**Château Les Charmes de** `16` `£7–10`
**Saint-Mayme,**
**Monbazillac 1995**
Interesting waxy fruit, the hallmark of
good Monbazillac, and what sets it
apart from Sauternes. Brilliant dessert
and blue cheese wine.

**Côtes de Provence 1999** `11` `−£5.00`
**(rosé)**

**Domaine de la Pouvraie** `14` `−£5.00`
**Vouvray 1999**
Woody richness typical of Chenin
from the Loire. Sweet edge to it.

**Gold Label Chardonnay** `15.5` `£5–7`
**Reserve 1998**

**Gold Label Chardonnay** `15` `−£5.00`
**VdP d'Oc 1999**
Nice plumpness and freshness here.

**Gold Label Sauvignon** `14` `−£5.00`
**Blanc VdP d'Oc 1999**
Very dry and uncompromisingly food
orientated.

**Gold Label Viognier 1999** `14` `−£5.00`
Very austere for a Viognier. The
apricot fruit is muted.

**Les Ruetttes Sancerre** `15.5` `£7–10`
**1999**
A crisp, deliciously mineral-edged
Sauvignon.

**Mâcon-Villages 1999** `15.5` `£5–7`
I like very much the typical vegetal
edge. It's a real white burgundy.

**Pouilly-Fumé 1999** `16` `£7–10`
An exceptional Fumé Sauvignon with
real lemon fruit and clean-finishing
elegance.

**Rivesaltes Ambre Hors** `15.5` `£7–10`
**d'Age 25 Year**
Baked fruit melee, crème brûlée,
sticky-toffee pudding and roasted nuts.
All in one glass!

**Rosé de Syrah VdP d'Oc** `14` `−£5.00`
**1999**
Good chewy cherry fruit.

**VdP des Côtes de** `14` `−£3.50`
**Gascogne 1999**

Light, playful, frisky with lemon/
pineapple fruit.

**Vin de Pays du Gers 1999**  14  −£3.50
Very crisp and molar clenching.

## MAJESTIC WHITE

**Bois de Lamothe**  15  −£3.50
**Sauvignon Blanc, VdP du**
**Lot et Garonne 1997**

**Bott-Geyl**  17.5  £10–13
**Gewürztraminer Grand**
**Cru Sonnenglanz 1998**
About as good as young Gewürz gets:
pears, peaches, rose petals, raspberries
and honey and intriguing acids. Left
for seven to eight years it'll rate
twenty.

**Bott-Geyl Riesling**  14.5  £7–10
**Burgreben de Zellenberg**
**1997**
Bit raw but will progress extremely
well if cellared for five or six years.
Possibly seventeen or eighteen points
in time.

**Bott-Geyl Riesling**  15  £7–10
**Grafenreben de**
**Zellenberg 1997**
More immediately fruity and subtly
rich and will develop if cellared – three
years?

**Bott-Geyl Tokay Pinot**  15  £7–10
**Gris 1998**
Two layers of apricot fruit now. Leave
it five or six years and it'll develop
even more.

**Bott-Geyl Tokay Pinot**  14  £13–20
**Gris Sonnenglanz**
**Vendages Tardives 1998**
Try it with foie gras or blue cheese. It
is intensely sweet.

**Cave de Ribeauville**  16  £5–7
**Gewürztraminer 1998**
Delicious rosy richness! Great quaffing
specimen. Concentrated and deeply
charming.

**Cave de Ribeauville**  15  £5–7
**Tokay Pinot Gris 1998**
Lovely dry edge to the firm peach/
apricot fruit. Excellent aperitif.

**Chablis 1er Cru Côte de**  12  £10–13
**Lechet La Chablisienne**
**1998**

**Chablis Domaine**  15.5  −£5.00
**Marguerite Carillon 1998**
A superbly well-tailored, rich Chablis
in the gentle New World mould of
textured softness yet crisp-to-finish
vivacity. Fantastic bargain. The label
will have wine buffs wetting their
pants.

**Chablis Domaine**  13.5  £7–10
**Vocoret 1998**

**Chablis Grand Cru Les**  10  £13–20
**Clos 1998**

**Chardonnay Jean**  15  −£5.00
**Belmont VdP du Jardin**
**de la France 1999**
Gooseberries, pears and plumpness.
Grand little quaffer.

**Chassagne-Montrachet**  10  £20+
**Fontaine-Gagnard 1er**
**Cru La Maltroie 1997**

**Château du Sours Rosé**  15  £5–7
**1999**
Delicious, food-friendly fruit. A lovely
summer barbecue wine.

**Château Haut Mazières**  16  £5–7
**Blanc, Bordeaux 1997**
Very classy. The hint of vegetality

FRENCH WHITE

only confirms it. Lovely food-friendly fruit.

**Château Méaume Rosé 1999**  14  £5–7
Sweet and rich.

**Chenin Blanc VdP du Jardin de la France, Rémy Pannier NV**  14.5  –£3.50

**Chinon Rosé Couly-Dutheil 1998**  13  £5–7

**Condrieu Guigal 1998**  15.5  £13–20
Very delicious if not entirely typical of the breed (Viognier grape = apricots). The finish is dry and nutty.

**Corton-Charlemagne, Bonneau du Martray 1996**  10  £20+

**Côtes du Rhône Rosé Guigal 1997**  14  £5–7

**Cuvée Apolline Tokay Pinot Gris 1997**  13  £10–13
Disappointing at the price.

**Domaine de Raissac CVM Barrique 1999**  15  –£5.00
Nice ripe gooseberry edge to it. Yummy stuff.

**Domaine de Raissac Viognier 1999**  15.5  –£5.00
Apricots and crisp appley acids. A terrific recipe.

**Domaine des Fontanelles Sauvignon Blanc 1999**  15  –£5.00
Simply terrific quaffing.

**Domaine Le Puts Blanc Michel Bordes 1999**  16  –£3.50
Brilliant value: has gorgeously amusing fruit combining pears, raspberries, lemons and crisp acids to refreshingly delicious effect.

**Gewürztraminer, Haegelin 1998**  14.5  £7–10
Great with Chinese and Thai food.

**Gewürztraminer Paul Zinck 1999**  13.5  £7–10
Sweet spicy finish. Needs oriental food.

**Givry Blanc Louis Latour 1996**  10  £7–10

**Grand Ardèche Chardonnay Louis Latour 1998**  15  £5–7
The best vintage yet of this Latour attempt to break out of the Burgundy mould. The wine is creamy and well-built, elegant yet rich.

**Le Fauve Chasan 1999**  15.5  –£5.00
Extremely fruity and very charming. Utterly quaffable and quaintly quirky.

**Le Fauve Marsanne 1999**  16  –£5.00
Gorgeous quaffing here of some quality. The fruit is rich, ripe, ready – yet elegant and handsomely textured. Has a peach/apricot/pear medley to it.

**Le Fauve Rosé de Syrah 1999**  14.5  –£5.00
Absolutely charming! Delicious dry cherries.

**Les Fontanelles Viognier Foncalieu 1999**  16  –£5.00
Has a very developed peachy richness which unfolds on the front, middle and back palate to excellent effect.

**Les Grands Clochers Chardonnay 1999**  14.5  £5–7
Ripe and mouthfilling, energetic and easy to glug.

**Moulin Touchais, Coteaux du Layon 1986**  16  £7–10

122

Very sweet but has a multiplicity of subtle soft fruit undertones.

**Muscadet Cuvée du Homard 1998** 14 −£3.50

**Muscadet Homard 1998** 13.5 −£3.50
Rather good for fish parties (schools?).

**Muscadet sur Lie Château la Touche 1998** 13.5 −£5.00

**Muscat Riquewihr, Bott-Geyl 1997** 15 £7–10
A very elegant aperitif. Individual and very incisive.

**Pinot Blanc Haegelin 1998** 13.5 £5–7
Bit basic.

**Quincy JC Bourguat 1999** 15 £5–7
Deliciously warm and plumply textured.

**Reuilly Beurdin 1999** 14 £5–7
I like it.

**Riesling Bollenberg, Haegelin 1998** 13 £5–7
Rather underdeveloped.

**Sancerre La Chaudillonne Fournier 1997** 10 £7–10
Quite remarkably fat and blowsily sweet.

**Sancerre Rosé Vacheron 1999** 10 £7–10
Bit thin and fruitless for nigh on ten quid.

**Sauvignon Lot 279, Bordeaux 1998** 13 −£5.00

**Sauvignon Touraine Delauney 1999** 12 −£5.00
Very sweet to finish.

**Sylvaner, Paul Zinck 1998** 14.5 −£5.00

**Tokay Pinot Gris, Haegelin 1998** 13.5 £7–10
Some pleasantries from the peaches found here.

**Vivian Ducourneau VdP des Côtes de Gascogne 1999** 15.5 −£5.00
Impish, irreverent, fun, clean, cheering, lively – a mix of lemon, lime, pineapple and the rare Hawaiian fruit, shaped like bovine genitalia, the kumquat.

**Vouvray Tris de Nobles Grain, Domaine Bourillon Dorléans 1995** 16 £10–13
(50cl)
Beautiful richness and ripeness. Put it down for a few years and it'll be even more complex.

## MORRISONS WHITE

**Bordeaux Blanc de Ginestet 1998** 15.5 −£5.00
Rather classy – woody, refined, stylish, excellent with rich fish and chicken dishes. Most stores.

**Château La Fage Bergerac Sec 1998** 13 −£5.00
Bit flat as it finishes.

**Château Loupiac Gaudiet, Loupiac 1996** 16 −£5.00
(50cl)
A really different pudding wine combining raw honey, limes, lychees, pawpaw and a touch of strawberry. Go for it!

**Falcon Ridge Chardonnay, VdP d'Oc 1999** 15 −£3.50
So warm and thick you could grease

an axle with it. Rich melon fruit of
unreserved lushness.

**Falcon Ridge Rosé VdP** `14` `–£3.50`
**d'Oc 1997**

**Falcon Ridge Sauvignon** `14` `–£3.50`
**Blanc, VdP d'Oc 1999**
The richer kind of Sauvignon, nothing
dry about it.

**Gewürztraminer Preiss** `15.5` `£5–7`
**Zimmer 1998**
Deliciously rich, gently honeyed and
lychee-fruited and great with oriental
food.

**Haut-Poitou Sauvignon** `14` `–£3.50`
**Blanc NV**

**James Herrick** `16` `–£5.00`
**Chardonnay 1999**
Very elegant, subtle, gently fruity,
stylish and well-priced. Lovely lemon
edge as it finishes.

**Mâcon-Villages Teissedre** `13` `–£5.00`
**1998**

**Pinot Blanc Preiss** `15.5` `–£5.00`
**Zimmer 1998**

**Rhône Valley White 1998** `14` `–£3.50`

**Saint-Véran 1998** `13` `£5–7`
Hint of butter, but it's thinly spread.

**Sancerre la Renardière** `12` `£7–10`
**1999**
Very fruity Sancerre, almost sweet.
Very untypical, even eccentric.

**Sichel Premières Côtes de** `12.5` `–£5.00`
**Bordeaux Blanc NV**
Far too clotted and sweet for this dry
old dog.

**Winter Hill White 1998** `14` `–£3.50`

## ODDBINS WHITE

**Burgundy Blanc 'Cuvée** `15` `–£5.00`
**Saint-Vincent', Vincent**
**Giradin 1998**

**Château de Fesles Rosé** `13.5` `–£5.00`
**d'Anjou 1998**

**Château Grand Escalion** `13.5` `£5–7`
**Rosé, Costières de Nîmes**
**1999**
Cherry bright but a touch pricey for
the style.

**Clos Petite Bellane, Côtes** `16` `£5–7`
**du Rhône 1999**
Superb control of acids and rich fruit
here. Melon/lime/pineapple and a
hint of peach – but it's dry-packed and
punchy on the finish.

**Clos Petite Bellane Rosé,** `13.5` `£5–7`
**Côtes du Rhône 1999**
Bit sour on the finish.

**Comte Cathare Domaine** `15` `–£5.00`
**Begude Chardonnay, VdP**
**d'Oc 1999**
Has some expressive sullen touches
but overall is seriously fruity.

**Comte Cathare Domaine** `15.5` `£7–10`
**Begude Limoux 1998**
Complex and concentrated,
accomplished richness, subtle ripeness,
good mineral edge to the acids.
Individual and hugely foodworthy.

**Comte Cathare** `15` `–£5.00`
**Marsanne/Viognier, VdP**
**d'Oc 1999**
Delicious apricot and lemon fruit.

**Domaine Borie de Maurel** `15.5` `£5–7`
**Chardonnay, VdP d'Oc**
**1999**
Individual approach to the chic variety

– has a sweet toffee edge which mingles deliciously with the pert acids.

**Domaine Borie de Maurel** `15` `£5–7`
**Cuvée Aude, Minervois**
**1999**
Has an odd bitter edge. Needs food.

**Domaine Cady Coteaux** `16.5` `£7–10`
**du Layon St-Aubin**
**'Cuvée Harmonie' 1997**
**(50cl)**
Sweet butterscotch, rum, a hint of wild artichoke, wild raspberry and lots of honey – did you pick up that lot? You might.

**Domaine de la Renaudie** `14` `–£5.00`
**Touraine Sauvignon 1999**
Very extruded and elongated. Needs fish to flow fully.

**Domaine de Montahuc** `15.5` `£5–7`
**Muscat, Muscat de Saint-**
**Jean de Minervois 1998**
**(50cl)**
Not as outrageously sweet as you might think as there's spicy lemon in there along with a hint of pear drop and toffee.

**Dourthe No 1 Bordeaux** `13.5` `–£5.00`
**1999**
An attractive fish wine.

**James Herrick** `16` `–£5.00`
**Chardonnay 1999**
Very elegant and controlled. A class act. One of the Languedoc's top Chardonnays.

**James Herrick Domaine** `16` `£5–7`
**Les Garrigues de Truilhas**
**Chardonnay VdP d'Oc**
**1998**
More French than anything Jim has turned out before – in the sense of the vegetality of the wine and the wood and herbs.

**Kiwi Cuvée Sauvignon** `15` `–£5.00`
**Blanc VdP du Jardin de la**
**France 1999**
Wow! The Kiwis shows the Frogs how to jump-start the Sauvignon. Delicious fruit here of elegance and concentration.

**Les Clos de Paulilles Rosé** `15` `£5–7`
**1999**
One of the most dynamic and lingering rosés I've tasted.

**Mâcon Davaye Domaine** `16` `£5–7`
**des Deux Roches 1998**
One of the best vintages from a rarely disappointing producer. Classic minor white Burgundy (by name) which manages to touch major Burgundy heights of texture and gentle fruit.

**Menetou-Salon Morogues** `13` `£7–10`
**'Clos de Ratier', Pelle**
**1998**

**Montagny 1er Cru,** `13` `£7–10`
**Domaine Maurice**
**Bertrand 1997**

**Pouilly-Fumé Le Champ** `12` `£7–10`
**des Vignes, Tabordet**
**1998**

**Sancerre Domaine de la** `12.5` `£7–10`
**Rossignole 1998**

**St-Romain 'Sous le** `13.5` `£10–13`
**Château' Baron de la**
**Charrière 1998**
Very expensive, lemony construct.

**St-Véran les Cras,** `12` `£13–20`
**Lassarat 1996**
Fine Wine Stores only.

## SAFEWAY WHITE

**Bourgogne Chardonnay** `15` `£5–7`
**Barrique Réserve 1998**
Very satisfying and collected. Good
rich fruit – not overbaked.

**Chablis Laroche 1999** `12` `£7–10`
Far too expensive for the rigidity of
the style.

**Chardonnay VdP de** `14` `–£5.00`
**l'Herault 1999, Safeway**
Rich, ripe, ready for any action. Even
Mission Impossible: tandoori octopus.

**Château de la Gravelle,** `14` `–£5.00`
**Muscadet de Sevre-et-**
**Maine Sur Lie 1998**
One of the more interesting and
attractively structured Muscadets
around.

**Château du Roc** `12` `–£5.00`
**Bordeaux Sauvignon 1999**
Humm . . .

**Château Magneau,** `15` `£5–7`
**Graves 1999**
A good fish wine, a solid quaffing
companion: a wine for dry
pursuits.

**Château Petit Roubie,** `13.5` `–£5.00`
**Coteaux du Languedoc**
**1999 (organic)**
Oddly agitated dryness.

**Domaine de Bosquet** `16` `£5–7`
**Chardonnay VdP d'Oc**
**1998**
Complex spread of flavours which
work from coriander and melon (with
a hint of raspberry) to pineapple
acidity.

**Domaine de Ciffre** `16` `£5–7`
**Viognier VdP d'Oc 1999**
Soft apricot fruit which lushly lingers

with hints of buttered raspberries and
yoghurt.

**Domaine de l'Ecu** `12` `–£5.00`
**Muscadet de Sevre-et-**
**Maine Sur Lie 1999**
**(biodynamic)**
Intensely lean and mean. Selected
stores.

**Domaine Lafage Muscat** `14` `–£5.00`
**Sec, VdP d'Oc 1999**
Not remotely sweet but coyly dry.

**Dourthe No 1 Bordeaux** `13.5` `–£5.00`
**1999**
An attractive fish wine.

**French Révolution Le** `13` `–£5.00`
**Blanc 1999**
Rather cosmetic edge to a wholly
gungo product.

**James Herrick** `16` `–£5.00`
**Chardonnay VdP d'Oc**
**1999**
Very elegant, subtle, gently fruity,
stylish and well-priced. Lovely lemon
edge as it finishes.

**L'If Grenache Blanc,** `15` `–£5.00`
**Elevé en Fûts de Chêne,**
**VdP d'Oc 1999**
Elegant, fruity, subtle, delicious.

**La Source Chardonnay/** `16` `–£5.00`
**Roussanne VdP d'Oc 1999**
Superb marriage of grapes: buttery yet
crisp, dry yet melony, deep yet
athletic, rich yet delicate.

**Montagny Premier Cru** `14` `£7–10`
**1998, Safeway**

**Pinot Blanc Alsace 1998,** `13.5` `–£5.00`
**Safeway**

**Sancerre 1999, Safeway** `12` `£5–7`
Cloying, annoying, expensive, very
blatant.

Sancerre 'Les Bonnes    13    £7–10
Bouches' 1999
Edge, very very edgy. Not quite
confident enough for me at nine
quid.

Sauvignon Blanc Cuvée   15.5   –£5.00
Réserve VdP d'Oc 1999
Not a classic lean Sauvignon, but a rich
softie. I like it lots.

St-Véran 1997    13    £5–7
Most stores.

VdP de l'Ardèche Rosé   14   –£3.50
1999, Safeway
Cherry-edged yet dry and food-
friendly.

Viognier Cuvée Réserve,   15.5   –£5.00
VdP d'Oc 1999
Deliciously serious, and apricotty and
nutty but very subtle richness.

## SAINSBURY'S WHITE

Alsace Gewürztraminer   16.5   £5–7
1999, Sainsbury's
Gorgeous rose/lychee/spicy fruit of
expressiveness and rich deliciousness.
Marvellous quaffing stuff and great
with oriental food. Most stores.

Blanc Anjou, Medium   12   –£3.50
Dry, Sainsbury's

Bordeaux Blanc de   15.5   –£5.00
Ginestet 1998
Rather classy – woody, refined, stylish,
excellent with rich fish and chicken
dishes. Most stores.

Bordeaux Blanc,   14.5   –£3.50
Sainsbury's

Bourgogne Blanc, Louis   14   £5–7
Max 1998
A real vegetal minor white Burgundy,

slightly coarse, gently austere. Not at
all stores.

Cabernet Rosé de Loire,   13.5   –£5.00
Lurton 1999
Refreshing and cherry-edged. Very
light and robust food will kill it. Most
stores.

Chablis 1er Cru Les   14   £13–20
Fourchaumes 1998
A very delicate, very authentic Chablis
of charm and eligibility (for pleasant
sipping). £17? Yes, but it has a crisp
classiness. Not at all stores.

Chardonnay VdP d'Oc,   15.5   –£5.00
Sainsbury's (3-litre box)
A Chardonnay which comes across
like a Burgundy – gently fat, vegetal,
dry, with both quaffability and food
matchability. The price band reflects
the equivalent price for a 75cl bottle.

Chardonnay VdP du   14.5   –£5.00
Jardin de la France,
Lurton 1999
Hints of plump melon but it's mainly
subtle citrus. Has a deal of charm, this
wine. Most stores.

Château Carsin, Cadillac   16   £5–7
1998 (half-bottle)
A wonderfully young yet completely
sweet Bordeaux with honey and a hint
of orange/lemon peel. Terrific with
pastry desserts. Selected stores.

Château du Sours Rosé   15   £5–7
1999
Delicious, food-friendly fruit. A lovely
summer barbecue wine.

Classic Selection   16   –£5.00
Muscadet de Sèvre-et-
Maine 1999, Sainsbury's
Astonishing! The highest-rating

Muscadet I've tasted in twenty years. Wonderfully minerally, knife-sharp fruit. Most stores.

**Classic Selection Pouilly-** `13.5` `£7–10`
**Fumé 1999, Sainsbury's**
Rather good, for a load of Pouilly. Very fat and New World-ish. Most stores.

**Classic Selection Sancerre** `13.5` `£7–10`
**1999, Sainsbury's**
Expensive, but decently crisp. A touch lean on the fruit for eight quid.

**Classic Selection Vouvray** `15` `£5–7`
**1999, Sainsbury's**
Half-sweet fruit, or demi-sec if you will. Makes an amusing warm weather aperitif. Most stores.

**Condrieu Guigal 1998** `15.5` `£13–20`
Very delicious if not entirely typical of the breed (Viognier grape = apricots). The finish is dry and nutty.

**Domaine de la Perrière** `13` `£7–10`
**Sancerre 1999**
Bit much, £8.50 for a four quid wine. Not at all stores.

**Domaine Leonce Cuisset,** `15` `£7–10`
**Saussignac 1996**

**French Révolution Le** `13` `–£5.00`
**Blanc 1999**
Rather cosmetic edge to a wholly gungo product.

**La Baume Sauvignon** `15` `–£5.00`
**Blanc, VdP d'Oc 1999**
Lovely warmth to the under-ripe melon fruit which is amply balanced by delicious acids. Most stores.

**LPA Côtes de St-Mont** `15` `–£5.00`
**Blanc 1998**

**Mâcon Chardonnay,** `16` `£5–7`

**Domaine les Ecuyers**
**1998**
A splendid minor white burgundy. Restrained vegetality, good acids, firm fruit on the finish. Selected stores.

**Mercurey Blanc Domaine** `13` `£13–20`
**la Marche les Rochelles**
**1998**
Finishes a bit short for fourteen quid. 50 stores.

**Montagny 'Les Rosiers'** `14` `£7–10`
**1998**
Very hard, clean, gunflinty fruit. Selected stores.

**Muscadet de Sèvre-et-** `13` `–£3.50`
**Maine Sur Lie NV,**
**Sainsbury's (3-litre box)**
The price band reflects the equivalent price for a 75cl bottle.

**Muscadet de Sèvre-et-** `14` `–£5.00`
**Maine Sur Lie, La**
**Goelette 1999**
Crisp and clean. Muscadet as more Muscadets ought to be but seldom are. Most stores.

**Orchid Vale Medium** `13.5` `–£5.00`
**French Chardonnay**
**Grenache Blanc, VdP**
**d'Oc 1999**
Very quirky and risibly packed (blue bottle). Young things will love it. Most stores.

**Petit Chablis 1999** `13` `£5–7`

**Pouilly-Fumé, Cuvée** `14.5` `£7–10`
**Pierre Louis 1999**
A fine steely specimen. Not at all stores.

**Réserve St-Marc** `16` `–£5.00`
**Sauvignon Blanc, VdP**
**d'Oc 1999**

Why doesn't the Sancerre, using the same grape, taste so elegant and powerful? Ah, the mysteries of French soil and sun (and bullshit – the customary manure). Most stores.

**Touraine Sauvignon** `15.5` `–£5.00`
**Blanc 1999**
Delicious nuttiness and concentrated grassy fruit. Most stores.

**Vin Blanc de France,** `12` `–£3.50`
**Sainsbury's (3-litre box)**
Old-fashioned rustic mustiness which makes little attempt to appear modern, well-cut, distinctive. The price band reflects the equivalent price for a 75cl bottle.

**Vin de Pays de l'Aude** `15` `–£3.50`
**Blanc, Sainsbury's**

**Vin de Pays des Côtes de** `15` `–£3.50`
**Gascogne NV,**
**Sainsbury's**

**Vin de Pays des Côtes de** `15` `–£3.50`
**Gascogne, Sainsbury's**
**(3-litre box)**
Delicious aperitif-style fruit uniting hard fruit (apple and pear) with soft fruit (mostly strawberry). It's not OTT fruit-wise, however, for there are solid, fresh acids. The price band reflects the equivalent price for a 75cl bottle.

**Vouvray la Couronne des** `15` `–£5.00`
**Plantagenets 1999**
Yes, it's a sweet-edged thing. And it's young. Give it a couple of years for the minerals to develop. I'm drinking the '95 of this wine at home now. Most stores.

**White Burgundy NV,** `14` `£5–7`
**Sainsbury's**

## SOMERFIELD WHITE

**Anjou Blanc 1999,** `13.5` `–£3.50`
**Somerfield**
Excellent with Thai food. Has a demi-sweet edge which really calms chillies and coriander.

**Bordeneuve Blanc VdP** `13` `–£5.00`
**des Côtes de Gascogne**
**1999**
Just a touch too fruity for me.

**Chablis 1998, Somerfield** `14` `£7–10`
Rather good edge of rich melon and thoroughly crisp minerals.

**Chablis Premier Cru 1997** `10` `£10–13`

**Chardonnay VdP d'Oc** `14.5` `–£5.00`
**1999, Somerfield**
Rich melon and sulky lemon.

**Chardonnay VdP du** `13` `–£5.00`
**Jardin de la France 1999**
Rather flat as it surges to the throat.

**Domaine d' Arain Muscat** `16` `–£5.00`
**de Frontignan (50cl)**
Wonderful honeyed, strawberry/peach-edged sweetness here. Great with pastry tarts and crème brûlée and ice cream. Terrific price and the size makes it perfect for a lovable pair of meal-ending hedonists.

**Domaine du Bois** `16` `–£5.00`
**Viognier VdP d'Oc,**
**Maurel Vedeau 1998**
It's the superb texture and faint smoky edge to the apricots which make the wine so palate-teasingly breezy.

**Entre-Deux-Mers 1998,** `12` `–£5.00`
**Somerfield**
Touch on the dull side.

**French Oak Aged** `16` `£5–7`
**Chardonnay, Domaine**
**Ste-Agathe 1998**

Very stylishly assembled from melons, figs, wood, sunshine and crisp, crisp apples and lemons.

**Gewürztraminer Caves de Turckheim 1999**   16   £5–7
Superb smoky, rose-petal, lychee and pawpaw richness with a very subtle undertone of coriander. A marvellous companion to all matters oriental.

**Goûts et Couleurs Chardonnay Viognier 1999**   15.5   −£5.00
Delicious apricot and melon richness with a touch of lemon and a lingering suggestion of mango.

**Goûts et Couleurs Cinsault Rosé 1999**   14   −£5.00
Goes a bit gooey and Marilyn Monroe-ish on the finish, but the fruit is a great performer with food.

**Hautes-Côtes de Beaune, Labouré-Roi 1998**   13   £5–7
Very lemony.

**James Herrick Chardonnay VdP d'Oc 1999**   16   −£5.00
Very elegant, subtle, gently fruity, stylish and well-priced. Lovely lemon edge as it finishes.

**Laperouse Chardonnay VdP d'Oc 1996**   16.5   −£5.00
A brilliant white Burgundy taste alike (if that doesn't insult it). Mature, vegetal, creamy, ripe, deep and hugely provocative. A fantastic bargain. Pour the wine into jugs and tell your friends it's Meursault.

**Les Marionettes Marsanne VdP d'Oc 1999**   15.5   −£5.00
Deliciously rich and generous: creamy, smoky, textured, good finish.

**Muscat de Frontignan NV (50 cl)**   17   −£5.00
Fantastic accompaniment to pastry desserts: it's creamy, toffeed, caramel-edged, hugely honeyed and husky and it tastes like a drink you could offer to a goddess (before you ask her to live with you).

**Rivers Meet Sauvignon Sémillon 1999**   13   −£5.00
Very firm and fruity.

**Sancerre Domaine les Grands Groux 1999**   13   £7–10
Too expensive for this pocket.

**VdP des Coteaux de l'Ardèche Blanc 1999, Somerfield**   14.5   −£3.50
Lemon and melon. Thoroughly different and drinkable.

**VdP du Comte du Tolosan, Les Chais Beaucarois 1998**   14   −£3.50
Great with moules marinières – it really hits those molluscs.

**Vouvray 1997, Somerfield**   14   −£5.00
Keep it for a few years, it'll liven up even more. But an interesting, off-dry aperitif, waxy honey and dry leaves, now.

**White Burgundy 1999, Somerfield**   13.5   £5–7
Trying hard. Oh so hard!

**Winter Hill White, VdP de l'Aude NV**   14   −£3.50
Good melon/pineapple/lemon attack – gentle of course.

## SPAR WHITE

**Chablis La Chablisienne 1998, Spar**   14   £7–10

Lot of money, but it's drinkable if not thrilling. Has some vague pretensions to class.

**French Country VdP de l'Hérault White NV**  `13`  `−£5.00`
Touch expensive for the fruit, which seems a little hollow on the finish.

**Grenache VdP d'Oc NV**  `10`  `−£3.50`

**La Côte Chasan Chardonnay 1999**  `13`  `−£5.00`
Touch muddy on the finish. Ill-defined structure.

**Muscat de St-Jean de Minervois, Spar (half-bottle)**  `15.5`  `−£3.50`
Honeyed, subtly waxy, hint of pineapple to sweet fruit. Ice cream? Strawberries? Yes – but it has the subtlety to serve as an aperitif – even though some palates will dismiss it as sweet – but for me a glass of such a wine as this is very uplifting before gossip round a dinner table.

**Oaked Chardonnay VdP d'Oc 1998, Spar**  `12.5`  `−£5.00`
Hmm . . . can't make up its mind, quite. Am I dry? Am I fresh? Or am I just loosely put together?

**Pouilly-Fuissé Les Vercheres Chardonnay 1996, Spar**  `10`  `£10–13`

**Salaison Chardonnay Sauvignon 1998, Spar**  `15`  `−£5.00`
Delicious: nuts, melons, lemons and a hint of raspberry.

**Sancerre Saget 1998**  `10`  `£7–10`
Dreadful stuff. Pretentious codswallop.

**Unoaked Chardonnay VdP d'Oc 1999, Spar**  `14`  `−£5.00`

Mild melon fruit and demure acids. A quiet wine, quite nice.

**Vin de Pays de l'Aude Blanc NV, Spar**  `12`  `−£3.50`

**White Burgundy Chardonnay 1996, Spar**  `13`  `£5–7`

## TESCO WHITE

**Alsace Gewürztraminer 1998, Tesco**  `16`  `£5–7`
Lovely rich, rosy fruit, hint of ripe lychee and a touch of pear, and the whole construct is designed to soothe the troubled mind or lubricate Thai food. At most stores.

**Alsace Riesling 1998, Tesco**  `14`  `£5–7`
Classy, typical, reluctant, dry, acquired testiness. Needs smoked salmon for the tender-palated. At most stores.

**Anjou Blanc NV, Tesco**  `13`  `−£3.50`
Slightly sweet, slightly yukky.

**Barrique Aged Marsanne Roussanne VdP d'Oc 1998**  `15.5`  `−£5.00`
The bottle I tasted was corked. That is to say there was a musty tang bequeathed by the cork which spoiled the fruit. Nevertheless – and I have never before done this – I will rate it as I have because I could still detect, from the colour, texture and acid balance, that here was an interesting wine – but for that plague-ridden twig in its neck.

**Cabernet de Saumur Rosé NV, Tesco**  `14.5`  `−£5.00`
A good dry summer rosé. Not remotely cosmetic or over-baked as too many rosés are.

**Celsius Dry Muscat 1999**  `13.5`  `−£5.00`

Interesting only, I feel, when the weather is humid, the wine cold, the company outrageous. Not at all stores.

**Chablis 1998, Tesco** `12.5` `£5–7`
Dull for seven quid.

**Coteaux du Layon Saint-Aubin Domaine Cady 1996** `16` `£5–7`
Gorgeous honey and straw-rich (and coloured) off-dry aperitif or a wine to gulp with fresh fruit. Laid down for ten years or more it might achieve a perfect twenty score for it has complex acids to the waxy fruit which will permit it to develop fascinatingly well into the next decade and beyond.

**Côtes du Rhône Blanc NV, Tesco** `15` `–£3.50`
Warm and gentle – not unlike the soft earth from which it has sprung.

**Domaine Cazal Viel Viognier 1999** `16` `£5–7`
The moment the beautiful golden liquid flows into the glass and you raise it to the eye, then the nose, you know you're in for a treat. And so it transpires as you raise the wine to the lips and the taste buds revel in subtle apricot fruit, lemon and a hint of nuttiness. A lovely, elegant wine of some class and smoothly textured delivery.

**Domaine de Montauberon Marsanne 1998** `12` `–£5.00`

**Domaine du Soleil Chardonnay VdP d'Oc NV** `14` `–£5.00`
Seems demure, almost shy, at first and then it puts in a lovely burst of rich nuttiness as it lingers on the finish.

**Domaine du Soleil Sauvignon/Chardonnay VdP d'Oc NV** `14` `–£5.00`
Very fat, sunny finish. Needs food.

**Entre-Deux-Mers NV, Tesco** `13.5` `–£5.00`
Simple, fruity, gently plump. Not typical (ie dry and fresh), but the lemon undertone augurs well for fish.

**French Chardonnay NV, Tesco** `13.5` `–£3.50`
Cheap enough, and reasonably cheerful.

**French Chenin Blanc NV, Tesco** `14.5` `–£3.50`
Impossible to complain, at £2.99, about this citrussy specimen with its keen finish and overall freshness. Also available in five litres.

**French Viognier VdP d'Oc 1999, Tesco** `15` `–£5.00`
The apricot depth of the fruit is controlled by the delicious lemon coating.

**Gaston d'Orléans Vouvray Demi Sec 1998** `12` `£5–7`

**James Herrick Chardonnay VdP d'Oc 1998** `16.5` `–£5.00`
Cracking performer: elegant toasty fruit, firm balance of fresh acid (lemon-edged) and an overall politeness of manner and form. Has well-established credentials which the '98 vintage only amplifies. Not at all stores.

**Les Estoiles Organic Chardonnay/Chenin VdP d'Oc NV** `13.5` `–£5.00`

**Les Quatre Clochers Chardonnay 1998** `15` `£5–7`
Fat, full, touch frolicsome on the

finish, and a different approach to the cloying melonosity of Chardonnay in that the fruit has a subtle pâtisserie edge on the finish.

| Mâcon Blanc Villages 1998, Tesco | 11 | −£5.00 |

| Meursault 1er Cru Les Genevrières 1988 | 10 | £20+ |

Oxidative and old hat. Top 85 stores.

| Montagny Oak Aged 1997 | 13.5 | £7–10 |

| Muscadet NV, Tesco | 13.5 | −£3.50 |

| Muscadet Sur Lie 1999, Tesco | 13 | −£5.00 |

| Oak Aged White Burgundy 1998, Tesco | 13.5 | £5–7 |

Plump and modern. That's an advance for Burgundy, I guess.

| Pouilly-Fuissé Louis Jadot 1998 | 11 | £10–13 |

Thirteen quid? Provocative – unlike the liquid itself.

| Pouilly-Fumé Cuvée Jules 1998 | 13 | £7–10 |

| Sancerre 1999, Tesco | 10 | £5–7 |

Raggedy baggedy fruit of minimal charm; indeed, it's a bit of a sourpuss.

| Vouvray, Tesco | 12 | −£5.00 |

Sweet.

| White Burgundy 1999, Tesco | 12 | −£5.00 |

Too fruitless, over-penceful.

## THRESHER WHITE

| Chablis Domaine de Bieville 1998 | 14 | £7–10 |

If you want classic clean Chablis, Chardonnay whistle fresh, you have to pay for it. Not at Wine Rack.

| Chablis Regional Classics 1997 | 13.5 | £7–10 |

Aficionados of Chablis will find attractive features in this style of Chardonnay and yet £7.99? Can't help wondering about life and relative values.

| Chablis Vieilles Vignes, Defaix 1996 | 11 | £10–13 |

| Chablis Vieilles Vignes, La Cuvée Exceptionelle, Defaix 1997 | 12.5 | £13–20 |

| Château Filhot Sauternes 1990 | 15 | £20+ |

| Château Petit Moulin Blanc, Bordeaux 1998 | 12.5 | £5–7 |

| Domaine Pré Baron Sauvignon de Touraine 1998 | 14.5 | £5–7 |

Very fresh-faced and keenly cut. Wine Rack only.

| Domaine Tariquert Sauvignon Blanc 1999 | 14 | £5–7 |

Incisive edge on the finish clinches the points. Wine Rack and Bottoms Up only.

| French Révolution Le Blanc 1999 | 13 | −£5.00 |

Rather cosmetic edge to a wholly gungo product.

| Le Vieux Mas Marsanne Viognier VdP d'Oc 1998 | 15 | −£5.00 |

| Les Pierres Blanches Sancerre 1998 | 12 | £7–10 |

Silly price really for basic fruit. Bottoms Up only.

| Old Bush Vines Grenache Blanc 1999 | 14 | −£5.00 |

Unusual dryness and nervous-sided

pertness here. Very good fish wine. Not at Wine Rack.

**Orchid Vale Medium** `10` `−£5.00`
**Chardonnay 1999**
Strictly as a reward for your great-grandma when she wins a packet at bingo.

**Petit Chablis de Maligny** `13.5` `£7–10`
**1996**
Warmth and some hint of activity from the fruit, but at the price . . . Wine Rack and Bottoms Up only.

**Riesling Wintzenheim** `14` `£7–10`
**Zind Humbrecht 1997**

**Riesling Zind Humbrecht** `14` `£13–20`
**Clos Hauserer 1997**

**Tequirat Côtes de** `14` `−£5.00`
**Gascogne 1998**
Delicious, crisp, ripe, cheerful. Not at Wine Rack.

**Tokay Pinot Gris** `16.5` `£13–20`
**Herrenweg, Zind**
**Humbrecht 1997**
So rich and roasted-honeyed that it whips the taste buds into peaks. Is it sweet? No. Is it dry? No way. Other categories refuse to accept it either. Perhaps goat's cheese and fruit are its best pals. Wine Rack only.

**Tokay Pinot Gris,** `15.5` `£5–7`
**Turckheim 1998**
It'll age for two or three years and mellow deliciously, but I like its subtle apricot freshness now. A real wine with individuality and soul.

**Turckheim Alsace Blanc** `13` `−£5.00`
**1998**
Dry, touch austere. Not at Wine Rack.

**Turckheim** `16` `£5–7`
**Gewürztraminer 1998**

Classic, spicy, rich, warm, immediate rosy/lychee/strawberry fruit. Great throat refresher and plate accompanist.

**Turckheim Pinot Blanc** `14.5` `−£5.00`
**1998**

**Zind Humbrecht Pinot** `16` `£7–10`
**d'Alsace 1997**
Deliciously impish richness, expensively furnished with decisive acidity, and the gentility of the wine, and its characterful freshness, make it a treat. It will age for a couple more years yet. Wine Rack only.

## UNWINS WHITE

**Anjou Blanc 1997** `11` `−£5.00`

**Ash Ridge Grenache/** `13` `−£5.00`
**Viognier 1999**

**Château Vieux** `16.5` `£13–20`
**Malveyren Monbazillac**
**Domaine Vilate 1990**
Magnificently textured, complex, honeyed fruit. A first-class dessert wine, better than many premier cru Sauternes.

**Condrieu Guigal 1998** `15.5` `£13–20`
Very delicious if not entirely typical of the breed (Viognier grape = apricots). The finish is dry and nutty.

**Corbières Les** `12` `−£5.00`
**Producteurs du Mont**
**Tauch**

**Côtes du Rhône Guigal** `14.5` `£7–10`
**1998**
Delicious texture, demure fruit with a very faint echo of earth.

**Cuvée Philippe VdP du** `12.5` `−£3.50`
**Comte Tolosan 1999**

Sweet-edged but dry. Strictly a curmudgeon's party wine.

**Domaine de Saubagnere** `14.5` `−£5.00`
**Côtes de Gascogne 1998**
Fresh, delicious, hint of tropicality.

**Domaine des Forges** `16` `£7–10`
**Coteaux du Layon-
Chaume 1997**
Pineapples, honey, wild strawberries and butterscotch. Complex enough for you? It is for me. To drink with fruit pastry desserts.

**Domaine Valette Pouilly-** `16` `£13–20`
**Vinzelles Vieilles Vignes
1997**
Expensive treat and quite remarkably concentrated and rich. Very elegant and untypical.

**La Chablisienne Chablis** `13` `£7–10`
**Vieilles Vignes 1997**

**Les Trois Herault Les** `13` `−£3.50`
**Chais Beaucarois NV**

**Mâcon Lugny Les** `14` `£5–7`
**Charmes 1998**
Always a decent drop, Chardonnay from this co-op.

**Marquis de Beausoleil NV** `15.5` `£5–7`
Delicious blue cheese wine.

**Marsanne/Roussanne** `14.5` `−£5.00`
**Frédéric Roger 1999**
Terrific food wine. Has energy, character and backbone.

**Muscadet Sur Lie Pierre** `13.5` `−£5.00`
**Brevin 1997**

**Petit Chablis Albert** `12` `£5–7`
**Bichot 1999**
Dull – not quite as ditchwater, that would be unfair, but it isn't a seven quid wine.

**Pinot Blanc d'Alsace** `14` `−£5.00`
**Cave de Turckheim 1999**
Hint of peach to the delicious freshness.

**Pouilly-Fumé Les** `10` `£7–10`
**Griottines 1998**

**Sancerre Harmonie Oak** `12` `£13–20`
**Aged 1997**
Hugely overpriced.

**Sancerre Les Roches** `13.5` `£10–13`
**Vacheron 1999**
Nice texture but eleven quid? No way.

**Sancerre Les Romains** `13.5` `£7–10`
**Vacherons 1999 (rosé)**
Very elegant, very expensive, very, very subtle.

**St-Véran Domaine des** `15.5` `£7–10`
**Deux Roches 1999**
Superb elegance and lingering fruit. Beautiful white burgundy for the money.

## VICTORIA WINE WHITE

**Bordeaux Sauvignon** `12` `−£5.00`
**Calvet 1997**

**Chablis Domaine de** `14` `£7–10`
**Bieville 1998**
If you want classic clean Chablis, Chardonnay whistle fresh, you have to pay for it.

**Chablis Regional Classics** `13.5` `£7–10`
**1997**
Aficionados of Chablis will find attractive features in this style of Chardonnay and yet £7.99? Can't help wondering about life and relative values.

Chablis Vieilles Vignes, **11** £10–13
Defaix 1996

Chablis Vieilles Vignes, **12.5** £13–20
La Cuvée Exceptionelle,
Defaix 1997

Château Filhot Sauternes **15** £20+
1990

Château Petit Moulin **12.5** £5–7
Blanc, Bordeaux 1998

Domaine Pré Baron **14.5** £5–7
Sauvignon de Touraine
1998
Very fresh-faced and keenly cut.

French Révolution Le **13** –£5.00
Blanc 1999
Rather cosmetic edge to a wholly
gungo product.

Le Vieux Mas Marsanne **15** –£5.00
Viognier VdP d'Oc 1998

Les Pierres Blanches **12** £7–10
Sancerre 1998
Silly price really for basic fruit.

Meursault, Les **12** £13–20
Chevaliers, Domaine
René Monnier 1996

Montagny Premier Cru **13.5** £5–7
Oak Aged Chardonnay
1997

Old Bush Vines Grenache **14** –£5.00
Blanc 1999
Unusual dryness and nervous-sided
pertness here. Very good fish wine.
Not at Wine Rack.

Rivers Meet White **11** –£5.00
Bordeaux 1997

Teuqirat Côtes de **14.5** –£5.00
Gascogne 1998
Delicious, crisp, ripe, cheerful.

Turckheim Alsace Blanc **13** –£5.00
1998
Dry, touch austere. Not at Wine Rack.

Turckheim **16** £5–7
Gewürztraminer 1998
Classic, spicy, rich, warm, immediate
rosy/lychee/strawberry fruit. Great
throat refresher and plate accompanist.

Turckheim Pinot Blanc **14.5** –£5.00
1998

## WAITROSE WHITE

Alsace Gewürztraminer **16.5** £5–7
1998, Waitrose
Superb plumpness and vivacity of
fruit. Not too spicy but oodles of
flavour.

Alsace Pinot Blanc, Paul **14** –£5.00
Blanck 1999
Deliciously different aperitif – hint of
wet wood and nuts.

Anjou Blanc Ackerman **13** –£3.50
1999
Almost sweet.

Bistro Blanc VdP d'Oc **13.5** –£5.00
1999
Oddly bitter on the finish. Expensive
for the style.

Bordeaux Blanc Medium **12** –£3.50
Dry, Yvon Mau NV
Medium it is, then.

Chablis Gaec des Reugnis **14.5** £7–10
1998
Some style here. Muted, compared to
Aus or NZ, but attractive.

Chablis Grand Cru Les **13** £13–20
Clos 1996
A lot of money for a wine which on
the sole evidence of the bottle I tasted,

sealed with heaven knows what variation in cork quality, is slightly less than exciting.

**Château Carsin Bordeaux** 15.5 £7–10
**Blanc Cuvée Prestige**
**1997**
Lovely woody undertone to crisp fresh gooseberries – tangy edge to it.

**Château de Caraghuiles** 15.5 £5–7
**Organic Rosé 1999**
Superb texture and assured class. If you are a real rosé fan, this is for you. It suits food or mood. Very versatile with food.

**Château Filhot Grand** 13.5 £20+
**Cru Classé Sauternes**
**1989**
Too expensive by a lot more than half.

**Château Vignal Labrie,** 17 £7–10
**Monbazillac 1997**
Most individual and exotic specimen. Has a gorgeous waxy texture and very ripe, complex undertones. Real whack of sweet fruit on the finish.

**Clos des Chenoves Blanc** 14 £5–7
**1998**
Interesting. Has some engaging mineral edges.

**Domaine de l'Olivette,** 15.5 –£5.00
**Corbières 1999**
Unusual finish to the wine of nuts and herb bread. Delicious, different, dainty, decisive.

**Domaine de Planterieu** 15 –£5.00
**VdP de Gascogne 1999**
Lovely exotic edge (subtle) underpinned by pineapple and pear freshness.

**French Connection** 15.5 –£5.00
**Viognier VdP d'Oc 1999**
The dry apricot fruit is very well

picked. It is a smooth, gently rich wine of some class.

**Gewürztraminer** 16.5 £7–10
**Wintzenheim Domaine**
**Zind Humbrecht 1998**
Wonderful dry spice here! Imperious class and concentration! Limited branches.

**Hermitage Le Chevalier** 17.5 £20+
**de Sterimberg 1997**
The acme of French arrogance. Has little fruit but mighty dry yet oily-textured richness. Only from Waitrose Direct.

**James Herrick** 16 –£5.00
**Chardonnay VdP d'Oc**
**1999**
Very elegant, subtle, gently fruity, stylish and well-priced. Lovely lemon edge as it finishes.

**L'Enclos Domeque Barrel** 16.5 –£5.00
**Fermented Marsanne/**
**Roussanne VdP d'Oc**
**1999**
What a smashing wine! Has wonderful crispness yet layers of baked fruit flavour and a hint of gelatinous richness as an undertone. Unusual, distinctive, very delicious.

**La Cité Chardonnay, VdP** 14.5 –£5.00
**d'Oc 1999**
Goes nicely ripe melony on the finish.

**'Les Fleurs' Chardonnay/** 16 £5–7
**Sauvignon VdP des Côtes**
**de Gascogne 1999**
What a cheeky brew! Lovely confident richness, almost serious, alongside rivulets of hard fruit freshness.

**Maury Vin Doux Naturel** 14 –£5.00
**NV**
Try it with chocolate.

Merchants Bay `14` `–£5.00`
Sauvignon/Sémillon 1998

Mercurey Blanc Château `14` `£10–13`
le Hardi 1998
Interesting. Cellar it for three years
and it'll be even more so.

Meursault Louis Jadot `12` `£13–20`
1997
Will develop, though, and '97 was a
decent enough vintage. Give it four
years, say?

Montagny 1er Cru `13` `£7–10`
Bouchard Père 1998

Muscadet Sur Lie 'Fief `14` `–£5.00`
Guerin' 1999
Has a lovely gripping texture and a
nutty edge to the fruit.

Muscat Sec Domaine de `16` `–£5.00`
Provenquière, VdP d'Oc
1999
Muscat sec is a difficult beast which
often shows two heads but fails to be
intimidating. Here there is integration
and the two heads, dry honey with
crisp freshness, work. A lovely, lovely
aperitif.

Muscat de Beaumes-de- `16` `–£5.00`
Venise NV (half-bottle)
A wonderful blue cheese wine – or
with fresh fruit.

Pinot Gris Grand Cru `18.5` `£20+`
Rangen de Thann Clos
St-Urbain, Domaine Zind
Humbrecht 1996
Stunning elegant spiciness and richness
here. Extraordinary depths of
deliciousness. Only from Waitrose
Direct.

Pouilly-Fumé Chatelain `12.5` `£7–10`
1999

Puligny-Montrachet 1er `13` `£20+`
Cru Champs Gains 1997

Quincy La Boissière 1999 `13` `£5–7`
Odd chewy finish.

Rosé d'Anjou 1999 `13` `–£5.00`
Sweet and loving.

Saint-Aubin Premier Cru `15` `£13–20`
Ropiteau 1998
Delicious, if expensive. Will age
extremely well for five or six years and
get really incisively Burgundyish.

Sancerre Blanc Domaine `13` `£7–10`
Naudet 1999
Oddly grassily fat edge.

Sancerre Réserve Alfonse `10` `£10–13`
Mellot 1998
Oh come on!! Thirteen quid!!!

Saumur Blanc 'les `14` `–£5.00`
Andides' Saint-Cyr-en-
Bourg 1999
Interesting oddity. Little charm or
concession to fruitiness. But fine with
a dozen Colchester natives.

Sauvignon Blanc 'Les `13.5` `–£5.00`
Rochers', VdP des Côtes
de Gascogne 1999
Curious fatness yet leanness on the
finish.

Sauvignon Bordeaux `13.5` `–£5.00`
Calvet 1999
Sealed with a real cork but a so-called
conglomerate, so expect variations
between bottles even greater than you
get with a whole natural cork. (Please.
Bring on screw caps.)

Tokay Pinot Gris `18` `£20+`
Vendanges Tardives,
Hugel 1990
Butterscotch richness yet calm acidic

# WINE CELLAR WHITE

complexity. A stunning aperitif wine.
Inner Cellar stores.

**Top 40 Chardonnay VdP** `17` `£5–7`
**d'Oc 1999**
Better than many a Meursault, this
creamy, woody wine. It has delicacy
yet lingering power and real deep
class.

**Touraine Sauvignon** `13.5` `–£5.00`
**1999, Waitrose**

**Vin Blanc Sec VdT** `12` `–£3.50`
**Français NV, Waitrose**

**Winter Hill Syrah Rosé,** `14` `–£3.50`
**VdP d'Oc 1999**
Great with food, this toffee and
cherries fruited rosé.

**Winter Hill VdP d'Oc** `15` `–£3.50`
**1999**
They add oak chips to this wine to
give it fatness which is a bit like
getting Kate Moss to drink water to
put on weight. In other words, you
taste no oak, thank goodness, but you
taste a real mean lean Ugni Blanc (the
grapes in this bottle). A great shellfish
wine here.

## WINE CELLAR WHITE

**Château l'Ermitage** `16` `–£5.00`
**Blanc, Costières de**
**Nîmes 1998**
Crackingly good peach/apricot/lemon
fruit, very subtle, beautifully textured.
A confident, very classy wine of wit
and style.

**Château l'Ermitage Rosé,** `15.5` `–£5.00`
**Costières de Nîmes 1998**
A superb, dry rosé of warmth and
richness. Really effective as a quaffer
and a food wine.

**Château Lacroix Rosé** `13` `£5–7`
**1999**
I want crispness with my fruit, not
out-of-focus cherries and plums.

**Château Lacroix** `13.5` `£5–7`
**Sémillon/Sauvignon 1998**
Muddy fruit, not crisply defined.
Suitable for rich fish dishes.

**Domaine l'Orgeril** `12` `£5–7`
**Réserve Chardonnay,**
**VdP d'Oc 1997**

**Orchid Vale Medium Dry** `13` `–£5.00`
**Chardonnay 1998**

**Rhône Valley White,** `11` `–£5.00`
**VdP de Vaucluse NV**

**Sancerre Seduction** `12` `£10–13`
**Vieilles Vignes 1998**
Very expensive and not especially
seductive. It is priced, as Sancerre
increasingly tends to be, three times
more than the fruit justifies.

139

# GERMANY

Going down the tubes fast as a mass producer, but not giving up without a fight. All those vineyards, all that fast-dying labour which can barely be persuaded to pick the grapes, no wonder the big players in the German wine industry are being squeezed by the changing tastes of UK wine drinkers. It is the single-estate Rieslings which are Germany's unique contribution to world culture (speaking vinously) and they are the greatest white wines in the world: unique, uncopyable, resplendently complex and mineral-tinged, and capable of inducing great happiness.

## CWS RED

**Devil's Rock Masterpiece Pinot Noir 1999** 10 −£5.00
Distinguished by being the feeblest red wine at the Co-op. Superstores only.

## ASDA WHITE

**Deidesheimer Hofstuck Riesling Kabinett 1997, Asda** 11 −£5.00

**Devil's Rock Riesling Kabinett 1997** 14 −£5.00

**Liebfraumilch Gold Seal 1997** 13.5 −£3.50

## BOOTHS WHITE

**Gau-Bickelheimer Kurfurstenstuck Auslese 1998** 13 −£5.00
Very mild for an Auslese. Well-chilled it's an acceptable aperitif.

**Liebfraumilch NV, Booths** 13 −£3.50

**Niersteiner Speigelberg Spatlese 1997** 12 −£5.00

**Piesporter Michelsberg NV, Booths** 13.5 −£5.00

**Riesling Louis Guntrum 1999** 14 −£5.00
A very pleasant aperitif – even better if cellared for five years.

## BUDGENS WHITE

**Flonheimer Adelberg Auslese 1997** 10 −£3.50

## CWS WHITE

**Bend in the River 1998** 12.5 −£5.00
Bit austere (unlike the name and the bottle).

**Bereich Bernkastel 1999, Co-op** 10 −£3.50

Very sweet and straight-in-yer-face.

**Bernkasteler Badstube** `16` `£5–7`
**Riesling Kabinett 1996**
Superb racy, mineralised acids. A dry
yet gently honey/melon (ogen) edged
wine of great class. Superstores only.

**Four Rs 1999, Co-op** `12` `–£5.00`
They forgot the fifth R: ah!

**Graacher Himmelreich** `14.5` `–£5.00`
**Riesling Spatlese 1997**
Nice tang to the minerals in the acids,
pleasant thwack to the gently honeyed
fruit. A most acceptable aperitif.
Superstores only.

**Kendermans Dry Riesling** `13.5` `–£5.00`
**1998**
Pleasant lemon edge on the finish.

**Kirchheimer Schwarzerde** `14` `–£5.00`
Beerenauslese 1998 (half-
bottle)

## KWIK SAVE WHITE

**Hock NV, Somerfield** `14.5` `–£2.50`
One of the great bargains on UK wine
shelves. A totally charming aperitif in
warm weather or a lush ingredient in a
spritzer.

**Niersteiner Spiegelberg** `13` `–£3.50`
**1999, Somerfield**
You might try laying it down – for
three or four years. Interesting fruit
should emerge.

## M&S WHITE

**Summer Spring Riesling** `12` `–£5.00`
**1999**
Expensive, tart, eccentrically-bottled
and rather pathetic – it seems to be
begging for attention.

## MAJESTIC WHITE

**Avelsbacher** `16.5` `–£5.00`
**Hammerstein Riesling**
**QbA 1992**
Amazing value: petroleum and
textured, ripe honeydew melon fruit.
Delicious aperitif.

**Bernkasteler Badstube** `13.5` `–£5.00`
**Riesling Kabinett,**
**Jacobus 1994**
Bit monodimensionally sweet on the
finish.

**Bernkasteler Badstube** `13` `£7–10`
**Riesling Kabinett**
**Thanisch Muller-**
**Burggrael 1998**
Too young and I'm uncertain as to
how well it will age. It has a very
uncertain, unMosel-like feel to its
sweetness.

**Domdechant Werner** `14.5` `–£5.00`
**Riesling Spatlese**
**Halbtrocken 1992**
Great aperitif. Delicious value.

**Erdener Treppchen** `16.5` `£5–7`
**Riesling Spatlese 1994**
I love the racy acids which flow so
purposefully with the rich fruit. At its
peak early.

**JL Wolf Forster Stiff** `14` `£5–7`
**Riesling Spatlese 1996**
Bare hints of the petroleum classicism
of old Pfalz Riesling, but then this is
young. Give it eight years and it'll rate
eighteen points.

**Kaseler Kehrnagel** `14` `–£5.00`
**Riesling Kabinett Bert**
**Simon 1990**
Interesting age for a Riesling from
Herr Simon. Simple? Not entirely.

Riesling QbA Friedrich-
Wilhelm-Gymnasium
1991
`14`  `-£5.00`

Great value thirst-quencher, very well
chilled, for warm firesides.

Riesling Ruppertsberger
1997
`13.5`  `-£5.00`

Serriger Vogelsang
Riesling Auslese (2nd
Barrel) 1989
`16.5`  `£5-7`

Petroleum, cherries, lemons, limes,
hint of pineapple – yet it's not too
fruity or remotely sweet. A sipping
wine for civilising effects on mood –
but not food.

Wehlener Sonnenuhr
Riesling Kabinett,
Jacobus 1992
`16`  `-£5.00`

Marvellous mineral dryness and
mature fruit.

Wehlener Sonnenuhr
Riesling Spatlese, Hauth-
Kerpen 1998
`15`  `£5-7`

Lush and lissom, lithe and lovely.

## MORRISONS WHITE

Kallstadter Beerenauslese
1998 (half-bottle)
`15`  `-£5.00`

Lovely honeyed richness which is not
OTT. Great with Greek pastries or
fresh fruit.

Kendermans Dry Riesling
1999
`13`  `-£5.00`

Brave stab at a brave new German
wine world.

Urziger Wurzgarten
Spatlese 1998
`12`  `£5-7`

Sweet, mono-dimensional, touch
flatulent.

Wehlener Sonnenuhr
Riesling Spatlese 1997
`11`  `£5-7`

## OODBINS WHITE

Durkheimer Fronhof
Scheurebe
Trockenbeerenauslese,
Kurt Darting 1998 (50cl)
`15.5`  `£13-20`

Lingfelder Bird Label
Riesling, Pfalz 1999
`13`  `-£5.00`

Can't quite make up its mind. Is it
sweet or dry?

Messmer Burrweiler
Riesling Spatlese
Trocken, Pfalz 1998
`13`  `£7-10`

Bit austere on the tongue.

Ruppertsberger
Reiterpfad Scheurebe
Beerenauslese, von Buhl
1994 (half-bottle)
`17`  `£20+`

Astonishing richness and honeyed
grapefruity lushness give it an unusual
multi-layered, dry effect in what is a
sweet wine. It will age for twenty
years, but you can enjoy it now with
fruit tarts.

Von Buhl Deidesheimer
Maushole Spatlese
Halbtrocken 1998
`14`  `£7-10`

Lay it down for five years.

Von Buhl Forster
Pechstein Riesling
Kabinett 1998
`14`  `£7-10`

Very sweet for a Kabinett. Best to let it
lie for a few more years.

## SAFEWAY WHITE

**Graacher Domprobst** 16 £7–10
**Riesling Spatlese, Mosel**
**Saar Ruwer 1996**
The ultimate Christmas lunch starter
wine – with the smoked salmon. The
complex acids buttress the rich fruit
beautifully. An immensely civilised
wine. Top 67 stores.

**Oppenheimer Sacktrager** 12 £5–7
**Riesling Kabinett,**
**Rheinhessen 1996**

**Peter Mertes Dry Riesling** 12 –£3.50
**1998**

## SAINSBURY'S WHITE

**Bereich Bernkastel** 12 –£3.50
**Riesling 1997**

**Dr Loosen Wehlener** 13 £13–20
**Sonnenuhr Riesling**
**Spatlese 1995**
Needs another five or six years to
really motor. At this price, now, you
are wasting your money. It needs
time. 10 stores.

**Fire Mountain Riesling** 13.5 –£5.00
**1999**
Some nice touches to the fruit.
Touches, mind. Selected stores.

**Hock NV, Sainsbury's** 11.5 –£3.50

**Hock, Sainsbury's (3 litre** 14.5 –£3.50
**box)**
A fantastic value aperitif and summer
thirst quencher. Not remotely sweet
or austere. The price band reflects the
equivalent price for a 75cl bottle.

**Kendermann Dry** 13 –£5.00
**Riesling 1999**

Brave stab at a brave new German
wine world. Selected stores.

**Liebfraumilch,** 14 –£3.50
**Sainsbury's (3 litre box)**
The perfect base for a spritzer or for
the honey-dentured crowd who like a
touch of honey in their wines. The
price band reflects the equivalent price
for a 75cl bottle.

**Mosel, Sainsbury's** 14 –£3.50

**Piesporter Michelsberg,** 12 –£3.50
**Sainsbury's**

**Zeltinger Himmelreich** 15 –£5.00
**Riesling Kabinett 1997**

## SOMERFIELD WHITE

**Baden Dry NV,** 13.5 –£5.00
**Somerfield**

**Hock NV, Somerfield** 14.5 –£2.50
One of the great bargains on UK wine
shelves. A totally charming aperitif in
warm weather or a lush ingredient in a
spritzer.

**Morio Muskat 1997** 15 –£3.50
Gamy, spicy, rich yet dry – this is a
great aperitif. Limited distribution.

**Mosel Riesling** 14 –£3.50
**Halbtrocken NV**

**Niersteiner Spiegelberg** 13 –£3.50
**1999, Somerfield**
You might try laying it down – for
three or four years. Interesting fruit
should emerge.

**Rheingau Riesling 1996,** 14 –£5.00
**Somerfield**
I wouldn't mind a glass of this – as a
well-chilled refresher on a honeyed
night.

143

**Rheinhessen Auslese** `14.5` `−£5.00`
**1997, Somerfield**
Delicious butterscotch/toffee edge to
the wine. Would work wonders with
fresh fruit and cheese. Limited
distribution.

**Rudesheimer** `13.5` `−£3.50`
**Rosengarten NV,**
**Somerfield**
Sweet-edged (of course) but very far
from yukky. Limited distribution.

**St Johanner Abtey** `14` `−£3.50`
**Kabinett NV, Somerfield**
Most acceptable, drunk with a bunch
of grapes, goat's cheese and bread.
Limited distribution.

**St Ursula Dry Riesling** `14` `−£5.00`
**NV**

## SPAR WHITE

**Grans Fassian Riesling** `16` `£5–7`
**1995**
The most elegant, most truly classic
white wine I've tasted at Spar. It is dry
and mineral, deliciously tinged with
freshness without tartness, and has a
subtle mix of dry honey and crisp
apple acidity. It will age with great
distinction for several years and
develop even more wonderful nuances
the riesling grape, uniquely, possesses.
A wine with true soul. An
uncompromised rebuke to the mass-
manufactured feel of other Spar
whites.

## TESCO WHITE

**Cark Erhard Rheingau** `14` `−£5.00`
**Riesling 1999**
Interesting aperitif here. Has hints of

melon, raspberry (on the finish as it
fades) and nuts.

**Devil's Rock Riesling** `14` `−£5.00`
**1998**

**Fire Mountain Riesling** `13.5` `−£5.00`
**1997**

**Grans Fassian** `14` `£7–10`
**Trittenheimer Riesling**
**Spatlese 1997**
So young! Cellar it for five to seven
years and a 17-point wine will emerge.
A Moselle like this needs time to let
the acids grow up in the bottle and cut
through the richness of the honey/
ogen melon fruit.

**Kendermans Dry Riesling** `13` `−£5.00`
**1999**
Brave stab at a brave new German
wine world.

**Liebfraumilch, Tesco** `12` `−£3.50`

**Steinweiler Kloster** `14` `−£5.00`
**Liebfrauenberg Kabinett,**
**Tesco**
Well chilled – what a lovely honeyed
aperitif (not too sweet).

**Steinweiler Kloster** `13` `−£5.00`
**Liebfrauenberg Spatlese,**
**Tesco**

**Villa Baden Chasselas** `12` `−£5.00`
**1998**

## THRESHER WHITE

**Piesporter Michelsberg** `10` `−£3.50`
**QbA 1997**

## UNWINS WHITE

**Fitz Riter Durkheimer** `13` `£5–7`
**Hochbenn Riesling**
**Kabinett 1997**

## VICTORIA WINE WHITE

**Kendermann Dry** `13.5` `−£5.00`
**Riesling 1998**
Touch expensive for the style.

## WAITROSE WHITE

**Devil's Rock Masterpiece,** `10.5` `−£5.00`
**St Ursula 1999**
Medium sweet anonymity.

**Johannisberger Klaus** `16.5` `£5–7`
**Riesling Spatlese, Schloss**
**Schonborn 1990**
Very ripe wine with lovely incut acids
which provide raciness to the richness.
Wonderful aperitif.

**Kendermann Vineyard** `13.5` `−£5.00`
**Selection Dry Riesling**
**1998**
Brave try.

**Liebfraumilch** `14` `−£3.50`
**Rheinhessen 1999,**
**Waitrose**
Totally respectable fruit. A charming
little aperitif.

**Piesporter Michelsburg** `13` `−£3.50`
**Mosel-Saar-Ruwer 1999,**
**Waitrose**
Good basis for spritzers.

**Ruppertsberger Dry** `13` `£5–7`
**Riesling Auslese 1996**
Neither fish nor fowl. Though it will
accompany the former well.

**Wehlener Sonnenuhr** `17` `£13–20`
**Riesling Auslese 1990**
One of the finest aperitifs in the world.
Trouble is, what follows? Only from
Waitrose Direct.

**Wehlener Sonnenuhr** `14` `£13–20`
**Riesling Spatlese, JJ Prum**
**1994**
Chewy, tangy aperitif – but best kept
for another twelve years to reach
eighteen points.

# GREECE

Macedonia seems to produce the most interesting, most soulful wines from this countrified mosaic which manages, with resinated Cretan reds, to produce the filthiest wine on the whole planet. The decent Greek stuff is expensive and purposeful, hugely well suited to robust dishes. Oddbins has some splendid examples.

## BOOTHS RED

**Vin de Crete Kourtaki 1998**   13   −£5.00
I have had my worst red-wine moments in Crete. This is not that bad but is not thrilling.

## BUDGENS RED

**Vin de Crete 1998**   12   −£3.50
Juicy and simplistic.

## KWIK SAVE RED

**Mavrodaphne of Patras NV**   14.5   −£5.00

## MORRISONS RED

**Mavrodaphne of Patras**   14   −£5.00

## ODDBINS RED

**Domaine Katsaros Red, Olympos 1997**   17   £13–20
One of the best red wines from Greece I've ever lingered over. Big, rich, spicy, deep and packed with layers of dry fruit. The tannins are awesome.

**Gaia Estate Agiorgitiko, Nemea 1998**   16   £10–13
Compares with great Rhône and Western Australian reds. Beautiful texture.

**Kosta Lazaridis Amethystos Cava, Drama 1995**   13   £13–20
Fine Wine Stores only.

**Ktima Domaine Mercouri, Peloponnese 1998**   16.5   £5–7
One of the most elevating Greek reds I've tasted. Beautiful fulfilling fruit and texture.

**Ktima Kyr-Yianni Ramnista, Naoussa 1997**   16   £5–7
Totally out of order: a Greek with muscles like a midi red, tannins like a very pricey Barolo and a finish which recalls a great Crozes-Hermitage. Yet for all these metaphors it writes in its own style.

Ktima Kyr-Yianni Syrah, 18 £7–10
Imathia 1997
A monumental syrah of such stunning
herby richness and power it has few
equals either in the Rhône or in the
Antipodes. The layers of fruit peel off
in delicious tannic frenzy and the finish
is like being kissed by a hallucinating
angel.

Ktima Kyr-Yianni 15.5 £7–10
Yianakahori, Imathia
1997

Ktima Voyatsi 1997 16 £7–10
Astonishingly savoury tannins and
chewy texture. Deep, black fruit of
style and richness. Fine Wine Stores
only.

Mavrodaphne of Patras 15.5 £5–7
NV (50 cl)

Papantonis Miden Agan, 16 £7–10
Peloponnese 1997
Stunning food wine! The ultimate
kleftiko red.

Tsantali Metoxi 16.5 £7–10
Agiorgitikos 1996
Wonderful multi-layered, lingering
lushness. Superb power of fruit and
balanced elements.

Tselepos Agiorgitikos, 15.5 £5–7
Nemea 1997
Juicy but dry, jammy but joyous!

Tselepos Cabernet 15.5 £7–10
Sauvignon, Peloponnese
1996

## SAFEWAY RED

Mavrodaphne of Patras 14.5 –£5.00
NV

## SAINSBURY'S RED

Kourtakis Vin de Crete 13 –£3.50
Red 1997

## TESCO RED

Grande Reserve Naoussa 13.5 £5–7
1995
Incredible raging tannins which attack
the teeth like piranhas. The fruit is
subdued under this austere overlord,
but with rich meat dishes this wine
would be a triumph. Very raisiny
aroma and colour.

Greek Red Wine 1999, 15 –£5.00
Tesco
A dry, rich, puddingy food wine.
Stalky, fruity, not sloppy and
overwarm.

## WAITROSE RED

Vin de Crete Kourtakis 14 –£3.50
1998
A sweet-raisin-edged wine of great
appeal to chillied food lovers.

## WINE CELLAR RED

Hatzimichalis Cabernet 16 £7–10
Sauvignon 1997
Most individual: rich, dry, herby,
warm, complex, multi-layered and full
of savoury surprises. An elegant,
authoritative Cabernet.

Sillogi Lafazanis Red 1997 13 £5–7

St George Skouras, 15.5 £5–7
Nemea 1996

## BOOTHS WHITE

Kretikos Vin de Crete `13` `−£5.00`
Blanc Boutari 1999

## KWIK SAVE WHITE

Kourtakis Retsina NV `14` `−£3.50`

## ODDBINS WHITE

Amethystos Fume, `14` `£7–10`
Drama 1999
Oddly attractive chewy edge to it, but
it is rather expensive.

Amethystos Rosé, `14` `£5–7`
Macedonia 1999
Very thick and rich and great with
robust food – you can't say that about
many rosés.

Boutari Visanto, `16` `£5–7`
Santorini 1993 (50cl)
Unusual pudding wine with hints of
nuts, honey, melon. Yet, curiously, it
finishes like dry apple skin.

Gerovassiliou White, `13` `£5–7`
Epanomi 1998

Kosta Lazaridis Château `13.5` `£5–7`
Julia Assyrtiko, Adriani
1998

Oenoforos Asprolithi, `13` `−£5.00`
Patras 1999
Bit sharp for me.

Spiropoulos White, `14` `−£5.00`
Mantinia 1998 (organic)

Strofilia Nafsika, `13.5` `£5–7`
Anavissos 1997

Thalassitis Santorini `15.5` `£5–7`
Assyrtiko 1998

Tsantali Ambelonas, `13.5` `£5–7`
Agios Pavlos 1999
Excellent white for take-away taverna
squid dishes.

Tsantali Chromitsa, `15` `£5–7`
Agiorgitikos 1999
Rich and creamy, slight crème brûlée
edge to it. Brilliant with food.

Tselepos Mantinia 1998 `13` `−£5.00`
Oddly ripe, tarty fruit.

## SOMERFIELD WHITE

Samos Greek Muscat NV `15.5` `−£3.50`
(half-bottle)

## TESCO WHITE

Greek White Wine 1999, `14` `−£5.00`
Tesco
Simple, dry fruit with a touch of
melon.

Santorini Dry White 1999 `13.5` `−£5.00`
Expensive but authentically Atlantean
and minerally.

## UNWINS WHITE

Samos Vin Doux Naturel `15.5` `−£5.00`
NV
Bargain! Sticky toffee fruit to pour
over ice cream.

## WINE CELLAR WHITE

Hatzimichalis `12` `£7–10`
Chardonnay 1998

Sillogi Lafazanis White `12` `£5–7`
1998

# HUNGARY

Probably hasn't gone as far as it might have, given its early flirtation with flying wine-makers, but the Merlots and Sauvignons (Cabernets and Blancs) can be brilliant. Even the odd Gewürztraminer is turning up, and turning out to be more than drinkable.

## ASDA RED

**River Route Cabernet** 15.5 −£3.50
**Sauvignon 1999**
Brilliant bargain. Great texture, ripeness and richness. Good dry edge to the finish.

## BUDGENS RED

**Spice Trail Zweigelt 1997** 10 −£5.00

## CWS RED

**Hungarian Country Wine** 13 −£3.50
**NV, Co-op**

## KWIK SAVE RED

**Chapel Hill Merlot 1997** 15.5 −£3.50

## SAFEWAY RED

**Chapel Hill Barrique** 16 −£5.00
**Aged Cabernet**
**Sauvignon, Balaton 1997,**
**Safeway**
A bargain whizzbang style cab of substance and dry wit. At most stores.

## SPAR RED

**Misty Mountain Merlot** 13 −£5.00
**NV, Spar**
Very forward and warmly jammy with slightly mismatched tannins. They protrude from the fruit rather than lying solidly beneath.

## TESCO RED

**Chapel Hill Barrique** 15 −£5.00
**Cabernet Sauvignon 1997**
Nods in the direction of Bordeaux. Smiles in the direction of South Australia. The result is highly drinkable. Not at all stores.

**Reka Valley Hungarian** 13 −£3.50
**Merlot, Tesco**
Dry but jammy – interesting paradox.

## ASDA WHITE

**Badger Hill Hungarian** 14 −£3.50
**Sauvignon 1999**
Very herbaceous and crisp. Great shellfish wine.

Hungarian Medium `12` `-£3.50`
Chardonnay 1999, Asda
Bit too sweet for me.

## BOOTHS WHITE

Chapel Hill Oaked `15.5` `-£3.50`
Chardonnay, Balaton
Boglar NV

## BUDGENS WHITE

Spice Trail Irsai Oliver/ `13.5` `-£5.00`
Pinot Grigio 1998

## CWS WHITE

Chapel Hill Irsai Oliver `14` `-£3.50`
1998
A wine for fish and chips with mushy
minted peas.

Hungarian Chardonnay `12` `-£3.50`
1999, Co-op
Lean and a touch mean. Superstores
only.

Hungarian White NV, `13.5` `-£3.50`
Co-op

## KWIK SAVE WHITE

Castle Ridge Pinot `14` `-£5.00`
Grigio, Neszmely 1999
Very subtle apricot fruit. Good food
wine (tuna salad). Limited distribution.

Hungarian Pinot Grigio, `15` `-£3.50`
Tolna Region 1998

Rhine Riesling, Mor `14` `-£3.50`
Region 1997

## MORRISONS WHITE

Ideal with Friends `12.5` `-£3.50`
Chardonnay NV
Well, my friends would like a little
more zip and more textured
melonosity with their Chardonnay.

'M' Ideal with Friends `13` `-£3.50`
Sauvignon Blanc NV
Very grassy and nervous. Choose your
friends carefully.

River Duna Pink Pinot `12.5` `-£5.00`
Noir 1998

## SAFEWAY WHITE

Hilltop Bianca 1999 `14.5` `-£3.50`
(organic)
Charmingly simple and fruity.

Hungarian Chardonnay `13` `-£3.50`
1999, Safeway

Irsai Oliver 1999, Safeway `13` `-£3.50`
Mildly entertaining aperitif style. Dry.

Karolyi Estate Private `13` `-£5.00`
Reserve 1998
Appley, simplistic.

Matra Mountain Oaked `13` `-£5.00`
Chardonnay, Nagyrede
1998, Safeway
Touch boyish.

Matra Mountain `15.5` `-£5.00`
Sauvignon Blanc 1999,
Safeway
Deliciously nervous edge to it. Great
refreshing sipping and fish dish
compatibility.

Matra Mountain Unoaked `14` `-£5.00`
Pinot Grigio 1998,
Safeway

Nagyrede Oaked Zenit `12` −£3.50
1998

Riverview Chardonnay `13.5` −£5.00
1999
Strains to make an impact.

Riverview Sauvignon `15.5` −£5.00
Blanc 1999
Excellent structure and touches of
class to the dry fruit.

Tokaji Aszu 5 Puttonyos `13.5` £7–10
1992 (50 cl)
A wine for crème brûlée or summer
pudding.

Woodcutter's White, `9` −£3.50
Neszmely 1999
Very cosmetic.

## SAINSBURY'S WHITE

Bin 66 Hilltop `14` −£5.00
Gewürztraminer 1999
Not like the fat, all-flowing Alsatian
kind, this is more crisp and modern.
Not at all stores.

Hilltop Chardonnay Bin `16` −£5.00
058 1997
Classy, restrained, dry yet fruity,
double-layered, nutty, not remotely
overdone or smug. Selected stores.

Hungarian Cabernet `11` −£3.50
Sauvignon Rosé NV,
Sainsbury's
Not as full of bravura as once it was.
It's a jejune little thing now, vaguely
cherryish in mode.

Zenit Sefir 1999 `13.5` −£5.00
A fish-party wine. Not at all stores.

## SOMERFIELD WHITE

Castle Ridge Pinot `14` −£5.00
Grigio, Neszmely 1999
Very subtle apricot fruit. Good food
wine (tuna salad). Limited distribution.

Castle Ridge Sauvignon `14` −£5.00
Blanc 1999
Very grassy and finely cut at that.
Limited distribution.

## SPAR WHITE

Misty Mountain `13` −£5.00
Chardonnay NV, Spar
Fruit's shrouded in mist too.

## TESCO WHITE

Chapel Hill Pinot Noir `15` −£3.50
Rosé 1998

Emerald Hungarian `14` −£5.00
Sauvignon Blanc 1999
The bones are poking through here, so
use it with smoked salmon. A very
attenuated dry wine. Not at all stores.

Hungarian Oaked `12` −£5.00
Chardonnay NV, Tesco
Curious ripe edge to it.

Hungarian Oaked `13.5` −£5.00
Chardonnay Reserve
1999, Tesco

Nagyrede Estate Barrel `16` −£5.00
Aged Pinot Grigio/Zenit
1998
Superb little throat charmer! Highly
stylised, rich/dry fruit, with a solidly
engaging finish. Terrific price for the
class. 100 selected stores.

Reka Valley Chardonnay `12` −£3.50
NV, Tesco

Somewhere between ho-hum and basic.

**Tokaiji Aszu 1990** `16` `£7–10`
Will age for ten to twelve years (and more) but it will go well with goose liver – which I drank it with. It lacks conventional sweetness but has a rich acidic vein like marmalade and lime. It has been bought in specially for Christmas at the top 85 stores, so please be aware that stocks may be limited.

## THRESHER WHITE

**AK 28 Sauvignon Blanc** `14.5` `–£5.00`
**1998**
Brilliant shellfish wine. Not at Wine Rack.

**Hilltop Gewürztraminer** `15.5` `–£5.00`
**1997**
A deft, gently spicy Gewürz with floods of fresh acidity to bolster the rich fruit. It's a lovely aperitif – quite individual and special. Not at Wine Rack or Bottoms Up.

**The Unpronounceable** `12` `–£3.50`
**Grape 1997**
Doesn't roll off the tongue.

## VICTORIA WINE WHITE

**AK 28 Sauvignon Blanc** `14.5` `–£5.00`
**1998**
Brilliant shellfish wine. Not at Wine Rack.

**Hilltop Gewürztraminer** `15.5` `–£5.00`
**1997**
A deft, gently spicy Gewürz with floods of fresh acidity to bolster the rich fruit. It's a lovely aperitif – quite individual and special.

**The Unpronounceable** `12` `–£3.50`
**Grape 1997**
Doesn't roll off the tongue.

## WAITROSE WHITE

**Deer Leap Dry White** `15.5` `–£3.50`
**1999**
Superbly fresh and crisp. Quite wonderful for the money.

**Deer Leap** `15.5` `–£5.00`
**Gewürztraminer, Mor**
**1999**
Think Sauvignon with spice. Not the usual rich roseate ferment but a clean, classy, very cool customer.

**Deer Leap Sauvignon** `16` `–£5.00`
**Blanc 1999**
Seriously demands of Kiwi Sauvignon: 'Why do you cost three times this to be as keen as a sushi-chef's knife edge?'

**Matra Springs 1999** `14` `–£3.50`
A fun party wine.

**Matra Springs Dry White** `15` `–£3.50`
**1999**
Fantastic screw-capped, taint-free fruit! It's dry, fresh, lemony and incisive.

# ITALY

The lira/pound sterling relationship and the waning interest in wine drinking among younger Italians means that for UK importers this is the promised land. Italy is desperate to export, has some tremendously fecund vineyards (especially in the south and Sicily) and flying wine-makers are all over the place. Of course, Barolo and Barbaresco remain its prized red jewels, but the silkiest of these are pricey and in meagre supply. Italy, like Italians, doesn't exist. It is merely a political and geographical expression. We must consider Italian wine, from its individual regions, in the same way.

## ASDA RED

**Barolo Veglio Angelo 1996**  `14`  `£7–10`
Good tannins here. Not much liquorice, though.

**Chianti 1999, Asda**  `12`  `−£3.50`

**Chianti Classico 1998, Asda**  `13.5`  `−£5.00`

**Chianti Classico Riserva 1997, Asda**  `14`  `£5–7`
Lovely savoury edge to the tannins as it finishes.

**La Vis Trentino Oak Aged Merlot 1998, Asda**  `14`  `−£5.00`
Very bright and rich and great with pasta.

**Organic Valpolicella 1999**  `13.5`  `−£5.00`
Very juicy and freshly cherried.

**Puccini Chianti Reserva 1997**  `14`  `−£5.00`
The juicy style.

**Sicilian Rosso NV, Asda**  `13.5`  `−£3.50`

**Trulli Primitivo del Salento 1999**  `14`  `−£5.00`
Very ripe. Needs chicken Dhansak.

**Tuscan Red 1999, Asda**  `13.5`  `−£3.50`
Bit rough. Very ready.

**Valpolicella Classico San Ciriaco 1998**  `15`  `£5–7`
Hugely funky. Wonderful! Lovely dry edge to jam. Typical Italian food/quaffing wine.

**Valpolicella NV, Asda**  `13`  `−£3.50`

## BOOTHS RED

**A Mano Primitivo Puglia 1999**  `15.5`  `£5–7`
Like putting your nose in an old ashtray, much used, much neglected by the pub's charlady. The fruit is vivid and it will develop well in bottle. It drinks well now with rich food.

## ITALIAN RED

**Amarone Classico** `15` `£13–20`
**Brigaldara 1994**

**Archidamo Pervini** `15.5` `£5–7`
**Primitivo di Manduria**
**1997**
Spreads like jam but stays just this side
of adulthood. Great with roasts and
casseroles.

**Barocco Rosso del** `15` `−£3.50`
**Salento 1998**

**Colli di Sasso Toscana** `14` `−£5.00`
**1998**
Unusually forward for a Tuscan red:
jam and judicious tannins which take
time to bite.

**I Promessa Sangiovese** `13.5` `−£5.00`
**Puglia 1999**
Good for pasta parties.

**La Piazza Rosso 1999** `15` `−£3.50`
**(Sicily)**
Delicious raspberry and blackcurrant
fruit with a hint of Sicilian sunshine
and olives.

**La Prendina Falcone** `14` `£10–13`
**Cabernet Sauvignon 1998**
Rather expensively tailored (and
priced) and lacks real tannic oomph
but it has a marvellous soft, giving
texture.

**Salice Salento Vallone** `14` `−£5.00`
**1997**

**Valpolicella Classico** `15.5` `£7–10`
**Superiore, Viviani 1996**
And superior it is, showing the dry
side of plums and blackberries with a
hint of savoury cherry.

**Valpolicella Classico,** `12` `£5–7`
**Viviani 1997**

**Valpolicella Ripasso** `14` `£7–10`
**Viviani 1994**

**Vigna Flaminio, Brindisi** `15` `£5–7`
**Rosso 1996**
Deliciously rich and ripe with
controlled earthy undertones. A terrific
quaffing specimen.

## BUDGENS RED

**Canaletto Merlot 1999** `14.5` `−£5.00`
Lovely leather textured cherries/plum
fruit. Warm, generous, great with
food.

**Fontella Chianti 1999** `13` `−£3.50`
Juicy and ripe.

**La Mura Rosso del** `14` `−£3.50`
**Salento 1999**
A food wine. Don't try it with
anything else. Pasta with bacon, garlic
and sun-dried tomatoes will do nicely.
The pruney earthiness of the wine will
suit this dish down to the ground.

**Merlot del Veneto Rocca** `9` `−£5.00`
**NV**
So spineless it can't walk.

## CWS RED

**Barolo, Terre del Barolo** `11` `£7–10`
**1995**
Thin, touch emaciated. Superstores
only.

**Barrelaia NV, Co-op** `13` `−£5.00`
Fades on the fruit, this juicy construct.

**IGT Merlot NV, Co-op** `11` `−£3.50`
So juicy!

**Il Padrino Rosso Sicilia** `15` `−£5.00`
**1999**
Delicious! Dee-licious – it's simple,
entertaining, cheering, warm and very
fruity. But it does not overstay its
welcome. Superstores only.

Melini Chianti 1998  14 −£5.00
Exceedingly juicy but it does possess
some tannic stealth. I would think
many Co-op palates lap it up like milk.
Superstores only.

Puglia Primitivo  16 −£5.00
Sangiovese 1999, Co-op
Wonderfully joyously fruity and fresh.
Combines a medley of fruit and fresh
acidity in compelling combination
with perfect, soft tannins.

Trulli Primitivo del  14.5 −£5.00
Salento 1998
Juicily ripe plums and peaches, a hint
of cherry and wild strawberry – so a
lot of sugar but it's not sweet. Good,
soft tannins, too. Overall, a wine for
spicy dishes.

Valpolicella NV, Co-op  12 −£3.50

## KWIK SAVE RED

Chianti Classico Conti  13.5 £5–7
Serristori 1998,
Somerfield
Sweet fruit, dry and earthy tannins.
Should be a quid cheaper.

Merlot Venezie 1997  14 −£3.50

Montepulciano  14 −£5.00
d'Abruzzo 1998,
Somerfield
Touch of spice is nice.

Solicella, VdT Umbria  15 −£3.50
NV

Terra Rossa Sangiovese  16 −£3.50
1997
Fantastic ripeness, clammy plums
sweating richly all over the tannins,
and the result is a gorgeous dry wine
of great class.

Valpolicella Venier NV  13 −£3.50

## M&S RED

Amarone Classico della  15.5 £10–13
Valpolicella 1995
The treat for Christmas lunch : wild
raspberries, figs, liquorice and earthy
tannins.

Barbera Piemonte 1998  16 −£5.00
Wonderful vigour and flushed-with-
youth freshness. Has huge drinkability
along with food friendliness. The
plump cherries in the wine are perfect.

Barolo 1996  13.5 £13–20
Not a full-blooded, liquorice-steeped
Barolo, but not a bad stab. Fifteen quid
though. That's hard to swallow.

Canfera 1997  14.5 £7–10
Exuberance and richness. Very soft,
integrated tannins.

Chianti Single Estate 1998  13 −£5.00
Real denture stripper.

Italian Table Red Wine  12 −£3.50
NV (1 litre)
Heavily earthy. Price band reflects the
75 cl equivalent.

Reggiano Rosso Single  10 −£5.00
Estate 1999
A liquefied lollipop. Maybe you should
freeze it (or make it into a sorbet at
least).

Rosso di Puglia 1998  13 −£3.50
Very dry and rustic.

Rosso Toscano 1997  16 £5–7
Joyous, gluggable and heart warming.
Perfect maturity and bite to the wine.
The fruit is rich and fresh, the tannins
in fine fettle.

155

ITALIAN RED

**Sangiovese di Puglia 1999**  `15.5`  `−£5.00`
Superb! Better than so many Chiantis
using the same sangiovese grape. It has
tenacious tannins.

**Valpolicella Classico**  `13`  `−£5.00`
**Single Estate 1999**
Sour dry cherries.

**Villa Cafagio Chianti**  `13.5`  `£7–10`
**Classico 1998**
I've always liked the tannins in this
wine but I do want fruit too. Here the
fruit is lean.

**Vino Montepulciano**  `13.5`  `£7–10`
**d'Abruzzo 1997**
Expensive, dry, earthy and herby and
highly amusing – except the price tag.

**Vino Nobile di**  `13.5`  `£7–10`
**Montepulciano 1995**

## MAJESTIC RED

**Aglianico del Vulture**  `18`  `£7–10`
**1997**
A real mineral-tinged treat. The
elegance, the concentrated ripeness,
the typical Vulture richness. A
beautiful, confident, stunning
mouthful.

**Amarone Valpolicella**  `18`  `£10–13`
**Tedeschi 1996**
One of the more perfect specimens of
this extravagant breed. Lively, serious,
hugely amusing, concentrated and
unites the joyous elements of wine
(sugar, acid, tannin) into something
original and very fine. Liquorice,
prunes and hedgerows. They're all
there.

**Barbera d'Asti Ca'Bianca**  `13.5`  `£5–7`
**1997**
Too juicy on the finish to rate higher.

**Centine Toscanna, Banfi**  `16`  `£5–7`
**1997**
Utterly compellingly quaffable richness
and controlled jamminess. Has loads
of freshness, good scaffolded tannins,
and a richly applied outer coat of
savoury fruit.

**Chianti Il Tasso 1998**  `14`  `−£5.00`

**Chianti Rufina Basciano**  `15.5`  `£5–7`
**1997**

**Colli di Sasso Banfi 1998**  `14`  `−£5.00`
Nice juice here and very good tannins.

**Conero Conti Cortesi**  `14.5`  `£5–7`
**1997**
More dry juice from the Italians. Very
sweet but rescued by its tannins.

**Dogajolo Toscana 1998**  `16`  `£5–7`
A most individualistic approach to
Tuscany, via a long winding road of
juicy soft-fruit hedgerows and fine
acidic hard-fruit orchards. Lovely
finish to it. Hugely quaffable.

**Dolcetto d'Alba de**  `16`  `£5–7`
**Forville 1998**
The spiky tannins stud the rich fruit
like spicy currants in a chocolate cake.

**Merlot del Veneto**  `14.5`  `−£3.50`
**Marchesini 1998**

**Merloti Marche**  `10`  `−£3.50`
**Marchesini 1999**
Total fruit juice. It's that scrawny.

**Montepulciano**  `11`  `−£5.00`
**d'Abruzzo Barone**
**Cornacchia 1998**
Very juicy and super-ripe.

**Primitivo del Salento**  `16`  `−£5.00`
**Antonini 1998**
Invigorating rush of sweet fruit which
then goes delightfully lush, then tannic
and gripping. A pungent food wine.

Primitivo del Salento `16` `–£5.00`
Sigillo Primo 1998
Big, rich, rousing, soft, cockle-
warming ( yet young and fresh),
cheeky and utterly drinkable.

Recioto Tedeschi 1996 `15` `£5–7`
(50cl)
Sweet and pruney, it defies
classification in terms of food. Curry?
Pasta with tomatoes and some rich
sausage? Casserole with prunes? It
does need food (it is cloyingly sweet-
edged) and it's worth experiencing. My
inclination is to try a salad of sweet
fruit and grilled vegetables.

Rosso di Sicilia La `15` `–£3.50`
Toricella 1998
Marvellous value for money: incisive,
stylishly well cut and has a firm, mildly
rich finish of roast nuts and dry fruit.

Salice del Salento Riserva `15.5` `£5–7`
1997
Delicious prune and liquorice richness,
dry earthiness and brilliant food-
matching possibilities.

Sangiovese Marchesini `13.5` `–£3.50`
1998
Very juicy. Great with Indian food
(rates 15.5 then).

Sassaiolo Rosso Piceno `14.5` `–£5.00`
1997

Valpolicella Classico, `12` `–£5.00`
Santepietre 1998

Valpolicella Classico `17` `£7–10`
Superiore 1996
Quite superb individuality here: spice,
cherries, leather, sweet blackberries,
soft tannins, and a hint of prune.
Terrific value for the ultimate Italian
dinner party.

Vino Nobile di `14.5` `£5–7`
Montepulciano 1996
Extremely arid to finish in spite of
some charm and sweet-natured fruit.

## MORRISONS RED

Casa di Monzi Merlot `13` `–£5.00`
1999
Juicy and super-ripe.

Chianti Uggiano 1997 `12` `–£5.00`
Ragged, rustic, dry.

Montepulciano Uggiano `12` `–£5.00`
1997
Has a whisky tang to it of considerable
oddity.

Puglia Primitivo 1999 `13` `–£5.00`
Odd clash of dryness and sweet
ripeness.

Valpolicella NV `12` `–£3.50`

Vino Rosso di Puglia NV `10` `–£3.50`

## ODDBINS RED

Barbera d'Asti Suri di `15.5` `£7–10`
Mu, Icardi 1998
Sweet plummy edge. Delicious food
wine.

Barbera d'Asti 'Tabarin', `14` `£5–7`
Icardi 1999
Sweet and soft.

Ca'Vergana Barbera `14.5` `–£5.00`
d'Asti 1997
Very ripe and juicy.

Castello Le Leccia `16` `£7–10`
Chianti Classico 1998
A most unusually richly tannic Chianti
of charm and concentrated
effortlessness. Outstanding of its type.

Cecchi La Gavina `17` `£7–10`
Cabernet Sauvignon,
Toscana 1997
Grandly gripping and multi-faceted.
Wonderful layers of figs, plums, spices
and tannins.

Dolcetto d'Alba `16.5` `£7–10`
'Rousori', Icardi 1999
Lovely tannins! Oh the tannins!

Felline 'Albarello' Rosso `16` `£7–10`
del Salento 1997
Dry yet rich and resoundingly full of
soft fruit flavours. Immensely food-
friendly.

Feudi di San Gregorio `16` `£5–7`
Rubrato, Irpinia 1997
Biscuity quality to the texture and
even a suggestion of some baked
currants in it. Terrific food wine.

Frescobaldi Campo Ai `14` `£7–10`
Sassi, Rosso di
Montalcino 1998
Has a very ripe fresh edge to the
finish.

Gagliardo Dolcetto `13.5` `£7–10`
d'Alba 1999
Bit too obvious and juicy for me.

Il Padrino Rosso Sicilia `15` `–£5.00`
1999
Delicious drinkability here – and it has
great tannins to give it real backbone.

Il Tarocco Chianti `15` `£7–10`
Classico 1997
A personality clash, resolved
deliciously, between firm tannins and
soft, jammy fruit.

Masi Modello delle `15.5` `–£5.00`
Venezie 1998
Lovely jammy fruit which is so soft it
oozes rather than flows.

Musella Rosso di Verona `15.5` `£7–10`
1996
Superbly juicy yet has great savoury
tannins.

Nolita Montepulciano `16` `–£5.00`
d'Abruzzo 1998
Biting tannins combine with
immensely chewy fruit to make a real
crunch mouthful of fruit.

Primitivo di Manduria, `15.5` `£7–10`
Felline 1998
Has blackcurrants and plums and
herbs and tannins. Really delicious.

Rosso di Spicca Le `15.5` `£5–7`
Velette 1999
Lovely richness of purpose. Brilliantly
food friendly.

San Crispino Primitivo `16` `–£5.00`
del Salento 1999
Striking richness and plump, ripe fruit.
Engaging, elastic, exhilarating.

San Crispino Sangiovese `14` `–£5.00`
di Romagna Superiore
1996
Juicy and ripe, typically Italianate and
gutsy. Good fresh grip to it.

San Fereolo Dolcetto di `14` `£7–10`
Dogliani 1998
Gushes over the taste buds leaving
behind touches of tannins and plums.

Scaranto, Colli Euganei `16` `£5–7`
1997
Warm and generous hint of jam to the
rich fruit and a lovely soft finish.

Tre Uve NV `14` `–£5.00`
Very jammy and ripe. Great with spicy
Indian food.

Tre Uve NV `14.5` `–£5.00`
Simple fresh cherry/plum fruit with a
delicious hint of tannin, savoury and

pureed, on the finish. Good to quaff. Excellent with pastas.

**Tre Uve Ultima NV**  15.5  £5–7
Chewiness to it, thanks to some tannins, and the fruit is alive to every possibility of the liaison – the result is a marvellously textured wine.

## SAFEWAY RED

**Amarone delle**  16.5  £10–13
**Valpolicella Classico,**
**Tedeschi 1995**
Expensive treat: prunes, liquorice, almonds, spicy cherries, and consummate smoothness yet alert tannins make for a lovely Christmas lunch wine of utter downability and food matchability.

**Barolo Castello Riserva**  10  £13–20
**1993**

**Farnio Rosso Piceno 1998**  13  –£5.00

**Inycon Merlot 1999**  13.5  –£5.00
**(Sicily)**
Very sweet and full and not typical but good with rich food.

**Sentiero NV**  13  –£3.50
Juicy with striking tannins.

**Serina Primitivo,**  15  –£5.00
**Tarantino, Puglia 1996**

**Tenuta San Vito 1998**  14  £5–7
**(organic)**
Certainly multi-layered but it goes up and down like a roller coaster. Most individual.

**Terriero Sangiovese di**  14.5  –£5.00
**Puglia 1998**

**Villa Mottura Squinzano**  11  –£5.00
**1997**

## SAINSBURY'S RED

**A Mano Primitivo Puglia**  15.5  £5–7
**1999**
Like putting your nose in an old ashtray, much used, much neglected by the pub's charlady. The fruit is vivid and it will develop well in bottle. It drinks well now with rich food.

**Allora Primitivo 1998**  15  –£5.00

**Amano Primitivo 1999**  15.5  £5–7
Juicy, jammy, joyous – all-fruit, all-dancing, all-singing, all over the taste buds like balsam. You can't spit it out. 100 stores.

**Barolo Cantine Rocca**  15  £10–13
**Ripalta 1995**
A liquorice-tinged, palate-expanding wine of classic Barolo brusqueness yet charm. That is to say it seems almost arid at first, after the tearing perfume the tannins, dissolving in the mouth, create. Not at all stores.

**Bright Brothers Roman**  16.5  –£5.00
**Vines Negroamaro**
**Cabernet Sauvignon 1999**
Dry, rich, incisive, savoury warm and very with it. Excellent tannins and tightly woven fruit. Most stores.

**Caramia Salice Salentino**  16.5  £5–7
**Riserva 1997**
Now here the raisiny, semi-sweet, oxidative style is hemmed in by great tannins. The wine pulsates to good purpose, parading cherries, plums and blackberries.

**Classic Selection Chianti**  15.5  £5–7
**Classico 1997, Sainsbury's**

**Emporio Nero d'Avola**  14  –£5.00
**Merlot 1999**
Very sweet, clinging and gravy-rich. A

wine for marinating beef and for marinating the tongues of larks and the young. Not at all stores.

**Inycon Syrah 1999**  16.5  −£5.00
Vibrant, saucy, sexy, beautifully harnessed tannins to the compressed fruit. A terrific fiver's worth of Sicilian style syrah.

**L'Arco Cabernet Franc, Friuli 1998**  14  −£5.00
Serious, almost glum cabernet franc with typical slate-and-charcoal dry fruit with a layering of black cherry. Most stores.

**Lambrusco Rosso, Sainsbury's**  10  −£3.50

**Merlot delle Venezie, Connubio 1998**  16.5  −£5.00
Quite brilliant. Has superbly plump, plummy texture, vivid tannins, soft leathery and blackcurrant fruit, and a flourishing finish. Great stuff. Most stores.

**Montepulciano d'Abruzzo 1999, Sainsbury's**  14  −£5.00
Very jammy and super-ripe but the tannins give it nobility. Most stores.

**Montepulciano d'Abruzzo, Connubio 1997**  15.5  −£5.00

**Morellino di Scansano Riserva 1997**  16  £7–10
A wonderful food wine of great energy and elongated, fruity richness. Warmly textured and extremely deep – like an old knitted cardigan worn by Isaiah Berlin. 100 stores.

**Natio Organic Chianti, Cecchi 1998**  13.5  £5–7
Claims to be made in the interests of

mankind. What about womankind? Ah, that's Italians for you. Selected stores.

**Nero d'Avola IGT Sicilia, Connubio 1998**  15.5  −£5.00

**Rosso di Provincia di Verona NV, Sainsbury's**  15  −£3.50

**Sangiovese di Toscana, Cecchi 1999**  13.5  −£5.00
Sweet natured and dry-finishing. Most stores.

**Serrano Rosso Conero 1999**  15.5  −£5.00
Very thick and linctus-textured, ripely fruity but not OTT (by a whisker). Very full and rich, it needs food. Not at all stores.

**Sicilia Red, Sainsbury's**  15  −£3.50
Bargain quaffing and food wine. Spice, cherries, plums, earth, sticky textured and toffeed richness and an urgency to please.

**Stowells Montepulciano del Molise NV (3 litre box)**  12  −£5.00
The price band reflects the equivalent price for a 75cl bottle.

**Teuzzo Chianti Classico, Cecchi 1997**  16  £5–7
One of the most gripping Chiantis at this price I've tasted of this vintage. Lovely Tuscan terracotta briskness, dryness and class of fruit. Most stores.

**The Full Montepulciano NV**  13  −£5.00
A good pun but a bit too full for me. A sweet, raisiny, overripe, nakedly all-embracing wine which would be great with curries. Not at all stores.

Valpantena Ripasso 14 £5–7
Valpolicella, Connubio
1997

Valpolicella NV, 13.5 –£3.50
Sainsbury's

Valpolicella, Sainsbury's 12 –£3.50
(3 litre box)
Bit arid and uninspiring as it finishes.
The price band reflects the equivalent
price for a 75cl bottle.

Via Nova Primitivo 1998 15 –£5.00
Brilliant spicy food wine: sweet and
dry, very fat and fit. Not at all stores.

Zagara Nero d'Avola 14 –£5.00
Sangiovese 1999
A ripe, raisiny, almost oxidised style –
it suits Indian food admirably. Most
stores.

## SOMERFIELD RED

Bright Brothers Roman 16.5 –£5.00
Vines Negroamaro
Cabernet Sauvignon 1998
Gorgeously sticky yet not overbaked
or overspiced. Has piles of flavour
buttressed by excellent tannins.
Flaunts blackcurrants, earth, plums
and strawberries.

Cabernet Sauvignon delle 14 –£5.00
Venezie 1999, Somerfield
Calm and collected, rich yet subtle,
very smooth tannins.

Caramia Primitivo 14 £5–7
Barrique 1998
Sweet primitivo-graped curry wine.
But six quid? Buy it for the BYOB
tandoori house.

Chianti Classico Conti 13.5 £5–7
Serristori 1998,
Somerfield

Sweet fruit, dry and earthy tannins.
Should be a quid cheaper.

D'Istinto Sangiovese 14 –£5.00
Merlot 1998 (Sicily)
One of the best examples of this
curate's egg of a wine range. Has fruit,
tannins and acidity in good order.

L'Arco Cabernet Franc, 14 –£5.00
Friuli 1998
Serious, almost glum Cabernet Franc
with typical slate-and-charcoal dry fruit
with a layering of black cherry.

Marano Amarone della 13.5 £10–13
Valpolicella 1996
I find thirteen quid for this cherry-ripe,
figgy-ish specimen a bit rich. Of
course, it's hugely individual and all-
enveloping and would be marvellous
with a festive fowl stuffed with fruit
and spices, but that price, unlike the
wine, is just too hard to swallow.
Selected stores.

Mimosa Maremma 15 –£5.00
Sangiovese 1998
Pure vinified hedgerows and herb
gardens. Brilliant with risottos and
mushroom dishes.

Montepulciano 14 –£5.00
d'Abruzzo 1998,
Somerfield
Touch of spice is nice.

Riparosso Montepulciano 13 –£5.00
d'Abruzzo 1998
Sweet and earthy. Great with pasta.

Terrale, Primitivo di 15 –£5.00
Puglia 1998, Somerfield
Brilliant, vivacious, cheering, warm,
herby, sunny, rich, delicious.

Tre Uve Ultima, 15 £7–10
Madonna dei Miracoli
1998

161

A construct of Montepulciano, Sangiovese and Primitivo, aged in oak. A deep rich wine with a touch of tarry sweetness on the finish. Selected stores.

**Trulli Chardonnay del** `15` `–£5.00`
**Salento 1999**
Elegant, thoughtful, precocious, solid from nose to throat.

**Trulli Primitivo Salento** `14.5` `–£5.00`
**1998**
Juicily ripe plums and peaches, a hint of cherry and wild strawberry – so a lot of sugar but it's not sweet. Good, soft tannins, too. Overall, a wine for spicy dishes.

**Valpolicella Classico** `15.5` `–£5.00`
**Vigneti Casterna 1997**
Sweet cherries and a touch of earth. Delicious pasta plonk. Selected stores.

## SPAR RED

**Barolo 'Costa di Bussia'** `16` `£13–20`
**1994**
Lot of money, a lot of wine. Has a lovely soft figgy richness, never too sweet, plus coffee and warmly spiced cherries. Gorgeous tannins fit perfectly.

**Chianti Chiantigiane** `12` `–£5.00`
**1997, Spar**
Juicy and jammy with a touch of tannic gravy.

**Chianti Classico Le** `11` `£7–10`
**Fioraie 1995**
Far too expensive to be sensibly paired with the curried food it requires. It's raisiny and getting near retirement.

**Montepulciano** `14` `–£5.00`
**d'Abruzzo 1999, Spar**

Raspberry and plum, earth and sunshine. Not a bad recipe to set beside a risotto.

**Pasta Red NV, Spar (1** `11` `–£3.50`
**litre)**
Been in a fight has it? Seems a bit shaky and bruised to me. Price band is for the 75cl equivalent.

**Riva Red NV, Spar** `13.5` `–£3.50`
Goes a bit flat on the finish. Has some sparky tannins, though.

## TESCO RED

**Barbera d'Asti Calissano** `15.5` `–£5.00`
**1997**

**Barolo Vigna dei Pola** `14` `£13–20`
**1995**
Wine Advisor Stores only.

**Chianti 1998, Tesco** `13` `–£3.50`

**L'Arco Cabernet Franc,** `14` `–£5.00`
**Friuli 1998**
Serious, almost glum cabernet franc with typical slate-and-charcoal dry fruit with a layering of black cherry.

**Melini Chianti 1998** `14` `–£5.00`
Exceedingly juicy but it does possess some tannic stealth. I would think many Tesco palates lap it up like milk.

**Merlot del Piave NV,** `11` `–£5.00`
**Tesco**
Very sullen. Needs to be blended with an overfruity Cape Merlot to achieve fire in its belly – and presence in the drinker's.

**Moncaro Sangiovese 1999** `13` `–£3.50`
A juicy wine to go with balti dishes.

**Monte d'Abro** `14` `–£5.00`
**Montepulciano Abruzzo**
**1999**

Juicy and earthy. Good with curries.

**Pendulum Zinfandel 1999** | 15.5 | −£5.00
Ignore the Marbella gold packaging.
Concentrate on the lovely soft
plummily plump fruit. Most stores.

**Pinot Noir del Veneto** | 11 | −£5.00
**NV, Tesco**
Not hugely overkeen. Very austere
fruit with little Pinot typicity nor a
single eccentric trait.

**Sicilian Red NV, Tesco** | 14 | −£3.50
The perfect curry companion – and it's
rated on that basis. The fruit is sweet
and sticky.

**Taruso Ripassato** | 16.5 | £5–7
**Valpolicella Valpentena**
**1997**
Wild strawberry, cherries, liquorice.
almonds and sweet lushness overall. A
wonderfully fruity wine of immense
charm. It also has smooth tannins
which will permit it to be aged for five
or six years and become even lovelier
(and perhaps reach 18/19 points). A
superb food wine with such plumpness
and depth it overrides the most robust
food. Top 80 stores.

**Terra Viva Vino da** | 15.5 | −£5.00
**Tavola Organic Red**

**Trulli Primitivo Salento** | 14.5 | −£5.00
**1998**
Juicily ripe plums and peaches, a hint
of cherry and wild strawberry – so a
lot of sugar but it's not sweet. Good,
soft tannins, too. Overall, a wine for
spicy dishes.

**Valpolicella Classico** | 13 | −£5.00
**1999, Tesco**
Cherry juiciness.

**Villa Pigna Rosso Piceno** | 14 | −£5.00
**1998**

**Amarone della** | 18 | £7–10
**Valpolicella Via Nova**
**1997**
Superb modern Amarone with classic
overtones of liquorice, fig, raspberry,
blackcurrant, herbs, jam, tannins and
rich acids. The texture is thick and
balsamic and lingering. Yet, withal,
this is not, in spite of 14.5% of alcohol,
a bruising experience. It is very elegant
and polished.

**Amarone della** | 17 | £13–20
**Valpolicella Zenato 1995**
Liquorice, figs, ripe cherries and
damsons, and marvellous tannins.
Even so, I'd cellar it for five or six
years and see it reach, perhaps,
perfection at twenty points. Wine
Rack and Bottoms Up only.

**Barbera Bricco del Bosco** | 14 | £5–7
**1997**
Juicy and ripe and very lap-uppable.
Wine Rack and Bottoms Up only.

**Barolo Terre da Vino** | 13 | £10–13
**1996**
Lot of money. Bitter ending, too.

**Brunello di Montalcino,** | 15.5 | £20+
**Casanova di Neri 1994**
Pulsates with ripeness and jammy
immediacy but then the gorgeous
tannins strike – and wham! we have a
serious mouthful on our hands (and
for that mixed metaphor, where this
wine is concerned, I make no
apologies).

**Cecchi Sangiovese 1998** | 14.5 | −£5.00

**Chianti Classico Riserva** | 16.5 | £7–10
**Rocca Guicciadia,**
**Ricasoli 1997**
Superb Tuscan masterwork of juicy

plums and cherries and exciting tannins. Wine Rack and Bottoms Up only.

**Chianti Grati Poggio** `13` `£7–10`
**Galiga, Banda Blu 1997**
Seems to give up the ghost before it reaches the finishing line. Wine Rack and Bottoms Up only.

**Formulae Sangiovese di** `13.5` `£5–7`
**Toscana, Ricasoli 1998**
Juicy with earthy tannins. Good with food.

**Graticciaia Puglia 1994** `17` `£13–20`
The smoothest, most integrated, most completely sophisticated Puglian red I've tasted. Concentrated and hugely classy, it shows local grapes a world class exhibition of richness and wit. Wine Rack only.

**La Bella Figura Merlot** `15.5` `–£5.00`
**Cabernet 1998**
Terrific pace and style here. Great tannins, good texture.

**Merlot Corvina** `13.5` `–£5.00`
**Fiordaliso 1998**
Light cherries.

**Montepulciano** `14` `–£5.00`
**d'Abruzzo Umani Ronchi 1999**
A jammy/earthy pasta party wine.

**Montepulciano Selva** `15.5` `£5–7`
**Torta 1998**
Energy and loads of fruit to carry it with. Good tannins and texture and a flourish on the finish.

**Rosso di Montalcino,** `15` `£10–13`
**Casanova di Neri 1998**
Great tannins (youthful yet) and rich, deep fruit.

**Salice Salento Vallone** `13.5` `£5–7`
**1997**
Very juicy and ripe but marvellous with spicy food.

**Trulli Primitivo 1997** `14` `–£5.00`
A soupy, very ripe wine, with tightly textured tannins underneath. It needs food – lots of it.

**Valpolicella Classico** `16` `–£5.00`
**Superiore Zenato 1997**
Marvellously fluent speaker of intense, soft, rich, harmonious Italian.

**Valpolicella Classico** `16.5` `–£5.00`
**Zenato 1997**
Valpol? Sixteen points? Something odd here. Yes, it's Signor Zenato who's the oddity. He turns Valpolicella into a world-class mouthful. At a fiver, this is a steal. One of the best reds on these shelves.

**Valpolicella Ripassa** `17` `£7–10`
**Superiore Zenato 1997**
Casual brilliance and effortlessly integrated fruity richness and textured, delicate tannined complexity. A wonderful wine. Wine Rack and Bottoms Up only.

**Vigna Flaminio, Brindisi** `15` `£5–7`
**Rosso 1996**
Deliciously rich and ripe with controlled earthy undertones. A terrific quaffing specimen. Wine Rack and Bottoms Up only.

## UNWINS RED

**Barocco Rosso del** `13` `–£5.00`
**Salento 1999**
Very very juicy and thickly spread.

**Chianti Classico Reserva** `14` `£7–10`
**Villa Antinori 1997**

A very fresh Chianti with good tannins.

**Ciro Classico 1998** `14` `−£5.00`
Sweet raisins and dry tannins.
Tandoori chicken step forward!

**La Mura Rosso Casa** `14` `−£5.00`
**Girelli 1999**
Raisiny and ripe. Terrific wine for
Indian food.

**Montepulciano** `15.5` `−£5.00`
**d'Abruzzo, Miglianico**
**1997**

**Primitivo Merum 1998** `13` `−£5.00`
So juicy!

**Villa Cafaggio Chianti** `13` `£5–7`
**Classico 1997**
Too jammy.

## VICTORIA WINE RED

**Amarone della** `18` `£7–10`
**Valpolicella Via Nova**
**1997**
Superb modern Amarone with classic
overtones of liquorice, fig, raspberry,
blackcurrant, herbs, jam, tannins and
rich acids. The texture is thick and
balsamic and lingering. Yet, withal,
this is not, in spite of 14.5% of alcohol,
a bruising experience. It is very elegant
and polished.

**Barolo Terre da Vino** `13` `£10–13`
**1996**
Lot of money. Bitter ending, too.

**Brunello di Montalcino,** `15.5` `£20+`
**Casanova di Neri 1994**
Pulsates with ripeness and jammy
immediacy but then the gorgeous
tannins strike – and wham! we have a
serious mouthful on our hands (and
for that mixed metaphor, where this

wine is concerned, I make no
apologies).

**Cecchi Sangiovese 1998** `14.5` `−£5.00`

**Formulae Sangiovese di** `13.5` `£5–7`
**Toscana, Ricasoli 1998**
Juicy with earthy tannins. Good with
food.

**La Bella Figura Merlot** `15.5` `−£5.00`
**Cabernet 1998**
Terrific pace and style here. Great
tannins, good texture.

**Merlot Corvina** `13.5` `−£5.00`
**Fiordaliso 1998**
Light cherries.

**Montepulciano** `14` `−£5.00`
**d'Abruzzo Umani Ronchi**
**1999**
A jammy / earthy pasta party wine.

**Montepulciano Selva** `15.5` `£5–7`
**Torta 1998**
Energy and loads of fruit to carry it
with. Good tannins and texture and a
flourish on the finish.

**Rosso di Montalcino,** `15` `£10–13`
**Casanova di Neri 1998**
Great tannins ( youthful yet) and rich,
deep fruit.

**Salice Salento Vallone** `13.5` `£5–7`
**1997**
Very juicy and ripe but marvellous
with spicy food.

**Trulli Primitivo 1997** `14` `−£5.00`
A soupy, very ripe wine, with tightly
textured tannins underneath. It needs
food – lots of it.

**Valpolicella Classico** `16` `−£5.00`
**Superiore Zenato 1997**
Marvellously fluent speaker of intense,
soft, rich, harmonious Italian.

# ITALIAN RED

**Valpolicella Classico** `16.5` `−£5.00`
**Zenato 1997**
Valpol? Sixteen points? Something odd
here. Yes, it's Signor Zenato who's the
oddity. He turns Valpolicella into a
world-class mouthful. At a fiver, this is
a steal. One of the best reds on these
shelves.

## WAITROSE RED

**Amarone della** `13` `£20+`
**Valpolicella Classico**
**Riserva 1990**
Too expensive. Only from Waitrose
Direct.

**Amarone della** `16` `£7–10`
**Valpolicella Classico**
**Vigneti Casterna 1995**
**(50cl)**
Lot of loot, lot of wine. Spicy, rich,
smooth, touch exotic and feral.
Delicious for the solo hedonist.

**Barolo Terre da Vino** `13` `£10–13`
**1996**
Lot of money. Bitter ending, too. Not
at all stores.

**Bonarda Sentito, Oltrepo** `15.5` `−£5.00`
**Pavese 1999**
Solid Italianate fruit here of great food
matching qualities.

**Brunello di Montalcino** `14` `£13–20`
**Tenuta Nova 1994**
Very savoury and ripely rich. Only
from Waitrose Direct.

**Emporio Barrel Aged** `16.5` `£5–7`
**Syrah 1998 (Sicilia)**
Remarkably toothsome and rich, dry,
savoury and deep. Terrific delivery of
eloquent fruit.

**Mezzomondo** `16` `−£5.00`
**Negroamaro 1999**
Brilliant value food wine with rich,
herby fruit and delicious spicy tannins.
Has a first-class texture and
concentration of flavours.

**Montepulciano** `16` `−£5.00`
**d'Abruzzo, Umani**
**Ronchi 1998**
Gorgeous tannins and rich red fruit.

**Nero d'Avola Syrah,** `14` `−£5.00`
**Firriato 1998**
Very juicy but has a meaty under-
edge, so it's a terrific pasta plonk.

**Pendulum Zinfandel 1999** `15.5` `−£5.00`
Ignore the Marbella gold packaging.
Concentrate on the lovely soft
plummily plump fruit.

**Sangiovese Marche,** `13` `−£3.50`
**Waitrose**
Very juicy.

**Summit Sangiovese di** `16` `£7–10`
**Maremma 1997**
Immensely stylish, Tuscan terroir-
riddled richness.

**Tenute Marchese** `16` `£10–13`
**Antinori Chianti Classico**
**1996**
Extremely civilised. Not at all stores.

**Tenute Marchese** `14.5` `£10–13`
**Antinori Chianti Classico**
**Riserva 1997**
Civilised baked-earth fruit, gently
tannic and fruitily teasing. Not at all
stores.

**Tenute Marchesi Chianti** `16` `£10–13`
**Classico Riserva 1996**
Perhaps it's *too* smooth. Blink and it
slithers down and you merely feel
warm inside. A stunning Chianti of
hauteur and class.

Teroldego Rotaliano, `14` `–£5.00`
Ca'Vit 1999
Warm, juicy, gently apple-edged with
a strong savoury plum overtone.

Terra Viva Merlot del `14` `–£5.00`
Veneto 1999 (organic)
Very dry but good with food.

Vigna Alta Merlot & `16.5` `–£5.00`
Cabernet Basilicata 1998
Superb multi-layered richness which
proceeds in deliciously textured layers
as it courses over the taste buds.
Compelling wine.

## WINE CELLAR RED

D'Istinto Sangiovese `14` `–£5.00`
Merlot 1998 (Sicily)
One of the best examples of this
curate's egg of a wine range. Has fruit,
tannins and acidity in good order.

## ASDA WHITE

La Vis Pinot Grigio 1999, `13.5` `–£5.00`
Asda
Not remotely harsh, as some p.g.s are.

Lambrusco Bianco NV, `13.5` `–£3.50`
Asda

Lambrusco Rosato NV, `13` `–£2.50`
Asda

Oaked Soave 1998, Asda `14` `–£5.00`

Soave NV, Asda `14` `–£3.50`

## BOOTHS WHITE

La Piazza Bianco 1999 `13.5` `–£3.50`
(Sicily)
Exceedingly fruity and a touch sweet.

Le Rime Pinot Grigio/ `13` `–£5.00`
Chardonnay 1999
Edging towards the dull.

Sentito Cortese DOC `13.5` `–£5.00`
Oltrepo Pavese 1998

Soave Classico Pra 1999 `15.5` `£5–7`
Shows how elegant, thrusting,
complex and entertaining Soave can
be.

Vin Suspo Rosado `13` `£5–7`
Capezza 1999

## BUDGENS WHITE

Canaletto Chardonnay `13` `–£5.00`
1999
Bright and lemony.

Marc Xero Chardonnay `15` `–£5.00`
NV
Very rich fruit, smoky and food-
friendly. Has delicious taint free
screwcap.

Pinot Grigio delle `14` `–£5.00`
Venezie 1999
Lovely little Italian fish wine.

## CWS WHITE

Marc Xero Chardonnay `14` `–£5.00`
1998
The fruit is respectable, the bottle
whacky, the idea delicious.

Puglia Chardonnay `12` `–£5.00`
Bombino 1999, Co-op
A little soapy – but no opera, alas.

Trulli Chardonnay 1998 `16` `–£5.00`
Delicate progression of richness yet
delicacy courses over the taste buds
here, leaving one refreshed and
panting for more. It would be easy to

quaff this wine too quickly and miss its abundant charms as it trips, with variegated steps, down the throat.

## KWIK SAVE WHITE

Bianco di Puglia 1998, Somerfield   13.5   −£3.50

Bright Brothers Roman Vines Sicilian Barrel-fermented Chardonnay 1999   16   −£5.00
Delicious sticky-toffee fruit which is not over the top. The hint of wood nicely counterpoints the strawberries, limes and melons. (And peach? Yes, I do believe peach too.)

Pinot Grigio/ Chardonnay Venezie 1997   15   −£3.50

Sicilian White 1999, Somerfield   15.5   −£3.50
Brilliant! One of Italy's and Somerfield's top bargain whites: soft, creamy yet crisp to finish, nutty and a touch elegant.

Soave 1998, Somerfield   14.5   −£3.50
Crisp, vaguely nutty, a nervous edge to it – classic Italian fish wine.

Villa Pani Frascati Superiore 1997   13   −£3.50

Vino da Tavola Bianco NV, Somerfield   14   −£3.50
Bargain fruit here. Subtle melon with a crisp undertone.

## M&S WHITE

Frascati Superiore 1999   12   −£5.00

Orvieto Single Estate 1999   13.5   −£5.00
Interesting edge to it. Only an edge though.

Pinot Grigio/Garganega 1999   12   −£5.00

Soave Superiore 1999   15.5   −£5.00
Superb fresh edge to it, like under-ripe melon. Has a nutty finish and a chewy texture. A delicious shellfish and fish wine.

Villa Masera Organic Wine 1999   11   −£5.00

## MAJESTIC WHITE

Bianco di Sicilia La Toricella 1998   15   −£3.50
Very dry with a finish which hints at vanilla. Terrific fish wine.

Ca'Visco Soave Classico Superiore Coffele 1998   16   £5–7
Intense concentration of texture and rich, serious fruit. Very elegant, very striking.

Castello di Tassarolo Gavi 1998   15.5   £7–10
Delicious, delicate, daring – it flaunts its differences and is a refreshing change from Chardonnay with its exciting sour/dryness and crisp melon spiciness.

Chardonnay di Puglia, Pasqua NV   14.5   −£3.50
Simply quaffable. Dry yet fruity and charmingly refreshing.

Chardonnay Pinot Grigio Pasqua 1999   13.5   −£5.00
Needs spaghetti a la vongole (not with tomato sauce) to make an impression.

Frascati Superiore,    15.5   −£5.00
Selciatella 1998

Garganega Garda DOC    14.5   −£5.00
Vigne Alte Fratelli Zeni
1999
Lovely melon and peach fruit.

Late Picked Gavi di Gavi   14   £7–10
Villa Lanata 1999
Unusual aperitif for a hot summer's
day.

Monte Tenda Vigneto    13   −£5.00
Soave Classico Tedeschi
1998

Orvieto Classico Secco   15.5   −£5.00
Vigneto Mortaro 1999
A lesson in how not to design a wine
label but this will only deter some
drinkers who will fail to reach the
lovely fruit in the bottle.

Piemonte Chardonnay de   15.5   £5–7
Forville 1998

Pinot Grigio Alois    16   £7–10
Lageder 1998
Astonishing level of nutty, peachy
fruit. Beautifully supple and textured.

Pinot Grigio San Angelo   10   £5–7
Vineyard, Banfi 1999
Very cosmetic and Barbie-dollish.

Verdicchio dei Castelli di   16   −£5.00
Jesi Coste del Molino
1999
Outstanding Italian richness,
quaffability and food friendliness. Goes
from ripe lemon to under-ripe melon.
Or is it the other way around? Ah well
. . . drink it!

## MORRISONS WHITE

Casa de Monzi    13   −£5.00
Chardonnay delle
Venezie 1999
Very ripe and off-dry.

Casa de Monzi Rosato   13   −£5.00
1999
Dry, touch austere.

Chardonnay di Puglia NV   13   −£3.50

Di Notte Pinot Grigio   14   −£5.00
1999
Pleasant apricot sensations.

Inycon Chardonnay 1999   15.5   −£5.00
(Sicily)
Delicious rich melon undertones,
slightly smoky. But it finishes clean
and fresh and very wholesome.

Ponte Vecchio Oaked   13.5   −£5.00
Soave 1997

Soave NV    13   −£3.50

Verdicchio di Jesi   15.5   −£3.50
Classico 1999
A bargain! Lovely teasing fruit, dry,
faintly peachy and nutty. Real elegance
here.

## ODDBINS WHITE

Arneis Roero Malvira   13.5   £5–7
1999

Cantine Gemma    13   −£5.00
Moscato, Piemonte 1999
Sweet riches for sweet-hearted
geriatrics.

Chiarlo Nivole Moscato   15   −£5.00
d'Asti NV (half-bottle)
Only 5.5% alcohol, but lovely with
fresh fruit and goat's cheese.

**Coffele Soave Classico** `14.5` `£5–7`
**1999**
Nutty and fresh. Delicious fish wine.

**Feudi di San Gregorio** `13` `£5–7`
**Falanghina, Sannio 1999**

**Gorgo Bianco di Custoza** `13` `–£5.00`
**1999**

**Histonium Chardonnay,** `15` `–£5.00`
**Abruzzo 1998**
Elegant, crisp and modern.

**Icardi Cortese 'Balera'** `14` `£5–7`
**Piemonte 1999**
An interesting aperitif, gently rich and polished.

**Il Padrino Greganico/** `14` `–£5.00`
**Chardonnay, Sicily 1999**
Clever combination of creamy fruit and lurking acids. Overall, rather plump.

**Pra Soave Classico** `14` `£5–7`
**Superiore 1999**
Very elegant.

**Tenuta le Velette** `13.5` `£5–7`
**'Lunato' Orvieto Classico**
**Superiore 1999**
Expensive for the style.

**Trulli Chardonnay** `16` `–£5.00`
**Salento 1998**
Delicate progression of richness yet delicacy courses over the taste buds here, leaving one refreshed and panting for more. It would be easy to quaff this wine too quickly and miss its abundant charms as it trips, with variegated steps, down the throat.

**Villa Felici Orvieto** `12` `£5–7`
**Classico Amabile 1999**
Bit on the sweet side yet insufficient to interest puds.

**Villa Felici 'Velette'** `12` `–£5.00`
**Orvieto Classico Secco**
**1999**
Very sullen and under-ripe.

## SAFEWAY WHITE

**Arcadia Veronese Rosato** `13.5` `–£5.00`
**1999**
Some agreeable nutty edginess.

**Ca'Bianca Gavi 1998** `14.5` `£5–7`
Dry, gripping, concentrated, charming. Selected stores.

**Cortechiara Soave** `13.5` `–£5.00`
**Classico 1999**
Odd finale.

**Inycon Chardonnay 1999** `15.5` `–£5.00`
**(Sicily)**
Delicious rich melon undertones, slightly smoky. But it finishes clean and fresh and very wholesome.

**Organic Soave 1999,** `12` `–£5.00`
**Safeway**
Bit too lean for me. Selected stores.

**Pinot Grigio Alto Adige** `16` `£5–7`
**1998**
Superbly couth texture, welcoming and civil, and a lovely dry yet warm finish. Very classy. Selected stores.

**Sentiero NV** `15.5` `–£3.50`
Totally charming: nutty, demurely rich, gently ripe and agreeably deep without being smothering.

**Sicilian Dry White 1998,** `13.5` `–£3.50`
**Safeway (1.5 litre)**
The price band reflects the equivalent price for a 75cl bottle.

**Terre Cortese Verdicchio** `14` `–£5.00`
**dei Castelli di Jesi 1999**

Great nuttiness and chewy-edged fruit. Very dry.

## SAINSBURY'S WHITE

Bianco di Provincia di Verona NV, Sainsbury's  `14` `–£3.50`

Cecchi Tuscan White NV  `13.5` `–£5.00`

Classic Selection Frascati Superiore 1998, Sainsbury's  `13.5` `£5–7`
Selected stores.

Connubio Pinot Grigio delle Venezie 1999  `14.5` `–£5.00`
Classic minerals and nuts. A terrific Italian fish wine. Works like a dream with spaghetti a la vongole and squid dishes. Selected stores.

Enofriulia Pinot Grigio Collio 1998  `16` `£5–7`
Extremely refined, yet purposefully rich and well balanced. Lovely apricot edge to it. Selected stores.

Inycon Chardonnay 1999 (Sicily)  `15.5` `–£5.00`
Delicious rich melon undertones, slightly smoky. But it finishes clean and fresh and very wholesome. Not at all stores.

Lambrusco dell'Emilia Bianco. Sainsbury's  `12` `–£5.00`

Lambrusco Rosato, Sainsbury's  `13` `–£3.50`

Lambrusco Secco, Sainsbury's  `11` `–£3.50`

Piave Organic Pinot Grigio 1999  `16` `–£5.00`
A deliciously compressed wine of dry peachiness and gentle nuttiness.

Extremely chic and well tailored. Most stores.

Pinot Bianco delle Venezie 1999, Sainsbury  `14` `–£5.00`
Great lemonic value. Has a pert brightness to it. Most stores.

Sartori Organic Soave 1999  `13.5` `–£5.00`
A clean and fruity Soave of medium-level excitement. Most stores.

Sicilian White, Sainsbury's  `13.5` `–£3.50`

Soave, Sainsbury's  `15.5` `–£3.50`

Soave, Sainsbury's (3 litre box)  `15` `–£3.50`
A solid Soave with the typically nutty credentials of the region. Good with fish and fish barbecues. The price band reflects the equivalent price for a 75cl bottle.

Verdicchio dei Castelli di Jesi Classico 1999, Sainsbury  `14.5` `–£5.00`
Very crisp, almost sushi-knife sharp. Most stores.

Villa Bianchi Verdicchio 1999  `13` `–£5.00`
Intensely dry. Not at all stores.

## SOMERFIELD WHITE

Bright Brothers Greganico Chardonnay 1999 (Sicily)  `13.5` `–£5.00`
If it was £2.99 it would rate fifteen.

Bright Brothers Roman Vines Sicilian Barrel-fermented Chardonnay 1999  `16` `–£5.00`
Delicious sticky-toffee fruit which is

not over the top. The hint of wood nicely counterpoints the strawberries, limes and melons. (And peach? Yes, I do believe peach too.)

**Chardonnay delle** 13.5 −£5.00
**Venezie 1998, Somerfield**
Getting a touch expensive, touching four quid. Drinkable, though.

**D'Istinto Trebbiano** 10 −£3.50
**Insolia 1998**

**L'Arco Chardonnay 1998** 16 −£5.00
Oh so delicate and delicious! Lovely fruit here.

**Marc Xero Chardonnay** 14 −£5.00
**1998**
Odd name, curious bottle, but the fruit's four-square melon and lemon.

**Sicilian White 1999,** 15.5 −£3.50
**Somerfield**
Brilliant! One of Italy's and Somerfield's top bargain whites: soft, creamy yet crisp to finish, nutty and a touch elegant.

**Soave 1998, Somerfield** 14.5 −£3.50
Crisp, vaguely nutty, a nervous edge to it – classic Italian fish wine.

**Vino da Tavola Bianco** 14 −£3.50
**NV, Somerfield**
Bargain fruit here. Subtle melon with a crisp undertone.

## SPAR WHITE

**Pasta White NV, Spar** 13 −£3.50
**(1 litre)**
Bit bony to accompany pasta, I would have thought. Price band is the 75cl equivalent.

**Riva White NV, Spar** 14.5 −£3.50
Bargain white with pleasantly soft

fruit, nothing harsh, and sympathetic acids.

## TESCO WHITE

**Antinori Orvieto Classico** 13 −£5.00
**Secco 1999**

**Asti NV, Tesco** 13 −£5.00

**Elegant Crisp White** 13.5 −£5.00
**1999, Tesco**
Seems to me, at a fiver, a tiny bit lacking in character.

**Frascati 1999, Tesco** 14 −£3.50
Hint of lemon peel, touch of chewy melon. Direct, uncomplicated, refreshing. Fantastic price.

**La Gioiosa Pinot Grigio** 13.5 −£5.00
**1999**
Slightly chunky in style. Suits fish dishes.

**Orvieto Classico** 13.5 −£5.00
**Abboccato 1999, Tesco**
Fat, mellow melon fruit. The sweet edge is for apprentice drinkers or occasional sippers.

**Soave Classico 1998,** 14.5 −£5.00
**Tesco**
A deliciously crisp and biting wine with a super nutty finish. Needs food, though, to really demonstrate its qualities.

**Trulli Dry Muscat 1999** 13.5 −£5.00
Aperitif style of muscat, dry and nervous.

**Verdicchio Classico 1999,** 14 −£5.00
**Tesco**
Lovely nutty finish.

**Villa del Borgo Pinot** 14 −£5.00
**Grigio 1999**
Good apricot edge to the steely fruit.

## THRESHER WHITE

**Falerio Pilastri Saladini** `15.5` `−£5.00`
**1999**
Has a lovely chewy edge and
remarkable subtle, crisp fruit.
Underfruited? Not a bit of it. It's classy.

**La Bella Figura** `14.5` `−£5.00`
**Chardonnay/Pinot**
**Grigio 1999**
Delicious lime and coconut fruit.

**Marc Xero Chardonnay** `15` `−£5.00`
**NV**
Very rich fruit, smoky and food-
friendly. Has delicious taint free
screwcap.

**Pinot Grigio Fiordaliso** `14.5` `−£5.00`
**1999**
Intensely lemony and fairly
memorable.

**Pinot Grigio Terrazze** `14` `£5−7`
**della Luna 1999**
Touch expensive, but clean and crisp
and curiously elegant. Wine Rack and
Bottoms Up only.

**Selva Torta Verdicchio** `14` `£5−7`
**1999**
Very smooth and accomplished.

**Soave Classico Zenato** `16.5` `−£5.00`
**1999**
The classiest Soave on the planet: rich,
controlled, stylishly acidic, beautifully
textured, very finely wrought and
terribly inexpensive.

**Verdicchio dei Castelli di** `15.5` `−£5.00`
**Jesi Verbacco 1999**
A delicious Verdicchio of some class
and precision. Has a nervous edge
typical of the breed, and lovely nutty
undertones. Not at Wine Rack.

## UNWINS WHITE

**Carato Barrique** `13.5` `£5−7`
**Chardonnay 1999**

**Chardonnay Mezzo** `14` `−£5.00`
**Mondo 1998**
Good thick, rich fruit.

**Moscato d'Asti Araldica** `10` `−£5.00`
**1998**
Hugely sweet. For the honey-dentured
crew it rates 20.

## VICTORIA WINE WHITE

**Falerio Pilastri Saladini** `13.5` `−£5.00`
**1998**

**Pinot Grigio Fiordaliso** `13.5` `−£5.00`
**1998**
Italian fish wine: dry.

**Verdicchio dei Castelli di** `15.5` `−£5.00`
**Jesi Verbacco 1999**
A delicious Verdicchio of some class
and precision. Has a nervous edge
typical of the breed, and lovely nutty
undertones.

## WAITROSE WHITE

**Catarratto Chardonnay** `16` `−£5.00`
**Firriato 1999 (Sicily)**
Splendid underpriced gooseberry,
lemon and melon fruited wine classily
assembled and so elegant it almost
defies belief.

**Frascati Superiore Tenuta** `15.5` `−£5.00`
**delle Marmorelle 1999**
Quite superbly clean Frascati and great
style. Crisp and very satisfying.

**Lugana Villa Flora 1999** `16.5` `£5−7`
Utterly lovely compressed
gooseberries, pears and melon (under-

ripe) with a hint of spice and a wonderful clean, crisp finish.

**Mezzo Mondo** 14 —£5.00
**Chardonnay 1998**
Good thick, rich fruit.

**Pinot Grigio Alto Adige** 14.5 £5–7
**San Michele-Appiano**
**1999**
Gentle apricot, touch of almond, delicious crisp, clean fruit.

**Verdicchio dei Castelli** 16 —£5.00
**Jesi, Moncaro 1999**
One of the more delicious of the breed, an extended, aromatic, very keen, nutty wine of huge quaffability and fish dish friendliness. Superb.

## WINE CELLAR WHITE

Monte Tenda Soave 1998 12 —£5.00

# LEBANON

Only Château Musar is widely known and from being, twenty years ago, the world's greatest red wine under a fiver made under fire, I find the wine has become less gripping (yet it's more expensive).

## BOOTHS RED

**Hochar Red 1995**   10   £5–7
Raisins and cranberry juice. Good for very hot curries but little else.

## UNWINS RED

**Château Musar 1994**   10   £10–13
So sour/sweet and overpriced it makes you weep for the wine it once was.

# MEXICO

L A Cetto, in Baja California, remains the most notable producer. As a nation it prefers beer, drugs and football to wine, so it will need to be encouraged to capitalise on its obvious charms as a potential producer of compelling bottles.

## MORRISONS RED

L A Cetto Zinfandel 1998    10    −£5.00
Far too sweet!

## SAFEWAY RED

L A Cetto Petite Sirah    16    −£5.00
1997
Hugely individual and dry –
fantastically alert tannins. An
exceptional wine. At most stores.

## TESCO RED

Mexican Cabernet    13    −£5.00
Sauvignon 1999, Tesco
Dry and stalky. Very peppery (green).

## WAITROSE RED

L A Cetto Petite Syrah    16    −£5.00
1997
Coffee and tobacco, juice and earth –
what a palate-prickling recipe for sheer
pleasure-giving vinosity.

## TESCO WHITE

Mexican Chardonnay    15    −£5.00
1999, Tesco
A superb spicy food wine. Most stores.

# MONTENEGRO

The lands of the once Yugoslavian Federation contain some of the most beautiful vineyards in the world, but beauty of site is not a guarantee of beauty of finished wine.

## SAFEWAY RED

Monte Cheval Vranac  10  −£5.00
1994
To be collected for its label – not its fruit.

# MOROCCO

Interesting, very interesting. Capable of some dazzlingly rich reds. Supermarket interest is vaguely increasing in this country's vineyards, and the potential is enormous.

## MORRISONS RED

Le Chameau Grenache  11  −£3.50
Cinsault NV

# NEW ZEALAND

Blame the grass. No grass, no cows. No cows, no dairy industry. No dairy industry, no cheap second-hand stainless-steel equipment and no know-how and technology going for a song to anyone who grows grapes and wants to make wine. No wonder the white Sauvignons from Marlborough used to smell of fresh-cut lawn. But the Merlots and Cabernets (but not some of those horribly jammy Pinots) from the other regions, especially Hawkes Bay, are also gutsy and interesting. There are exemplary growers in Nelson (like the Finns with their world-class Chardonnay from their Neudorf vineyards), Gisborne and the Auckland area.

## ASDA RED

**Montana Cabernet Merlot 1998**  | 16 | £5–7
Spreads, or perhaps oozes is a better word, slowly over the taste buds with great rich fruit.

## BUDGENS RED

**Corbans White Label Dry Red NV**  | 14 | –£5.00
Very ripe and raucous. It really does deafen the tongue and so it needs the balancing charms of a plate of bangers and mash with roasted garlic gravy.

**Helderberg Pinotage 1998**  | 15 | –£5.00
Marvellous fluency and spice here. Perfect with mild Indian food. Great to take to that friendly Tandoori BYOB joint.

**Montana Cabernet Sauvignon/Merlot 1999**  | 15 | £5–7

Deliciously rich tannins, gently savoury, allied to beautifully warm fruit.

## CWS RED

**Terrace View Cabernet Merlot 1997**  | 16 | –£5.00
Yes, it's difficult and a touch grouchy, but these personality traits (from the peppery Cab and the vegetal Merlot) make it a terrific, dry food wine of some class. Fantastic price for such quality of fruit.

## M&S RED

**Kaituna Hills Cabernet Merlot 1998**  | 13 | £5–7

**Kaituna Hills Reserve Cabernet Merlot 1998**  | 15.5 | £7–10
Deliciously direct and warm. Real depth to it, yet finesse too. The dry

vegetal Cabernet married to the richer, leatherier Merlot make for a very harmonious union.

## ODDBINS RED

**Delegat's Reserve** `15.5` `£7–10`
**Cabernet Sauvignon,**
**Hawkes Bay 1998**
Distinguished and not delicate. Has fine tannins and firm blackcurrant depth.

**Montana Fairhall Estate** `13` `£10–13`
**Cabernet Sauvignon,**
**Marlborough 1996**

## SAFEWAY RED

**Alpha Domus Merlot/** `15` `£7–10`
**Cabernet 1998**
Silky fruit rudely interrupted by down-to-earth tannins. Great! 70 stores.

**Delegat's Reserve** `15.5` `£7–10`
**Cabernet Sauvignon**
**Barrique Matured 1998**
Soft and savoury, sweet yet dry. 70 stores.

**Ninth Island Pinot Noir,** `11` `£7–10`
**Tasmania 1999**
Not like real Pinot. A pale juicy shadow.

**Villa Maria Cellar** `14` `£7–10`
**Selection Cabernet/**
**Merlot, Hawkes Bay 1997**
Very juicy for Michelle. This winemaker is usually more subtle. Is she in love? With an Aussie? 70 stores.

## SAINSBURY'S RED

**Shingle Peak Pinot Noir** `13` `£5–7`
**1999**
Falls short of fruit at the end, although, curiously, the tannins are intact. 135 stores.

## TESCO RED

**Babich Winemaker's** `15` `£7–10`
**Reserve Syrah 1998**
Dry style of Syrah, not Aussie, more Rhone-like, but, overall, it's its own creature. Needs a few hours of opening to gather its wits. Selected stores.

**Montana Cabernet** `16` `£5–7`
**Sauvignon/Merlot 1998**
A deep, rich, dark chocolate and raspberry/blackcurrant construct of fine tannins and finish. 85 stores.

**Montana Reserve Merlot** `16.5` `£7–10`
**1998**
A superb mouthful of richness with gorgeous woody undertones – the fruit, though, is firmly in command and offers a great texture and a tightly woven finish of power, substance and great style. An impressively compact Merlot of dryness and class. Nine quid well spent here.

**Montana Reserve Pinot** `12` `£7–10`
**Noir 1998**
Almost good. The aroma is pleasant, straining to be fruity and rich, but the fruit is not a tenner's worth by a long chalk.

**New Zealand Cabernet** `13.5` `–£5.00`
**Sauvignon NV, Tesco**

**Waimanu Red 1998** `13` `–£5.00`

## THRESHER RED

**Awatea Cabernet Sauvignon/Merlot 1997** `13.5` `£13–20`
Very disappointingly juicy and obvious for this price.

**Church Road Cabernet Sauvignon/Merlot 1998** `15` `£7–10`
The tannins get there in the end, finishing off some engaging, spicy and generous fruit.

**Felton Road Pinot Noir, Otago 1998** `13.5` `£13–20`
Terrific Pinot aroma of wild raspberry and even a very subtle suggestion of truffle but disappoints thereafter. If you blend it with the Palliser Estate Pinot you get a 16.5 point wine and I recommend this to any well heeled Pinot lover looking for really interesting, concentrated, aromatic Pinot. Wine Rack and Bottoms Up only.

**Martinborough Pinot Noir 1998** `13.5` `£13–20`
Good firm texture and decent tannins.

**Montana Cabernet Sauvignon Merlot 1999** `15` `£5–7`
Good rich Cabernet pepperiness and the usual clichéd leather from the Merlot.

**Montana Reserve Merlot 1998** `16.5` `£7–10`
A superb mouthful of rich fruit with gorgeous woody undertones – the fruit, though, is firmly in command and offers a great texture and a tightly woven finish of power, substance and great style. An impressively compact Merlot of dryness and class. Nine quid well spent here.

**Palliser Pinot Noir 1998** `14` `£10–13`

Lovely texture and hint of classic wild strawberry. Might do better if it was aged for two or three years more. Wine Rack and Bottoms Up only.

**Sacred Hill Basket Press Cabernet Sauvignon 1998** `16` `£7–10`
Juicy and rounded and stylistically between Bordeaux and McLaren Vale. The plumpness of the soft fruit is its theme. Wine Rack and Bottoms Up only.

**Te Mata Estate Cabernet Merlot 1998** `16.5` `£7–10`
Superb texture and subtle tensions between the grape varieties. This is as it should be in a fine wine which this is, for the drinker is guaranteed plot, character, wit and a stunning climax. Wine Rack and Bottoms Up only.

**Timara Cabernet/Merlot 1998** `14` `−£5.00`
Respectable rather than striking but with food it'll rate much higher (in the mouth).

## UNWINS RED

**Rippon Pinot Noir 1998** `10` `£13–20`
Rippoff more like.

**Sacred Hill Basket Press Merlot/Cabernet, Hawkes Bay 1996** `14` `£7–10`
Juicy yet dry. Too much money, though.

## VICTORIA WINE RED

**Awatea Cabernet Sauvignon/Merlot 1997** `13.5` `£13–20`
Very disappointingly juicy and obvious for this price.

Church Road Cabernet `15` `£7–10`
Sauvignon/Merlot 1998
The tannins get there in the end,
finishing off some engaging, spicy and
generous fruit.

Montana Cabernet `15` `£5–7`
Sauvignon Merlot 1999
Good rich Cabernet pepperiness and
the usual clichéd leather from the
Merlot.

Montana Reserve Merlot `16.5` `£7–10`
1998
A superb mouthful of rich fruit with
gorgeous woody undertones – the
fruit, though, is firmly in command
and offers a great texture and a tightly
woven finish of power, substance and
great style. An impressively compact
Merlot of dryness and class. Nine quid
well spent here.

Timara Cabernet/Merlot `14` `–£5.00`
1998
Respectable rather than striking but
with food it'll rate much higher (in the
mouth).

## WAITROSE RED

Grove Mill Marlborough `11` `£10–13`
Pinot Noir 1998
Smells okay – don't like what follows
(for twelve quid!). Not at all stores.

Jackson Estate `15` `£10–13`
Marlborough Pinot Noir
1998
Good aroma and texture.

Montana Cabernet `15` `£5–7`
Merlot 1999
Delicious nutty and grassy overtone to
leather and blackcurrants.

Unison Selection, `13.5` `£13–20`
Hawkes Bay 1998
Absurd price for the juice on offer.

## ASDA WHITE

Montana Sauvignon `16` `£5–7`
Blanc 1999
Supremely drinkable and charming.
Sauvignon as comfort wine: soft, ripe,
cool, not tart or too dry as many
Sauvignons. Delicious.

Nobilo Sauvignon Blanc `15` `£5–7`
1999
The best Nobilo I've tasted. Fruity
with a hint of custard cream.

## BOOTHS WHITE

Jackson Estate Riesling `13.5` `£5–7`
1998

Jackson Estate Sauvignon `15` `£7–10`
Blanc 1999
Such a good vineyard for some years
now and the '99 is typically ripe and
rich.

Vavasour Sauvignon `15` `£7–10`
Blanc 1999
Better, by far, if cellared for eighteen
months or so. It will concentrate
better then.

## BUDGENS WHITE

Corbans Sauvignon Blanc `15.5` `–£5.00`
1999
Lovely mineralised, crisp and precise,
food-friendly acids. A class act.

## CWS WHITE

**Explorer's Vineyard Sauvignon Blanc 1999, Co-op**  `16`  `£5-7`
Very dry and a touch schoolmasterly in this respect but its purity of intention is flawless.

**Fat Cat Chardonnay 1998**  `14`  `-£5.00`
And very fat it is – indeed, it's positively obese with folds of rich, fleshy, sunburnt fruit. Needs food to stay drinkable over a long period. Exceedingly juicy but it does possess some rich stealth. I would think many Co-op palates lap it up like milk.

**Oyster Bay Sauvignon Blanc 1999**  `16.5`  `£5-7`
Deliciously compressed gooseberries, a hint of nuts and grass, and a lovely chewy edge. A gently nervous wine, possibly feline in character, and it bristles rather than soothes.

## M&S WHITE

**Kaituna Blue Sauvignon Semillon 1999**  `11`  `-£5.00`

**Kaituna Hills Chardonnay 1999**  `15`  `£5-7`
Some agreeable richness rising to the surface here.

**Kaituna Hills Reserve Chardonnay 1999**  `14.5`  `£7-10`
Chewy richness here.

**Kaituna Hills Reserve Sauvignon Blanc 1999**  `14`  `£7-10`
Expensive companion to oysters.

**Kaituna Hills Sauvignon Blanc 1999**  `12.5`  `£5-7`
The herbaceousness bites back.

## MAJESTIC WHITE

**Jackson Estate Sauvignon Blanc 1999**  `15`  `£7-10`
Such a good vineyard for some years now and the '99 is typically ripe and rich.

**Marlborough Gold Chardonnay 1998**  `13`  `£5-7`

**Marlborough Gold Sauvignon 1999**  `14.5`  `£5-7`
Very grassy and ripe – as if buttercups, daisies and grass are herbal elements. Overall, a thick, ripe wine of no elegance but great with food.

**Oyster Bay Chardonnay 1999**  `16.5`  `£5-7`
Immense elegance and spread-easy fruit which stretches itself languorously over the taste buds, exposing layers of delicious fruit and acids.

**Oyster Bay Sauvignon 1999**  `16.5`  `£5-7`
Gorgeous! Controlled grassiness and herby richness. A handsomely tailored specimen of some class.

## MORRISONS WHITE

**Cooks Sauvignon Blanc, Marlborough 1999**  `13`  `-£5.00`
Bit saline on the finish. Might be all right with shellfish.

**Montana Chardonnay, Marlborough 1999**  `15.5`  `£5-7`
Very jolly and lemon/melon/raspberry fruited.

**Montana Sauvignon Blanc 1999**  `15.5`  `£5-7`

Grassy and a touch green but superb with shellfish.

## ODDBINS WHITE

**Church Road** `16` `£7–10`
**Chardonnay 1998**
Gorgeous price, true, but then so is the fruit. It has great smoky flavour and texture.

**Dashwood Sauvignon** `16` `£5–7`
**Blanc 1999**
Superb ripe gooseberries, lemon and a faraway echo of melon. Superb texture.

**Hawkesbridge** `15.5` `£5–7`
**'Willowbank Vineyard'**
**Sauvignon Blanc,**
**Marlborough 1999**
Very ripe and progressive. Not stately, this progression, but very entertaining.

**Hunter's Sauvignon** `16` `£7–10`
**Blanc 1999**
Expressive and elegant.

**Jackson Estate Sauvignon** `15` `£7–10`
**Blanc 1999**
Such a good vineyard for some years now and the '99 is typically ripe and rich.

**McDonald Church Road** `16` `£7–10`
**Chardonnay, Hawkes**
**Bay 1998**
Stylish and finely wrought with a lingering creamy richness on the finish – almost yoghurty.

**Villa Maria Reserve** `16.5` `£7–10`
**'Clifford Bay' Sauvignon**
**Blanc, Marlborough 1999**
Grassy aroma leads to a richness and ripeness on the finish.

## SAFEWAY WHITE

**Delegat's Reserve** `14.5` `£7–10`
**Chardonnay, Barrel**
**Fermented 1998**
Very chewy. Great with scallop and crab dishes. 77 stores.

**Grove Mill Sauvignon** `16.5` `£7–10`
**Blanc 1999**
Superb clean fruit, compressed gooseberries and minerals.

**Montana Chardonnay** `15.5` `£5–7`
**1999**
Warm and deep. Great for complex fish and poultry.

**Montana Reserve** `16.5` `£7–10`
**Chardonnay 1998**
Exceptional style of fruit where the depth remains dry, retains complexity, finishes with rich promise. Top 60 stores.

**Montana Sauvignon** `15.5` `£5–7`
**Blanc 1999**
Deliciously citrus, hint of fresh mown lawn, earth and warm fruit – all with a crisp finish. Very stylish stuff.

**Oyster Bay Chardonnay,** `16.5` `£5–7`
**Marlborough 1999**
Immense elegance and spread-easy fruit which stretches itself languorously over the taste buds, exposing layers of delicious fruit and acids. Top 145 stores.

**Oyster Bay Sauvignon** `16.5` `£5–7`
**Blanc 1999**
Superb rich grassy fruit which is wildly inaustere and quaffable. Very classy and fine. Not at all stores.

**Villa Maria Reserve** `17` `£7–10`
**Wairau Valley Sauvignon**
**Blanc 1999**

The tastiest Sauvignon in the store and the most expensive. But by gum, it motors smoothly and excitingly.

## SAINSBURY'S WHITE

**Cooks Sauvignon Blanc,** 13.5 −£5.00
**Marlborough 1998**

**Grove Mill Sauvignon** 16.5 £7–10
**Blanc 1999**
Superb clean fruit, compressed gooseberries and minerals.

**Millton New Zealand** 13.5 £5–7
**Organic Chardonnay
1999**
Falls a bit short on the finish – it fades just as it seems about to say something interesting. 50 stores.

**Montana 'B' Brancott** 16 £10–13
**Estate Sauvignon Blanc
1998**
Severely elegant and classy. 20 stores.

**Montana Reserve** 16 £7–10
**Barrique Fermented
Chardonnay 1998**
Compelling style here of great class. Combines an impish directness of freshness with a suggestion of rich maturity. Selected stores.

**Montana Sauvignon** 16 £5–7
**Blanc 1998**
A rich vintage – fewer cold nights to build up acids – has resulted in Marlborough's Sauvignons for '98 being fatter than normal, but there is good balancing acidity. A very elegant wine.

**Shingle Peak** 16.5 £5–7
**Chardonnay,
Marlborough 1998**
Superb richness and depth of gentle

smoky melon fruit. Really stylish and fine. 52 selected stores.

**Shingle Peak Pinot Gris,** 16.5 £5–7
**Marlborough 1999**
A superb specimen of an underrated grape. It offers apricots, pineapple, a hint of raspberry and gentle lemonosity. A triumph of a fruity yet elegant specimen. 135 selected stores.

**Shingle Peak Sauvignon** 16 £5–7
**Blanc, Marlborough 1998**
Gorgeous concentration of fruit here, with a lovely zippy finish. 123 selected stores.

**Stoneleigh Vineyard** 15.5 £5–7
**Chardonnay,
Marlborough 1997**

**The Sanctuary** 16 £5–7
**Chardonnay,
Marlborough 1997**
Gorgeous, luscious, full of finesse yet flavoursome and exhibits both polish and depth. How can Chablis compete with it? Selected stores.

**The Sanctuary Sauvignon** 15.5 £5–7
**Blanc 1999**
Very grassy and greengage-fruited. Crisp, clean, fresh, very dry – a terrific fish wine. Not at all stores.

**Villa Maria East Coast** 14 £5–7
**Chardonnay 1998**
Very untypical freshness. Needs to age a year. Selected stores.

**Villa Maria Private Bin** 17 £5–7
**Sauvignon, Marlborough
1998**
Back to the form of a few years back when it was the least grassy style of NZ Sauvignon yet the most elegant.

## SOMERFIELD WHITE

**Coopers Creek** `15.5` `£7–10`
**Sauvignon Blanc,**
**Marlborough 1999**
Wonderful energy to the wine which
is compacted gooseberries and a hint
of pineapple and lime.

**Montana Sauvignon** `15.5` `£5–7`
**Blanc 1999**
Sancerre? Knocks it into a cocked hat
at this money. Great elegance and
elongated fruit here.

## TESCO WHITE

**Azure Bay Chardonnay/** `13` `–£5.00`
**Semillon 1999**
It commences work with a biting
freshness, then goes a bit bruised,
blatant and over-ripe on the finish.

**Cooks Chardonnay,** `13` `£5–7`
**Gisborne 1998**

**Jackson Estate Sauvignon** `15` `£7–10`
**Blanc 1999**
Such a good vineyard for some years
now and the '99 is typically ripe and
rich. Selected stores.

**Lawsons Dry Hills** `16.5` `£7–10`
**Sauvignon Blanc 1999**
Immensely classy – the Sauvignon
coats the taste buds like delicate
emulsion: tense, dry, mineralised, and
very delicious. 330 selected stores.

**Montana Reserve** `17` `£7–10`
**Chardonnay 1999**
Intensely classy and enormously
creamy and rich without being too
ripe and obvious. A provocative blend
of smoky melon and fine acids. Has
elegance, elongation and ease of effort.

**Montana Riesling 1999** `16` `–£5.00`
A beautifully opulent Riesling with
great texture and subtle acidity. The
theme is warm, well-spoken, mannerly
and polite and the finish has flair. A
delicious mouthful.

**Montana Sauvignon** `15.5` `£5–7`
**Blanc 1999**
Deliciously citrus, hint of fresh mown
lawn, earth and warm fruit – all with a
crisp finish. Very stylish stuff. Not at
all stores.

**New Zealand Dry White,** `13.5` `–£5.00`
**Tesco**

**New Zealand Sauvignon** `13.5` `–£5.00`
**Blanc 1998, Tesco**
Not typically Kiwi or typical
Sauvignon blanc.

**Stoneleigh Chardonnay** `15.5` `£5–7`
**1997**

## THRESHER WHITE

**Azure Bay Sauvignon/** `13.5` `–£5.00`
**Semillon 1999**
Green wine, blue bottle.

**Babich Pinot Gris,** `16` `£5–7`
**Marlborough 1999**
Interesting complexity here as the
apricot fruit deepens, then goes crisp
and chewy, then spreads itself to
reveal nuts and white peaches. Wine
Rack only.

**Church Road** `16` `£7–10`
**Chardonnay 1998**
Gorgeous price, true, but then so is
the fruit. It has great smoky flavour
and texture.

**Church Road Reserve** `17` `£10–13`
**Chardonnay 1998**
Such extreme elegance and controlled

fruitiness make the taste buds weep with pleasure. Marvellous texture and big finish. Wine Rack and Bottoms Up only.

**Craggy Range Old Renwick Vineyard Sauvignon Blanc 1999**   `15`  `£7–10`
Very nervous on the finish, but the wine will age wonderfully because of this acidic paranoia. Let it rest for two or three years and a seventeen- or eighteen-pointer might emerge. Wine Rack only.

**Dashwood Sauvignon Blanc 1999**   `16`  `£5–7`
Superb ripe gooseberries, lemon and a faraway echo of melon. Superb texture.

**Elston Chardonnay 1998**   `16.5`  `£13–20`
A lot of money but a lot of wine. It has old fashioned vegetality of the Montrachet kind and limpid acids of the Kiwi kind. The marriage is superb: angular, classy, finely wrought and outstandingly, compactly balanced. Wine Rack and Bottoms Up only.

**Framingham Pinot Noir 1998**   `12`  `£10–13`
Thick juice, little Pinot pertinacity. Wine Rack only.

**In the Black Chardonnay 1998**   `16.5`  `£5–7`
Wonderful clash of baked melon/ pineapple with fresh lemon acids. They impact gorgeously.

**Montana Chardonnay 1999**   `15.5`  `£5–7`
Warm and deep. Great for complex fish and poultry.

**Montana 'O' Ormond Estate Chardonnay 1998**   `15.5`  `£10–13`

Very rich and ripe and ready with a curious woody/nutty edge on the finish. Touch yoghurty too. Wine Rack and Bottoms Up only.

**Montana Reserve Chardonnay 1999**   `17`  `£7–10`
Intensely classy and enormously creamy and rich without being too ripe and obvious. A provocative blend of smoky melon and fine acids. Has elegance, elongation and ease of effort.

**Montana Reserve Gewürztraminer 1999**   `16`  `£7–10`
Gorgeous spicy fruit, concentrated and multi-layered.

**Montana Reserve Sauvignon Blanc, Marlborough 1999**   `16`  `£7–10`
Brilliant hints of cut grass are subsumed under terrific fruit.

**Montana Sauvignon Blanc 1999**   `15.5`  `£5–7`
Sancerre? Knocks it into a cocked hat at this money. Great elegance and elongated fruit here.

**Oyster Bay Chardonnay, Marlborough 1999**   `16.5`  `£5–7`
Immense elegance and spread-easy fruit which stretches itself languorously over the taste buds, exposing layers of delicious fruit and acids.

**Oyster Bay Sauvignon Blanc 1999**   `16.5`  `£5–7`
The model for modern Sancerre: crisp, clean, gooseberryish, lingering, longish finish. An exemplary Sauvignon.

**Oyster Bay Sauvignon Blanc 2000**   `16`  `£5–7`
Richer, riper and, of course, less mature than the '99 but it has its own

charms and these include pineapple and apple richness.

**Palliser Estate Sauvignon** `14` `£7–10`
**Blanc, Martinborough**
**1999**
Very plump and svelte and a touch self-satisfied.

**Quartz Reef Pinot Gris** `13.5` `£10–13`
**1999**
Amusing pretension, at eleven quid, which is entertaining, but the price of admission is hard to swallow. Wine Rack only.

**Te Mata Estate** `17` `£7–10`
**Chardonnay 1999**
A lot of money but a lot of wine. It has old fashioned vegetality of the Montrachet kind and limpid acids of the Kiwi kind. The marriage is superb: angular, classy, finely wrought and outstandingly, compactly balanced. Wine Rack and Bottoms Up only.

**Timara Dry White 1999** `13` `–£5.00`
A little mule-loaded on the finish.

**Tohu Sauvignon Blanc,** `16` `£7–10`
**Marlborough 1999**
Remarkable nutty richness with a hint of smoky melon plus silky acids.

**Villa Maria Lightly Oaked** `16` `£5–7`
**Chardonnay 1999**
Plump but not fat, lithe yet not thin, fruity yet not full – it has, then, classic virtues of the old world and the purity of the grapes shines through.

**Villa Maria Private Bin** `16` `£5–7`
**Riesling 1999**
Young, as yet, but deliciously drinkable. Not like Riesling as you know it, and maybe loathe for its grouchiness – this one has smooth acids to help it age gracefully for years.

**Villa Maria Private Bin** `16` `£5–7`
**Sauvignon Blanc 1999**
Gorgeous texture and warmth of welcome. Quite quite delicious.

**Villa Maria Reserve** `15.5` `£7–10`
**Sauvignon Blanc, Wairau**
**Valley 1998**
Very rich and melony with the acidity lurking deliciously. Wine Rack and Bottoms Up only.

**Villa Maria Reserve** `17` `£7–10`
**Sauvignon Blanc, Wairau**
**Valley 1999**
The tastiest Sauvignon in the store and the most expensive. But by gum, it motors smoothly and excitingly. Wine Rack and Bottoms Up only.

## UNWINS WHITE

**De Redcliffe** `15` `£7–10`
**Mangatawhiri**
**Chardonnay 1997**
Gentle melon fruit which finishes exotically.

**Hunter's Sauvignon** `16` `£7–10`
**Blanc 1999**
Expressive and elegant.

**Kim Crawford Sauvignon** `16` `£7–10`
**Blanc 1999**
Lovely touch of ripe grass to the steely edge.

**Kumeu River** `16` `£10–13`
**Chardonnay 1998**
Expensive but exceedingly elegant. Very finely wrought fruit.

**Marlborough Gold** `14.5` `£5–7`
**Sauvignon 1999**
Very grassy and ripe – as if buttercups, daisies and grass are herbal elements.

Overall, a thick, ripe wine of no elegance but great with food.

**Oyster Bay Chardonnay,** `16.5` `£5-7`
**Marlborough 1999**
Always one of Kiwi's most delicately decisive, deliciously dainty exports.

**Oyster Bay Sauvignon** `16.5` `£5-7`
**Blanc 1999**
Extremely elongated and energetic fruit – lovely, dry and minerally. Terrific fish wine.

## VICTORIA WINE WHITE

**Church Road** `16` `£7-10`
**Chardonnay 1998**
Gorgeous price, true, but then so is the fruit. It has great smoky flavour and texture.

**Montana Reserve** `16.5` `£7-10`
**Chardonnay 1998**
Exceptional style of fruit where the depth remains dry, retains complexity, finishes with rich promise.

**Timara Dry White 1998** `13.5` `-£5.00`
Leaves a parched note in the back of the throat. Not at Wine Rack.

**Villa Maria Lightly Oaked** `16` `£5-7`
**Chardonnay 1999**
Plump but not fat, lithe yet not thin, fruity yet not full – it has, then, classic virtues of the old world and the purity of the grapes shines through.

**Villa Maria Private Bin** `16` `£5-7`
**Riesling 1999**
Young, as yet, but deliciously drinkable. Not like Riesling as you know it, and maybe loathe for its grouchiness – this one has smooth acids to help it age gracefully for years.

## WAITROSE WHITE

**Craggy Range Winery** `16` `£10-13`
**Chardonnay, Hawkes**
**Bay 1999**
Splendid treat of a wine, nutty, caramely, rich and lingering. Individual and very stylish.

**Jackson Estate Sauvignon** `15` `£7-10`
**Blanc 1999**
Such a good vineyard for some years now and the '99 is typically ripe and rich.

**Missionvale Chardonnay** `14` `£10-13`
**1997**
Very chewy and woody. Fine, but pricey. Only from Waitrose Direct.

**Montana Reserve** `16` `£7-10`
**Barrique Fermented**
**Chardonnay 1998**
Compelling style here of great class. Combines an impish directness of freshness with a suggestion of rich maturity.

**Oyster Bay Marlborough** `16.5` `£5-7`
**Sauvignon Blanc 1999**
The model for modern Sancerre: crisp, clean, gooseberryish, lingering, longish finish. An exemplary Sauvignon.

**Tiki Ridge Dry White** `12.5` `-£5.00`
**1999**
The dullest white at Waitrose? Egregious fruit anyway.

**Villa Maria Private Bin** `14` `£5-7`
**Chardonnay, Gisborne**
**1998**

**Villa Maria Private Bin** `16` `£5-7`
**Riesling 1999**
Young, as yet, but deliciously drinkable. Not like Riesling as you know it, and maybe loathe for its

grouchiness – this one has smooth acids to help it age gracefully for years.

## WINE CELLAR WHITE

**Delegat's Reserve Chardonnay, Barrel Fermented 1998**  14.5  £7–10
Very chewy. Great with scallop and crab dishes.

**Matua Valley Chardonnay 1999**  14  £5–7
Big and rich and a touch of a bully on the taste buds as it muscles in with little deftness.

**Matua Valley Sauvignon Blanc 1999**  16  £5–7

A rich, not classically dry Sauvignon but none the worse for that. It is forward and well textured, layered and polished and it has a good, firm finish.

**Montana Reserve Barrique Fermented Chardonnay 1998**  16  £7–10
Compelling style here of great class. Combines an impish directness of freshness with a suggestion of rich maturity.

**Oyster Bay Sauvignon Blanc 1999**  16.5  £5–7
The model for modern Sancerre: crisp, clean, gooseberryish, lingering, longish finish. An exemplary Sauvignon.

# PORTUGAL

The dullest food in Europe and the sloppiest drivers and there was a time, vintage port aside, when there was nothing worth sniffing at whatsoever on the table wine scene. Vinho Verde can be a delicious tipple, when the weather is warm and the sardines are fresh, but there are now some tenaciously tannic reds coming out of here and they have an engaging personality all of their own.

## ASDA RED

Bright Brothers Baga 1997 — 14 — −£5.00

Douro 1997 — 13 — −£5.00

Duro Douro 1997 — 13.5 — −£5.00

## BOOTHS RED

Alfrocheiro Preto Dao 1996 — 10 — £10–13

Alianca Floral Douro Reserva 1997 — 15.5 — −£5.00
Lovely dry-edged raspberry/plum/blackcurrant fruit. Good fresh textured tenacity.

Alta Mesa Red 1998 — 15 — −£3.50

Bela Fonte Baga 1998 — 14 — −£5.00
Intense plum/cherry fruit with mild tannins. Good, soft/solid glugging here.

Cartuxa Evora Alentejo 1995 — 16 — £7–10
Superb texture, totally gripping yet (paradoxically) relaxed and non-meshing. Terrific rich fruit and fine tannins.

Dao Dom Ferraz 1998 — 16.5 — −£5.00
Superb vintage of this old warhorse of a brand. It's thicker, more complex, finer tannically and with a wonderfully complex, lingering finish.

Espiga 1998 — 15.5 — −£5.00

Foral Alianca Reserva, Douro 1997 — 14.5 — −£5.00
Dry yet gently jammy. Needs food.

Portada Red Estremadura 1999 — 13.5 — −£5.00
Very ripe and juicy – in spite of the tannins.

Quinta da Villa Freire Douro 1996 — 15 — £5–7

Quinta das Setencostas 1998 — 16.5 — −£5.00
From the great '98 vintage comes such texture, such richness, such satin-sided aplomb. Very elegant stuff.

Quinta de la Rosa Douro 1998 — 14 — £5–7

Very juicy and energetic. Needs strong food.

## BUDGENS RED

**Alta Mesa Red 1999**   13  −£3.50
Good for curries, with its sweet prune-like fruit.

**Dao Dom Ferraz 1999**   15  −£5.00
A rich, blackcurranty specimen perfect for vegetable casseroles laden with spices and herbs.

**Segada Trincadeira Preta-**   14  −£5.00
**Castelao 1999**
Juicy and full of interest – especially if you've got a plate of robust victuals in front of you.

## CWS RED

**Big Baga 1999, Co-op**   13.5  −£5.00
A big bag of juice. Great with curries and their ilk.

**Ramada Vinho Regional**   13  −£3.50
**Estremadura 1998**

**Star Mountain Touriga**   14  −£5.00
**Nacional 1997**
Invigorating tannins with ripe, raw, plummy fruit.

**Terra Boa Portuguese**   16.5  −£5.00
**Red 1998**
Terrific personality, this wine: dry yet full of savoury, gently spicy richness and lovely tannins. I drank it with garlic and mozzarella omelettes with a touch of cardamom.

## KWIK SAVE RED

**Ramada Red 1999**   13  −£5.00

Very ripe and sweet. Terrific with Indian food.

**Vila Regia 1995**   15  −£3.50

## MAJESTIC RED

**Contes de Cima Vinho**   14  £7–10
**Regional Alentejano 1997**

**Duas Quintas 1997**   16  £5–7
Chewy, rich, dry, elegant ( yet faintly rustic and characterful) and it has a lovely surge of warm fruit on the finish which, though subtle, is telling.

**Tuella Douro Tinto 1997**   15.5  −£5.00
Very juicy and figgy – tastes like young raw (unfortified) port. Great with Chinese food.

## MORRISONS RED

**Dom Ferraz Dao 1998**   16.5  −£5.00
Lovely herbiness and lingering richness. Great tannins and tense, dramatic fruit.

**Tamara Red Vinho**   13  −£3.50
**Regional Ribatejo 1999**
Rustic? It goes deeper than that.

## ODDBINS RED

**Foral Douro Grande**   15.5  £5–7
**Escolha 1997**
A warm, subtly spicy, tobacco-tinged wine of charm, character and yielding richness.

**Pegos Claros, Palmela**   15.5  £7–10
**1994**

**Quinta da Lagoalva,**   15  £5–7
**Ribatejo 1995**

**Quinta das Setencostas,** `16.5` `£5–7`
**Alenquer 1998**
Huge generosity of fruit, warmth of
disposition, weight of personality and
panache of fruit. An exciting wine.

**Quinta do Crasto** `17` `£7–10`
**Reserva, Doura 1997**
Beautifully cultured and plummy
voiced but it has lovely slang
expressions: tannin and earth for one.

**Segada Tinto, Ribatejano** `16` `–£5.00`
**1999**
Deliciously different: sensual texture,
spicy plum/blackcurrant fruit and very
deep tannins.

**Terra Boa Portuguese** `16.5` `–£5.00`
**Red 1998**
Terrific personality, this wine: dry yet
full of savoury, gently spicy richness
and lovely tannins. I drank it with
garlic and mozzarella omelettes with a
touch of cardamom.

## SAFEWAY RED

**Bright Brothers** `14` `–£5.00`
**Trincadeira Preta 1997**
Rich as a game sauce. Need I say
more?

**Falcoaria, Almeira 1997** `14.5` `£5–7`
Fruity yet earthy, sweet yet dry, subtle
yet impactful. A cultured food wine.

**Miradouro, Terras do** `12` `–£3.50`
**Sado 1999**
Very jammy and rich.

**Palmela 1998** `14.5` `–£5.00`
Piles it on deliciously, this ripe and
very ready red. Soft, concentrated,
tannic.

**Tamara Ribetajo 1999** `13` `–£5.00`

Great for curries. A sweet natural wine
of cherry-dispositioned fruit.

**Quinta de Bons-Ventos** `14` `–£5.00`
**1999**
Sweet plums and a hint of earth.
Needs spicy food. Not at all stores.

## SAINSBURY'S RED

**Ramada 1999** `13` `–£3.50`
Very sweet and curry-friendly.

**Segada Trincadeira Preta-** `14` `–£5.00`
**Castelao 1999**
Juicy and full of interest – especially if
you've got a plate of robust victuals in
front of you.

**Senda do Vale** `15.5` `£5–7`
**Trincadeira Cabernet**
**Sauvignon 1999**
Easily the best of Sainsbury's
Portuguese reds but even so it's sweet-
layered and ripe. But the tannins save
it. Needs food. Not at all stores.

## SOMERFIELD RED

**Bright Brothers Atlantic** `14` `–£5.00`
**Vines Baga 1999**
Real bruising fruit. Nothing subtle
here.

**Fiuza Bright Cabernet** `14.5` `–£5.00`
**Sauvignon 1998**
Sweet but engagingly rich. Great food
wine. Selected stores.

**Portuguese Red NV,** `14` `–£3.50`
**Somerfield**
Oh yes! With a curry, it's a perfect
marriage.

**Ramada Red 1999** `13` `–£5.00`
Very ripe and sweet. Terrific with
Indian food.

## TESCO RED

**Alianca Particular Palmela 1995** `17` `£5-7`
Such sweetness and emulsion-thick texture yet it's dry, herby, very rich and classy on the finish. A terrific wine. Top 85 stores.

**Bela Fonte Baga 1998** `14` `−£5.00`
Intense plum/cherry fruit with mild tannins. Good, soft/solid glugging here.

**Dao, Tesco 1998** `14` `−£5.00`
Juicy, fruity and hugely food friendly.

**Dom Ferraz Bairrada 1997** `16` `−£5.00`
Old Dom's back on form and sprightlier than ever! Terrific juice here – and serious underlying tannin. A tenacious wine of substance and style. Top 80 stores.

**Dom Ferraz Dao 1997** `15` `−£5.00`
Juicy hints of rusticity and earthiness, good bold strokes on the finish.

**Portuguese Red NV, Tesco** `14.5` `−£3.50`
Totally convincing fruit with a pleasant earthy tang to tightly assembled plums and raspberries (these under-ripe). A brilliant bargain for bangers and mash.

**Vinha Nove Tras-os-Montes 1998** `15.5` `−£5.00`

## THRESHER RED

**Dom Ferraz Dao 1997** `15` `−£5.00`
Juicy hints of rusticity and earthiness, good bold strokes on the finish.

**Fiuza Cabernet Sauvignon 1997** `14` `−£5.00`

**Pedras do Monte 1998** `16` `−£5.00`
Very tarry and ripe, hugely well ameliorated tannins; the whole effect is balsamic and bursting with fruit. It really smacks the taste buds, this wine. Not at Wine Rack or Bottoms Up.

**Segada Tinto 1998** `15.5` `−£5.00`
Very rich and multi-layered ripeness. Great with food.

## UNWINS RED

**Bela Fonte Jaen 1998** `16` `−£5.00`
Superb texture, biting fresh tannins, soft ripe fruit and galloping, zesty finish. Classy yet irreverent.

**Dao Dom Ferraz Reserva Caves Primavera 1999** `15.5` `−£5.00`
Full of fun, juicy, jammy, jaw-breakingly fruity.

**Pedras do Monte 1999** `15` `−£5.00`
Oh! What a wine for curried meat and veg!

**Portada Vinho Regional Estremadura 1999** `13.5` `−£5.00`
Sweet undertone.

**Quinta das Setencostas, Alenquer 1998** `16.5` `£5-7`
Huge generosity of fruit, warmth of disposition, weight of personality and panache of fruit. An exciting wine.

**Quinta do Crasto Reserva 1997** `17` `£7-10`
Beautifully cultured and plummy voiced but it has lovely slang expressions: tannin and earth for one.

**Segada Red 1998** `15.5` `−£5.00`
Juicy, ripe, delicious, rich yet not OTT, good tannins, gently tenacious.

## VICTORIA WINE RED

**Dom Ferraz Dao 1997**  `15`  −£5.00
Juicy hints of rusticity and earthiness, good bold strokes on the finish.

**Fiuza Cabernet Sauvignon 1997**  `14`  −£5.00

**Pedras do Monte 1998**  `16`  −£5.00
Very tarry and ripe, hugely well ameliorated tannins; the whole effect is balsamic and bursting with fruit. It really smacks the taste buds, this wine. Not at Wine Rack or Bottoms Up.

**Segada Tinto 1998**  `15.5`  −£5.00
Very rich and multi-layered ripeness. Great with food.

## WAITROSE RED

**Terra de Lobos, Quinta do Casal Branco 1999**  `14`  −£5.00
Rich almost soupy fruit but has good, ripe tannins to provide balance.

**Trincadeira Joao Portugal Ramos 1999**  `16`  £7–10
One of the most civilised tipples from Portugal – beautifully smooth, aromatic, plump and lingering.

**Vila Santa Alentejo 1998**  `16.5`  £7–10
Superb multi-layered richness and velvet textured tightness (ie concentration) of fruit.

**Vinho do Monte, Alentejo 1998**  `13.5`  −£5.00
Very ripe.

## WINE CELLAR RED

**Belafonte Baga, Beiras 1998**  `14`  −£5.00
Intense plum/cherry fruit with mild

tannins. Good, soft/solid glugging here.

**Portada Tinto Estremadura 1995**  `16`  −£5.00
Great value here. An aromatic, gorgeously soft, rich, ripe wine with a walloping fruity finish.

**Terra Boa 1997**  `12`  −£5.00
Sweet red for curries.

## ASDA WHITE

**Vinho Verde 1999, Asda**  `10`  −£3.50

## CWS WHITE

**Fiuza Chardonnay 1999**  `16`  −£5.00
Rather dainty at first and then it really surges into fruity action. Captivating final richness here.

**Ramada Vinho Regional Estremadura 1998**  `15.5`  −£3.50

## KWIK SAVE WHITE

**Falua 1998**  `13.5`  −£3.50

**Portuguese White 1999, Somerfield**  `15`  −£3.50
A rich and very ready food wine – suits a whole range of dishes from tuna salad to chicken tikka.

## MORRISONS WHITE

**Sinfonia White Alentejo 1998**  `13`  −£5.00

**Tamara White Ribatejo 1998**  `12`  −£3.50
Jolie laide, as the French have it. That is to say, it's a contradiction.

## ODDBINS WHITE

**Bela Fonte Bical 1999**   15.5   −£5.00
Very pert and fleshy, great for mergers with robust dishes, and a lush acidity.

**Segada Branco,**   15   −£5.00
**Ribatejano 1999**
Slightly fat edge gives it character and the edgy acids food compatibility.

## SAFEWAY WHITE

**Globus Ribetajo 1999**   11   −£5.00
Rather clotted and sullen.

**Tamara Ribetajo White**   14.5   −£3.50
**1999**
Lovely ripe melon fruit.

## SAINSBURY'S WHITE

**Portuguese Rosé,**   13.5   −£3.50
**Sainsbury's**

**Vinho Verde, Sainsbury's**   13.5   −£3.50

## SOMERFIELD WHITE

**Fiuza Bright Chardonnay**   16   −£5.00
**1999**
Rather dainty at first and then it really surges into fruity action. Captivating final richness here.

**Portuguese White 1999,**   15   −£3.50
**Somerfield**
A rich and very ready food wine – suits a whole range of dishes from tuna salad to chicken tikka.

## TESCO WHITE

**Bela Fonte Bical 1998**   15   −£5.00
Good clean fun – for fish. Very good price for such purposeful fruit. 200 stores.

**Dry Vinho Verde, Tesco**   13.5   −£5.00

## UNWINS WHITE

**Bical Bela Fonte 1998**   15   −£5.00
Good clean fun – for fish. Very good price for such purposeful fruit.

**Segada White 1998**   13   −£5.00

## WAITROSE WHITE

**Quinta de Simaens Vinho**   10   −£5.00
**Verde 1998**

**Terras do Rio Quinta de**   15   −£3.50
**Abrigada 1998**

# ROMANIA

What happened, readers so often ask me, to the magical, cheap Pinot Noirs of the late 1980s and early 1990s? I wish I knew. Romania itself doesn't know. It just remains puzzled at why UK professional wine buyers have lost their appetite for Romanian wines. The country has not progressed as it could have done, though it has some marvellous vines and creditable grape-growers and wine-makers. Needs another revolution probably.

## BUDGENS RED

**Romanian Classic Pinot Noir 1998**   13.5   −£5.00
Classic? Nope. But drinkable and dry.

**Romanian Young Cabernet Sauvignon 1998**   14   −£5.00
Delicious warmth and soft peppery blackcurrants.

**Sahateni Merlot 1998**   15   −£5.00
Hugely slurpable and food-friendly. Leather, herbs and subtly spicy plums.

## CWS RED

**Romanian Prairie Merlot 1999, Co-op**   14.5   −£3.50
A party wine for ripe throats and warm hearts.

## MORRISONS RED

**Romanian Classic Pinot Noir 1998**   11   −£3.50
Classic? Hardly. It's too toffeed for that.

**Special Reserve Pinot Noir 1998**   10   −£5.00
Very raw tannins. They skin the cheeks.

**Special Reserve Sangiovese 1998**   10   −£5.00
More raw tannins. My granny would choke to death on them.

## SAFEWAY RED

**Idle Rock Merlot 1998**   12   −£5.00

## SOMERFIELD RED

**Pietroasa Young Vatted Cabernet Sauvignon 1998**   16   −£5.00
Try it as an alternative to Beaujolais. It has similar cheeky freshness but more character, bite and tannins. And a rich finish.

## TESCO RED

**Reka Valley Romanian Pinot Noir, Tesco**   15.5   −£3.50

Terrific! Best blend yet of this Pinot. Has bitter cherry richness, a hint of ripe plum, but the winning ingredient is the brilliant tannic edge. Classic Pinot? No, but a brilliant bargain of wrap-around-your-palate fruit.

## THRESHER RED

River Route Limited     13.5  −£5.00
Edition Cabernet
Sauvignon 1997
Juicy and ripe.

River Route Pinot Noir     12  −£5.00
1998
Odd cough mixture undertone.

## VICTORIA WINE RED

River Route Limited     13.5  −£5.00
Edition Cabernet
Sauvignon 1997
Juicy and ripe.

River Route Pinot Noir     12  −£5.00
1998
Odd cough mixture undertone.

## BUDGENS WHITE

Romanian Classic     11  −£5.00
Gewürztraminer 1998
Very odd and vegetal. Hardly a classic Gewürz.

Romanian Classic Pinot     13  −£5.00
Gris 1999
Dry, faint tang of dried apricot.

## MORRISONS WHITE

Romanian Special     16  −£5.00
Reserve Barrel

Fermented Chardonnay
1996
Catch it while it's at its peak of maturity: creamy, textured, deliciously firm and fruity.

## SAFEWAY WHITE

Château Cotnari, Blanc     10  −£5.00
de Cotnari 1998
Very bland and boring.

## SAINSBURY'S WHITE

Romanian Merlot Rosé     14  −£3.50
NV, Sainsbury's

## THRESHER WHITE

River Route Limited     15.5  −£5.00
Edition Chardonnay 1997
The first Chardonnay made on this section of the Danube! Delicious.

## VICTORIA WINE WHITE

River Route Limited     15.5  −£5.00
Edition Chardonnay 1997
The first Chardonnay made on this section of the Danube! Delicious.

## WAITROSE WHITE

Willow Ridge     15.5  −£3.50
Sauvignon/Feteasca 1999
Unusual and very pretty aperitif with a light floral/honey undertone. Overall, crisp and fresh.

# RUSSIA

If only Russian wine danced as beautifully on the tongue as Safin and Kournekova dance around a tennis court, we'd have wine to rave about.

## SAFEWAY RED

**Caucasus Valley, Matrassa, Georgia 1998**  15  −£5.00
Great fun. A real Russian doll here as it unwraps one dry flavour after another.

**Odessos Steppe Cabernet Sauvignon, Ukraine 1998**  13  −£5.00
Quirky, bold, tannic, yet very juicy.

**Tamada Saperavi, Georgia 1998**  13.5  −£5.00
Dry and jammy.

# SOUTH AFRICA

There was a huge surge of enthusiasm when the Cape wine industry, nearly 350 years old now, had its export fetters removed, at the time South Africa was considered to have become a civilised country again with the abolition of apartheid. But where are those dazzling bottles we expected to come pouring out year after year? True, there are some high spots, like Kim Warwick's Chardonnay at Waitrose, and the Spice Route wines (lots of places), and there are others, but overall I admit to feeling disappointed that the Cape hasn't gone from strength to strength as I anticipated. Most individual red grape is Pinotage (young and feisty and best drunk not more than two years old because it goes soppy with age). Chenin Blanc shines most characterfully among the whites, the odd splendidly quirky Chardonnay apart (like Jordan). The Chenin grape exhibits a wonderful subtle spiciness and gooseberryness lacking in the often flaccid specimens from France.

## ASDA RED

**Cape Merlot 1999, Asda** `13.5` `–£5.00`
Very juicy. Needs pasta.

**Dumisani Ruby** `15.5` `–£5.00`
**Cabernet/Merlot 1999**
Juicy with good tannins to relieve the palate from the all-fruit attack.

**Kumala Cabernet** `14` `–£5.00`
**Sauvignon/Shiraz 1997**

**Landskroon Merlot** `16` `£5–7`
**Reserve 1999**
Gigantic hedgerow fruitiness. The wine simply swims with flavours. Utterly seductive from nose to throat.

**Long Mountain Red NV** `14` `–£5.00`

**Pinotage Reserve 1999,** `14` `–£5.00`
**Asda**
Very sweet and juicy – perfect for . . . curries? ('fraid so.)

**Porcupine Ridge Syrah** `16` `£5–7`
**1999**
There used to be two styles of Syrah: the Rhone's (dry) and the Aussie's (very rich). Now comes the Cape's Crusader. And it makes a very strong, rich case for itself.

**South African Cabernet** `14` `–£5.00`
**Sauvignon 1999, Asda**
The dry, stalky edge, subtle, of the peppery Cabernet gives the wine some added character.

South African Pinotage `13.5` `–£5.00`
1999, Asda
Again, it's so juicy!

Van Loveren Cabernet `13` `–£5.00`
Shiraz 1999
Too juicy.

## BOOTHS RED

Helderberg Shiraz 1999 `15` `–£5.00`
Hint of cigar box to the plum and
blackcurrant fruit.

Spice Route Andrew's `16.5` `£5–7`
Hope 1998
Thundering riches abound here:
blackcurrants, tar, violets, rosewater,
leather and a subtle spicy tang. Great
stuff.

Stormy Cape Cinsault/ `16` `–£5.00`
Shiraz 1998
Wonderfully offensive stuff: dog-eared,
cheroot-stained. rubber-necked, spicy,
fruit, utterly quaffable and food
friendly. A storm in a glass.

Welmoed Merlot 1998 `15.5` `£5–7`
Juicy plums, raisins, hint of herb and
tobacco. Brilliant for roast dinner party
meats.

Wide River Pinotage `15.5` `£5–7`
1999
Curious grassy undertone to the
cheroot-tinged juice. Great food wine.

## BUDGENS RED

Cape Medium Fruity Red `11` `–£3.50`
NV, Budgens

Long Mountain Merlot `13.5` `£5–7`
Shiraz 1998
Another excellent curry red.

## CWS RED

Arniston Bay Ruby `13.5` `–£5.00`
Cabernet-Merlot 1998

Birdfield Shiraz 1998 `14` `–£5.00`

Cape American Oak `14` `–£5.00`
Pinotage 1999, Co-op
Oddly ripe and rich, almost baked in
its warmth and depth of flavour, but
the tannins are a real presence.

Cape Indaba Pinotage `13` `–£5.00`
1998

Cape Ruby Cabernet, `13.5` `–£5.00`
Oak Aged 1999, Co-op
Loads of juice. Perfect with Indian
food.

Elephant Trail Cinsault/ `15` `–£5.00`
Merlot 2000, Co-op
Good jammy richness with terrifically
vivacious tannins which spark a riot of
flavours on the finish.

Goats Do Roam `15.5` `–£5.00`
Fairview, Paarl 1999
Great pun, great fruit. Though it isn't
so much Côtes-du-Rhône as juicy
Bandol-style. Great quaffing style.
Superstores only.

Natural State Cape Soleil `15` `£5–7`
Organic Shiraz 1999
Expensive but ultimately deeply
satisfying. The fruit is rounded yet dry,
rich yet not over-ripe, full yet delicate
in parts. It is its own wine, not a copy
of Rhône or McLaren Vale.
Superstores only.

Oak Village Cabernet `15` `–£5.00`
Sauvignon 1998
Delicious Cab – it takes you from nose
to throat in great comfort.

Pinnacle Merlot 1998 `16` `£5–7`

Very thrusting style, taking no prisoners, and it has something to say for itself. 'I am utterly hedonistic and delicious.' Amen to that. Superstores only.

**Railroad Cabernet Sauvignon Shiraz 1999** `15.5` `−£5.00`
Pulsates with an interesting duo-level of Cabernet dryness and hint of spice (pepper) and the soft, saddle-weary richness of the Shiraz. Superstores only.

**Three Worlds Pinotage Shiraz Zinfandel 1999, Co-op** `15.5` `£5–7`
Has immense chutzpah which does not overstay its welcome. The fruit is certainly ripe but it has little nooks and crannies of intrigue where odd fruits, acids, nuts and earthy bits lurk.

**Winds of Change Pinotage/Cabernet Sauvignon 1998** `16` `−£5.00`
Superb elegance and dry richness here. Has a savoury biscuit quality to its texture and a quietly thrilling climax of spicy plums and berries. Superstores only.

**South African Cape Red 1999, Somerfield** `15` `−£3.50`
Beautifully soft and luminous as it courses, cherries and plums, over the taste buds.

**South African Cinsault Ruby Cabernet 1999, Somerfield** `15` `−£5.00`
Delicious layers of ripe, rich fruit. Baked, yes. But not overdone.

**Bin 121 Merlot Ruby Cabernet 1998** `15.5` `−£5.00`

**Cape Country Cinsault/ Ruby Cabernet 1999** `13.5` `−£5.00`
Juicy and very forward.

**Rock Ridge Pinotage 1999** `16.5` `−£5.00`
Brilliant spicy warmth and wit here. The tobacco and rubber, the smoke and the basket of leathery fruit, all hang together sexily.

**Rockridge Cabernet Sauvignon 1998** `14` `−£5.00`
Jammy with dry overtones.

**Drosty-Hof Merlot 1998** `16` `£5–7`
Dark and crunchy fruit, richly leathery, faintly spicy, chocolatey and deep. It's dry for all this and the tannins are warm and savoury.

**Fairview Merlot 1998** `16.5` `£5–7`
Lovely lingering, non-leathery Merlot with startlingly glamorous tannins of the younger Zsa-Zsa Gabor variety: cheeky, finely boned and exuberant. The finish is gripping.

**Goats Do Roam Fairview, Paarl 1999** `15.5` `−£5.00`
Great pun, great fruit. Though it isn't so much Côtes-du-Rhône as juicy Bandol-style. Great quaffing style.

**Cathedral Cellars Merlot 1996** `13` `£7–10`

**Fairview Malbec 1999** `16.5` `£5–7`

Juicy but Fairview's wines are always elegant and purposeful on the finish, as this one is, and so what seems forward is only, in the final analysis, rich friendliness.

**Namaqua Classic Red NV** 11.5 £5-7
**(3 litre box)**
Sweet and basic. Price band is for a 75cl equivalent.

**South African Red NV** 13 −£3.50

**Spice Route Andrew's** 16.5 £5-7
**Hope 1998**
Thundering riches abound here: blackcurrants, tar, violets, rosewater, leather and a subtle spicy tang. Great stuff.

**Van Loveren Merlot 1999** 13 −£5.00
Too sweet for me.

## ODDBINS RED

**Beyerskloof Pinotage,** 16 £5-7
**Stellenbosch 1999**
The ultimate pizza and savoury tart red. Tobacco, cassis, herbs and tannins is the recipe.

**Blaauwklippen Shiraz** 13.5 £5-7
**1997**

**Boschkloof Cabernet** 15.5 £5-7
**Sauvignon 1997**

**Boschkloof Reserve** 14 £7-10
**Cabernet Sauvignon/**
**Merlot 1997**
Fine Wine Stores only.

**Fairview Carignan,** 13 £5-7
**Coastal Region 1998**

**Fairview Shiraz** 17.5 £5-7
**Mourvedre 1998**
The aroma is initially of fine Cuban cigars from tobacco grown on the plain overlooking the Baie de Cerdos. This finesse, powerfully augmented by the nigh 15% of alcohol as the ripe, spicy fruit floods the mouth, breaks up into a variety of soft fruits with light, soft tannins. A big yet lithe wine of rugged charms (yet smooth).

**Fairview Zinfandel** 17.5 £5-7
**Cinsault 1999**
Such energy and delivery of complex acids and fruits is remarkable. Very savoury and deep, it has to be appreciated with rich food.

**Glen Carlou Pinot Noir** 13.5 £7-10
**1998**
Fine Wine Stores only.

**Kanonkop, Paul Sauer,** 14 £13-20
**Stellenbosch 1995**
Juicy, ripe, teeth-tremblingly gushing. Needs food.

**Kumala Reserve** 16.5 £7-10
**Cabernet Sauvignon 1998**
Curious ambivalence here: youthful exuberance with seasoned mellowness. The wine offers ripe plum, subtle tobacco nuances, hint of chocolate and tea (lapsang souchong) and a smoothness of almost smug hauteur. For all that, nine quid is a lot of money. It can be opened and decanted five to six hours beforehand.

**Longridge Bay View** 14 £5-7
**Cabernet Sauvignon 1998**

**Longridge Bay View** 14 £5-7
**Merlot 1998**

**Longridge Bay View** 15 £5-7
**Pinotage 1998**

**Radford Dale Merlot,** 14 £7-10
**Stellenbosch 1999**
Very juicy and ripe on the finish. Expensive for what it is.

Savanha Shiraz, Western 13 £5–7
Cape 1997

Saxenberg Cabernet 17 £10–13
Sauvignon, Stellenbosch
1997
Stunning! Quite stunning: raisins, figs,
spicy cherries, liquorice and herbs.

Stellenzicht Pinotage 17 £7–10
1998
Astonishingly richly textured, as
clotted as a hawser, and it's difficult to
unravel the fruit from the tannins. But
the complexity is considerable – it
includes tobacco and chocolate – and
the finish manages, paradoxically, to
achieve elegance in spite of the
dynamic, galloping fruit.

Stellenzicht Shiraz 1998 15 £7–10

Vinum Cabernet 14 £5–7
Sauvignon, Stellenbosch
1999
A juicy, curry-friendly red of great
richness.

Yonder Hill Cabernet 16 £7–10
Merlot, Stellenbosch 1998
Stupendously soft and ripe but not
soppy or stodgy. Wonderful texture
here.

Yonder Hill Cabernet 16.5 £7–10
Sauvignon, Stellenbosch
1998
Utterly compelling in its argument
that Cape Cabernet can be just as
textured as claret but far more
hedgerow-like in its wonderful fruit.

## SAFEWAY RED

Apostle's Falls Cabernet 16.5 £5–7
Sauvignon 1998
What wouldn't they give in Bordeaux

for such ripeness, such texture, such
savoury richness with austerity. A
beautiful performer, this specimen, on
every front.

Arniston Bay Ruby 13 –£5.00
Cabernet/Merlot 1999
Very juicy.

Cape Soleil Organic 9 –£5.00
Pinotage 1998
Thin and insubstantial. Why sell
organic wine as puny as this just to see
the word organic on shelf?

Fairview Malbec 1999 16.5 £5–7
Wonderfully generous and
hedonistically textured fruit here. So
soft (yet not gooey), so ripe (yet not
puerile), so all-engagingly rich (yet not
over-friendly or falsely hospitable).

Kanonkop 'Kadette' 15.5 £5–7
Estate Wine 1998
Brilliant value. Has character and
backbone, good tannins, firm plummy
fruit.

Kleinbosch Reserve 14 £5–7
Cabernet Sauvignon 1999
Cabernet as happy juice. Very soft and
ripe. 29 stores.

Kleinbosch Young Vatted 15 –£5.00
Pinotage, Paarl 1999
Lovely dry tannins add the cutting
edge to rich, deep fruit.

Landskroon Cinsault/ 15.5 £5–7
Shiraz, Paarl 1999
Firmly ripe and soft-hitting fruit of
gentle spice, posh plums and lush
finishing herbs.

Landskroon Shiraz, Paarl 15.5 £5–7
1998
Very jammy but the texture holds firm
(and ripe) and the wondrous

generosity of the fruit is thrilling. Selected stores.

**Simsberg Pinot Noir,** `13.5` `£5–7`
**Paarl 1998**
Good Pinot aroma and some hint of mystery in the fruit but lacks the impact to intrigue the brain for very long.

**Stellenbosch Cabernet** `14` `–£5.00`
**Sauvignon 1999**
Very very dry. Lovely with undercooked red meats.

**Stellenbosch Merlot 1999** `15.5` `–£5.00`
Deliciously sunny and savoury. Nicely textured. Most stores.

## SAINSBURY'S RED

**African Legend Shiraz** `15` `–£5.00`
**The Quivering Spear \***
**1998**
A spicy, intensely warm wine of immense savouriness. Excellent with chillied pastas and vegetable dishes. Most stores. \* No joke – it's actually got this on the label. It does not refer to many South Africans' preferred method of cork removal.

**Bellingham Merlot 1998** `16` `£5–7`
Curious pear-drop undertone to rich, dry fruit. But delicious? It redefines Merlot's mouthwatering deliciousness. Most stores.

**Bellingham Premium** `14` `£7–10`
**Pinotage 1998**
Dry and more than a touch expensive for the level of fruit on offer. 50 stores.

**Bellingham Shiraz 1998** `16` `£5–7`
Cheeky fruit for it seems aromatically Aussie but Chilean in finish. Lovely dark riches here. Fullness and flavour

but not OTT or puerile. Not at all stores.

**Clos Malverne Cabernet** `15` `£5–7`
**Pinotage 1998**
Curious marriage of unlikely grapes. The old fart Cabernet meets the whizz kid Pinotage. Imagine Denis Thatcher sleeping with Britney Spears. Fruity? yes. Enormously so and very entertaining. Not at all stores.

**Fairview Carignan 1999** `15.5` `£5–7`
Intensely plummy and polished with a layered, double-effect finish combining spice with baked fruit. 85 stores.

**Fairview Pinotage 1999** `17` `£5–7`
One of South Africa's, perhaps the world's, most joyously juicy yet seriously delicious and multi-layered wines. It has wonderful graduated texture, a middle wallop of berries and a striking, witty finish. Selected stores.

**Hidden Valley Limited** `13` `£13–20`
**Release Pinotage 1997**
I don't think it's worth fifteen quid when it offers fruit less gripping than six quid Sainsbury Cape reds. 50 stores.

**Kumala Cabernet** `16` `–£5.00`
**Sauvignon Shiraz 1998**
Delicious as both a throat charmer and food companion. It has layers of textured fruit, warm, touch spicy, hint of pepper, good tannins. Lush, luxurious, lissom, lovely to down!

**Middlevlei Shiraz 1999** `15.5` `£5–7`
A food wine. Has a celeriac edge to the firm tannins and a hint of some Indian spice on the finish. A serious wine of dry, complex, elegant quirkiness. Not at all stores.

**Milton Grove Cabernet** `16` `£5–7`
**Franc 1999**
Mouthfilling and mindfilling – the fruit
is almost gung-ho but not, thankfully,
fully so. The delicious restraint is
courtesy of the civilising tannins. A
delicious, sunny, joyful wine. Not at
all stores.

**Railroad Cabernet** `15.5` `–£5.00`
**Sauvignon Shiraz 1999**
Pulsates with an interesting duo-level
of Cabernet dryness and hint of spice
(pepper) and the soft, saddle-weary
richness of the Shiraz. Most stores.

**South African Cabernet** `15.5` `–£5.00`
**Sauvignon NV,**
**Sainsbury's**
Utterly unpretentious and deliciously
soft, ripe and rich. It makes few
demands on the intellect, true, but as a
slab of fruit it is marvellously
quaffable. Most stores.

**South African Pinotage** `16` `–£5.00`
**NV, Sainsbury's**
Terrific modernity and chutzpah here.
Hint of civilised boy-racer rubber,
spice (cinnamon? cardamom?
coriander?) and a lovely dry tannic
finish to the cassis/plum fruit.

**South African Red NV,** `15` `–£3.50`
**Sainsbury's**
An eager-to-please glugging red of
some dignity and wit. Most stores.

**South African Reserve** `16.5` `£5–7`
**Selection Pinotage 1998,**
**Sainsbury's**
A high class Pinotage which manages
to put a brave face on burnt rubber,
cassis, pepper, blackberries and
dry earthy tannins. 155 selected
stores.

**Spice Route Andrew's** `16.5` `£5–7`
**Hope Cabernet Merlot**
**1999**
Great opening of spice and leather
(aromatically) and then it turns more
petit château and dry and then it goes
full frontal rich and ripe. Good
integrated tannins on the final flourish.
Most stores.

**Spice Route Flagship** `17` `£13–20`
**Merlot 1998**
A big, rich special occasion Merlot of
massive depth, lingering tannins and
huge food compatibility. 50 stores.

**Stowells of Chelsea** `15.5` `–£5.00`
**Cinsault Pinotage**
**Sainsbury (3 litre box)**
Lots of smoky, ripe fruit, fluid and full.
Hint of spiced plum to it plus good
earthy tannins. But mostly it's all rich,
flowing fruit which comes to a very
satisfying climax. The price band
reflects the equivalent price for a 75cl
bottle.

**Winds of Change** `16` `–£5.00`
**Pinotage Cabernet**
**Sauvignon 1998**
Superb elegance and dry richness here.
Has a savoury biscuit quality to its
texture and a quietly thrilling climax of
spicy plums and berries. Most stores.

**Yonder Hill Inanda 1997** `17` `£7–10`
A powerful Bordeaux blend of Cab
Sauv, Merlot and Cab Franc which is
exotic, warm, spicy, thick and deep,
and very sustaining. A marvellous
wine for game dishes. Selected stores.

## SOMERFIELD RED

**Bellingham Pinotage 1999** `17` `£5–7`
Stunning tannins! Even Lafite doesn't

get tannins this exciting, this tasty, this deep. Limited distribution.

**Bush Vines Pinotage** 16 −£5.00
**1999, Somerfield**
Those spicy, exotic tannins! Or is it the fruit? Either way, this is a roller-coaster experience.

**Kumala Cinsault** 15 −£5.00
**Pinotage 1999**
Drink it with chicken dhansak.

**Kumala Reserve** 16.5 £7−10
**Cabernet Sauvignon 1998**
Curious ambivalence here: youthful exuberance with seasoned mellowness. The wine offers ripe plum, subtle tobacco nuances, hint of chocolate and tea (lapsang souchong) and a smoothness of almost smug hauteur. For all that, nine quid is a lot of money. It can be opened and decanted five to six hours beforehand. Limited distribution.

**South African Cabernet** 16 −£5.00
**Sauvignon 1999,**
**Somerfield**
A lovely specimen of Cape warmth and wit. A dry, tobacco-edged red of huge charm and commitment.

**South African Cape Red** 15 −£3.50
**1999, Somerfield**
Beautifully soft and luminous as it courses, cherries and plums, over the taste buds.

**South African Cinsault** 15 −£5.00
**Ruby Cabernet 1999,**
**Somerfield**
Delicious layers of ripe, rich fruit. Baked, yes. But not overdone.

**South African Pinotage** 16.5 −£5.00
**1998, Somerfield**
Superb! Spice, sustaining fruit, great

active tannins, finely knit acids – all in one fabulous experience.

**Winds of Change** 16 −£5.00
**Pinotage Cabernet 1998**
Superb elegance and dry richness here. Has a savoury biscuit quality to its texture and a quietly thrilling climax of spicy plums and berries. Limited distribution.

## SPAR RED

**Chiwara Cinsault/Ruby** 13 −£5.00
**Cabernet 1998**
Goes a bit walkabout on the finish. Starts off well, if very ripely, but then . . .

**Chiwara Pinotage 1998,** 14.5 −£5.00
**Spar**

**Chiwara Ruby Cabernet/** 11 −£5.00
**Pinotage 1998, Spar**

**Table Mountain Pinot** 10 −£5.00
**Noir NV**

## TESCO RED

**African Legend Pinotage** 14 −£5.00
**1998**
Not at all stores.

**Beyers Truter Pinotage** 16.5 −£5.00
**1998, Tesco**
Stunning bargain for Christmas lunch. Really hums with aromatic richness, hint of spice, touch of chocolate and cassis, but it's fresh, the tannins are alert, the whole surging flavoursome construct is eager to delight the palate. At most stores.

**Cape Cinsault NV, Tesco** 15.5 −£3.50

**Cape Cinsault/Pinotage** 15.5 −£5.00
**NV, Tesco**

**Clos Malverne Pinotage** 16 £5–7
**1999**
Always a solid hitter, this vintage has
violet/plum overtones to its very free-
flowing fruit. Aromatic, exotic, spicy,
delicious. 100 selected stores.

**Diemersdal Shiraz 1998** 15 £5–7

**Goats Do Roam** 15.5 −£5.00
**Fairview, Paarl 1999**

**Goiya Glaan 1999** 15 −£5.00
Most individual. The fruit is far more
serious and complex than the hysteria
of the label would suggest.

**International Winemaker** 15 −£5.00
**Cabernet/Merlot, Tesco**
Very generous and soft. Really
cheering tippling.

**Kumala Cabernet** 15 −£5.00
**Sauvignon/Shiraz 1999**
Bounces with personality without
being trying or too puerile. Has a
gentle pepperiness from the Cabernet
and a touch of leather and hedgerow
fruitiness from the Shiraz.

**Kumala Cinsault/** 13.5 −£5.00
**Cabernet Sauvignon 1999**
Juicy with a hint of an exotic herb.
Touch of tobacco is good but its
overall jamminess suits spicy food
best.

**Landskroon Premier** 14 £5–7
**Reserve Cabernet**
**Sauvignon 1998**
Most stores.

**Long Mountain Cabernet** 13.5 −£5.00
**Sauvignon 1998**

**Oak Village Pinotage/** 13 −£5.00
**Merlot 1999**

Juicy and super-ripe. Good with . . .
curries etc.

**South African Cabernet** 14 −£5.00
**Sauvignon/Shiraz 1999,**
**Tesco**
Has a dry beefiness and richness which
demands to be fed.

**South African Red NV,** 14.5 −£3.50
**Tesco**
Terrific quaffing here. Even throws
sophisticated tannins.

**South African Reserve** 12 −£5.00
**Cabernet NV, Tesco**
Very jammy and sweet. Like
experiencing one of those continental
cigars with cherries and kirsch in the
leaves.

**Spice Route Andrew's** 16.5 £5–7
**Hope Merlot/Cabernet,**
**Malmesbury 1998**
The essence of new world cheekiness
– it dares to be utterly unashamedly
immediate and all-embracing. It's got
so much jammy richness, which never
goes gooey or blowsy. It's great,
gorgeous and grandly underpriced.
Top 80 stores.

**Spice Route Cabernet** 16.5 £7–10
**Merlot 1998**
Aromatic, very ripe and uplifting, full
of deep fruit and beautifully finished
off. 100 selected stores.

**Winds of Change** 16 −£5.00
**Cabernet/Pinotage 1999**
Superb jammy richness balanced by
dry, earthy tannins. Lovely
quaffability. Has a savoury undertone
to its exuberance which keeps it
serious. Remarkable New World wine.
100 selected stores.

SOUTH AFRICAN RED

## THRESHER RED

**Cape View Cinsault/ Shiraz 1998**  `12`  `–£5.00`
Curious lack of personality on the finish. It starts with a brash note but hits a trough on the way to the throat.

**Capells Court Cabernet 1998**  `14`  `£5–7`
Very ripe, very curry friendly. Wine Rack and Bottoms Up only.

**Oak Village Cabernet Sauvignon 1998**  `15`  `–£5.00`
Delicious Cab – it takes you from nose to throat in great comfort.

**The Pinotage Company Pinotage 1999**  `13.5`  `£5–7`
Touch expensive for the style of juice. Wine Rack only.

**Villiera Pinot Noir G & G Reserve 1997**  `13`  `£7–10`

**Winelands Cabernet Sauvignon/Franc, Stellenbosch 1997**  `13.5`  `£5–7`

## UNWINS RED

**African Legend Pinotage 1998**  `14`  `–£5.00`

**Bellingham Pinotage 1998**  `16`  `£5–7`
Perfect mature amalgam of spicy fruit and brisk, savoury tannins. Drink it with roast game.

**Cape Cinsault/Merlot 1999**  `13`  `–£5.00`
Sheer juice – only the lolly stick is missing.

**Cathedral Cellar Cabernet Sauvignon 1995**  `15`  `£7–10`
At its peak of fruitiness. The tannins

are holding out well against the glucose.

**Clos Malverne Cabernet/ Shiraz, Stellenbosch 1997**  `14.5`  `£5–7`

**Clos Malverne Pinotage, Stellenbosch 1999**  `16`  `£5–7`
One of the lushest, most aromatic, most tannically teasing of Pinotages. Gushes with tobacco and spicy plum personality.

**Jordan Cabernet Sauvignon 1997**  `16`  `£7–10`
Beautifully concentrated and smooth. Great elegance and depth here.

**Leef Op Hoop Cabernet Sauvignon/Merlot, Stellenbosch 1998**  `14`  `£5–7`
Jammy, savoury, very ripe. Needs rich food.

**Millbrook Cinsault 1998**  `14`  `–£5.00`
Very juicy and ripe, Needs food.

**Neil Joubert Cabernet Sauvignon 1998**  `13`  `£5–7`
Goes a bit tutti-frutti on the finish.

**Spice Route Shiraz 1998**  `16`  `£7–10`
Very meaty and dark. Lovely richness and exuberance without pretentious show-offness.

## VICTORIA WINE RED

**Cape View Cinsault/ Shiraz 1998**  `12`  `–£5.00`
Curious lack of personality on the finish. It starts with a brash note but hits a trough on the way to the throat.

**Oak Village Cabernet Sauvignon 1998**  `15`  `–£5.00`
Delicious Cab – it takes you from nose to throat in great comfort.

The Pinotage Company  13.5  £5–7
Pinotage 1999
Touch expensive for the style of juice.

## WAITROSE RED

Avontuur Estate  13  –£5.00
Cabernet Sauvignon/
Merlot 1998

Clos Malverne Basket  16  £7–10
Pressed Pinotage,
Stellenbosch 1999
Tobacco richness – fresh and delicious.

Goats Do Roam  15.5  –£5.00
Fairview, Paarl 1999

Hamilton Russell Pinot  13  £13–20
Noir 1997
Only from Waitrose Direct.

Hidden Valley Pinotage,  15  £13–20
Devon Valley 1996
Nothing hidden about the hideous
Marbella beach bum medallion-laden
label.

Kumala Reserve  16.5  £7–10
Cabernet Sauvignon 1998
Curious ambivalence here: youthful
exuberance with seasoned mellowness.
The wine offers ripe plum, subtle
tobacco nuances, hint of chocolate and
tea (lapsang souchong) and a
smoothness of almost smug hauteur.
For all that, nine quid is a lot of
money. It can be opened and decanted
five to six hours beforehand.

Spice Route Cabernet  16.5  £7–10
Sauvignon/Merlot 1998
Aromatic, very ripe and uplifting, full
of deep fruit and beautifully finished
off.

Spice Route Flagship  17  £13–20
Merlot 1998

A big, rich special occasion Merlot of
massive depth, lingering tannins and
huge food compatibility. Not at all
stores.

Steenberg Merlot,  15  £7–10
Constantia 1998
A very collected, finely textured
Merlot of warmth and substance.
Classy finish to it.

Thelema Mountain  14  £13–20
Vineyards Cabernet
Sauvignon 1996
Lingering finish but the overture is
demure.

## WINE CELLAR RED

Jordan Merlot 1998  16  £7–10
Most unusual Merlot (no leather) but
it compels the palate to like it because
it's so blatantly deliciously rich, ripe
and ready.

L'Avenir Cabernet  13  £7–10
Sauvignon 1996

Neil Joubert Cabernet  13  £5–7
Sauvignon 1998
Goes a bit tutti-frutti on the finish.

Neil Joubert Pinotage  16  £5–7
1998
Very subtle tobacco hint to the creamy
fruit. Great texture and tension
between fruit and acids. Terrific food
wine.

Paradyskloof Cabernet  13.5  £5–7
Sauvignon/Merlot 1997

Simonsig Pinotage 1998  16  £5–7
A raucous wine which has,
nevertheless, something to shout
about: tannins! A brilliant, exotic food
wine of style.

## ASDA WHITE

**Cape Chardonnay 1999, Asda** `15.5` −£3.50
Terrific richness of fruit and depth of flavour. Needs food, so fulsome is it.

**Cape Sauvignon Blanc 1999, Asda** `15.5` −£5.00
Deliciously rich and calm. Very classy, touch warm on the finish for the classicist, but I like it.

**First Vintage 2000** `13.5` −£5.00

**Van Loveren Blanc de Noirs 2000** `14` −£5.00
A delicious cherry/raspberry aperitif.

## BOOTHS WHITE

**Altus Sauvignon Blanc, Paarl 1999** `13` −£5.00
Odd ragged edge.

**Jordan Chardonnay 1998** `16.5` £7–10
Melon and lime yoghurt with a hint of walnut. An individual approach to the Chardonnay riddle and an original solution. Deliciously so.

**Landema Falls Colombard Chardonnay NV** `15` −£3.50
A chewy food wine. Tastes slightly baked.

**Springfield Estate 'Life from Stone' Sauvignon Blanc 1999** `16` £5–7
Very impressively minerally gooseberryish, grassy (rich and ripe, not tart and fresh) plus complex acids.

**Welmoed Sauvignon Blanc 1999** `14` −£5.00
Tight and grassy. Terrific with crustacea.

## BUDGENS WHITE

**Cape White NV, Budgens** `11` −£3.50

**Clear Mountain Chenin Blanc NV** `13.5` −£3.50
Will do justice to large fish and chip parties (as long as the wallies aren't too vinegary).

**Glen Eden Chardonnay 1998** `14` −£5.00
Good with an oriental take-away.

**Long Mountain Sauvignon Blanc 1999** `13` −£5.00
The fruit overwhelms the acids.

**Long Mountain Semillon Chardonnay 1999** `14.5` −£5.00
Has some character and charm. Ripe and forward but far from uncontrolled.

**Stowells of Chelsea Chenin Blanc NV** `13` −£5.00
Soapy and ripely rich. Needs food.

## CWS WHITE

**Cape Chenin Blanc, Oak Aged 1999, Co-op** `13` −£5.00

**Cape French Oak Chardonnay 1999, Co-op** `13` −£5.00

**Cape Indaba Chardonnay 1998** `13` −£5.00
Superstores only.

**Elephant Trail Colombard/Chardonnay 2000, Co-op** `14` −£3.50
Odd effect, but oddly appealing fruitwise. It is a little blatant, true, so it needs rich food – scallops perhaps with a creamy curry sauce (mild).

**Fairview Chardonnay 1998** `16.5` £5–7

Hints of woodsmoke, oak, yoghurt and fresh under-ripe melon. A classic new world Chardy in a rich textured cardie. Superstores only.

**First Release Chardonnay 2000**  13.5  −£5.00
Very ripe and obvious, but food will tame it – oriental food especially. Superstores only.

**French Quarter Semillon 1999, Co-op**  14.5  −£5.00
Delicious nutty riches. Lingering, warm, refreshing and energetic.

**Goiya Kgeisje Chardonnay Sauvignon Blanc 2000**  15  −£5.00
A lovely blend of soft fruit and crisp acids where ogen melon and pineapple/lemon freshness connect well.

**Long Mountain Semillon Chardonnay 1998**  14  −£5.00
Very dry finish. Needs fish.

**Oak Village Sauvignon Blanc 1999**  13  −£5.00
Odd almost-stalkiness and grassiness which doesn't quite ignite the taste buds. Superstores only.

**Spice Route Chenin Blanc 1998**  16  £7–10
Fat but far from out of condition or flabby. Has a lush peachy ripeness relieved by a lovely texture and nutty-edged acidity. Not at all stores.

**Stowells South African Chenin Blanc NV**  13  −£5.00
Soapy and ripely rich. Needs food.

**Waterside White Colombard Chardonnay 1999**  15.5  −£5.00
Bargain elegance and subtle richness here. Superstores only.

**Cape Country Chenin Blanc 2000**  14.5  −£5.00
Crisp and gooseberryish to open, then goes soft and ripe as it finishes. Dry and engagingly fruity.

**Cape Country Colombard 2000**  13.5  −£5.00
Extremely gung-ho fruity.

**Perdeberg Sauvignon Blanc 2000**  14  −£5.00
Very clean and engagingly fresh and charming.

**De Wetshof Estate 'Lesca' Chardonnay 1999**  16.5  £5–7
Great elegance and gently woody, creamy richness here – of lingering depth and style. The best Lesca for some years. A fine Cape Chardonnay of complexity and real worth.

**Franschoek Barrel Fermented Chenin Blanc 1998**  12  −£5.00
Bit odd. Touch crazy. Bit fantastical. Nor normal enough for me.

**Kumala Semillon Chardonnay 1999**  16  −£5.00
Bargain richness and stealth here. Has melony ripeness well balanced by fresh hard-fruit acids.

**Danie de Wet Chardonnay Surlie 1999**  15  −£5.00
Strikes a delicate balance between dryness and melony richness.

**Faircape Chenin Blanc** `15.5` `–£3.50`
**2000**
A thundering great bargain: apricot
edged, lemon touched, tightly knitted
texture.

**Fairview Chardonnay** `16.5` `£5–7`
**1998**
Has a burnt rubber aroma, lovely
creamy fruit with a hint of lemon and
ripe ogen melon, and a beautiful finish.

**Namaqua Classic Dry** `15` `£5–7`
**White NV (3 litre box)**
Delicious, crisp gooseberry and lemon
fruit. A real class act: refreshing, bold,
well tailored. Price band is for the 75cl
equivalent.

**Spice Route Abbotsdale** `16` `–£5.00`
**Colombard / Chenin**
**Blanc 1998**
Very subtle but vibrant and sensual in
its delicious fruity finish.

**Van Loveren Blanc de** `14` `–£5.00`
**Noirs 2000**
A delicious cherry / raspberry aperitif.

**Van Loveren Pinot Gris** `14` `–£5.00`
**1999**
Touch of peach to the very dry fruit.

**Van Loveren Semillon** `14` `–£5.00`
**1999**
Dry and fish friendly.

## ODDBINS WHITE

**Boschkloof Chardonnay** `13` `£5–7`
**Reserve 1997**

**Buitenverwachting** `16` `£7–10`
**Chardonnay, Constantia**
**1998**
Very lingering and ambitious.
Constraint by the fruit permits lovely
acidic intrusion. Delicate overall.

**Buitenverwachting Rhine** `15` `£5–7`
**Riesling, Constantia 1999**
Lovely honey and mineral fruit.
Wonderful fish wine.

**Buitenverwachting** `16` `£7–10`
**Sauvignon Blanc,**
**Constantia 1999**
A brilliant fish wine when the occasion
calls for elegance, grassiness and
perfect balance.

**Danie de Wet** `15` `–£5.00`
**Chardonnay sur Lie,**
**Robertson 2000**
One of Oddbins' bargain elegances.
Lovely demure melon / lemon fruit.

**Eikendal Chardonnay,** `14` `£7–10`
**Stellenbosch 1998**

**Fair Valley Bush Vine** `15.5` `–£5.00`
**Chenin Blanc, Coastal**
**Region 1999**

**Fairview Akkerbos** `16.5` `£7–10`
**Chardonnay, Paarl 1999**
Seems fat and buttery then goes
meltingly crisp and subtly lemony with
a hint of yoghurt. Lovely wine.

**Fairview Chardonnay** `16.5` `£5–7`
**1999**
The most elegant Chardonnay in the
Cape for the money. Beautiful balance
of elements and a lingering, yoghurty
finish.

**Fairview Cyril Back** `16` `£5–7`
**Semillon, Paarl 1998**
Hugely lingering yoghurt / raspberry /
melon / lime fruit. Quite delicious. The
delicacy of the impact is impressive
and very, very classy.

**Fairview Goats do Roam** `16` `–£5.00`
**Rosé 2000**
The best rosé under a fiver in the land.

**Fairview 'Oom Pagel'** 16.5 £5–7
**Semillon, Paarl 1999**
Utterly compelling fruit, rather
magical for 100% Semillon, a little
mysterious and richly engaging.

**Fairview Viogner, Paarl** 16 £7–10
**2000**
Tinged with peach and apricot and a
hint of pineapple plus lemony acids.
Terrific stuff. Fine Wine Stores only.

**Glen Carlou Chardonnay** 14 £7–10
**1999**
Fat, very fat. Waddles across the taste
buds.

**Glen Carlou Reserve** 12 £10–13
**Chardonnay 1997**

**Ken Forrester** 14 £5–7
**Scholtzenhof Chenin**
**Blanc, Stellenbosch 1998**

**Klein Constantia** 15.5 £7–10
**Chardonnay 1998**

**Klein Constantia Riesling** 13.5 –£5.00
**1998**

**Klein Constantia** 15.5 £5–7
**Sauvignon Blanc 1998**

**Longridge Bay View** 14 –£5.00
**Chardonnay, Western**
**Cape 1998**

**Longridge Chardonnay,** 13.5 £7–10
**Stellenbosch 1998**

**Radford Dale** 16 £7–10
**Chardonnay,**
**Stellenbosch 1999**
How to impress by stealth not wealth.

**Saxenburg Private** 16.5 £7–10
**Collection Chardonnay,**
**Stellenbosch 1998**
Has a croissant-edged richness of huge
charm. Lovely texture here.

**Scholtzenhof Petit** 15.5 –£5.00
**Chenin, Stellenbosch**
**1999**

**Slayley Chardonnay 1997** 15.5 £7–10
Fine Wine Stores only.

**Stellenzicht Sauvignon** 13.5 £5–7
**Blanc, Stellenbosch 1998**

**Stellenzicht Semillon** 15 £7–10
**Reserve, Stellenbosch**
**1998**

**Ten Fifty Six Blanc** 13.5 –£5.00
**Fume, Franschoek 1998**
Odd acids. Don't quite add up to the
fruit.

**Ten Fifty Six** 14 £5–7
**Chardonnay, Paarl 1998**
Lovely aroma and initial attack but
goes a bit walkabout on the finish.

**Vergelegen Reserve** 16.5 £7–10
**Chardonnay 1997**
Always one of the Cape's most elegant
Chardonnays statements. A magical
Meursault-like wine!!

**Von Ortloff Chardonnay** 16 £5–7
**1998**
Very thickly textured and smooth and
has an effortless richness to it.

## SAFEWAY WHITE

**Douglas Green** 15.5 –£5.00
**Sauvignon 2000**
Has a gentle elegance with a hint of
gooseberry fool.

**First Release Chardonnay** 13.5 –£5.00
**2000**
A dry but coy Chardonnay.

**First Release Chenin** 14 –£5.00
**Blanc 2000**
Fresh and full of charm.

**Sea of Serenity Dry** `14` `−£3.50`
**Muscat 2000**
Exactly what it says: serene, dry, muscat-edged fruit. A fine little aperitif.

**Vale of Peace Colombard** `14` `−£5.00`
**2000**
Charming, low key, but charming.

**Versus 1999 (1 litre)** `16` `−£5.00`
Very classy and collected. Lovely subtle fleshy fruit with incisive acids. Price bracket adjusted to the 75cl equivalent.

## SAINSBURY'S WHITE

**Call of the African Eagle** `17` `£5–7`
**Chardonnay 1999**
Beautifully natural and pure-seeming – as elegant as a nun's wimple. The fruit is quite remarkably refined and rich, complex, seamlessly stitched and elegant. 120 stores.

**Gioya Kgeisje** `14` `−£5.00`
**Chardonnay/Sauvignon 2000**
Very fruity! So fruity it begs for Thai/Chinese food. Most stores.

**Rhona Muscadel 1996** `16` `£5–7`
Wonderful textured syrupy richness of concentrated sweetness and ripeness. Pour it over ice cream or drink it with raspberries and cream. 70 stores.

**South African** `14` `−£5.00`
**Chardonnay NV, Sainsbury's**
Demure and rather restrained.

**South African Chenin** `15` `−£3.50`
**Blanc NV, Sainsbury's**
Very modern so it's a little flushed but it isn't embarrassing. Most stores.

**South African Chenin** `14.5` `−£3.50`
**Blanc NV, Sainsbury's (3 litre box)**
Not your big rich Chenin but a good dry mouthful of solid fruitiness which never tires or goes flabby. The price band reflects the equivalent price for a 75cl bottle.

**South African Colombard** `14` `−£5.00`
**NV, Sainsbury's**

**South African Medium** `13` `−£3.50`
**White NV, Sainsbury's**
Strictly for those seeking an alternative to Liebfraumilch. Most stores.

**South African Reserve** `15.5` `£5–7`
**Selection Chardonnay 1999, Sainsbury's**
Warm and very comfortable for the tongue to wear. Richly textured and thickly knitted. Most stores.

**Springfield Estate** `15.5` `£10–13`
**Methode Ancienne Chardonnay 1999**
Very warm and unabrasively forward but relents on the finish to provide some understated easy-going richness. 30 stores.

**Vergelegen Chardonnay** `16` `£5–7`
**1999**
Really lingers lushly. A finger-lickin' good Chardonnay but not, for all that richness, OTT or inelegant. It's just unconscionably gluggable. 100 selected stores.

**Vergelegen Chardonnay** `16.5` `£7–10`
**Reserve 1998**
Superb aplomb and buttery, gently smoky richness. A lush yet delicate wine of great class and concentrated style. 30 selected stores.

Vergelegen Reserve    17.5   £7–10
Sauvignon Blanc 1999
Outpoints Sancerre at the same price
by ten to one. It's subtly grassy, very
concentrated (melon and soft, spiced
gooseberry) and the finish is sublime.
30 stores.

Waterside White    15.5   –£5.00
Chardonnay Colombard
1999
Great blend of exuberance and
delicacy. Has rich melon fruit and
quiet acids well knitted in.

## SOMERFIELD WHITE

Bellingham Sauvignon    15.5   –£5.00
Blanc 1999

Bush Vines Semillon    14   –£5.00
1999, Somerfield
Very rich and well textured. Great
with robust food.

Kumala Sauvignon    15.5   –£5.00
Blanc/Colombard 1999
An impressive blend of grapes
providing depth and deftness. Well
tailored, perfectly under-ripe and fresh-
edged yet fruity. Limited distribution.

Millennium Early Release   14   –£3.50
Chenin Blanc 2000
Very crisp and refreshing.

South African    14   –£5.00
Chardonnay 1999,
Somerfield
Warm and rich and very satisfyingly
packed with flavour.

South African Colombard   14.5   –£5.00
1999, Somerfield
Tasty undertone of ripe melon
harnessed to neat acids. Excellent fish
wine.

## SPAR WHITE

Chiwara Colombard/    12.5   –£5.00
Sauvignon 1998, Spar

South African Classic    12   £5–7
Chardonnay 1998, Spar
Classic? In what way? Rather ragged
fruit which fades fast.

## TESCO WHITE

African Legend    14   –£5.00
Colombard 1999
Slightly spicy approach, good with
oriental food.

Arniston Bay Chenin/    13   –£5.00
Chardonnay 1999
Touch gooey on the finish – oddly
defined.

Arniston Bay Rosé 2000   13   –£5.00
Dry but straining at the cherries to be
riper.

Boschendal Grande    13.5   £5–7
Cuvee Sauvignon Blanc
1998

Cape Chenin Blanc NV,    15   –£3.50
Tesco
Brilliant nutty and ripe melon and
gooseberry fruit. Has a delicious
creamy finish. Superb for drinks parties
and for first courses at nose-in-the-air
dinner parties.

Fairview Chardonnay    16.5   £5–7
1998
Hints of woodsmoke, oak, yoghurt
and fresh under-ripe melon. A classic
new world Chardy in a rich textured
cardie.

Firefinch Sauvignon    16   –£5.00
Blanc 1999
Interesting herbaceous richness. Very

215

dry and slightly intimidating with its compressed, stalky, under-ripe gooseberry fruit. But great with fish, smoked or poached, and superb with shellfish. Amazing price for such class. 100 selected stores only.

**Goiya Kgeisje 2000**  `15`  `–£5.00`
A lovely blend of soft fruit and crisp acids where ogen melon and pineapple/lemon freshness connect well.

**Kumala Colombard/**  `14.5`  `–£5.00`
**Chardonnay 1999**
Hint of agreeable fatness to the ripe melon gives it an easy drinking feel of no pretension but to refresh the palate for more.

**Oak Village Sauvignon**  `13`  `–£5.00`
**Blanc 1999**
Odd almost-stalkiness and grassiness which doesn't quite ignite the taste buds.

**Ryland's Grove Barrel**  `16`  `–£5.00`
**Fermented Chenin Blanc**
**1999**
One of the best value whites on Tesco's shelves: rich, dry, balanced, peachy/melony/nutty and with a generous finish. At most stores.

**Rylands Grove Dry**  `13.5`  `–£5.00`
**Muscat 1999**
Most stores.

**Rylands Grove**  `14.5`  `–£5.00`
**Sauvignon Blanc 2000**
Good fresh edge of pressed gooseberries with an undertone of lemon. Pet little performer.

**South African**  `14`  `–£5.00`
**Chardonnay/Colombard**
**NV, Tesco**
Charmingly bumptious and full of

itself (which is ripe melon with a hint of woodsmoke).

**South African Medium**  `13`  `–£3.50`
**Sweet White NV, Tesco**
Anyone who likes Liebfraumilch can cheerfully spend less on this.

**South African Reserve**  `13.5`  `–£5.00`
**Chardonnay 1999, Tesco**
Good up front but falls away a touch on the finish, then gathers momentum and just about sneaks home. I must say I find the reserve designation hyperbole.

**South African White,**  `14`  `–£3.50`
**Tesco**

**Spice Route Long Walk**  `16`  `£5–7`
**Sauvignon Blanc 1998**
Hint of earthy minerals and concentrated gooseberries. Excellent structure and depth.

**Third Millennium Chenin**  `13`  `–£5.00`
**Chardonnay 1999**
Blue bottle though the fruit is a little lacking in sting.

**Van Loveren Blanc de**  `14`  `–£3.50`
**Noir Red Muscadel Rosé**
**2000**
A very delicate aperitif showing ripe cherries in spouting form.

## THRESHER WHITE

**African Legend**  `13`  `£5–7`
**Sauvignon Blanc 1998**
Touch musty. Bottoms Up only.

**Capells Court**  `14`  `£5–7`
**Chardonnay 1998**
Needs Thai food, I fancy. The creamy richness plus the energy of the acids are made for grilled flying fish on a

bed of Ojumpula nettles. Wine Rack
and Bottoms Up only.

| Carisbrook Chenin/ Chardonnay 1999 | 14 | −£5.00 |
|---|---|---|

| Hartenberg 'Occasional' Auxerrois 1997 | 16 | £5–7 |
|---|---|---|

Tremendous flavour and style here. A
quirkily rich, Chardonnay-style wine
of complexity and real lengthy flavour.
A thought-provokingly fruity wine.
Not at Thresher Wine Shops.

| Hartenberg 'Occasional' Bush Vine Chenin Blanc 1997 | 15.5 | £5–7 |
|---|---|---|

| Hartenberg 'Occasional' Pinot Blanc 1997 | 15 | £5–7 |
|---|---|---|

| Hartenberg Weisser Riesling,Stellenbosch 1997 | 13 | £5–7 |
|---|---|---|

| Oak Village Chardonnay 1999 | 13.5 | −£5.00 |
|---|---|---|

Chewy finish which dissipates the hard
work of the fruit.

| Villiera Chenin Blanc 1997 | 15 | −£5.00 |
|---|---|---|

## UNWINS WHITE

| Bellingham Chardonnay 1999 | 15 | £5–7 |
|---|---|---|

Very forward, creamy, smoky and
hugely food friendly.

| Cape Chardonnay 1999 | 13 | −£5.00 |
|---|---|---|

Too adolescent, obvious and unsubtle
for me. Like the juice from a fruit
salad.

| Cape White 1999 | 13.5 | −£5.00 |
|---|---|---|

| Cathedral Cellar Chardonnay 1997 | 15.5 | £7–10 |
|---|---|---|

Perfectly delicious and unpretentious.
Has superb unfussy melony fruit.

| Coastline Chenin Blanc 2000 | 13.5 | −£5.00 |
|---|---|---|

| Fairview Chardonnay 1999 | 16.5 | £5–7 |
|---|---|---|

The most elegant Chardonnay in the
Cape for the money. Beautiful balance
of elements and a lingering, yoghurty
finish.

| Jordan Barrel Fermented Chenin Blanc, Stellenbosch 1999 | 16.5 | £5–7 |
|---|---|---|

Bargain apricot richness and
plumpness of expression. Rarely does
Chenin perform such tricks.

| Jordan Chardonnay, Stellenbosch 1998 | 16.5 | £7–10 |
|---|---|---|

Very complex, modern, creamy and
rich – but subtle and polished with it.
Beautiful texture and class here.

| L'Avenir Chenin Blanc 1998 | 15.5 | £5–7 |
|---|---|---|

Impish, decisive, richly chiming, fluted
fruit.

| Vergelegen Chardonnay 1998 | 16 | £5–7 |
|---|---|---|

Has a hard edge but a soft heart. The
effect is glorious, entertaining, rich,
stylish, deep, delicious.

## VICTORIA WINE WHITE

| African Legend Sauvignon Blanc 1998 | 13 | £5–7 |
|---|---|---|

Touch musty.

| Capells Court Chardonnay 1998 | 16 | £5–7 |
|---|---|---|

Hint of spicy melon on the finish
rounds off a rousing performance from
a gorgeously textured and tightly

woven specimen of top notch quaffing.

**Oak Village Chardonnay** 13.5 −£5.00
**1999**
Chewy finish which dissipates the hard work of the fruit.

## WAITROSE WHITE

**Culemborg Cape Dry** 14 −£3.50
**White 1999**
Bargain party plonk.

**Culemborg Unwooded** 15 −£5.00
**Chardonnay, Western**
**Cape 1999**
Great value here, especially if fish is on your plate.

**Fairview Barrel** 16 −£5.00
**Fermented Chenin Blanc**
**1999**
Superb style and acidity meet Cape richness and fruity depth.

**Spice Route Abbotsdale** 15 £7–10
**Colombard/Chenin**
**Blanc 1999**
Rich and very fit for food.

**Springfield Sauvignon** 15.5 £5–7
**Blanc Special Cuvee 1999**

**Steenberg Sauvignon** 16 £7–10
**Blanc 1999**
Either a Sauvignon lover's nightmare or a complex wet dream come true. The wine has celery, gooseberry, hashish and buttercup overtones and it's crisp to finish.

**Thelema Mountain** 17 £10–13
**Vineyard Sauvignon**
**Blanc 1999**
Perfect herbaceous undertone to beautifully multi-layered fruit of massive charm. Only from Waitrose Direct.

**Warwick Estate** 17.5 £5–7
**Chardonnay,**
**Stellenbosch 1999**
The best value Chardonnay in the world. Lovely creamy woodiness, alert acids underpinning good melon/ vegetal fruit and it'll get more like Montrachet as it ages over the next five years.

## WINE CELLAR WHITE

**Jordan Chardonnay 1998** 16.5 £7–10
Melon and lime yoghurt with a hint of walnut. An individual approach to the Chardonnay riddle and an original solution. Deliciously so.

# SOUTH AMERICA

Please see Chile and Argentina for the two partners in this sort of wine which, though not common, does offer a few examples created by blending wines from each of these Andean neighbours.

| TESCO RED | | | TESCO WHITE | | |
|---|---|---|---|---|---|
| Two Tribes Red | 13.5 | −£5.00 | Two Tribes White | 13.5 | −£5.00 |

# SPAIN

Spain is suffering from similar social upheavals as Italy. In 1999 a wine producer in the Toro region told me that when he was a boy the average per capita wine consumption was nearly seventy litres a year and now it was less than thirty. This is why so many UK wine pros are touring the vineyards and snapping up bargains. Spain must export to survive as a meaningful world-class exporter and producer. It is easily the most creatively dynamic of the European superpowers (and not just in football and architecture); it is in tremendous form as a creator of complex, fascinating red and white wines. Its full potential in these respects is far away from being realised. Even greater days, and affordable wines, are ahead.

## ASDA RED

| | | |
|---|---|---|
| Baron de Ley Reserva Rioja 1994 | 13 | £5–7 |
| Conde de Navasques 1997 | 15.5 | –£5.00 |
| Don Darias Tinto NV | 15.5 | –£3.50 |

Off to the Greek taverna? Going to a dinner party in Hampstead? Bring along the Don – he's getting soft and fruity with age and his tannic side is well developed.

| | | |
|---|---|---|
| Fuentespina Crianza 1996 | 15.5 | £7–10 |
| Mont Marcal Crianza 1997 | 14 | –£5.00 |

Very cheering fruit. Puts a smile on your face.

| | | |
|---|---|---|
| Oaked Tempranillo 1998, Asda | 16 | –£5.00 |

Superb value here. Really engaging tannins, expensively furnished and upholstered, and the fruit is warm, ripe, aromatic and deliciously soft.

| | | |
|---|---|---|
| Rioja NV, Asda | 14.5 | –£5.00 |
| Spanish Oaked Red NV, Asda | 13 | –£3.50 |
| Valdepeñas Crianza 1995 | 15.5 | –£5.00 |
| Viña Albali Gran Reserva 1991 | 16 | £5–7 |

Terrific grilled meat wine – anything from boar to Toulouse sausage. It's ripe, vanilla-tinged, dry yet full, nicely textured, warmly tannin-undertoned and very friendly. Better than many Riojas.

## BOOTHS RED

| | | |
|---|---|---|
| Amant Tinto de Toro 1999 | 15.5 | –£5.00 |

Delicious savoury fruit, plump texture, and a wonderful smooth finish.

Casa de la Viña
Valdepeñas 1999
14.5 −£5.00
A juicy creamy wine – has tannins but
the fruit rules.

Casa Morena, Valdepeñas 14 −£3.50
NV

Castillo de Almansa 15.5 −£5.00
Reserva Bodegas
Piqueras 1994
Perfect weight and maturity of very
gently burned plum fruit with a very
subtle touch of spice.

Mas Collet Capcanes 16.5 £5−7
Tarragona 1998
Delicious personality where ripe
tannins and rich fruit and great acids
combine rather thrillingly.

Mas Donis Capcanes 16 −£5.00
Taragona 1999
Huge, mouthfilling, soft (yet gently
dry and rich), beautifully textured and
finishes with style and wit. Very
smooth overall.

Ochoa Tempranillo 15 −£5.00
Garnacha 1999
Lovely tobacco-edged fruit with a
warm undertone of baked bread.

Rioja Crianza Amezola 12 £7−10
1996
Super-ripe and raisiny. Only food can
give it stature.

Scraping the Barrel 14.5 −£3.50
Tempranillo, Utiel-
Requena NV

Simply Spanish Soft Red 9 −£2.50
NV
Quite revolting.

Viña Alarba, Calatayud 15.5 −£3.50
1998

Viña Albali Gran Reserva 15 £5−7
1993
Very ripe, raisiny and deep and a great
red for game dishes.

## BUDGENS RED

Diego de Almagro 15 −£5.00
Valdepeñas 1996
Wonderful pasta and pizza red: sunny,
ripe, thick and generous.

Palacio de la Vega 15.5 −£5.00
Cabernet Sauvignon/
Tempranillo 1996

Palacio de la Vega 15.5 £5−7
Crianza 1997
Getting ripe but perfect for that
Christmas fowl, gravy sodden and
spicily stuffed (just like the wine).

Viña Albali Gran Reserva 15 £5−7
1993
Very ripe, raisiny and deep and a great
red for game dishes.

## CWS RED

Berberana Dragon 15 −£5.00
Tempranillo 1998
Brilliant food wine with its plummy
directness and ascendant tannins.

Berberana Rioja Reserva 12 £7−10
1995
Very juicy and creamy.

Berberana Rioja Viura 13.5 −£5.00
1997
A little on the boring side for four fifty.
Superstores only.

Chestnut Gully 15.5 −£5.00
Monastrell-Merlot 1998

Rioja Tinto, Viña Gala  `13.5`  `−£5.00`
NV, Co-op
A juicy red for Indian non-delicacies.

Tempranillo Oak Aged  `13`  `−£3.50`
NV, Co-op

Tierra Sana Organic  `17`  `−£5.00`
Wine 1999, Co-op
A thrilling organic, unfiltered wine of
huge substance and thrillingly deep
and all-enveloping fruit which is
absurdly inexpensive. Lovely savoury
bouquet, big blackcurrant and cherry
fruit and a lushly tannic finish. A real
beaut of a bargain.

Torres Gran Sangre de  `16`  `£5−7`
Toro Reserva 1996
Delicious, dry, classic, elegant (yet
robust), complex as it dies out in the
throat, and a lot of richness and warm
character. Superstores only.

## KWIK SAVE RED

Bodegas Castano  `16.5`  `−£5.00`
Monastrell Merlot 1999
Totally convincing! Utterly
extraordinary quality tannins and
velvet and leather fruit.

d'Avalos Tempranillo  `15`  `−£3.50`
1997

Don Darias Red NV  `15.5`  `−£5.00`
Off to the Greek taverna? Going to a
dinner party in Hampstead? Bring
along the Don – he's getting soft and
fruity with age and his tannic side is
well developed.

Flamenco Red NV  `11`  `−£3.50`

Los Molinos  `15.5`  `−£3.50`
Tempranillo,
Valdepeñas/Oak Aged
1993

Modernista Tempranillo  `16`  `−£3.50`
1997
Brilliant summer bargain for the
barbecue! Has rich fluid fruit,
developed and deep, and terrific
tannins. Modern indeed!

Pergola Tempranillo  `15`  `−£5.00`
1999, Somerfield
Gorgeous texture and ripeness. Surges
with flavour and interesting nuances.

Rioja Crianza 1997,  `14`  `−£5.00`
Somerfield
Juicy yet earthy. Great with a chicken
stew with choriza.

Teja Tempranillo  `14.5`  `−£3.50`
Cabernet 1997

## M&S RED

Campo Ran 1999  `14`  `−£5.00`
A great party wine. Give 'em
something rich and ripe to talk
about.

Las Falleras 1999  `14`  `−£3.50`
A bargain for large parties of pasta
eaters. Dry, earthy but a little
pleasingly plump, and properly
balanced.

Marisa 1999  `16`  `−£5.00`
Baked, savoury fruit with a tobacco
undertone. Lovely warmth to the
texture. Terrific food wine.

Rioja Roseral 1996  `13.5`  `£5−7`
Dry yet fruitily jammy. Not a typical
rioja (a good thing).

Sotelo 1996  `15.5`  `£5−7`
Delicious earthy/mineral richness and
ripeness here. A wine for candlelight
and soft music.

## MAJESTIC RED

**Artadi Viñas de Gain** 15 £7–10
**Rioja 1997**
A food wine because it has a quirky
imbalance in its personality where a
certain sourness predominates. With
food however, it would be impressive.

**Arva Vitis Tempranillo** 15.5 –£5.00
**1998**
Strictly for tannin lovers or those
needing to summon up the blood.

**Berberana Dragon** 15 –£5.00
**Tempranillo 1998**
Brilliant food wine with its plummy
directness and ascendant tannins.

**Costers del Gravet Celler** 17 £7–10
**de Capcanes 1998**
Huge yet delicate, expansive yet lithe,
effortless yet eager-to-delight. A very
concentrated, compelling amalgam of
multi-layered fruit, fine tannins and
superb acids which all work
dynamically to produce a rousing,
tenacious finish.

**Finca Lasendal, Celler de** 15.5 –£5.00
**Capcanes 1999**
Stewed fruitiness gives way to dry,
tannin richness on the finish.

**'G' Dehesa Gago Telmo** 16 £5–7
**Rodriguez 1998**
The bullish wit of the label does
nothing to prepare you for the surprise
of the earthy riches in the bottle.
Rustic? Only a touch. Knitted edges
yet power.

**Marques de Grinon Rioja** 15 £5–7
**1997**

**Marques de Murietta** 14 £7–10
**Rioja Reserva 1995**

**Mas Collet Celler de** 16.5 £5–7
**Capcanes 1998**
Stunning heaviness of effect, like
Wagner. Wonderful richness and
glamorous tannins so well-knitted that
the seams are invisible. A moving,
soulful experience.

**Muga Rioja Reserva 1995** 13 £7–10
Bit juicy for ten quid.

**Ochoa Tempranillo** 15 –£5.00
**Garnache Navarra 1998**

**Viña Armantes Garnacha** 15 –£5.00
**1999**
Sweet baked edge of plummy fruit is a
perfect pasta accompaniment.

**Viña El Salado** 15 –£5.00
**Extremadura 1998**

## MORRISONS RED

**Conforrales Tinto** 15 –£3.50
**Cencibel 1998**
Bargain acidity. Lush tannins and a dry
charcoal edge.

**De Muller Pinot Noir** 13 £7–10
**1996**
Not typical Pinot, very rich and sticky.

**Gran Feudo Navarra** 13 –£5.00
**Crianza 1997**
Very juicy and bruised fruity.

**'M' Red Rioja NV** 13 –£5.00
Sweet and sour sauce for Indian food.

**Rio Rojo Tinto NV** 14 –£3.50

**Stowells Tempranillo NV** 12.5 –£3.50
**(3 litre box)**
Price bracket reflects 75cl equivalent.

**Torres Sangre de Toro** 14 £5–7
**1998**
Ripe yet dry.

Vega del Rio Reserve
Rioja 1994
`13` `£7–10`
Very mature, too pricey.

Viña Albali Gran Reserva
1991
`16` `£5–7`
Vanillary, spicy, nicely warmly
textured and softly, savourily tannic.
Has an almost yoghurt touch on the
finish.

Viña Albali Tempranillo
1999
`15.5` `–£3.50`
Slightly creamy, very subtly vanillary
fruit with assertive tannins. Excellent
roast meat / veg / casserole wine.
Terrific price.

## ODDBINS RED

Artadi Orobio
Tempranillo, Rioja 1999
`16` `£5–7`
One of the more gripping riojas.
Distinguished and deliciously tannic.

Bodegas Palacio Glorioso
Crianza Rioja 1997
`14.5` `£5–7`
Very smooth on the finish.

Cosme Palacio y
Hermanos, Rioja 1997
`16` `£5–7`
Always one of the more elegantly
compact Riojas.

Costers del Gravet Red,
Capcanes 1998
`17.5` `£7–10`
Quite stunning ripeness and tannic
tenacity of very complex richness
offering a variety of delightful
sensations from its medley of fruit to
its final bequest of lingering herbiness.

Dardell Negre, Gandesa
1999
`15.5` `–£5.00`
Gorgeous rich tannins, deep burned
fruit and a very generous finish.

La Cata Tempranillo, La
Mancha 1998
`14` `–£5.00`

La Vicalanda de Viña
Pomal Reserva, Rioja
1995
`13` `£10–13`

Olivares Dulce
Monastrell 1996
`16` `£13–20`
'Almost tastes like a dish in itself,' said
Karen at Oddbins, and she's right. This
is a stickily sweet red which will go
with fruit cake, a hangover, a hospital
cure for a blue mood, and it'll even
waken the dead palate. It is never
monodimensional and simply gooey –
rather, it's textured, multi-layered and
teasing. Great with blue cheese.

Piedemonte Merlot/
Cabernet Sauvignon,
Navarra 1998
`15` `–£5.00`

Raimat Tempranillo,
Costers del Segre 1997
`16.5` `£7–10`
Ripe, stylishly smooth and rounded,
delicious plum / strawberry / blackberry
undertones and a gorgeous textured
finish.

Taja Gran Reserva,
Jumilla 1994
`16` `£7–10`
Very juicy and ripe but with lovely
lingering tannins. Huge presence on
the taste buds. Great food wine.

Taja Jumilla 1999
`16` `–£5.00`
Bargain fruit here – deep, herby, rich,
strikingly dry and tannic – and very
lingering richness.

## SAFEWAY RED

Ceremonia, Utiel
Requena 1996
`16.5` `£7–10`
Stunning class here. Loads of woody
flavours, hedgerow and orchard fruits

and superb tannins. It's a very potent red. 48 stores.

**Cruz de Piedra Garnacha** `14` `−£5.00`
**Calatayud 1999**
A superb wine for all Indian meat and fish dishes. It's slightly sweet and very deeply textured.

**Navasques Navarra 1999** `14` `−£5.00`
Sweet and dry. The usual suspects can be rounded up to accompany it.

**Valdepeñas Reserva Aged** `15` `−£5.00`
**in Oak 1995, Safeway**
Very creamy, woody fruit which suits highly spiced food.

## SAINSBURY'S RED

**Alteza 600 Old Vines** `16` `−£5.00`
**Garnacha NV**
Burnt leaves and ripe plums, dry tannins, vivid acidity and fruit balance. Superb for food or mood. Selected stores.

**Alteza 750 Tempranillo** `16` `−£5.00`
**NV**
Why drink expensive Rioja when there is this compelling reason to spend so much less? Gorgeously rich fruit which stays firm and dry even as it strikes with such vivacity. Most stores.

**Alteza 775 Tempranillo** `16` `−£5.00`
**Cabernet Sauvignon NV**
The juicy style of Cabernet, vivacious and deep, but it has solid tannins to give it serious presence in the mouth. Most stores.

**Classic Selection Rioja** `12` `£7–10`
**Reserva 1996, Sainsbury's**
Too old and raisiny for me. Most stores.

**Dama de Toro 1999** `16.5` `−£5.00`

Stunning tenacity to the fruit – it won't leave hold of the molars. Thus, you feel your soul is lifted. Most stores.

**Enate Cabernet Merlot** `16.5` `£5–7`
**1998**
Sweet cherries and plums (gently warmed through) on the finish – and they linger. But the overture is beautifully savoury and ripe – and stylishly smooth and finely textured. Not at all stores.

**Jumilla NV, Sainsbury's** `15.5` `−£5.00`

**Marques de Vitoria Rioja** `13.5` `£7–10`
**Crianza 1995 (organic)**
Very juicy. Great with Indian food. Selected stores.

**Navarra NV, Sainsbury's** `16` `−£5.00`
Superb bargain. Lovely tobacco-edged fruit, classy and rich, with loads of freshness and depth behind it. Terrific quaffing wine.

**Navarra Tempranillo/** `16` `−£5.00`
**Cabernet Sauvignon**
**Crianza 1995, Sainsbury's**
Wonderful mature fruit here: tobaccoey, ripe, rich, deep, woody, balanced and very eager to please. Loads of class.

**Old Vines Garnacha,** `15.5` `−£5.00`
**Navarra NV**

**Stowells of Chelsea** `13` `−£3.50`
**Tempranillo NV (3 litre box)**
Has a hint of unshaven stubble still left on the cheeks of the fruit and it tickles as it quits the throat. Very dry. The price band reflects the equivalent price for a 75cl bottle.

**Torres Gran Sangre de** `16` `£5–7`
**Toro 1996**

The fruit has a lovely coating of tannins which restrains its friskiness. A jammy wine of paradoxically dry, serious, almost glumly joyous finish. Delicious, compelling, hugely friendly.

**Valencia Oak Aged NV,** `13.5` `−£5.00`
**Sainsbury's**

**Viña Albali Gran Reserva** `15` `£5–7`
**1993**
Vanillary and super-ripe, dry and tenacious, it excels with robust foods. Most stores.

**Viña Ardanza Rioja** `13.5` `£10–13`
**Reserva 1994**
Expensive, raisiny, very ripe, very old-fashioned, very expensive. Selected stores.

## SOMERFIELD RED

**Bodegas Castano** `16.5` `−£5.00`
**Monastrell Merlot 1999**
Totally convincing! Utterly extraordinary quality tannins and velvet and leather fruit.

**Bright Brothers Old** `14` `−£5.00`
**Vines Navarra Garnacha**
**1998**
Very ripe and all-embracing. Has a touch of peach and strawberry yoghurt on the finish.

**Don Darias Red NV** `15.5` `−£5.00`
Off to the Greek taverna? Going to a dinner party in Hampstead? Bring along the Don – he's getting soft and fruity with age and his tannic side is well developed.

**Pergola Tempranillo** `15` `−£5.00`
**1999, Somerfield**
Gorgeous texture and ripeness. Surges with flavour and interesting nuances.

**Rioja Crianza 1997,** `14` `−£5.00`
**Somerfield**
Juicy yet earthy. Great with a chicken stew with choriza.

**Sierra Alta Cabernet** `16` `−£5.00`
**Sauvignon 1998**
Terrific! Lovely rich ripe cherry/ blackcurrant fruit. Great texture and warmth of finish. Terrifically soft and quaffable.

**Valencia Red NV,** `14` `−£3.50`
**Somerfield**
Brilliantly thick and chewy fruit, rich and clinging. Even dares to fling tannins at you.

## SPAR RED

**Perfect for Parties Red** `10` `−£3.50`
**NV, Spar (1 litre)**
Willy Hague's wine (his party will love it): insignificant, not hair-raising, squeaky voiced and pretending to something it isn't. Price band is for the 75cl equivalent.

**Valencia Soft Red NV,** `14` `−£3.50`
**Spar**
Good plummy fruit, soft texture, alert tannins. A pleasant mouthful.

## TESCO RED

**Campillo Gran Reserva** `10` `£13–20`
**Rioja 1989**
Absurd price, which only a madman would pay. Yes, the wine's very mature and ripely slurpable but it does not possess the wit to demand fifteen pounds. To think you can buy five bottles of Tesco's Reka Valley Pinot Noir for the same money, and receive a much more thrilling mouthful, only

makes my point with greater emphasis.

**Campillo Reserva Rioja 1995**  `13`  `£10–13`
Immensely pleasurable to drink, but not to splash out eleven quid on.

**Carmesi Garnacha/ Tempranillo Calatayud 1998**  `16`  `−£5.00`
Superb richness of the earthy variety. Great gobbets of blackcurrant and plum. 100 selected stores.

**Don Darias NV**  `15.5`  `−£5.00`
Off to the Greek taverna? Going to a dinner party in Hampstead? Bring along the Don – he's getting soft and fruity with age and his tannic side is well developed.

**Espiral Moristel Tempranillo/Cabernet Sauvignon 1998**  `16`  `−£5.00`
It's the blackcurrant jam richness which startles – but it's dry and herby. Tannins and tenacity, style and utter drinkability – a lovely wine.

**Huge Juicy Red, Tesco**  `13.5`  `−£5.00`
Doesn't quite live up to its billing since it is medium sized rather than huge, but it is juicy. Best drunk with curries where its sweetness is best appreciated.

**Marques de Chive Reserva 1994, Tesco**  `14.5`  `−£5.00`

**Marques de Chive Tempranillo NV, Tesco**  `15`  `−£3.50`
The tannins give the coconut-edged fruit some real backbone. An excellent food wine. Great with anything from fish stew to chicken casserole.

**Marques de Grinon Rioja 1997**  `15`  `−£5.00`

**Muruve Crianza 1996**  `15.5`  `£5–7`

**Orobio Tempranillo Rioja 1998**  `13`  `£5–7`

**Piedmonte Merlot Tempranillo 1998**  `14`  `−£5.00`

**Priorat l'Agnet 1998**  `14`  `£5–7`
Top 85 stores.

**Senorio de los Llanos Valdepeñas Gran Reserva 1994**  `14`  `−£5.00`
Rioja taste-alike with the woody and vanillary fruit being so forward. This kind of attack I can only find drinkable with robust food, at which encounter the wine comes into its own.

**Senorio de los Llanos Valdepeñas Reserva 1996**  `14`  `−£5.00`
Nicely mature and ripe but the tannins ensure it stays on track. So much better value than so many Riojas.

**Viña Azbache Rioja 1998**  `15.5`  `−£5.00`
Terrific gentle fruit with loads of stylish tannins and a complex layered finish.

**Viña Mara Gran Reserva Rioja 1990, Tesco**  `13.5`  `£7–10`
Very jammy and creamy for a tenner.

**Viña Mara Rioja Alavesa 1998, Tesco**  `16`  `£5–7`
A simply terrific Rioja. It just bounces with ripe, plump, dark fruit with lovely attendant tannins of savoury richness.

**Viña Mara Rioja Reserva 1995, Tesco**  `15`  `£7–10`
Very dry on the finish. Almost austerely so. At most stores.

**Viña Mara Rioja, Tesco**  `14`  `−£5.00`

## SPANISH RED

Viña Montana `16` `−£5.00`
Monastrell/Merlot 1998
Superb texture here, classy, ripe and all-enveloping and the soft tannins are yielding up meaty undertones.

## THRESHER RED

Abadia Retuerta Rivola, `16.5` `£5–7`
Duero 1996
One of the smartest red wines in Spain. Real elongated fruit, elegant reach, great balance of elements. Dry, delicious, decisive. Wine Rack only.

Alvaro Palacios Finca `18` `£20+`
Dofi Priorat 1996
£60! Sixty quid!? Yes, but it may well be one of the most nigh-perfect red wines in Spain. It is hugely elegant and forceful. The tannins are like gold dust and the finish is sublime. A truly exciting world-class wine, the unique product of an obsessed individual. Wine Rack and Bottoms Up only.

Alvaro Palacios 'Les `13.5` `£13–20`
Terrasses' DO Priorat
1997
Struggles to be good value and fails, but the tannins are outstanding – like biceps on a supermodel. Wine Rack and Bottoms Up only.

Baron de Ley Rioja `13` `£7–10`
Reserva 1996
Begins well, then gets lost. Eight quid? Oh, come on.

Casa Rural Tinto NV `14.5` `−£3.50`
Rural!? Oh yes. Rusticity vinified . . . but great with bouncy dishes.

Castillo Ygay Rioja Gran `10` `£13–20`
Reserva 1989
So juicy the molars wince. Bottoms Up only.

Chivite Reserva, Gran `13.5` `£5–7`
Feudo, Navarra 1995
Juicy with jaded tannins.

Conde de Valdemar Rioja `13.5` `£5–7`
Crianza 1997
Needs food. It's very juicy and the tannins are quite raw.

Conde de Valdemar Rioja `14` `£7–10`
Reserva 1995
Getting old and juicy as the tannins slip away.

Contino Rioja Reserva `15` `£20+`
1995
Very expensive but with such sveltely textured and finely wrought tannins and fruit that it is of great quality. It has the feel of luxury cashmere. And it costs. Bottoms Up only.

Cune Reserva 1995 `13.5` `£7–10`
Very odd woody edge to it. Nakedly arboreal. Needs food to explode into life. Bottoms Up only.

Dominio di Montalvo `13` `£5–7`
Rioja 1998
I find it a touch sour as it sprints down the throat. Not as open as rioja could, or perhaps ought to, be.

El Meson Rioja NV `15` `£5–7`
Very juicy but has a finish with a hint of cigarillo. Needs food.

Finca Valpiedra Rioja `12` `£13–20`
1995
A seriously drinkable £5 wine, but at £19 it takes your breath and too much of your money away. Wine Rack and Bottoms Up only.

Jumilla Senorio de Robles `16` `−£3.50`
1998
A bargain wine for summer barbecues as well as winter firesides. It's dry,

plummy, soft, characterful and hugely quaffable – and it'll go with loads of foods. Not at Wine Rack or Bottoms Up.

**Marques de Aragon Garnacha 1998**  15  −£5.00
A marvellous curry wine: sweet/dry, plummy, rich, full of deep, delicious riches.

**Marques de Grinon Rioja 1998**  15.5  £5–7
As usual, the Marques continues to make benchmark Rioja at a sane price. A dry, serious, rich, elegant wine. Wine Rack and Bottoms Up only.

**Marques de Grinon Rioja Reserva 1996**  14  £7–10
For three pounds less, the non-reserva is a better wine (though less unashamedly tannic). Wine Rack and Bottoms Up only.

**Marques de Grinon Valdepusa Cabernet Sauvignon 1997**  16.5  £7–10
Stunning development as it courses its way over the tongue. Complex, plump, soft, polished, dry yet full of charms. Wine Rack and Bottoms Up only.

**Marques de Grinon Valdepusa Syrah 1997**  17  £10–13
Makes many an Aussie construct via Shiraz seem junior league. A wonderfully exuberant, spiky wine which is seriously multi-faceted. Wine Rack and Bottoms Up only.

**Marques de Murrieta Rioja Reserva Especial 1995**  13  £13–20
Too brutal to rate any more at £15. Bottoms Up only.

**Marques de Riscal Reserva 1996**  14  £7–10
Claret with a touch of the sun and spice.

**Navajas Rioja Crianza 1997**  13.5  £5–7
Touch thin. For Navajas, this is most odd.

**Ochoa Gran Reserva, Navarra 1992**  14  £10–13
A lot of money, almost a lot of wine. Bottoms Up only.

**Raimat Cabernet Sauvignon 1996**  15  £7–10
Dry, vegetal edge, savoury richness to the fruit, decent, textured tightness of expression. Sounds grim? Gorgeous – with food. Wine Rack and Bottoms Up only.

**Raimat Merlot 1996**  15.5  £7–10
Develops on the taste buds as a fine wine has to, slowly evolving layers of texture, fruit and rich interest. Wine Rack and Bottoms Up only.

**Remonte Cabernet Sauvignon 1996**  15.5  −£5.00
Combines a dry, vegetal side with a plummy ripe dimension. Gushes with flavour and urgency but still manages to keep respectably Cabernet.

**Torres Gran Coronas 1996**  17  £7–10
It combines the frisky tannins of a Haut-Medoc, the terracotta tension of a Chianti, the pulse of a Cornas and the richness, sunnyness and depth of a sub-Pyreneean Cabernet. Perfect age to catch its boldness yet finesse. Wine Rack and Bottoms Up stores only.

**Torres Gran Sangre de Toro 1996**  16  £5–7

The fruit has a lovely coating of tannins which restrains its friskiness. A jammy wine of paradoxically dry, serious, almost glumly joyous finish. Delicious, compelling, hugely friendly. Wine Rack and Bottoms Up stores only.

**Viña Real Gran Reserva 1988**    `13`  `£13–20`
Has some pleasing tobacco touches but the price . . . Ouch! Bottoms Up only.

**Viña Real Gran Reserva 1991**    `13.5`  `£13–20`
Overpriced, underexciting. Bottoms Up only.

## UNWINS RED

**Castillo Perelada Cabernet Sauvignon 1997**    `13.5`  `£7–10`
Touch expensive for the theme.

**Conde de Valdemar Reserva 1995**    `14`  `£7–10`
Getting old and juicy as the tannins slip away.

**Cosme Palacio y Hermanos Rioja 1997**    `16`  `£5–7`
Always one of the more elegantly compact Riojas.

**Gran Vos Reserva 1995**    `15`  `£7–10`

**Marques de Grinon Tempranillo 1998**    `15`  `£5–7`
One of the more confident Riojas and marvellous with chillied vegetable dishes with coriander and cardamom.

**Martinez Bujanda Gran Reserva 1993**    `13.5`  `£13–20`
Expensive, ripe, ancient – yet nicely throat-tickling.

**Nekeas Barrel Fermented Merlot 1997**    `13.5`  `£5–7`
Oddly raisiny-ripe edge suggests it'll only really amount to anything with rich food in the mouth.

**Ochoa Tempranillo 1997**    `15`  `£5–7`
Superb tannins here allied to strawberries and plums.

**Tapon de Oro Garnacha 1998**    `12.5`  `£5–7`

**Valdepusa Cabernet Sauvignon Marques de Grinon 1997**    `16.5`  `£7–10`
Sublime, if getting juicy, yet it has presence and impactful plummy fruit and well-cut tannins.

**Viña Albali Reserva 1995**    `13`  `–£5.00`

**Viñas del Vero Cabernet Sauvignon 1998**    `16.5`  `£5–7`
The tannins and the fruit in perfect harmony progress in stately yet vivid elegance over the taste buds creating delicious havoc.

## VICTORIA WINE RED

**Abadia Retuerta Rivola, Duero 1996**    `16.5`  `£5–7`
One of the smartest red wines in Spain. Real elongated fruit, elegant reach, great balance of elements. Dry, delicious, decisive.

**Baron de Ley Rioja Reserva 1996**    `13`  `£7–10`
Begins well, then gets lost. Eight quid? Oh, come on.

**Casa Rural Tinto NV**    `14.5`  `–£3.50`
Rural!? Oh yes. Rusticity vinified . . . but great with bouncy dishes.

Chivite Navarra Viña    13   −£5.00
Marcos 1997

Chivite Reserva, Gran    13.5   £5–7
Feudo, Navarra 1995
Juicy with jaded tannins.

Conde de Valdemar Rioja    13.5   £5–7
Crianza 1997
Needs food. It's very juicy and the
tannins are quite raw.

Conde de Valdemar Rioja    14   £7–10
Reserva 1995
Getting old and juicy as the tannins
slip away.

Dominio di Montalvo    13   £5–7
Rioja 1998
I find it a touch sour as it sprints down
the throat. Not as open as Rioja could,
or perhaps ought to, be.

El Meson Rioja NV    15   £5–7
Very juicy but has a finish with a hint
of cigarillo. Needs food.

Jumilla Senorio de Robles    16   −£3.50
1998
A bargain wine for summer barbecues
as well as winter firesides. It's dry,
plummy, soft, characterful and hugely
quaffable – and it'll go with loads of
foods.

Marques de Aragon    15   −£5.00
Garnacha 1998
A marvellous curry wine: sweet/dry,
plummy, rich, full of deep, delicious
riches.

Marques de Riscal    14   £7–10
Reserva 1996
Claret with a touch of the sun and
spice.

Navajas Rioja Crianza    13.5   £5–7
1997

Touch thin. For Navajas, this is most
odd.

Remonte Cabernet    15.5   −£5.00
Sauvignon 1996
Combines a dry, vegetal side with a
plummy ripe dimension. Gushes with
flavour and urgency but still manages
to keep respectably Cabernet.

## WAITROSE RED

Agramont Tempranillo/    14.5   £5–7
Cabernet Sauvignon,
Navarra 1996
Good alertness of tannins, decent
cherry edge to the fruit.

Espiral Oaked    15   £5–7
Tempranillo 1998
Rich and juicy, very modern and
throat-teasing.

Espiral Tempranillo/    16   −£5.00
Cabernet Sauvignon 1998
Tobacco, tannins, concentration, class
– plus character and bite. Terrific stuff.

La Rioja Alta Gran    13.5   £13–20
Reserve 904, 1989

Torres Gran Sangre de    16   £5–7
Toro Reserva 1996
Wonderful vintage of the old warhorse
– the best for some time. Great
tannins, herbs, richness of layered fruit
and a striking finish.

Totally Tinto    15   −£3.50
Tempranillo, La Mancha
NV

Totally Two Thousand    15.5   −£3.50
Tempranillo NV
(magnum)
Superbly adult brew of warmth and
wit. Plummy fruit allied to great
tannins. Fresh-edged and full of fun.

Viña Fuerte Garnacha, 16 −£5.00
Calatayud 1999
Astonishingly cultured, soft and
yieldingly textured. Gorgeously ripe
yet not over the top.

## WINE CELLAR RED

Montalvo Reserva Rioja 14.5 £7–10
1994

Ondarre Reserva Rioja 13 £7–10
1994

Ondarre 'Rivallana' 13 £5–7
Crianza Rioja 1996

Valdetore Calatayud 15 −£5.00
Grenache 1998
Delicious calm fruit, plum mostly with
a touch of raspberry and appleskin.
Excellent food wine.

Viñas del Vero Merlot 15.5 £5–7
1997
Juicy yet memorably rich and plump
as it finishes, where it develops
lingering nuances of vanilla, plum,
spice and saccharin.

## ASDA WHITE

Bodegas Cerrosol 15 −£5.00
Sauvignon Rueda 1998
Interesting and unusually soft
Sauvignon which finishes crisply of
concentrated gooseberries. Great with
food.

Moscatel de Valencia NV, 16 −£3.50
Asda
Brilliant sweet wine for crème brûlées,
ice creams and fruit salad. Has a
delicious undertone of marmalade.

Spanish Oaked White 15.5 −£3.50
NV, Asda

Castillo de Almansa 1998 16 −£5.00
Huge presence and charisma here:
crisp, clean, collected, consummately
dry and delicate.

## BOOTHS WHITE

Estrella, Moscatel de 16 −£5.00
Valencia NV
Superb muscat sweetness and hints of
marmalade. Marvellous with ice
cream.

Palacio de Bornos Rueda 13 −£5.00
1999

Santa Lucia Viura, Vino 14 −£3.50
de la Tierra Manchuela
1998

Simply Spanish White 12 −£2.50
NV

## BUDGENS WHITE

Castillo de Liria Moscatel 15.5 −£5.00
de Valencia NV
Delicious! Try it with ice cream – or
even just pour it over it. Very subtly
spiced honeyed fruit.

Viña Albali Rosado 13 −£5.00
Tempranillo 1999
Cherry-edged freshness.

## CWS WHITE

Jaume Serra Chardonnay 16 −£5.00
1999
From one of the unsung heroes of
Catalan winemaking. A ridiculously
well priced, rich, handsomely textured,
charming wine of mannered
complexity and style.

## KWIK SAVE WHITE

Castillo Imperial Blanco   13.5   −£3.50
NV, Somerfield
Hint of unfortunate sugar.

Muscatel de Valencia,   16   −£3.50
Somerfield
Hint of marmalade, lashings of honey
and hint of strawberry jam. What a
bargain pud wine this is. And its
screwcap ensures it stays fresh and
frisky.

## M&S WHITE

Moscatel de Valencia   14.5   −£5.00
1999
A delicious sweet pudding wine. Great
with ice cream.

## MAJESTIC WHITE

Albarino Martin Codax   13.5   £5–7
Rias Maixas 1999

Rueda Blanco, Vinos   15   −£5.00
Sanz 1999
Very steely and crisp with an
underlying fruitiness of gooseberry
and pear.

Vionta Albarino 1999   13   £7–10
Very pleasant and mildly amusing but
eight quid?

## MORRISONS WHITE

De Muller Chardonnay   13   −£5.00
1999
Oily, medicinal, very balsamic in
texture and mighty peculiar as it
finishes – like sour butter. A very
creamy food wine.

Sanz Rueda Superior   14   −£5.00
1998
Something a little different from
Chardonnay, has a hint of minerals to
the ripe fruit.

Viña Albali Rosado   13   −£3.50
Tempranillo 1999
Cherry-edged freshness.

## ODDBINS WHITE

Burgans Albarino, Rias   12.5   £5–7
Baixas 1999

Chivite Gran Feudo Rosé,   14   −£5.00
Navarra 1999
Brilliant food wine!

Marques de Caceres   13   £5–7
Rosé, Rioja 1999
Bit tart.

Torres Viña Esmeralda   14   £5–7
1999
A charming aperitif. Full of interesting
edges: peaches, pears, pineapples.

Viñas del Vero   15   −£5.00
Chardonnay, Somontano
1999
A food Chardonnay in that it has a
crisp, nutty, demurely fruity style to it.

## SAFEWAY WHITE

Cruz de Piedra Garnacha   15   −£5.00
Macabeo 1999
Individual, dry, vaguely gooseberryish
and gently nutty. Makes a delicious
change from Chardonnay.

El Velero Valdepeñas   13.5   −£3.50
1999
Gentle fruit, dry, with a faint musty
tang.

Northern Block Macabeo, `15` `−£3.50`
Lozano Estate, La
Mancha 1999
Has a delicious fat edge of melon and
raspberry with a touch of butter.

Orange Grove 1999 `12` `−£5.00`

Viña Malea Viura 1999 `12.5` `−£5.00`
A bleak fish wine.

## SAINSBURY'S WHITE

Dry White NV, `14` `−£3.50`
Sainsbury's
A party wine for New Labour:
compromised, tight, very steely, suave,
finishes with a sullen dryness. Most
stores.

Lagar de Cervera 1999 `13` `£7–10`
Too pricey except for aficionados of
the breed. Not at all stores.

Oaked Viura, Alteza 640 `15.5` `−£5.00`
NV
Deliciously up to standard, the new
blend of this wine. Most stores.

## SOMERFIELD WHITE

Castillo Imperial Blanco `13.5` `−£3.50`
NV, Somerfield
Hint of unfortunate sugar.

Don Darias White NV `14` `−£5.00`
Lemons, lemons, lemons – plus a hint
of lime.

Muscatel de Valencia, `16` `−£3.50`
Somerfield
Hint of marmalade, lashings of honey
and hint of strawberry jam. What a
bargain pud wine this is. And its screw
cap ensures it stays fresh and frisky.

Pergola Oaked Viura `14` `−£5.00`
1999, Somerfield
A delicious thirst-quencher.

Viña Cana Rioja Blanco `12.5` `−£5.00`
1998, Somerfield
Loses its grip towards the end of its
act.

## SPAR WHITE

Perfect for Parties White `10` `−£3.50`
NV, Spar (1 litre)
Dull. Not for any party I'd like to
attend. Price band is the 75cl
equivalent.

Valencia Dry White NV, `13.5` `−£3.50`
Spar
Fresh and fruity with an earthy
undertone.

## TESCO WHITE

Moscatel de Valencia, `16` `−£3.50`
Tesco
Quite superb! Has an overtone of
orange marmalade to the honey and
the raspberry and pear sweetness.
Wonderful taint-free screwcap!

## THRESHER WHITE

Albarino Condes de `14.5` `£5–7`
Alberei 1999
You have to love the crisp
individuality of this wine (Albarino is
one of Europe's great individuals), to
find six quid worth paying. Worth it?
Just about.

Albarino Enexebre 1997 `15.5` `£7–10`
A more compressed and complex
version of the '99 wine – more texture

and teasing. Wine Rack and Bottoms Up only.

**Campo Viejo Barrel** | 13 | £5–7
**Fermented Viura 1998**
Odd and vegetal. Needs a spicy fish stew to work.

**Casa Rural White NV** | 15.5 | –£3.50

**Castillo de Liria Rosé NV** | 15 | –£3.50
Cherry-ripe and flirtatious. Terrific charm to its fruit.

**Conde de Valdemar** | 16 | £7–10
**Barrique Fermented Rioja 1996**
One of the spraunciest white Riojas I've tasted. The vanilla undertone is very attractive and controlled by rich fruit and balanced acids. Wine Rack and Bottoms Up only.

**Conde de Valdemar** | 12 | £7–10
**Barrique Fermented Rioja 1998**
Very oaky and non-orgasmic. Wine Rack and Bottoms Up only.

**Conde de Valdemar** | 14 | –£5.00
**Rosado 1999**
A terrific rosé to go with grilled fish.

**Dominio di Montalvo** | 15.5 | £5–7
**White Rioja 1998**
Seriously elegant and subtly rich. Has real style to its fruit, which is gently chewy, and the finish has flourish and wit.

**Enexbre Albarino Condes** | 15 | £5–7
**de Albarei 1997**

**Torres Viña Esmeralda** | 14 | £5–7
**1999**
A charming aperitif. Full of interesting edges: peaches, pears, pineapples.

**Torres Viña Sol 1999** | 14 | –£5.00
Not as vivid as previous vintages the

'99, but it will develop over the next year – if anyone keeps it that long.

## UNWINS WHITE

**Nekeas Barrel Fermented** | 15 | £5–7
**Chardonnay 1998**
Rich, creamy, immensely good news for gently spicy chicken dishes.

**Viñas del Vero** | 14 | –£5.00
**Chardonnay 1998**

**Viñas del Vero Clarion,** | 13 | £7–10
**Somontano 1997**

## VICTORIA WINE WHITE

**Albarino Condes de** | 14.5 | £5–7
**Alberei 1999**
You have to love the crisp individuality of this wine (Albarino is one of Europe's great individuals), to find six quid worth paying. Worth it? Just about.

**Campo Viejo Barrel** | 13 | £5–7
**Fermented Viura 1998**
Odd and vegetal. Needs a spicy fish stew to work.

**Casa Rural White NV** | 15.5 | –£3.50

**Castillo de Liria Rosé NV** | 15 | –£3.50
Cheery-ripe and flirtatious. Terrific charm to its fruit.

**Conde de Valdemar** | 14 | –£5.00
**Rosado 1999**
A terrific rosé to go with grilled fish.

**Dominio di Montalvo** | 15.5 | £5–7
**White Rioja 1998**
Seriously elegant and subtly rich. Has real style to its fruit, which is gently chewy, and the finish has flourish and wit.

Moscatel de Valencia NV  `16`  `–£5.00`
The best value dessert wine in the
world. Rich honey fruit with a flowing
undertone of sweet orange
marmalade.

Torres Viña Esmeralda  `14`  `£5–7`
1999
A charming aperitif. Full of interesting
edges: peaches, pears, pineapples.

Torres Viña Sol 1999  `14`  `–£5.00`
Not as vivid as previous vintages the
'99, but it will develop over the next
year – if anyone keeps it that long.

## WAITROSE WHITE

Albarino Pazo de Seoane,  `15.5`  `£7–10`
Rias Baixas 1999
Unusual, complex (great double-
change of gear on the finish) and very
rewarding to sip and muse on.

Espiral Macabeo/  `15.5`  `–£5.00`
Chardonnay 1998

Lustau Moscatel de  `15`  `–£5.00`
Chipiona NV
Honey and muted marmalade
richness. A superb bargain pudding
wine.

Viñas del Vero  `14`  `–£5.00`
Chardonnay 1998

# SWITZERLAND

The most marvellous thing about many Swiss wines is the absence of a cork seal. The sad thing is that there are very few Swiss wines on our major retailers' shelves. Could it be cost? Yes. Might it be the image of a country associated with cows, chocolate, cuckoo clocks and ski-slopes? Partly. Is it those screw caps? Undoubtedly. Swiss wine, however, is a secret worth investigating; native varieties, beautifully clean fruit, individual approach – all from 36,000 acres of well-tended vines. I only wish I found more bottles in the UK to taste and rate. The wine I like best, when I find a rare bottle in the UK, is white and it's made from the Chasselas grape.

## WINE CELLAR RED

Pinot Noir Trilogy 1996    12    £5–7

# URUGUAY

Fascinating bijou ornamentation to the continent, growing the stupendous Tannat grape. This is the Costa Brava for Argentinians, but for us it can be the source of some richly individual and concentrated red wines. As well as the Basque-derived Tannat, there are fulsome Cabernets and Merlots. I expect to see an increasing demand among UK wine buyers for reds from here.

## SAINSBURY'S RED

Bright Brothers Merlot/ — 14 —£5.00
Tannat 1998

## SOMERFIELD RED

Bright Brothers Tannat — 16 —£5.00
Cabernet Franc 2000
Wow! It explodes with flavour and personality. Great food wine.

## WAITROSE RED

Pisano Family Reserve — 14.5 £7–10
Tannat 1998
Lovely juicy richness with class-preserving tannins and acids.

## SOMERFIELD WHITE

Bright Brothers — 15.5 —£5.00
Uruguayan Sauvignon/
Semillon 2000
Loads of energy and flavour here.
Excellent acids underpinning firm fruit.

# USA

What happened to Washington State's Cabernets? To Oregon's Pinot Noirs? Well, we still have California to keep our thirsts in check, and it is from this state that most of the interesting stuff emanates. Ridge, the former dazzling producer in the mountains, isn't as fantastic as it was ten years ago – maybe it's the Japanese owners – but Fetzer continues to make some magical organic wines, and there are also some cheapies, under-a-fiver wines, creeping in. Overall, California's Pinots and Chardonnays, from operations like Torres, are benchmarks of their kind

## ASDA RED

**Arius Zinfandel 1998**   `12`   `-£5.00`
Intensely fruity. Like a game sauce rather than a wine.

**Bonterra Cabernet**   `17`   `£7–10`
**Sauvignon 1997 (organic)**
Superbly California-style: warm, rich, pulsating, brilliant tannins, great ripe yet serious dry-sweet fruit. Absolutely marvellous stuff.

**California Red 1999, Asda**   `14`   `-£3.50`
Even has a hint of the Californian lifestyle. Great little glugging wine.

**California Syrah 1997,**   `14.5`   `-£5.00`
**Asda**

**Turning Leaf Cabernet**   `12`   `£5–7`
**Sauvignon 1997**
Very juicy and sloppy. Not good for the brain.

**Turning Leaf Zinfandel**   `12.5`   `£5–7`
**1996**
Very overpriced and, sadly, over here.

## BOOTHS RED

**Redwood Trail Pinot**   `13`   `£5–7`
**Noir 1998**
Not as charmingly old-hat as previous vintages.

**Stonybrook Merlot 1998**   `16`   `£5–7`
Yes, it's soft and ripe, too ripe for old farts, but it's wonderfully jammy yet not OTT.

**Turning Leaf Cabernet**   `12`   `£5–7`
**Sauvignon 1997**
Very juicy and sloppy. Not good for the brain.

**Turning Leaf Zinfandel**   `12.5`   `£5–7`
**1996**
Very overpriced and, sadly, over here.

## BUDGENS RED

**Glen Ellen Cabernet**   `13`   `£5–7`
**Sauvignon 1998**
Huge. Sheer skyscraper juice.

Marc Xero Merlot NV `15` `−£5.00`
Most agreeable tannin which will help the blackcurrant fruit to go brilliantly with roast lamb.

Sutter Home Merlot 1998 `13` `−£5.00`
Merlot? Really?

Turning Leaf Cabernet `12` `£5–7`
Sauvignon 1997
Very juicy and sloppy. Not good for the brain.

Turning Leaf Zinfandel `12.5` `£5–7`
1996
Very overpriced and, sadly, over here.

## CWS RED

Blossom Hill Cabernet `11` `−£5.00`
Sauvignon 1997

Eagle Peak Merlot, Fetzer `15.5` `£5–7`
Vineyards 1998
Very elegant yet characterful. Resounds with flavoursome fruit, gently leathery and black cherryish. The finish is striking.

Fetzer Eagle Peak Merlot `15` `£5–7`
1997
Very expensive as it flattens out its leathery richness on the taste buds. Superstores only.

'Laid Back Ruby' `15` `−£5.00`
California Ruby Cabernet
1999, Co-op
Bristles with food-friendly fruit. A bravura performance from dear old much-despised ruby Cabernet grapes.

Sebastiani Sonoma Cask `14.5` `£7–10`
Old Vine Zinfandel 1998
Too expensive but with a Christmas turkey, with that fruity stuffing and that rich gravy, this extravagantly

fruity specimen would be a rare but fitting companion. Superstores only.

## KWIK SAVE RED

E & J Gallo Cabernet `13` `−£5.00`
Sauvignon 1997

E & J Gallo Ruby `11` `−£5.00`
Cabernet 1997

## M&S RED

Clear Lake Cabernet `15` `−£5.00`
Franc 1999
If you can get over the reek of sulphur you reach some interesting fruit of cherry-rich charms.

Freedom Ridge Shiraz `15` `£5–7`
1999
Very juicy, almost smoked jammy in its ripeness. Needs food.

Live Oak Road Zinfandel `15` `£7–10`
1999
Hugely generous, relaxed warmth here. The texture is like tufted carpet – you sink up to your ears in it.

Zamora Zinfandel 1998 `14` `£5–7`
For lovers of baked fruit tarts only. It's an extremely self-consciously rich and ripe wine.

## MAJESTIC RED

Beringer Appellation `14` `£7–10`
Zinfandel 1996

Beringer Valdeguie 1998 `15` `£5–7`
Astonishingly elegant and untypically European in style. It's dry, mild, blackcurrany yet not sweet, and it has casual confidence on the finish.

Firestone Old Vine | 17 | £7–10
Cucmunga Zinfandel
1997
Wonderful unfiltered, natural wine of substance and spiciness. Gorgeous tannins sweep the taste buds in a tide of buttressed flavour of plums/cherries and blackberries.

Foxen Pinot Noir Santa | 14 | £13–20
Maria 1997
Typical Californian sweetness and almost-elegance. Good Pinot perfume.

Ironstone Vineyards | 15.5 | £5–7
Cabernet Franc 1996

Ironstone Vineyards | 15 | £5–7
Cabernet Franc 1997
Hugely juicy but saved from a fate worse than death (OTTness) by its alert tannins.

Ironstone Vineyards | 16 | £5–7
Merlot 1997
Very jammy and textured but has lovely tannins which make for a balanced mouthful of ripeness, not too dry or over-fruity, and a lingering finish.

Kautz-Ironstone Shiraz | 16 | £5–7
1997
A very vibrant personality of meaty depth and resounding richness. Not typically California or Shiraz but that's its charm. It has character, control and calmness.

Prosperity Red NV | 16 | –£5.00
The label is worth the price of admission and what you get is dry, savoury fruit of pizzazz and purpose. Huge serious fun quaffing.

## MORRISONS RED

Blossom Hill California | 10 | –£5.00
Red NV

Californian Red NV | 10 | –£3.50

Fetzer Bonterra Cabernet | 14 | £7–10
Sauvignon 1997
Getting very dry as it matures and begins to lose its composure. Needs a casserole to spark it into life.

Glen Ellen Pinot Noir | 9 | £5–7
1997
Ugh!

Glen Ellen Proprietor's | 12 | –£5.00
Reserve Zinfandel 1997

Glen Ellen Zinfandel | 11 | £5–7
1997
Very candy-like in its richness.

Ironstone Vineyards | 15 | £5–7
Cabernet Franc 1997
Hugely juicy but saved from a fate worse than death (OTTness) by its alert tannins.

Ironstone Vineyards | 14.5 | –£5.00
Shiraz 1998
Vigorous attack of spicy plums and berries, very smooth texture and a deep finish.

Turning Leaf Cabernet | 12 | £5–7
Sauvignon 1997
Very juicy and sloppy. Not good for the brain.

Turning Leaf Zinfandel | 12.5 | £5–7
1996
Very overpriced and, sadly, over here.

## ODDBINS RED

Bonterra Zinfandel, | 16.5 | £7–10
Mendocino 1996

---

---

**AMERICAN RED**

A wonderfully exotic specimen of warmth and immediacy. Spicy, chewy, softly tannic, hedgerow fruited, it has immense charm and forwardness.

**Canyon Road Cabernet Sauvignon 1998** — 14 £5–7

**Canyon Road Merlot, Geyserville 1997** — 13.5 £5–7

**Clos LaChance Cabernet Sauvignon, Santa Cruz Mountains 1997** — 13 £13–20
Lot of money, lot of juice.

**Clos LaChance Zinfandel, El Dorado County 1997** — 16.5 £10–13
Ripe, jammy, savoury, tannic – huge credentials for a formidably rich and engaging Zin. Has a lovely layer of subtle spice.

**Fetzer Syrah 1997** — 14 £7–10
Very juicy and ripe.

**Fetzer Valley Oaks Cabernet Sauvignon 1997** — 15.5 £5–7
Sunny, warmly engaging fruit, little tannin to give it grip but the lushness of the fruit is spot on. A modern, pacy wine of controlled charms.

**Fetzer Vineyards Home Ranch Zinfandel 1996** — 15.5 £5–7

**Fetzer Vineyards Select Zinfandel 1997** — 16.5 £7–10
Jammy, spicy, very ripe but awesomely delicious.

**Ravenswood Vintners Blend Zinfandel 1997** — 15 £7–10
Juicy and rich. Lovely spicy food wine.

**Ravenswood Zinfandel, Napa Valley 1997** — 16 £10–13
The tannins! The tannins! The tannins! Quite yummy.

**Ravenswood Zinfandel, Sonoma County 1997** — 14 £10–13
Touch too juicy to sip over a long afternoon. Needs chicken tikka.

**Sterling Vineyards Cabernet Sauvignon, Napa Valley 1996** — 15 £7–10
Ripe and raisiny, very ready to drink. Tannins beginning to absorb the glucose and turn super dry.

## SAFEWAY RED

**Echelon Merlot 1998** — 15 £7–10
Tastes barbecues, so rich and burned-crusty is it.

**Fetzer Bonterra Zinfandel 1997 (organic)** — 16.5 £7–10
The acme of rip-roaring fruit: sunny ripe, soft, urgent-to-please, individual, pure, natural and massively quaffable. A superb modern mouthful. 70 stores.

**Pacific Coast Ruby Cabernet 1998** — 15 –£5.00
California in a bottle! Like a genie, the fruit escapes very happily. Selected stores.

**Turning Leaf Cabernet Sauvignon 1997** — 12 £5–7
Very juicy and sloppy. Not good for the brain.

**Turning Leaf Zinfandel 1996** — 12.5 £5–7
Very overpriced and, sadly, over here.

## SAINSBURY'S RED

**Bonterra Cabernet Sauvignon 1997 (organic)** — 17 £7–10
Superbly California-style: warm, rich, pulsating, brilliant tannins, great ripe

yet serious dry-sweet fruit. Absolutely
marvellous stuff. Not at all stores.

**Bonterra Zinfandel 1997** | 16 | £7–10
**(organic)**
Buzzes with rich, deep, subtly spicy
fruit. Selected stores.

**Coastal Pinot Noir,** | 16 | £7–10
**Robert Mondavi 1996**
To be preferred to a hundred Volnays.
Superb texture, with raspberry and
truffle fruit, hint of plum jam, great
tannins and big, beetle-browed length
of finish. Selected stores.

**Eagle Peak Merlot, Fetzer** | 15.5 | £5–7
**Vineyards 1998**
Very elegant yet characterful.
Resounds with flavoursome fruit,
gently leathery and black cherryish.
The finish is striking.

**Fetzer Valley Oaks** | 15.5 | £5–7
**Cabernet Sauvignon 1997**
Sunny, warmly engaging fruit, little
tannin to give it grip but the lushness
of the fruit is spot on. A modern, pacy
wine of controlled charms.

**Ironstone Vineyards** | 10 | £5–7
**Cabernet Sauvignon 1997**
Like a baked fruit tart. Make a good
gravy base.

**Mondavi Coastal Merlot** | 16 | £7–10
**1997**
Not a typical Merlot – it's not leathery
or biting at first sip – but it is hugely
civilised and with some pretensions to
class. The texture is plummy, polished
and poised. Exceedingly quaffable. Not
at all stores.

**Stonybrook Vineyard** | 16 | £5–7
**Merlot 1998**
Yes, it's soft and ripe, too ripe for old

farts, but it's wonderfully jammy yet
not OTT. Selected stores.

**Sutter Home Merlot 1998** | 13 | –£5.00
So juicy you can drink it through a
straw – though there are some tannins
which might clog it up. Most stores.

**Sutter Home Pinot Noir** | 13 | £5–7
**1997**
Has some real Pinot charm but not
enough to rate higher. Selected
stores.

**Turning Leaf Cabernet** | 12 | £5–7
**Sauvignon 1997**
Very juicy and sloppy. Not good for
the brain.

**Turning Leaf Zinfandel** | 12.5 | £5–7
**1996**
Very overpriced and, sadly, over here.

**Californian Dry Red NV,** | 14 | –£5.00
**Somerfield**
Juicy and super-ripe. A curry wine.

**Laguna Canyon** | 12 | –£5.00
**Zinfandel 1998**
Very cosmetic aroma, exceedingly
juicy fruit.

**Turning Leaf Cabernet** | 12 | £5–7
**Sauvignon 1997**
Very juicy and sloppy. Not good for
the brain.

**Turning Leaf Zinfandel** | 12.5 | £5–7
**1996**
Very overpriced and, sadly, over here.

**Fetzer Valley Oaks** | 15.5 | £5–7
**Cabernet Sauvignon 1997**

Sunny, warmly engaging fruit, little tannin to give it grip but the lushness of the fruit is spot on. A modern, pacy wine of controlled charms.

## TESCO RED

**California Old Vine Estate Carignane 1996** `13.5` `£5–7`

**Colombia Crest Cote de Colombia Grenache 1997** `15` `–£5.00`
Terrific performer with TV dinners: sweet, saucy, commercial, a good laugh.

**Edgewood Estate Napa Valley Malbec 1997** `16` `£10–13`
Extremely cool and collected in style by virtue of its smoothness of delivery and highly evolved, soft tannins. It is expensive but it is rewardingly rich and elegant and in a perfect state of healthy drinkability.

**Ehlers Grove Syrah 1998** `13` `£7–10`
Selected stores.

**Mondavi Coastal Merlot 1997** `16` `£7–10`
Not a typical Merlot – it's not leathery or biting at first sip – but it is hugely civilised and with some pretensions to class. The texture is plummy, polished and poised. Exceedingly quaffable. Not at all stores.

**Robert Mondavi Coastal Cabernet Sauvignon 1995** `14` `£7–10`

**Turning Leaf Cabernet Sauvignon 1997** `12` `£5–7`
Very juicy and sloppy. Not good for the brain.

**Turning Leaf Zinfandel 1996** `12.5` `£5–7`
Very overpriced and, sadly, over here.

**West Coast Ruby Cabernet/Merlot 1999, Tesco** `15` `–£5.00`
Strikingly rich, herby, and with subtle yet characterful tannins.

## THRESHER RED

**Clos du Bois Merlot 1996** `14.5` `£13–20`
Not necessarily classic Merlot but the clash here between the sweet fruit and the ripe tannins is highly drinkable and well-meaning. A curiously delicate Merlot of some finesse, it is expensive but it is delicious. Only at Wine Rack and Bottoms Up.

**E & J Gallo Ruby Cabernet 1999** `14` `–£5.00`
Joyously plump and ripe with enough tannins to keep it from going OTT. Great with pasta dishes.

**Eagle Peak Merlot, Fetzer Vineyards 1998** `15.5` `£5–7`
Very elegant yet characterful. Resounds with flavoursome fruit, gently leathery and black cherryish. The finish is striking.

**Fetzer Valley Oaks Cabernet Sauvignon 1997** `15.5` `£5–7`
Sunny, warmly engaging fruit, little tannin to give it grip but the lushness of the fruit is spot on. A modern, pacy wine of controlled charms.

**Redwood Trail Pinot Noir 1997** `13.5` `£5–7`
Getting long in the tooth, fruitwise, and the taste buds feel the reluctance of the wine to move with any energy.

**Robert Mondavi North Coast Cellars Zinfandel 1995** `15` `£7–10`

**Talus Zinfandel 1997** `13` `£5–7`
Juicy with a savoury finish.

**Turning Leaf Cabernet** `12` `£5–7`
**Sauvignon 1997**
Very juicy and sloppy. Not good for
the brain.

**Turning Leaf Zinfandel** `12.5` `£5–7`
**1996**
Very overpriced and, sadly, over here.

**Vendange Californian** `14` `–£5.00`
**Red 1998**
Party wine! This party, at least, feels it
needs lots of company. Only at
Thresher Wine Stores.

**Woodbridge Mondavi** `14` `£5–7`
**Zinfandel 1996**

## UNWINS RED

**Beaulieu Vineyard** `14` `£5–7`
**Coastal Pinot Noir 1998**
Nice nose tickle on the Pinot aroma
(wild raspberry) and cherryish
thereafter.

**Blossom Hill NV** `10` `–£5.00`

**De Loach Zinfandel** `10` `£7–10`
**Platinum 1996**
Too old and treacly. Was good and
tannic two years ago. Wines age fast in
California. Good for marinating dead
meat but not live tongues.

**Delicato Cabernet** `14` `£5–7`
**Sauvignon 1998**
Deliciously rich and gently savoury
with polished tannins.

**Delicato Zinfandel 1998** `13` `£5–7`
Very juicy and simpering.

**Fetzer Private Collection** `15` `£13–20`
**Cabernet Sauvignon 1994**

Highly drinkable. At its peak and it
won't keep.

**Fetzer Syrah 1997** `14` `£5–7`
Very juicy for Fetzer. Possibly ageing
too fast.

**Ironstone Vineyards** `15` `£5–7`
**Cabernet Franc 1997**
Hugely juicy but saved from a fate
worse than death (OTTness) by its
alert tannins.

**King Estate Pinot Noir** `12` `£13–20`
**1995**
Absurd price for a vaguely absurd
Pinot.

**R H Phillips Cabernet** `15` `£5–7`
**Sauvignon 1997**
Handsome sweet fruit with excellent
tannic backbone.

**Saintsbury Garnet** `13.5` `£10–13`
**Carneros Pinot Noir 1998**
Bitter cherries at Fortnum & Mason
prices.

**Schug Pinot Noir 1996** `11` `£10–13`
Starts well and alertly but descends
into farce.

**Seven Peaks Cabernet** `16.5` `£7–10`
**Sauvignon 1996**
Outstanding chocolate, coffee and
cassis-edged fruit. A perfectly mature
specimen with lovely tannins.

**Stonehedge Merlot 1998** `15` `£5–7`
Has a sweet figgy finish but it's got a
dry underbelly of herbs and a very
thick texture – so it coagulates
pleasantly in the throat.

**Thornhill Pinot Noir 1996** `12` `–£5.00`
Extremely juicy and curry friendly.

**Turning Leaf Cabernet** `12` `£5–7`
**Sauvignon 1997**

Very juicy and sloppy. Not good for the brain.

**Turning Leaf Zinfandel 1996**  `12.5`  `£5–7`
Very overpriced and, sadly, over here.

**Wente Cabernet Sauvignon 1996**  `16`  `£7–10`
Catch it and drink it before Christmas – it'll age fast and its lovely tannins will loosen quickly.

**Wente Charles Wetmore Reserve Cabernet Sauvignon 1995**  `12.5`  `£10–13`
Or rather, 12.5 to 15 points. Just beginning to turn juicy. The aroma is breaking up. The variation in rating refers to the variation in the bottle.

**Wente Crane Ridge Reserve Merlot 1997**  `13.5`  `£10–13`
Juicy fruit, warm tannins.

**Wente Reliz Creek Reserve Pinot Noir 1996**  `14`  `£10–13`
Soft and ripe and expensive.

**Wente Zinfandel 1998**  `11`  `£5–7`
So fruit juicy.

## VICTORIA WINE RED

**Blossom Hill Californian Red NV**  `10`  `–£5.00`

**E & J Gallo Ruby Cabernet 1999**  `14`  `–£5.00`
Joyously plump and ripe with enough tannins to keep it from going OTT. Great with pasta dishes.

**Eagle Peak Merlot, Fetzer Vineyards 1998**  `15.5`  `£5–7`
Very elegant yet characterful. Resounds with flavoursome fruit,

gently leathery and black cherryish. The finish is striking.

**Fetzer Valley Oaks Cabernet Sauvignon 1997**  `15.5`  `£5–7`
Sunny, warmly engaging fruit, little tannin to give it grip but the lushness of the fruit is spot on. A modern, pacy wine of controlled charms.

**Redwood Trail Pinot Noir 1997**  `13.5`  `£5–7`
Getting long in the tooth, fruitwise, and the taste buds feel the reluctance of the wine to move with any energy.

**Talus Zinfandel 1996**  `13.5`  `£5–7`

**Talus Zinfandel 1997**  `13`  `£5–7`
Juicy with a savoury finish.

**Turning Leaf Cabernet Sauvignon 1997**  `12`  `£5–7`
Very juicy and sloppy. Not good for the brain.

**Turning Leaf Zinfandel 1996**  `12.5`  `£5–7`
Very overpriced and, sadly, over here.

**Vendange Californian Red 1998**  `14`  `–£5.00`
Party wine! This party, at least, feels it needs lots of company.

**Woodbridge Mondavi Zinfandel 1996**  `14`  `£5–7`

## WAITROSE RED

**Bonterra Vineyards Merlot 1997 (organic)**  `16.5`  `£7–10`
Great class and polish here, with outstanding tannins and acids to balance so brilliantly the lashings of sweet fruit. It finishes dryly and decisively.

Fetzer Valley Oaks 15.5 £5–7
Cabernet Sauvignon 1997
Sunny, warmly engaging fruit, little
tannin to give it grip but the lushness
of the fruit is spot on. A modern, pacy
wine of controlled charms.

Shafer Cabernet 13 £20+
Sauvignon 1995
The ripeness subsumes the tannins.
Only from Waitrose Direct.

Stags Leap Cabernet 16 £20+
Sauvignon 1995
Lot of money, but a mountain of
moody fruit. Only from Waitrose
Direct.

Stonebridge Cellars 13 £5–7
Zinfandel 1997
Very jammy and creamy finishing.

Yorkville Cellars 14 £7–10
Cabernet Franc 1997
(organic)
Juicy yet dry.

Yorkville Petit Verdot 16 £7–10
1997
Much more like it, Yorkville!
Brilliantly bustling tannins to lovely
purple damson fruit. Spicy, deep,
warm.

## WINE CELLAR RED

Clos du Val Le Clos NV 14 £7–10

Fetzer Pinot Noir, Santa 13 £5–7
Barbara 1996

Fetzer Valley Oaks 16.5 £5–7
Cabernet Sauvignon 1996
Warm, all-embracing, deep, broad,
and most charmingly well-textured
and ripe on the finish.

Gallo Sonoma Barrelli 15.5 £10–13
Creek Cabernet
Sauvignon 1994

Gallo Sonoma County 13.5 £7–10
Pinot Noir 1995

Gallo Sonoma Frei Ranch 14 £10–13
Cabernet Sauvignon 1994

Mondavi Coastal Merlot 16 £7–10
1997
Not a typical Merlot – it's not leathery
or biting at first sip – but it is hugely
civilised and with some pretensions to
class. The texture is plummy, polished
and poised. Exceedingly quaffable. Not
at all stores.

## ASDA WHITE

Arius Californian Chenin 13 –£5.00
Blanc 1998, Asda
Odd, very odd. But with Thai food, it
would be fine.

Bonterra Chardonnay 15.5 £7–10
1998 (organic)
Very rich and aromatic. Not OTT, but
close, but with oriental food it would
be a winner.

Californian White 1999, 13.5 –£3.50
Asda
Amazing price for a Hollywood style
wine.

## BOOTHS WHITE

Stonybrook Chardonnay 16 –£5.00
1998
Lovely plump ripe fruit which does
not turn blowsy. Gorgeous demure
melonosity here.

## BUDGENS WHITE

**Glen Ellen Chardonnay 1998** `15` `£5-7`
Lovely throbbing melon fruit. A real throat charmer as a welcome-home-from-the-coalface pick-me-up.

## CWS WHITE

**Garnet Point Chardonnay-Chenin 1997** `15.5` `-£5.00`

**'The Big Chill' California Colombard Chardonnay 1999, Co-op** `13.5` `-£5.00`
A minor chill in fact.

## KWIK SAVE WHITE

**E & J Gallo Chardonnay 1997** `10` `-£5.00`

## M&S WHITE

**Clear Lake Chardonnay 1999** `13.5` `-£5.00`
Goes a bit gooey-lemon and sentimental on the finish.

**Clear Lake Rosé 1999** `13` `-£5.00`
Very sweet and cloying.

**Dunnigan Lane Fume Blanc 1999** `13.5` `£5-7`

**Gardeners Grove Chardonnay 1999** `13.5` `£5-7`

## MAJESTIC WHITE

**Beringer Californian Sauvignon Blanc 1997** `15.5` `£5-7`

**Beringer Californian Zinfandel Blush 1998** `6` `£5-7`

Repulsive mush. It is a sin to turn Zin into fruit juice.

**Beringer Napa Valley Fume Blanc 1998** `15` `£7-10`
Very woody beginning and a very smoothly sandpapered finish. A superb wine for complex fish dishes and poultry dishes with cream sauces.

**Essencia Orange Muscat 1996 (half-bottle)** `16` `£5-7`
Gorgeously rich and sweet and takes no prisoners – however boisterously rich the pud.

**Fetzer Barrel Select Chardonnay 1997** `15` `£7-10`
Very tropical and ripe.

**Fetzer Viognier 1999** `15` `£7-10`
Delicious! And what an apricot-scented change from melony Chardonnay.

**Foxen Bien Nacido Vineyard Chardonnay 1996** `14` `£13-20`
More lemon to leaven the balsam here and very drinkable but absurdly priced for a medium-complex wine. It has good woody notes.

**Foxen Tinaquaic Vineyard Chardonnay 1996** `13.5` `£13-20`
Very thick and rich – like balsam – but goes with food (which it needs). The price is outrageous. Rather overbearing.

**Ironstone Chardonnay 1998** `10` `£5-7`
Hugely fruity and woody. Too OTT for this drinker.

**Ironstone Semillon Chardonnay 1998** `15` `£5-7`
Has delicacy with power in a way

typical of whites from the sublime vineyards of Western Australia. It combines under-ripe melons and a thrusting nuttiness. Dry and hugely food-friendly.

**Kautz-Ironstone** 13.5 £5–7
**Chardonnay 1998**
A very muddled Chardonnay which has to be drunk with food to be effective. It is ripe, very full, very loquacious and has no counterpoint to its fruity fulsomeness.

**Prosperity White NV** 15 –£5.00

## MORRISONS WHITE

**Californian White NV** 12 –£3.50

**Ironstone Chardonnay** 15.5 £5–7
**1997**

**Ironstone Chardonnay** 10 £5–7
**1998**
Hugely fruity and woody. Too OTT for this drinker.

**Ironstone Obsession 1998** 10 –£5.00
Extremely puerile and off-sweet.

**Wente Johannesburg** 16.5 –£5.00
**Riesling 1997**
Terrific spice and lime sherbet fruit here. Not wholly dry, to be sure, but it bounces with life and would be terrific with Thai food.

## ODDBINS WHITE

**Canyon Road** 14 £5–7
**Chardonnay 1998**

**Clos LaChance** 13.5 £13–20
**Chardonnay, Santa Cruz Mountains 1997**
Very expensive and almost delicious

but the elements are so loosely knit I query its impact and value. It does not carry through the promise of its bouquet.

**Fetzer Bonterra Muscat** 15 £5–7
**1999 (half-bottle)**
Delicious sweet aperitif.

**Fetzer Vineyards** 16 £7–10
**Bonterra Viognier 1998**
One of the most sophisticated Viogniers around. Lovely sophisticated fruit.

**Fetzer Viognier 1999** 15 £7–10
Delicious! And what an apricot-scented change from melony Chardonnay.

**Landmark Overlook** 17 £13–20
**Chardonnay 1998**
Like a Meursault, no Montrachet, in a magic vintage. Brilliant wood and fruit marriage. Polished seduction.

**Mariquita White 1996** 14 –£5.00
Very sweet and full but a must-have wine for Indian and rich Thai/Chinese dishes. Fine Wine Stores only.

## SAFEWAY WHITE

**Bonterra Muscat 1997** 15.5 £5–7
**(half-bottle)**
A delicious half-sweet aperitif which tastes of grapes. Yes! Grapes! Not plums or grass or strawberries or orchards, but rich muscat grapes. Isn't that what we pay our money for?

**Fetzer Unoaked** 16 £5–7
**Chardonnay 1998**
A finely wrought but not overwrought specimen: gentle, understated yet warm and Californian. It's relaxed,

soft, supple and hugely drinkable. Has a lovely chewiness on the finish.

**Ironstone Chardonnay** 10 £5–7
**1998**
Hugely fruity and woody. Too OTT for this drinker.

**Pacific Coast Chardonnay** 15.5 –£5.00
**1999**
Delicious! Hints of smoke, lime, strawberry and melon.

**Pyramid Lake Napa** 8 –£5.00
**Gamay Rosé NV**
Revoltingly cosmetic and 'manufactured'. An insult to the grape.

**Sutter Home Unoaked** 13.5 –£5.00
**Chardonnay 1998**
Very sticky so it will adhere to a spicy fish stew.

## SAINSBURY'S WHITE

**Bonterra Chardonnay** 15.5 £7–10
**1998 (organic)**
So elegant it walks on tiptoe where other Chardonnays stride. If this minimalist deliciousness is your style, wear it. Even at £8.50. Not at all stores.

**Bonterra Muscat (half-** 15.5 £5–7
**bottle) (organic)**
A delicious half-sweet aperitif which tastes of grapes. Yes! Grapes! Not plums or grass or strawberries or orchards, but rich muscat grapes. Isn't that what we pay our money for? Selected stores.

**Coastal Chardonnay,** 17 £7–10
**Robert Mondavi 1997**
Beautiful biscuity texture, subtle vegetal fruit, and very elegant on the finish. 60 stores.

**Fetzer Barrel Select** 15 £7–10
**Chardonnay 1997**
Very tropical and ripe.

**Gallo Colombard NV** 11 –£5.00

**Stonybrook Vineyards** 16 –£5.00
**Chardonnay 1997**
Staggeringly good value here. Loads of richness and flavour without being remotely overbaked or clumsy. Selected stores.

## SOMERFIELD WHITE

**Talus Chardonnay 1998** 16.5 £5–7
Superb value fruit for you get authentic California all-surfin' fruit and sunshine. Deep and delicious.

## TESCO WHITE

**Fetzer Barrel Select** 15 £7–10
**Chardonnay 1997**
Very tropical and ripe.

**Fetzer Viognier 1999** 15 £7–10
Delicious! And what an apricot-scented change from melony Chardonnay.

**Hogue Chenin Blanc 1998** 11 £5–7
Flouncy and frivolous (not a six quid wine). Most stores.

**West Coast California** 14.5 –£5.00
**Chardonnay 1999, Tesco**
Some good rich touches to the urgent and unguent fruit which stays the civilised side of gushing.

## THRESHER WHITE

**Columbia Crest** 15.5 £5–7
**Chardonnay 1997**

**Dunnewood Chardonnay** 16 £7–10
**1998**
Delightfully uncluttered yet richly
endowed, balanced, bonny
Chardonnay.

**Fetzer Barrel Select** 17 £7–10
**Viognier 1997**
More attractively fruity yet subtle
(apricots and warm wood) than many
a forty-quid Condrieu – the bijou
French vineyard area which first
planted the Viognier grape. Wine Rack
and Bottoms Up only.

**Fetzer Sundial** 16 £5–7
**Chardonnay, 1998**
Always as full of sun as the face of a
California beachbum, this is fruit
modelled on richness, warmth, and the
flavours of the tropics. This vintage
has a lovely freshness to it.

**Fetzer Syrah Rosé 1999** 13 £5–7
Very clammy and humid. Needs
mackerels from the barbecue to leaven
its richness.

**Fetzer Viognier 1999** 15 £7–10
Delicious! And what an apricot-
scented change from melony
Chardonnay.

**Jekel Chardonnay,** 15.5 £7–10
**Gravelstone Vineyards**
**1996**
Meaty and ripe. Great with robust fish
dishes. Wine Rack and Bottoms Up
stores only.

**St Supery Sauvignon** 15.5 £7–10
**Blanc 1997**
Very unusual and possibly repellent
(to an old world wine soak). But the
sheer fluidity of the rich fruit, textured
and softly sticky, is remarkable. Wine
Rack and Bottoms Up only.

**Vendange Californian** 11 –£5.00
**Dry White 1998**
Struggles to make an impact. Like a
one-legged centre-forward. Not at
Wine Rack.

**Vendanges White** 9 –£5.00
**Zinfandel 1998**
Utterly revolting confection: sweet,
rosy, clotted, jejune. Thresher Wine
Shops only.

**Wente Riva Ranch** 16 £7–10
**Chardonnay 1996**
Big and a touch blistering in its
richness and spicy pear and pastry
fruitiness but I love its quirkiness and
food compatibility. Wine Rack and
Bottoms Up only.

**Woodbridge Californian** 13 £5–7
**Sauvignon Blanc, Robert**
**Mondavi 1996**
Odd sticky texture. Wine Rack and
Bottoms Up only.

## UNWINS WHITE

**Blossom Hill NV** 10 –£5.00

**Bonterra Viognier 1998** 15 £7–10
**(organic)**
Chewy apricots.

**Byron Chardonnay, Santa** 13.5 £13–20
**Barbara 1996**
Far too much to ask for the limitations
of the fruit.

**Coastal Chardonnay,** 17 £10–13
**Robert Mondavi 1997**
Beautiful biscuity texture, subtle
vegetal fruit, and very elegant on the
finish.

**Fetzer Sundial** 16 £5–7
**Chardonnay 1997**

251

## AMERICAN WHITE

One of the best Californian Chardonnays around for the money.

**Redwood Trail** 15.5 £5–7
**Chardonnay 1998**
Delicious sticky fruit. Gums up the molars something marvellous.

**Seven Oaks Reserve** 14.5 £10–13
**Chardonnay 1997**
Very expressive and exceptionally creamy fruit.

**Seven Peaks Chardonnay** 15 £7–10
**1997**
Pricey but plump and ripe with promise.

**Sutter Home Chardonnay** 14 −£5.00
**1997**

**Sutter Home White** 8 −£5.00
**Zinfandel 1998**
An abomination. Zinfandel is a red wine not a sweet pink gunge. An act of criminality.

**Wente Chardonnay 1998** 14 £5–7
Chewy, very chewy.

**Wente Riva Ranch** 14 £7–10
**Reserve Chardonnay**
**1996**
Expensive though elegant and expressive.

**Wente Sauvignon Blanc** 13 £5–7
**1998**
Lacks freshness and zip.

**Wente White Zinfandel** 10 £5–7
**1998**
Too sweet.

### VICTORIA WINE WHITE

**Columbia Crest** 15.5 £5–7
**Chardonnay 1997**

**Fetzer Sundial** 16 £5–7
**Chardonnay, 1998**
Always as full of sun as the face of a California beachbum, this is fruit modelled on richness, warmth, and the flavours of the tropics. This vintage has a lovely freshness to it. Selected stores.

**Fetzer Syrah Rosé 1999** 13 £5–7
Very clammy and humid. Needs mackerels from the barbecue to leaven its richness.

**Vendange Californian** 11 −£5.00
**Dry White 1998**
Struggles to make an impact. Like a one-legged centre-forward. Not at Wine Rack.

**Vendanges White** 9 −£5.00
**Zinfandel 1998**
Utterly revolting confection: sweet, rosy, clotted, jejune.

**Wente Riva Ranch** 16 £7–10
**Chardonnay 1996**
Big and a touch blistering in its richness and spicy pear and pastry fruitiness but I love its quirkiness and food compatibility.

### WAITROSE WHITE

**Acacia Chardonnay 1995** 14.5 £10–13
Thundering richness and leafy depth. Only from Waitrose Direct.

**Fetzer Unoaked** 14.5 £5–7
**Chardonnay 1999**
Nutty richness and warm throughout of fruit. Not elegant but good with food.

**Fetzer Viognier 1999** 15 £7–10
Delicious! And what an apricot-

scented change from melony
Chardonnay.

Gallo Sonoma County    10    £7–10
Chardonnay 1995

Quady Essensia Orange    16    £5–7
Muscat, California 1996
(half-bottle)

Excellent keeping qualities with its
waxy, candied orange peel fruit and
rich acidity – say ten years or so – but
great now with fresh fruit – or a crème
brûlée.

Quady Starboard Batch    15    −£5.00
88, California (half-bottle)

# PART 2

# FORTIFIED AND
# SPARKLING WINES

# FORTIFIED WINES

## ASDA

**Fine Ruby Port, Asda** `14` `£5–7`

**Manzanilla, Asda** `17` `£5–7`
A staggeringly well-endowed,
aromatic, yet subtle sherry of immense
charm and richness. Unusually well
textured and soft (uniquely so, I
suggest) and so warm and
approachable it must convert those
who previously found the tealeaf and
hard edge of this style of wine too
austere.

**Tawny Port, Asda** `15` `£5–7`

## BOOTHS

**Amontillado del Puerto,** `16` `£7–10`
**Lustau**
Sure, it smells mouldy and too ripe for
comfort but imagine a glass, well
chilled, with a bowl of almonds and an
absorbing book. Great combination.

**Banyuls Chapoutier 1996** `16` `£7–10`
**(50cl)**
A red wine of wonderful sweet
richness. It's like liquid Christmas
cake.

**Churchills Dry White** `13` `£7–10`
**Port**
Labelled like an invitation to a
memorial service, this is rich and
sticky and fine in the Douro, ice-cold,

in 140-degree heat and with comedic
companions. In other circumstances it
may fail to ignite your soul.

**Finest Reserve Port,** `14.5` `£7–10`
**Booths**
Very sweet and simpering and again
fruit cakes get top billing.

**Fino, Booths** `14` `–£5.00`

**Henriques & Henriques** `15` `£10–13`
**5 year Old Madeira**

**Lustau Old East India** `17` `£7–10`
**Sherry**
Magnificent name, recalling the
excesses of empire, just as the intense
sweet fruit (molasses and butterscotch
with crème brûlée overtones) is
redolent of excess around Victorian
dinner tables. A taste of history. Quite
marvellous stuff.

**Manzanilla Sherry,** `15` `–£5.00`
**Booths**
Classic tealeaf and saline-edged, bone-
dry fruit – or rather, not fruit so much
as decayed vegetable matter.

**Medium Amontillado** `15.5` `–£5.00`
**NV, Booths**
Delicious rich crème brûlée-edged rich
fruit which is never sweet. A
marvellous winter warmer.

**Niepoort LBV 1994** `13` `£10–13`
Sweet, and you can taste the alcohol.

Niepoort Ruby Port  14  £7–10
Sweet and rich and great with fruit
cakes (Uncle Eustace, for example).

Taylors Quinta de  15.5  £13–20
Vargellas Port 1986

## M&S

Pale Dry Fino Sherry  16  –£5.00
One of the best finos around, blended
specifically to M&S's instructions, in
which the bone-dry salinity of classic
fino has a background echo of gentle
fruit so the result is a lingering
pleasure, still very dry, of residual
richness. A fino of exceptional style –
and still a great wine for grilled
prawns.

Vintage Character Port  15  £5–7

## MAJESTIC

Amontillado Seco  16  £7–10
Napoleon, Hidalgo
Pour it over ice cream or simply use a
spoon to lap it up. It's molasses-rich
but not sweet. Wonderful treat for the
in-laws.

Pedro Ximénez Viejo  15  £7–10
Napoleon, Hidalgo

Taylor's Quinta de Terra  17  £13–20
Feita 1986
Like taking a draught of liquidised
hedgerow plus sun, an allotment of
herbs and even a hint of very soft,
beautifully developed tannins. The
texture is balsamic and gripping, the
effect is heady, the residual memory is
of doing something rather naughty.

## ODDBINS

Bodegas Don Tomas  16  –£5.00
'Zingara' Manzanilla,
Sanlúcar Du Barrameda
NV (half-bottle)
An acquired taste, this bone-dry,
tealeaf-flavoured, saline-tangy aperitif.
Please acquire it. It will be difficult.
The way will be fraught. But one day
you will be able to say I am, my
children, a real Manzanilla lover.

Classic Fino, Valdespino  16  £7–10
NV
Intense fruit of such dryness it puckers
the molars. Remarkable austerity in a
world of so much sweet fruit. Terrific
with grilled prawns,

Classic Manzanilla,  16  £5–7
Valdespino NV
Dry as above, tealeaf-edged, beautiful.
One of the planet's great pre-prandial
tipples.

## SAFEWAY

Amontillado, Safeway  13  –£5.00

Blandy's Duke of  16  £7–10
Clarence Rich Madeira
Wonderful old-fashioned plot:
Dickensian, warm, sweet, sentimental.
Drink it with Christmas cake. At most
stores.

Fino, Safeway  14  –£5.00

González Byass Tio Pepe  14  £7–10
Fino Muy Sec NV
Very dry and old uncle-y.

Marsala Superiore,  16  £5–7
Garibalde Dolce NV (18%
vol)
Staggeringly rich and figgy. Wonderful

for desserts of all descriptions (even if they all come served at once on the same grand plate). Or pour it over ice cream.

Vintage Character Port, Safeway `13` `£5–7`

Warre's Warrior Finest Reserve Port NV `13` `£7–10`

## SAINSBURY'S

Blandy's Duke of Clarence Madeira `15.5` `£7–10`

González Byass Matusalem NV (half-bottle) `17.5` `£10–13`
Wonderful! One of the world's great dessert wines. The texture and the colour of engine oil, it has a butterscotch and crème brûlée sweetness and a complex smoky honeyed edge. Selected stores.

Medium Dry Montilla, Sainsbury's `13.5` `–£3.50`

Pale Cream Montilla, Sainsbury's `14` `–£3.50`

Pale Cream Sherry, Sainsbury's `15.5` `–£5.00`

Pale Dry Amontillado, Sainsbury's `15` `–£5.00`

Pale Dry Fino Sherry, Sainsbury's `15` `£5–7`

Pale Dry Manzanilla, Sainsbury's `15` `–£5.00`

Pale Dry Montilla, Sainsbury's `14` `–£3.50`

Ruby Port, Sainsbury's `13` `£5–7`

Sainsbury's LBV Port 1992 `15.5` `£7–10`

Tawny Port, Sainsbury's `13.5` `£5–7`

Ten Year Old Tawny Port, Sainsbury's `15` `£7–10`

## SOMERFIELD

Amontillado Sherry, Somerfield `17.5` `–£5.00`
Quite magnificent richness and honeyed dryness with a sweet edge which is unusually rich yet not ripe. A lovely wine of great class.

Cream Sherry, Somerfield `16` `–£5.00`
A bargain wine for chocolate biscuit lovers. The biscuits and the wine is a marriage made not on this earth.

Fino Sherry, Somerfield `16` `–£5.00`
Remarkable lilt on the finish which stops the wine being characterised as austere. A remarkably toothsome experience.

Manzanilla Sherry, Somerfield `16` `–£5.00`
Superb nutty Earl Grey (subtle) tealeaf edge. A wonderful aperitif wine of great distinction.

## SPAR

Old Cellar LBV Port 1996, Spar `14` `£7–10`
Very rich and ripe and puzzling to match with food. Fruit cake? Stilton? Doesn't have the crustiness of fine vintage port but it's forward enough to raise the spirits.

Old Cellar Ruby Port NV, Spar `14.5` `£5–7`
Rich, sweet and generous – just like

the perfect maiden aunt. A perfect fireside cockle-warmer.

## TESCO

**10 Year Old Tawny Port, Tesco** `13.5` `£10–13`

**Finest Madeira, Tesco** `15.5` `£7–10`

**Mick Morris Rutherglen Liqueur Muscat (half-bottle)** `17` `–£5.00`
A miraculously richly textured pud wine of axle-grease texture and creamy figginess. Huge, world class.

**Superior Oloroso Seco, Tesco** `16` `–£3.50`
Contemplating that lush amber hue, like the eyes of a rare snake, the promise of great things is evident and so it proves. It is dry yet it has burned butter, molasses (dry), and a wonderful spread of flavours as it stretches itself over the palate. A quite superb drink, well chilled, by itself, as an aperitif with nuts etc, and, supremely, as a bottle to read by. An Anita Brookner hero would drink this wine and smile at life.

**Superior Palo Cortado, Tesco** `16` `–£5.00`
For a pound more you get more life to the bouquet and a rich, plumper texture than Tesco's Superior Oloroso . . . but the wine has many similar features. The Palo, perhaps, is more elegant and individual.

## UNWINS

**Calem 10 Year Old Port** `11` `£13–20`

**Calem Colheita Tawny Port 1987** `10` `£20+`
Not good value. Many other tawnies are more vigorous at half the price.

**Calem Late Bottled Vintage Port 1994** `14` `£7–10`
Sweet yet biscuity. Rich yet layered and not obvious. Ripe yet capable of subtle surprises.

**Calem Quinta da Foz Port 1987** `13` `£13–20`

**Calem Vintage Port 1983** `10` `£20+`
Load of rubbish for fifty quid. Defies belief that anyone could see any complexity in this straightforwardly rich, sweet wine. The LBV from the same lodge is loads better.

**Cockburns 1991** `13` `£20+`

**Croft 1991** `13` `£20+`

**Dos Cortados Dry Old Oloroso Sherry** `14` `£7–10`

**Henriques & Henriques Aged 10 Years Malmsey Madeira** `16` `£13–20`
To sip while watching an OTT Bond movie over Christmas week. It's not very sweet but it is fruitcake vinified. Utterly delicious and heart-stopping.

**Henriques & Henriques Aged 5 Years Finest Medium Dry Madeira** `15` `£10–13`
Wonderful Christmas aperitif: rich, not sweet but hugely fruity, curranty, ripe, thick and hedonistic.

**Lustau Old East India Sherry** `17` `£7–10`
Magnificent name, recalling the excesses of empire, just as the intense sweet fruit (molasses and butterscotch with crème brûlée overtones) is

redolent of excess around Victorian dinner tables. A taste of history. Quite marvellous stuff.

**Matusalem Sweet Old Oloroso Sherry** `14.5` `£7–10`

**Quinta do Noval 1991** `13` `£20+`

**Warres 1991** `16` `£20+`
The best of the '91s. Hugely delicious figgy richness and grip.

## VICTORIA WINE

**Dows LBV 1992** `13.5` `£10–13`

**Quinta de Vargellas Vintage Port 1986** `15` `£13–20`

**Taylors Quinta de Terra Feita 1986** `17` `£13–20`
Like taking a draught of liquidised hedgerow plus sun, an allotment of herbs and even a hint of very soft, beautifully developed tannins. The texture is balsamic and gripping, the effect is heady, the residual memory is of doing something rather naughty.

## WAITROSE

**10 Year Old Tawny Port, Waitrose** `14` `£10–13`
Very rich and sympathetic (to a slice of Christmas cake).

**Apostoles Palo Cortado Muy Viejo (half-bottle)** `18.5` `£10–13`
The ultimate bookworm's, lone hedonist treat: a wine of huge treacly texture (but not sweetness), baked apple and cobnut crumble-edged fruit with touches of liquorice, and a stunningly gripping finish.

**Apostoles Palo Cortado Oloroso (half-bottle)** `15.5` `£7–10`

**Comte de Lafont Pineau des Charentes** `15` `£5–7`

**Dry Fly Amontillado** `12` `£5–7`

**Fino Sherry, Waitrose** `15.5` `–£5.00`
Bone-dry, saline, demanding, clean –has a lovely lingering marzipan echo.

**Fonseca Traditional LBV 1983** `15` `£13–20`

**Matusalem Oloroso Dulce Muy Viejo (half-bottle)** `16.5` `£10–13`
Brilliant wine to clog the throats of carol singers. Has a rich toffeed undertone of burned treacle.

**Oloroso Sherry, Waitrose** `13` `–£5.00`

**Solera Jerezana Dry Amontillado, Waitrose** `16` `£5–7`
Stunning rich, dry, crème brûlée edge. Marvellous cockle-warmer.

**Solera Jerezana Dry Oloroso, Waitrose** `16.5` `£5–7`
Fabulous chilled as an aperitif. Dry toffee fruit with a hint of almond.

**Solera Jerezana Old Oloroso, Waitrose** `16.5` `£5–7`
Roast walnuts, herbs, molasses, malt whisky (very subtle) – what a marvellous wine.

**Vintage Warre Quinta da Cavadinha 1987** `17.5` `£13–20`
A magnificently complete port. It has a chewy texture (vibrant tannins), lovely complex fruit of immense depths and sunny ripeness, and lovely balance. It is a wine to stiffen the sinews, summon up the blood, stun the soul.

# SPARKLING WINES

## ASDA

Asti Spumante NV, Asda `11` `−£5.00`

Cava Brut, Asda `16.5` `−£5.00`
Utterly superb. It's better than Krug at £100. More authentic value for money, unpretentious freshness and classic dryness.

Cava Medium Dry, Asda `13` `−£5.00`

Cava Rosado 1998, Asda `13.5` `−£5.00`
Very flinty and rich.

Champagne Brut NV, Asda `13.5` `£10–13`

Champagne Brut Rosé NV, Asda `13` `£10–13`

Charles Lafitte Cuvée 2000 NV `13` `£13–20`

Crémant de Bourgogne 1997 `14` `£5–7`

De Bregille Vintage 1995 `14` `£13–20`

Nicholas Feuillate Blanc de Blancs NV `13` `£13–20`

Nottage Hill Sparkling Chardonnay 1996 `15` `£5–7`

Rondel Cava NV `14` `£5–7`
Very soft and subtly rich.

Seaview Sparkling NV `14.5` `£5–7`
One of the best-value bubblies on the planet. Defeats the idea of Champagne at twice the price.

Stamps Sparkling 1999 `15` `£5–7`
Delicately delicious. Lovely hint of raspberry fruit on the finish.

Three Choirs Cuvée Brut (England) `10` `£5–7`

Vintage Cava 1996, Asda `15.5` `£5–7`

Vintage Champagne 1993, Asda `14.5` `£13–20`

## BOOTHS

Bollinger Grande Année 1990 `11` `£20+`

Brossault Rosé Champagne NV `13` `£13–20`

Bruno Paillard Champagne NV `15` `£13–20`

Champagne Barone-Fuenté Brut NV `15` `£10–13`
Rather grand in its rich croissant-edged fruitiness yet dryness.

Champagne Fleurie NV (organic) `10` `£13–20`

Champagne Gremillet NV `14` `£13–20`

Chandon Argentina Brut NV `15` `£7–10`

Brilliant alternative to Champagne.
Great aperitif style.

**Chapelle de Cray Brut** 13 –£5.00
**Rosé 1993 (France)**

**Concerto Lambrusco** 16 £5–7
**1998 (Italy)**
Sparkling red wine? From Italy? Called
Lambrusco? Ah! But this is the real
thing. Magically yet impishly fruity, it
is marvellous with charcuterie at the
start of a meal.

**Crémant d'Alsace Cuvée** 13 £7–10
**Prestige (France)**

**Deutz NV (New Zealand)** 15 £10–13
Better than a thousand Champagnes.

**Hunter's Miru Miru 1996** 15 £10–13
**(New Zealand)**

**Palau Brut Cava NV** 10 –£5.00

**Pétillant de Listel,** 12 –£2.50
**Traditional**

**Piper Heidsieck Brut** 15 £13–20
**Champagne NV**
Very fine and classy.

**Prosecco Zonin NV** 16 –£5.00
**(Italy)**
One of the world's great unsung
bubbly wine bargains. Deliciously dry
with a hint of strawberry.

## BUDGENS

**Budgens Brut** 12 £13–20
**Champagne NV**
Not in the same league as the Cava.

**Budgens Rosé** 10 £13–20
**Champagne NV**
Rather feeble as it finishes.

**Cava la Vuelta NV** 14 –£5.00
Very lemony and thick.

**Hardys Stamp Sparkling** 14 £5–7
**Chardonnay Pinot Noir**
**NV**
Richer than most.

**Lindauer Brut NV** 15 £5–7
An excellent, sane alternative to
overpriced Champagnes.

## CWS

**Australian Quality** 14 –£5.00
**Sparkling Wine, Co-op**

**Blossom Hill NV (USA)** 13 £5–7

**Brut Sparkling** 13.5 –£5.00
**Chardonnay NV, Co-op**
**(France)**

**Cava Brut NV, Co-op** 14 –£5.00

**De Bracieux Champagne** 11 £10–13
**NV**

**Jacob's Creek Sparkling** 15 £5–7
**Chardonnay/Pinot Noir**
**NV (Australia)**

**Moscato Spumante NV,** 11 –£5.00
**Co-op**
Very sweet.

**Sparkling Saumur NV,** 13 £5–7
**Co-op**
Very earthy.

**Tempranillo Brut Red** 13.5 £5–7
**NV, Co-op**
I like sparkling red but Tempranillo
lacks the weight to counterpoint the
crisp bubbles. Still, it's a brave stab.
Might work best with tandoori dishes.

**Y2K Champagne NV** 13 £13–20

## KWIK SAVE

**Asti Spumante NV, Somerfield**   `14`  `£5–7`
Very, very sweet and old grandadish.

**Cava Brut NV, Somerfield**   `14.5`  `–£5.00`
Not bone-dry, but not overly fruity either. Delicious aperitif.

**Cava Rosado NV, Somerfield**   `14`  `–£5.00`
A solid rosé, if not an exciting one.

**Moscato Fizz, Somerfield**   `14`  `–£2.50`
Sweet and Muscaty. Makes a pleasant summer tipple.

**Prince William Blanc de Noirs Champagne NV, Somerfield**   `14`  `£10–13`
Very fruity, has hints of wild strawberries. Delicious aperitif. Limited distribution.

## M&S

**Bluff Hill Sparkling Wine (New Zealand)**   `13`  `£5–7`

**Cava Brut NV (Spain)**   `13.5`  `£5–7`

**Cava Medium Dry NV (Spain)**   `12`  `£5–7`

**Champagne de St-Gall Blanc de Blancs NV**   `15`  `£13–20`

**Champagne de St-Gall Brut NV**   `13.5`  `£13–20`

**Champagne Desroches NV**   `13.5`  `£13–20`

**Champagne Oudinot Grand Cru 1993**   `13`  `£13–20`

**Cuvée Orpale Grand Cru 1990**   `12`  `£20+`

Charming! Love it! But at £5.99 not £25.

**Gold Label Sparkling Chardonnay NV**   `16`  `£5–7`
Excellent, dry, subtly fruity bubbly – elegance and classic tailoring at a third of the price of a comparable Champagne.

**Oudinot Brut Champagne**   `13`  `£10–13`
Stewed apple edge to it.

**Vintage Cava 1994**   `15`  `£7–10`

**Veuve Truffeau Colombard/Chardonnay Brut**   `13.5`  `–£5.00`

## MAJESTIC

**Ayala Champagne NV**   `15`  `£13–20`
Decidedly prim and very French.

**Ayala Champagne Rosé NV**   `11`  `£13–20`

**Bouvet-Ladubay Saumur NV**   `10`  `£7–10`
I just find the fruit so gauche and ripe.

**Cava Verano, Freixenet NV**   `15.5`  `–£5.00`

**Conde de Caralt Cava Brut NV**   `16.5`  `£5–7`
As elegant a Cava as they come. Knocks a thousand Champagnes into oblivion.

**De Telmont Grande Réserve Champagne NV**   `14.5`  `£13–20`
Very elegant and a touch hoity-toity.

**Freixenet Cuvée DS 1996**   `16.5`  `£10–13`
Stunning complexity and crispness here. A great sparkling wine. Better than Krug.

Gloria Ferrer Royal `13` `£13–20`
Cuvée 1991
Very sweaty aroma.

Jacquart Brut Mosaïque `12` `£13–20`
Champagne NV

Jacquart Champagne 1992 `12` `£20+`
Very warm. Not overkeen on warm
Champagne.

Lamberhurst Brut NV `8` `£7–10`
(England)
One of the more repulsive bubblies
made. Why bother with grapes so
uncongenial?

Langlois Crémant de `15` `£7–10`
Loire NV (France)
Charming muted richness and crisp
acid attack.

Langlois Crémant de `16` `£7–10`
Loire Rosé NV (France)
Terrific! A real excuse to make a rosé
bubbly. Better than a thousand
Champagnes.

Lindauer Special Reserve `16` `£7–10`
NV (New Zealand)
Very elegant and classically cut. Very
smart on the taste buds.

Oeil de Perdrix `16` `£13–20`
Champagne NV
A delicious new blend of the well-
established Majestic bubbly. It's an
onion-skin colour, or partridge's eye,
and it's extremely dry and well
wrought.

Taittinger Champagne `12` `£20+`
Brut NV

Yellowglen Pinot Noir `13.5` `£7–10`
Chardonnay NV
(Australia)

## MORRISONS

Asti Spumante Gianni `14` `−£5.00`
(Italian)

Barramundi Sparkling `15` `−£5.00`
NV (Australia)
Hugely slurpable and entertaining.

Brut de Channay NV `11` `£5–7`
(France)

Champagne Philippe Prie `13` `£10–13`
NV
Lemony and dry.

Chapel Hill Chardonnay `12` `−£5.00`
Pinot Noir NV (Hungary)

'M' Vintage Cava 1996 `15.5` `£5–7`
Very thick and rich but not cloying.
Great with smoked salmon.

Mumm Cuvée Napa Brut `14` `£7–10`
NV (California)
Expensive elegance, but better value
than so many Champagnes.

Paul Herard Champagne `12` `£10–13`
Brut NV

Paul Herard Demi Sec `13.5` `£5–7`
Champagne (half-bottle)

Reminger Sparkling Brut `10` `−£5.00`
NV (France)

Santa Carolina `13` `£5–7`
Chardonnay Brut 1996
(Chile)
A touch feeble as it dries out on the
tongue.

Seaview Brut NV `14` `£5–7`
(Australia)

Seaview Brut Rosé `13.5` `£5–7`
(Australia)
Very rich and ripe.

Sparkling Zero (alcohol-free)   0   −£2.50
And zero is what it scores. Why? It isn't wine. It's a crime.

## ODDBINS

Billecart-Salmon Cuvée Nicholas-François Billecart Brut 1991   14   £20+
Fine Wine Stores only.

Bonnet Brut Heritage NV   13.5   £13–20
Very fruity for a champers.

Cuvee Napa by Mumm Blanc de Blancs NV   15.5   £10–13

Deutz Marlborough Cuvée (New Zealand)   13.5   £7–10

Henri Harlin Brut NV   15   £13–20

Lindauer Special Reserve Brut NV   14.5   £7–10

Mumm Cordon Rouge Cuvée Limitée 1990   13   £20+

Pierre Gimonnet et Fils Brut Gastronome 1995   13.5   £13–20
Not as incisive as its cheaper sister.

Pierre Gimonnet et Fils 'Cuis 1er Cru' Blanc de Blancs Brut NV   16   £13–20
Hugely elegant and civilised. Beats many a bubbly costing three times more.

Ployez-Jacquemart Brut NV   13   £13–20
Lot of money for the style.

Yellowglen Vintage Brut 1995 (Australia)   14   £7–10

## SAFEWAY

Albert Etienne Champagne Brut Rosé NV, Safeway   13   £13–20

Albert Etienne Champagne Vintage 1993, Safeway   13   £13–20

Canard Duchene Champagne Brut NV   14   £13–20

Chandon Argentina NV   15   £7–10
Brilliant alternative to Champagne. Great aperitif style.

Chandon Australia NV   15.5   £7–10
Elegant and rich – not always a combination which is apparent in fine bubbly but here it works.

Chenin Brut, Vin Mousseux de Qualité (France)   14   −£5.00

Conde de Caralt Cava Brut NV   16.5   £5–7
As elegant a Cava as they come. Knocks a thousand Champagnes into oblivion. Top 280 stores from mid-June.

Cuvée Signe Champagne, Nicolas Feuillate NV   14.5   £13–20

Freixenet Cava Rosada Brut NV   13.5   £5–7

Graham Beck Brut NV (South Africa)   14   £5–7

Lambrusco Rosé Light, Safeway (4% vol)   13.5   −£2.50

Lanson Champagne Demi-Sec Ivory Label NV   12   £13–20

Le Bron de Monceny
Chardonnay Brut NV
`12` `−£5.00`

Le Bron de Monceny
Merlot/Gamay Brut NV
`15.5` `−£5.00`
Superb juicy bubbly red for game
dishes. Exuberant, sweet, gushing.
Selected stores.

Le Monferrine Moscato
d'Asti 1999 (5%)
`13` `−£3.50`
Deliciously Muscat and ripe melon
sweetness and bubbles. That's the
recipe. Great chilled in summer. Great
for sweet talking to the neighbours.

Lindauer Brut NV (New
Zealand)
`14` `£7−10`
I'd prefer it under a fiver but then I ask
the impossible.

Louis Roederer
Champagne Brut Premier
NV
`13` `£20+`

Merlot/Gamay Brut NV
(France)
`14` `−£5.00`

Nicolas Feuillate
Champagne Blanc de
Blancs NV
`14` `£13−20`

Piper Heidsieck
Champagne Vintage 1990
`10` `£20+`
Thirty quid? I'd rather put it on a
horse.

Pommery Brut Royal
Champagne NV
`12` `£20+`

Sélection XXI,
Champagne, Nicolas
Feuillate NV
`13` `£13−20`

## SAINSBURY'S

Asti, Sainsbury's (Italy)
`13` `−£5.00`

Australian Sparkling
Wine, Sainsbury's
`13` `−£5.00`

Blanc de Noirs
Champagne NV,
Sainsbury's
`16` `£10−13`
One of the best-value Champagnes
around. Really elegant.

Cava Brut NV,
Sainsbury's
`16.5` `−£5.00`
Still a flagship sparkling wine: crisp,
clean, fresh, classic. Better than
hundreds of Champagnes.

Cava Rosado Brut,
Sainsbury's
`15` `−£5.00`

Champagne Canard
Duchene NV
`14` `£13−20`

Champagne Chanoine
1990
`15.5` `£13−20`

Champagne Charles
Heidsieck Mis en Cave
1995
`14.5` `£20+`

Champagne Demi-Sec
NV, Sainsbury's
`14` `£10−13`

Champagne Jeanmaire
Brut 1990
`14` `£13−20`

Champagne Krug Grande
Cuvée
`10` `£20+`

Champagne Lanson Black
Label Brut NV
`13.5` `£13−20`

Champagne Laurent-
Perrier NV
`13.5` `£20+`

Champagne Louis
Roederer NV
`13` `£20+`

Champagne Nicolas
Feuillate Premier Cru NV
`14` `£13−20`

Champagne Perrier-Jouët
NV
`14` `£13−20`

Champagne Pol Roger
1990
`13` `£20+`

Champagne Pommery Brut Royal NV | 13 | £20+

Champagne Premier Cru Extra Dry, Sainsbury's | 15 | £13–20
Extra dry? Don't you believe it. It hums with soft, raspberry-scented fruit. Also available in 1.5 litres. Most stores.

Champagne Veuve Clicquot Grande Dame 1990 | 12 | £20+

Chardonnay Brut, Méthode Traditionelle, Sainsbury's (France) | 15 | £5–7

Freixenet Cava Rosada NV | 13.5 | £5–7

Grand Cru Millennium Champagne 1995, Sainsbury's | 13 | £13–20
To be drunk only by those born in the year of the vintage.

Hardys Nottage Hill Chardonnay Brut 1998 | 15 | £5–7
Dry, subtly nutty and rich. Most stores.

Hardys Stamp of Australia Chardonnay/ Pinot Noir Brut NV | 14 | £5–7
Selected stores.

Jacobs Creek Chardonnay/Pinot Noir Brut NV (Australia) | 13 | £5–7

Lindauer Special Reserve NV (New Zealand) | 16 | £7–10
Very elegant and classically cut. Very smart on the taste buds. Selected stores.

Millennium Vintage Cava 1997, Sainsbury's | 13 | £5–7

Mumm Champagne Brut NV | 13 | £13–20
Most stores.

Piper Heidsieck Brut NV | 15 | £13–20
Very fine and classy. Most stores.

Sekt, Medium Dry, Sainsbury's (Germany) | 13 | –£5.00

Vin Mousseux Brut, Sainsbury's (France) | 13 | –£5.00

Vintage Blanc de Blancs Champagne 1993, Sainsbury's | 14 | £13–20
Most stores.

## SOMERFIELD

Asti Spumante NV, Somerfield | 14 | £5–7
Very very sweet and old grandadish.

Australian Quality Sparkling NV, Somerfield | 14 | £5–7

Australian Sparkling Chardonnay 1995, Somerfield | 14 | £5–7
A very fruity bubbly, not subtle but equally not OTT.

Cava Brut NV, Somerfield | 14.5 | –£5.00
Not bone-dry, but not overly fruity either. Delicious aperitif.

Cava Rosada NV, Somerfield | 14 | –£5.00
A solid rosé, if not an exciting one.

Crémant de Bourgogne, Caves de Bailly 1998, Somerfield | 13.5 | £5–7

Devauzelle Champagne NV | 13.5 | £10–13

Lindauer Brut NV (New Zealand) | 14 | £7–10

I'd prefer it under a fiver but then I ask the impossible.

**Millennium Champagne** `13` `£13–20`
**1990, Somerfield**

**Moscato Fizz, Somerfield** `14` `–£2.50`
Sweet and Muscaty. Makes a pleasant summer tipple.

**Mumm Cuvee Napa Brut** `14` `£7–10`
**NV (California)**
Expensive elegance, but better value than so many Champagnes.

**Nicolas Feuillate Brut** `14` `£13–20`
**Premier Cru NV**

**Nottage Hill Sparkling** `14.5` `£5–7`
**Chardonnay**

**Pierre Larousse** `16` `–£5.00`
**Chardonnay Brut NV**
**(France)**
Superb value for money. Has good rich fruit but it's serious and dry and not remotely tart or blowsy. Real bargain elegance here.

**Prince William Blanc de** `13.5` `£13–20`
**Blancs Champagne NV,**
**Somerfield**

**Prince William Blanc de** `14` `£10–13`
**Noirs Champagne NV,**
**Somerfield**
Very fruity, has hints of wild strawberries. Delicious aperitif. Limited distribution.

**Prince William** `15.5` `£13–20`
**Champagne 1er Cru,**
**Somerfield**
A very classy blend of Chardonnay and Pinot Noir.

**Prince William** `13` `£13–20`
**Champagne Rosé NV,**
**Somerfield**

**Prince William** `13` `£13–20`
**Millennium Champagne**
**1990, Somerfield**

**Seaview Brut Rosé** `13.5` `£5–7`
Very rich and ripe.

**Seaview Pinot Noir/** `15` `£7–10`
**Chardonnay 1995**
**(Australia)**

**South African Sparkling** `16` `£5–7`
**Sauvignon, Somerfield**
Gorgeous, just gorgeous! Loads of personality and flavour – yet it's stylish withal.

**Vintage Cava 1996,** `15.5` `£5–7`
**Somerfield**
Real classy bubbly. Better than so many Champagnes. Limited distribution.

## SPAR

**Cava Brut NV, Spar** `15` `–£5.00`
Very rich and creamy but the firm structure holds the fruit well in. A bubbly for food, what's more.

**Marqúes de Prevel** `10` `£13–20`
**Champagne NV, Spar**
Blatant, overpriced, murky. The Cava at a third of the price is a much tastier beast.

## TESCO

**Australian Sparkling** `13` `–£5.00`
**Wine NV, Tesco**
Very corpulent and sluggishly fruity. For a bubbly it's too fruity for me.

**Blanc de Blancs** `13.5` `£13–20`
**Champagne NV, Tesco**

**Blanc de Noirs** `14` `£13–20`
**Champagne NV, Tesco**

Cava NV, Tesco   `15`  `-£5.00`
Deliciously dry and deftly interwoven
fruit and acid.

Chapel Down Epoch Brut  `11`  `£5-7`
NV (England)

Charles Duret Blanc de  `13`  `-£5.00`
Blancs Brut NV

Charles Duret Blanc de  `12`  `-£5.00`
Blancs Demi-Sec NV
Too sweet for me.

Cockatoo Ridge Black  `16.5`  `£7-10`
Sparkling NV
One of the best sparkling reds around.
It has great dry richness and loads of
energy. A terrific wine for game
dishes. 100 selected stores.

Demi-Sec Champagne,  `13`  `£10-13`
Tesco

Hardys Stamp of  `14`  `£5-7`
Australia Chardonnay/
Pinot Noir Sparkling NV
Very fruity but not overbaked.

Hungarian Sparkling  `13.5`  `-£5.00`
Chardonnay NV, Tesco
Touch of florid fruit on the finish.

Jacob's Creek Sparkling  `15`  `£5-7`
Chardonnay/Pinot Noir
NV (Australia)

Laurent-Perrier Cuvée  `11`  `£20+`
Rosé Brut NV

Laurent-Perrier Vintage  `13`  `£20+`
1990

Les Etoiles Organic  `12`  `£5-7`
Sparkling Wine NV
Very soft/dry approach and sullen –
though fruity, it's not happy. Not at all
stores.

Lindauer Brut NV (New  `14`  `£7-10`
Zealand)

I'd prefer it under a fiver but then I ask
the impossible.

Lindauer Special Reserve  `16`  `£7-10`
NV (New Zealand)
Very elegant and classically cut. Very
smart on the taste buds.

Moët Vintage 1993  `13.5`  `£20+`

Nicolas Feuillate Brut NV  `13.5`  `£13-20`

Pirie 1996  `13`  `£13-20`
Overpriced for the leanness of the
style. Wine Advisor Stores only.

Premier Cru Champagne  `15`  `£10-13`
Brut NV

Rosé Cava NV, Tesco  `15.5`  `-£5.00`

South African Sparkling  `14.5`  `-£5.00`
Sauvignon Blanc 1998,
Tesco

Taittinger Champagne  `12`  `£20+`
Brut NV

Valdivieso Sparkling  `16`  `£5-7`
Merlot 1998
What fun! Mellow, ripe, rich, hugely
fruity and great with spicy food. Try it
with a vindaloo. It's a triumph. 30
stores only.

Veuve du Vernay Brut  `14`  `£7-10`
NV
Soft and elegant. Most stores.

## THRESHER

Bollinger RD 1985  `13`  `£20+`

Bollinger Special Cuvée  `14`  `£20+`
NV

Canard Duchene Charles  `14.5`  `£20+`
VII NV

Charles Heidsieck 'Mis en  `13`  `£20+`
Caves 1995' NV

Cool Ridge Sparkling Chardonnay/Pinot Noir Brut NV (Hungary) | 12 | −£5.00

Deutz NV (New Zealand) | 15 | £10–13
Better than a thousand Champagnes.

Gosset Grande Millésime 1989 | 15 | £20+

Gosset Grande Réserve NV | 14 | £20+

Green Point Brut 1996 | 15 | £10–13

Krug Grande Cuvée NV | 13 | £20+

Krug Vintage 1989 | 13.5 | £20+

La Corunna Cava NV | 15 | −£5.00

Lanson Vintage Gold Label 1993 | 13.5 | £20+

Lindauer Brut NV (New Zealand) | 14 | £7–10
I'd prefer it under a fiver but then I ask the impossible.

Lindauer Brut Rosé NV (New Zealand) | 15 | £7–10
A truly delicious rosé of real style.

Lindauer Special Reserve NV (New Zealand) | 16 | £7–10
Very elegant and classically cut. Very smart on the taste buds.

Louis Roederer Brut Vintage 1993 (magnum) | 13 | £20+

Mumm Cuvee Napa Brut (California) | 16 | £7–10
So much more assertive, refined, tasty and sanely priced than its French cousin I'm surprised there aren't serious riots in Reims.

Out of the Blue Lightly Sparkling (Italy) (4%) | 10 | −£3.50

Perrier-Jouët Brut Vintage 1992 | 12 | £20+

Pinot Grigio Frizzante NV (Italy) | 15 | −£5.00
Crisp and elegant with a subtle hint of underripe apricot.

Piper Heidsieck Rare 1985 | 17 | £20+
My favourite: toast, nuts, fruit, finesse, dry, liveliness, not too old – perfect maturity. Bottoms Up only.

Pol Roger Sir Winston Churchill Cuvée 1988 | 16 | £20+
Immensely proud, dry, witty, plump yet fleet of foot. Goes extremely well with cucumber sandwiches with mint. Also smoked salmon. Bottoms Up only.

Pommery Vintage 1991 | 12 | £20+

Veuve Clicquot La Grande Dame 1990 | 16 | £20+
Rather lovely – achieves dryness yet texture and a suggestion of fruit.

## UNWINS

Alain Thienot Brut 1990 | 10 | £20+
Worth a tenner at most. It's highly drinkable but far too highly priced.

Cuvée Princesse de Aimery Blanquette de Limoux 1997 | 13 | £5–7
Odd stale nut finish.

Duchatel Blanc de Blancs Brut NV | 12.5 | £13–20

Duchatel Brut Champagne NV | 13 | £10–13
Tarty stuff.

Duchatel Champagne Brut 1994 | 13.5 | £13–20
Elegance here. The best by far of the Duchatel wines at Unwins.

Duchatel Rosé Brut Champagne NV | 11 | £13–20
Nowt much for £16.

Freixenet Cava Brut NV | 15.5 | £5–7

Graham Beck Brut NV (South Africa) | 14 | £5–7

Jacob's Creek Sparkling Chardonnay/Pinot Noir NV (Australia) | 15 | £5–7

Lindauer Brut NV (New Zealand) | 14.5 | £7–10

Pelorus Brut 1995 | 18 | £10–13
Better than Krug. It's got beautifully smoky fruit, richness with elegance, bite with delicacy.

## VICTORIA WINE

Blossom Hill Sparkling NV (USA) | 13 | £5–7

Bollinger RD 1985 | 13 | £20+

Bollinger Special Cuvée NV | 14 | £20+

Canard Duchene Charles VII NV | 14.5 | £20+

Charles Heidsieck Mis en Caves 1995 | 13 | £20+

Cool Ridge Sparkling Chardonnay/Pinot Noir Brut NV (Hungary) | 12 | –£5.00

Cuvée Napa Brut, Mumm NV | 16 | £7–10
So much more assertive, refined, tasty and sanely priced than its French cousin I'm surprised there aren't serious riots in Reims.

Deutz Marlborough Cuvée NV | 13.5 | £10–13

Gosset Grande Millésime 1989 | 15 | £20+

Gosset Grande Réserve NV | 14 | £20+

Green Point Brut 1996 | 15 | £10–13

Krug Grande Cuvée NV | 13 | £20+

Krug Vintage 1989 | 13.5 | £20+

La Corunna Cava NV | 15 | –£5.00

Lanson Vintage Gold Label 1993 | 13.5 | £20+

Louis Roederer Brut Vintage 1993 (magnum) | 13 | £20+

Marquis de la Tour Demi-Sec NV (France) | 8 | –£5.00
A touch revolting.

Marquis de la Tour Rosé NV (France) | 14 | –£5.00

Piper Heidsieck Rare 1985 | 17 | £20+
My favourite: toast, nuts, fruit, finesse, dry, liveliness, not too old – perfect maturity. Martha's Vineyard only.

Pol Roger Sir Winston Churchill Cuvée 1988 | 16 | £20+
Immensely proud, dry, witty, plump yet fleet of foot. Goes extremely well with cucumber sandwiches with mint. Also smoked salmon. Martha's Vineyard only.

Pommery Vintage 1991 | 12 | £20+

Seaview Brut Rosé | 14 | £5–7

Veuve Clicquot La Grande Dame 1990 | 16 | £20+
Rather lovely – achieves dryness yet texture and a suggestion of fruit.

## WAITROSE

**Alexandre Bonnet Brut Rosé NV (France)** 12 £13–20

**Banrock Station Sparkling Shiraz NV (Australia)** 17 £7–10

One of the most delicious sparkling Shirazes I've tasted. Concentrated blackcurrant fruit, with spicy plums and a hint of savoury leather, with huge but elegant tannins, and a rousing finish. A magnificent wine for the festive fowl.

**Brut Vintage 1990, Waitrose** 13 £13–20

**Cava Brut NV, Waitrose** 15.5 –£5.00
Terrific blend of local grapes produces individuality and bite.

**Champagne Blanc de Blancs NV, Waitrose** 15 £13–20

**Champagne Blanc de Noirs NV, Waitrose** 15 £10–13
One of the more refined and finesseful successful Blanc de Noirs at the own-label level.

**Champagne Brut NV, Waitrose** 12.5 £13–20

**Champagne Fleury 1993** 13 £20+
At this price, this organic Champagne seems vastly under-exciting and overpriced. Clean and crisp but not great.

**Champagne Fleury Brut NV** 18.5 £13–20
A biodynamic Champagne? How did someone wean the vignerons off pesticides and herbicides and on to the astrologic ideas of Rudolf Steiner? In Reims? With that weird climate? It's a miracle akin to discovering John Major

campaigning for the Red Brigade. The wine? Superb. All Pinot grapes (fifteen acres of), loads of calm, controlled fruit, immense class (without pretension – no Krug tobacco edging), beautiful fruit, and a lovely finish. It has wonderful texture which, as with all outstanding Champagnes, combines a seemingly soft fruitiness (hint of wild strawberry from the Pinot Noir grapes) with a crisp yet warm finish. One of the best Champagnes I've tasted – ever. For the money, it's a steal. Waitrose has it exclusively, and they have only 1,600 cases of it (yet all Waitrose branches have it). It knocks Moët (which is pricier) into the most cocked of cocked chapeaux.

**Chandon Argentina Brut NV** 15 £7–10
Brilliant alternative to Champagne. Great aperitif style.

**Chandon Australia Brut NV** 15.5 £7–10
Elegant and rich – not always a combination which is apparent in fine bubbly but here it works.

**Chapel Hill Pinot Noir/ Chardonnay NV** 15 –£5.00
Nicely calm fruit here. Finishes well and confidently (like a poem by Robert Graves).

**Charles Heidsieck Champagne Blanc de Blancs 1982** 20 £20+
Perfect Champagne. As good as it is possible for Chardonnay to get with bubbles. It is perfectly mature, rich and complex but finally dry and delicate. It is so elegant it defines what Champagne is. Only from Waitrose Direct.

Charles Heidsieck Réserve Mise en Cave en 1993 — 13.5 — £20+

Clairette de Die Tradition (half-bottle) (France) — 14 — £5–7

Crémant de Bourgogne Blanc de Noirs, Lugny — 14 — £5–7

Crémant de Bourgogne Rosé NV (France) — 14 — £7–10
Lollipop richness here.

Cuvée Royale Blanquette de Limoux NV — 13 — £5–7
Odd nutty richness.

Duc de Marre Special Cuvée Champagne Brut Non-Vintage — 13.5 — £13–20

Jacob's Creek Sparkling Chardonnay/Pinot Noir NV (Australia) — 15 — £5–7
Great new entrant to the Aussie sparkling wine stakes. Has fruit and essential crispness of attack.

Le Mesnil Blanc de Blancs Grand Cru Champagne Brut Non-Vintage — 14 — £13–20
Rich hints of cherry and pastry.

Lindauer Brut NV (New Zealand) — 14 — £7–10
I'd prefer it under a fiver but then I ask the impossible.

Saumur Brut NV, Waitrose — 14 — £5–7

Seaview Brut NV — 14 — £5–7

Seaview Brut Rosé NV — 13.5 — £5–7
Very rich and ripe.

Sparkling Burgundy NV (France) — 13 — £5–7
Curious jam-tart rich middle to the fruit.

Taittinger Comtes de Champagne Blanc de Blancs 1990 — 13 — £20+
Lot of money here. Not worth it by five times. Only from Waitrose Direct.

## WINE CELLAR

Jansz Tasmanian NV — 12 — £7–10
Very fat and florid and a touch out of breath. Had the grapes been exercising overmuch?

Pelorus NV (New Zealand) — 17 — £10–13
One of the most richly elegant bubblies on the planet in this blend (almost all Chardonnay). It has to be compared with absurdities like Krug to get some idea of the value here.

# PART 3

# A TO Z OF RETAILERS

# ASDA

When I was invited to organise a wine tasting in the cellars of the Café Royal for a small group of citizens, all financial advisers forsooth, I anticipated, rather naïvely, that I could include the venerable vintages the Café has in its cellars. But only the wines on the restaurant's list were available and I was horrified: they were highly priced, in some cases obscenely so, and desperately uninspiring. Asda came to my rescue, insisted on providing for free some of its own wines for the tasting, and two of them were marvellous 17-pointers.

The first was Asda's own-label Manzanilla (17 out of 20, £4.97), which is individually fruity – or perhaps vegetal is a more accurate simile – with a tealeaf edginess. It is an aromatic sherry of charm and unusual, if subtle, richness. Well textured and soft (not as bone dry as most Manzanillas but no less characterful), it is so approachable it might convert those who have found the uncompromising style of this wine austere in the past. This specimen is one of the planet's most civilised summer aperitifs, well chilled in the glass. One of the most popular reds at the Café tasting was 35 Sur Cabernet Sauvignon 1999 (17 points, £4.49) from Chile, which went down gloriously with the audience, more so when the price tag was revealed. Dark, rich, firm yet supple, wonderfully seriously fruity (leather, spice, blackcurrants) and hugely lingering, it provides a generous mouthful.

Of course, the financial advisers were gently gobsmacked, not only by the fruit in the wines but by the chutzpah of Asda, which they conceived as a place at which no civilised individual, pinstriped and bow-tied, would be seen dead buying wine. They are, sadly, right. You don't see hordes of wine buffs in Asda with the exception of the odd, perceptive *Guardian* reader. I say this because Asda's average bottle price is around £3, a touch less perhaps, and this compares with £3.49 for Tesco and a little higher at Sainsbury's. In other words (and pro wine buyers at supermarkets worry about these figures a great deal), the average price which Asda customers are prepared to pay for a bottle of wine is less than at its competitors.

Asda would like to raise this average price. It wants to encourage its customers to try more expensive wines, but two-thirds of them aren't biting. But Asda is still putting great efforts into some great inexpensive wine ranges around the £3.50/£4.99 mark – witness the Tramontane range – and it has an excellent set of buyers. Russell Burgess and Alistair Morrell have been doing a first-rate job for some years now and in 1999 they pulled off something of a coup when they hired the extremely experienced and enthusiastic Sarah Marsay to join them. Indeed, so excited was she at landing the job that she changed her name to Marsh (via a new husband in order to effect the change in the simplest way).

Asda is an old hand at marriage. It was set to wed Woolworth at one stage, only to jilt this retailer prior to striding down the aisle. It is now, as everyone in the UK must surely know by now, the bride of the massive US outfit, Wal-Mart – the retailer which is sending shudders, so the tabloid press make out, down the backs of every retailer in the land. Wal-Mart will do nothing to lift the average price people spend on a bottle of wine at Asda but surely all those folk buying their cheap TVs at an Asda/Wal-Mart superduperstore will be tempted to add a few bottles of wine to their trolleys, will they not?

The conclusion of the successful £6.7 billion takeover of Asda by Wal-Mart was patently the highlight of Asda's year and this has undoubtedly added a new competitive atmosphere to UK shopping. *Retail Week* magazine rather blandly put it that 'Wal-Mart's entry into the UK will dramatically change the face of retailing in this country'. Wal-Mart said that it intended to double Asda's profits (to around £1 billion) within five years.

Asda are a feisty lot, with or without Wal-Mart. They got up Sainsbury's nose by claiming that it now occupied the number-two slot in the grocery league table headed by Tesco (16.53% of the market to Sainsbury's 16.50%). Sainsbury's said Asda had misrepresented the research data by Taylor Nelson Sofres. In the same issue, *Retail Week* reported that Archie Norman, the man who once ran Asda full-time and who is now the Tory's Shadow Minister for Europe, was frustrated by being in opposition. It was said Sainsbury's wanted him to run their show. But he's stayed where he was. Maybe he should persuade Wal-Mart to buy Europe for him to run. They can probably afford it. (Mr Norman, in spite of being a mere shadow, came nineteenth in one of those fatuous lists, this one in *The Sunday Times*, of the Top 20 most powerful men in British business.)

It was from Mr Norman that Asda learned how to spring newsworthy surprises. It found a radical way to attract customers into its stores by staging pop concerts. The rock band Younger Younger 28s described by *Melody Maker* as 'the best new band in Britain', was signed up to go on a six-date tour of Asda supermarkets.

Asda has, though, a solid sense of its social commitments. *The Times* reported that Asda and Tesco have asked toy-maker Mattel to manufacture Barbie dolls with a fuller figure following worries that Barbie's skinny frame was an unhealthy image for young girls and could encourage eating disorders. At the same time, Asda launched a 'value range' of organic products and announced plans to open fifteen home-delivery centres across southern England by 2004.

Asda was said to be recruiting some 27,000 new staff over the next five years and that it was considering replacing its in-store hair salons with mobile phone concessions. (For the life of me I can't see why they can't combine the two. Perfect fit, aren't they?) It also launched a domestic phone-call service offering a pre-paid programme saving customers 62% on domestic and up to 85% on international calls. More imaginatively, it also launched a 'speakers corner in very town' idea encouraging customers as well as anyone else to use Asda car parks to voice their opinions. This idea might well require policing if it gets out of hand.

Most intriguing of all (to my mind) was the report in *Supermarketing* magazine that Asda was to increase its job-sharing programme, a key factor behind this initiative being the need to persuade more female staff to apply for store manager jobs. Only 15 of Asda's 233 stores are run by women, yet it is, of course, women who make up the majority of the customers.

Except, in my limited experience, for the wine shelves. On all my visits to this retailer I would say that men outnumber women by five to three, and that the majority of the women who are there browsing around the wines have a male consort firmly in tow (usually pushing the trolley). These happy-couple trolleys are almost invariably full or half-full of groceries, whereas the trolleys of the single men, that is to say the men shopping solo, are empty or have just a few cans of something or other rattling around. What does this reveal about Asda customers? Only that men head straight for what's on their minds, whereas women take a more leisurely approach. The Freudian implications of this are, of course, enormous.

Does the Asda male / female bias also tell us something deep and meaningful? I really have no idea. I do know that at other supermarkets the male / female bias is slightly different. Safeway seems to have more single men (on my visits); Sainsbury's more single women; Tesco I can't come to a view either way. At Waitrose I once saw a very tall fellow wearing a pink shirt, a psychedelic bow tie, a rose in the lapel of his blue pin-striped suit, perspiring as he filled his trolley to overflowing with bottles of wine. He

ASDA

had a marvellous and very expensively acquired paunch, too. It stuck out like a torpedo.

Asda needs more wine customers like him. All the supermarkets need more customers like him.

Asda Stores Limited
Asda House
Great Wilson Street
Leeds
LS11 5AD

Tel 0500 100055 Customer Service Line
Fax 0113 241 8666
www.asda.co.uk

## ARGENTINIAN RED

Argentinian Bonarda 1999, Asda — 14.5 −£5.00

Argentinian Pinot Noir Oak Aged 1997, Asda — 12 −£5.00

Argentinian Red 1998, Asda — 15.5 −£3.50

Argentinian Sangiovese 1999, Asda — 15.5 −£5.00

Argentinian Syrah 1999, Asda — 16 −£5.00

Far Flung Malbec 1999 — 14 −£5.00

Santa Julia Tempranillo Reserva 1999 — 16.5 £5–7

Santa Julia Tempranillo Selection 1999 — 16 £5–7

## ARGENTINIAN WHITE

Argentinian Chardonnay 1998, Asda — 15.5 −£5.00

Argentinian White NV, Asda — 14 −£3.50

Far Flung Viognier 1999 — 16 −£5.00

## AUSTRALIAN RED

Andrew Peace Cabernet Merlot 1999 — 15 £5–7

Andrew Peace Mighty Murray 1999 — 13 −£5.00

Andrew Peace Shiraz 1999 — 13 £5–7

Fox River Pinot Noir 1998 — 13 £5–7

Hardys Nottage Hill Cabernet Sauvignon/ Shiraz 1997 — 14 £5–7

Hardys Stamp Cabernet Shiraz Merlot 1997 — 15 £5–7

Houghtons Shiraz 1998 — 15 £5–7

Karalta Cabernet 1999, Asda — 12 −£5.00

280

| | | |
|---|---|---|
| Karalta Red 1999, Asda | 13.5 | −£3.50 |
| Karalta Shiraz/Cabernet 1999, Asda | 13 | −£3.50 |
| Lindemans Bin 50 Shiraz 1998 | 14.5 | −£5.00 |
| Maglieri Shiraz 1998 | 15.5 | £7–10 |
| Mount Hurtle Grenache 1997 | 16 | £5–7 |
| Peter Lehmann Seven Surveys Mourvedre/ Shiraz/Grenache 1997 | 16 | £5–7 |
| Rochcombe Pinot Noir 1998 | 12 | £5–7 |
| Rosemount Estate Shiraz 1997 | 15 | £7–10 |
| Rosemount Estate Shiraz Cabernet 1998 | 15.5 | £5–7 |
| Rymill Merlot/Cabernet Sauvignon/Cabernet Franc 1996 | 15.5 | £7–10 |
| Secession Xanadu Shiraz/ Cabernet 1999 | 14.5 | £5–7 |
| South Australia Cabernet Sauvignon 1996, Asda | 14 | −£5.00 |
| Vine Vale Grenache 1998 (Peter Lehmann) | 15 | £5–7 |

## AUSTRALIAN WHITE

| | | |
|---|---|---|
| Andrew Peace Chardonnay 1999 | 15.5 | −£5.00 |
| Cranswick Nine Pines Vineyard Marsanne 1998 | 16.5 | −£5.00 |
| Hardys Chardonnay Semillon 1999 | 16 | £5–7 |
| Hardys Nottage Hill Chardonnay 1997 | 16.5 | −£5.00 |

| | | |
|---|---|---|
| Hardys Stamp Riesling Traminer 1997 | 15 | −£5.00 |
| Houghton HWB 1998 | 16 | £5–7 |
| Karalta Chardonnay 1998, Asda | 15.5 | −£5.00 |
| Karalta Chardonnay/ Semillon 1999, Asda | 13.5 | −£3.50 |
| Karalta Semillon 1999, Asda | 14 | −£5.00 |
| Karalta White 1999, Asda | 14 | −£3.50 |
| Maglieri Semillon 1999 | 16.5 | £5–7 |
| Mount Hurtle Chenin Blanc 1999 | 15.5 | −£5.00 |
| Penfolds Rawson's Retreat Bin 21 Semillon Chardonnay Colombard 1997 | 15 | −£5.00 |
| Peter Lehmann Eden Valley Riesling 1999 | 15.5 | £5–7 |
| Peter Lehmann The Barossa Semillon, 1998 | 16 | £5–7 |
| Rosemount Estate Semillon/Chardonnay 1997 | 15 | £5–7 |
| Rymill Sauvignon Blanc 1999 | 15.5 | £5–7 |
| Temple Bruer Chenin Blanc 1999 | 15.5 | £5–7 |

## BULGARIAN RED

| | | |
|---|---|---|
| Bulgarian Cabernet Sauvignon, Svichtov 1995, Asda | 14 | −£5.00 |
| Bulgarian Country Red, Asda | 14 | −£3.50 |

ASDA

Bulgarian Oak Aged | 15 | −£5.00
Cabernet Sauvignon,
Svichtov 1993, Asda

## CHILEAN RED

35 Sur Cabernet | 17 | −£5.00
Sauvignon 1999

Casas del Bosque Merlot | 14 | £5–7
1999

Castillo de Molina | 15.5 | £5–7
Cabernet Sauvignon 1998

Chilean Cabernet | 16.5 | −£5.00
Sauvignon 1999, Asda

Chilean Red 1997, Asda | 14.5 | −£3.50

Cono Sur Merlot 1999 | 16 | −£5.00

Cono Sur Merlot Reserve | 16.5 | £5–7
1999

Cono Sur Pinot Noir 1999 | 16 | −£5.00

## CHILEAN WHITE

35 Sur Sauvignon Blanc | 15.5 | −£5.00
1999

Casas del Bosque | 15 | £5–7
Sauvignon Blanc 1999

Chilean Sauvignon Blanc | 15.5 | −£5.00
1999, Asda

Chilean White 1999, Asda | 16 | −£3.50

Cono Sur Chardonnay | 14 | −£5.00
1999

## CYPRIOT RED

Ancient Isle Red 1998 | 15.5 | −£3.50

## ENGLISH WHITE

Three Choirs Coleridge | 12 | −£5.00
Hill English White 1998

## FRENCH RED

Beaujolais Villages 1998, | 14 | −£5.00
Asda

Bourgueil Domaine de | 13.5 | £5–7
l'Ereau 1999

Buzet Cuvée 44 1997 | 15 | −£5.00

Château de Parenchere | 16.5 | £5–7
Bordeaux Superieure
1997

Château Guerin Bellevue | 16 | £5–7
Saint Emilion 1997

Château Haut | 16.5 | £7–10
Canteloupe Medoc 1998

Château Lahore Bergez, | 16.5 | −£5.00
Fitou 1998

Château Vieux Gabiran | 14 | −£5.00
1999 (organic)

Chenas 1997, Asda | 14 | −£5.00

Claret NV, Asda | 14.5 | −£3.50

Comte de Gasparin, | 16 | £5–7
Côtes du Rhône 1997

Domaine de Picheral VdP | 15 | −£5.00
d'Oc 1999 (organic)

Domaine des Hardiers | 16.5 | −£5.00
Anjou Villages 1999

Domaine Pont Pinot Noir | 13 | £5–7
1996

La Domeque 'Vieilles | 16 | £5–7
Vignes' Syrah 1997

Merlot, Vin de Pays d'Oc | 15 | −£3.50
1998, Asda

282

| | | |
|---|---|---|
| Moulin a Vent Oak Aged 1997, Asda | 13.5 | £5–7 |
| Oak Aged Côtes du Rhône 1999, Asda | 15 | –£5.00 |
| Organic Claret Château Vieux Georget, Bordeaux 1998 | 15.5 | £5–7 |
| Reserve du Mouton 1997 | 13.5 | £5–7 |
| Tramontane Grenache VdP d'Oc 1998, Asda | 16 | –£5.00 |
| Tramontane Merlot VdP d'Oc 1999, Asda | 16 | –£5.00 |
| Tramontane Red VdP de l'Aude 1999, Asda | 16 | –£3.50 |
| Tramontane Reserve Oak Aged Cabernet Sauvignon VdP d'Oc 1998, Asda | 14.5 | –£5.00 |
| Tramontane Reserve Syrah VdP d'Oc 1996, Asda | 16.5 | £5–7 |
| Tramontane Syrah VdP d'Oc 1997, Asda | 13.5 | –£5.00 |
| Tramontane Syrah/ Merlot VdP d'Oc 1997, Asda | 14.5 | –£3.50 |
| Vacqueyras Domaine de l'Oiselet 1999 | 16.5 | £5–7 |

## FRENCH WHITE

| | | |
|---|---|---|
| Baron de Turckheim Gewürztraminer 1998 | 16 | £7–10 |
| Chablis Grand Cru Bougros 1996 | 13 | £13–20 |
| Chardonnay, Jardin de la France 1999 | 14 | –£3.50 |

| | | |
|---|---|---|
| Chateauneuf-du-Pape Blanc 1997 | 13 | £13–20 |
| Chenin Blanc Loire 1999, Asda | 14 | –£3.50 |
| La Domeque 'Tete de Cuvee' Vieilles Vignes VdP d'Oc 1998 | 16.5 | –£5.00 |
| Muscadet 1999, Asda | 13 | –£3.50 |
| Oak Aged Côtes du Rhône Blanc 1998, Asda | 12 | –£3.50 |
| Rosé d'Anjou 1998, Asda | 12.5 | –£3.50 |
| Sancerre 1999 | 12 | £5–7 |
| St Veran Domaine des Deux Roches 1998 | 15 | £5–7 |
| Tramontane Chardonnay VdP d'Oc 1999, Asda | 16 | –£5.00 |
| Tramontane Chardonnay/ Vermentino 1999, Asda | 13.5 | –£5.00 |
| Tramontane Reserve Oak Aged Chardonnay 1997, Asda | 14 | –£5.00 |
| Tramontane Sauvignon Blanc 1999, Asda | 15 | –£5.00 |
| Tramontane Viognier 1999, Asda | 15.5 | –£5.00 |
| Vouvray Denis Marchais 1999 | 10 | –£5.00 |

## GERMAN WHITE

| | | |
|---|---|---|
| Deidesheimer Hofstuck Riesling Kabinett 1997, Asda | 11 | –£5.00 |
| Devil's Rock Riesling Kabinett 1997 | 14 | –£5.00 |

Liebfraumilch Gold Seal 1997   13.5   −£3.50

## HUNGARIAN RED

River Route Cabernet Sauvignon 1999   15.5   −£3.50

## HUNGARIAN WHITE

Badger Hill Hungarian Sauvignon 1999   14   −£3.50

Hungarian Medium Chardonnay 1999, Asda   12   −£3.50

## ITALIAN RED

Barolo Veglio Angelo 1996   14   £7–10

Chianti 1999, Asda   12   −£3.50

Chianti Classico 1998, Asda   13.5   −£5.00

Chianti Classico Riserva 1997, Asda   14   £5–7

La Vis Trentino Oak Aged Merlot 1998, Asda   14   −£5.00

Organic Valpolicella 1999   13.5   −£5.00

Puccini Chianti Reserva 1997   14   −£5.00

Sicilian Rosso NV, Asda   13.5   −£3.50

Trulli Primitivo del Salento 1999   14   −£5.00

Tuscan Red 1999, Asda   13.5   −£3.50

Valpolicella Classico San Ciriaco 1998   15   £5–7

Valpolicella NV, Asda   13   −£3.50

## ITALIAN WHITE

La Vis Pinot Grigio 1999, Asda   13.5   −£5.00

Lambrusco Bianco NV, Asda   13.5   −£3.50

Lambrusco Rosato NV, Asda   13   −£2.50

Oaked Soave 1998, Asda   14   −£5.00

Soave NV, Asda   14   −£3.50

## NEW ZEALAND RED

Montana Cabernet Merlot 1998   16   £5–7

## NEW ZEALAND WHITE

Montana Sauvignon Blanc 1999   16   £5–7

Nobilo Sauvignon Blanc 1999   15   £5–7

## PORTUGUESE RED

Bright Brothers Baga 1997   14   −£5.00

Douro 1997   13   −£5.00

Duro Douro 1997   13.5   −£5.00

## PORTUGUESE WHITE

Vinho Verde 1999, Asda   10   −£3.50

## SOUTH AFRICAN RED

Cape Merlot 1999, Asda   13.5   −£5.00

Dumisani Ruby Cabernet/Merlot 1999   15.5   −£5.00

Kumala Cabernet Sauvignon/Shiraz 1997 `14` `–£5.00`

Landskroon Merlot Reserve 1999 `16` `£5–7`

Long Mountain Red NV `14` `–£5.00`

Pinotage Reserve 1999, Asda `14` `–£5.00`

Porcupine Ridge Syrah 1999 `16` `£5–7`

South African Cabernet Sauvignon 1999, Asda `14` `–£5.00`

South African Pinotage 1999, Asda `13.5` `–£5.00`

Van Loveren Cabernet Shiraz 1999 `13` `–£5.00`

## SOUTH AFRICAN WHITE

Cape Chardonnay 1999, Asda `15.5` `–£3.50`

Cape Sauvignon Blanc 1999, Asda `15.5` `–£5.00`

First Vintage 2000 `13.5` `–£5.00`

Van Loveren Blanc de Noirs 2000 `14` `–£5.00`

## SPANISH RED

Baron de Ley Reserva Rioja 1994 `13` `£5–7`

Conde de Navasques 1997 `15.5` `–£5.00`

Don Darias Tinto NV `15.5` `–£3.50`

Far Flung Cabernet Merlot 1999 `13` `–£5.00`

Fuentespina Crianza 1996 `15.5` `£7–10`

Mont Marcal Crianza 1997 `14` `–£5.00`

Oaked Tempranillo 1998, Asda `16` `–£5.00`

Rioja NV, Asda `14.5` `–£5.00`

Spanish Oaked Red NV, Asda `13` `–£3.50`

Valdepeñas Crianza 1995 `15.5` `–£5.00`

Vina Albali Gran Reserva 1991 `16` `£5–7`

## SPANISH WHITE

Bodegas Cerrosol Sauvignon Rueda 1998 `15` `–£5.00`

Moscatel de Valencia NV, Asda `16` `–£3.50`

Spanish Oaked White NV, Asda `15.5` `–£3.50`

## USA RED

Arius Zinfandel 1998 `12` `–£5.00`

Bonterra Cabernet Sauvignon 1997 (organic) `17` `£7–10`

California Red 1999, Asda `14` `–£3.50`

California Syrah 1997, Asda `14.5` `–£5.00`

Turning Leaf Cabernet Sauvignon 1997 `12` `£5–7`

Turning Leaf Zinfandel 1996 `12.5` `£5–7`

## USA WHITE

Arius Californian Chenin Blanc 1998, Asda `13` `–£5.00`

ASDA

Bonterra Chardonnay 1998 (organic) | 15.5 | £7–10

Californian White 1999, Asda | 13.5 | –£3.50

## FORTIFIED WINES

Fine Ruby Port, Asda | 14 | £5–7

Manzanilla, Asda | 17 | £5–7

Tawny Port, Asda | 15 | £5–7

## SPARKLING WINES

Asti Spumante NV, Asda | 11 | –£5.00

Cava Brut, Asda | 16.5 | –£5.00

Cava Medium Dry, Asda | 13 | –£5.00

Cava Rosado 1998, Asda | 13.5 | –£5.00

Champagne Brut NV, Asda | 13.5 | £10–13

Champagne Brut Rosé NV, Asda | 13 | £10–13

Charles Lafitte Cuvée 2000 NV | 13 | £13–20

Cremant de Bourgogne 1997 | 14 | £5–7

De Bregille Vintage 1995 | 14 | £13–20

Nicolas Feuillate Blanc de Blancs NV | 13 | £13–20

Nottage Hill Sparkling Chardonnay 1996 | 15 | £5–7

Rondel Cava NV | 14 | £5–7

Seaview Sparkling NV | 14.5 | £5–7

Stamps Sparkling 1999 | 15 | £5–7

Three Choirs Cuvée Brut (England) | 10 | £5–7

Vintage Cava 1996, Asda | 15.5 | £5–7

Vintage Champagne 1993, Asda | 14.5 | £13–20

**SEE STOP PRESS SECTION AT END OF BOOK FOR LAST-MINUTE ADDITIONS OR UPDATES TO THIS RETAILER'S RANGE.**

# BOOTHS

There were a few reports doing the rounds in summer 2000 about Tesco reverting to pounds and ounces because customers preferred this Britannic nostalgia to Continental litres and kilos, but I dismissed this as a practical joke. Tesco? Surely not. Booths? Absolutely. If any retailer listed in this book was going to turn the clock deliciously back, then Booths would be the one. Even the title 'supermarket' sits oddly on this retailer's head, even though its stores are set up as such, though confined to the northern shires. It does not lack ambition, however. In 1999 it set to roll out home shopping across Lakeland. Another move, indeed innovation, reported at that time was that Booths was stocking what was thought to be the first range of branded organic frozen vegetables in the UK.

The millennium began with the death of John Booth, father of Edwin, the current eponym running the show. He was seventy-six and entered the business in 1946 as a shop assistant, later becoming chairman. The spirit of Booths – which revolves around a committed sense of grocery excellence and service to customers – is very alive, and with the passing of the personal Sainsbury's presence at that supermarket may well mean that Booths, which was formed in 1847, is not only the oldest such establishment of its kind but the only one, along with Morrisons, where a descendant of the founder still has a hand on the tiller.

This tiller has turned in new and excitingly modern directions. Booths now has a huge and magnificently ambitious wine sales website master-minded by director of technology Chris Dee, who was, before Sally Holloway's arrival, the wine buyer here. I say 'has', and I hope 'has'; but I write these words the day after I enjoyed a pleasant pub lunch in August 2000 with Mr Dee and the launch date of the site is November, after the book goes to press.

(It isn't all wine at Booths. It was voted Beer Supermarket of the Year Award by the British Guild of Beer Writers on the eminently appropriate grounds that it stocks some 295 different beers, including some 119 bottled ales.)

Sally is the new pride of the Booths wine aisles and you can readily see, from the entries that follow, that the range has both widened and deepened.

It will never have the resources, unlike the giants, to invest vast amounts in many own-label wine ranges from the main producing countries, but shrewdness and taste are evident in the examples I have tasted, lending considerable weight to the claim that Booths may not be big but it's a jolly good place at which to buy wine.

Booths Supermarkets
4–6 Fishergate
Preston
Lancs
PR1 3LJ

Tel 01772 251701
Fax 01772 255669
sholloway@booths-supermarkets.co.uk
www.booths-supermarkets.co.uk

## ARGENTINIAN RED

| | | |
|---|---|---|
| El Montonero Bonarda Barbera 1999 | 15.5 | −£5.00 |
| Finca el Retiro Malbec, Mendoza 1999 | 15 | £5–7 |
| Libertad Malbec Bonarda 1999 | 15 | −£5.00 |
| Libertad Sangiovese Malbec 1998 | 15 | −£5.00 |
| Mission Peak Red NV | 15.5 | −£3.50 |
| Terrazas Alto Cabernet Sauvignon 1999 | 14.5 | £5–7 |

## ARGENTINIAN WHITE

| | | |
|---|---|---|
| El Montonero Torrontes 1999 | 15 | −£5.00 |
| Libertad Chenin Sauvignon 1999 | 14.5 | −£5.00 |

| | | |
|---|---|---|
| Terrazas Alto Chardonnay 1999 | 15.5 | £5–7 |

## AUSTRALIAN RED

| | | |
|---|---|---|
| Australian Red Shiraz Cabernet Sauvignon NV, Booths | 14 | −£5.00 |
| Australian Red, South Eastern Australia NV, Booths | 11 | −£3.50 |
| Brown Brothers Tarrango 1998 | 13 | −£5.00 |
| CV Capel Vale Shiraz 1997 | 14.5 | £7–10 |
| d'Arenberg d'Arrys Original Shiraz/Grenache 1998 | 15 | £5–7 |
| Ironstone Shiraz Grenache 1998 | 16.5 | £5–7 |

Knappstein Cabernet | 15 | £7–10
Franc 1998

Marktree Premium Red | 11 | −£5.00
1998

Penfolds Bin 407 | 15 | £10–13
Cabernet Sauvignon 1996

Rosemount Estate | 15.5 | £5–7
Shiraz/Cabernet
Sauvignon 1998

Wakefield Estate | 16 | £5–7
Cabernet Sauvignon 1998

Yaldara Grenache 1998 | 13.5 | £5–7

## AUSTRALIAN WHITE

Château Tahbilk | 15.5 | £5–7
Marsanne 1998

Cranswick Botrytis | 15 | £10–13
Semillon 1996 (half-
bottle)

CV Capel Vale | 16 | £7–10
Unwooded Chardonnay
1998

CV Capel Vale Verdelho | 16.5 | £7–10
1998

d'Arenberg The Olive | 16 | £5–7
Grove Chardonnay 1998

d'Arenberg White Ochre | 13 | £5–7
1999

Deakin Estate | 15.5 | −£5.00
Chardonnay 1999

Hardys Stamp Riesling | 15.5 | −£5.00
Gewürztraminer 1999

Ironstone Semillon | 17 | £5–7
Chardonnay 1999

Marktree White SE | 13.5 | −£5.00
Australia 1999

Ninth Island Chardonnay | 13 | £7–10
1999

Oxford Landing Viognier | 16 | £5–7
1998

Penfolds Bin 21 Rawson's | 14 | −£5.00
Retreat Semillon/
Colombard/Chardonnay
1999

Penfolds Clare Valley | 15.5 | £7–10
Organic Chardonnay/
Sauvignon Blanc 1998

Riddoch Coonawarra | 15 | £5–7
Chardonnay 1998

Shaw & Smith Sauvignon | 15 | £7–10
Blanc 1998

## BULGARIAN RED

Boyar Cabernet Merlot | 12.5 | −£3.50
1998

## CHILEAN RED

Carmen Grande Vidure | 16.5 | £7–10
Cabernet Sauvignon 1998

Cono Sur Pinot Noir 1998 | 16.5 | −£5.00

Vistasur Cabernet Malbec | 14 | −£5.00
1998

## CHILEAN WHITE

Isla Negra Chardonnay | 16 | £5–7
1998

Tocornal White NV | 13.5 | −£3.50

Via Vina Chardonnay | 14 | −£5.00
1999

Vistasur Chardonnay | 13 | −£5.00
Sauvignon Vistamar 1999

## FRENCH RED

| | | |
|---|---|---|
| Bergerac Organic Red 1998 | 14 | −£5.00 |
| Bergerac Rouge NV, Booths | 13 | −£3.50 |
| Bourgogne Rouge Jean-Luc Joillet 1998 | 12.5 | £5–7 |
| Bourgueil Domaine Pierre Gautier 1995 | 15 | −£5.00 |
| Cahors 1998 | 14 | −£5.00 |
| Chapoutier La Ciboise Coteaux du Tricastin 1998 | 15.5 | −£5.00 |
| Château Ducla, Bordeaux 1997 | 15 | £5–7 |
| Château l'Euziere Pic St Loup 1997 | 14.5 | £5–7 |
| Château Mayne-Vieil, Fronsac 1996 | 16.5 | −£5.00 |
| Château Pierrail Bordeaux Superieur 1996 | 15 | £5–7 |
| Château Pouchaud-Larquey, Bordeaux 1996 | 15.5 | £5–7 |
| Chaume Arnaud Domaine Côtes du Rhône Villages 1998 (organic) | 17 | £7–10 |
| Côtes du Rhône Villages Georges Darriaud 1998 | 13.5 | £5–7 |
| Domaine du Trillol Corbieres 1996 | 15.5 | −£5.00 |
| Faugeres Gilbert Alquier 1997 | 15 | £7–10 |
| Fitou Madame Parmentier 1998 | 13.5 | −£5.00 |
| Gigondas Domaine Paillere et Pied 1998 | 16 | £7–10 |
| Julienas Paul Boutinot 1997 | 11 | £5–7 |
| La Passion Rouge VdP de Vaucluse 1999 | 14 | −£3.50 |
| La Reserve du Reverend Corbieres 1999 | 13.5 | −£5.00 |
| Marcillac 1997 | 15 | £5–7 |
| Oak Aged Claret Bordeaux Superieur NV, Booths | 14 | −£5.00 |
| Old Git Grenache Syrah 1999 | 15.5 | −£5.00 |
| Pernands Vergelesses, Cornu 1997 | 10 | £7–10 |
| Rasteau Domaine des Coteaux des Travers 1998 | 16.5 | £5–7 |
| Vin Rouge NV, Booths | 11 | −£3.50 |

## FRENCH WHITE

| | | |
|---|---|---|
| Bergerac Blanc NV, Booths | 14 | −£3.50 |
| Bordeaux Blanc Sec NV, Booths | 13.5 | −£3.50 |
| Bourgogne Chardonnay Domaine Joseph Matrot NV | 12 | £5–7 |
| Chablis Domaine de l'Eglantiere 1998 | 10 | £7–10 |
| Château d'Angludet Rosé 1997 | 13 | £5–7 |
| Château Lamothe Vincent, Bordeaux 1999 | 14 | −£5.00 |
| Château Petit Roubie, Coteaux du Pinet 1999 (organic) | 13 | −£5.00 |

| | | |
|---|---|---|
| Château Pierrail Blanc Prestige 1996 | 15.5 | £5–7 |
| Château Pique-Segue, Montravel 1999 | 15 | −£5.00 |
| Clos de Monestier Bergerac Blanc 1999 | 13.5 | −£5.00 |
| Clos de Monestier Bergerac Rosé 1999 | 14.5 | −£5.00 |
| Côtes du Rhône Chaume Arnaud 1998 | 16 | £7–10 |
| Domaine de Pellehaut Côtes de Gascogne 1999 | 15 | −£5.00 |
| Domaine de Petit Roubie, Marsanne 1999 (organic) | 15 | −£5.00 |
| Edelzwicker Aimé Stentz 1998 | 14.5 | −£5.00 |
| Gewürztraminer d'Alsace Turckheim 1999 | 15.5 | £5–7 |
| James Herrick Chardonnay VdP d'Oc 1999 | 16 | −£5.00 |
| La Passion Blanc VdP de Vaucluse 1999 | 15 | −£3.50 |
| Louis Chatel Sur Lie VdP d'Oc 1999 | 14 | −£3.50 |
| Muscadet Sur Lie La Roche Renard 1998 | 13.5 | −£5.00 |
| Pouilly Fume les Cornets, Cailbourdin 1997 | 10 | £7–10 |
| Riesling d'Alsace Aimé Stentz 1997 | 13 | £5–7 |
| Sancerre Domaine du Petit Roy, Dezat 1998 | 14.5 | £7–10 |
| Vermentino Les Yeuses VdP d'Oc 1999 | 15.5 | −£3.50 |
| Vin Blanc NV, Booths | 12 | −£3.50 |

## GERMAN WHITE

| | | |
|---|---|---|
| Gau-Bickelheimer Kurfurstenstuck Auslese 1998 | 13 | −£5.00 |
| Liebfraumilch NV, Booths | 13 | −£3.50 |
| Niersteiner Speigelberg Spatlese 1997 | 12 | −£5.00 |
| Piesporter Michelsberg NV, Booths | 13.5 | −£5.00 |
| Riesling Louis Guntrum 1999 | 14 | −£5.00 |

## GREEK RED

| | | |
|---|---|---|
| Vin de Crete Kourtaki 1998 | 13 | −£5.00 |

## GREEK WHITE

| | | |
|---|---|---|
| Kretikos Vin de Crete Blanc Boutari 1999 | 13 | −£5.00 |

## HUNGARIAN WHITE

| | | |
|---|---|---|
| Chapel Hill Oaked Chardonnay, Balaton Boglar NV | 15.5 | −£3.50 |

## ITALIAN RED

| | | |
|---|---|---|
| A Mano Primitivo Puglia 1999 | 15.5 | £5–7 |
| Amarone Classico Brigaldara 1994 | 15 | £13–20 |
| Archidamo Pervini Primitivo di Manduria 1997 | 15.5 | £5–7 |

BOOTHS

| Barocco Rosso del Salento 1998 | 15 | −£3.50 |

| Colli di Sasso Toscana 1998 | 14 | −£5.00 |

| I Promessa Sangiovese Puglia 1999 | 13.5 | −£5.00 |

| La Piazza Rosso 1999 (Sicily) | 15 | −£3.50 |

| La Prendina Falcone Cabernet Sauvignon 1998 | 14 | £10–13 |

| Salice Salento Vallone 1997 | 14 | −£5.00 |

| Valpolicella Classico Superiore, Viviani 1996 | 15.5 | £7–10 |

| Valpolicella Classico, Viviani 1997 | 12 | £5–7 |

| Valpolicella Ripasso Viviani 1994 | 14 | £7–10 |

| Vigna Flaminio, Brindisi Rosso 1996 | 15 | £5–7 |

## ITALIAN WHITE

| La Piazza Bianco 1999 (Sicily) | 13.5 | −£3.50 |
| Le Rime Pinot Grigio/ Chardonnay 1999 | 13 | −£5.00 |
| Sentito Cortese DOC Oltrepo Pavese 1998 | 13.5 | −£5.00 |
| Soave Classico Pra 1999 | 15.5 | £5–7 |
| Vin Suspo Rosado Capezza 1999 | 13 | £5–7 |

## LEBANESE RED

| Hochar Red 1995 | 10 | £5–7 |

## NEW ZEALAND WHITE

| Jackson Estate Riesling 1998 | 13.5 | £5–7 |
| Jackson Estate Sauvignon Blanc 1999 | 15 | £7–10 |
| Vavasour Sauvignon Blanc 1999 | 15 | £7–10 |

## PORTUGUESE RED

| Alfrocheiro Preto Dao 1996 | 10 | £10–13 |
| Alianca Floral Douro Reserva 1997 | 15.5 | −£5.00 |
| Alta Mesa Red 1998 | 15 | −£3.50 |
| Bela Fonte Baga 1998 | 14 | −£5.00 |
| Cartuxa Evora Alentejo 1995 | 16 | £7–10 |
| Dao Dom Ferraz 1998 | 16.5 | −£5.00 |
| Espiga 1998 | 15.5 | −£5.00 |
| Foral Alianca Reserva, Douro 1997 | 14.5 | −£5.00 |
| Portada Red Estremadura 1999 | 13.5 | −£5.00 |
| Quinta da Villa Freire Douro 1996 | 15 | £5–7 |
| Quinta das Setencostas 1998 | 16.5 | −£5.00 |
| Quinta de la Rosa Douro 1998 | 14 | £5–7 |

## SOUTH AFRICAN RED

| Helderberg Shiraz 1999 | 15 | −£5.00 |
| Spice Route Andrew's Hope 1998 | 16.5 | £5–7 |

| Stormy Cape Cinsault/ Shiraz 1998 | 16 | −£5.00 |
| Welmoed Merlot 1998 | 15.5 | £5–7 |
| Wide River Pinotage 1999 | 15.5 | £5–7 |

## SOUTH AFRICAN WHITE

| Altus Sauvignon Blanc, Paarl 1999 | 13 | −£5.00 |
| Jordan Chardonnay 1998 | 16.5 | £7–10 |
| Landema Falls Colombard Chardonnay NV | 15 | −£3.50 |
| Springfield Estate 'Life from Stone' Sauvignon Blanc 1999 | 16 | £5–7 |
| Welmoed Sauvignon Blanc 1999 | 14 | −£5.00 |

## SPANISH RED

| Amant Tinto de Toro 1999 | 15.5 | −£5.00 |
| Casa de la Vina Valdepeñas 1999 | 14.5 | −£5.00 |
| Casa Morena, Valdepeñas NV | 14 | −£3.50 |
| Castillo de Almansa Reserva Bodegas Piqueras 1994 | 15.5 | −£5.00 |
| Mas Collet Capcanes Tarragona 1998 | 16.5 | £5–7 |
| Mas Donis Capcanes Taragona 1999 | 16 | −£5.00 |
| Ochoa Tempranillo Garnacha 1999 | 15 | −£5.00 |

| Rioja Crianza Amezola 1996 | 12 | £7–10 |
| Scraping the Barrel Tempranillo, Utiel-Requena NV | 14.5 | −£3.50 |
| Simply Spanish Soft Red NV | 9 | −£2.50 |
| Vina Alarba, Calatayud 1998 | 15.5 | −£3.50 |
| Vina Albali Gran Reserva 1993 | 15 | £5–7 |

## SPANISH WHITE

| Castillo de Almansa 1998 | 16 | −£5.00 |
| Estrella, Moscatel de Valencia NV | 16 | −£5.00 |
| Palacio de Bornos Rueda 1999 | 13 | −£5.00 |
| Santa Lucia Viura, Vino de la Tierra Manchuela 1998 | 14 | −£3.50 |
| Simply Spanish White NV | 12 | −£2.50 |

## USA RED

| Redwood Trail Pinot Noir 1998 | 13 | £5–7 |
| Stonybrook Merlot 1998 | 16 | £5–7 |
| Turning Leaf Cabernet Sauvignon 1997 | 12 | £5–7 |
| Turning Leaf Zinfandel 1996 | 12.5 | £5–7 |

BOOTHS

## USA WHITE

| | | |
|---|---|---|
| Stonybrook Chardonnay 1998 | 16 | –£5.00 |

## FORTIFIED WINES

| | | |
|---|---|---|
| Amontillado del Puerto, Lustau | 16 | £7–10 |
| Banyuls Chapoutier 1996 (50cl) | 16 | £7–10 |
| Churchills Dry White Port | 13 | £7–10 |
| Finest Reserve Port, Booths | 14.5 | £7–10 |
| Fino, Booths | 14 | –£5.00 |
| Henriques & Henriques 5 year Old Madeira | 15 | £10–13 |
| Lustau Old East India Sherry | 17 | £7–10 |
| Manzanilla Sherry, Booths | 15 | –£5.00 |
| Medium Amontillado NV, Booths | 15.5 | –£5.00 |
| Niepoort LBV 1994 | 13 | £10–13 |
| Niepoort Ruby Port | 14 | £7–10 |
| Taylors Quinta de Vargellas Port 1986 | 15.5 | £13–20 |

## SPARKLING WINES

| | | |
|---|---|---|
| Bollinger Grande Annee 1990 | 11 | £20+ |
| Brossault Rosé Champagne NV | 13 | £13–20 |
| Bruno Paillard Champagne NV | 15 | £13–20 |
| Champagne Barone-Fuenté Brut NV | 15 | £10–13 |
| Champagne Fleurie NV (organic) | 10 | £13–20 |
| Champagne Gremillet NV | 14 | £13–20 |
| Chandon Argentina Brut NV | 15 | £7–10 |
| Chapelle de Cray Brut Rosé 1993 (France) | 13 | –£5.00 |
| Concerto Lambrusco 1998 (Italy) | 16 | £5–7 |
| Cremant d'Alsace Cuvée Prestige (France) | 13 | £7–10 |
| Deutz NV (New Zealand) | 15 | £10–13 |
| Hunter's Miru Miru 1996 (New Zealand) | 15 | £10–13 |
| Palau Brut Cava NV | 10 | –£5.00 |
| Petillant de Listel, Traditional | 12 | –£2.50 |
| Piper Heidsieck Brut Champagne NV | 15 | £13–20 |
| Prosecco Zonin NV (Italy) | 16 | –£5.00 |

# BUDGENS

Budgens! Ah yes, Budgens. Isn't that the outfit which discovered in 1999 that it had been trading, unknowingly, in fake Rioja for two years? That's right. Some 300,000 Rioja labels were found in a Spanish police raid on a winery in La Mancha, labels it was said were about to be stuck on bottles of local red destined for Budgens (among other UK retail destinations), and suspicions were aroused because, well, Rioja isn't in La Mancha, is it? Caught red-wine-handed is putting it precisely.

Budgens took the wine off its shelves, but its customers, I imagine, didn't bat an eye. Neither did I. The wine, called Don Marino, rated 10 points in the previous two *Superplonk* books and I always felt I was being generous in rating it that highly.

Budgens is an old-fashioned establishment in certain ways, illustrated by the fact that Ms Christine Sandys is Senior Buyer, Wines, Spirits & Tobacco. No other wine buyer I deal with buys fags, though their ancient counterparts, a few decades ago, routinely did. Budgens hired Christine from the Co-op to replace Mr Tony Finnerty and, though we are yet to see the full effects of her regime, the wines that follow amply demonstrate that she is a smart new broom.

Christine has, no doubt about it, joined a growing company now 208 branches strong. Profits leaped by 20% to £12.6 million in 1999. The company launched a home-delivery service from thirty stores, delivering free to customers spending more than £20. It unveiled a new-look town-centre format designed to compete with similar concepts from Sainsbury's and Tesco, and new MD Martin Hyson announced that the company intended to buy as many convenience sites in the south of England as it could.

It also said that its b2 refits of the old 711 chain would be designed to 'be female-friendly', according to a report in *Supermarketing* magazine.

Well, I said Budgens was old-fashioned, but even I didn't think they'd be saying something that American retail gurus first proclaimed in 1885.

Budgens Stores Limited
PO Box 9
Stonefield Way

BUDGENS

Ruislip
Middlesex
HA4 0JR

Tel 020 8422 9511
Fax 020 8864 2800
www.budgens.co.uk

## ARGENTINIAN RED

| Etchart Rio de Plata Tempranillo/Malbec 1998 | 14 | −£5.00 |

## ARGENTIAN WHITE

| Etchart Rio de Plata Torrontes 1999 | 13.5 | −£3.50 |
| Etchart Rio de Plata Torrontes/Chardonnay 1998 | 13 | −£5.00 |

## AUSTRALIAN RED

| Oxford Landing Cabernet Sauvignon Shiraz 1999 | 14 | £5−7 |
| Wolf Blass Yellow Label Cabernet Sauvignon 1998 | 15 | £7−10 |
| Wynns Coonawarra Shiraz 1997 | 16.5 | £5−7 |

## AUSTRALIAN WHITE

| Hardys Stamp Grenache Shiraz Rosé 1999 | 13.5 | −£5.00 |
| Oxford Landing Chardonnay 1999 | 15.5 | £5−7 |

| Rawsons Retreat Bin 202 Riesling 1999 | 15 | −£5.00 |
| Rosemount Estate Chardonnay 1999 | 16 | £5−7 |
| Rosemount Estate Semillon/Chardonnay 1997 | 15 | £5−7 |
| Rosemount GTR 2000 | 14 | £5−7 |
| White Pointer 2000 | 13 | −£5.00 |

## CHILEAN RED

| Antu Mapu Merlot 1998 | 15 | −£5.00 |
| Antu Mapu Merlot Reserva 1998 | 14 | £5−7 |
| Millaman Cabernet Malbec 1998 | 13 | £5−7 |
| Millaman Merlot 1999 | 14 | £5−7 |
| Stowells of Chelsea Cabernet Merlot NV | 14.5 | −£5.00 |
| Terra Andina Cabernet Merlot 1999 | 14 | −£5.00 |
| Terra Andina Cabernet Sauvignon 1998 | 14 | −£5.00 |
| Vina Gracia Cabernet Sauvignon 1998 | 15 | −£5.00 |

## CHILEAN WHITE

| | | |
|---|---|---|
| Antu Mapu Sauvignon Blanc 1999 | 12.5 | −£5.00 |
| Terra Andina Chardonnay 1998 | 14 | −£5.00 |
| Terra Andina Semillon Chardonnay 1999 | 14 | −£5.00 |

## FRENCH RED

| | | |
|---|---|---|
| Bourgogne Rouge Vienot 1996 | 12 | £5−7 |
| Château de Malijay Côtes du Rhône 1996 | 13.5 | −£5.00 |
| Corbieres Château Saint-Louis 1997 | 13 | −£5.00 |
| Côtes du Rhône Villages Cuvée Reserve 1997 | 14 | −£5.00 |
| Côtes Marmandais, Beaupuy 1996 | 13.5 | −£5.00 |
| Domaine St Roche VdP de l'Aude NV | 12 | −£3.50 |
| Gargantua Côtes du Rhône 1997 | 14 | −£5.00 |
| Organic Red VdP du Pays du Gard NV | 13 | −£3.50 |
| Premium Oaked Cabernet Franc/Syrah VdP d'Oc, Devereux NV | 15.5 | −£3.50 |

## FRENCH WHITE

| | | |
|---|---|---|
| Bordeaux Blanc Sec 1998 | 15 | −£3.50 |
| Bordeaux Sauvignon NV, Budgens | 13.5 | −£5.00 |

| | | |
|---|---|---|
| Chablis Delaroche 1999 | 11 | £7−10 |
| Domaine Villeroy-Castellas Sauvignon 1998 | 14 | −£5.00 |
| French Organic White NV | 13 | −£5.00 |
| James Herrick Chardonnay 1999 | 16 | −£5.00 |
| 'L' Grande Cuvée VdP d'Oc 1999 | 15.5 | £5−7 |
| Premium Oaked Chardonnay VdP d'Oc, Devereux NV | 14 | −£5.00 |

## GERMAN WHITE

| | | |
|---|---|---|
| Flonheimer Adelberg Auslese 1997 | 10 | −£3.50 |

## GREEK RED

| | | |
|---|---|---|
| Vin de Crete 1998 | 12 | −£3.50 |

## HUNGARIAN RED

| | | |
|---|---|---|
| Spice Trail Zweigelt 1997 | 10 | −£5.00 |

## HUNGARIAN WHITE

| | | |
|---|---|---|
| Spice Trail Irsai Oliver/ Pinot Grigio 1998 | 13.5 | −£5.00 |

## ITALIAN RED

| | | |
|---|---|---|
| Canaletto Merlot 1999 | 14.5 | −£5.00 |
| Fontella Chianti 1999 | 13 | −£3.50 |
| La Mura Rosso del Salento 1999 | 14 | −£3.50 |

Merlot del Veneto Rocca NV | 9 | −£5.00

Sahateni Merlot 1998 | 15 | −£5.00

## ITALIAN WHITE

Canaletto Chardonnay 1999 | 13 | −£5.00

Marc Xero Chardonnay NV | 15 | −£5.00

Pinot Grigio delle Venezie 1999 | 14 | −£5.00

## NEW ZEALAND RED

Corbans White Label Dry Red NV | 14 | −£5.00

Helderberg Pinotage 1998 | 15 | −£5.00

Montana Cabernet Sauvignon/Merlot 1999 | 15 | £5–7

## NEW ZEALAND WHITE

Corbans Sauvignon Blanc 1999 | 15.5 | −£5.00

## PORTUGUESE RED

Alta Mesa Red 1999 | 13 | −£3.50

Dao Dom Ferraz 1999 | 15 | −£5.00

Segada Trincadeira Preta-Castelao 1999 | 14 | −£5.00

## ROMANIAN RED

Romanian Classic Pinot Noir 1998 | 13.5 | −£5.00

Romanian Young Cabernet Sauvignon 1998 | 14 | −£5.00

## ROMANIAN WHITE

Romanian Classic Gewürztraminer 1998 | 11 | −£5.00

Romanian Classic Pinot Gris 1999 | 13 | −£5.00

## SOUTH AFRICAN RED

Cape Medium Fruity Red NV, Budgens | 11 | −£3.50

Long Mountain Merlot Shiraz 1998 | 13.5 | £5–7

## SOUTH AFRICAN WHITE

Cape White NV, Budgens | 11 | −£3.50

Clear Mountain Chenin Blanc NV | 13.5 | −£3.50

Glen Eden Chardonnay 1998 | 14 | −£5.00

Long Mountain Sauvignon Blanc 1999 | 13 | −£5.00

Long Mountain Semillon Chardonnay 1999 | 14.5 | −£5.00

Stowells of Chelsea Chenin Blanc NV | 13 | −£5.00

## SPANISH RED

Diego de Almagro Valdepeñas 1996 | 15 | −£5.00

Palacio de la Vega Cabernet Sauvignon/ Tempranillo 1996 | 15.5 | −£5.00

Palacio de la Vega Crianza 1997 `15.5` `£5–7`

Vina Albali Gran Reserva 1993 `15` `£5–7`

## SPANISH WHITE

Castillo de Liria Moscatel de Valencia NV `15.5` `–£5.00`

Vina Albali Rosado Tempranillo 1999 `13` `–£5.00`

## USA RED

Glen Ellen Cabernet Sauvignon 1998 `13` `£5–7`

Marc Xero Merlot NV `15` `–£5.00`

Sutter Home Merlot 1998 `13` `–£5.00`

Turning Leaf Cabernet Sauvignon 1997 `12` `£5–7`

Turning Leaf Zinfandel 1996 `12.5` `£5–7`

## USA WHITE

Glen Ellen Chardonnay 1998 `15` `£5–7`

## SPARKLING WINES

Budgens Brut Champagne NV `12` `£13–20`

Budgens Rosé Champagne NV `10` `£13–20`

Cava la Vuelta NV `14` `–£5.00`

Hardys Stamp Sparkling Chardonnay Pinot Noir NV `14` `£5–7`

Lindauer Brut NV `15` `£5–7`

# CO-OP

This is the only retailer for whom I don a collar and tie, a jacket and smart slacks ('jeans and casual trews not permitted') in order to get my lips on its wines. This is because Mr Paul Bastard, the man who buys the Co-op's wines, likes his bottles to be tasted at a swanky West End club, sited between Berkeley Square and Marco Pierre White's opulent Mirabelle restaurant (£11,000 for a bottle of 1986 burgundy is one entry on the restaurant wine list). Why this insistence on sartorial uniformity? Because the club's fee for renting a large room for the day, a room suitable for entertaining a *Guardian* journalist (who has since removed his tie and jacket upon getting past reception) is incredibly cheap. This approach entirely sums up Mr Bastard's approach to wine: value for money. He is then a chap after my own heart.

The CWS and CRS are rapidly becoming a retailer after more people's hearts. The merger of the two groups' buying strengths will not only result in less confusion but has the professed aim to boost sales by standardising ranges and store design, and by sharing customer information. Following CRS's decision last year to join the CWS-run Co-operative Retail Trading Group, the sixth largest buying force in UK food retailing was created. CWS is testing its 'Market Town' and 'Welcome' formats for roll-out in autumn 2000, and CRS said it might adopt these formats if they were successful.

The Co-op's roots are in fair trading. It supported the Jubilee 2000 movement, which aimed to persuade Western governments about the unacceptability (I would say obscenity) of Third World debt. Badges were offered to customers in stores.

Modern thinking and expansive ideas were, at this time, modestly popping up everywhere at the Co-op. It updated the design of its own brands and expanded the range from 3,200 to 4,200 lines. It acquired the six-store Penny's chain in Perthshire, a Costcutter store in Invernesshire and a Londis outlet in Northamptonshire.

It launched a full on-line off-licence offer under the Grape and Grain brand which it also uses in some of its stores. Some 300 wines and 30 whiskies are available from the website.

For the pre-millennium Christmas, the Co-op vowed to continue selling bargain-price Champagne sourced on the grey market. The result of this was that CWS claimed 6.1% of the total UK Champagne market over this period and said that its sales over the festive season had shown a 48% rise.

As the year got under way, CWS put drinks merchandising at the heart of its in-store revamp. The redesigned drinks sections will feature stainless-steel shelving and much-enhanced drinks ranges. Some 230 market-town stores are supposedly being given this facelift, with the larger stores carrying 350 wines. The move follows the redesign of the drinks sections in the Co-op Lateshop outlets, now cosily badged 'Welcome' stores.

The CWS said that its merger with CRS would lead to more consistent drinks ranges throughout the merged operation (according to a report in the *Off Licence News* trade journal). This was followed by a series of regional consultation meetings across the CRS chain which showed major support for a full merger with CWS. The merged group would have 1,000 stores and food sales of around £2.5 billion (total sales £4.7 billion). Analysts say the merger is long overdue, and if it did not go ahead it could jeopardise the future of the Co-operative movement – a sentiment I heartily and sentimentally endorse. (As a young kid I had the family Co-op dividend number indelibly written on my wrist. Nowadays, any mother who sent a five-year-old child out to buy a cauliflower and a pound of spuds from a Co-op greengrocer would probably be arrested for child abuse or negligence.)

In those days organic produce was an exotic neverheardof (no one realised that all those allotments London had during the war were all organic – who could afford synthetic fertilisers and pesticides?). Now, like most everyone else, the Co-op is on the organic bandwagon, seeking to introduce organic fruit and vegetables to its 342 convenience stores, currently being rebranded under the aforementioned cheery 'Welcome' fascia. This sort of titular cheeriness is admired at this retailer.

In April the North-Eastern and Cumbrian Co-op rebranded its home-delivery service under the name 'Take It Easy' and announced its extension to two more stores. The scheme is free to customers spending more than fifteen quid.

Do all these new ideas mean that old-fashioned value for money gets overshadowed? Decidedly not. In an *Off Licence News* price survey in spring 2000, the Co-op and Unwins were identified as the retailers with the lowest drinks prices in the UK.

This was the time the marriage was formally and finally announced: the

CWS and CRS will merge to form a new £4.65 billion operation. In a separate report in *Retail Week* magazine, it was revealed that the merged group intended to take market share from the ailing Somerfield operation. Indeed, the Co-op bought several Somerfield stores, six of which it converted in, apparently, world record time. The half-dozen, all in Scotland, were converted from Somerfields to Co-ops in exactly 36 hours.

Let us hope this kind of pace reaches every corner of the Co-op estate. Mr Bastard is already doing a fine job, but if he had more time and money (i.e. more management hands) he could develop some cracking own-label Co-op wine ranges to compete with the best.

Watch this space? My fingers are crossed. My Co-op divi number, alas, has long disappeared, but not my goodwill towards this retailer and its commercial ethos.

Co-operative Wholesale Society Limited
PO Box 53
New Century House
Manchester
M60 4ES

Tel 0800 068 6727 Customer Careline
Fax 0161 827 6604
www.grapeandgrain.co.uk
www.co-op.co.uk (online wine and spirit ordering)

## ARGENTINIAN RED

| | | |
|---|---|---|
| Adiseno Cabernet Sauvignon Shiraz 1999 | 16 | −£5.00 |
| Adiseno Tempranillo 1999 | 15 | −£5.00 |
| Argentine Malbec 1999, Co-op | 15.5 | −£5.00 |
| Argento Malbec 1999 | 16.5 | −£5.00 |
| Balbi Malbec 1999 | 13.5 | −£5.00 |
| Bianchi Cabernet Sauvignon 1996 | 17 | £7–10 |
| First Ever Shiraz 2000 | 16 | −£5.00 |
| La Nature Organic Barbera 2000 | 14.5 | −£5.00 |
| Lost Pampas Cabernet Malbec 1999, Co-op | 14 | −£5.00 |
| Malbec/Bonarda Mendoza Soft Red Wine 1998 | 14 | −£3.50 |
| Mission Peak Argentine Red NV | 15.5 | −£3.50 |
| Weinert Malbec 1994 | 16 | £7–10 |
| Y2K Shiraz 1999 | 16 | £5–7 |

## ARGENTINIAN WHITE

| | | |
|---|---|---|
| Argentine Sauvignon/ Chenin Blanc 1998 | 15 | −£3.50 |
| Balbi Shiraz Rosé 1999 | 14 | −£5.00 |
| Bright Brothers Viognier Reserve 1999 | 15 | £5–7 |
| Etchart Rio de Plata Torrontes 1999 | 13.5 | −£5.00 |
| First Ever Chardonnay 2000 | 13.5 | −£5.00 |
| La Nature Organic Torrontes 2000 | 15.5 | −£5.00 |
| Lost Pampas Oaked Chardonnay 1999, Co-op | 16 | −£5.00 |
| Mission Peak Argentine White NV | 15.5 | −£3.50 |
| Y2K Chardonnay, San Juan 1999 | 16 | −£5.00 |

## AUSTRALIAN RED

| | | |
|---|---|---|
| Australian Cabernet Sauvignon 1998, Co-op | 14 | −£5.00 |
| Australian Grenache 1999, Co-op | 14 | −£5.00 |
| Australian Merlot 1999, Co-op | 13.5 | −£5.00 |
| Brown Brothers Tarrango 1999 | 13.5 | £5–7 |
| Château Reynella Basket Press Cabernet Merlot 1996 | 16.5 | £10–13 |
| E & E Black Pepper Shiraz 1996 | 16 | £20+ |
| Hardys Coonawarra Cabernet Sauvignon 1996 | 16 | £10–13 |

| | | |
|---|---|---|
| Hardys Stamp Cabernet Shiraz Merlot 1997 | 15 | £5–7 |
| Leasingham Cabernet Sauvignon/Malbec 1996 | 16.5 | £7–10 |
| Rosemount Estate Grenache/Shiraz 1998 | 15 | £5–7 |

## AUSTRALIAN WHITE

| | | |
|---|---|---|
| Australian Chardonnay 1999, Co-op | 15.5 | −£5.00 |
| Bethnay Chardonnay 1998 | 16 | £5–7 |
| Hardys Chardonnay Sauvignon Blanc 1998 | 15 | £5–7 |
| Jacaranda Hill Semillon 1999, Co-op | 14 | −£5.00 |
| Lindemans Bin 65 Chardonnay 1999 | 16.5 | −£5.00 |
| Lindemans Cawarra Chardonnay 1999 | 15.5 | −£5.00 |
| Rosemount GTR 2000 | 14 | £5–7 |

## BULGARIAN RED

| | | |
|---|---|---|
| Plovdiv Cabernet Sauvignon Rubin 1996 | 15.5 | −£3.50 |
| Pomorie Country Cabernet Merlot 1998 | 15.5 | −£3.50 |
| Sliven Merlot/Pinot Noir NV | 13.5 | −£3.50 |

## CHILEAN RED

| | | |
|---|---|---|
| Antares Merlot 1998 | 16 | −£5.00 |
| Casa Lapostolle Merlot Cuvée Alexandre 1997 | 17.5 | £10–13 |

Chilean Cabernet Sauvignon, Co-op — 15 — −£5.00

Chilean Fair Trade Carmenere 2000, Co-op — 15.5 — −£5.00

La Palmeria Cabernet Sauvignon 1998 — 16 — −£5.00

La Palmeria Merlot Gran Reserva 1998 — 17 — £7–10

Las Lomas Cot Rouge Reserva 1998 — 15 — £5–7

Las Lomas Organic Chilean Red, Vinas Viejas 1998 — 16 — £5–7

Long Slim Cabernet Merlot 1999 — 16 — −£5.00

Old Vines Carignan 1999, Co-op — 14 — −£5.00

Terramater Malbec 1999 — 15.5 — −£5.00

Vina Gracia Cabernet Sauvignon Reserve 1999 — 15.5 — £5–7

Vina Gracia Carmenere Reserve Especial 1999 — 16 — −£5.00

Vina Gracia Merlot 1998 — 16 — −£5.00

## CHILEAN WHITE

Four Rivers Chardonnay 1998 — 14 — −£5.00

Long Slim Chardonnay Semillon 1999 — 14.5 — −£5.00

Santa Carolina Chardonnay 1999 — 16.5 — −£5.00

## CYPRIOT RED

Mountain Vines Reserve — 16 — −£5.00

Cabernet/Maratheftiko 1999, Co-op

## CYPRIOT WHITE

Island Vines White Wine 1998, Co-op — 15.5 — −£3.50

Mountain Vines Semillon 1999, Co-op — 13 — −£5.00

## FRENCH RED

Beloup St Chinian 1998 — 14.5 — −£5.00

Château Laurencon Bordeaux Superieur 1998 — 14 — −£5.00

Château Pierrousselle Bordeaux 1999 — 14 — −£5.00

Chevaliere Reserve Grenache Vieilles Vignes 1998 — 14 — −£5.00

Claret NV, Co-op — 15 — −£3.50

Corbieres Rouge NV, Co-op — 15 — −£3.50

Corso Merlot 1999 — 15.5 — −£5.00

Domaine les Combelles Minervois 1998 — 13.5 — −£5.00

Fleurie Pierre Leduc 1998 — 13.5 — £7–10

La Baume Syrah 1997 — 15.5 — −£5.00

Louis Mousset Crozes Hermitage 1997 — 15 — £5–7

Oak Aged Claret NV, Co-op — 13 — −£5.00

Rhône Valley Red 1999 — 14.5 — −£3.50

Valreas Domaine de la Grande Bellane 1998 (organic) — 16.5 — £5–7

| | | |
|---|---|---|
| Vin de Pays d'Oc Cabernet Merlot NV, Co-op | 15 | −£5.00 |
| Vin de Pays d'Oc Cabernet Sauvignon, Co-op | 14 | −£3.50 |
| Vin de Pays d'Oc Merlot NV, Co-op | 14.5 | −£3.50 |
| Vin de Pays d'Oc Syrah, Co-op | 14 | −£3.50 |
| Vin de Pays d'Oc Syrah/ Malbec, Co-op (vegetarian) | 14 | −£5.00 |

## FRENCH WHITE

| | | |
|---|---|---|
| Alsace Gewürztraminer Producteurs A. Eguisheim 1997 | 16.5 | £5–7 |
| Chablis, Les Vignerons de Chablis 1998 | 13.5 | £7–10 |
| Chardonnay VdP du Jardin Pierre Guery 1998 | 15 | −£5.00 |
| Chardonnay-Chenin Vegetarian NV, Co-op | 12.5 | −£5.00 |
| Château Pierrousselle Blanc, Entre Deux Mers 1998 | 13 | −£5.00 |
| Domaine des Perruches Vouvray 1998 | 15.5 | £5–7 |
| Fortant VdP d'Oc Sauvignon Blanc 1999 | 13 | −£5.00 |
| James Herrick Chardonnay 1999 | 16 | −£5.00 |
| Monbazillac Domaine du Haut-Rauly 1995 (half-bottle) | 14.5 | −£5.00 |

| | | |
|---|---|---|
| Montagny 1er Cru 1998 | 13 | £7–10 |
| Orchid Vale Chardonnay Grenache Blanc 1999 | 13.5 | −£5.00 |
| Rhône Valley White 1999 | 14 | −£3.50 |
| Sancerre Domaine Raimbault 1998 | 13 | £7–10 |
| VdP d'Oc Sauvignon Blanc NV, Co-op | 14 | −£5.00 |
| Vin de Pays d'Oc Chardonnay 1999, Co-op | 13 | −£5.00 |
| Vin de Pays d'Oc Chardonnay Chenin Blanc NV, Co-op | 14.5 | −£5.00 |
| Vin de Pays des Cotes de Gascogne, Co-op | 14.5 | −£3.50 |

## GERMAN RED

| | | |
|---|---|---|
| Devil's Rock Masterpiece Pinot Noir 1999 | 10 | −£5.00 |

## GERMAN WHITE

| | | |
|---|---|---|
| Bend in the River 1998 | 12.5 | −£5.00 |
| Bereich Bernkastel 1999, Co-op | 10 | −£3.50 |
| Bernkasteler Badstube Riesling Kabinett 1996 | 16 | £5–7 |
| Four Rs 1999, Co-op | 12 | −£5.00 |
| Graacher Himmelreich Riesling Spatlese 1997 | 14.5 | −£5.00 |
| Kendermans Dry Riesling 1998 | 13.5 | −£5.00 |
| Kirchheimer Schwarzerde Beerenauslese 1998 (half-bottle) | 14 | −£5.00 |

CO-OP

## HUNGARIAN RED

Hungarian Country Wine NV, Co-op — 13 — -£3.50

## HUNGARIAN WHITE

Chapel Hill Irsai Oliver 1998 — 14 — -£3.50

Hungarian Chardonnay 1999, Co-op — 12 — -£3.50

Hungarian White NV, Co-op — 13.5 — -£3.50

## ITALIAN RED

Barolo, Terre del Barolo 1995 — 11 — £7–10

Barrelaia NV, Co-op — 13 — -£5.00

IGT Merlot NV, Co-op — 11 — -£3.50

Il Padrino Rosso Sicilia 1999 — 15 — -£5.00

Melini Chianti 1998 — 14 — -£5.00

Puglia Primitivo Sangiovese 1999, Co-op — 16 — -£5.00

Trulli Primitivo del Salento 1998 — 14.5 — -£5.00

Valpolicella NV, Co-op — 12 — -£3.50

## ITALIAN WHITE

Marc Xero Chardonnay 1998 — 14 — -£5.00

Puglia Chardonnay Bombino 1999, Co-op — 12 — -£5.00

Trulli Chardonnay 1998 — 16 — -£5.00

## NEW ZEALAND RED

Terrace View Cabernet Merlot 1997 — 16 — -£5.00

## NEW ZEALAND WHITE

Explorer's Vineyard Sauvignon Blanc 1999, Co-op — 16 — £5–7

Fat Cat Chardonnay 1998 — 14 — -£5.00

Oyster Bay Sauvignon Blanc 1999 — 16.5 — £5–7

## PORTUGUESE RED

Big Baga 1999, Co-op — 13.5 — -£5.00

Ramada Vinho Regional Estremadura 1998 — 13 — -£3.50

Star Mountain Touriga Nacional 1997 — 14 — -£5.00

Terra Boa Portuguese Red 1998 — 16.5 — -£5.00

## PORTUGUESE WHITE

Fiuza Chardonnay 1999 — 16 — -£5.00

Ramada Vinho Regional Estremadura 1998 — 15.5 — -£3.50

## ROMANIAN RED

Romanian Prairie Merlot 1999, Co-op — 14.5 — -£3.50

## SOUTH AFRICAN RED

Arniston Bay Ruby Cabernet-Merlot 1998 — 13.5 — -£5.00

| | | |
|---|---|---|
| Birdfield Shiraz 1998 | 14 | −£5.00 |
| Cape American Oak Pinotage 1999, Co-op | 14 | −£5.00 |
| Cape Indaba Pinotage 1998 | 13 | −£5.00 |
| Cape Ruby Cabernet, Oak Aged 1999, Co-op | 13.5 | −£5.00 |
| Elephant Trail Cinsault/ Merlot 2000, Co-op | 15 | −£5.00 |
| Goats Do Roam Fairview, Paarl 1999 | 15.5 | −£5.00 |
| Natural State Cape Soleil Organic Shiraz 1999 | 15 | £5–7 |
| Oak Village Cabernet Sauvignon 1998 | 15 | −£5.00 |
| Pinnacle Merlot 1998 | 16 | £5–7 |
| Railroad Cabernet Sauvignon Shiraz 1999 | 15.5 | −£5.00 |
| Three Worlds Pinotage Shiraz Zinfandel 1999, Co-op | 15.5 | £5–7 |
| Winds of Change Pinotage/Cabernet Sauvignon 1998 | 16 | −£5.00 |

## SOUTH AFRICAN WHITE

| | | |
|---|---|---|
| Cape Chenin Blanc, Oak Aged 1999, Co-op | 13 | −£5.00 |
| Cape French Oak Chardonnay 1999, Co-op | 13 | −£5.00 |
| Cape Indaba Chardonnay 1998 | 13 | −£5.00 |
| Elephant Trail Colombard/Chardonnay 2000, Co-op | 14 | −£3.50 |

| | | |
|---|---|---|
| Fairview Chardonnay 1998 | 16.5 | £5–7 |
| First Release Chardonnay 2000 | 13.5 | −£5.00 |
| French Quarter Semillon 1999, Co-op | 14.5 | −£5.00 |
| Goiya Kgeisje Chardonnay Sauvignon Blanc 2000 | 15 | −£5.00 |
| Long Mountain Semillon Chardonnay 1998 | 14 | −£5.00 |
| Oak Village Sauvignon Blanc 1999 | 13 | −£5.00 |
| Spice Route Chenin Blanc 1998 | 16 | £7–10 |
| Stowells South African Chenin Blanc NV | 13 | −£5.00 |
| Waterside White Colombard Chardonnay 1999 | 15.5 | −£5.00 |

## SPANISH RED

| | | |
|---|---|---|
| Berberana Dragon Tempranillo 1998 | 15 | −£5.00 |
| Berberana Rioja Reserva 1995 | 12 | £7–10 |
| Berberana Rioja Viura 1997 | 13.5 | −£5.00 |
| Chestnut Gully Monastrell-Merlot 1998 | 15.5 | −£5.00 |
| Rioja Tinto, Vina Gala NV, Co-op | 13.5 | −£5.00 |
| Tempranillo Oak Aged NV, Co-op | 13 | −£3.50 |
| Tierra Sana Organic Wine 1999, Co-op | 17 | −£5.00 |

| | | |
|---|---|---|
| Torres Gran Sangre de Toro Reserva 1996 | 16 | £5–7 |

## SPANISH WHITE

| | | |
|---|---|---|
| Jaume Serra Chardonnay 1999 | 16 | –£5.00 |

## USA RED

| | | |
|---|---|---|
| Blossom Hill Cabernet Sauvignon 1997 | 11 | –£5.00 |
| Eagle Peak Merlot, Fetzer Vineyards 1998 | 15.5 | £5–7 |
| Fetzer Eagle Peak Merlot 1997 | 15 | £5–7 |
| 'Laid Back Ruby' California Ruby Cabernet 1999, Co-op | 15 | –£5.00 |
| Sebastiani Sonoma Cask Old Vine Zinfandel 1998 | 14.5 | £7–10 |

## USA WHITE

| | | |
|---|---|---|
| Garnet Point Chardonnay-Chenin 1997 | 15.5 | –£5.00 |
| 'The Big Chill' California Colombard Chardonnay 1999, Co-op | 13.5 | –£5.00 |

## SPARKLING WINES

| | | |
|---|---|---|
| Australian Quality Sparkling Wine, Co-op | 14 | –£5.00 |
| Blossom Hill NV (USA) | 13 | £5–7 |
| Brut Sparkling Chardonnay NV, Co-op (France) | 13.5 | –£5.00 |
| Cava Brut NV, Co-op | 14 | –£5.00 |
| De Bracieux Champagne NV | 11 | £10–13 |
| Jacob's Creek Sparkling Chardonnay/Pinot Noir NV (Australia) | 15 | £5–7 |
| Moscato Spumante NV, Co-op | 11 | –£5.00 |
| Sparkling Saumur NV, Co-op | 13 | £5–7 |
| Tempranillo Brut Red NV, Co-op | 13.5 | £5–7 |
| Y2K Champagne NV | 13 | £13–20 |

**SEE STOP PRESS SECTION AT END OF BOOK FOR LAST-MINUTE ADDITIONS OR UPDATES TO THIS RETAILER'S RANGE.**

# KWIK SAVE

See Somerfield/Kwik Save, page. 390.

## ARGENTINIAN RED

Maranon Malbec NV    13    −£3.50

## AUSTRALIAN RED

Australian Dry Red 1999,    14.5    −£5.00
Somerfield

Australian Shiraz    15    −£5.00
Cabernet 1999,
Somerfield

Banrock Station Shiraz    15    −£5.00
Mataro 1999

Hardys Stamp Shiraz    14    −£5.00
Cabernet 1999

## AUSTRALIAN WHITE

Banrock Station    14    −£5.00
Chardonnay 1999

Banrock Station    15    −£5.00
Colombard Chardonnay
1999

Lindemans Bin 65    16.5    −£5.00
Chardonnay 1999

Pelican Bay Medium Dry    14    −£3.50
White

Penfolds Rawsons
Retreat Semillon/

Chardonnay/Colombard    15    −£5.00
1999

## BULGARIAN RED

Boyar Merlot 1999    15    −£3.50

Bulgarian Cabernet    13.5    −£3.50
Sauvignon 1999.
Somerfield

Bulgarian Country Red    14    −£3.50
NV, Somerfield

## BULGARIAN WHITE

Bulgarian Country White    14.5    −£3.50
1999, Somerfield

## CHILEAN RED

Chilean Cabernet    16.5    −£5.00
Sauvignon Vina La Rosa
1999, Somerfield

## CHILEAN WHITE

Chilean White 1999,    15.5    −£3.50
Somerfield

Vina Morande Chilean    15.5    −£5.00
Chardonnay 1999,
Somerfield

## FRENCH RED

| Wine | Score | Price |
|------|-------|-------|
| Brouilly Les Celliers de Bellevue 1998 | 12 | £5–7 |
| Cabernet Malbec VdP d'Oc 1997 | 15.5 | −£3.50 |
| Cabernet Sauvignon d'Oc Val d'Orbieu 1998, Somerfield | 14 | −£3.50 |
| Claret NV, Somerfield | 13.5 | −£3.50 |
| Corbieres Rouge Val d'Orbieu 1998, Somerfield | 15 | −£3.50 |
| Fitou Rocher d'Ambree 1998, Somerfield | 14.5 | −£5.00 |
| Les Oliviers VdT Francais Red NV | 12 | −£2.50 |
| March Hare VdP d'Oc 1997 | 15.5 | −£5.00 |
| Minervois Château la Reze 1996 | 16 | −£3.50 |
| Morgon 1998 | 12.5 | −£5.00 |
| Rivers Meet Merlot/ Cabernet, Bordeaux 1997 | 14 | −£5.00 |
| Skylark Hill Merlot, VdP d'Oc 1997 | 15.5 | −£3.50 |
| Skylark Hill Syrah VdP d'Oc 1997 | 15.5 | −£3.50 |
| Skylark Hill Very Special Red VdP d'Oc 1997 | 14 | −£3.50 |
| St Didier VdP du Tarn 1997 | 15.5 | −£3.50 |
| VdP des Coteaux de l'Ardeche Rouge 1999, Somerfield | 14 | −£3.50 |

## FRENCH WHITE

| Wine | Score | Price |
|------|-------|-------|
| Blanc de France Vin de Table NV | 15.5 | −£3.50 |
| Chablis Domaine de Bouchots Cuvée Boissonneuse 1998 | 12.5 | £5–7 |
| Chardonnay en Sol Oxfordien, Bourgogne 1998 | 14 | £5–7 |
| Chardonnay VdP du Jardin de la France 1999 | 13 | −£5.00 |
| Chenin Blanc VdP du Jardin de la France 1997 | 15.5 | −£2.50 |
| James Herrick Chardonnay VdP d'Oc 1999 | 16 | −£5.00 |
| Les Marionettes Marsanne VdP d'Oc 1999 | 15.5 | −£5.00 |
| Les Oliviers du Jardin Vin de Table NV | 15.5 | −£2.50 |
| VdP des Coteaux de l'Ardeche Blanc 1999, Somerfield | 14.5 | −£3.50 |
| VdP du Comte du Tolosan, Les Chais Beaucarois 1998 | 14 | −£3.50 |
| Wild Trout VdP d'Oc 1997 | 15.5 | −£5.00 |

## GERMAN WHITE

| Wine | Score | Price |
|------|-------|-------|
| Hock NV, Somerfield | 14.5 | −£2.50 |
| Niersteiner Spiegelberg 1999, Somerfield | 13 | −£3.50 |

## GREEK RED

Mavrodaphne of Patras NV   14.5   −£5.00

## GREEK WHITE

Kourtakis Retsina NV   14   −£3.50

## HUNGARIAN RED

Chapel Hill Merlot 1997   15.5   −£3.50

## HUNGARIAN WHITE

Castle Ridge Pinot Grigio, Neszmely 1999   14   −£5.00

Hungarian Pinot Grigio, Tolna Region 1998   15   −£3.50

Rhine Riesling, Mor Region 1997   14   −£3.50

## ITALIAN RED

Chianti Classico Conti Serristori 1998, Somerfield   13.5   £5–7

Merlot Venezie 1997   14   −£3.50

Montepulciano d'Abruzzo 1998, Somerfield   14   −£5.00

Solicella, VdT Umbria NV   15   −£3.50

Terra Rossa Sangiovese 1997   16   −£3.50

Valpolicella Venier NV   13   −£3.50

## ITALIAN WHITE

Bianco di Puglia 1998, Somerfield   13.5   −£3.50

Bright Brothers Roman Vines Sicilian Barrel-fermented Chardonnay 1999   16   −£5.00

Pinot Grigio/Chardonnay Venezie 1997   15   −£3.50

Sicilian White 1999, Somerfield   15.5   −£3.50

Soave 1998, Somerfield   14.5   −£3.50

Villa Pani Frascati Superiore 1997   13   −£3.50

Vino da Tavola Bianco NV, Somerfield   14   −£3.50

## PORTUGUESE RED

Ramada Red 1999   13   −£5.00

Vila Regia 1995   15   −£3.50

## PORTUGUESE WHITE

Falua 1998   13.5   −£3.50

Portuguese White 1999, Somerfield   15   −£3.50

## SOUTH AFRICAN RED

South African Cape Red 1999, Somerfield   15   −£3.50

South African Cinsault Ruby Cabernet 1999, Somerfield   15   −£5.00

311

KWIK SAVE

## SPANISH RED

Bodegas Castano Monastrell Merlot 1999 — 16.5 −£5.00

d'Avalos Tempranillo 1997 — 15 −£3.50

Don Darias Red NV — 15.5 −£5.00

Flamenco Red NV — 11 −£3.50

Los Molinos Tempranillo, Valdepeñas/Oak Aged 1993 — 15.5 −£3.50

Modernista Tempranillo 1997 — 16 −£3.50

Pergola Tempranillo 1999, Somerfield — 15 −£5.00

Rioja Crianza 1997, Somerfield — 14 −£5.00

Teja Tempranillo Cabernet 1997 — 14.5 −£3.50

## SPANISH WHITE

Castillo Imperial Blanco NV, Somerfield — 13.5 −£3.50

Muscatel de Valencia, Somerfield — 16 −£3.50

## USA RED

E & J Gallo Cabernet Sauvignon 1997 — 13 −£5.00

E & J Gallo Ruby Cabernet 1997 — 11 −£5.00

## USA WHITE

E & J Gallo Chardonnay 1997 — 10 −£5.00

## SPARKLING WINES

Asti Spumante NV, Somerfield — 14 £5–7

Cava Brut NV, Somerfield — 14.5 −£5.00

Cava Rosado NV, Somerfield — 14 −£5.00

Moscato Fizz, Somerfield — 14 −£2.50

Prince William Blanc de Noirs Champagne NV, Somerfield — 14 £10–13

312

# MAJESTIC

As someone who was once called 'a traitor' on BBC television by a representative of the English wine industry (because I disparaged the majority of English wine and said it was a conceit which would never catch on), I am sensitive where the subject of that strange liquid called English wine is concerned. I am, however, always prepared to accept evidence that will force me to eat my words, and over Christmas 1999 Majestic came up with this humbling dish. It reported that sales of English wine, principally Chapel Down Summerhill Dry (£3.99) and Chapel Down Bacchus (£4.99), had shot up 50% in its stores.

Majestic is increasing, indeed, on many fronts. It opened 12 branches in the past 12 months, planning eventually to end up with some 150 stores 'in the near future'. It also continued to persuade its customers to spend more than the national average on wine. The average price of a bottle of wine sold in Majestic has broken the £5 barrier, according to a report in *Retail Week* magazine, a figure to make a supermarket wine department chief weep with envy.

In May 2000 it launched its new website, allowing customers to buy on-line for the first time. It offered a core range of 450 wines. Orders will be referred to local branches and delivery carried out by the retailer's own vans.

Majestic also succeeds, unlike any other retailer, in carrying out daring raids on the Scandinavians. Its forays into Sweden, as a buyer of surplus wine stock, have been brilliantly successful for some years, and the latest one, in July 2000, saw Majestic clear out a state-owned warehouse, due for closure, on the outskirts of Stockholm. Such opportunities come about because of absurd overstocking in Sweden, cripplingly high alcohol taxes, and a sluggish retail market.

Over 400 different wines were picked up, retail value around £2.5 million. Much of it was 1997 vintage Bordeaux, and Majestic claimed that all the 'prices are way below what you would pay at auction or a traditional merchants, some up to 40% cheaper, and they are unrepeatable'. Many of the wines were in small case lots and included famous stuff like Pétrus and Yquem, so not every branch could get every wine. I heard of the wines'

MAJESTIC

arrival immediately, via e-mail, and wanted to taste the less expensive
bottles to see if any were suitable for my Saturday column, but the wines
were selling faster than 1999 vintage dot.com shares. I ended up getting my
lips around just four of the '97s, but wasn't impressed with them, the most
disappointing being the priciest, Château Lagrange, the Japanese-owned
St-Julien, at £19.99. Any one of several Majestic Côtes du Rhône or Languedoc reds would have been a deeper, more meaningful experience – at
around a third of the price.

Such wines apart, Majestic employs charming people running no-
nonsense stores.

Majestic Wine Warehouses
Majestic House
Otterspool Way
Watford
Herts
WD25 8WW

Tel 01923 298200
Fax 01923 819105
info@majestic.co.uk
www.majestic.co.uk

## ARGENTINIAN RED

| | | |
|---|---|---|
| Carrascal Cavas de Weinert 1996 | 14 | £5–7 |

## AUSTRALIAN RED

| | | |
|---|---|---|
| Bethany Cabernet Merlot 1998 | 14 | £7–10 |
| Bethany Grenache 1998 | 13 | £5–7 |
| Capel Vale 'CV' Pinot Noir 1998 | 13 | £7–10 |
| Capel Vale 'CV' Shiraz 1998 | 14.5 | £7–10 |
| Capel Vale Howecroft Cabernet 1996 | 15.5 | £13–20 |
| Ironstone Shiraz Grenache, Margaret River and Swan Valley 1996 | 16.5 | £5–7 |
| Kangarilla Road Cabernet, Cabernet Franc, Malbec 1998 | 14 | £7–10 |
| Kangarilla Road Shiraz 1998 | 15.5 | £7–10 |
| Mamre Brook Cabernet Shiraz 1996 | 16 | £5–7 |
| Mirrabrook Shiraz Cabernet 1999 | 14 | −£3.50 |
| Mount Langi Ghiran Shiraz Grenache 1997 | 13 | £7–10 |

314

| | | |
|---|---|---|
| Oxford Landing Cabernet Sauvignon Shiraz 1999 | 15.5 | £5–7 |
| Penfolds Bin 128 Coonawarra Shiraz 1996 | 15.5 | £7–10 |
| Penfolds Bin 28 Kalimna Shiraz 1996 | 15.5 | £7–10 |
| Penfolds Bin 389 Coonawarra Cabernet Shiraz 1996 | 16 | £10–13 |
| Penfolds Bin 407 Coonawarra Cabernet 1996 | 15 | £10–13 |
| Penfolds Old Vine Syrah Grenache Mourvedre, Barossa 1996 | 13.5 | £7–10 |
| Penfolds Rawsons Retreat Bin 35 Cabernet Sauvignon/Shiraz/Ruby Cabernet 1998 | 14 | £5–7 |
| Pirramimma Cabernet Sauvignon 1998 | 17 | £7–10 |
| Pirramimma Petit Verdot 1997 | 17 | £7–10 |
| Pirramimma Premium Shiraz 1997 | 15.5 | £7–10 |
| Pirramimma Stocks Hill Shiraz 1998 | 16 | £5–7 |
| Rymill Coonawarra Cabernet 1996 | 12.5 | £7–10 |
| Rymill Coonawarra Shiraz 1996 | 12 | £7–10 |
| Tatachilla Breakneck Creek Cabernet Sauvignon 1999 | 14 | £5–7 |
| Tatachilla Breakneck Creek Merlot 1999 | 15 | £5–7 |
| Woodstock McLaren Vale Grenache 1997 | 13 | £7–10 |
| Woodstock 'The Stocks' McLaren Shiraz 1996 | 10 | £10–13 |

## AUSTRALIAN WHITE

| | | |
|---|---|---|
| Bethany Riesling 1998 | 16.5 | £5–7 |
| Bethany Semillon Riesling Chardonnay 1998 | 16 | £5–7 |
| Capel Vale Riesling 1999 | 15 | £7–10 |
| Capel Vale Verdelho 1999 | 16 | £7–10 |
| Lindemans Bin 65 Chardonnay 1998 | 16 | −£5.00 |
| Mamre Brook Chardonnay 1997 | 14 | £5–7 |
| Mirrabrook Chardonnay 1999 | 15 | −£3.50 |
| Noble Road Verdelho 1998 | 14.5 | £5–7 |
| Oxford Landing Limited Release Viognier 1999 | 17 | £5–7 |
| Oxford Landing Sauvignon Blanc 1999 | 15 | −£5.00 |
| Penfolds Koonunga Hill Chardonnay 1999 | 16 | £5–7 |
| Pirramimma Chardonnay 1997 | 17 | £5–7 |
| Pirramimma Late Harvest Riesling 1998 (half-bottle) | 15 | £5–7 |
| Rosemount Estate Diamond Semillon 1997 | 16 | £5–7 |
| Rosemount GTR 1998 | 16 | £5–7 |

Tatachilla Breakneck Creek Chardonnay 1999 — 16 — −£5.00

Wynns Coonawarra Riesling 1998 — 16 — −£5.00

Yalumba Griffith-Barossa Botrytis Semillon Sauvignon Blanc 1997 (half-bottle) — 16 — £7–10

Yalumba Growers Chardonnay 1999 — 17 — £5–7

## CHILEAN RED

Luis Felipe Edwards Pupilla Cabernet Sauvignon 1999 — 14 — −£5.00

Montes Alpha Merlot 1997 — 14 — £7–10

Santa Rita Reserva Cabernet Sauvignon, Maipo 1997 — 16 — £5–7

Santa Rita Triple C 1997 — 17 — £10–13

Valdivieso Barrel Selection Malbec 1999 — 16 — £5–7

Valdivieso Barrel Selection Merlot 1998 — 17 — £5–7

Vistasur Cabernet Sauvignon 1998 — 15.5 — −£5.00

## CHILEAN WHITE

Chardonnay Reserve Cono Sur 1998 — 16.5 — £5–7

Luis Felipe Edwards Chardonnay 1998 — 14 — −£5.00

Santa Rita Cabernet Sauvignon Rosé 1999 — 16 — −£5.00

Santa Rita Dona Paula Cabernet Sauvignon Rosé 1998 — 14 — −£5.00

Vistasur Sauvignon Blanc 1999 — 15.5 — −£5.00

## FRENCH RED

Beaune 1er Cru Les Chauacheaux 1997 — 12 — £13–20

Beaune Louis Latour 1997 — 11 — £7–10

Beaune-Epenotes 1979 — 10 — £20+

Bois de Lamothe Cabernet Franc, Cotes de Duras 1997 — 16 — −£3.50

Bott-Geyl Pinot Noir Beblenheim 1997 — 15.5 — £7–10

Bourgeuil La Vernelle 1997 — 16 — −£5.00

Bouton d'Or Cairanne, Côtes du Rhône Villages 1998 — 14 — −£5.00

Calvet Reserve Claret 1998 — 14.5 — £5–7

Cave de Ribeauville Pinot Noir 1998 — 14 — £5–7

Chambolle-Musigny Jaffelin 1996 — 10 — £10–13

Château de Bosc Côtes du Rhône 1997 — 11 — £5–7

Château de Candale, Haut Medoc 1996 — 14 — £10–13

Château de Gaudou Cuvée Tradition Cahors 1998 — 15.5 — −£5.00

| Wine | Score | Price |
|---|---|---|
| Château de Haute Serre Cahors 1989 | 13 | £7–10 |
| Château de Nardon 1998 | 14 | £5–7 |
| Château de Sales, Pomerol 1996 | 13.5 | £20+ |
| Château Flauguergues Coteaux du Languedoc 1998 | 17.5 | £5–7 |
| Château Guiot Costieres de Nimes 1999 | 15.5 | −£5.00 |
| Château Haut Mazieres, Bordeaux 1997 | 14 | £5–7 |
| Château l'Abbaye de St Ferme Bordeaux Superieur 1998 | 15.5 | £5–7 |
| Château Lamartine, Cotes de Castillon 1997 | 15 | £5–7 |
| Château Ludon Pomies Agassac, Bordeaux 1997 | 12 | £10–13 |
| Château Meaume Bordeaux Superieur 1997 | 16 | £5–7 |
| Château Morin, St Estephe 1997 | 16.5 | £7–10 |
| Château Tour Saint Paul, Bordeaux Superieur 1997 | 13 | £5–7 |
| Châteauneuf-du-Pape Domaine Cailloux 1997 | 13 | £10–13 |
| Châteauneuf-du-Pape Domaine Pegau 1997 | 14.5 | £13–20 |
| Chinon les Garous, Couly-Dutheil 1997 | 16 | £5–7 |
| Claret Cuvée 090 1998 | 14 | −£5.00 |
| Claret Lot 278 1998 | 14 | −£5.00 |
| Corbieres Domaine Madelon 1999 | 14 | −£5.00 |
| Corton Grancey Grand Cru 1995 | 12.5 | £20+ |
| Coteaux de Tricastin Domaine Saint Remy 1997 | 15 | −£5.00 |
| Côtes de Nuits Villages Louis Latour 1996 | 10 | £7–10 |
| Côtes du Rhône Guigal 1997 | 14 | £5–7 |
| Côtes du Rhône Guigal 1998 | 16 | £7–10 |
| Côtes du Rhône Les Chevaliers aux Lys d'Or 1998 | 13 | −£3.50 |
| Côtes du Ventoux Vidal-Fleury 1998 | 14 | −£5.00 |
| Crozes-Hermitage Cave Tain l'Hermitage 1998 | 14 | £5–7 |
| Domaine de l'Ile St-Pierre Cabernet Franc 1998 | 16.5 | −£5.00 |
| Domaine de la Closerie St Nicholas de Bourgueil 1997 | 13 | £5–7 |
| Domaine de Rodes Grenache VdP d'Oc 1998 | 15 | −£5.00 |
| Domaine de Rodes Syrah VdP d'Oc 1998 | 16.5 | −£5.00 |
| Domaine des Bois du Garn Côtes du Vivarais 1998 | 16 | −£5.00 |
| Fixin Jaffelin 1996 | 12 | £7–10 |
| Gigondas Guigal 1997 | 16.5 | £10–13 |
| Givry 1er Cru Steinmaier 1998 | 15 | £7–10 |
| Givry Louis Latour 1997 | 11 | £7–10 |

| | | |
|---|---|---|
| Grenache/Cabernet VdP de l'Ardeche 1998 | 16 | −£3.50 |
| Hautes Côtes de Beaune Cave Co-op 1997 | 13.5 | £5–7 |
| La Fauve Merlot VdP d'Oc 1998 | 15 | −£5.00 |
| La Fauve Syrah VdP d'Oc 1998 | 15.5 | −£5.00 |
| La Ramillade Gigondas 1998 | 15 | £7–10 |
| Lirac Domaine de la Rocaliere 1997 | 16 | £5–7 |
| Macon St Gengoux 1998 | 14 | −£5.00 |
| Madiran Meinjarre Alain Brumont 1997 | 15 | £5–7 |
| Mas de Bressades Cabernet Syrah VdP du Gard 1998 | 17 | £5–7 |
| Mas de Guiot Cabernet Syrah VdP du Gard 1998 | 17.5 | £5–7 |
| Merlot VdP de la Haute Vallee de l'Aude 1998 | 14 | −£3.50 |
| Morgon Jean Descombes 1998 | 13 | £7–10 |
| Pernand-Vergelesses Jaffelin 1996 | 12.5 | £7–10 |
| Regnie Vallieres 1998 | 14 | −£5.00 |
| Sancerre Rouge Les Belles Dames Vacheron 1997 | 14.5 | £13–20 |
| Sancerre Rouge Vacheron 1998 | 15.5 | £7–10 |
| Syrah Collines Rhodaniennes, Co-op de Tain Hermitage 1998 | 13.5 | −£5.00 |
| Syrah VdP du Cave Tain l'Hermitage 1998 | 13 | −£5.00 |

## FRENCH WHITE

| | | |
|---|---|---|
| Bois de Lamothe Sauvignon Blanc, VdP du Lot et Garonne 1997 | 15 | −£3.50 |
| Bott-Geyl Gewürztraminer Grand Cru Sonnenglanz 1998 | 17.5 | £10–13 |
| Bott-Geyl Riesling Burgreben de Zellenberg 1997 | 14.5 | £7–10 |
| Bott-Geyl Riesling Grafenreben de Zellenberg 1997 | 15 | £7–10 |
| Bott-Geyl Tokay Pinot Gris 1998 | 15 | £7–10 |
| Bott-Geyl Tokay Pinot Gris Sonnenglanz Vendages Tardives 1998 | 14 | £13–20 |
| Cave de Ribeauville Gewürztraminer 1998 | 16 | £5–7 |
| Cave de Ribeauville Tokay Pinot Gris 1998 | 15 | £5–7 |
| Chablis 1er Cru Côte de Lechet La Chablisienne 1998 | 12 | £10–13 |
| Chablis Domaine Marguerite Carillon 1998 | 15.5 | −£5.00 |
| Chablis Domaine Vocoret 1998 | 13.5 | £7–10 |
| Chablis Grand Cru Les Clos 1998 | 10 | £13–20 |
| Chardonnay Jean Belmont VdP du Jardin de la France 1999 | 15 | −£5.00 |

| | | |
|---|---|---|
| Vacqueyras Beaumes de Venise 1999 | 16.5 | £5–7 |

Chassagne-Montrachet Fontaine-Gagnard 1er Cru La Maltroie 1997 — 10 — £20+

Château du Sours Rosé 1999 — 15 — £5–7

Château Haut Mazieres Blanc, Bordeaux 1997 — 16 — £5–7

Château Meaume Rosé 1999 — 14 — £5–7

Chenin Blanc VdP du Jardin de la France, Remy Pannier NV — 14.5 — –£3.50

Chinon Rosé Couly-Dutheil 1998 — 13 — £5–7

Condrieu Guigal 1998 — 15.5 — £13–20

Corton-Charlemagne, Bonneau du Martray 1996 — 10 — £20+

Côtes du Rhône Rosé Guigal 1997 — 14 — £5–7

Cuvée Apolline Tokay Pinot Gris 1997 — 13 — £10–13

Domaine de Raissac CVM Barrique 1999 — 15 — –£5.00

Domaine de Raissac Viognier 1999 — 15.5 — –£5.00

Domaine des Fontanelles Sauvignon Blanc 1999 — 15 — –£5.00

Domaine Le Puts Blanc Michel Bordes 1999 — 16 — –£3.50

Gewürztraminer, Haegelin 1998 — 14.5 — £7–10

Gewürztraminer Paul Zinck 1999 — 13.5 — £7–10

Givry Blanc Louis Latour 1996 — 10 — £7–10

Grand Ardeche Chardonnay Louis Latour 1998 — 15 — £5–7

Le Fauve Chasan 1999 — 15.5 — –£5.00

Le Fauve Marsanne 1999 — 16 — –£5.00

Le Fauve Rosé de Syrah 1999 — 14.5 — –£5.00

Les Fontanelles Viognier Foncalieu 1999 — 16 — –£5.00

Les Grands Clochers Chardonnay 1999 — 14.5 — £5–7

Moulin Touchais, Coteaux du Layon 1986 — 16 — £7–10

Muscadet Cuvée du Homard 1998 — 14 — –£3.50

Muscadet Hommard 1998 — 13.5 — –£3.50

Muscadet sur Lie Château la Touche 1998 — 13.5 — –£5.00

Muscat Riquewihr, Bott-Geyl 1997 — 15 — £7–10

Pinot Blanc Haegelin 1998 — 13.5 — £5–7

Quincy JC Bourguat 1999 — 15 — £5–7

Reuilly Beurdin 1999 — 14 — £5–7

Riesling Bollenberg, Haegelin 1998 — 13 — £5–7

Sancerre La Chaudillonne Fournier 1997 — 10 — £7–10

Sancerre Rosé Vacheron 1999 — 10 — £7–10

Sauvignon Lot 279, Bordeaux 1998 — 13 — –£5.00

Sauvignon Touraine Delauney 1999 — 12 — –£5.00

Sylvaner, Paul Zinck 1998 — 14.5 — –£5.00

| | | |
|---|---|---|
| Tokay Pinot Gris, Haegelin 1998 | 13.5 | £7–10 |
| Vivian Ducourneau VdP des Côtes de Gascogne 1999 | 15.5 | –£5.00 |
| Vouvray Tris de Nobles Grain, Domaine Bourillon Dorleans 1995 (50cl) | 16 | £10–13 |

| | | |
|---|---|---|
| Serriger Vogelsang Riesling Auslese (2nd Barrel) 1989 | 16.5 | £5–7 |
| Wehlener Sonnenuhr Riesling Kabinett, Jacobus 1992 | 16 | –£5.00 |
| Wehlener Sonnenuhr Riesling Spatlese, Hauth-Kerpen 1998 | 15 | £5–7 |

## GERMAN WHITE

| | | |
|---|---|---|
| Avelsbacher Hammerstein Riesling QbA 1992 | 16.5 | –£5.00 |
| Bernkasteler Badstube Riesling Kabinett, Jacobus 1994 | 13.5 | –£5.00 |
| Bernkasteler Badstube Riesling Kabinett Thanisch Muller-Burggrael 1998 | 13 | £7–10 |
| Domdechant Werner Riesling Spatlese Halbtrocken 1992 | 14.5 | –£5.00 |
| Erdener Treppchen Riesling Spatlese 1994 | 16.5 | £5–7 |
| JL Wolf Forster Stiff Riesling Spatlese 1996 | 14 | £5–7 |
| Kaseler Kehrnagel Riesling Kabinett Bert Simon 1990 | 14 | –£5.00 |
| Riesling QbA Friedrich-Wilhelm-Gymnasium 1991 | 14 | –£5.00 |
| Riesling Ruppertsberger 1997 | 13.5 | –£5.00 |

## ITALIAN RED

| | | |
|---|---|---|
| Aglianico del Vulture 1997 | 18 | £7–10 |
| Amarone Valpolicella Tedeschi 1996 | 18 | £10–13 |
| Barbera d'Asti Ca'Bianca 1997 | 13.5 | £5–7 |
| Centine Toscanna, Banfi 1997 | 16 | £5–7 |
| Chianti Il Tasso 1998 | 14 | –£5.00 |
| Chianti Rufina Basciano 1997 | 15.5 | £5–7 |
| Colli di Sasso Banfi 1998 | 14 | –£5.00 |
| Conero Conti Cortesi 1997 | 14.5 | £5–7 |
| Dogajolo Toscana 1998 | 16 | £5–7 |
| Dolcetto d'Alba de Forville 1998 | 16 | £5–7 |
| Merlot del Veneto Marchesini 1998 | 14.5 | –£3.50 |
| Merloti Marche Marchesini 1999 | 10 | –£3.50 |
| Montepulciano d'Abruzzo Barone Cornacchia 1998 | 11 | –£5.00 |

| | | |
|---|---|---|
| Primitivo del Salento Antonini 1998 | 16 | −£5.00 |
| Primitivo del Salento Sigillo Primo 1998 | 16 | −£5.00 |
| Recioto Tedeschi 1996 (50cl) | 15 | £5–7 |
| Rosso di Sicilia La Toricella 1998 | 15 | −£3.50 |
| Salice del Salento Riserva 1997 | 15.5 | £5–7 |
| Sangiovese Marchesini 1998 | 13.5 | −£3.50 |
| Sassaiolo Rosso Piceno 1997 | 14.5 | −£5.00 |
| Valpolicella Classico, Santepietre 1998 | 12 | −£5.00 |
| Valpolicella Classico Superiore 1996 | 17 | £7–10 |
| Vino Nobile di Montepulciano 1996 | 14.5 | £5–7 |

## ITALIAN WHITE

| | | |
|---|---|---|
| Bianco di Sicilia La Toricella 1998 | 15 | −£3.50 |
| Ca'Visco Soave Classico Superiore Coffele 1998 | 16 | £5–7 |
| Castello di Tassarolo Gavi 1998 | 15.5 | £7–10 |
| Chardonnay di Puglia, Pasqua NV | 14.5 | −£3.50 |
| Chardonnay Pinot Grigio Pasqua 1999 | 13.5 | −£5.00 |
| Frascati Superiore, Selciatella 1998 | 15.5 | −£5.00 |
| Garganega Garda DOC | 14.5 | −£5.00 |

| | | |
|---|---|---|
| Vigne Alte Fratelli Zeni 1999 | | |
| Late Picked Gavi di Gavi Villa Lanata 1999 | 14 | £7–10 |
| Monte Tenda Vigneto Soave Classico Tedeschi 1998 | 13 | −£5.00 |
| Orvieto Classico Secco Vigneto Mortaro 1999 | 15.5 | −£5.00 |
| Piemonte Chardonnay de Forville 1998 | 15.5 | £5–7 |
| Pinot Grigio Alois Lageder 1998 | 16 | £7–10 |
| Pinot Grigio San Angelo Vineyard, Banfi 1999 | 10 | £5–7 |
| Verdicchio dei Castelli di Jesi Coste del Molino 1999 | 16 | −£5.00 |

## NEW ZEALAND WHITE

| | | |
|---|---|---|
| Jackson Estate Sauvignon Blanc 1999 | 15 | £7–10 |
| Marlborough Gold Chardonnay 1998 | 13 | £5–7 |
| Marlborough Gold Sauvignon 1999 | 14.5 | £5–7 |
| Oyster Bay Chardonnay 1999 | 16.5 | £5–7 |
| Oyster Bay Sauvignon 1999 | 16.5 | £5–7 |

## PORTUGUESE RED

| | | |
|---|---|---|
| Contes de Cima Vinho Regional Alentejano 1997 | 14 | £7–10 |
| Duas Quintas 1997 | 16 | £5–7 |

Tuella Douro Tinto 1997 | 15.5 | −£5.00

## SOUTH AFRICAN RED

Drosty-Hof Merlot 1998 | 16 | £5–7

Fairview Merlot 1998 | 16.5 | £5–7

Goats Do Roam | 15.5 | −£5.00
Fairview, Paarl 1999

## SOUTH AFRICAN WHITE

De Wetshof Estate | 16.5 | £5–7
'Lesca' Chardonnay 1999

Franschoek Barrel | 12 | −£5.00
Fermented Chenin Blanc
1998

Kumala Semillon | 16 | −£5.00
Chardonnay 1999

## SPANISH RED

Artadi Vinas de Gain | 15 | £7–10
Rioja 1997

Arva Vitis Tempranillo | 15.5 | −£5.00
1998

Berberana Dragon | 15 | −£5.00
Tempranillo 1998

Costers del Gravet Celler | 17 | £7–10
de Capcanes 1998

Finca Lasendal, Celler de | 15.5 | −£5.00
Capcanes 1999

'G' Dehesa Gago Telmo | 16 | £5–7
Rodriguez 1998

Marques de Grinon Rioja | 15 | £5–7
1997

Marques de Murietta | 14 | £7–10
Rioja Reserva 1995

Mas Collet Celler de | 16.5 | £5–7
Capcanes 1998

Muga Rioja Reserva 1995 | 13 | £7–10

Ochoa Tempranillo | 15 | −£5.00
Garnache Navarra 1998

Vina Armantes Garnacha | 15 | −£5.00
1999

Vina El Salado | 15 | −£5.00
Extremadura 1998

## SPANISH WHITE

Albarino Martin Codax | 13.5 | £5–7
Rias Maixas 1999

Rueda Blanco, Vinos | 15 | −£5.00
Sanz 1999

Vionta Albarino 1999 | 13 | £7–10

## USA RED

Beringer Appellation | 14 | £7–10
Zinfandel 1996

Beringer Valdeguie 1998 | 15 | £5–7

Firestone Old Vine | 17 | £7–10
Cucmunga Zinfandel
1997

Foxen Pinot Noir Santa | 14 | £13–20
Maria 1997

Ironstone Vineyards | 15.5 | £5–7
Cabernet Franc 1996

Ironstone Vineyards | 15 | £5–7
Cabernet Franc 1997

Ironstone Vineyards | 16 | £5–7
Merlot 1997

Kautz-Ironstone Shiraz | 16 | £5–7
1997

Prosperity Red NV | 16 | −£5.00

## USA WHITE

| | | |
|---|---|---|
| Beringer Californian Sauvignon Blanc 1997 | 15.5 | £5–7 |
| Beringer Californian Zinfandel Blush 1998 | 6 | £5–7 |
| Beringer Napa Valley Fume Blanc 1998 | 15 | £7–10 |
| Essencia Orange Muscat 1996 (half-bottle) | 16 | £5–7 |
| Fetzer Barrel Select Chardonnay 1997 | 15 | £7–10 |
| Fetzer Viognier 1999 | 15 | £7–10 |
| Foxen Bien Nacido Vineyard Chardonnay 1996 | 14 | £13–20 |
| Foxen Tinaquaic Vineyard Chardonnay 1996 | 13.5 | £13–20 |
| Ironstone Chardonnay 1998 | 10 | £5–7 |
| Ironstone Semillon Chardonnay 1998 | 15 | £5–7 |
| Kautz-Ironstone Chardonnay 1998 | 13.5 | £5–7 |
| Prosperity White NV | 15 | −£5.00 |

## FORTIFIED WINES

| | | |
|---|---|---|
| Amontillado Seco Napoleon, Hidalgo | 16 | £7–10 |
| Pedro Ximenez Viejo Napoleon, Hidalgo | 15 | £7–10 |
| Taylor's Quinta de Terra Feita 1986 | 17 | £13–20 |

## SPARKLING WINES

| | | |
|---|---|---|
| Ayala Champagne NV | 15 | £13–20 |
| Ayala Champagne Rosé NV | 11 | £13–20 |
| Bouvet Ladubay Saumur NV | 10 | £7–10 |
| Cava Verano, Freixenet NV | 15.5 | −£5.00 |
| Conde de Caralt Cava Brut NV | 16.5 | £5–7 |
| De Telmont Grande Reserve Champagne NV | 14.5 | £13–20 |
| Freixenet Cuvée DS 1996 | 16.5 | £10–13 |
| Gloria Ferrer Royal Cuvée 1991 | 13 | £13–20 |
| Jacquart Brut Mosaique Champagne NV | 12 | £13–20 |
| Jacquart Champagne 1992 | 12 | £20+ |
| Lamberhurst Brut NV (England) | 8 | £7–10 |
| Langlois Cremant de Loire NV (France) | 15 | £7–10 |
| Langlois Cremant de Loire Rosé NV (France) | 16 | £7–10 |
| Lindauer Special Reserve NV (New Zealand) | 16 | £7–10 |
| Oeil de Perdrix Champagne NV | 16 | £13–20 |
| Oeil de Perdrix NV | 14 | £13–20 |
| Taittinger Champagne Brut NV | 12 | £20+ |
| Yellowglen Pinot Noir Chardonnay NV (Australia) | 13.5 | £7–10 |

**SEE STOP PRESS SECTION AT END OF BOOK FOR LAST-MINUTE ADDITIONS OR UPDATES TO THIS RETAILER'S RANGE.**

# MARKS & SPENCER

Considerable distraction was endured while tasting El Padruell 1998, a monumentally cheeky Spanish red from Señor Jaume Serra in Penedès, since I tasted it in a mausoleum-cum-art gallery. This unique establishment is the new tasting arena on the top floor of Marks & Spencer's head office in Baker Street in London's West End. The area was once the directors' executive suite, where exhausted retail moguls could gather their wits in fat armchairs, take in the chintz-curtain-framed views, and regard with awe the abundance of framed daubs on the walls (taking exceptional encouragement, no doubt, from Terence Cuneo's cutsie beach scene and Lowry's stick insect townsfolk). Marks & Spencer, however, doesn't have any armchaired moguls any more; they've passed away in all the 'reorganis-ations' of the recent past. But the memoria remain; as does the space which has been given to the company's wine buyers to use.

The bad news about El Padruell is that M&S bought it as a one-off 'special parcel' and so there is not likely to be much, if anything, left on any shelf. Nevertheless, I discovered many other interesting things at that tasting, Lowry's emaciated populace notwithstanding, as the wines which follow show.

I would particularly point to the following: Marisa 1999 (16 points, £4.99) from Spain, with its baked, savoury fruit with a tobacco undertone and a lovely warmth to the texture. Sierra Los Andes Merlot Cabernet 1999 (16 points, £4.99) from Chile, which has a curious strawberry fool aroma but don't let this kid you, for this is serious stuff with piles of flavour courtesy of resoundingly rich fruit of vivacity and pace. La Tour du Prevot Côtes du Ventoux 1999 (16 points, £5.99) is what terrific under-a-fiver French country reds are all about: deep, herby, rich, warm, drinkable, unpretentious, food-friendly, full of character, and, less typical of the handsomest of its kind, Sangiovese di Puglia 1999 (15.5 points, £3.99), which, with its tenacious tannins, is so much more lip-smackingly savoury and entertaining than many Chiantis using the same Sangiovese grape. Barbera Piemonte 1998 (16 points, £4.49), with its plump cherry fruit, is more typical of its kind, but it does have a wonderful vigour and flushed-with-youth freshness on the finish that is not entirely classic. And lastly in this mini-peek at the M&S

range there is Rock Ridge Pinotage 1999 (16.5 points, £4.99), from the Cape, a wine of brilliant spicy warmth and wit. The tobacco and rubber, the smoke and the basket of leathery fruit – all the usual Pinotage pleasures – hanging together extremely sensuously.

Chris Murphy (who's had to endure a horrible year as a Leeds supporter) runs the wine department with Jane Masters, who's actually made wine (and so knows all about horrible years too).

On the business front, M&S announced the expansion of its flagship French store on the Boulevard Haussmann in Paris even though the company had just put a halt to its expansion in Europe and the Far East. In the UK, it was said M&S planned to 'rethink' food stores and redesign and rebrand, whatever that means, 40 neighbourhood food stores. In June 2000 the store announced the radical idea that it was extending its refund policy to food, so that consumers can return food they haven't enjoyed. The move was expected to cost the retailer about £1 million a year because such returned goods can obviously not be resold. Personally, I expect it to cost a lot more because there are a lot of shifty blighters out there who will cheerfully cough up £30 for a load of Indian dishes, say, scoff half, and then return the remainder as unsatisfactory and demand a refund.

No such returns for that amiable Greenbury chap, who was chairman. He retired last year. Brian Baldock took over as chairman until a 'permanent replacement can be found'. Mr Greenbury had been with M&S for 46 years. Mr Baldock said that he would not be staying on permanently but as attempts to find a replacement, at that time, seemed deadlocked it appeared he might be there for some time, but a certain Luc Vandevelde finally landed the job. (More of whom in a moment.)

There was a launch in 1999 of M&S's new wine shop format (called Wine Shop 2000), which was basically just a rebranding and merchandising initiative. Wines were merchandised under twelve different taste styles, colour-coded by country. There was also a display of the current top ten best-sellers, and tastings were held at zinc counters at prearranged times (the zinc counter was particularly stressed – as no doubt were the tasters behind it). I've visited a dozen M&S stores over the past year and I've yet to come across a single zinc counter but I don't doubt they exist or did exist.

Some months later I learned that the moves to roll out M&S's Wine Shop 2000 format had stalled. It had been feebly extended to seven outlets from its initial two pilot versions (in Oxford and Tolworth). It was now being incorporated into a wider rebranding scheme for its combined food and wine shelves (where the food has the lion's share, of course).

M&S's summer sales flagged in 1999. Like-for-like sales were rumoured to be down 12% for clothing, and rumours of another profits warning were rife. It was revealed in *The Times* that M&S was looking to recruit a marketing director from outside the company to succeed James Benfield. Mr Benfield, in the job just six months, had been the company's first marketing director and been with the company 30 years. Alan McWalter was eventually recruited as marketing director from Kingfisher.

In 1999 M&S reported a 12.9% drop in sales over April, May and June, the largest in its 115-year history. But it wasn't taking these reverses lying down. It opened food and lingerie concessions in stores overseas and offered cash incentives to staff to promote better customer service. Then *The Times* revealed that M&S was planning to sell clothes brands other than St Michael, while the *Independent on Sunday* reported that in a survey by Western International Media M&S was still the retailer most trusted by consumers.

But only in the UK. In the wider landscapes of Europe, M&S closed six of its forty-two Continental European outlets at a cost of three hundred jobs but resulting in a £10 million annual saving. Rumours were rife at this time about thirty top staff cuts. These were dismissed as 'pure speculation'. *The Times* reported that M&S was considering a mass property sell-off.

Nothing daunted, M&S expanded its home shopping format, increasing the number of catalogues distributed from 21 million to nearly 50 million and offering 3,000 lines on the Internet. It was reported in *Retail Week* magazine to be considering the launch of its own credit card. This followed the decision, long, long overdue, to accept credit cards (a move which finally took effect in April 2000). M&S currently has 5 million chargecard holders and these moves surely enhance its chances to acquire many more.

M&S was, however, according to the *Guardian*, still the fifth most profitable retailer in the UK – so what was it doing wrong? Well, it wasn't sucking up to its UK suppliers. *The Times* carried the doleful news that M&S, once the undisputed champion of British-made merchandise, will eventually import up to 75% of the garments it sells. Parallel to this, M&S was seeking a summary court judgment to dismiss a £53 million lawsuit from clothing manufacturer, and long-time and once trusted British supplier, William Baird. The basis of the M&S case was that there was no formal contract. Later, the GMB Union urged M&S to pay £35 million to textile workers who faced unemployment as a result of the firm's decision to source clothes from abroad.

Hard on the heels of this report, the *Sunday Telegraph* wrote that M&S had appointed a 'change tsar' to oversee the retailer's battles to adapt itself to today's market. A certain Nigel Robertson has 'a licence to challenge and sanction at all levels', just like the tsars of old. The *Sunday Telegraph* also reported in February that M&S was to adapt its ranges to suit the needs of local markets and consumers.

Finally, in February, Mr Luc Vandevelde was named as the new M&S chairman (to take up the post in March). *Retail Week* magazine reported that the chairman's office was being redecorated and refurbished in his honour. He was also getting a £2.2 million golden hello. The trade paper observed that he shared his name with the golfer who famously snatched defeat from the jaws of victory at last year's Open in the most bizarre and farcical of circumstances. Analysts, at this time, speculated that chief executive Peter Salsbury's position was now under threat.

Matters now began to gather pace and heat. M&S launched its new Autograph designer range, which did indeed bear designers' names rather than the legendary St Michael, and it was reported in the *Sun*, of all places, that M&S was to drop the legendary label from all its own-label clothing and simply use the Marks & Spencer label. According to the *Mail on Sunday*, M&S asked 450 senior managers at its head office to reapply for their jobs as part of a strategy to split the group into seven units.

In spring 2000 M&S appointed Ms Cheri Lofland as their first-ever director of communications. This fact, allied to the appointment of the store's first-ever outside marketing director (the Mr McWalter referred to above), tells you more about the reasons for the state which M&S got itself into than any amount of statistics and columns of sagging sales figures.

Last I heard, M&S was going to open its first outlet in Croatia. Since I don't have any plans to visit this country, may I ask any reader who does to see if s(he) finds any zinc counters in the M&S in Zagreb?

Marks & Spencer Plc
Michael House
57 Baker Street
London
W1U 8EP

Tel 020 7268 1234
Fax 020 7268 2380
www.marksandspencer.com

## ARGENTINIAN RED

| | | |
|---|---|---|
| Rio Santos Bonarda Barbera 1999 | 13.5 | −£5.00 |
| Rio Santos Cabernet Syrah 1999 | 13.5 | −£5.00 |
| Rio Santos Malbec 1999 | 14 | −£5.00 |

## ARGENTINIAN WHITE

| | | |
|---|---|---|
| Rio Santos Torrontes 1999 | 13.5 | −£5.00 |

## AUSTRALIAN RED

| | | |
|---|---|---|
| Australian Shiraz 1999 | 15 | £5–7 |
| Fusion Shiraz 1998 | 16 | £5–7 |
| HoneyTree Grenache Shiraz 1999 | 13 | £5–7 |
| HoneyTree Reserve Pinot Noir 1998 | 13 | £7–10 |
| HoneyTree Shiraz Cabernet 1999 | 15.5 | £5–7 |
| HoneyTree Shiraz Reserve 1998 | 14 | £7–10 |
| Shiraz Ruby Cabernet Merlot Bin 312 1999 | 12.5 | −£5.00 |
| South East Australian Cabernet 1999 | 14 | −£5.00 |
| South East Australian Merlot 1999 | 13.5 | −£5.00 |

## AUSTRALIAN WHITE

| | | |
|---|---|---|
| Fusion Riesling 1999 | 15 | −£5.00 |
| HoneyTree Gewürztraminer Riesling 1999 | 12 | £5–7 |

| | | |
|---|---|---|
| HoneyTree Semillon Chardonnay 1999 | 15 | £5–7 |
| Hunter Valley Chardonnay Bin 109 1999 | 14.5 | −£5.00 |
| Lindemans Bin 65 Chardonnay 1999 | 16.5 | −£5.00 |
| Semillon Bin 381 1999 | 13 | −£5.00 |
| South East Australian Medium Dry 1999 | 13 | −£5.00 |
| South Eastern Australian Chardonnay 1999 | 15 | −£5.00 |
| South Eastern Australian Riesling 1999 | 12 | −£5.00 |
| Verdelho 1999 | 12 | −£5.00 |

## CHILEAN RED

| | | |
|---|---|---|
| Casa Leona Cabernet Sauvignon 1999 | 16.5 | −£5.00 |
| Casa Leona Merlot 1999 | 16 | £5–7 |
| Sierra Los Andes Merlot Cabernet 1999 | 16 | £5–7 |
| Sierra Los Andes Merlot Cabernet Reserve 1998 | 15 | £5–7 |

## CHILEAN WHITE

| | | |
|---|---|---|
| Alta Mira Chilean White 1999 | 15 | −£5.00 |
| Casa Leona Chardonnay 1999 | 16.5 | −£5.00 |
| Casa Leona Merlot/ Cabernet Sauvignon Rosé 2000 | 14 | −£5.00 |
| Sierra Los Andes Chardonnay 1999 | 16 | −£5.00 |

Sierra Los Andes Chardonnay Reserve 1999 — 16 £5–7

Sierra Los Andes Gewürztraminer 1999 — 16 –£5.00

## FRENCH RED

Abbaye de Tholomies Minervois 1996 — 16.5 £5–7

Burgundy Pinot Noir 1998 — 12 £7–10

Château de Sauvanes Faugeres 1997 — 15.5 £5–7

Château de Surville Costieres de Nimes 1998 — 16 £5–7

Château des Lanes, Corbieres 1998 — 16 £5–7

Château Planezes, Cotes du Roussillon Villages 1998 — 16.5 £5–7

Côtes du Parc, Coteaux du Languedoc 1999 (organic) — 15.5 –£5.00

Devois des Agneaux Coteaux du Languedoc 1998 — 15.5 £7–10

Domaine St Pierre VdP de l'Herault 1999 — 11 –£3.50

Gold Label Cabernet Sauvignon VdP d'Oc 1998 — 15 –£5.00

Gold Label Reserve Barrel Aged Syrah VdP d'Oc 1998 — 16.5 £5–7

Gold Label Syrah VdP d'Oc 1999 — 16 –£5.00

House Red Wine, VdP du Comte Tolosan 1999 — 12 –£3.50

La Tour du Prevot Côtes de Ventoux 1999 — 16 –£5.00

Margaux 1997 — 13.5 £10–13

Merlot Cave de Rauzan 1998 — 13.5 –£5.00

Oak Aged Bordeaux 1997 — 13 £5–7

## FRENCH WHITE

Bordeaux Sauvignon 1999 — 13.5 –£5.00

Chablis 1997 — 13.5 £7–10

Chablis Grand Cru Grenouille 1994 — 12 £13–20

Chablis Premier Cru 1996 — 13 £10–13

Château Les Charmes de Saint-Mayme, Monbazillac 1995 — 16 £7–10

Côtes de Provence 1999 (rosé) — 11 –£5.00

Domaine de la Pouvraie Vouvray 1999 — 14 –£5.00

Gold Label Chardonnay Reserve 1998 — 15.5 £5–7

Gold Label Chardonnay VdP d'Oc 1999 — 15 –£5.00

Gold Label Sauvignon Blanc VdP d'Oc 1999 — 14 –£5.00

Gold Label Viognier 1999 — 14 –£5.00

Les Ruetttes Sancerre 1999 — 15.5 £7–10

Macon Villages 1999 — 15.5 £5–7

Pouilly Fume 1999 — 16 £7–10

| | | |
|---|---|---|
| Rivesaltes Ambre Hors d'Age 25 Year | 15.5 | £7–10 |
| Rosé de Syrah VdP d'Oc 1999 | 14 | –£5.00 |
| VdP des Côtes de Gascogne 1999 | 14 | –£3.50 |
| Vin de Pays du Gers 1999 | 14 | –£3.50 |

## GERMAN WHITE

| | | |
|---|---|---|
| Summer Spring Riesling 1999 | 12 | –£5.00 |

## ITALIAN RED

| | | |
|---|---|---|
| Amarone Classico della Valpolicella 1995 | 15.5 | £10–13 |
| Barbera Piemonte 1998 | 16 | –£5.00 |
| Barolo 1996 | 13.5 | £13–20 |
| Canfera 1997 | 14.5 | £7–10 |
| Chianti Single Estate 1998 | 13 | –£5.00 |
| Italian Table Red Wine NV (1 litre) | 12 | –£3.50 |
| Reggiano Rosso Single Estate 1999 | 10 | –£5.00 |
| Rosso di Puglia 1998 | 13 | –£3.50 |
| Rosso Toscano 1997 | 16 | £5–7 |
| Sangiovese di Puglia 1999 | 15.5 | –£5.00 |
| Valpolicella Classico Single Estate 1999 | 13 | –£5.00 |
| Villa Cafagio Chianti Classico 1998 | 13.5 | £7–10 |
| Vino Montepulciano d'Abruzzo 1997 | 13.5 | £7–10 |
| Vino Nobile di Montepulciano 1995 | 13.5 | £7–10 |

## ITALIAN WHITE

| | | |
|---|---|---|
| Frascati Superiore 1999 | 12 | –£5.00 |
| Orvieto Single Estate 1999 | 13.5 | –£5.00 |
| Pinot Grigio/Garganega 1999 | 12 | –£5.00 |
| Soave Superiore 1999 | 15.5 | –£5.00 |
| Villa Masera Organic Wine 1999 | 11 | –£5.00 |

## NEW ZEALAND RED

| | | |
|---|---|---|
| Kaituna Hills Cabernet Merlot 1998 | 13 | £5–7 |
| Kaituna Hills Reserve Cabernet Merlot 1998 | 15.5 | £7–10 |

## NEW ZEALAND WHITE

| | | |
|---|---|---|
| Kaituna Blue Sauvignon Semillon 1999 | 11 | –£5.00 |
| Kaituna Hills Chardonnay 1999 | 15 | £5–7 |
| Kaituna Hills Reserve Chardonnay 1999 | 14.5 | £7–10 |
| Kaituna Hills Reserve Sauvignon Blanc 1999 | 14 | £7–10 |
| Kaituna Hills Sauvignon Blanc 1999 | 12.5 | £5–7 |

## SOUTH AFRICAN RED

| | | |
|---|---|---|
| Bin 121 Merlot Ruby Cabernet 1998 | 15.5 | –£5.00 |
| Cape Country Cinsault/ Ruby Cabernet 1999 | 13.5 | –£5.00 |

| | | |
|---|---|---|
| Rock Ridge Pinotage 1999 | 16.5 | −£5.00 |
| Rockridge Cabernet Sauvignon 1998 | 14 | −£5.00 |

## SOUTH AFRICAN WHITE

| | | |
|---|---|---|
| Cape Country Chenin Blanc 2000 | 14.5 | −£5.00 |
| Cape Country Colombard 2000 | 13.5 | −£5.00 |
| Perdeberg Sauvignon Blanc 2000 | 14 | −£5.00 |

## SPANISH RED

| | | |
|---|---|---|
| Campo Ran 1999 | 14 | −£5.00 |
| Las Falleras 1999 | 14 | −£3.50 |
| Marisa 1999 | 16 | −£5.00 |
| Rioja Roseral 1996 | 13.5 | £5–7 |
| Sotelo 1996 | 15.5 | £5–7 |

## SPANISH WHITE

| | | |
|---|---|---|
| Moscatel de Valencia 1999 | 14.5 | −£5.00 |

## USA RED

| | | |
|---|---|---|
| Clear Lake Cabernet Franc 1999 | 15 | −£5.00 |
| Freedom Ridge Shiraz 1999 | 15 | £5–7 |
| Live Oak Road Zinfandel 1999 | 15 | £7–10 |
| Zamora Zinfandel 1998 | 14 | £5–7 |

## USA WHITE

| | | |
|---|---|---|
| Clear Lake Chardonnay 1999 | 13.5 | −£5.00 |
| Clear Lake Rosé 1999 | 13 | −£5.00 |
| Dunnigan Lane Fume Blanc 1999 | 13.5 | £5–7 |
| Gardeners Grove Chardonnay 1999 | 13.5 | £5–7 |

## FORTIFIED WINES

| | | |
|---|---|---|
| Pale Dry Fino Sherry | 16 | −£5.00 |
| Vintage Character Port | 15 | £5–7 |

## SPARKLING WINES

| | | |
|---|---|---|
| Veuve Truffeau Colombard/Chardonnay Brut | 13.5 | −£5.00 |
| Bluff Hill Sparkling Wine (New Zealand) | 13 | £5–7 |
| Cava Brut NV (Spain) | 13.5 | £5–7 |
| Cava Medium Dry NV (Spain) | 12 | £5–7 |
| Champagne de St Gall Blanc de Blancs NV | 15 | £13–20 |
| Champagne de St Gall Brut NV | 13.5 | £13–20 |
| Champagne Desroches NV | 13.5 | £13–20 |
| Champagne Oudinot Grand Cru 1993 | 13 | £13–20 |
| Cuvee Orpale Grand Cru 1990 | 12 | £20+ |
| Gold Label Sparkling Chardonnay NV | 16 | £5–7 |

## MARKS & SPENCER

Oudinot Brut Champagne    13    £10–13

Vintage Cava 1994    15    £7–10

# MORRISONS

Stuart Purdie, the sturdy, stoical, sole wine buyer of this chain, is the only major British supermarket wine professional who has not visited Australia. What does this tell us about Morrisons? That they don't like unnecessary expense and to contemplate a staff member taking twenty-four hours to reach a vineyard, twenty-fours hours during which he would be doing nothing more profitable than twiddling his thumbs and swigging free Champagne on an aeroplane, sends shivers up the management's collective spine. Pennies count at Morrisons. But so does freshness. Morrisons are a family-centred business and a multi-millionaire knight called Morrison will still pitch up at a branch and prowl the fresh-fruit counters to see if the pears are up to scratch.

Eleven years ago, when I started wine scribbling, I'd never heard of Morrisons. But even if *Guardian* readers hadn't insisted I go and taste their wines, I would know about them now because from being a resolutely northern chain they have been spreading south in the past few years. Letchworth in Hertfordshire, Erith in Kent, Banbury in Oxfordshire, Ipswich – it can't be long before it sets up stall (and setting up a stall is very much what Morrisons still does, since it began that way in Bradford in 1899) outside my own front door in central London.

The money they save on not sending wine buyers abroad (though Stuart did manage to sneak off to Chile and do some good business there while the boys at the top were distracted by planning the company's centenary celebrations) ends up in the staff's pockets. 22,000 employees shared a £9.9 million windfall in a profit-share scheme which was, said fresh-fruit prowler Sir Ken Morrison, 'a much deserved reward for a terrific contribution to the group's continuing success'.

Being mean with the wine buyer also means being mean with the wine. Prices can be as low as they come on Mr Purdie's shelves. Wines at £2.99 are to be found here, and these are not discounted special offers but regular lines. In spite of this, the company makes loads of dosh. It announced pre-tax profits for the year to Jan 2000 of £189.2 million (up 11%), a spokesman remarking 'it would continue to eschew convenience stores and home shopping in order to concentrate on its core supermarket business' and that it would leave 'short-term PR stunts' to its rivals (I thank the business journal *Supermarketing* for these titbits).

Morrisons was also actively breathing down its competitors' necks in other ways. It has pressed for changes in planning legislation to allow it to open more out-of-town stores in the south of England and thus to hot up its war with Sainsbury's and Tesco. The legislation, Morrisons says, is anti-competitive.

What does all this add up to? A very buoyant business. Overall sales are running 17.3% ahead of last year and Morrisons' market share is up from 3.9% to 4.8%. Over the next two years the company expects to create 3,500 new jobs.

One of which will be a wine buyer to assist Stuart. Until she departed in the summer of 2000, he employed the extremely able Fiona Smith. Ms Smith, having distinguished herself as president of the boozers' club at Edinburgh University, got fed up, I suspect, with number-crunching. She wanted to do what Mr Ken does: go about feeling fruit. This fruit would, of course, be on the vine, rather than on the shelf, and be growing in exotic climes, not in Erith or Harrogate. You can see Ms Smith's point. If Morrisons has a weakness it is surely here. It is no coincidence that the company's smartest own-label range of wines is the Australian-inspired Falcon Ridge setup, which is sourced in France. Fantastic wines at fantastic prices, oh yes (see the ratings). But then France is only across the Channel. It's cheap to visit, whereas New World countries are not.

Stuart does a great job, but he won't be able to assemble a mouth-wateringly inexpensive, own-label Australian range, for example, until he can feel the vineyard soil under his feet. Romantic tosh? Well, other supermarkets don't think so. They pour considerable management resources into wine and many buyers collect record Air Miles. At Morrisons there is just Stuart – at the time of going to press – his bum on his office chair or in the driving seat of his company car ('100,000 miles in three years' he told me), but not in a business-class seat on Qantas.

Let's hope he gets an early Christmas present of a return air ticket to Adelaide from our Ken along with a new assistant wine buyer. Any reader interested in the job should write to Stuart at Morrison HQ at the address below. I know it would be easier to give you his e-mail address, but he doesn't have one.

He doesn't have an e-mail address? In the year 2000? Nope. As far as I know he doesn't even have a computer.

Eeh, lad, computers cost money. Stick to stamps.

Wm Morrison Supermarkets
Hilmore House
Thornton Road
Bradford
West Yorkshire
BD8 9AX

Tel 01924 870000
Fax 01924 821300
www.morereasons.co.uk (under construction at the time of going to press)

## ARGENTINIAN RED

| | | |
|---|---|---|
| Balbi Barbaro 1997 | 16 | £7–10 |
| Balbi Malbec 1999 | 13.5 | –£5.00 |
| Balbi Shiraz 1999 | 13.5 | –£5.00 |
| Santa Julia Sangiovese Bonarda 1999 | 15.5 | –£5.00 |

## AGENTINIAN WHITE

| | | |
|---|---|---|
| Etchart Rio de Plata Torrontes/Chardonnay 1998 | 13 | –£5.00 |
| Rio de Plate Chardonnay 1997 | 13.5 | –£5.00 |

## AUSTRALIAN RED

| | | |
|---|---|---|
| Barramundi Shiraz/Merlot NV | 15.5 | –£5.00 |
| Cranswick Kidman Way Cabernet Sauvignon 1998 | 14 | –£5.00 |
| Cranswick Nine Pines Cabernet Sauvignon 1998 | 14 | –£5.00 |
| Deakin Estate Merlot 1998 | 15 | £5–7 |
| Hardys Cabernet Shiraz Merlot 1998 | 15 | £5–7 |
| Jindalee Shiraz 1998 | 13 | –£5.00 |
| Lindemans Bin 45 Cabernet Sauvignon 1999 | 15 | £5–7 |
| 'M' Australian Shiraz Cabernet NV | 10 | –£5.00 |
| Nottage Hill Cabernet Sauvignon Shiraz 1998 | 14 | £5–7 |
| Rosemount Estate Shiraz 1998 | 15.5 | £7–10 |
| Thomas Mitchell Shiraz 1998 | 13 | £5–7 |

## AUSTRALIAN WHITE

| | | |
|---|---|---|
| Barramundi Semillon/Chardonnay NV | 16 | –£5.00 |
| Brown Brothers Chenin Blanc 1998 | 14 | –£5.00 |
| Cranswick Kidman Way Chardonnay 1998 | 15.5 | –£5.00 |

| | |
|---|---|
| Deakin Estate Chardonnay 1999 | 15.5 −£5.00 |
| Jindalee Chardonnay 1998 | 16 −£5.00 |
| Lindemans Bin 65 Chardonnay 1999 | 16.5 −£5.00 |
| Nottage Hill Chardonnay 1999 | 15.5 −£5.00 |
| Penfolds Koonunga Hill Chardonnay 1998 | 16.5 £5−7 |
| Rosemount Estate Chardonnay 1998 | 16.5 £5−7 |
| Rosemount Estate GTR 1999 | 15 £5−7 |

## BULGARIAN RED

| | |
|---|---|
| Boyar Bulgarian Gamza 1998 | 14 −£3.50 |
| Boyar Iambol Cabernet Sauvignon 1999 | 14.5 −£3.50 |
| Boyar Premium Oak Merlot 1997 | 13.5 −£5.00 |
| Danube Red 1999 | 13.5 −£3.50 |

## BULGARIAN WHITE

| | |
|---|---|
| Boyar Pomorie Chardonnay 1998 | 10 −£3.50 |

## CHILEAN RED

| | |
|---|---|
| 35 Sur Cabernet Sauvignon 1998 | 15 −£5.00 |
| Antares Merlot 1999 | 13.5 −£5.00 |
| Castillo de Molina Reserve Cabernet Sauvignon 1998 | 16 £5−7 |

| | |
|---|---|
| Curioso Gracia de Chile Merlot 1998 | 16 −£5.00 |
| 'M' Chilean Cabernet Sauvignon 1999 | 15 −£5.00 |
| Undurraga Merlot 1999 | 13 −£5.00 |
| Villa Montes Cabernet Sauvignon 1999 | 15.5 −£5.00 |
| Vina Gracia Cabernet Sauvignon 1998 | 15 −£5.00 |
| Vina Gracia Merlot 1998 | 16 −£5.00 |

## CHILEAN WHITE

| | |
|---|---|
| 35 Sur Chardonnay 1999 | 14.5 −£5.00 |
| 35 Sur Sauvignon Blanc 1999 | 15 −£5.00 |
| Antares Santa Carolina Chardonnay 1999 | 16 −£5.00 |
| Antu Mapu Reserva Rosé 1999 | 13 −£5.00 |
| Antu Mapu Sauvignon Blanc 1999 | 13 −£3.50 |
| Castillo de Molina Reserve Chardonnay 1998 | 16 £5−7 |
| Montes Alpha Chardonnay 1998 | 17.5 £7−10 |
| Stowells Chilean Sauvignon Blanc NV (3 litre box) | 13 −£3.50 |
| Villa Montes Sauvignon Blanc 1999 | 14 −£5.00 |

## FRENCH RED

| | |
|---|---|
| Beaujolais NV | 13 −£5.00 |
| Bouches du Rhone Merlot NV | 15 −£3.50 |

336

Château Cadillac
Legourgues Bordeaux
1997 — 15 — £5–7

Château de Candale Haut
Medoc 1996 — 15 — £7–10

Château La Fage Cotes
de Bergerac 1997 — 13.5 — –£5.00

Château Saint Galier
Graves 1997 — 14.5 — –£5.00

Chinon Domaine de
Briancon 1997 — 16 — –£5.00

Claret Bordeaux NV,
Morrisons — 13.5 — –£3.50

Falcon Ridge Cabernet
Sauvignon, VdP d'Oc
1999 — 16 — –£3.50

Falcon Ridge Merlot VdP
d'Oc 1999 — 15 — –£3.50

Falcon Ridge Syrah VdP
d'Oc 1999 — 15.5 — –£3.50

Fitou NV — 13 — –£5.00

Heritage des Caves des
Papes Côtes du Rhône
1998 — 15.5 — –£5.00

La Chasse du Pape
Reserve Côtes du Rhône
1998 — 16 — –£5.00

Les Planels Minervois
1997 — 14 — –£5.00

'M' Côtes du Rhône NV — 13 — –£3.50

'M' Cotes du Roussillon
Red NV — 13 — –£3.50

Minervois Cellier la
Chouf NV — 13 — –£3.50

Oak Matured Bordeaux
1997 — 13 — –£5.00

Rhone Valley Red 1998 — 14 — –£3.50

Saint Emilion NV,
Morrisons — 14 — £5–7

Sichel Medoc NV — 13 — £5–7

Vacqueyras Domaine de
Ameleraies 1998 — 14.5 — £5–7

Vin de Pays de
l'Hauterive NV — 12 — –£3.50

Winter Hill Red VdP
d'Oc 1999 — 14 — –£3.50

## FRENCH WHITE

Bordeaux Blanc de
Ginestet 1998 — 15.5 — –£5.00

Château La Fage
Bergerac Sec 1998 — 13 — –£5.00

Château Loupiac
Gaudiet, Loupiac 1996
(50cl) — 16 — –£5.00

Falcon Ridge
Chardonnay, VdP d'Oc
1999 — 15 — –£3.50

Falcon Ridge Rosé VdP
d'Oc 1997 — 14 — –£3.50

Falcon Ridge Sauvignon
Blanc, VdP d'Oc 1999 — 14 — –£3.50

Gewürztraminer Preiss
Zimmer 1998 — 15.5 — £5–7

Haut Poitou Sauvignon
Blanc NV — 14 — –£3.50

James Herrick
Chardonnay 1999 — 16 — –£5.00

Macon Villages Teissedre
1998 — 13 — –£5.00

Pinot Blanc Preiss
Zimmer 1998 — 15.5 — –£5.00

Rhone Valley White 1998 `14` −£3.50

Saint Veran 1998 `13` £5–7

Sancerre la Renardiere 1999 `12` £7–10

Sichel Premieres Côtes de Bordeaux Blanc NV `12.5` −£5.00

Winter Hill White 1998 `14` −£3.50

## GERMAN WHITE

Kallstadter Beerenauslese 1998 (half-bottle) `15` −£5.00

Kendermans Dry Riesling 1999 `13` −£5.00

Urziger Wurzgarten Spatlese 1998 `12` £5–7

Wehlener Sonnenuhr Riesling Spatlese 1997 `11` £5–7

## GREEK RED

Mavrodaphne of Patras `14` −£5.00

## HUNGARIAN WHITE

Ideal with Friends Chardonnay NV `12.5` −£3.50

'M' Ideal with Friends Sauvignon Blanc NV `13` −£3.50

River Duna Pink Pinot Noir 1998 `12.5` −£5.00

## ITALIAN RED

Casa di Monzi Merlot 1999 `13` −£5.00

Chianti Uggiano 1997 `12` −£5.00

Montepulciano Uggiano 1997 `12` −£5.00

Puglia Primitivo 1999 `13` −£5.00

Valpolicella NV `12` −£3.50

Vino Rosso di Puglia NV `10` −£3.50

## ITALIAN WHITE

Casa de Monzi Chardonnay delle Venezie 1999 `13` −£5.00

Casa de Monzi Rosato 1999 `13` −£5.00

Chardonnay di Puglia NV `13` −£3.50

Di Notte Pinot Grigio 1999 `14` −£5.00

Inycon Chardonnay 1999 (Sicily) `15.5` −£5.00

Ponte Vecchio Oaked Soave 1997 `13.5` −£5.00

Soave NV `13` −£3.50

Verdicchio di Jesi Classico 1999 `15.5` −£3.50

## MEXICAN RED

L A Cetto Zinfandel 1998 `10` −£5.00

## MOROCCAN RED

Le Chameau Grenache Cinsault NV `11` −£3.50

## NEW ZEALAND WHITE

Cooks Sauvignon Blanc, Marlborough 1999 `13` −£5.00

| | | |
|---|---|---|
| Montana Chardonnay, Marlborough 1999 | 15.5 | £5–7 |
| Montana Sauvignon Blanc 1999 | 15.5 | £5–7 |

## PORTUGUESE RED

| | | |
|---|---|---|
| Dom Ferraz Dao 1998 | 16.5 | –£5.00 |
| Tamara Red Vinho Regional Ribatejo 1999 | 13 | –£3.50 |

## PORTUGUESE WHITE

| | | |
|---|---|---|
| Sinfonia White Alentejo 1998 | 13 | –£5.00 |
| Tamara White Ribatejo 1998 | 12 | –£3.50 |

## ROMANIAN RED

| | | |
|---|---|---|
| Romanian Classic Pinot Noir 1998 | 11 | –£3.50 |
| Special Reserve Pinot Noir 1998 | 10 | –£5.00 |
| Special Reserve Sangiovese 1998 | 10 | –£5.00 |

## ROMANIAN WHITE

| | | |
|---|---|---|
| Romanian Special Reserve Barrel Fermented Chardonnay 1996 | 16 | –£5.00 |

## SOUTH AFRICAN RED

| | | |
|---|---|---|
| Cathedral Cellars Merlot 1996 | 13 | £7–10 |

| | | |
|---|---|---|
| Fairview Malbec 1999 | 16.5 | £5–7 |
| Namaqua Classic Red NV (3 litre box) | 11.5 | £5–7 |
| South African Red NV | 13 | –£3.50 |
| Spice Route Andrew's Hope 1998 | 16.5 | £5–7 |
| Van Loveren Merlot 1999 | 13 | –£5.00 |

## SOUTH AFRICAN WHITE

| | | |
|---|---|---|
| Danie de Wet Chardonnay Surlie 1999 | 15 | –£5.00 |
| Faircape Chenin Blanc 2000 | 15.5 | –£3.50 |
| Fairview Chardonnay 1998 | 16.5 | £5–7 |
| Namaqua Classic Dry White NV (3 litre box) | 15 | £5–7 |
| Spice Route Abbotsdale Colombard/Chenin Blanc 1998 | 16 | –£5.00 |
| Van Loveren Blanc de Noirs 2000 | 14 | –£5.00 |
| Van Loveren Pinot Gris 1999 | 14 | –£5.00 |
| Van Loveren Semillon 1999 | 14 | –£5.00 |

## SPANISH RED

| | | |
|---|---|---|
| Viña Albali Tempranillo 1999 | 15.5 | –£3.50 |
| Conforrales Tinto Cencibel 1998 | 15 | –£3.50 |
| De Muller Pinot Noir 1996 | 13 | £7–10 |

| | | |
|---|---|---|
| Gran Feudo Navarra Crianza 1997 | 13 | −£5.00 |
| 'M' Red Rioja NV | 13 | −£5.00 |
| Rio Rojo Tinto NV | 14 | −£3.50 |
| Stowells Tempranillo NV (3 litre box) | 12.5 | −£3.50 |
| Torres Sangre de Toro 1998 | 14 | £5–7 |
| Vega del Rio Reserve Rioja 1994 | 13 | £7–10 |
| Vina Albali Gran Reserva 1991 | 16 | £5–7 |

## SPANISH WHITE

| | | |
|---|---|---|
| De Muller Chardonnay 1999 | 13 | −£5.00 |
| Sanz Rueda Superior 1998 | 14 | −£5.00 |
| Vina Albali Rosado Tempranillo 1999 | 13 | −£3.50 |

## USA RED

| | | |
|---|---|---|
| Blossom Hill California Red NV | 10 | −£5.00 |
| Californian Red NV | 10 | −£3.50 |
| Fetzer Bonterra Cabernet Sauvignon 1997 | 14 | £7–10 |
| Glen Ellen Pinot Noir 1997 | 9 | £5–7 |
| Glen Ellen Proprietor's Reserve Zinfandel 1997 | 12 | −£5.00 |
| Glen Ellen Zinfandel 1997 | 11 | £5–7 |
| Ironstone Vineyards Cabernet Franc 1997 | 15 | £5–7 |

| | | |
|---|---|---|
| Ironstone Vineyards Shiraz 1998 | 14.5 | −£5.00 |
| Turning Leaf Cabernet Sauvignon 1997 | 12 | £5–7 |
| Turning Leaf Zinfandel 1996 | 12.5 | £5–7 |

## USA WHITE

| | | |
|---|---|---|
| Californian White NV | 12 | −£3.50 |
| Ironstone Chardonnay 1997 | 15.5 | £5–7 |
| Ironstone Chardonnay 1998 | 10 | £5–7 |
| Ironstone Obsession 1998 | 10 | −£5.00 |
| Wente Johannesburg Riesling 1997 | 16.5 | −£5.00 |

## SPARKLING WINES

| | | |
|---|---|---|
| Asti Spumante Gianni (Italian) | 14 | −£5.00 |
| Barramundi Sparkling NV (Australia) | 15 | −£5.00 |
| Brut de Channay NV (France) | 11 | £5–7 |
| Champagne Philippe Prie NV | 13 | £10–13 |
| Chapel Hill Chardonnay-Pinot Noir NV (Hungary) | 12 | −£5.00 |
| 'M' Vintage Cava 1996 | 15.5 | £5–7 |
| Mumm Cuvee Napa Brut NV (California) | 14 | £7–10 |
| Paul Herard Champagne Brut NV | 12 | £10–13 |
| Paul Herard Demi Sec Champagne (half-bottle) | 13.5 | £5–7 |

Reminger Sparkling Brut `10` `−£5.00`
NV (France)

Santa Carolina `13` `£5–7`
Chardonnay Brut 1996
(Chile)

Seaview Brut NV `14` `£5–7`
(Australia)

Seaview Brut Rosé `13.5` `£5–7`
(Australia)

Sparkling Zero (alcohol `0` `−£2.50`
free)

**SEE STOP PRESS SECTION AT END OF BOOK FOR LAST-MINUTE
ADDITIONS OR UPDATES TO THIS RETAILER'S RANGE.**

# ODDBINS

On my first visit to an Oddbins shop, the year the England football team was managed by an extremely successful bald bloke in a macintosh, I paid 24 shillings for three half-bottles of Château Smith-Haut-Lafitte 1933. I wasted my money and didn't get any of it back (one bottle oxidised, one bottle corked, one bottle boring). Oddbins has come on a lot since then, but one thing which has never changed is how seriously it takes its wine.

Let me illustrate what I mean with this single incident involving a single *Guardian* reader. I received, at the newspaper, this e-mail from Mr Loxton of Milton Keynes.

> *Dear Malcolm Gluck: I have often in the past taken your advice given in your* Superplonk *column in the* Guardian. *I have never previously had cause to regret doing so, but now feel so strongly about one particular wine that I have been moved to write a letter of complaint (a very rare occurrence). Several weeks ago (exact date not known) you recommended a red wine available from Oddbins, Domaine Remaury Cabernet Sauvignon Vin de Pays d'Oc, and gave it 17 points. On the strength of that advice I have today purchased (after having asked my local Milton Keynes branch of Oddbins to obtain it) 12 bottles. This evening I opened the first bottle, and was very disappointed in it. It has no character, has very little fruit flavour, and is distinctly 'chemical' in taste. I am not a wine connoisseur, but I can recognise a bad wine when I taste it. It is so bad that I intend returning the 11.5 bottles to Oddbins as soon as I am able. I do not hold you responsible for my poor purchase, but I do want you to know that what is being sold in Oddbins as Domaine Remaury Cabernet Sauvignon Vin de Pays d'Oc is clearly not what was provided to you for tasting prior to your recommendation. Clearly, if others have received wine similar to mine, your reputation as a wine critic could be severely damaged. If you can reply to this e-mail quickly, I would happily make some of the wine available to you for tasting before I return it to Oddbins. I realise you must be a very busy man, but if you can find time to reply to this missive I would appreciate your comments.*

I replied immediately:

*Dear Mr Loxton: Appalled to get your e-mail. Have you opened other bottles? The wine is patently faulty. Please try more bottles. You can still send the lot back to Oddbins and get a refund. I will send your e-mail to Oddbins HQ who may get in touch. Let me know what happens. I take complaints very seriously. Since I give advice I expect it to be seriously swallowed. My readers cannot open the same bottle of wine as me, it is true, but they should approximate the same experience. Please keep me informed of developments – especially if all the other bottles are equally vile! Thanks for getting in touch. Malcolm Gluck.*

I also contacted Karen Wise and Natashia Bartlett at Oddbins. They promised to look into it and alerted Steve Daniel, Oddbins wine-buying supremo. They also sent me, within the hour, two bottles of Remaury so I could check them for myself and Steve insisted that he would try to get Mr Loxton's bottles back and send them to a laboratory for testing to see what could be wrong with them. I tasted the two bottles I received, rather pleased to have them with Sunday lunch, as a matter of fact, and I found them as gorgeous as previously. I immediately thought Mr Loxton should hear of this and so I contacted him again:

*Dear Mr Loxton: While we await the Oddbins boffin's report to see what caused the first of your Cabernets to be so repulsively sick and undrinkable I thought you might like to hear of my reaction to two Remaury '98 bottles I tasted, and then drank, over the weekend, which Oddbins sent to me. They were marvellous; more or less as before when I awarded the wine 17 points, though each offered an individual experience. Both bottles had good corks with no taint. Colour of both wines was excellent, full red, no browning or oxidation. Bottle one offered rich fruit and good tannins, slightly earthy. At £3.99, still 17 points. Bottle two was plumper, less dry, and the tannins more subsumed under the sweetness of the fruit. It had a little less character than the first bottle. I conjectured whether to knock half a point off but, nope, still 17 points. The lesson here was one I have been teaching for years: it isn't so much that corks spoil so many wines (as one did yours) but that the corks cause variation even on so young a wine as a 1998. I offered my wife, prior to roast duck for Sunday lunch, a glass of each and she definitely preferred bottle number one, saying it was more like her preferred earthy Rhône style. We drank most of both bottles with the duck and the cheese which followed. In sum, then, I think the wine is remarkable value for the quality of its fruit, and my wife, spontaneously, upon being apprised of this price said 'I wouldn't have believed it'. What does all this prove? Our tastes are our own and if you don't like Remaury that's fine by me, though I must say I wish you'd opened more bottles to find one in perfect condition. Best wishes, yours sincerely Malcolm Gluck.*

What were the results of the lab test? Three of the bottles returned by Mr Loxton (who got his money back), that is to say already opened samples, were sent to Geoff Taylor, who runs the analytic chemists Corkwise, and he found, as one would expect, oxidation in varying degrees with all three. But that was all. There was nothing else wrong with the wines.

What does all this prove? It proves how seriously Oddbins takes its wine, it proves how one bad experience with an 'off' bottle can spoil a wine's reputation, and it strengthens my belief that if all wines were screwcapped my readers would run no risk of finding themselves with faulty or oxidised wine on their hands.

On other fronts, Oddbins has had an interesting year. In 1999 it cut staff overtime to four hours per week, according to *Off Licence News*. It was also reported that a more individual feel would be achieved in individual branches via a radical programme of refits. Although the stores will retain Oddbins' branding, the fascias, internal fixtures and the ranges will be customised according to the local environment and clientele. I've visited a dozen Oddbins in the past year and they look just the same to me, but that is often the secret of a 'radical programme of refits' – you can't tell that anything's changed.

Genuinely radical, though, was Oddbins victory in Parliament. It beat eleven other wine companies to win the contract to supply the House of Commons with an own-label Champagne. (So the hangovers you see evident on some of the jowls of elected Members during the TV broadcasts can be firmly laid at Oddbins' door.)

Oddbins also announced that the Irish side of its internet activities would be up and running by spring. The full UK service, at that time geared only to Champagne sales, became fully operational at the end of the summer. Expect to see several current e-commerce wine sites suffering as a result of this and, along with this, further chatter about a buyer for the whole Oddbins wine chain.

Indeed, this old chestnut came out of the fire in no uncertain terms. Who *would* buy the chain, wondered the gossips in the wine trade? This speculation was refuelled by the probability that Seagram, which owns Oddbins, would withdraw totally from the drinks business (made speculatively probable by the Canadian group's dive into an embrace with the Vivendi company). The new price on Oddbins' head, £75 million a few years back, was said to be £50 million.

One idea no one broaches (except, perhaps, behind doors firmly closed ) is the prospect of a management buyout. If Oddbins can become the most dynamic of e-commerce retailers over the next eighteen months, this is not a wholly romantic fiction.

I have no doubt that the brightest individuals at Oddbins, like Mr Steve Daniel, the dynamic and extraordinarily able director in charge of buying and marketing, are trying not to be seduced by these exotic, mind-numbing possibilities. Oddbins has never been one to be swayed by pie-in-the-sky recipes, but it does have loads of marvellous wines to accompany such fanciful fare.

Oddbins
31–32 Weir Road
Wimbledon
London
SW19 8UG

Tel 020 8944 4400
Fax 020 8944 4411
www.oddbins.com

## ARGENTINIAN RED

| Wine | Score | Price |
|------|------|------|
| Alamos Ridge Bonarda, Mendoza 1998 | 16 | £5–7 |
| Alamos Ridge Merlot, Mendoza 1997 | 16 | £5–7 |
| Bodegas Rosca Malbec, Mendoza 1999 | 15 | –£5.00 |
| Bodegas Rosca Shiraz, Mendoza 1999 | 16.5 | £5–7 |
| Bodegas Rosca Shiraz Reserve, Mendoza 1999 | 16 | £5–7 |
| Famiglia Bianchi Cabernet Sauvignon, San Rafael 1996 | 17 | £13–20 |
| Las Lilas Malbec Sangiovese, Mendoza 1997 | 15.5 | –£5.00 |
| Norton Reserve Syrah Cabernet, Mendoza 1997 | 15.5 | £5–7 |
| Valentin Bianchi Cabernet Sauvignon, San Rafael 1996 | 16.5 | £7–10 |
| Valentin Bianchi Malbec Reserve, San Rafael 1996 | 15 | £7–10 |
| Valentin Bianchi Malbec, San Rafael 1997 | 16 | –£5.00 |
| Valentin Bianchi Merlot Reserve, San Rafael 1997 | 16.5 | £7–10 |

## ARGENTINIAN WHITE

| | | |
|---|---|---|
| Alamos Ridge Chardonnay 1997 | 16 | £5–7 |
| Bodegas Rosca Dry White, Mendoza 1999 | 15 | –£3.50 |
| Catena Chardonnay 1997 | 14 | £7–10 |

## AUSTRALIAN RED

| | | |
|---|---|---|
| Annie's Lane Shiraz, Clare Valley 1997 | 13 | £7–10 |
| Baileys Shiraz 1997 | 14 | £5–7 |
| Brokenwood Shiraz 1998 | 15 | £7–10 |
| Cape Jaffa Mount Benson Shiraz 1998 | 13 | £7–10 |
| Church Block Cabernet Shiraz Merlot, Wirra Wirra Vineyards 1998 | 17 | £7–10 |
| d'Arenberg The Footbolt Old Vine Shiraz, McLaren Vale 1998 | 15.5 | £5–7 |
| d'Arry's Original Shiraz Grenache, McLaren Vale 1997 | 16 | £5–7 |
| Deakin Estate Cabernet Sauvignon, Victoria 1999 | 15.5 | £5–7 |
| Deakin Estate Shiraz Cabernet Sauvignon, Victoria 1999 | 15 | –£5.00 |
| Deakin Estate Shiraz, Victoria 1999 | 15 | £5–7 |
| E & C Cabernet Sauvignon, McLaren Vale 1998 | 16 | £5–7 |
| E & C Shiraz, McLaren Vale 1998 | 15.5 | £5–7 |
| Elderton Cabernet Sauvignon, Barossa 1996 | 16 | £10–13 |
| Elderton Merlot, Barossa 1996 | 14 | £13–20 |
| Elderton Shiraz, Barossa 1996 | 17 | £10–13 |
| Elderton Tantalus Shiraz/Cabernet Sauvignon 1998 | 16 | £5–7 |
| Hillstowe 'Buxton' Cabernet Merlot, McLaren Vale 1998 | 15 | £7–10 |
| Hillstowe Udy's Mill Pinot Noir, Lenswood 1997 | 14 | £7–10 |
| Mamre Brook Cabernet Shiraz 1996 | 16 | £5–7 |
| Merrill's Mount Hurtle Bush Vine Grenache, McLaren Vale 1996 | 13.5 | £5–7 |
| Normans White Label Cabernet Sauvignon, South Eastern Australia 1998 | 13 | £5–7 |
| Normans White Label Merlot, South Australia 1998 | 13 | £5–7 |
| Oxford Landing Cabernet Sauvignon Shiraz 1999 | 15.5 | £5–7 |
| Penny's Hill Shiraz, McLaren Vale 1998 | 16 | £7–10 |
| Peter Lehmann The Barossa Shiraz 1998 | 17 | £5–7 |
| Preece Shiraz 1997 | 15.5 | £5–7 |
| Rufus Stone Heathcote Shiraz, Victoria 1998 | 14.5 | £10–13 |

Rufus Stone Shiraz, `16.5` `£7–10`
McLaren Vale 1998

Tatachilla Shiraz, South `15.5` `£5–7`
Australia 1998

Wirra Wirra Original `16.5` `£7–10`
Blend Grenache Shiraz,
McLaren Vale 1997

Wirra Wirra Vineyards `13` `£10–13`
The Angelus Cabernet
Sauvignon 1996

Wirra Wirra W2 `15` `£5–7`
Grenache Shiraz
Cabernet 1999

Yarra Valley Hills `15` `£10–13`
Cabernet Sauvignon 1996

Yarra Valley Hills `14` `£7–10`
Warranwood Pinot Noir
1998

## AUSTRALIAN WHITE

Annie's Lane Riesling, `15` `£5–7`
Clare Valley 1999

Antipodean Unwooded `15` `£5–7`
Chardonnay 1999

Bleasdale 'Sandhill `13` `£5–7`
Vineyard' Verdelho,
Langhorne Creek 1999

Brokenwood Cricket `16` `£7–10`
Pitch Sauvignon/
Semillon 1999

Campbells Liqueur `16.5` `£5–7`
Muscat, Rutherglen NV
(half-bottle)

Cranswick Estate Zirilli `16.5` `£7–10`
Vineyard Botrytis
Semillon, Riverina 1996

d'Arenberg The Olive `16` `£5–7`
Grove Chardonnay,
McLaren Vale 1998

d'Arenberg White Ochre, `13` `–£5.00`
McLaren Vale 1999

Deakin Estate `15.5` `–£5.00`
Chardonnay 1999

E & C Chardonnay, `13.5` `£5–7`
McLaren Vale 1999

Hillstowe Sauvignon `13.5` `£5–7`
Blanc, Adelaide Hill 1999

Killawarra Chardonnay `15.5` `–£5.00`
1999

Knappstein Riesling, `16` `£5–7`
Clare Valley 1998

Lindemans Bin 65 `16.5` `–£5.00`
Chardonnay 1999

Nepenthe Vineyards `15.5` `£7–10`
Lenswood Unwooded
Chardonnay 1999

Oxford Landing `15` `–£5.00`
Sauvignon Blanc 1999

Penny's Hill Chardonnay, `16` `£7–10`
McLaren Vale 1999

Peter Lehmann Semillon, `16` `£5–7`
Barossa 1999

Rothbury Estate Hunter `16` `£5–7`
Valley Verdelho 1998

Rufus Stone Sauvignon `13.5` `£5–7`
Blanc 1999

Seaview Chardonnay, `14` `–£5.00`
McLaren Vale 1998

Tatachilla Sauvignon `15.5` `£5–7`
Semillon, McLaren Vale
& Adelaide Hills 1998

ODDBINS

| | | |
|---|---|---|
| Wirra Wirra 'Sexton's Acre' Unwooded Chardonnay, McLaren Vale 1999 | 15 | £5–7 |
| Wirra Wirra W2 Riesling 1998 | 14 | –£5.00 |
| Wolf Blass South Australia Barrel Fermented Chardonnay 1999 | 16 | £7–10 |
| Wolf Blass South Australia Chardonnay 1999 | 16 | £7–10 |
| Yarra Valley Hills Kiah Yallambee Chardonnay 1998 | 12.5 | £7–10 |

## CHILEAN RED

| | | |
|---|---|---|
| Carmen Reserve Grande Vidure Cabernet, Maipo 1997 | 16 | £5–7 |
| Carmen Reserve Merlot, Rapel 1998 | 16.5 | £7–10 |
| Carmen Reserve Pinot Noir 1998 | 16 | £7–10 |
| Casa Lapostolle Cabernet Sauvignon 1997 | 17 | £5–7 |
| Casa Lapostolle Cuvee Alexandre Cabernet Sauvignon 1997 | 16.5 | £7–10 |
| Casa Lapostolle Cuvée Alexandre Merlot, Rapel 1998 | 17.5 | £13–20 |
| Casa Lapostolle Merlot 1998 | 16.5 | £5–7 |
| Cono Sur Reserve Cabernet Sauvignon 1999 | 16 | £5–7 |

| | | |
|---|---|---|
| Errazuriz Merlot, Curico Valley 1999 | 16.5 | £5–7 |
| Isla Negra Cabernet Sauvignon, Rapel 1998 | 15.5 | –£5.00 |
| La Palmeria Merlot Cabernet Gran Reserva 1998 | 16.5 | £7–10 |
| La Palmeria Reserve Cabernet Sauvignon/ Merlot 1998 | 16.5 | £5–7 |
| Santa Rita Medalla Real Cabernet Sauvignon 1998 | 16 | £7–10 |
| Santa Rita Reserva Cabernet 1998 | 16.5 | £5–7 |
| Santa Rita Reserva Merlot Unfiltered, 1999 | 16.5 | £5–7 |
| Veramonte Cabernet Sauvignon, Alto de Casablanca 1997 | 16 | £5–7 |
| Veramonte Merlot 1998 | 14 | £5–7 |
| Vina Porta Cabernet Sauvignon, Maipo 1999 | 16.5 | –£5.00 |
| Vina Porta Reserva Unfiltered Cabernet Sauvignon 1995 | 17 | £7–10 |

## CHILEAN WHITE

| | | |
|---|---|---|
| Carmen Chardonnay, Central Valley 1998 | 16.5 | –£5.00 |
| Casa Lapostolle Chardonnay 1998 | 17 | £5–7 |
| Casa Lapostolle Cuvée Alexandre Chardonnay 1997 | 18.5 | £7–10 |
| Casa Lapostolle Sauvignon Blanc 1999 | 17 | £5–7 |

| | | |
|---|---|---|
| Casablanca Neblus Botrytis Chardonnay 1997 (half-bottle) | 16 | −£5.00 |
| Casablanca Santa Isabel Chardonnay 1998 | 16.5 | £5–7 |
| Casablanca Santa Isabel Gewürztraminer 1999 | 14 | £5–7 |
| Cono Sur Gewürztraminer 1999 | 16 | −£5.00 |
| Errazuriz La Escultura Estate Chardonnay, Casablanca 1998 | 17.5 | £5–7 |
| Errazuriz Wild Ferment Chardonnay, Casablanca 1998 | 17 | £7–10 |
| Isla Negra Chardonnay 1998 | 16 | £5–7 |
| La Palmeria Chardonnay Gran Reserva 1998 | 15.5 | £7–10 |
| Veramonte Chardonnay, Alto de Casablanca 1998 | 14 | £5–7 |
| Villard Chardonnay, Casablanca Valley 1998 | 16 | £7–10 |
| Villard Reserve Chardonnay, Casablanca Valley 1998 | 15.5 | £7–10 |
| Vina Porta Chardonnay, Cachapoal 1998 | 14 | −£5.00 |

## FRENCH RED

| | | |
|---|---|---|
| Abbotts Ammonite Côte du Roussillon 1999 | 15 | −£5.00 |
| Baron Saint-Pierre, Coteaux du Languedoc 1998 | 14.5 | −£3.50 |

| | | |
|---|---|---|
| Château de Combebelle Saint-Chinian 1998 (bio-dynamic) | 15.5 | £5–7 |
| Château de Valcombe, Costieres de Nimes 1998 | 17 | £5–7 |
| Château de Valcombe Prestige, Costieres de Nimes 1998 | 16 | £5–7 |
| Château Depaule, Cabardes 1998 | 16.5 | −£5.00 |
| Château Grand Escalion, Costieres de Nimes 1998 | 17 | £5–7 |
| Château Lamarche Canon 'Candelaire', Canon Fronsac 1998 | 15 | £7–10 |
| Château Maris Minervois 1998 (bio-dynamic) | 16 | £5–7 |
| Château Ollieux Romanis, Corbieres 1998 | 17 | £5–7 |
| Château St Jean de Conques, Saint Chinian 1998 | 13 | −£5.00 |
| Château Vaugelas Cuvée Prestige Corbieres 1998 | 15.5 | −£5.00 |
| Comte Cathare Fitou 1998 | 16 | £5–7 |
| Comte Cathare Le Clot La Clap Coteaux du Languedoc 1999 | 16.5 | £5–7 |
| Côte Rotie Guigal 1996 | 17 | £20+ |
| Côtes du Rhône, Clos Petite Bellane 1999 | 16 | £5–7 |
| Côtes du Rhône, Domaine d'Andezon 1999 | 15 | £5–7 |
| Côtes du Rhône Guigal 1998 | 16 | £7–10 |

Côtes du Rhône Les Arbousiers, Remejeanne 1997 — 14 — £5–7

Crozes Hermitage Domaine du Pavillion-Mercurol 1998 — 15 — £7–10

Crozes Hermitage Les Pierrelles, Belle 1996 — 13 — £7–10

Crozes Hermitage Meysonniers, Chapoutier 1998 — 15.5 — £7–10

Domaine Borie de Maurel Belle de Nuit, Minervois 1999 — 17.5 — £7–10

Domaine Borie de Maurel Esprit d'Automne, Minervois 1999 — 17 — £5–7

Domaine Borie de Maurel Reve de Carignan, Minervois 1999 — 14 — £5–7

Domaine de la Vistoule Cabernet Sauvignon, VdP d'Oc 1998 — 16 — £5–7

Domaine de la Vistoule Merlot, VdP d'Oc 1998 — 15.5 — £5–7

Domaine de Montine Coteaux du Tricastin 1998 — 16 — £5–7

Domaine de Saint Antoine Syrah, Costieres de Nimes 1999 — 15 — £5–7

Domaine l'Aigueliere Grenat, VdP du Mont Baudile 1998 — 16.5 — £7–10

Domaine Lafage Cuvée Les Cotes du Roussillon 1998 — 15 — £5–7

Domaine Remaury Cabernet Sauvignon VdP d'Oc 1998 — 17 — −£5.00

Domaine Saint Jullien Coteaux du Languedoc 1998 — 15.5 — −£5.00

Dourthe No 1 Bordeaux 1998 — 13 — £5–7

Enclave des Papes Cuvée Speciale, Côtes du Rhône 1999 — 16 — −£5.00

Grangeneuve Vieilles Vignes Coteaux du Tricastin 1998 — 17 — £5–7

James Herrick Millia Passum Syrah, VdP d'Oc 1998 — 16.5 — £5–7

La Maquis Coteaux du Languedoc 1998 — 16 — −£5.00

Le Grand Verdier, Minervois 1998 — 17 — £5–7

Les Bories Blanques, Minervois 1998 — 15 — −£5.00

Les Grandes Vignes, Côtes du Rhône 1999 — 16 — £5–7

Mas Saint-Vincent Coteaux du Languedoc 1998 — 16.5 — −£5.00

Mosaique Grenache Syrah VdP d'Oc 1999 — 14 — −£5.00

Mosaique Syrah, VdP d'Oc 1999 — 14 — −£5.00

Pavillion de l'Escalion, Costieres de Nimes 1998 — 16.5 — −£5.00

Plan Macassan, Costieres de Nimes 1998 — 16.5 — −£5.00

| | | |
|---|---|---|
| Ptomaine de Blageurs Syrah, VdP de l'Ardeche 1997 | 14 | −£5.00 |
| Santenay 1er Cru Les Gravieres, Domaine Bourgeot 1998 | 13 | £10–13 |

## FRENCH WHITE

| | | |
|---|---|---|
| Burgundy Blanc 'Cuvée Saint-Vincent', Vincent Giradin 1998 | 15 | −£5.00 |
| Château de Fesles Rosé d'Anjou 1998 | 13.5 | −£5.00 |
| Château Grand Escalion Rosé, Costieres de Nimes 1999 | 13.5 | £5–7 |
| Clos Petite Bellane, Côtes du Rhône 1999 | 16 | £5–7 |
| Clos Petite Bellane Rosé, Côtes du Rhône 1999 | 13.5 | £5–7 |
| Comte Cathare Domaine Begude Chardonnay, VdP d'Oc 1999 | 15 | −£5.00 |
| Comte Cathare Domaine Begude Limoux 1998 | 15.5 | £7–10 |
| Comte Cathare Marsanne/Viognier, VdP d'Oc 1999 | 15 | −£5.00 |
| Domaine Borie de Maurel Chardonnay, VdP d'Oc 1999 | 15.5 | £5–7 |
| Domaine Borie de Maurel Cuvée Aude, Minervois 1999 | 15 | £5–7 |
| Domaine Cady Coteaux du Layon St-Aubin 'Cuvee Harmonie' 1997 (50cl) | 16.5 | £7–10 |

| | | |
|---|---|---|
| Domaine de la Renaudie Touraine Sauvignon 1999 | 14 | −£5.00 |
| Domaine de Montahuc Muscat, Muscat de Saint Jean de Minervois 1998 (50cl) | 15.5 | £5–7 |
| Dourthe No 1 Bordeaux 1999 | 13.5 | −£5.00 |
| James Herrick Chardonnay 1999 | 16 | −£5.00 |
| James Herrick Domaine Les Garrigues de Truilhas Chardonnay VdP d'Oc 1998 | 16 | £5–7 |
| Kiwi Civee Sauvignon Blanc VdP du Jardin de la France 1999 | 15 | −£5.00 |
| Les Clos de Paulilles Rosé 1999 | 15 | £5–7 |
| Macon Davaye Domaine des Deux Roches 1998 | 16 | £5–7 |
| Menetou-Salon Morogues 'Clos de Ratier', Pelle 1998 | 13 | £7–10 |
| Montagny 1er Cru, Domaine Maurice Bertrand 1997 | 13 | £7–10 |
| Pouilly-Fume Le Champ des Vignes, Tabordet 1998 | 12 | £7–10 |
| Sancerre Domaine de la Rossignole 1998 | 12.5 | £7–10 |
| St Romain 'Sous le Château' Baron de la Charriere 1998 | 13.5 | £10–13 |
| St Veran les Cras, Lassarat 1996 | 12 | £13–20 |

## GERMAN WHITE

| | | |
|---|---|---|
| Durkheimer Fronhof Scheurebe Trockenbeerenauslese, Kurt Darting 1998 (50cl) | 15.5 | £13–20 |
| Lingfelder Bird Label Riesling, Pfalz 1999 | 13 | –£5.00 |
| Messmer Burrweiler Riesling Spatlese Trocken, Pfalz 1998 | 13 | £7–10 |
| Polz Grassnitzberg Grauburgunder 1998 | 11 | £7–10 |
| Ruppertsberger Reiterpfad Scheurebe Beerenauslese, von Buhl 1994 (half-bottle) | 17 | £20+ |
| Von Buhl Deidesheimer Maushole Spatlese Halbtrocken 1998 | 14 | £7–10 |
| Von Buhl Forster Pechstein Riesling Kabinett 1998 | 14 | £7–10 |

## GREEK RED

| | | |
|---|---|---|
| Domaine Katsaros Red, Olympos 1997 | 17 | £13–20 |
| Gaia Estate Agiorgitiko, Nemea 1998 | 16 | £10–13 |
| Kosta Lazaridis Amethystos Cava, Drama 1995 | 13 | £13–20 |
| Ktima Domaine Mercouri, Peloponnese 1998 | 16.5 | £5–7 |
| Ktima Kyr-Yianni Ramnista, Naoussa 1997 | 16 | £5–7 |
| Ktima Kyr-Yianni Syrah, Imathia 1997 | 18 | £7–10 |
| Ktima Kyr-Yianni Yianakahori, Imathia 1997 | 15.5 | £7–10 |
| Ktima Voyatsi 1997 | 16 | £7–10 |
| Mavrodaphne of Patras NV (50 cl) | 15.5 | £5–7 |
| Papantonis Miden Agan, Peloponnese 1997 | 16 | £7–10 |
| Tsantali Metoxi Agiorgitikos 1996 | 16.5 | £7–10 |
| Tselepos Agiorgitikos, Nemea 1997 | 15.5 | £5–7 |
| Tselepos Cabernet Sauvignon, Peloponnese 1996 | 15.5 | £7–10 |

## GREEK WHITE

| | | |
|---|---|---|
| Amethystos Fumé, Drama 1999 | 14 | £7–10 |
| Amethystos Rosé, Macedonia 1999 | 14 | £5–7 |
| Boutari Visanto, Santorini 1993 (50cl) | 16 | £5–7 |
| Gerovassiliou White, Epanomi 1998 | 13 | £5–7 |
| Kosta Lazaridis Château Julia Assyrtiko, Adriani 1998 | 13.5 | £5–7 |
| Oenoforos Asprolithi, Patras 1999 | 13 | –£5.00 |
| Spiropoulos White, Mantinia 1998 (organic) | 14 | –£5.00 |
| Strofilia Nafsika, Anavissos 1997 | 13.5 | £5–7 |

| | | |
|---|---|---|
| Thalassitis Santorini Assyrtiko 1998 | 15.5 | £5–7 |
| Tsantali Ambelonas, Agios Pavlos 1999 | 13.5 | £5–7 |
| Tsantali Chromitsa, Agiorgitikos 1999 | 15 | £5–7 |
| Tselepos Mantinia 1998 | 13 | –£5.00 |

## ITALIAN RED

| | | |
|---|---|---|
| Barbera d'Asti Suri di Mu, Icardi 1998 | 15.5 | £7–10 |
| Barbera d'Asti 'Tabarin', Icardi 1999 | 14 | £5–7 |
| Ca'Vergana Barbera d'Asti 1997 | 14.5 | –£5.00 |
| Castello Le Leccia Chianti Classico 1998 | 16 | £7–10 |
| Cecchi La Gavina Cabernet Sauvignon, Toscana 1997 | 17 | £7–10 |
| Dolcetto d'Alba 'Rousori', Icardi 1999 | 16.5 | £7–10 |
| Felline 'Albarello' Rosso del Salento 1997 | 16 | £7–10 |
| Feudi di San Gregorio Rubrato, Irpinia 1997 | 16 | £5–7 |
| Frescobaldi Campo Ai Sassi, Rosso di Montalcino 1998 | 14 | £7–10 |
| Gagliardo Dolcetto d'Alba 1999 | 13.5 | £7–10 |
| Il Padrino Rosso Sicilia 1999 | 15 | –£5.00 |
| Il Tarocco Chianti Classico 1997 | 15 | £7–10 |

| | | |
|---|---|---|
| Masi Modello delle Venezie 1998 | 15.5 | –£5.00 |
| Musella Rosso di Verona 1996 | 15.5 | £7–10 |
| Nolita Montepulciano d'Abruzzo 1998 | 16 | –£5.00 |
| Primitivo di Manduria, Felline 1998 | 15.5 | £7–10 |
| Rosso di Spicca Le Velette 1999 | 15.5 | £5–7 |
| San Crispino Primitivo del Salento 1999 | 16 | –£5.00 |
| San Crispino Sangiovese di Romagna Superiore 1996 | 14 | –£5.00 |
| San Fereolo Dolcetto di Dogliani 1998 | 14 | £7–10 |
| Scaranto, Colli Euganei 1997 | 16 | £5–7 |
| Tre Uve NV | 14.5 | –£5.00 |
| Tre Uve Ultima NV | 15.5 | £5–7 |

## ITALIAN WHITE

| | | |
|---|---|---|
| Arneis Roero Malvira 1999 | 13.5 | £5–7 |
| Cantine Gemma Moscato, Piemonte 1999 | 13 | –£5.00 |
| Chiarlo Nivole Moscato d'Asti NV (half-bottle) | 15 | –£5.00 |
| Coffele Soave Classico 1999 | 14.5 | £5–7 |
| Feudi di San Gregorio Falanghina, Sannio 1999 | 13 | £5–7 |
| Gorgo Bianco di Custoza 1999 | 13 | –£5.00 |

| | | |
|---|---|---|
| Histonium Chardonnay, Abruzzo 1998 | 15 | −£5.00 |
| Icardi Cortese 'Balera' Piemonte 1999 | 14 | £5–7 |
| Il Padrino Greganico/ Chardonnay, Sicily 1999 | 14 | −£5.00 |
| Pra Soave Classico Superiore 1999 | 14 | £5–7 |
| Tenuta le Velette 'Lunato' Orvieto Classico Superiore 1999 | 13.5 | £5–7 |
| Trulli Chardonnay Salento 1998 | 16 | −£5.00 |
| Villa Felici Orvieto Classico Amabile 1999 | 12 | £5–7 |
| Villa Felici 'Velette' Orvieto Classico Secco 1999 | 12 | −£5.00 |

## NEW ZEALAND RED

| | | |
|---|---|---|
| Delegat's Reserve Cabernet Sauvignon, Hawkes Bay 1998 | 15.5 | £7–10 |
| Montana Fairhall Estate Cabernet Sauvignon, Marlborough 1996 | 13 | £10–13 |

## NEW ZEALAND WHITE

| | | |
|---|---|---|
| Church Road Chardonnay 1998 | 16 | £7–10 |
| Dashwood Sauvignon Blanc 1999 | 16 | £5–7 |
| Hawkesbridge 'Willowbank Vineyard' Sauvignon Blanc, Marlborough 1999 | 15.5 | £5–7 |

| | | |
|---|---|---|
| Hunter's Sauvignon Blanc 1999 | 16 | £7–10 |
| Jackson Estate Sauvignon Blanc 1999 | 15 | £7–10 |
| McDonald Church Road Chardonnay, Hawkes Bay 1998 | 16 | £7–10 |
| Villa Maria Reserve 'Clifford Bay' Sauvignon Blanc, Marlborough 1999 | 16.5 | £7–10 |

## PORTUGUESE RED

| | | |
|---|---|---|
| Foral Douro Grande Escolha 1997 | 15.5 | £5–7 |
| Pegos Claros, Palmela 1994 | 15.5 | £7–10 |
| Quinta da Lagoalva, Ribatejo 1995 | 15 | £5–7 |
| Quinta das Setencostas, Alenquer 1998 | 16.5 | £5–7 |
| Quinta do Crasto Reserva, Doura 1997 | 17 | £7–10 |
| Segada Tinto, Ribatejano 1999 | 16 | −£5.00 |
| Terra Boa Portuguese Red 1998 | 16.5 | −£5.00 |

## PORTUGUESE WHITE

| | | |
|---|---|---|
| Bela Fonte Bical 1999 | 15.5 | −£5.00 |
| Segada Branco, Ribatejano 1999 | 15 | −£5.00 |

## SOUTH AFRICAN RED

| | | |
|---|---|---|
| Beyerskloof Pinotage, Stellenbosch 1999 | 16 | £5–7 |
| Blaauwklippen Shiraz 1997 | 13.5 | £5–7 |
| Boschkloof Cabernet Sauvignon 1997 | 15.5 | £5–7 |
| Boschkloof Reserve Cabernet Sauvignon/ Merlot 1997 | 14 | £7–10 |
| Fairview Carignan, Coastal Region 1998 | 13 | £5–7 |
| Fairview Shiraz Mourvedre 1998 | 17.5 | £5–7 |
| Fairview Zinfandel Cinsault 1999 | 17.5 | £5–7 |
| Glen Carlou Pinot Noir 1998 | 13.5 | £7–10 |
| Kanonkop, Paul Sauer, Stellenbosch 1995 | 14 | £13–20 |
| Kumala Reserve Cabernet Sauvignon 1998 | 16.5 | £7–10 |
| Longridge Bay View Cabernet Sauvignon 1998 | 14 | £5–7 |
| Longridge Bay View Merlot 1998 | 14 | £5–7 |
| Longridge Bay View Pinotage 1998 | 15 | £5–7 |
| Radford Dale Merlot, Stellenbosch 1999 | 14 | £7–10 |
| Savanha Shiraz, Western Cape 1997 | 13 | £5–7 |
| Saxenberg Cabernet Sauvignon, Stellenbosch 1997 | 17 | £10–13 |

| | | |
|---|---|---|
| Stellenzicht Pinotage 1998 | 17 | £7–10 |
| Stellenzicht Shiraz 1998 | 15 | £7–10 |
| Vinum Cabernet Sauvignon, Stellenbosch 1999 | 14 | £5–7 |
| Yonder Hill Cabernet Merlot, Stellenbosch 1998 | 16 | £7–10 |
| Yonder Hill Cabernet Sauvignon, Stellenbosch 1998 | 16.5 | £7–10 |

## SOUTH AFRICAN WHITE

| | | |
|---|---|---|
| Boschkloof Chardonnay Reserve 1997 | 13 | £5–7 |
| Buitenverwachting Chardonnay, Constantia 1998 | 16 | £7–10 |
| Buitenverwachting Rhine Riesling, Constantia 1999 | 15 | £5–7 |
| Buitenverwachting Sauvignon Blanc, Constantia 1999 | 16 | £7–10 |
| Danie de Wet Chardonnay sur Lie, Robertson 2000 | 15 | –£5.00 |
| Eikendal Chardonnay, Stellenbosch 1998 | 14 | £7–10 |
| Fair Valley Bush Vine Chenin Blanc, Coastal Region 1999 | 15.5 | –£5.00 |
| Fairview Akkerbos Chardonnay, Paarl 1999 | 16.5 | £7–10 |
| Fairview Chardonnay 1999 | 16.5 | £5–7 |

| | | |
|---|---|---|
| Fairview Cyril Back Semillon, Paarl 1998 | 16 | £5–7 |
| Fairview Goats do Roam Rosé 2000 | 16 | –£5.00 |
| Fairview 'Oom Pagel' Semillon, Paarl 1999 | 16.5 | £5–7 |
| Fairview Viogner, Paarl 2000 | 16 | £7–10 |
| Glen Carlou Chardonnay 1999 | 14 | £7–10 |
| Glen Carlou Reserve Chardonnay 1997 | 12 | £10–13 |
| Ken Forrester Scholtzenhof Chenin Blanc, Stellenbosch 1998 | 14 | £5–7 |
| Klein Constantia Chardonnay 1998 | 15.5 | £7–10 |
| Klein Constantia Riesling 1998 | 13.5 | –£5.00 |
| Klein Constantia Sauvignon Blanc 1998 | 15.5 | £5–7 |
| Longridge Bay View Chardonnay, Western Cape 1998 | 14 | –£5.00 |
| Longridge Chardonnay, Stellenbosch 1998 | 13.5 | £7–10 |
| Radford Dale Chardonnay, Stellenbosch 1999 | 16 | £7–10 |
| Saxenburg Private Collection Chardonnay, Stellenbosch 1998 | 16.5 | £7–10 |
| Scholtzenhof Petit Chenin, Stellenbosch 1999 | 15.5 | –£5.00 |
| Slayley Chardonnay 1997 | 15.5 | £7–10 |

| | | |
|---|---|---|
| Stellenzicht Sauvignon Blanc, Stellenbosch 1998 | 13.5 | £5–7 |
| Stellenzicht Semillon Reserve, Stellenbosch 1998 | 15 | £7–10 |
| Ten Fifty Six Blanc Fume, Franschoek 1998 | 13.5 | –£5.00 |
| Ten Fifty Six Chardonnay, Paarl 1998 | 14 | £5–7 |
| Vergelegen Reserve Chardonnay 1997 | 16.5 | £7–10 |
| Von Ortloff Chardonnay 1998 | 16 | £5–7 |

## SPANISH RED

| | | |
|---|---|---|
| Artadi Orobio Tempranillo, Rioja 1999 | 16 | £5–7 |
| Bodegas Palacio Glorioso Crianza Rioja 1997 | 14.5 | £5–7 |
| Cosme Palacio y Hermanos, Rioja 1997 | 16 | £5–7 |
| Costers del Gravet Red, Capcanes 1998 | 17.5 | £7–10 |
| Dardell Negre, Gandesa 1999 | 15.5 | –£5.00 |
| La Cata Tempranillo, La Mancha 1998 | 14 | –£5.00 |
| La Vicalanda de Vina Pomal Reserva, Rioja 1995 | 13 | £10–13 |
| Olivares Dulce Monastrell 1996 | 16 | £13–20 |
| Piedemonte Merlot/ Cabernet Sauvignon, Navarra 1998 | 15 | –£5.00 |

| Raimat Tempranillo, Costers del Segre 1997 | 16.5 | £7–10 |
| Taja Gran Reserva, Jumilla 1994 | 16 | £7–10 |
| Taja Jumilla 1999 | 16 | –£5.00 |

## SPANISH WHITE

| Burgans Albarino, Rias Baixas 1999 | 12.5 | £5–7 |
| Chivite Gran Feudo Rosé, Navarra 1999 | 14 | –£5.00 |
| Marques de Caceres Rosé, Rioja 1999 | 13 | £5–7 |
| Torres Vina Esmeralda 1999 | 14 | £5–7 |
| Vinas del Vero Chardonnay, Somontano 1999 | 15 | –£5.00 |

## USA RED

| Bonterra Zinfandel, Mendocino 1996 | 16.5 | £7–10 |
| Canyon Road Cabernet Sauvignon 1998 | 14 | £5–7 |
| Canyon Road Merlot, Geyserville 1997 | 13.5 | £5–7 |
| Clos LaChance Cabernet Sauvignon, Santa Cruz Mountains 1997 | 13 | £13–20 |
| Clos LaChance Zinfandel, El Dorado County 1997 | 16.5 | £10–13 |
| Fetzer Syrah 1997 | 14 | £7–10 |
| Fetzer Valley Oaks Cabernet Sauvignon 1997 | 15.5 | £5–7 |
| Fetzer Vineyards Home Ranch Zinfandel 1996 | 15.5 | £5–7 |

| Fetzer Vineyards Select Zinfandel 1997 | 16.5 | £7–10 |
| Ravenswood Vintners Blend Zinfandel 1997 | 15 | £7–10 |
| Ravenswood Zinfandel, Napa Valley 1997 | 16 | £10–13 |
| Ravenswood Zinfandel, Sonoma County 1997 | 14 | £10–13 |
| Sterling Vineyards Cabernet Sauvignon, Napa Valley 1996 | 15 | £7–10 |

## USA WHITE

| Canyon Road Chardonnay 1998 | 14 | £5–7 |
| Clos LaChance Chardonnay, Santa Cruz Mountains 1997 | 13.5 | £13–20 |
| Fetzer Bonterra Muscat 1999 (half-bottle) | 15 | £5–7 |
| Fetzer Vineyards Bonterra Viognier 1998 | 16 | £7–10 |
| Fetzer Viognier 1999 | 15 | £7–10 |
| Landmark Overlook Chardonnay 1998 | 17 | £13–20 |
| Mariquita White 1996 | 14 | –£5.00 |

## FORTIFIED WINES

| Bodegas Don Tomas 'Zingara' Manzanilla, Sanlucar Du Barrameda NV (half bottle) | 16 | –£5.00 |
| Classic Fino, Valdespino NV | 16 | £7–10 |
| Classic Manzanilla, Valdespino NV | 16 | £5–7 |

## SPARKLING WINES

Billecart-Salmon Cuvée Nicholas Francois Billecart Brut 1991 — 14 — £20+

Bonnet Brut Heritage NV — 13.5 — £13–20

Cuvée Napa by Mumm Blanc de Blancs NV — 15.5 — £10–13

Deutz Marlborough Cuvée (New Zealand) — 13.5 — £7–10

Henri Harlin Brut NV — 15 — £13–20

Lindauer Special Reserve Brut NV — 14.5 — £7–10

Mumm Cordon Rouge Cuvée Limitee 1990 — 13 — £20+

Pierre Gimonnet et Fils Brut Gastronome 1995 — 13.5 — £13–20

Pierre Gimonnet et Fils 'Cuis 1er Cru' Blanc de Blancs Brut NV — 16 — £13–20

Ployez-Jacquemart Brut NV — 13 — £13–20

Yellowglen Vintage Brut 1995 (Australia) — 14 — £7–10

SEE STOP PRESS SECTION AT END OF BOOK FOR LAST-MINUTE ADDITIONS OR UPDATES TO THIS RETAILER'S RANGE.

# SAFEWAY

The big event in this enigmatic retailer's year was the departure of Ms Elizabeth Robertson, who had been its strength, as controller of wine buying, for many years. Liz had an unruffled, quirkily humorous intelligence, not so much typical of supermarket wine buyers as chemistry teachers and lexicographers. She has not been replaced – a gap has been created which has not been filled – and as a result Safeway, though staffed with some highly professional buyers, has carried on much as before rather than made any startling advances.

However, on the non-wine front, Safeway innovated. It mounted trials of coupon machines, in 1999, offering instant discounts on branded goods. Each pilot store had about twenty machines positioned alongside branded-goods displays.

At about this time it appointed Roger Ramsden as its new marketing director. Mr Ramsden joined Safeway in 1995 and had been on the board since 1997. Mr Ramsden's appointment follows the departure of Roger Partington, who was reckoned by the supermarket wine press to have resigned as a result of this appointment. At the same time Carlos Criado-Perez, previously chief operating officer of Wal-Mart's international division, joined Safeway as chief operating officer. It was thought that he is being groomed to succeed Colin Smith as Safeway's chief executive.

Change was much in the air, at this time, at Safeway. According to the *Grocer* magazine, the retailer and BP were 'racing ahead with forecourt development'. The store also tested a new generation of personal hand-held scanners in a pilot scheme at its Malden store in Surrey. New gizmos on the new scanners include a voice intercom which allows shoppers to ask a helpdesk about the location of a certain product. It also has a sixteen-line graphic display which can be used to inform customers about promotions.

In spring 2000 it reckoned to be introducing in-store radio in all its superstores within a few weeks. Hard on the heels of this news (a step backwards in my view, for I loathe supermarkets which play loud music and constantly plague the ear with puerile announcements like 'Martin Fluck, the world-famous wine celebrity, is now telling jokes and signing copies of his latest *Superplonk* paperback next to the bottle bank in the main car park'), Safeway was reported to have suffered a sharp fall in the level of favourable price coverage it receives – in the second 'Food and Drug Retailer's Reputation Monthly' report – according to *Supermarketing* magazine. The reasons given were a fall in its share price and the potential impact on Safeway of a price war between Tesco and the Wal-Mart-generated Asda.

Nothing daunted, Safeway belatedly jumped on the sushi bandwagon, offering it in chilled counters to take away, and it also unveiled the first phase of its new look. Layout and presentation were changed in areas such as bakery goods and produce, though the wine shelves were untouched (they'd had enough tweaks and redesigns, unsuccessfully, over the past few years).

Then Safeway announced its 'new' logo. Well, you could have fooled me. The 'tweak' this so-called new logo represented did indeed appear not much different from the old one, but Safeway management apparently described the new image as 'passionate, vibrant, and contemporary'. In keeping with this, the 'lightening the load' slogan has been dumped. It was anodyne, to speak flattering of it, and the ad agency that dreamed it up must have been desperate when they presented it and even more astonished when their desperate client bought it. The new branding is to be carried on all products and delivery vehicles and was introduced in all the company's 482 stores over the summer. Safeway did not reveal how much the redesign cost, but one anonymous authority I spoke to said 'millions, millions, think of all that paint and the hourly rate of the painters'.

Little of all this bravura enterprise brushed the wine shelves or changed much the wine buyers' lives. Just as well from our point of view because Safeway has an interesting range of wines well up there with the best in the business. The Australians, especially the reds around the £5/£7 mark, are quite brilliant, as testified by the high ratings awarded these wines in the pages that follow.

Safeway plc
Safeway House
6 Millington Road
Hayes
Middlesex
UB3 4AY

Tel 020 8848 8744
Fax 020 8573 1865
www.safeway.co.uk

## ARGENTINIAN RED

| | | |
|---|---|---|
| Adiseno Bonarda 1999 | 15.5 | −£5.00 |
| Adiseno Reserve Malbec 1999 | 15 | £5–7 |
| Argentinian Bonarda 1999, Safeway | 14 | −£5.00 |
| Argentinian Cabernet Sauvignon 1999, Safeway | 14 | −£5.00 |
| Argentinian Red 1999, Safeway | 14 | −£3.50 |
| Caballo de Plata Bonarda/Barbera 2000 | 13 | −£3.50 |
| Diego Murillo Malbec, Patagonia 1997 | 17 | £5–7 |
| Rafael Estate Malbec, Mendoza 1997 | 16 | £5–7 |
| Simonassi Lyon Barbera 1998 | 14 | £5–7 |
| Weinert Malbec 1994 | 16 | £7–10 |

## ARGENTINIAN WHITE

| | | |
|---|---|---|
| Argentinian Chardonnay 1999, Safeway | 16 | −£5.00 |
| Caballo de Plata Torrontes 2000 | 13.5 | −£3.50 |

## AUSTRALIAN RED

| | | |
|---|---|---|
| Australian Oaked Cabernet Sauvignon 1999, Safeway | 14.5 | −£5.00 |
| Australian Oaked Shiraz 1999, Safeway | 14 | −£5.00 |
| Australian Shiraz 1999, Safeway | 15 | −£5.00 |
| Australian Shiraz/Ruby Cabernet 1999, Safeway | 14 | −£5.00 |
| Basedow Bush Vine Grenache 1998 | 15 | £5–7 |
| Capel Vale Shiraz 1998 | 14 | £7–10 |
| Clancy's Shiraz/Cabernet Sauvignon/Merlot/ Cabernet Franc 1998 | 17 | £7–10 |
| Dawn Ridge Australian Red (3 litre box) | 15 | −£3.50 |
| Endeavour Cabernet Sauvignon 1998 | 13 | £7–10 |
| Evans & Tate Shiraz 1999 | 16.5 | £7–10 |
| Geoff Merrill Reserve Cabernet Sauvignon 1995 | 15 | £10–13 |
| Hardys Stamp of Australia Shiraz Cabernet 1999 | 14 | −£5.00 |
| Haselgrove 'Bentwing' Shiraz, Wrattonbully 1998 | 14 | £7–10 |
| Haselgrove Shiraz, McLaren Vale 1998 | 14 | £7–10 |
| Jindalee Shiraz, Murray-Darling Region 1998 | 13 | −£5.00 |
| Knappstein Cabernet/ Merlot 1998 | 16.5 | £7–10 |
| Koltz LFD Shiraz 1998 | 16 | £7–10 |
| Lindemans Pyrus Cabernet Sauvignon/ Merlot/Cabernet France 1997 | 16.5 | £13–20 |
| Mamre Brook Cabernet Sauvignon 1997 | 15 | £7–10 |
| Mamre Brook Cabernet Shiraz 1996 | 16 | £5–7 |

| | | |
|---|---|---|
| Masterpeace Shiraz Malbec 2000 | 14 | £5–7 |
| Metala Shiraz/Cabernet Sauvignon 1997 | 14 | £5–7 |
| Oxford Landing Limited Release Shiraz 1998 | 13.5 | £5–7 |
| Penfolds Bin 128 Coonawarra Shiraz 1996 | 15.5 | £7–10 |
| Penfolds Bin 389 Cabernet Shiraz 1996 | 16 | £10–13 |
| Penfolds Organic Merlot Shiraz Cabernet 1998 | 15.5 | £7–10 |
| Peter Lehmann The Barossa Shiraz 1998 | 17 | £5–7 |
| Riddoch Cabernet Shiraz 1998 | 16 | £7–10 |
| Rosemount Estate Grenache Shiraz 1998 | 15 | £5–7 |
| Rosemount Estate Merlot 1998 | 13 | £7–10 |
| Rosemount Estate Shiraz 1998 | 15.5 | £7–10 |
| Rosemount Estate Show Reserve Cabernet Sauvignon 1996 | 13 | £13–20 |
| Rosemount 'Hill of Gold' Shiraz, Mudgee 1998 | 17.5 | £7–10 |
| Tatachilla Breakneck Creek Cabernet Sauvignon 1999 | 14 | £5–7 |
| Tatachilla Breakneck Creek Merlot 1999 | 15 | £5–7 |
| Tatachilla 'Foundation' Shiraz 1998 | 16 | £13–20 |
| Tatachilla Padthaway Cabernet Sauvignon 1998 | 16.5 | £7–10 |

| | | |
|---|---|---|
| Wirrega Vineyards Cabernet Sauvignon/ Petit Verdot 1999 | 16 | £5–7 |
| Wirrega Vineyards Shiraz 1999 | 16.5 | £5–7 |
| Woolshed Cabernet/ Shiraz/Merlot, Coonawarra 1998 | 17 | £5–7 |

## AUSTRALIAN WHITE

| | | |
|---|---|---|
| Annie's Lane Semillon, Clare Valley 1999 | 15.5 | £5–7 |
| Australian Chardonnay/ Colombard 1999, Safeway | 12 | –£5.00 |
| Australian Oaked Chardonnay 1999, Safeway | 15 | –£5.00 |
| Basedow Semillon, Barossa Valley 1998 | 16.5 | £5–7 |
| Capel Vale Unwooded Chardonnay 1999 | 15 | £7–10 |
| Capel Vale Verdelho 1999 | 16 | £7–10 |
| CV Chenin Blanc 2000 | 16 | £5–7 |
| Endeavour Barrel- fermented Chardonnay 1998 | 14.5 | £7–10 |
| Goundrey Reserve Selection Chardonnay 1998 | 16.5 | £10–13 |
| Hardys Nottage Hill Chardonnay 1999 | 15 | –£5.00 |
| Jindalee Chardonnay, Murray-Darling Region 1998 | 16 | –£5.00 |
| Lindemans Bin 65 Chardonnay 1999 | 16.5 | –£5.00 |

| | | |
|---|---|---|
| Loxton Low Alcohol Chardonnay (1.2% vol) | 11 | −£3.50 |
| Mamre Brook Chardonnay 1999 | 16 | £5–7 |
| Ninth Island Sauvignon Blanc, Tasmania 1999 | 14 | £7–10 |
| Penfolds Bin 21 Rawson's Retreat Semillon/ Colombard/Chardonnay 1999 | 14 | −£5.00 |
| Penfolds Eden Valley Reserve Riesling 1999 | 13.5 | £7–10 |
| Peter Lehmann 'The Barossa' Semillon 1999 | 16 | £5–7 |
| Peter Lehmann Vine Vale Riesling, Barossa Valley 2000 | 13 | −£5.00 |
| Riddoch Coonawarra Chardonnay 1998 | 15 | £5–7 |
| Robertson Barrel Fermented Colombard 1999 | 13 | −£5.00 |
| Rosemount Show Reserve Chardonnay 1998 | 15 | £7–10 |
| Rothbury Estate Hunter Valley Verdelho 1999 | 16 | £5–7 |
| Taltarni Sauvignon Blanc, Victoria 1999 | 15.5 | £5–7 |
| Tatachilla Breakneck Creek Chardonnay 1999 | 16 | −£5.00 |
| Tatachilla Chardonnay 1998 | 16 | £7–10 |
| Tatachilla Padthaway Chardonnay 1999 | 16 | £5–7 |
| Woolshed Chardonnay, Coonawarra 1998 | 16 | £5–7 |

## AUSTRIAN WHITE

| | | |
|---|---|---|
| Cat's Leap Gruner Veltliner 1999 | 12 | −£5.00 |

## BULGARIAN RED

| | | |
|---|---|---|
| Azbuka Merlot 1996 | 15 | £5–7 |
| Bulgarian Country Red, Merlot/Gamza 1999, Safeway | 15.5 | −£3.50 |
| Nazdrave Cabernet Sauvignon 1999 | 15.5 | −£5.00 |
| Sapphire Cove NV | 14.5 | −£3.50 |
| Suhindol Merlot Reserve 1996 | 14 | −£5.00 |
| Young Vatted Cabernet Sauvignon 1999, Safeway | 14 | −£3.50 |
| Young Vatted Merlot 1999, Safeway | 14.5 | −£3.50 |

## BULGARIAN WHITE

| | | |
|---|---|---|
| Bulgarian Chardonnay, Rousse 1999, Safeway | 13 | −£3.50 |
| Bulgarian Country Wine, Welschrizling/Rikat 1999, Safeway | 12.5 | −£3.50 |
| Bulgarian Oaked Chardonnay Reserve 1998, Safeway | 10 | −£5.00 |
| Preslav, Barrel Fermented Chardonnay 1997 | 16 | −£5.00 |
| Valley of the Roses Cabernet Sauvignon Rosé 1999 | 13 | −£3.50 |

## CHILEAN RED

| | | |
|---|---|---|
| 35 Sur Cabernet Sauvignon 1998 | 15 | −£5.00 |
| Acacias Estate Merlot, Maipo Valley 1998, Safeway | 14 | −£5.00 |
| Carta Vieja Merlot 1999 | 14 | −£5.00 |
| Castillo de Molina Cabernet Sauvignon Reserva, Lontue 1998 | 16 | £5–7 |
| Chilean Cabernet Sauvignon 1999, Safeway | 16.5 | −£5.00 |
| Chilean Red 1999, Safeway | 15 | −£5.00 |
| Concha y Toro Casillero del Diablo Cabernet Sauvignon, Maipo 1998 | 16.5 | −£5.00 |
| Cono Sur Cabernet Sauvignon, Rapel Valley 1999 | 14 | −£5.00 |
| Cono Sur Reserva Merlot 1999 | 16.5 | £5–7 |
| Errazuriz Cabernet Sauvignon, El Ceibo Estate, Aconcagua 1998 | 17.5 | £5–7 |
| Errazuriz Merlot Reserva, Don Maximiano Estate Aconcagua, 1997 | 16 | £7–10 |
| Errazuriz Syrah Reserva 1998 | 16 | £7–10 |
| Isla Negra Merlot 1998 | 16.5 | £5–7 |
| Santa Rita Reserva Cabernet Sauvignon, Alto Jahull Vineyards Maipo 1997 | 16 | £5–7 |
| TerraMater Zinfandel/ Syrah, Maipo 1998 | 16.5 | −£5.00 |

| | | |
|---|---|---|
| Valdivieso Cabernet Franc Reserve 1997 | 17.5 | £7–10 |
| Valdivieso Malbec Reserve, Lontue 1996 | 15.5 | £7–10 |
| Valdivieso Single Vineyard Merlot Reserve, Lontue 1998 | 16.5 | £7–10 |
| Villard Estate Cabernet Sauvignon, Central Valley 1997 | 16 | £5–7 |
| Vina Morande Merlot 1999 | 15.5 | −£5.00 |
| Vina Morande Pinot Noir 1998 | 14 | −£5.00 |
| Vina Morande Syrah 1998 | 10 | −£5.00 |

## CHILEAN WHITE

| | | |
|---|---|---|
| 35 Sur Sauvignon Blanc 1999 | 15.5 | −£5.00 |
| Chilean Dry White 2000, Safeway | 16 | −£3.50 |
| Chilean Sauvignon Blanc Lontue 1999, Safeway | 16 | −£5.00 |
| Chilean Sauvignon Blanc/Chardonnay 1999, Safeway | 15.5 | −£5.00 |
| Cono Sur Chardonnay 1999 | 14 | −£5.00 |
| Cordillera Estate Oak Aged Chardonnay Reserva 1997, Safeway | 15.5 | −£5.00 |
| Errazuriz La Escultura Estate Chardonnay, Casablanca 1998 | 17.5 | £5–7 |
| TerraMater Estates Sauvignon Blanc, Select Cuvée, 1999 | 15.5 | £5–7 |

## FRENCH RED

Anciennes Vignes Carignan, VdP de l'Aude 1998 — 15.5 −£5.00

Baron de Lestac, Bordeaux 1998 — 15 −£5.00

Beaujolais Villages 'Combes aux Jacques' 1998 — 12 £5–7

Bourgogne Pinot Noir 'Reserve de la Famille' 1996 — 12 £5–7

Cabernet Sauvignon VdP d'Oc 1998, Safeway — 16 −£5.00

Calvet St Emilion 1997 — 13 £5–7

Château Clos de la Chesnaie, Lalande de Pomerol 1998 — 14 £7–10

Château de Coulaine, Chinon 1998 (organic) — 16 £5–7

Château de Lausieres, Coteaux du Languedoc 1998 — 15.5 −£5.00

Château de Villenouvette, Cuvée Marcel Barsalou Corbieres 1998 — 16 £7–10

Château Grand Champs Bordeaux 1998 — 13.5 £5–7

Château Jouanin Cuvée Prestige, Côtes du Castillon 1998 — 15 £5–7

Château La Rose Brisson St Emilion Grand Cru 1998 — 16 £10–13

Château Limonier, Bordeaux 1998 — 15.5 −£5.00

Château Liversan, Cru Bourgeois, Haut-Medoc 1997 — 12 £7–10

Château Maison Neuve Montagne St Emilion 1998 — 15.5 £7–10

Château Montbrun Corbieres 1999 — 16.5 −£5.00

Château Montbrun de Gautherius Corbieres 1999 — 15 −£5.00

Château Philippe de Vessiere, Costieres de Nimes 1997 — 15.5 −£5.00

Château Pourchaud-Larquey, Bordeaux 1998 (organic) — 15.5 £5–7

Château Rozier, St Emilion Grand Cru 1996 — 13 £10–13

Château Tour du Mont, Haut Medoc 1998 — 13.5 £5–7

Chevalier de Malle, Graves 1998 — 14 £7–10

Claret NV, Safeway — 13 −£5.00

Corbieres 1999, Safeway — 14 −£3.50

Côtes du Rhône 1999, Safeway — 14 −£3.50

Crozes-Hermitage Etienne Barret 1999 — 14.5 £5–7

Domaine Chris Limouzi, Corbieres 1998 — 16.5 £5–7

Domaine de Contenson Merlot, VdP d'Oc 1998 — 16 −£5.00

Domaine des Bruyeres, Côtes de Malepere 1998 — 16.5 −£5.00

| | | |
|---|---|---|
| Domaine des Lauriers, Faugeres 1997 | 16.5 | £5–7 |
| Domaine Montmija, Corbieres 1999 (organic) | 15.5 | –£5.00 |
| Domaine Vieux Manoir de Maransan Cuvée Speciale 1998, Safeway | 15.5 | –£5.00 |
| Enclos des Cigales Merlot, VdP d'Oc 1999 | 14 | –£5.00 |
| Enclos des Cigales Syrah, VdP d'Oc 1999 | 15.5 | –£5.00 |
| Fleurie Domaine des Raclets 1998 | 13 | £7–10 |
| French Revolution Le Rouge 1999 | 16 | –£5.00 |
| Hautes Côtes de Nuits Cuvée Speciale 1996 | 10 | £7–10 |
| James Herrick Millia Passum Syrah, VdP d'Oc 1998 | 16.5 | £5–7 |
| Jean Louis Denois Mourvedre/Grenache, VdP d'Oc 1998 | 17 | £5–7 |
| L'If Merlot/Carignan, VdP d'Oc 1999 | 14.5 | –£5.00 |
| La Chasse du Pape 'Reserve Barrique' Côtes du Rhône 1999 | 16.5 | –£5.00 |
| La Cuvée Mythique VdP d'Oc 1998 | 16 | £5–7 |
| La Provincia Cabernet Sauvignon/Syrah, VdP d'Oc 1998 | 15.5 | £5–7 |
| La Source Merlot/Syrah VdP d'Oc 1999 | 15 | –£5.00 |
| 'Les Tourelles' Cahors 1999 | 15.5 | –£5.00 |

| | | |
|---|---|---|
| Mercurey Raoul Clerget 1996 | 12 | £7–10 |
| Merlot Vin de Pays d'Oc 1999, Safeway | 14 | –£3.50 |
| Minervois 1999, Safeway | 14 | –£3.50 |
| Mont Tauch Merlot, Barrel Matured, VdP du Torgan 1998 | 17 | £7–10 |
| Moulin de Ciffre Faugeres 1998 | 16.5 | £5–7 |
| No 2 Château Lafon-Rochet, St Estephe 1996 | 13.5 | £13–20 |
| Oak-aged Côtes du Rhône 1999, Safeway | 13.5 | –£5.00 |
| Organic French Red VdP du Gard 1999, Safeway | 13 | –£5.00 |
| Pinot Noir d'Autrefois VdP d'Oc 1999 | 13 | –£5.00 |
| Pommard Premier Cru Le Clos Blanc 1997 | 11 | £13–20 |
| Pommard Premier Cru Les Arvelets 1996 | 12 | £13–20 |
| Reserve Valseque VdP de l'Aude 1999 | 14 | –£3.50 |
| Savigny du Domaine du Château de Meursault 1996 | 11 | £7–10 |
| Syrah VdP d'Oc 1999, Safeway | 15 | –£3.50 |
| Valreas Cuvée Prestige, Côtes du Rhône Villages 1999 | 16 | –£5.00 |
| Young Vatted Grenache VdP de l'Ardeche 1999 | 15 | –£3.50 |
| Young Vatted Syrah VdP de Vaucluse 1999, Safeway | 15 | –£5.00 |

## FRENCH WHITE

Bourgogne Chardonnay | 15 | £5–7
Barrique Reserve 1998

Chablis Laroche 1999 | 12 | £7–10

Chardonnay VdP de | 14 | –£5.00
l'Herault 1999, Safeway

Château de la Gravelle, | 14 | –£5.00
Muscadet de Sevres et
Maine Sur Lie 1998

Château du Roc | 12 | –£5.00
Bordeaux Sauvignon 1999

Château Magneau, | 15 | £5–7
Graves 1999

Château Petit Roubie, | 13.5 | –£5.00
Coteaux du Languedoc
1999 (organic)

Domaine de Bosquet | 16 | £5–7
Chardonnay VdP d'Oc
1998

Domaine de Ciffre | 16 | £5–7
Viognier VdP d'Oc 1999

Domaine de l'Ecu | 12 | –£5.00
Muscadet de Sevre et
Maine Sur Lie 1999
(biodynamic)

Domaine Lafage Muscat | 14 | –£5.00
Sec, VdP d'Oc 1999

Dourthe No 1 Bordeaux | 13.5 | –£5.00
1999

French Revolution Le | 13 | –£5.00
Blanc 1999

James Herrick | 16 | –£5.00
Chardonnay VdP d'Oc
1999

L'If Grenache Blanc, | 15 | –£5.00
Eleve en Futs de Chene,
VdP d'Oc 1999

La Source Chardonnay/ | 16 | –£5.00
Roussanne VdP d'Oc
1999

Montagny Premier Cru | 14 | £7–10
1998, Safeway

Pinot Blanc Alsace 1998, | 13.5 | –£5.00
Safeway

Sancerre 1999, Safeway | 12 | £5–7

Sancerre 'Les Bonnes | 13 | £7–10
Bouches' 1999

Sauvignon Blanc Cuvée | 15.5 | –£5.00
Reserve VdP d'Oc 1999

St Veran 1997 | 13 | £5–7

VdP de l'Ardeche Rosé | 14 | –£3.50
1999, Safeway

Viognier Cuvée Reserve, | 15.5 | –£5.00
VdP d'Oc 1999

## GERMAN WHITE

Graacher Domprobst | 16 | £7–10
Riesling Spatlese, Mosel
Saar Ruwer 1996

Oppenheimer Sacktrager | 12 | £5–7
Riesling Kabinett,
Rheinhessen 1996

Peter Mertes Dry Riesling | 12 | –£3.50
1998

## GREEK RED

Mavrodaphne of Patras | 14.5 | –£5.00
NV

## HUNGARIAN RED

Chapel Hill Barrique Aged Cabernet Sauvignon, Balaton 1997, Safeway — 16 — £5.00

## HUNGARIAN WHITE

Hilltop Bianca 1999 (organic) — 14.5 — £3.50

Hungarian Chardonnay 1999, Safeway — 13 — £3.50

Irsai Oliver 1999, Safeway — 13 — £3.50

Karolyi Estate Private Reserve 1998 — 13 — £5.00

Matra Mountain Oaked Chardonnay, Nagyrede 1998, Safeway — 13 — £5.00

Matra Mountain Sauvignon Blanc 1999, Safeway — 15.5 — £5.00

Matra Mountain Unoaked Pinot Grigio 1998, Safeway — 14 — £5.00

Nagyrede Oaked Zenit 1998 — 12 — £3.50

Riverview Chardonnay 1999 — 13.5 — £5.00

Riverview Sauvignon Blanc 1999 — 15.5 — £5.00

Tokaji Aszu 5 Puttonyos 1992 (50 cl) — 13.5 — £7–10

Woodcutter's White, Neszmely 1999 — 9 — £3.50

## ITALIAN RED

Amarone delle Valpolicella Classico, Tedeschi 1995 — 16.5 — £10–13

Barolo Castello Riserva 1993 — 10 — £13–20

Farnio Rosso Piceno 1998 — 13 — £5.00

Inycon Merlot 1999 (Sicily) — 15 — £5.00

Sentiero NV — 13 — £3.50

Serina Primitivo, Tarantino, Puglia 1996 — 15 — £5.00

Tenuta San Vito 1998 (organic) — 14 — £5–7

Terriero Sangiovese di Puglia 1998 — 14.5 — £5.00

Villa Mottura Squinzano 1997 — 11 — £5.00

## ITALIAN WHITE

Arcadia Veronese Rosato 1999 — 13.5 — £5.00

Ca'Bianca Gavi 1998 — 14.5 — £5–7

Cortechiara Soave Classico 1999 — 13.5 — £5.00

Inycon Chardonnay 1999 (Sicily) — 15.5 — £5.00

Organic Soave 1999, Safeway — 12 — £5.00

Pinot Grigio Alto Adige 1998 — 16 — £5–7

Sentiero NV — 15.5 — £3.50

Sicilian Dry White 1998, Safeway (1.5 litre) — 13.5 — £3.50

Terre Cortese Verdicchio dei Castelli di Jesi 1999 — 14  −£5.00

## MONTENEGRAN RED

Monte Cheval Vranac 1994 — 10  −£5.00

## NEW ZEALAND RED

Alpha Domus Merlot/ Cabernet 1998 — 15  £7–10

Delegat's Reserve Cabernet Sauvignon Barrique Matured 1998 — 15.5  £7–10

Ninth Island Pinot Noir, Tasmania 1999 — 11  £7–10

Villa Maria Cellar Selection Cabernet/ Merlot, Hawkes Bay 1997 — 14  £7–10

## NEW ZEALAND WHITE

Delegat's Reserve Chardonnay, Barrel Fermented 1998 — 14.5  £7–10

Grove Mill Sauvignon Blanc 1999 — 16.5  £7–10

Montana Chardonnay 1999 — 15.5  £5–7

Montana Reserve Chardonnay 1998 — 16.5  £7–10

Montana Sauvignon Blanc 1999 — 15.5  £5–7

Oyster Bay Chardonnay, Marlborough 1999 — 16.5  £5–7

Oyster Bay Sauvignon Blanc 1999 — 16.5  £5–7

Villa Maria Reserve Wairau Valley Sauvignon Blanc 1999 — 17  £7–10

## PORTUGUESE RED

Bright Brothers Trincadeira Preta 1997 — 14  −£5.00

Falcoaria, Almeira 1997 — 14.5  £5–7

Miradouro, Terras do Sado 1999 — 12  −£3.50

Palmela 1998 — 14.5  −£5.00

Tamara Ribetajo 1999 — 13  −£5.00

## PORTUGUESE WHITE

Globus Ribetajo 1999 — 11  −£5.00

Tamara Ribetajo White 1999 — 14.5  −£3.50

## ROMANIAN RED

Idle Rock Merlot 1998 — 12  −£5.00

## ROMANIAN WHITE

Château Cotnari, Blanc de Cotnari 1998 — 10  −£5.00

## RUSSIAN RED

Caucasus Valley, Matrassa, Georgia 1998 — 15  −£5.00

Odessos Steppe Cabernet Sauvignon, Ukraine 1998 — 13  −£5.00

Tamada Saperavi, Georgia 1998 — 13.5  −£5.00

SAFEWAY

## SOUTH AFRICAN RED

| | | |
|---|---|---|
| Apostle's Falls Cabernet Sauvignon 1998 | 16.5 | £5–7 |
| Arniston Bay Ruby Cabernet/Merlot 1999 | 13 | –£5.00 |
| Cape Soleil Organic Pinotage 1998 | 9 | –£5.00 |
| Fairview Malbec 1999 | 16.5 | £5–7 |
| Kanonkop 'Kadette' Estate Wine 1998 | 15.5 | £5–7 |
| Kleinbosch Reserve Cabernet Sauvignon 1999 | 14 | £5–7 |
| Kleinbosch Young Vatted Pinotage, Paarl 1999 | 15 | –£5.00 |
| Landskroon Cinsault/ Shiraz, Paarl 1999 | 15.5 | £5–7 |
| Landskroon Shiraz, Paarl 1998 | 15.5 | £5–7 |
| Simsberg Pinot Noir, Paarl 1998 | 13.5 | £5–7 |
| Stellenbosch Cabernet Sauvignon 1999 | 14 | –£5.00 |
| Stellenbosch Merlot 1999 | 15.5 | –£5.00 |

## SOUTH AFRICAN WHITE

| | | |
|---|---|---|
| Douglas Green Sauvignon 2000 | 15.5 | –£5.00 |
| First Release Chardonnay 2000 | 13.5 | –£5.00 |
| First Release Chenin Blanc 2000 | 14 | –£5.00 |
| Sea of Serenity Dry Muscat 2000 | 14 | –£3.50 |
| Vale of Peace Colombard 2000 | 14 | –£5.00 |

| | | |
|---|---|---|
| Versus 1999 (1 litre) | 16 | –£5.00 |

## SPANISH RED

| | | |
|---|---|---|
| Ceremonia, Utiel Requena 1996 | 16.5 | £7–10 |
| Cruz de Piedra Garnacha Calatayud 1999 | 14 | –£5.00 |
| Navasques Navarra 1999 | 14 | –£5.00 |
| Valdepeñas Reserva Aged in Oak 1995, Safeway | 15 | –£5.00 |

## SPANISH WHITE

| | | |
|---|---|---|
| Cruz de Piedra Garnacha Macabeo 1999 | 15 | –£5.00 |
| El Velero Valdepeñas 1999 | 13.5 | –£3.50 |
| Northern Block Macabeo, Lozano Estate, La Mancha 1999 | 15 | –£3.50 |
| Orange Grove 1999 | 12 | –£5.00 |
| Vina Malea Viura 1999 | 12.5 | –£5.00 |

## USA RED

| | | |
|---|---|---|
| Echelon Merlot 1998 | 15 | £7–10 |
| Fetzer Bonterra Zinfandel 1997 (organic) | 16.5 | £7–10 |
| L A Cetto Petite Sirah 1997 | 16 | –£5.00 |
| Pacific Coast Ruby Cabernet 1998 | 15 | –£5.00 |
| Turning Leaf Cabernet Sauvignon 1997 | 12 | £5–7 |
| Turning Leaf Zinfandel 1996 | 12.5 | £5–7 |

## USA WHITE

Bonterra Muscat 1997 (half-bottle) — 15.5 £5–7

Fetzer Unoaked Chardonnay 1998 — 16 £5–7

Ironstone Chardonnay 1998 — 10 £5–7

Pacific Coast Chardonnay 1999 — 15.5 –£5.00

Pyramid Lake Napa Gamay Rosé NV — 8 –£5.00

Sutter Home Unoaked Chardonnay 1998 — 13.5 –£5.00

## FORTIFIED WINES

Amontillado, Safeway — 13 –£5.00

Blandy's Duke of Clarence Rich Madeira — 16 £7–10

Fino, Safeway — 14 –£5.00

Gonzales Byass Tio Pepe Fino Muy Sec NV — 14 £7–10

Marsala Superiore, Garibalde Dolce NV (18% vol) — 16 £5–7

Vintage Character Port, Safeway — 13 £5–7

Warre's Warrior Finest Reserve Port NV — 13 £7–10

## SPARKLING WINES

Albert Etienne Champagne Brut Rosé NV, Safeway — 13 £13–20

Albert Etienne Champagne Vintage 1993, Safeway — 13 £13–20

Canard Duchene Champagne Brut NV — 14 £13–20

Chandon Argentina NV — 15 £7–10

Chandon Australia NV — 15.5 £7–10

Chenin Brut, Vin Mousseux de Qualite (France) — 14 –£5.00

Conde de Caralt Cava Brut NV — 16.5 £5–7

Cuvée Signe Champagne, Nicolas Feuillate NV — 14.5 £13–20

Freixenet Cava Rosada Brut NV — 13.5 £5–7

Graham Beck Brut NV (South Africa) — 14 £5–7

Lambrusco Rosé Light, Safeway (4%vol) — 13.5 –£2.50

Lanson Champagne Demi-Sec Ivory Label NV — 12 £13–20

Le Bron de Monceny Chardonnay Brut NV — 12 –£5.00

Le Bron de Monceny Merlot/Gamay Brut NV — 15.5 –£5.00

Le Monferrine Moscato d'Asti 1999 (5%) — 13 –£3.50

Lindauer Brut NV (New Zealand) — 14 £7–10

Louis Roederer Champagne Brut Premier NV — 13 £20+

Merlot/Gamay Brut NV (France) — 14 –£5.00

Nicolas Feuillate
Champagne Blanc de
Blancs NV
`14` `£13–20`

Piper Heidsieck
Champagne Vintage 1990
`10` `£20+`

Pommery Brut Royal
Champagne NV
`12` `£20+`

Selection XXI,
Champagne, Nicolas
Feuillate NV
`13` `£13–20`

**SEE STOP PRESS SECTION AT END OF BOOK FOR LAST-MINUTE ADDITIONS OR UPDATES TO THIS RETAILER'S RANGE.**

# SAINSBURY'S

There have been two big events in the life of this retailer's wine department and they both involved the same man. In summer 1999 Mr Allan Cheesman, director of wine buying, chucked it in to work as marketing director for the Australian wine producers BRL Hardy. He'd been at Sainsbury's nearly three decades. The department regrouped, around the efficient and extremely likeable Mr Allan Webb (perhaps the board thought that if they replaced one Allan with another Allan, complete with two ells, no one would notice), and made some important surges forward.

However, a year later and the first Allan is back, in a newly styled job as Director of Wine, but with day-to-day responsibilities for wine buying firmly retained by the second Allan. There is a new regime at Sainsbury's helm, the purposeful Sir Peter Davis (the ex-Man from the Pru) now top tiller, and the company seems determined to make every effort to put itself back where it belongs: as Britain's number-one supermarket and food retailer. The return of Allan Cheesman in a more fluid role (ouch! unintentional punning) – a role concerned with long-term strategy, e-commerce and the like – only adds to these strengths. Too many Allans, though, spoiling the broth?

I don't think so. We shall have to wait to see the evidence of our own eyes and tongues (and pockets), but Sainsbury's has been clawing back some of its lost share of the wine market vis-à-vis Tesco and the Wal-Mart-charged Asda, and surely the return of Mr Cheesman can only enhance this progress.

The estimable Claire Gordon-Brown MW also left, deciding that seven children and a husband in advertising meant that she really wanted to spend more time on part-time business pursuits at home. This was a blow for me because she was the epitome of efficiency and good sense and my main point of contact for checking wines, readers' complaints, and many of the sundry matters which add spice, and occasional dementia, to my life. However, in time-honoured Sainsbury's fashion, the department found itself another Claire (Whitehead, this time) and the transition from one Claire t'other Claire has not upset my routine one jot.

One aspect of Sainsbury's wine shelves over the past year has been the increasing number of bargains and special offers. The following e-mail I received from a *Guardian* reader in Canterbury illustrates the nature of these bargains perfectly:

> *Having enjoyed the* Superplonk *column since it started and having been wonderfully entertained by you at a wine tasting at the Waterstone's branch in Canterbury some years past, I cannot resist the temptation, by way of a thank you, of alerting you to an offer that Sainsbury's is currently running. To my mind their Agramont Crianza 1997 would be a bargain at the original £4.99, but at £2.49 (or less if bought in bulk – £2.35-ish) it must scandalise any upright capitalist who's invested in Sainsbury's shares. I drink far too little wine and without the discernment that I ought, but it's the best sub-£5 bottle I ever glugged – even the best £5–10 bottle although I have far less experience at such heady prices. At the ludicrous price of under £2.50 it has to be nudging 19 or 20 points on the Gluck Scale. Thanks for all the splendid bottles of wine I've enjoyed as a result of your informative and, not least, entertaining column. I must cut this note short, however, Sainbury's is only a couple of hundred yards from here and I've got another half-dozen bottles to get before I reach the limit of 12 per customer . . . then again with a wife and both daughters over 18, I make that 48 bottles. Perhaps you'd better ignore this e-mail as there shan't be any left come Saturday. You're wrong about plastic corks though – I just regard the odd bad bottle as a minor, if annoying, 'conservation tax' to preserve all the superb wildlife of the Spanish cork oak forests. I do hope that you will be supporting the campaign by the RSPB to give like-minded folk the option to pick wines corked with the real thing by having it plainly stated on the bottle. With warmest regards and an apology for the closing polemic, John Cantelo.*

I replied as follows:

> *My dear sir: I remember Canterbury and not just from the time we met. I was once chased by a small group of violent squaddies, me and my beauty contest-winning girl, through the streets of Canterbury before I lost them, when I used to stay near the town on a farm as a teenager. Ah, those lost opportunities. I never saw her again after rescuing her. I was only fourteen. Alas, we shall not see the like of the Sainsbury's wine either. Too late to get it in the column, but thank you for telling me about it, though I did know it was on offer. I haven't tasted it for a while. Thank you for your kind words also about my column. As long as there is a breath left in my body, so will the column, Matthew Fort and God willing (I'll leave it to you to decide who is the most awesome editor of the two), continue. Thanks, best wishes, Malcolm Gluck.*

Sainsbury's, then, is not going to be outdone by the Morrisons and the Somerfields or even the Tescos of this world. Its bargains can rank up there with the best of them, though I balk at 20 points for that Agramont Crianza 1997 (17? perhaps 17.5?).

Behind such bargains, Sainsbury's has endured quite a year, though its problems were summed up, to my mind, by a committee-compiled new advertising campaign carrying the feeble slogan, 'Making life taste better'. You might say this of a soy sauce, or perhaps a cute brand of rock salt, but is this really the juiciest promise you can make to customers?

On other fronts, JS got back to its roots – in city centres. It announced it was to expand its 'Local' convenience concept by opening a further two hundred stores within the next three years. It eventually plans to have 1,000 such outlets, and I can testify personally to the difference such a 'Local' store has made to the life of Westbourne Grove where I live. My neighbours have been crying out for a terrific local mini-supermarket since the local Sainsbury's closed down years ago when the superstore was built a pound's bus-ride away. Sainsbury's decision to close such local smaller branches years ago and concentrate on superstores I believe was ill-judged and unfriendly – especially to elderly shoppers.

It was the accumulation of such dubious decisions which last October caused investors in Sainsbury's, according to a report in *The Sunday Times*, to accuse chairman Sir George Bull of failing to tackle the supermarket chain's problems. According to another report, this one in the *Guardian*, Archie Norman, who is credited with turning Asda around, declined an approach to take over at the Sainsbury's helm.

A little later *Retail Week* magazine reported that it was not just Mr Dino Adriano, then MD of JS, who was returning to the shop floor (to participate in a BBC2 documentary in which bosses of major companies returned to the sharp end). Some 4,000 head office staff were also being encouraged to pitch in at stores as part of a 'company bonding exercise'.

Then, in spring 2000, things really hotted up when the new chief executive, Sir Peter Davis, arrived and hardly got his feet under his desk before he pulled a very sharp axe out of his briefcase. According to *Retail Week*, JS store managers were 'shocked and amazed' when their new boss ousted directors David Bremner and Kevin McCarten only 'one week after taking up his position' as supremo. Sir Peter said he wanted to assume direct responsibility for the supermarket business. Mr Bremner had been managing director for just two months. Mr McCarten, who as marketing director had approved the least appealing TV commercials ever written for a supermarket (those dreadful episodes starring John Cleese), had been moved sideways to a position as stores director. But he was now replaced by corporate development director Robin Whitbread, a former colleague of Sir Peter during his ten-year stint at Sainsbury's between 1976 and 1986. The following month, four more senior directors left. Sir Peter was not hanging around and can take the whole credit for persuading the Mr Allan Cheesman referred to above to return.

There were, it seemed, no longer any Sainsburys running Sainsbury's. But the family fortunes are closely linked with the group's performance. Lord Sainsbury slipped from second to fourth in *The Sunday Times* list of fattest capitalist cats. The family fortunes declined by some £900 million as a result of the fall in Sainsbury's shares.

Down today, up tomorrow. The nature of the casino; the law of the bourse. And Sainsbury's had to be seen to be making more assured strides, in an attempt to up its share price, by impressing City analysts. One way to do this, thought the wily Sir Peter, would be to employ a public relations person who knows the City inside, outside and backwards and no one, further conjectured Sir Peter, knows these configurations better than Jan Shawe, Mr Allan Cheesman's wife. Versatile family, the Cheesmans (more versatile, so it has transpired, than the Sainsburys). So Sir Peter has brought this estimable woman on board as well.

In another bold move, Sainsbury's also joined the Association of Convenience Stores (ACS). Clearly, the 'Local' concept qualified it for membership though since supermarket chains began to extend their shopping hours it was pointed out that most supermarkets were already convenience stores anyway. To which I would riposte that when I see how many of my neighbours are thronging my 'Local' Sainsbury's in preference to trogging over to the Sainsbury's superstore a 23 bus-ride away, I know what convenience really means. Sainsbury's is getting back to talking to, and listening to, its customers.

Inevitably, then, it introduced a person-to-person communication facility for shop-floor staff. The so-called 'Quail' system was trialled at the Greenwich store and is now being introduced in 200 branches. The hands-free system allows supervisors to call shop-floor staff to the checkout to help with price checks or to assist customers with their packing, the aim being to cut queuing at checkouts to a minimum.

The suggestion, anonymously put forward, that Mr Cheesman might care to extend this facility to wine department staff so they could contact selected leading members of the Circle of Wine Writers when a customer had a particular tricky wine question is not, as far as I know, being actively pursued. However, with the new Sainsbury's which is slowly but surely emerging as a result of its scourging travails over the past few years, no one should put anything beyond the enterprising Mr Cheesman or the passionate Sir Peter Davis.

Sainsbury's Supermarkets Limited
Stamford House
Stamford Street
London
SE1 9LL

Tel 0800 636262 Customer Careline
www.sainsburys.co.uk

## ARGENTINIAN RED

| | | |
|---|---|---|
| Alamos Ridge Cabernet Sauvignon 1997 | 16.5 | £5–7 |
| Argento Malbec 1999 | 16 | –£5.00 |
| Bright Brothers Reserve Shiraz 1999 | 15.5 | –£5.00 |
| Bright Brothers Vistalba Malbec 1999 | 14.5 | –£5.00 |
| Catena Cabernet Sauvignon 1997 | 16.5 | £7–10 |
| First Ever Shiraz 2000 | 16 | –£5.00 |
| Mendoza Cabernet Sauvignon/Malbec NV, Sainsbury's | 15.5 | –£5.00 |
| Mendoza Country Red NV, Sainsbury's | 15 | –£3.50 |
| Santa Julia Oak Aged Tempranillo 1999 | 15.5 | –£5.00 |
| Trapiche Oak Cask Reserve Cabernet Sauvignon 1995 | 17 | £5–7 |

## ARGENTINIAN WHITE

| | | |
|---|---|---|
| Bright Brothers San Juan Chardonnay Reserve 1999 | 15.5 | –£5.00 |
| First Ever Chardonnay 2000 | 13.5 | –£5.00 |
| Mendoza Country White NV, Sainsbury's | 14.5 | –£3.50 |
| Tupungato Chardonnay NV, Sainsbury's | 13 | –£5.00 |

## AUSTRALIAN RED

| | | |
|---|---|---|
| Australian Shiraz 1999, Sainsbury's | 15.5 | –£5.00 |
| Banrock Station Mataro Shiraz NV, (3 litre box) | 14.5 | –£5.00 |
| Banrock Station Shiraz Mataro 1999 | 15 | £5–7 |
| Brown Brothers Tarrango 1999 | 13.5 | £5–7 |

Hardys Cabernet Shiraz Merlot 1998 — 15 — £5–7

Hardys Coonawarra Cabernet Sauvignon 1996 — 16 — £10–13

Hardys Stamp of Australia Shiraz Cabernet 1999 — 14 — –£5.00

Leasingham Domaine Shiraz 1996 — 15 — £7–10

Lindemans Bin 45 Cabernet Sauvignon 1999 — 15 — £5–7

Lindemans Cawarra Merlot 1999 — 12 — –£5.00

Lindemans Cawarra Merlot Shiraz Ruby Cabernet 1999 — 12 — –£5.00

Lindemans Limestone Coast Shiraz 1998 — 15.5 — £5–7

Oxford Landing Cabernet Sauvignon Shiraz 1999 — 15.5 — £5–7

Penfolds Bin 389 Cabernet Shiraz 1997 — 16.5 — £10–13

Petaluma Bridgewater Mill Shiraz 1997 — 15 — £7–10

Petaluma Coonawarra Cabernet Merlot 1997 — 16.5 — £13–20

Rosemount Estate Cabernet Merlot 1999 — 15 — £5–7

Rosemount Estate Grenache/Shiraz 1999 — 15 — £5–7

Rosemount Estate Shiraz 1998 — 15.5 — £7–10

Rosemount Estate Shiraz Cabernet 1999 — 15.5 — £5–7

Tatachilla Breakneck Creek Cabernet Sauvignon 1999 — 14 — £5–7

Tatachilla Breakneck Creek Merlot 1999 — 15 — £5–7

Tyrrells Old Winery Cabernet Merlot 1998 — 13.5 — £5–7

Wynns Coonawarra Shiraz 1997 — 16.5 — £5–7

## AUSTRALIAN WHITE

Australian Chardonnay NV, Sainsbury's — 16 — –£5.00

Brown Brothers Late Harvested Orange Muscat & Flora 1999 (half-bottle) — 16.5 — £5–7

Hardys Chardonnay Sauvignon Blanc 1999 — 15.5 — £5–7

Hardys Stamp of Australia Chardonnay Semillon (3 litre box) — 15.5 — –£5.00

Hardys Stamp of Australia Riesling Gewürztraminer 1999 — 15.5 — –£5.00

Lindemans Limestone Coast Chardonnay 1999 — 16.5 — £5–7

Penfolds Botrytis Semillon 1998 (half-bottle) — 15 — £5–7

Penfolds Koonunga Hill Chardonnay 1999 — 16 — £5–7

Penfolds Organic Chardonnay Sauvignon Blanc 1999 — 15.5 — £7–10

Penfolds Rawsons Retreat Bin 202 Riesling 1999 — 15 — –£5.00

Penfolds Rawsons Retreat Semillon/ — 15 — –£5.00

Chardonnay/Colombard
1999

Petaluma Bridgewater | 16 | £7–10
Mill Chardonnay 1998

Petaluma Chardonnay | 13 | £13–20
1998

Peter Lehmann The | 16.5 | £5–7
Barossa Semillon 1999

Rosemount Estate | 16 | £5–7
Diamond Label
Chardonnay 1999

Rosemount Estate Show | 14 | £7–10
Reserve Chardonnay
1999

Stowells of Chelsea | 15.5 | –£5.00
Australian Chardonnay
NV (3 litre box)

Tatachilla Breakneck | 16 | –£5.00
Creek Chardonnay 1999

Tyrrells Old Winery | 14 | £5–7
Chardonnay 1999

## BULGARIAN RED

Bulgarian Cabernet | 15.5 | –£3.50
Sauvignon, Sainsbury's (3
litre box)

Bulgarian Country Dry | 14.5 | –£3.50
Red, Russe, Sainsbury's
(1.5 litre)

Bulgarian Merlot NV, | 15.5 | –£3.50
Sainsbury's

Domaine Boyar Premium | 14 | –£5.00
Oak Barrel Aged Merlot
1997

Domaine Boyar Premium | 14.5 | –£5.00
Reserve Cabernet
Sauvignon 1997

Domaine Boyar Premium | 15 | –£5.00
Reserve Merlot 1997

## CHILEAN RED

35 Sur Cabernet | 17 | –£5.00
Sauvignon 1999

Chilean Cabernet Merlot | 16 | –£5.00
NV, Sainsbury's (3 litre
box)

Chilean Merlot, | 16.5 | –£5.00
Sainsbury's

Chilean Red, Sainsbury's | 13 | –£5.00

La Palma Merlot Gran | 17 | £7–10
Reserva 1998

Los Robles Carmenere | 16.5 | –£5.00
1999

MontGras Cabernet | 15.5 | £5–7
Sauvignon Reserva 1998

MontGras Carmenere | 14 | £5–7
Reserva 1998

MontGras Single | 16 | £5–7
Vineyard Syrah 1999

MontGras Single | 15 | £5–7
Vineyard Zinfandel 1999

Terra Mater Zinfandel | 16.5 | –£5.00
Shiraz 1999

Valdivieso Malbec 1998 | 16 | –£5.00

Valdivieso Malbec | 16.5 | £7–10
Reserve 1998

Valdivieso Merlot 1999 | 15.5 | –£5.00

## CHILEAN WHITE

35 Sur Sauvignon Blanc | 15.5 | –£5.00
1999

| | | |
|---|---|---|
| Canepa Winemaker's Selection Gewürztraminer 1999 | 16.5 | −£5.00 |
| Casablanca Sauvignon Blanc 1998 | 14.5 | −£5.00 |
| Chilean Cabernet Sauvignon Rosé NV, Sainsbury's | 15.5 | −£5.00 |
| Chilean Chardonnay NV, Sainsbury's | 15 | −£5.00 |
| Chilean Sauvignon Blanc NV, Sainsbury's | 15.5 | −£5.00 |
| Chilean Semillon Sauvignon NV, Sainsbury's (3 litre box) | 13.5 | −£3.50 |
| La Palmeria Chardonnay Gran Reserva 1998 | 15.5 | £7–10 |
| MontGras Reserve Chardonnay 1998 | 15 | £5–7 |
| Santa Carolina Chardonnay 1999 | 16.5 | −£5.00 |
| Stowells Chilean Sauvignon Blanc NV (3 litre box) | 15.5 | −£3.50 |

## ENGLISH WHITE

| | | |
|---|---|---|
| Denbies Estate English table Wine NV | 10 | −£5.00 |

## FRENCH RED

| | | |
|---|---|---|
| Beaujolais NV, Sainsbury's | 13.5 | −£5.00 |
| Beaujolais Villages Les Roches Grillees 1999 | 12 | £5–7 |
| Bordeaux Rouge, Sainsbury's | 13 | −£3.50 |

| | | |
|---|---|---|
| Cabernet Sauvignon d'Oc NV, Sainsbury's | 15.5 | −£3.50 |
| Cabernet Sauvignon d'Oc NV, Sainsbury's (3 litre box) | 14.5 | −£3.50 |
| Château Beaumont Cru Bourgeois, Haut Medoc 1995 | 15 | £13–20 |
| Château Clement-Pichon, Haut-Medoc 1995 | 13 | £10–13 |
| Château Coufran Cru Bourgeois, Haut Medoc 1996 | 13 | £10–13 |
| Château de la Grande Gandiole Châteauneuf-du-Pape 1997 | 16.5 | £10–13 |
| Château de la Tour Bordeaux Rouge 1998 | 14 | £5–7 |
| Château Haut Bergey, Pessac-Leognan 1995 | 14 | £10–13 |
| Château Haut de la Pierriere Côtes de Castillon 1998 | 16 | £5–7 |
| Château Memoires, Bordeaux Rouge 1996 | 14 | £5–7 |
| Château Semeillan Mazeau Cru Bourgeois, Listrac 1996 | 14 | £13–20 |
| Château Tassin Premieres Côtes de Bordeaux 1999 | 15 | −£5.00 |
| Châteauneuf-du-Pape Château de la Grande Gardiole 1998 | 17 | £10–13 |
| Châteauneuf-du-Pape, Domaine Michel Bernard 1997 | 15.5 | £10–13 |

| | | | |
|---|---|---|---|
| Chinon Domaine de du Colombier 1999 | 16.5 | -£5.00 | |
| Claret Cuvée Prestige NV, Sainsbury's | 14 | -£5.00 | |
| Claret, Sainsbury's | 14.5 | -£5.00 | |
| Classic Selection Brouilly 1997, Sainsbury's | 14 | £5-7 | |
| Classic Selection Châteauneuf-du-Pape 1998, Sainsbury's | 15 | £7-10 | |
| Classic Selection St Emilion 1996, Sainsbury's | 14 | £7-10 | |
| Clos Magne Figeac, St Emilion 1997 | 16 | £7-10 | |
| Clos Rene, Pomerol 1994 | 16.5 | £20+ | |
| Côtes du Rhône NV, Sainsbury's | 13.5 | -£3.50 | |
| Crozes Hermitage Petite Ruche 1997 | 15.5 | £7-10 | |
| Cuvee Prestige Côtes du Rhône 1998, Sainsbury's | 15 | -£5.00 | |
| French Revolution Le Rouge 1999 | 16 | -£5.00 | |
| Hautes Côtes de Nuits 1998 | 12 | £7-10 | |
| Hautes Côtes de Nuits Dames Huguettes 1998 | 13.5 | £7-10 | |
| Jacques Frelin Organic Crozes Hermitage 1998 | 13 | £7-10 | |
| La Chasse du Pape Côtes du Rhône 1998 | 16.5 | -£5.00 | |
| La Demoiselle de Sociando Mallet, Haut Medoc 1996 | 10 | £13-20 | |

| | | | |
|---|---|---|---|
| LPA Côtes de St Mont 1997 | 14.5 | -£5.00 | |
| Marsannay Domaine Bertagna 1998 | 15 | £7-10 | |
| Mercurey Clos la Marche 1997 | 13 | £13-20 | |
| Merlot VdP d'Oc NV, Sainsbury's (1.5 litre) | 15.5 | £5-7 | |
| Merlot VdP de la Cite de Carcassonne, Caroline de Beaulieu 1999 | 16.5 | -£5.00 | |
| Minervois, Sainsbury's | 15 | -£3.50 | |
| Old Git Grenache Syrah 1999 | 15.5 | -£5.00 | |
| Red Burgundy NV, Sainsbury's | 12 | £5-7 | |
| Santenay, Château de Mercey 1996 | 12 | £10-13 | |
| Stowells Claret NV (3 litre box) | 10 | -£5.00 | |
| Stowells of Chelsea Merlot VdP d'Oc (3 litre box) | 15 | -£3.50 | |
| Syrah VdP d'Oc NV, Sainsbury's | 15 | -£3.50 | |
| Valreas Domaine de la Grande Bellane 1998 (organic) | 16.5 | £5-7 | |
| Vieux Château Landon, Medoc 1996 | 13 | £7-10 | |
| Vin de Pays de l'Aude Rouge, Sainsbury's | 16 | -£3.50 | |
| Vin de Pays des Bouches du Rhône NV, Sainsbury's | 14.5 | -£3.50 | |

Vin Rouge de France NV, `13` −£3.50
Sainsbury's (3 litre box)

Vougeot Domaine `13` £13–20
Bertagna 1995

## FRENCH WHITE

Alsace Gewürztraminer `16.5` £5–7
1999, Sainsbury's

Blanc Anjou, Medium `12` −£3.50
Dry, Sainsbury's

Bordeaux Blanc de `15.5` −£5.00
Ginestet 1998

Bordeaux Blanc, `14.5` −£3.50
Sainsbury's

Bourgogne Blanc, Louis `14` £5–7
Max 1998

Cabernet Rosé de Loire, `13.5` −£5.00
Lurton 1999

Chablis 1er Cru Les `14` £13–20
Fourchaumes 1998

Chardonnay VdP d'Oc, `15.5` −£5.00
Sainsbury's (3 litre box)

Chardonnay VdP du `14.5` −£5.00
Jardin de la France,
Lurton 1999

Château Carsin, Cadillac `16` £5–7
1998 (half-bottle)

Château du Sours Rosé `15` £5–7
1999

Classic Selection `16` −£5.00
Muscadet Sevre et Maine
1999, Sainsbury

Classic Selection Pouilly `13.5` £7–10
Fume 1999, Sainsbury's

Classic Selection Sancerre `13.5` £7–10
1999, Sainsbury's

Classic Selection Vouvray `15` £5–7
1999, Sainsbury

Condrieu Guigal 1998 `15.5` £13–20

Domaine de la Perriere `13` £7–10
Sancerre 1999

Domaine Leonce Cuisset, `15` £7–10
Saussignac 1996

French Revolution Le `13` −£5.00
Blanc 1999

La Baume Sauvignon `15` −£5.00
Blanc, VdP d'Oc 1999

LPA Cotes de St Mont `15` −£5.00
Blanc 1998

Macon Chardonnay, `16` £5–7
Domaine les Ecuyers
1998

Mercurey Blanc Domaine `13` £13–20
la Marche les Rochelles
1998

Montagny 'Les Rosiers' `14` £7–10
1998

Muscadet de Sevre et `13` −£3.50
Maine sur Lie NV,
Sainsbury's (3 litre box)

Muscadet Sevre et Maine `14` −£5.00
Sur Lie, La Goelette 1999

Orchid Vale Medium `13.5` −£5.00
French Chardonnay
Grenache Blanc, VdP
d'Oc 1999

Petit Chablis 1999 `13` £5–7

Pouilly Fume, Cuvée `14.5` £7–10
Pierre Louis 1999

Reserve St Marc `16` −£5.00
Sauvignon Blanc, VdP
d'Oc 1999

| | | |
|---|---|---|
| Touraine Sauvignon Blanc 1999 | 15.5 | –£5.00 |
| Vin Blanc de France, Sainsbury's (3 litre box) | 12 | –£3.50 |
| Vin de Pays de l'Aude Blanc, Sainsbury's | 15 | –£3.50 |
| Vin de Pays des Côtes de Gascogne NV, Sainsbury's | 15 | –£3.50 |
| Vin de Pays des Côtes de Gascogne, Sainsbury's (3 litre box) | 15 | –£3.50 |
| Vouvray la Couronne des Plantagenets 1999 | 15 | –£5.00 |
| White Burgundy NV, Sainsbury's | 14 | £5–7 |

## GERMAN WHITE

| | | |
|---|---|---|
| Bereich Bernkastel Riesling 1997 | 12 | –£3.50 |
| Dr Loosen Wehlener Sonnenuhr Riesling Spatlese 1995 | 13 | £13–20 |
| Fire Mountain Riesling 1999 | 13.5 | –£5.00 |
| Hock NV, Sainsbury's | 11.5 | –£3.50 |
| Hock, Sainsbury's (3 litre box) | 14.5 | –£3.50 |
| Kendermann Dry Riesling 1999 | 13 | –£5.00 |
| Liebfraumilch, Sainsbury's (3 litre box) | 14 | –£3.50 |
| Mosel, Sainsbury's | 14 | –£3.50 |
| Piesporter Michelsberg, Sainsbury's | 12 | –£3.50 |

| | | |
|---|---|---|
| Zeltinger Himmelreich Riesling Kabinett 1997 | 15 | –£5.00 |

## GREEK RED

| | | |
|---|---|---|
| Kourtakis Vin de Crete Red 1997 | 13 | –£3.50 |

## HUNGARIAN WHITE

| | | |
|---|---|---|
| Bin 66 Hilltop Gewürztraminer 1999 | 14 | –£5.00 |
| Hilltop Chardonnay Bin 058 1997 | 16 | –£5.00 |
| Hungarian Cabernet Sauvignon Rosé NV, Sainsbury's | 11 | –£3.50 |
| Zenit Sefir 1999 | 13.5 | –£5.00 |

## ITALIAN RED

| | | |
|---|---|---|
| Amano Primitivo Puglia 1999 | 15.5 | £5–7 |
| Allora Primitivo 1998 | 15 | –£5.00 |
| Amano Primitivo 1999 | 15.5 | £5–7 |
| Barolo Cantine Rocca Ripalta 1995 | 15 | £10–13 |
| Bright Brothers Roman Vines Negroamaro Cabernet Sauvignon 1999 | 15 | –£5.00 |
| Caramia Salice Salentino Riserva 1997 | 16.5 | £5–7 |
| Classic Selection Chianti Classico 1997, Sainsbury's | 15.5 | £5–7 |
| Emporio Nero d'Avola Merlot 1999 | 14 | –£5.00 |

| | | |
|---|---|---|
| Inycon Syrah 1999 (Sicily) | 16.5 | −£5.00 |
| L'Arco Cabernet Franc, Friuli 1998 | 14 | −£5.00 |
| Lambrusco Rosso, Sainsbury's | 10 | −£3.50 |
| Merlot delle Venezie, Connubio 1998 | 16.5 | −£5.00 |
| Montepulciano d'Abruzzo 1999, Sainsbury's | 14 | −£5.00 |
| Montepulciano d'Abruzzo, Connubio 1997 | 15.5 | −£5.00 |
| Morellino di Scansano Riserva 1997 | 16 | £7–10 |
| Natio Organic Chianti, Cecchi 1998 | 13.5 | £5–7 |
| Nero d'Avola IGT Sicilia, Connubio 1998 | 15.5 | −£5.00 |
| Rosso di Provincia di Verona NV, Sainsbury's | 15 | −£3.50 |
| Sangiovese di Toscana, Cecchi 1999 | 13.5 | −£5.00 |
| Serrano Rosso Conero 1999 | 15.5 | −£5.00 |
| Sicilia Red, Sainsbury's | 15 | −£3.50 |
| Stowells Montepulciano del Molise NV (3 litre box) | 12 | −£5.00 |
| Teuzzo Chianti Classico, Cecchi 1997 | 16 | £5–7 |
| The Full Montepulciano NV | 13 | −£5.00 |
| Valpantena Ripasso Valpolicella, Connubio 1997 | 14 | £5–7 |
| Valpolicella NV, Sainsbury's | 13.5 | −£3.50 |
| Valpolicella, Sainsbury's (3 litre box) | 12 | −£3.50 |
| Via Nova Primitivo 1998 | 15 | −£5.00 |
| Zagara Nero d'Avola Sangiovese 1999 | 14 | −£5.00 |

## ITALIAN WHITE

| | | |
|---|---|---|
| Bianco di Provincia di Verona NV, Sainsbury's | 14 | −£3.50 |
| Cecchi Tuscan White NV | 13.5 | −£5.00 |
| Classic Selection Frascati Superiore 1998, Sainsbury's | 13.5 | £5–7 |
| Connubio Pinot Grigio delle Venezie 1999 | 14.5 | −£5.00 |
| Enofriulia Pinot Grigio Collio 1998 | 16 | £5–7 |
| Inycon Chardonnay 1999 (Sicily) | 15.5 | −£5.00 |
| Lambrusco dell'Emilia Bianco. Sainsbury's | 12 | −£5.00 |
| Lambrusco Rosato, Sainsbury's | 13 | −£3.50 |
| Lambrusco Secco, Sainsbury's | 11 | −£3.50 |
| Piave Organic Pinot Grigio 1999 | 16 | −£5.00 |
| Pinot Bianco delle Venezie 1999, Sainsbury | 14 | −£5.00 |
| Sartori Organic Soave 1999 | 13.5 | −£5.00 |
| Sicilian White, Sainsbury's | 13.5 | −£3.50 |

| | | |
|---|---|---|
| Soave, Sainsbury's | 15.5 | −£3.50 |
| Soave, Sainsbury's (3 litre box) | 15 | −£3.50 |
| Verdicchio dei Castelli di Jesi Classico 1999, Sainsbury | 14.5 | −£5.00 |
| Villa Bianchi Verdicchio 1999 | 13 | −£5.00 |

## NEW ZEALAND RED

| | | |
|---|---|---|
| Shingle Peak Pinot Nor 1999 | 13 | £5–7 |

## NEW ZEALAND WHITE

| | | |
|---|---|---|
| Cooks Sauvignon Blanc, Marlborough 1998 | 13.5 | −£5.00 |
| Grove Mill Sauvignon Blanc 1999 | 16.5 | £7–10 |
| Millton New Zealand Organic Chardonnay 1999 | 13.5 | £5–7 |
| Montana 'B' Brancott Estate Sauvignon Blanc 1998 | 16 | £10–13 |
| Montana Reserve Barrique Fermented Chardonnay 1998 | 16 | £7–10 |
| Montana Sauvignon Blanc 1998 | 16 | £5–7 |
| Shingle Peak Chardonnay, Marlborough 1998 | 16.5 | £5–7 |
| Shingle Peak Pinot Gris, Marlborough 1999 | 16.5 | £5–7 |
| Shingle Peak Sauvignon Blanc, Marlborough 1998 | 16 | £5–7 |

| | | |
|---|---|---|
| Stoneleigh Vineyard Chardonnay, Marlborough 1997 | 15.5 | £5–7 |
| The Sanctuary Chardonnay, Marlborough 1997 | 16 | £5–7 |
| The Sanctuary Sauvignon Blanc 1999 | 15.5 | £5–7 |
| Villa Maria East Coast Chardonnay 1998 | 14 | £5–7 |
| Villa Maria Private Bin Sauvignon, Marlborough 1998 | 17 | £5–7 |

## PORTUGUESE RED

| | | |
|---|---|---|
| Quinta de Bons-Ventos 1999 | 14 | −£5.00 |
| Ramada 1999 | 13 | −£3.50 |
| Segada Trincadeira Preta-Castelao 1999 | 14 | −£5.00 |
| Senda do Vale Trincadeira Cabernet Sauvignon 1999 | 15.5 | £5–7 |

## PORTUGUESE WHITE

| | | |
|---|---|---|
| Portuguese Rosé, Sainsbury's | 13.5 | −£3.50 |
| Vinho Verde, Sainsbury's | 13.5 | −£3.50 |

## ROMANIAN WHITE

| | | |
|---|---|---|
| Romanian Merlot Rosé NV, Sainsbury's | 14 | −£3.50 |

## SOUTH AFRICAN RED

| | | |
|---|---|---|
| African Legend Shiraz The Quivering Spear 1998 | 15 | −£5.00 |
| Bellingham Merlot 1998 | 16 | £5–7 |
| Bellingham Premium Pinotage 1998 | 14 | £7–10 |
| Bellingham Shiraz 1998 | 16 | £5–7 |
| Clos Malverne Cabernet Pinotage 1998 | 15 | £5–7 |
| Fairview Carignan 1999 | 15.5 | £5–7 |
| Fairview Pinotage 1999 | 17 | £5–7 |
| Hidden Valley Limited Release Pinotage 1997 | 13 | £13–20 |
| Kumala Cabernet Sauvignon Shiraz 1998 | 16 | −£5.00 |
| Middlevlei Shiraz 1999 | 15.5 | £5–7 |
| Milton Grove Cabernet Franc 1999 | 16 | £5–7 |
| Railroad Cabernet Sauvignon Shiraz 1999 | 15.5 | −£5.00 |
| South African Cabernet Sauvignon NV, Sainsbury's | 15.5 | −£5.00 |
| South African Pinotage NV, Sainsbury's | 16 | −£5.00 |
| South African Red NV, Sainsbury's | 15 | −£3.50 |
| South African Reserve Selection Pinotage 1998, Sainsbury's | 16.5 | £5–7 |
| Spice Route Andrew's Hope Cabernet Merlot 1999 | 16.5 | £5–7 |
| Spice Route Flagship Merlot 1998 | 17 | £13–20 |
| Stowells of Chelsea Cinsault Pinotage Sainsbury (3 litre box) | 15.5 | −£5.00 |
| Winds of Change Pinotage Cabernet Sauvignon 1998 | 16 | −£5.00 |
| Yonder Hill Inanda 1997 | 17 | £7–10 |

## SOUTH AFRICAN WHITE

| | | |
|---|---|---|
| Call of the African Eagle Chardonnay 1999 | 17 | £5–7 |
| Gioya Kgeisje Chardonnay/Sauvignon 2000 | 14 | −£5.00 |
| Rhona Muscadel 1996 | 16 | £5–7 |
| South African Chardonnay NV, Sainsbury's | 14 | −£5.00 |
| South African Chenin Blanc NV, Sainsbury's | 15 | −£3.50 |
| South African Chenin Blanc NV, Sainsbury's (3 litre box) | 14.5 | −£3.50 |
| South African Colombard NV, Sainsbury's | 14 | −£5.00 |
| South African Medium White NV, Sainsbury's | 13 | −£3.50 |
| South African Reserve Selection Chardonnay 1999, Sainsbury's | 15.5 | £5–7 |
| Springfield Estate Methode Ancienne Chardonnay 1999 | 15.5 | £10–13 |
| Vergelegen Chardonnay 1999 | 16 | £5–7 |
| Vergelegen Chardonnay Reserve 1998 | 16.5 | £7–10 |

| Vergelegen Reserve Sauvignon Blanc 1999 | 17.5 | £7–10 |
|---|---|---|
| Waterside White Chardonnay Colombard 1999 | 15.5 | –£5.00 |

## SPANISH RED

| Alteza 600 Old Vines Garnacha NV | 16 | –£5.00 |
|---|---|---|
| Alteza 750 Tempranillo NV | 16 | –£5.00 |
| Alteza 775 Tempranillo Cabernet Sauvignon NV | 16 | –£5.00 |
| Classic Selection Rioja Reserva 1996, Sainsbury's | 12 | £7–10 |
| Dama de Toro 1999 | 16.5 | –£5.00 |
| Enate Cabernet Merlot 1998 | 16.5 | £5–7 |
| Jumilla NV, Sainsbury's | 15.5 | –£5.00 |
| Marques de Vitoria Rioja Crianza 1995 (organic) | 13.5 | £7–10 |
| Navarra NV, Sainsbury's | 16 | –£5.00 |
| Navarra Tempranillo/ Cabernet Sauvignon Crianza 1995, Sainsbury's | 16 | –£5.00 |
| Old Vines Garnacha, Navarra NV | 15.5 | –£5.00 |
| Stowells of Chelsea Tempranillo NV (3 litre box) | 13 | –£3.50 |
| Torres Gran Sangre de Toro 1996 | 16 | £5–7 |
| Valencia Oak Aged NV, Sainsbury's | 13.5 | –£5.00 |
| Vina Albali Gran Reserva 1993 | 15 | £5–7 |

| Vina Ardanza Rioja Reserva 1994 | 13.5 | £10–13 |
|---|---|---|

## SPANISH WHITE

| Dry White NV, Sainsbury's | 14 | –£3.50 |
|---|---|---|
| Lagar de Cervera 1999 | 13 | £7–10 |
| Oaked Viura, Alteza 640 NV | 15.5 | –£5.00 |

## URUGUAYAN RED

| Bright Brothers Merlot/ Tannat 1998 | 14 | –£5.00 |
|---|---|---|

## USA RED

| Bonterra Cabernet Sauvignon 1997 (organic) | 17 | £7–10 |
|---|---|---|
| Bonterra Zinfandel 1997 (organic) | 16 | £7–10 |
| Coastal Pinot Noir, Robert Mondavi 1996 | 16 | £7–10 |
| Eagle Peak Merlot, Fetzer Vineyards 1998 | 15.5 | £5–7 |
| Fetzer Valley Oaks Cabernet Sauvignon 1997 | 15.5 | £5–7 |
| Ironstone Vineyards Cabernet Sauvignon 1997 | 10 | £5–7 |
| Mondavi Coastal Merlot 1997 | 16 | £7–10 |
| Stonybrook Vineyard Merlot 1998 | 16 | £5–7 |
| Sutter Home Merlot 1998 | 13 | –£5.00 |
| Sutter Home Pinot Noir 1997 | 13 | £5–7 |

| | | |
|---|---|---|
| Turning Leaf Cabernet Sauvignon 1997 | 12 | £5–7 |
| Turning Leaf Zinfandel 1996 | 12.5 | £5–7 |

## USA WHITE

| | | |
|---|---|---|
| Bonterra Chardonnay 1998 (organic) | 15.5 | £7–10 |
| Bonterra Muscat (half-bottle) (organic) | 15.5 | £5–7 |
| Coastal Chardonnay, Robert Mondavi 1997 | 17 | £7–10 |
| Fetzer Barrel Select Chardonnay 1997 | 15 | £7–10 |
| Gallo Colombard NV | 11 | –£5.00 |
| Stonybrook Vineyards Chardonnay 1997 | 16 | –£5.00 |

## FORTIFIED WINES

| | | |
|---|---|---|
| Blandy's Duke of Clarence Madeira | 15.5 | £7–10 |
| Gonzales Byass Matusalem NV (half-bottle) | 17.5 | £10–13 |
| Medium Dry Montilla, Sainsbury's | 13.5 | –£3.50 |
| Pale Cream Montilla, Sainsbury's | 14 | –£3.50 |
| Pale Cream Sherry, Sainsbury's | 15.5 | –£5.00 |
| Pale Dry Amontillado, Sainsbury's | 15 | –£5.00 |
| Pale Dry Fino Sherry, Sainsbury's | 15 | £5–7 |

| | | |
|---|---|---|
| Pale Dry Manzanilla, Sainsbury's | 15 | –£5.00 |
| Pale Dry Montilla, Sainsbury's | 14 | –£3.50 |
| Ruby Port, Sainsbury's | 13 | £5–7 |
| Sainsbury's LBV Port 1992 | 15.5 | £7–10 |
| Tawny Port, Sainsbury's | 13.5 | £5–7 |
| Ten Year Old Tawny Port, Sainsbury's | 15 | £7–10 |

## SPARKLING WINES

| | | |
|---|---|---|
| Asti, Sainsbury's (Italy) | 13 | –£5.00 |
| Australian Sparkling Wine, Sainsbury's | 13 | –£5.00 |
| Blanc de Noirs Champagne NV, Sainsbury's | 16 | £10–13 |
| Cava Brut NV, Sainsbury's | 16.5 | –£5.00 |
| Cava Rosado Brut, Sainsbury's | 15 | –£5.00 |
| Champagne Canard Duchene NV | 14 | £13–20 |
| Champagne Chanoine 1990 | 15.5 | £13–20 |
| Champagne Charles Heidsieck Mis en Cave 1995 | 14.5 | £20+ |
| Champagne Demi-Sec NV, Sainsbury's | 14 | £10–13 |
| Champagne Jeanmaire Brut 1990 | 14 | £13–20 |
| Champagne Krug Grande Cuvée | 10 | £20+ |

| | | |
|---|---|---|
| Champagne Lanson Black Label Brut NV | 13.5 | £13–20 |
| Champagne Laurent Perrier NV | 13.5 | £20+ |
| Champagne Louis Roederer NV | 13 | £20+ |
| Champagne Nicolas Feuillate Premier Cru NV | 14 | £13–20 |
| Champagne Perrier-Jouet NV | 14 | £13–20 |
| Champagne Pol Roger 1990 | 13 | £20+ |
| Champagne Pommery Brut Royal NV | 13 | £20+ |
| Champagne Premier Cru Extra Dry, Sainsbury's | 15 | £13–20 |
| Champagne Veuve Clicquot Grande Dame 1990 | 12 | £20+ |
| Chardonnay Brut, Methode Traditionelle, Sainsbury's (France) | 15 | £5–7 |
| Freixenet Cava Rosada NV | 13.5 | £5–7 |
| Grand Cru Millennium Champagne 1995, Sainsbury's | 13 | £13–20 |
| Hardys Nottage Hill Chardonnay Brut 1998 | 15 | £5–7 |
| Hardys Stamp of Australia Chardonnay/ Pinot Noir Brut NV | 14 | £5–7 |
| Jacobs Creek Chardonnay/Pinot Noir Brut NV (Australia) | 13 | £5–7 |
| Lindauer Special Reserve NV (New Zealand) | 16 | £7–10 |
| Millennium Vintage Cava 1997, Sainsbury's | 13 | £5–7 |
| Mumm Champagne Brut NV | 13 | £13–20 |
| Piper Heidsieck Brut NV | 15 | £13–20 |
| Sekt, Medium Dry, Sainsbury's (Germany) | 13 | –£5.00 |
| Vin Mousseux Brut, Sainsbury's (France) | 13 | –£5.00 |
| Vintage Blanc de Blancs Champagne 1993, Sainsbury's | 14 | £13–20 |

**SEE STOP PRESS SECTION AT END OF BOOK FOR LAST-MINUTE ADDITIONS OR UPDATES TO THIS RETAILER'S RANGE.**

# SOMERFIELD/KWIK SAVE

The current range at Mrs Mount's supermarket (I prefer this appellation to Somerfield or Kwik Save) is the finest it has ever been. Just look at the ratings of the wines which follow. Yet this is a woman who operates from home Mondays and Thursdays so she can spend time with her two children. Never, in all my time wine range tasting and commentating, has a supermarket more successfully gathered together, at one time, such a tasty set of wine ranges from all countries, covering all styles of wines at several prices points (though the £3.29 to £4.99 bracket dominates, as it must).

Ange, my readers love you (I cannot pretend to be unmoved myself). And not just because of the abundance of sanely priced, richly fruity wines but also because of the monthly wine offers where that beast I thought would become extinct a decade ago still breathes: the £1.99 and £2.29 bottle.

In spite of Mrs Mount's heroic efforts, Somerfield has a fight to stay competitive. In 1999 it announced plans to woo 'one million time-poor consumers' with the launch of its 24–7 home-shopping service to be backed by a multi-million-pound marketing campaign. Dinner-for-two, wine and beer selections and other specially grouped products are featured as '24–7' solutions, featured prominently in 24–7 catalogues to be distributed to a million households. This Somerfield offer carried some 5,000 lines and made it the first supermarket home-shopping offer which could be accessed by the internet, interactive TV, telephone or fax. How's it feel to be the Queen of the Couch Potato wine market, Angela?

Famously, Somerfield purchased Kwik Save in 1999. *Off Licence News* reported that Somerfield was bidding to arrest the decline in the fortunes of this new acquisition by redesigning the chain's off-licence sections. Seven key Kwik Save stores were quickly revamped and some 140 further ones were scheduled for change over the year. The overhaul features a greater range of Somerfield's own label wines together with a bigger selection of beers and spirits.

At this time, Mrs Mount was already sowing the seeds of the ranges we now see on shelf. She doubled the store's range of wines from Iberia and introduced a number of new additions from South America in a bid to cater for changing tastes in drinking patterns. Red wines from Spain and Portugal priced between £3.50 and £5 were among some forty newcomers and the newer vintages of these, as you can readily see from the ratings which follow, give Somerfield and Kwik Save one of the most competitive wine ranges around.

Yet in October 1999 Somerfield was denying a report in the *Independent on Sunday* that it was considering selling off all its stores and reinventing itself as a home-delivery company. Somerfield was reportedly looking for a friendly takeover or a merger. *Retail Week* magazine reported that discount chains such as Aldi, Netto and Lidl would be the most likely buyers for the 350 Kwik Save stores now put on the market by Somerfield. These stores, 'in secondary and tertiary' locations, so it was said, are of interest only to the toughest of the so-called 'hard' discounters.

Come the dawn of the new millennium, Somerfield insisted that its tighter focus on smaller stores and home shopping guaranteed it a long-term future. This statement came as the retailer announced a halving of its interim pre-tax profits from £113.8 million to £63.9 million.

In March 2000 it launched Somerfield Link, a free delivery service to village shops and small stores around the UK. The scheme, similar to the Sainsbury's SAVE initiative, will offer some 12,000 lines and hardly endear it to the likes of the Spar franchised chain which can't, where wine is concerned, compete with supermarket pricing. At this time, speculation was rife about a possible takeover of Somerfield. Venture capitalists, buyout specialists and banks, and other assorted vultures, were all rumoured to be looking at ways to pick the bones of the ailing retailer (when, of course, it was very far from being dead). Somerfield admitted that it had received offers but nothing more.

Alan Smith then took over from David Simons as chief executive. Mr Smith was formerly chief executive of Punch Taverns and managing director of Kingfisher's B&Q and Superdrug chains, so his pedigree was, and is, excellent. He quickly announced a reprieve for the 350 Kwik Save stores put up for sale by his predecessor, planning to resurrect the discount chain and giving it its own management team under managing director Simon Hughes. The programme to convert some 400 Kwik Save stores to the Somerfield format was also cancelled with only a small number of stores 'in certain locations' being converted to the Somerfield identity.

Somerfield now conducted an in-depth review of its 24–7 home-shopping business which could result in its being sold off. On the other hand, the review could lead to more investment for 24–7 or the offer of equity to strategic partners in the scheme. At the time of writing, it is not certain which way this particular nut will be cracked.

Yet through all these twists and turns in the Somerfield saga, Mrs Angela Mount enthusiastically beavers away, putting all these terrific wine ranges together. I simply don't know how she does it. Frankly, I can't for the life of me understand why a competitor doesn't snap her up, put her on the board as Director of Off-Licensed Trading, give her a yellow Ferrari, and pay her £250,000 a year. A day and a half a fortnight should be sufficient I would have thought, not counting, of course, all those trips to the south of France, Sydney and Adelaide, Cape Town, Santiago, Beunos Aires, Puglia and La Mancha. Let's hope the children like travelling.

Somerfield/Kwik Save
Somerfield House
Hawkfield Business Park
Whitchurch Lane
Bristol
BS14 0TJ

Tel 0117 935 6669 Customer Services
Fax 0117 978 0629
www.somerfield.co.uk

## ARGENTINIAN RED

| | | |
|---|---|---|
| Argentine Tempranillo 1999, Somerfield | 16 | −£5.00 |
| Bright Brothers San Juan Cabernet Sauvignon 1999 | 16.5 | −£5.00 |
| First Ever Shiraz 2000 | 16 | −£5.00 |
| Santa Julia Sangiovese 1999, Somerfield | 15.5 | −£5.00 |
| Trivento Syrah 1999 | 15.5 | −£5.00 |

## ARGENTINIAN WHITE

| | | |
|---|---|---|
| Argentine Chardonnay 1999, Somerfield | 16 | −£5.00 |
| Bright Brothers Argentine Chardonnay 1999, Somerfield | 16 | −£5.00 |
| Bright Brothers San Juan Chardonnay Reserve 1999 | 15.5 | −£5.00 |
| First Ever Chardonnay 2000 | 13.5 | −£5.00 |
| Santa Julia Syrah Rosé 2000 | 15.5 | −£5.00 |

## AUSTRALIAN RED

Australian Cabernet Sauvignon 1999, Somerfield — 15.5 — −£5.00

Australian Dry Red 1999, Somerfield — 14.5 — −£5.00

Australian Shiraz Cabernet 1999, Somerfield — 15 — −£5.00

Banrock Station Shiraz Mataro 1999 — 15 — −£5.00

Hardys Cabernet Shiraz Merlot 1998 — 15 — £5–7

Hardys Nottage Hill Cabernet Sauvignon/ Shiraz 1999 — 16.5 — £5–7

Hardys Stamp Shiraz Cabernet 1999 — 14 — −£5.00

Penfolds Bin 28 Kalimna Shiraz 1997 — 17 — £7–10

Penfolds Coonawarra Bin 128 Shiraz 1996 — 15.5 — £7–10

Penfolds Koonunga Hill Shiraz Cabernet Sauvignon 1998 — 16.5 — £5–7

Rosemount Estate Shiraz 1998 — 15.5 — £7–10

Rosemount Estate Shiraz Cabernet 1998 — 15.5 — £5–7

## AUSTRALIAN WHITE

Australian Chardonnay 1999, Somerfield — 15.5 — −£5.00

Australian Semillon/ Chardonnay 1999, Somerfield — 14.5 — −£5.00

Banrock Station Chardonnay 1999 — 14 — −£5.00

Banrock Station Colombard Chardonnay 1999 — 15 — −£5.00

Hardys Chardonnay Sauvignon Blanc 1998 — 15 — £5–7

Hardys Padthaway Chardonnay 1996 — 16 — £7–10

Hardys Stamp of Australia Chardonnay Semillon 1999 — 15 — −£5.00

Hardys Stamp of Australia Riesling Gewürztraminer 1999 — 15.5 — −£5.00

Hardys Stamp Semillon/ Chardonnay 1999 — 15 — −£5.00

Jacobs Creek Semillon/ Chardonnay 1999 — 15.5 — −£5.00

Jindalee Chardonnay 1999 — 16 — −£5.00

Lindemans Bin 65 Chardonnay 1999 — 16.5 — −£5.00

Lindemans Padthaway Chardonnay 1999 — 16.5 — £7–10

Loxton Lunchtime Light Chardonnay (4% vol) — 12 — −£3.50

Penfolds Koonunga Hill Chardonnay 1999 — 16 — £5–7

Penfolds Rawsons Retreat Semillon/ Chardonnay/Colombard 1999 — 15 — −£5.00

## BULGARIAN RED

Boyar Merlot 1999 — 15 — −£3.50

Bulgarian Cabernet 13.5 −£3.50
Sauvignon 1999,
Somerfield

Bulgarian Country Red 14 −£3.50
NV, Somerfield

Isla Negra Chardonnay 16.5 −£5.00
1999

Vina Morande Chilean 15.5 −£5.00
Chardonnay 1999,
Somerfield

## BULGARIAN WHITE

Bulgarian Chardonnay 14 −£3.50
1998, Somerfield

Bulgarian Country White 14.5 −£3.50
1999, Somerfield

## CHILEAN RED

Chilean Cabernet 16.5 −£5.00
Sauvignon Vina La Rosa
1999, Somerfield

Chilean Cabernet 16.5 −£5.00
Sauvignon/Merlot Vina
La Rosa 1999, Somerfield

Chilean Merlot 1999, 17 −£5.00
Somerfield

Cono Sur Cabernet 17 £5–7
Sauvignon Reserve 1998

Cono Sur Pinot Noir 1999 16 −£5.00

Isla Negra Merlot 1999 16.5 £5–7

## CHILEAN WHITE

Chilean Sauvignon Blanc, 16 −£5.00
Canepa 1999, Somerfield

Chilean Semillon 16 −£5.00
Chardonnay 1999,
Somerfield

Chilean White 1999, 15.5 −£3.50
Somerfield

Cono Sur Viognier 1999 16 −£5.00

## FRENCH RED

Buzet Cuvée 44 1997 15 −£5.00

Cabernet Sauvignon d'Oc 14 −£3.50
Val d'Orbieu 1998,
Somerfield

Château Blanca, 15.5 −£5.00
Bordeaux 1999

Château Cazal Cuvée des 16 £5–7
Fees Vieilles Vignes,
St Chinian 1998

Château Plaisance, 15.5 £5–7
Montagne St Emilion
1996

Château Valoussiere 16.5 −£5.00
Coteaux de Languedoc
1997

Château Verdignan Haut 13.5 £10–13
Medoc 1996

Claret NV, Somerfield 13.5 −£3.50

Corbieres Rouge Val 15 −£3.50
d'Orbieu 1998,
Somerfield

Côtes du Rhône Villages 14 −£5.00
1999, Somerfield

Côtes du Roussillon 15 −£3.50
Rouge 1998, Somerfield

Crozes Hermitage 1998 14.5 −£5.00

Domaine de Bisconte 15 −£5.00
Côtes du Roussillon 1998

394

FRENCH WHITE

Domaine de Courtilles Côte 125 Corbieres 1998 — 15.5 — £5–7

Domaine Haut St Georges Corbieres 1998 — 16 — –£5.00

Domaine la Tuque Bel Air, Côtes de Castillon 1997 — 14 — £5–7

Fitou Rocher d'Ambree 1998, Somerfield — 14.5 — –£5.00

Gouts et Couleurs Cabernet Sauvignon VdP d'Oc 1998 — 16 — –£5.00

Gouts et Couleurs Syrah Mourvedre VdP d'Oc 1999 — 16 — –£5.00

Hautes Côtes de Beaune Rouge, G. Desire 1999 — 12 — £5–7

James Herrick Cuvêe Simone VdP d'Oc 1998 — 16.5 — –£5.00

Medoc NV, Somerfield — 13 — –£5.00

Oak Aged Claret NV, Somerfield — 15 — –£5.00

Red Burgundy 1997, Somerfield — 12 — £5–7

Vacqueyras Côtes du Rhône 1999 — 15.5 — –£5.00

Vacqueyras Domaine de la Soleiade 1998 — 15 — –£5.00

VdP des Coteaux de l'Ardeche Rouge 1999, Somerfield — 14 — –£3.50

VdP des Côtes de Gascogne Rouge 1998, Somerfield — 15 — –£3.50

Winter Hill Rouge, VdP de l'Aude 1999 — 14 — –£3.50

Brouilly Les Celliers de Bellevue 1998 — 12 — £5–7

## FRENCH WHITE

Anjou Blanc 1999, Somerfield — 13.5 — –£3.50

Bordeneuve Blanc VdP des Côtes de Gascogne 1999 — 13 — –£5.00

Chablis 1998, Somerfield — 14 — £7–10

Chablis Premier Cru 1997 — 10 — £10–13

Chardonnay VdP d'Oc 1999, Somerfield — 14.5 — –£5.00

Chardonnay VdP du Jardin de la France 1999 — 13 — –£5.00

Domaine d' Arain Muscat de Frontignan (50cl) — 16 — –£5.00

Domaine du Bois Viognier VdP d'Oc, Maurel Vedeau 1998 — 16 — –£5.00

Entre Deux Mers 1998, Somerfield — 12 — –£5.00

French Oak Aged Chardonnay, Domaine Ste Agathe 1998 — 16 — £5–7

Gewürztraminer Caves de Turckheim 1999 — 16 — £5–7

Gouts et Couleurs Chardonnay Viognier 1999 — 15.5 — –£5.00

Gouts et Couleurs Cinsault Rosé 1999 — 14 — –£5.00

Hautes Côtes de Beaune, Laboure Roi 1998 — 13 — £5–7

James Herrick Chardonnay VdP d'Oc 1999 — 16 −£5.00

Laperouse Chardonnay VdP d'Oc 1996 — 16.5 −£5.00

Les Marionettes Marsanne VdP d'Oc 1999 — 15.5 −£5.00

Muscat de Frontignan NV (50 cl) — 17 −£5.00

Rivers Meet Sauvignon Semillon 1999 — 13 −£5.00

Sancerre Domaine les Grands Groux 1999 — 13 £7–10

VdP des Coteaux de l'Ardeche Blanc 1999, Somerfield — 14.5 −£3.50

VdP du Comte du Tolosan, Les Chais Beaucarois 1998 — 14 −£3.50

Vouvray 1997, Somerfield — 14 −£5.00

White Burgundy 1999, Somerfield — 13.5 £5–7

Winter Hill White, VdP de l'Aude NV — 14 −£3.50

## GERMAN WHITE

Baden Dry NV, Somerfield — 13.5 −£5.00

Hock NV, Somerfield — 14.5 −£2.50

Morio Muskat 1997 — 15 −£3.50

Mosel Riesling Halbtrocken NV — 14 −£3.50

Niersteiner Spiegelberg 1999, Somerfield — 13 −£3.50

Rheingau Riesling 1996, Somerfield — 14 −£5.00

Rheinhessen Auslese 1997, Somerfield — 14.5 −£5.00

Rudesheimer Rosengarten NV, Somerfield — 13.5 −£3.50

St Johanner Abtey Kabinett NV, Somerfield — 14 −£3.50

St Ursula Dry Riesling NV — 14 −£5.00

## GREEK WHITE

Samos Greek Muscat NV (half-bottle) — 15.5 −£3.50

## HUNGARIAN WHITE

Castle Ridge Pinot Grigio, Neszmely 1999 — 14 −£5.00

Castle Ridge Sauvignon Blanc 1999 — 14 −£5.00

## ITALIAN RED

Bright Brothers Roman Vines Negroamaro Cabernet Sauvignon 1998 — 16.5 −£5.00

Cabernet Sauvignon delle Venezie 1999, Somerfield — 14 −£5.00

Caramia Primitivo Barrique 1998 — 14 £5–7

Chianti Classico Conti Serristori 1998, Somerfield — 13.5 £5–7

D'Istinto Sangiovese Merlot 1998 (Sicily) — 14 −£5.00

L'Arco Cabernet Franc, Friuli 1998 — 14 −£5.00

Marano Amarone della | 13.5 | £10–13
Valpolicella 1996

Mimosa Maremma | 15 | –£5.00
Sangiovese 1998

Montepulciano | 14 | –£5.00
d'Abruzzo 1998,
Somerfield

Riparosso Montepulciano | 13 | –£5.00
d'Abruzzo 1998

Terrale, Primitivo di | 15 | –£5.00
Puglia 1998, Somerfield

Tre Uve Ultima, | 15 | £7–10
Madonna dei Miracoli
1998

Trulli Chardonnay del | 15 | –£5.00
Salento 1999

Trulli Primitivo Salento | 14.5 | –£5.00
1998

Valpolicella Classico | 15.5 | –£5.00
Vigneti Casterna 1997

## ITALIAN WHITE

Bright Brothers | 13.5 | –£5.00
Greganico Chardonnay
1999 (Sicily)

Bright Brothers Roman | 16 | –£5.00
Vines Sicilian Barrel-
fermented Chardonnay
1999

Chardonnay delle | 13.5 | –£5.00
Venezie 1998, Somerfield

D'Istinto Trebbiano | 10 | –£3.50
Insolia 1998

L'Arco Chardonnay 1998 | 16 | –£5.00

Marc Xero Chardonnay | 14 | –£5.00
1998

Sicilian White 1999, | 15.5 | –£3.50
Somerfield

Soave 1998, Somerfield | 14.5 | –£3.50

Vino da Tavola Bianco | 14 | –£3.50
NV, Somerfield

## NEW ZEALAND WHITE

Coopers Creek | 15.5 | £7–10
Sauvignon Blanc,
Marlborough 1999

Montana Sauvignon | 15.5 | £5–7
Blanc 1999

## PORTUGUESE RED

Bright Brothers Atlantic | 14 | –£5.00
Vines Baga 1999

Fiuza Bright Cabernet | 14.5 | –£5.00
Sauvignon 1998

Portuguese Red NV, | 14 | –£3.50
Somerfield

Ramada Red 1999 | 13 | –£5.00

## PORTUGUESE WHITE

Fiuza Bright Chardonnay | 16 | –£5.00
1999

Portuguese White 1999, | 15 | –£3.50
Somerfield

## ROMANIAN RED

Pietroasa Young Vatted | 16 | –£5.00
Cabernet Sauvignon 1998

SOMERFIELD/KWIK SAVE

## SOUTH AFRICAN RED

Bellingham Pinotage 1999 | 17 | £5–7

Bush Vines Pinotage 1999, Somerfield | 16 | –£5.00

Kumala Cinsault Pinotage 1999 | 15 | –£5.00

Kumala Reserve Cabernet Sauvignon 1998 | 16.5 | £7–10

South African Cabernet Sauvignon 1999, Somerfield | 16 | –£5.00

South African Cape Red 1999, Somerfield | 15 | –£3.50

South African Cinsault Ruby Cabernet 1999, Somerfield | 15 | –£5.00

South African Pinotage 1998, Somerfield | 16.5 | –£5.00

Winds of Change Pinotage Cabernet 1998 | 16 | –£5.00

## SOUTH AFRICAN WHITE

Bellingham Sauvignon Blanc 1999 | 15.5 | –£5.00

Bush Vines Semillon 1999, Somerfield | 14 | –£5.00

Kumala Sauvignon Blanc/Colombard 1999 | 15.5 | –£5.00

Millennium Early Release Chenin Blanc 2000 | 14 | –£3.50

South African Chardonnay 1999, Somerfield | 14 | –£5.00

South African Colombard 1999, Somerfield | 14.5 | –£5.00

## SPANISH RED

Bodegas Castano Monastrell Merlot 1999 | 16.5 | –£5.00

Bright Brothers Old Vines Navarra Garnacha 1998 | 14 | –£5.00

Don Darias Red NV | 15.5 | –£5.00

Pergola Tempranillo 1999, Somerfield | 15 | –£5.00

Rioja Crianza 1997, Somerfield | 14 | –£5.00

Sierra Alta Cabernet Sauvignon 1998 | 16 | –£5.00

Valencia Red NV, Somerfield | 14 | –£3.50

## SPANISH WHITE

Castillo Imperial Blanco NV, Somerfield | 13.5 | –£3.50

Don Darias White NV | 14 | –£5.00

Muscatel de Valencia, Somerfield | 16 | –£3.50

Pergola Oaked Viura 1999, Somerfield | 14 | –£5.00

Vina Cana Rioja Blanco 1998, Somerfield | 12.5 | –£5.00

## URUGUAYAN RED

Bright Brothers Tannat Cabernet Franc 2000 | 16 | –£5.00

Bright Brothers Uruguayan Sauvignon/ Semillon 2000 | 15.5 | –£5.00

## USA RED

Californian Dry Red NV, Somerfield — 14 — −£5.00

Laguna Canyon Zinfandel 1998 — 12 — −£5.00

Turning Leaf Cabernet Sauvignon 1997 — 12 — £5–7

Turning Leaf Zinfandel 1996 — 12.5 — £5–7

## USA WHITE

Talus Chardonnay 1998 — 16.5 — £5–7

## FORTIFIED WINES

Amontillado Sherry, Somerfield — 17.5 — −£5.00

Cream Sherry, Somerfield — 16 — −£5.00

Fino Sherry, Somerfield — 16 — −£5.00

Manzanilla Sherry, Somerfield — 16 — −£5.00

## SPARKLING WINES

Asti Spumante NV, Somerfield — 14 — £5–7

Australian Quality Sparkling NV, Somerfield — 14 — £5–7

Australian Sparkling Chardonnay 1995, Somerfield — 14 — £5–7

Cava Brut NV, Somerfield — 14.5 — −£5.00

Cava Rosado NV, Somerfield — 14 — −£5.00

Cremant de Bourgogne, Caves de Bailly 1998, Somerfield — 13.5 — £5–7

Devauzelle Champagne NV — 13.5 — £10–13

Lindauer Brut NV (New Zealand) — 14 — £7–10

Millennium Champagne 1990, Somerfield — 13 — £13–20

Moscato Fizz, Somerfield — 14 — −£2.50

Mumm Cuvée Napa Brut NV (California) — 14 — £7–10

Nicolas Feuillate Brut Premier Cru NV — 14 — £13–20

Nottage Hill Sparkling Chardonnay — 14.5 — £5–7

Pierre Larousse Chardonnay Brut NV (France) — 16 — −£5.00

Prince William Blanc de Blancs Champagne NV, Somerfield — 13.5 — £13–20

Prince William Blanc de Noirs Champagne NV, Somerfield — 14 — £10–13

Prince William Champagne 1er Cru, Somerfield — 15.5 — £13–20

Prince William Champagne Rosé NV, Somerfield — 13 — £13–20

Prince William Millennium Champagne 1990, Somerfield — 13 — £13–20

Seaview Brut Rosé — 13.5 — £5–7

Seaview Pinot Noir/      `15`  `£7–10`      Vintage Cava 1996,      `15.5`  `£5–7`
Chardonnay 1995                              Somerfield
(Australia)

South African Sparkling   `16`  `£5–7`
Sauvignon, Somerfield

**SEE STOP PRESS SECTION AT END OF BOOK FOR LAST-MINUTE
ADDITIONS OR UPDATES TO THIS RETAILER'S RANGE.**

# SPAR

What has been happening over the past year at this retailer? Nothing to set the world alight? Well, let's see.

In July 1999 there were the thrills attached to the report of its considering 24-hour opening for its off-licences on Millennium Eve. Wow, thought I! Same month, it said it was spending £2 million on advertising. (About what Tesco spends a week? Something like that.)

Things hotted up in September when eight Spar outlets in Aberdeen had to shut their off-licences after the group failed to inform licensing authorities of changes of the names of licensees. Staff promotions had led to new store managers being put in place, but someone forgot to inform the local magistrates. Spar does, in fact, claim to have more off-licences than any other retail group, so it's quite understandable if small admin details are overlooked. It was later reported in the Aberdeen press that all the Spar branches, to great local relief, had regained their licences.

Spar likes Scotland. It intends, so it said, to consolidate its position north of the border with a spate of new store openings before the end of 1999. It plans to increase its share of the Scottish convenience market from 42% to 50% in that time. The group predicted £2 billion-worth of sales for its UK operations in the year 2000.

This was the year it announced the arrival of the Eurospar supermarket format. The stores (of about 5,000 square feet) are widely used by International Spar on the Continent. The first UK Eurospar opened in Warren Point in Belfast (operated by Spar wholesaler John Henderson).

It is at this point that I am required to explain that Spar, which you see all over Europe, is not so much a store chain as an international franchise. Stores are owned by individuals, not the group. It is only the buying which is centrally controlled, which is posited on the basis that this helps these individuals, as Spar franchisees, to compete with the prices in supermarkets. They don't, of course, and they can't. A £2.29 wine bargain at Spar is an impossibility. A drinkable one, that is.

This requires of Spar that it offers new ideas and services to its customers, and in all the Spar stores I've visited in the past year I've been struck by the modernity of the layout and the eagerness of the staff to help. This should be greatly enhanced in the future if Spar's plans for in-store banking in rural areas become a reality. At a time when certain clearing banks are attracting a lot of adverse publicity for closing smaller branches, the idea of banking at Spar is quite brilliant.

However, the biggest benefit as far as wine drinkers are concerned would be for Spar's wine buyer, Liz Aked, to have an even playing field to compete on. By this I mean that Spar shops are not compelled to take the wines she so assiduously tracks down and offers to the Spar wholesalers who trade with these shops. Spar shops can buy their wines elsewhere and many do, though there would be hugely communal benefits if all Spar shops had the same wines.

It would help if the Spar shops were offered a continuing flow of great bargains at £3.50 and under, but this is Spar's great area of weakness. As the following ratings show, there are few decently rated wines at this price point, yet this is surely the one where the competition is hottest. The me-too initiatives (if that isn't a contradiction) like Spar's Party Wines and Pasta Wine (echoing Tesco and Morrisons) are fine if the wines are superbly fruity, work well within the context of their labels, and are darned cheap. I do not find the crucial first two of these constraints to have been met, and the third is debatable.

One reason for the all-round higher pricing at Spar is because Spar has to trade with wholesalers who then trade with the individual franchisees. This inevitably, unlike a supermarket, involves two further tiers of profit-taking.

Spar, then, can never compete with supermarkets, yet it could, I feel, concentrate on the £3.99/£4.29 sector but with a far greater array of wines of genuine interest and fruitiness. There are some, notably from southern France, but the dynamic wineries capable of supplying such wines have more important customers than Spar, and these are inevitably the supermarkets. Thus, Spar is doomed for ever to be the poor relation in this regard. Liz, who must bite her lips in frustration at times, cannot even deal in last-minute bargains or buy in large one-off amounts of cut-price wine, for she cannot be guaranteed that the shops would take the wine, nor could she build in sufficient margin to convey profit to everyone involved.

Spar's professed commitment, therefore, to the local community, as exemplified by its 'Keep It Local' campaign, the aim of which is 'to fight back against the destruction of the local community, highlight the plight of the small businessman and keep local shops and businesses open for the local customer', has immense internal contradictions which frustrate its success. Where wine is concerned, these problems are nigh insoluble.

I heartily approve of Spar's drive to expand its network (of 2,700 UK stores) and to provide 'additional services such as post offices and chemists' as well as such things as the rural banking facilities mentioned earlier.

If only, however, there were solid ranges of £3 to £4 wines, outstandingly fruity and rich and food-friendly, which ensured that customers made these a compelling reason to visit a Spar shop – rather than simply picking up some wine because they happen to be on the premises – then Spar could become a real force in UK wine retailing.

I became interested in Spar because a few *Guardian* readers wrote and told me they found such shops useful for picking up the odd bottle to bring along to friends' suppers. This was before the supermarkets opened at all hours and before people cottoned on to the idea that they ought to buy wine for the month ahead rather than just stocking up for the weekend. If there were many more great bottles on Spar's shelves, like some of the high-rating southern French reds I have found (all worth a detour to find, I might add), then this retailer would have more competitive presence.

As a group, not just as wine departments, Spar might find it useful to devote more senior managerial time to solving this problem. Because if it can solve it, then many of the group's other ambitions would be more smoothly realisable. I wish them, and Liz, all the luck in the world.

Spar (UK) Limited
32–40 Headstone Drive
Harrow
Middlesex
HA3 5QT

Tel 020 8863 5511
Fax 020 8863 0603
webside under construction at time of going to press

| AUSTRALIAN RED | | |
|---|---|---|
| Australian Shiraz Cabernet 1998, Spar | 13.5 | −£5.00 |
| Hardys Bankside Shiraz 1997 | 16.5 | £7–10 |

| AUSTRALIAN WHITE | | |
|---|---|---|
| Australian Semillon Chardonnay 1999, Spar | 16 | −£5.00 |
| Burraburra Hill Chardonnay 1999, Spar | 15.5 | −£5.00 |
| Lindemans Bin 65 Chardonnay 1999 | 16.5 | −£5.00 |

SPAR

## BULGARIAN RED

Bulgarian Country Wine Cabernet Sauvignon & Merlot NV, Spar — 13 — −£3.50

## BULGARIAN WHITE

Bulgarian Country White NV, Spar — 11 — −£3.50

## CHILEAN RED

Canepa Cabernet Sauvignon 1998, Spar — 10 — −£5.00

Canepa Merlot 1998, Spar — 15 — −£5.00

## CHILEAN WHITE

Canepa Chilean Chardonnay 1999, Spar — 14.5 — −£5.00

Canepa Chilean Sauvignon Blanc 1998, Spar — 14 — −£5.00

Chilean Sauvignon Blanc 1998 — 15.5 — −£5.00

## FRENCH RED

Claret NV, Spar — 15 — −£5.00

Cordier Château Le Cadet de Martinens, Margaux 1995 — 15.5 — £7–10

Coteaux du Languedoc NV — 13 — −£3.50

Côtes du Ventoux Le Rossignol, Spar 1998 — 15.5 — −£5.00

Fitou NV, Spar — 16 — −£5.00

French Country VdP de l'Herault NV, Spar (1 litre) — 13 — −£3.50

Gevrey-Chambertin Les Caves des Hautes Côtes 1994 — 12 — £13–20

Hautes Côtes de Beaune 1995, Spar — 10 — £5–7

La Côte Syrah Merlot VdP d'Oc 1998, Spar — 15.5 — −£5.00

Lussac St Emilion 1997 — 11 — £5–7

Merlot VdP d'Oc 1998, Spar — 15.5 — −£5.00

Salaison Shiraz/Cabernet VdP d'Oc 1998, Spar — 15.5 — −£5.00

Vin de Pays de l'Aude NV, Spar — 12 — −£3.50

## FRENCH WHITE

Chablis La Chablisienne 1998, Spar — 14 — £7–10

French Country VdP de l'Herault White NV — 13 — −£5.00

Grenache VdP d'Oc NV — 10 — −£3.50

La Côte Chasan Chardonnay 1999 — 13 — −£5.00

Muscat de St Jean de Minervois, Spar (half-bottle) — 15.5 — −£3.50

Oaked Chardonnay VdP d'Oc 1998, Spar — 12.5 — −£5.00

Pouilly Fuisse Les Vercheres Chardonnay 1996, Spar — 10 — £10–13

Salaison Chardonnay Sauvignon 1998, Spar — 15 — −£5.00

Sancerre Saget 1998 · 10 · £7–10

Unoaked Chardonnay VdP d'Oc 1999, Spar · 14 · –£5.00

Vin de Pays de l'Aude Blanc NV, Spar · 12 · –£3.50

White Burgundy Chardonnay 1996, Spar · 13 · £5–7

## GERMAN WHITE

Grans Fassian Riesling 1995 · 16 · £5–7

## HUNGARIAN RED

Misty Mountain Merlot NV, Spar · 13 · –£5.00

## HUNGARIAN WHITE

Misty Mountain Chardonnay NV, Spar · 13 · –£5.00

## ITALIAN RED

Barolo 'Costa di Bussia' 1994 · 16 · £13–20

Chianti Chiantigiane 1997, Spar · 12 · –£5.00

Chianti Classico Le Fioraie 1995 · 11 · £7–10

Montepulciano d'Abruzzo 1999, Spar · 14 · –£5.00

Pasta Red NV, Spar (1 litre) · 11 · –£3.50

Riva Red NV, Spar · 13.5 · –£3.50

## ITALIAN WHITE

Pasta White NV, Spar (1 litre) · 13 · –£3.50

Riva White NV, Spar · 14.5 · –£3.50

## SOUTH AFRICAN RED

Chiwara Cinsault/Ruby Cabernet 1998 · 13 · –£5.00

Chiwara Pinotage 1998, Spar · 14.5 · –£5.00

Chiwara Ruby Cabernet/ Pinotage 1998, Spar · 11 · –£5.00

Table Mountain Pinot Noir NV · 10 · –£5.00

## SOUTH AFRICAN WHITE

Chiwara Colombard/ Sauvignon 1998, Spar · 12.5 · –£5.00

South African Classic Chardonnay 1998, Spar · 12 · £5–7

## SPANISH RED

Perfect for Parties Red NV, Spar (1 litre) · 10 · –£3.50

Valencia Soft Red NV, Spar · 14 · –£3.50

## SPANISH WHITE

Perfect for Parties White NV, Spar (1 litre) · 10 · –£3.50

Valencia Dry White NV, Spar · 13.5 · –£3.50

SPAR

## USA RED

Fetzer Valley Oaks    15.5    £5–7
Cabernet Sauvignon 1997

## FORTIFIED WINES

Old Cellar LBV Port    14    £7–10
1996, Spar

Old Cellar Ruby Port NV,    14.5    £5–7
Spar

## SPARKLING WINES

Cava Brut NV, Spar    15    −£5.00

Marques de Prevel    10    £13–20
Champagne NV, Spar

# TESCO

The fastest act in the west is Tesco. No retailer thinks faster on its feet, and none is more concerned to keep prices as low as humanly possible (in some cases inhumanly low, say its green-eyed competitors). The wines and the ratings which follow speak for themselves. Tesco has an immense range of wines, would like to stock everything, has excellent own-label ranges at the cheaper end of the spectrum as well as some solid contenders priced more highly. Its wine department is efficient and widely spread (it exiled Phil Reedman to Australia, where he has a crucial role in coordinating, as product development manager, Tesco's myriad purchases of wine from this immensely ambitious island).

It is also tough (ruthless say its competitors), no-nonsense and highly focused. It is, I think, the largest department of its kind, comprising managers, buyers, marketing and PR people whose roles, to the casual observer, seem to overlap, but at the last count there were Alex Austin, Kevin Smith, Charles Clowes and Eleanor Beatty buying; Lindsay Talas, Helen McGinn and Sara Pattinson product developing; Anne-Marie Bostock producing babies; and Sara Archer and Nicky Walden marketing and wine critic feather-smoothing. I can report the department for only one delicious bribe this year when Nicky sent me a packet of fudge (eight ounces). I devoured it in a single sitting and felt suitably corrupted. It rated 18 points out of 20.

In the ten years I have been writing the Superplonk column I would say the biggest change has been in the number of readers who shopped for wine at Sainsbury's who have now switched to Tesco. It can't just be the wine, of course. Tesco is innovative and dynamic in many areas.

For example, it was Tesco which launched in 1999 a pet insurance scheme in fifty of its stores. The insurance service (£7 for a dog, £4 for a cat) included a twenty-four-hour helpline and an emergency vet service.

This was the month that reminiscences about Jack 'Slasher' Cohen, the founder of Tesco, were given prominence via Lord MacLaurin's memoirs melodramatically entitled *Tiger by the Tail*. Lord MacLaurin is an ex-chairman of Tesco. One particular anecdote, surely apocryphal, concerned Slasher – so called because the man loved slashing prices – acquiring a consignment of tinned milk from stock that had run aground at sea. The milk was sent to the stores with the following note: 'Managers are allowed to use Duraglit to remove the rust from the tins.'

Amiable nonsense, perhaps, but Tesco is deadly serious about maintaining a competitive edge with its prices. In 1999 it launched a price comparison website which allows customers to compare immediately prices on 1,000 lines at Tesco, Safeway, Sainsbury's and Asda. What a fantastic idea. Slasher was doubtless chortling with glee at that one, up there on his celestial cloud doing deals in second-hand harps.

Tesco also emerged as a really serious internationalist on several fronts. It trounced its competitors in the Hungarian hypermarket sector, expanding faster in the sector than its Euro-retailing rivals, Auchan and Cora, by employing Hungarians as departmental and store managers. Tesco (at time of report) had four hypermarkets in Hungary and had plans to open seven new stores in 2000 – each at a cost of £15 million. Tesco is also active in Poland, and the Czech and Slovak Republics. According to the trade magazine *Supermarketing*, Tesco also gained a foothold in Trinidad. When offers are invited to set up a supermarket on the moon, you may be sure that Tesco will be the first to consider the practicalities.

On the other hand, it quietly withdraws from situations that don't add up. In 1999 it quit as a drinks specialist in Northern Ireland with the sale of its eighteen off-licences as well as two larger drinks stores.

The company patently takes account of differing national retail characteristics. It is, as far as I know, the only supermarket to appoint a marketing manager solely for Scotland, to take account of differing tastes north of the border. It announced, at the same time, plans for a massive 97,000-square-feet store in Glasgow.

Small wonder there was, with so much going on, speculation about a possible bid by Tesco for the troubled M&S chain. Nothing came of this, as surely no informed observer thought there would.

The millennium got under way with plans to triple its home-shopping outlets, and Tesco Express added 150 forecourt sites to its growing portfolio. Tesco retained its position as the UK supermarket group 'receiving the most favourable press coverage', according to a report in *Supermarketing*. The findings came from the second Food and Drug Retailers' Reputation Monthly.

Tesco was also reportedly bullish about opening stores in China, according to a report in *Retail Week*. It was also set to open its first 24-hour discount store in Bangkok. Tesco also launched its own credit card in Thailand (to increase 'brand awareness', it was said). Such initiatives are, apparently, a vital step in gaining loyalty in emerging markets where it is difficult for consumers to get credit. If successful, Tesco may, apparently, introduce a similar scheme in central Europe.

Money is certainly on Tesco's mind right now. A few months back it announced that customers would soon be able to pay in cheques to their bank accounts at Tesco checkouts. The scheme, which was piloted in 100 stores in July, could be rolled out nationally if successful. Holders of Tesco savings accounts and Clubcard Plus will also be able to pay in cheques; previously customers had only been able to pay in cheques at the personal finance kiosks in nine stores.

If I were running Barclays or one of the bigger bank/building societies, I'd take note of these initiatives. The day can't be far off when Tesco puts financial advisers in stores and starts to offer mortgages and savings accounts. If this were linked to Tesco share ownership in some ground-breaking way, it could produce a massive flood of retailer-loyal new stock-holders. It would represent cooperative retailing of a dynamic new kind altogether. (So the Co-operative movement needs to consider such ideas as well.)

Indeed, the only retailer which doesn't appear concerned at Tesco's competitiveness and eager ideas is Wal-Mart. But then they haven't been around long enough to know the scene. Certainly many of Tesco's ideas, both big and small, are scrutinised by rivals and often shamelessly pinched. One such is the Tesco's Finest neck label which has been appearing on selected wine bottles over the past year. This does nothing more than 'halo' a wine, yet on some lines the increase in sales has been phenomenal. An unbelievable 7,000% increase in sales, so I learned, occurred on one German wine which was neck-labelled Tesco's Finest, and on other lines, like the superb own-label Gewürztraminer, the increase in sales has been a more modest, but still dramatic, 400%.

Patently, Tesco customers trust the store. It is now expected that Tesco's competitors will follow this neck-label idea, and already I hear rumours that Sainsbury's is experimenting with a similar idea.

Tesco has now achieved an aloofness from its rivals which was once the preserve of Sainsbury's and Marks & Spencer. Part of the inheritance which comes with this air of disdain of the top dog is to ignore com-petitors rather than publicly knocking them. I never hear of Tesco slagging a rival off or saying nasty things about another supermarket, even in private. The company merely gets on with delivering the goods, minding its own business. Possibly it follows the precept of the Roman emperor Marcus

Aurelius that 'the noblest form of retribution is not to become like your enemy'.

Only accidental knocks, it would appear, occur. I learned from the invaluable *Retail Week* magazine that a Tesco Direct van delivering to the house of Steven Round, an executive at Woolworths/Kingfisher, rammed into Mr Round's car, causing a certain amount of damage. But then I'm told that Tesco now has 500,000 customers using Tesco Direct services via the Internet, so the odd scrape is perhaps inevitable.

Personally, though, I prefer trundling my own trolley round a Tesco store, and I especially like the smiling faces wandering up and down the wine aisles. These belong to the customers who find the range huge, the bargains many, and the opportunities to find something individual (but not expensive) irresistible.

Tesco
Tesco House
PO Box 18 Delamare Road
Cheshunt
EN8 9SL

Tel 0800 505555 Customer Careline
www.tesco.co.uk

## ARGENTINIAN RED

| | | |
|---|---|---|
| Anubis Tempranillo 1999 | 16 | £5–7 |
| Argentinian Bonarda/ Barbera 1999, Tesco | 13 | −£3.50 |
| Argento Malbec 1999 | 16.5 | −£5.00 |
| Bright Brothers Barrica Reserve Cabernet Sauvignon/Syrah 1998 | 15 | £5–7 |
| Bright Brothers Barrica Reserve Syrah 1998 | 16 | £5–7 |
| Bright Brothers San Juan Reserve Cabernet/Shiraz 1998 | 14 | −£5.00 |
| Bright Brothers San Juan Reserve Shiraz 1998 | 14.5 | −£5.00 |
| Catena Cabernet Sauvignon 1996 | 17 | £7–10 |
| Monster Spicy Red Syrah, Tesco | 16 | −£5.00 |
| Picajuan Peak Bonarda NV | 15.5 | −£5.00 |
| Picajuan Peak Malbec 1999, Tesco | 14.5 | −£5.00 |
| Picajuan Peak Sangiovese 1998, Tesco | 16 | −£5.00 |
| 'Q' Cabernet Sauvignon 1998 | 17 | £7–10 |

Q Tempranillo 1998 — 16.5 — £7–10

Santa Julia Oaked Tempranillo 1997 — 16 — −£5.00

## ARGENTINIAN WHITE

Argentinian Torrontes 1999, Tesco — 13 — −£3.50

Argento Chardonnay 1999 — 17 — −£5.00

Picajuan Peak Viognier 1999 — 15 — −£5.00

## AUSTRALIAN RED

Australian Cabernet/ Merlot NV, Tesco — 14 — −£5.00

Australian Red, Tesco — 14 — −£3.50

Australian Ruby Cabernet, Tesco — 14 — −£5.00

Australian Shiraz NV, Tesco — 13 — −£5.00

Australian Shiraz/ Cabernet NV, Tesco — 14 — −£5.00

Banrock Station Shiraz 1999 — 13 — £5–7

Banrock Station Shiraz/ Mataro 1999 — 15 — −£5.00

Barramundi Shiraz/ Merlot NV — 15.5 — −£5.00

Best's Great Westner Dolcetto 1998 — 15.5 — £5–7

Blue Pyrenees Estate Red 1996 — 14 — £10–13

Brown Brothers Tarrango 1999 — 13.5 — £5–7

Buckleys Grenache/ Shiraz/Mourvedre 1998 — 14 — £7–10

Chapel Hill Cabernet Sauvignon 1997 — 14 — £7–10

Coonawarra Cabernet Sauvignon 1998, Tesco — 16 — £5–7

Hardys Nottage Hill Cabernet Sauvignon/ Shiraz 1999 — 16.5 — £5–7

Lindemans Bin 50 Shiraz 1998 — 14.5 — £5–7

Lindemans Cawarra Shiraz/Cabernet 1999 — 14 — −£5.00

McLaren Vale Grenache 1998, Tesco — 13.5 — £5–7

McLaren Vale Shiraz 1997, Tesco — 14 — £5–7

Miranda 'Left Field' Tinta Cao 1998 — 13 — −£5.00

Oxford Landing Cabernet Sauvignon Shiraz 1999 — 15.5 — £5–7

Penfold Koonunga Hill Shiraz/Cabernet Sauvignon 1998 — 16.5 — £5–7

Rosemount Estate Grenache/Shiraz 1999 — 15 — £5–7

Rosemount Estate Shiraz Cabernet 1999 — 15.5 — £5–7

Rosemount Shiraz 1998 — 15.5 — £7–10

Sunstone Fresh Spicy Red NV — 12 — −£5.00

Temple Bruer Cornucopia Grenache 1997 — 14 — £5–7

Tim Adams Shiraz 1997 — 14.5 — £7–10

Woolpunda Cabernet Sauvignon 1998 — `15` `−£5.00`

Woolpunda Shiraz 1998 — `16` `−£5.00`

## AUSTRALIAN WHITE

Australian Chardonnay, Tesco — `16` `−£3.50`

Banrock Station Chardonnay 1999 — `14` `−£5.00`

Barramundi Semillon/ Chardonnay NV — `16` `−£5.00`

Blue Pyrenees Estate Chardonnay 1997 — `16.5` `£10–13`

Blues Point Semillon/ Chardonnay 1998 — `12.5` `£5–7`

Brown Brothers Dry Muscat 1999 — `15` `£5–7`

Chapel Hill Unwooded Chardonnay 1998 — `15.5` `£5–7`

Clare Valley Riesling 1999, Tesco — `15.5` `−£5.00`

Geoff Merrill Chardonnay Reserve 1995 — `17` `£7–10`

Hardys Grenache/Shiraz Rosé 1999 — `14` `−£5.00`

Hardys Stamp of Australia Chardonnay Semillon 1999 — `15` `−£5.00`

Hunter Valley Semillon 1999, Tesco — `13.5` `£5–7`

Jacobs Creek Dry Riesling 2000 — `14` `−£5.00`

Langhorne Creek Verdelho 1998, Tesco — `15.5` `−£5.00`

Limited Release Barramundi Marsanne 1998 — `16.5` `£5–7`

Lindemans Bin 65 Chardonnay 1999 — `16.5` `−£5.00`

Lindemans Cawarra Chardonnay 1999 — `15.5` `−£5.00`

McLaren Vale Chardonnay 1999, Tesco — `15` `£5–7`

Miranda White Pointer 1999 — `15` `−£5.00`

Mount Pleasant Elizabeth Semillon 1994 — `15.5` `£7–10`

Ninth Island Chardonnay 1998 — `14` `£7–10`

Normans Unwooded Chardonnay 1999 — `16.5` `−£5.00`

Oxford Landing Sauvignon Blanc 1999 — `15` `−£5.00`

Pendulum Chardonnay 1999 — `15` `−£5.00`

Penfolds Koonunga Hill Chardonnay 1999 — `16` `£5–7`

Pewsey Vale Eden Valley Riesling 1999 — `15.5` `£5–7`

Provenance Chardonnay 1997 — `13.5` `£10–13`

Rosemount Chardonnay 1999 — `16` `£5–7`

Rosemount Sauvignon Blanc 2000 — `15` `£5–7`

Rosemount Semillon/ Sauvignon 1999 — `14` `£5–7`

Smithbrook Chardonnay 1998 — `15` `£7–10`

| | | |
|---|---|---|
| Smooth Voluptuous White NV, Tesco | 15 | −£5.00 |
| St Hallett Poachers Blend 1998 | 16 | −£5.00 |
| Tasmanian Chardonnay 1999, Tesco | 13 | £5–7 |
| Tim Adams Riesling 1998 | 16 | £7–10 |
| Woolpunda Blue Rock Chardonnay 1998 | 15.5 | −£5.00 |
| Yendah Vale Chardonnay/Merlot Rosé 1999 | 12 | −£5.00 |

## AUSTRIAN RED

| | | |
|---|---|---|
| Blauer Zweigelt Lenz Moser 1997 | 14.5 | −£5.00 |
| Lenz Moser's Prestige Beerenauslese 1995 (half-bottle) | 15 | £5–7 |

## BULGARIAN RED

| | | |
|---|---|---|
| Azbuka Cabernet Sauvignon 1994 | 14 | £5–7 |
| Bulgarian Cabernet Sauvignon Reserve 1995, Tesco | 14 | −£5.00 |
| Reka Valley Bulgarian Cabernet Sauvignon NV, Tesco | 14.5 | −£3.50 |

## CHILEAN RED

| | | |
|---|---|---|
| Altum Cabernet Sauvignon Reserve 1997 | 14 | £7–10 |
| Altum Merlot Reserve 1997 | 14 | £7–10 |
| Canepa Zinfandel 1998 | 14 | −£5.00 |
| Chilean Cabernet Sauvignon NV, Tesco | 16 | −£5.00 |
| Chilean Cabernet Sauvignon Reserve 1999, Tesco | 16 | −£5.00 |
| Chilean Merlot Reserve 1999, Tesco | 16 | −£5.00 |
| Chilean Red NV, Tesco | 15 | −£3.50 |
| Cono Sur Pinot Noir 1999 | 16 | −£5.00 |
| Cono Sur Pinot Noir Reserve 1996 | 14 | £5–7 |
| Errazuriz Cabernet Sauvignon Reserva 1998 | 16.5 | £7–10 |
| Errazuriz Merlot 1999 | 16.5 | £5–7 |
| Errazuriz Syrah Reserva 1998 | 16 | £7–10 |
| Isla Negra Cabernet Sauvignon 1998 | 16 | −£5.00 |
| Isla Negra Merlot 1999 | 16.5 | £5–7 |
| Mont Gras Quatro 1998 | 15 | £5–7 |
| Montgras Merlot 1998 | 16 | −£5.00 |
| Salsa Cabernet Sauvignon 1999 | 14 | −£5.00 |
| Santa Catalina Cabernet Sauvignon 1999 | 15.5 | −£5.00 |
| Santa Catalina Merlot 1999 | 16 | −£5.00 |
| Santa Ines Cabernet/ Carmenere Reserva, Legado de Armida 1999 | 17.5 | £5–7 |
| Santa Ines Cabernet/ Merlot 1998 | 16 | −£5.00 |
| Stowells Chilean Cabernet/Merlot NV | 14.5 | −£5.00 |

413

| | | |
|---|---|---|
| TerraMater Cabernet Sauvignon 1998 | 16 | −£5.00 |
| Undurraga Familia Cabernet Sauvignon 1995 | 14 | £7−10 |
| Undurraga Pinot Noir 1999 | 14 | −£5.00 |
| Valdivieso Cabernet Franc Reserve 1997 | 17.5 | £7−10 |
| Valdivieso Carignan 1999 | 16 | −£5.00 |
| Valdivieso Malbec Reserve 1997 | 16.5 | £7−10 |

| | | |
|---|---|---|
| Undurraga Gewürztraminer 1998 | 13.5 | −£5.00 |
| Vina Casablanca Santa Isabel Sauvignon Blanc 1998 | 16 | £5−7 |

## ENGLISH WHITE

| | | |
|---|---|---|
| Chapel Down Bacchus 1997 | 12 | −£5.00 |
| Chapel Down Summerhill Oaked NV | 12 | −£5.00 |

## CHILEAN WHITE

| | | |
|---|---|---|
| Chilean Chardonnay Reserve 1998, Tesco | 15.5 | −£5.00 |
| Chilean Chardonnay, Tesco | 14 | −£5.00 |
| Chilean Sauvignon Blanc NV, Tesco | 14.5 | −£5.00 |
| Chilean White NV, Tesco | 14.5 | −£5.00 |
| Cono Sur Gewürztraminer 1999 | 16 | −£5.00 |
| Errazuriz Chardonnay 1999 | 16 | £5−7 |
| Errazuriz Chardonnay Reserva 1997 | 16 | £7−10 |
| Santa Ines Sauvignon Blanc 1999 | 16 | −£5.00 |
| Stowells Chilean Sauvignon Blanc NV | 12 | −£5.00 |
| TerraMater Chardonnay 1999 | 15.5 | −£5.00 |
| Undurraga Chardonnay/ Sauvignon Blanc 1999 | 15 | −£5.00 |

## FRENCH RED

| | | |
|---|---|---|
| Beaujolais NV, Tesco | 11 | −£3.50 |
| Beaujolais Villages 1999, Tesco | 12 | −£5.00 |
| Burgundy Pinot Noir 1998, Tesco | 13.5 | £5−7 |
| Buzet Cuvée 44 1997 | 15 | −£5.00 |
| Cabernet Sauvignon VdP d'Oc NV, Tesco | 14 | −£3.50 |
| Chartron la Fleur Château La Grave Bordeaux 1997 | 13 | −£5.00 |
| Château Clement Pichon, Cru Bourgeois Haut Medoc 1996 | 13 | £13−20 |
| Château de Côte de Montpezat, Côtes de Castillon 1997 | 15.5 | £5−7 |
| Château de Goelane Bordeaux Superieur 1997 | 13 | £5−7 |
| Château Ginestiere Coteaux du Languedoc 1997 | 15.5 | −£5.00 |

| | | | | | | |
|---|---|---|---|---|---|---|
| Château Haut-Chaigneau Lalande de Pomerol 1996 | 14 | £13–20 | | Dark Horse Barrique Aged Cahors 1998 | 14 | −£5.00 |
| Château la Fleur Bellevue Premieres Côtes de Blaye 1998 | 14 | £5–7 | | Domaine du Soleil Syrah/Malbec VdP d'Oc NV | 14.5 | −£5.00 |
| Château La Raze Beauvalet Haut Medoc 1997 | 14 | £5–7 | | Fitou NV, Tesco | 14.5 | −£3.50 |
| | | | | Fitou Reserve Baron de la Tour NV, Tesco | 15.5 | −£5.00 |
| Château la Tour de Mons Bordeaux 1996 | 13.5 | £13–20 | | French Grenache Prestige, Tesco | 14.5 | −£5.00 |
| Château Lafarque Pessac Leognan 1996 | 12 | £13–20 | | French Grenache, Tesco | 14 | −£3.50 |
| Château Liliane-Ladouys Cru Bourgeois Superieur Saint-Estephe 1996 | 12 | £13–20 | | French Merlot VdP d'Oc NV, Tesco | 14.5 | −£3.50 |
| | | | | Gamay, Tesco | 10 | −£3.50 |
| Château Maucaillou, Cru Bourgeois Moulis en Medoc 1996 | 12 | £20+ | | Gevrey Chambertin 1997 | 12 | £13–20 |
| Château Maurel Fonsalade, St Chînian 1997 | 14.5 | −£5.00 | | Gouts et Couleurs Premium Cuvée Cabernet Sauvignon VdP d'Oc 1998 | 16 | −£5.00 |
| Château Tour de l'Esperance Bordeaux Superieur 1997 | 16 | −£5.00 | | Graves 1996, Tesco | 14 | £7–10 |
| | | | | Les Etoiles French Organic Red Wine NV | 13 | −£5.00 |
| Claret, Tesco | 12.5 | −£3.50 | | Louis Jadot Combe aux Jacques Beaujolais Villages 1998 | 13 | £5–7 |
| Clarity Bordeaux Rouge 1998 | 14 | −£5.00 | | | | |
| Corbieres NV, Tesco | 13.5 | −£3.50 | | Margaux 1997, Tesco | 12 | £7–10 |
| Corbieres Reserve La Sansoure 1999, Tesco | 15 | −£5.00 | | Medoc 1997, Tesco | 13 | −£5.00 |
| | | | | Minervois NV, Tesco | 14 | −£3.50 |
| Côte Rotie Guigal 1996 | 17 | £20+ | | Nuits St Georges, Les Chezeaux 1996 | 13 | £13–20 |
| Côtes du Rhône NV, Tesco | 13.5 | −£3.50 | | Oak Aged Red Burgundy 1998, Tesco | 13.5 | £5–7 |
| Côtes du Rhône Villages Domaine de la Grande Retour 1999, Tesco | 14 | −£5.00 | | Oaked Côtes du Rhône NV | 13.5 | −£5.00 |

| | | |
|---|---|---|
| Pommard 1er Cru, Clos des Verger 1996 | 13.5 | £13–20 |
| Rasteau Côtes du Rhône Villages 1998 | 16.5 | −£5.00 |
| St Emilion 1997, Tesco | 12.5 | £7–10 |
| Syrah VdP d'Oc, Tesco | 13.5 | −£3.50 |
| Valreas Domaine de la Grande Bellane 1998 (organic) | 16.5 | £5–7 |
| Yvecourt Claret Bordeaux 1998 | 12 | −£5.00 |

## FRENCH WHITE

| | | |
|---|---|---|
| Alsace Gewürztraminer 1998, Tesco | 16 | £5–7 |
| Alsace Riesling 1998, Tesco | 14 | £5–7 |
| Anjou Blanc NV, Tesco | 13 | −£3.50 |
| Barrique Aged Marsanne Roussanne VdP d'Oc 1998 | 15.5 | −£5.00 |
| Cabernet de Saumur Rosé NV, Tesco | 14.5 | −£5.00 |
| Celsius Dry Muscat 1999 | 13.5 | −£5.00 |
| Chablis 1998, Tesco | 12.5 | £5–7 |
| Coteaux du Layon Saint-Aubin Domaine Cady 1996 | 16 | £5–7 |
| Côtes du Rhône Blanc NV, Tesco | 15 | −£3.50 |
| Domaine Cazal Viel Viognier 1999 | 16 | £5–7 |
| Domaine de Montauberon Marsanne 1998 | 12 | −£5.00 |
| Domaine du Soleil Chardonnay VdP d'Oc NV | 14 | −£5.00 |
| Domaine du Soleil Sauvignon/Chardonnay VdP d'Oc NV | 14 | −£5.00 |
| Entre Deux Mers NV, Tesco | 13.5 | −£5.00 |
| French Chardonnay NV, Tesco | 13.5 | −£3.50 |
| French Chenin Blanc NV, Tesco | 14.5 | −£3.50 |
| French Viognier VdP d'Oc 1999, Tesco | 15 | −£5.00 |
| Gaston d'Orleans Vouvray Demi Sec 1998 | 12 | £5–7 |
| James Herrick Chardonnay VdP d'Oc 1998 | 16.5 | −£5.00 |
| Les Estoiles Organic Chardonnay/Chenin VdP d'Oc NV | 13.5 | −£5.00 |
| Les Quatre Clochers Chardonnay 1998 | 15 | £5–7 |
| Macon Blanc Villages 1998, Tesco | 11 | −£5.00 |
| Meursault 1er Cru Les Genevrieres 1988 | 10 | £20+ |
| Montagny Oak Aged 1997 | 13.5 | £7–10 |
| Muscadet NV, Tesco | 13.5 | −£3.50 |
| Muscadet Sur Lie 1999, Tesco | 13 | −£5.00 |
| Oak Aged White Burgundy 1998, Tesco | 13.5 | £5–7 |
| Pouilly Fuisse Louis Jadot 1998 | 11 | £10–13 |

Pouilly Fume Cuvée Jules 1998 — 13 — £7–10

Sancerre 1999, Tesco — 10 — £5–7

Vouvray, Tesco — 12 — –£5.00

White Burgundy 1999, Tesco — 12 — –£5.00

## GERMAN WHITE

Carl Erhard Rheingau Riesling 1999 — 14 — –£5.00

Devil's Rock Riesling 1998 — 14 — –£5.00

Fire Mountain Riesling 1997 — 13.5 — –£5.00

Grans Fassian Trittenheimer Riesling Spatlese 1997 — 14 — £7–10

Kendermans Dry Riesling 1999 — 13 — –£5.00

Liebfraumilch, Tesco — 12 — –£3.50

Steinweiler Kloster Liebfrauenberg Kabinett, Tesco — 14 — –£5.00

Steinweiler Kloster Liebfrauenberg Spatlese, Tesco — 13 — –£5.00

Villa Baden Chasselas 1998 — 12 — –£5.00

## GREEK RED

Grande Reserve Naoussa 1995 — 13.5 — £5–7

Greek Red Wine 1999, Tesco — 15 — –£5.00

## GREEK WHITE

Greek White Wine 1999, Tesco — 14 — –£5.00

Santorini Dry White 1999 — 13.5 — –£5.00

## HUNGARIAN RED

Chapel Hill Barrique Cabernet Sauvignon 1997 — 15 — –£5.00

Reka Valley Hungarian Merlot, Tesco — 13 — –£3.50

## HUNGARIAN WHITE

Chapel Hill Pinot Noir Rosé 1998 — 15 — –£3.50

Emerald Hungarian Sauvignon Blanc 1999 — 14 — –£5.00

Hungarian Oaked Chardonnay NV, Tesco — 12 — –£5.00

Hungarian Oaked Chardonnay Reserve 1999, Tesco — 13.5 — –£5.00

Nagyrede Estate Barrel Aged Pinot Grigio/Zenit 1998 — 16 — –£5.00

Reka Valley Chardonnay NV, Tesco — 12 — –£3.50

Tokaiji Aszu 1990 — 16 — £7–10

## ITALIAN RED

Barbera d'Asti Calissano 1997 — 15.5 — –£5.00

Barolo Vigna dei Pola 1995 — 14 — £13–20

Chianti 1998, Tesco — 13 — –£3.50

417

TESCO

| L'Arco Cabernet Franc, Friuli 1998 | 14 | −£5.00 |
| Melini Chianti 1998 | 14 | −£5.00 |
| Merlot del Piave NV, Tesco | 11 | −£5.00 |
| Moncaro Sangiovese 1999 | 13 | −£3.50 |
| Monte d'Abro Montepulciano Abruzzo 1999 | 14 | −£5.00 |
| Pendulum Zinfandel 1999 | 15.5 | −£5.00 |
| Pinot Noir del Veneto NV, Tesco | 11 | −£5.00 |
| Sicilian Red NV, Tesco | 14 | −£3.50 |
| Taruso Ripassato Valpolicella Valpentena 1997 | 16.5 | £5–7 |
| Terra Viva Vino da Tavola Organic Red | 15.5 | −£5.00 |
| Trulli Primitivo Salento 1998 | 14.5 | −£5.00 |
| Valpolicella Classico 1999, Tesco | 13 | −£5.00 |
| Villa Pigna Rosso Piceno 1998 | 14 | −£5.00 |

## ITALIAN WHITE

| Antinori Orvieto Classico Secco 1999 | 13 | −£5.00 |
| Asti NV, Tesco | 13 | −£5.00 |
| Elegant Crisp White 1999, Tesco | 13.5 | −£5.00 |
| Frascati 1999, Tesco | 14 | −£3.50 |
| La Gioiosa Pinot Grigio 1999 | 13.5 | −£5.00 |

| Orvieto Classico Abboocato 1999, Tesco | 13.5 | −£5.00 |
| Soave Classico 1998, Tesco | 14.5 | −£5.00 |
| Trulli Dry Muscat 1999 | 13.5 | −£5.00 |
| Verdicchio Classico 1999, Tesco | 14 | −£5.00 |
| Villa del Borgo Pinot Grigio 1999 | 14 | −£5.00 |

## MEXICAN RED

| Mexican Cabernet Sauvignon 1999, Tesco | 13 | −£5.00 |

## MEXICAN WHITE

| Mexican Chardonnay 1999, Tesco | 15 | −£5.00 |

## NEW ZEALAND RED

| Babich Winemaker's Reserve Syrah 1998 | 15 | £7–10 |
| Montana Cabernet Sauvignon/Merlot 1998 | 16 | £5–7 |
| Montana Reserve Merlot 1998 | 16.5 | £7–10 |
| Montana Reserve Pinot Noir 1998 | 12 | £7–10 |
| New Zealand Cabernet Sauvignon NV, Tesco | 13.5 | −£5.00 |
| Waimanu Red 1998 | 13 | −£5.00 |

## NEW ZEALAND WHITE

| | | |
|---|---|---|
| Azure Bay Chardonnay/ Semillon 1999 | 13 | −£5.00 |
| Cooks Chardonnay, Gisborne 1998 | 13 | £5−7 |
| Jackson Estate Sauvignon Blanc 1999 | 15 | £7−10 |
| Lawsons Dry Hills Sauvignon Blanc 1999 | 16.5 | £7−10 |
| Montana Reserve Chardonnay 1999 | 17 | £7−10 |
| Montana Riesling 1999 | 16 | −£5.00 |
| Montana Sauvignon Blanc 1999 | 15.5 | £5−7 |
| New Zealand Dry White, Tesco | 13.5 | −£5.00 |
| New Zealand Sauvignon Blanc 1998, Tesco | 13.5 | −£5.00 |
| Stoneleigh Chardonnay 1997 | 15.5 | £5−7 |

## PORTUGUESE RED

| | | |
|---|---|---|
| Alianca Particular Palmela 1995 | 17 | £5−7 |
| Bela Fonte Baga 1998 | 14 | −£5.00 |
| Dao, Tesco 1998 | 14 | −£5.00 |
| Dom Ferraz Bairrada 1997 | 16 | −£5.00 |
| Dom Ferraz Dao 1997 | 15 | −£5.00 |
| Portuguese Red NV, Tesco | 14.5 | −£3.50 |
| Vinha Nove Tras-os-Montes 1998 | 15.5 | −£5.00 |

## PORTUGUESE WHITE

| | | |
|---|---|---|
| Bela Fonte Bical 1998 | 15 | −£5.00 |
| Dry Vinho Verde, Tesco | 13.5 | −£5.00 |

## ROMANIAN RED

| | | |
|---|---|---|
| Reka Valley Romanian Pinot Noir, Tesco | 15.5 | −£3.50 |

## SOUTH AFRICAN RED

| | | |
|---|---|---|
| African Legend Pinotage 1998 | 14 | −£5.00 |
| Beyers Truter Pinotage 1998, Tesco | 16.5 | −£5.00 |
| Cape Cinsault NV, Tesco | 15.5 | −£3.50 |
| Cape Cinsault/Pinotage NV, Tesco | 15.5 | −£5.00 |
| Clos Malverne Pinotage 1999 | 16 | £5−7 |
| Diemersdal Shiraz 1998 | 15 | £5−7 |
| Goats Do Roam Fairview, Paarl 1999 | 15.5 | −£5.00 |
| Goiya Glaan 1999 | 15 | −£5.00 |
| International Winemaker Cabernet/Merlot, Tesco | 15 | −£5.00 |
| Kumala Cabernet Sauvignon/Shiraz 1999 | 15 | −£5.00 |
| Kumala Cinsault/ Cabernet Sauvignon 1999 | 13.5 | −£5.00 |
| Landskroon Premier Reserve Cabernet Sauvignon 1998 | 14 | £5−7 |
| Long Mountain Cabernet Sauvignon 1998 | 13.5 | −£5.00 |

TESCO

| | | |
|---|---|---|
| Oak Village Pinotage/ Merlot 1999 | 13 | −£5.00 |
| South African Cabernet Sauvignon/Shiraz 1999, Tesco | 14 | −£5.00 |
| South African Red NV, Tesco | 14.5 | −£3.50 |
| South African Reserve Cabernet NV, Tesco | 12 | −£5.00 |
| Spice Route Andrew's Hope Merlot/Cabernet, Malmesbury 1998 | 16.5 | £5–7 |
| Spice Route Cabernet Merlot 1998 | 16.5 | £7–10 |
| Winds of Change Cabernet/Pinotage 1999 | 16 | −£5.00 |

## SOUTH AFRICAN WHITE

| | | |
|---|---|---|
| African Legend Colombard 1999 | 14 | −£5.00 |
| Arniston Bay Chenin/ Chardonnay 1999 | 13 | −£5.00 |
| Arniston Bay Rosé 2000 | 13 | −£5.00 |
| Boschendal Grande Cuvée Sauvignon Blanc 1998 | 13.5 | £5–7 |
| Cape Chenin Blanc NV, Tesco | 15 | −£3.50 |
| Fairview Chardonnay 1998 | 16.5 | £5–7 |
| Firefinch Sauvignon Blanc 1999 | 16 | −£5.00 |
| Goiya Kgeisje 2000 | 15 | −£5.00 |
| Kumala Colombard/ Chardonnay 1999 | 14.5 | −£5.00 |

| | | |
|---|---|---|
| Oak Village Sauvignon Blanc 1999 | 13 | −£5.00 |
| Ryland's Grove Barrel Fermented Chenin Blanc 1999 | 16 | −£5.00 |
| Rylands Grove Dry Muscat 1999 | 13.5 | −£5.00 |
| Rylands Grove Sauvignon Blanc 2000 | 14.5 | −£5.00 |
| South African Chardonnay/Colombard NV, Tesco | 14 | −£5.00 |
| South African Medium Sweet White NV, Tesco | 13 | −£3.50 |
| South African Reserve Chardonnay 1999, Tesco | 13.5 | −£5.00 |
| South African White, Tesco | 14 | −£3.50 |
| Spice Route Long Walk Sauvignon Blanc 1998 | 16 | £5–7 |
| Third Millennium Chenin Chardonnay 1999 | 13 | −£5.00 |
| Van Loveren Blanc de Noir Red Muscadel Rosé 2000 | 14 | −£3.50 |

## SOUTH AMERICAN RED

| | | |
|---|---|---|
| Two Tribes Red | 13.5 | −£5.00 |

## SOUTH AMERICAN WHITE

| | | |
|---|---|---|
| Two Tribes White | 13.5 | −£5.00 |

## SPANISH RED

| | | |
|---|---|---|
| Campillo Gran Reserva Rioja 1989 | 10 | £13–20 |

| | | |
|---|---|---|
| Campillo Reserva Rioja 1995 | 13 | £10–13 |
| Carmesi Garnacha/ Tempranillo Calatayud 1998 | 16 | –£5.00 |
| Don Darias NV | 15.5 | –£5.00 |
| Espiral Moristel Tempranillo/Cabernet Sauvignon 1998 | 16 | –£5.00 |
| Huge Juicy Red, Tesco | 13.5 | –£5.00 |
| Marques de Chive Reserva 1994, Tesco | 14.5 | –£5.00 |
| Marques de Chive Tempranillo NV, Tesco | 15 | –£3.50 |
| Marques de Grinon Rioja 1997 | 15 | –£5.00 |
| Muruve Crianza 1996 | 15.5 | £5–7 |
| Orobio Tempranillo Rioja 1998 | 13 | £5–7 |
| Piedmonte Merlot Tempranillo 1998 | 14 | –£5.00 |
| Priorat l'Agnet 1998 | 14 | £5–7 |
| Senorio de los Llanos Valdepeñas Gran Reserva 1994 | 14 | –£5.00 |
| Senorio de los Llanos Valdepeñas Reserva 1996 | 14 | –£5.00 |
| Vina Azbache Rioja 1998 | 15.5 | –£5.00 |
| Vina Mara Gran Reserva Rioja 1990, Tesco | 13.5 | £7–10 |
| Vina Mara Rioja Alavesa 1998, Tesco | 16 | £5–7 |
| Vina Mara Rioja Reserva 1995, Tesco | 15 | £7–10 |
| Vina Mara Rioja, Tesco | 14 | –£5.00 |

| | | |
|---|---|---|
| Vina Montana Monastrell/Merlot 1998 | 16 | –£5.00 |

## SPANISH WHITE

| | | |
|---|---|---|
| Moscatel de Valencia, Tesco | 16 | –£3.50 |

## USA RED

| | | |
|---|---|---|
| California Old Vine Estate Carignane 1996 | 13.5 | £5–7 |
| Colombia Crest Côte de Colombia Grenache 1997 | 15 | –£5.00 |
| Edgewood Estate Napa Valley Malbec 1997 | 16 | £10–13 |
| Ehlers Grove Syrah 1998 | 13 | £7–10 |
| Mondavi Coastal Merlot 1997 | 16 | £7–10 |
| Robert Mondavi Coastal Cabernet Sauvignon 1995 | 14 | £7–10 |
| Turning Leaf Cabernet Sauvignon 1997 | 12 | £5–7 |
| Turning Leaf Zinfandel 1996 | 12.5 | £5–7 |
| West Coast Ruby Cabernet/Merlot 1999, Tesco | 15 | –£5.00 |

## USA WHITE

| | | |
|---|---|---|
| Fetzer Barrel Select Chardonnay 1997 | 15 | £7–10 |
| Fetzer Viognier 1999 | 15 | £7–10 |
| Hogue Chenin Blanc 1998 | 11 | £5–7 |
| West Coast California Chardonnay 1999, Tesco | 14.5 | –£5.00 |

## FORTIFIED WINES

| | | |
|---|---|---|
| 10 Year Old Tawny Port, Tesco | 13.5 | £10–13 |
| Finest Madeira, Tesco | 15.5 | £7–10 |
| Mick Morris Rutherglen Liqueur Muscat (half-bottle) | 17 | –£5.00 |
| Superior Oloroso Seco, Tesco | 16 | –£3.50 |
| Superior Palo Cortado, Tesco | 16 | –£5.00 |

## SPARKLING WINES

| | | |
|---|---|---|
| Australian Sparkling Wine NV, Tesco | 13 | –£5.00 |
| Blanc de Blancs Champagne NV, Tesco | 13.5 | £13–20 |
| Blanc de Noirs Champagne NV, Tesco | 14 | £13–20 |
| Cava NV, Tesco | 15 | –£5.00 |
| Chapel Down Epoch Brut NV (England) | 11 | £5–7 |
| Charles Duret Blanc de Blancs Brut NV | 13 | –£5.00 |
| Charles Duret Blanc de Blancs Demi Sec NV | 12 | –£5.00 |
| Cockatoo Ridge Black Sparkling NV | 16.5 | £7–10 |
| Demi-Sec Champagne, Tesco | 13 | £10–13 |
| Hardys Stamp of Australia Chardonnay/ Pinot Noir Sparkling NV | 14 | £5–7 |
| Hungarian Sparkling Chardonnay NV, Tesco | 13.5 | –£5.00 |
| Jacob's Creek Sparkling Chardonnay/Pinot Noir NV (Australia) | 15 | £5–7 |
| Laurent-Perrier Cuvée Rosé Brut NV | 11 | £20+ |
| Laurent-Perrier Vintage 1990 | 13 | £20+ |
| Les Etoiles Organic Sparkling Wine NV | 12 | £5–7 |
| Lindauer Brut NV (New Zealand) | 14 | £7–10 |
| Lindauer Special Reserve NV (New Zealand) | 16 | £7–10 |
| Moet Vintage 1993 | 13.5 | £20+ |
| Nicolas Feuillate Brut NV | 13.5 | £13–20 |
| Pirie 1996 | 13 | £13–20 |
| Premier Cru Champagne Brut NV | 15 | £10–13 |
| Rosé Cava NV, Tesco | 15.5 | –£5.00 |
| South African Sparkling Sauvignon Blanc 1998, Tesco | 14.5 | –£5.00 |
| Taittinger Champagne Brut NV | 12 | £20+ |
| Valdivieso Sparkling Merlot 1998 | 16 | £5–7 |
| Veuve du Vernay Brut NV | 14 | £7–10 |

**SEE STOP PRESS SECTION AT END OF BOOK FOR LAST-MINUTE ADDITIONS OR UPDATES TO THIS RETAILER'S RANGE.**

# THRESHER/BOTTOMS UP/ WINE RACK/VICTORIA WINE – 1ST QUENCH

It used to be Ms Arabella Woodrow of the Co-op who was the one retail wine buyer with whom I could have an intelligent conversation about marathon running, but she has left and gone elsewhere. Luckily, however, I now have Jonathan Butt of 1st Quench, as the umbrella name of this massive retailer (2,600 shops) has it. Why 1st Quench? Not because of Jonathan's athletic prowess (he narrowly failed to win the millennium London Marathon only by some several thousand places), but because this astonishing hybrid, a coming together of many once-competitive wine shops, is in love with acronyms.

Think of this. Qu = quality, en = enjoyment, ch = choice. No, I did not make this up. I lack the talent. But someone who attended the Thresher and Victoria Wine marriage did. From this initial conjugal bliss, much has transpired.

At Christmas 1999 a company pay review was reported to have axed Victoria Wine employees' Christmas bonus of a week's extra pay. A new rewards and incentives scheme was being introduced, it was said, and the company announced that staff across the whole chain were now on an equal footing and on the same pay and bonus structure. The following month the retailer announced that a further 110 Victoria Wine and 70 Thresher outlets would close in the second round of its 'rationalisation programme', with job losses as high as 600 according to the union USDAW. This follows the 150 store closures announced at the beginning of 1999.

The company said that it was prepared to give stores earmarked for closure a second chance to show their worth after two stores were granted reprieves. The two stores (one in London and one in Somerset) were given a second chance after store managers convinced bosses they could reverse the stores' fortunes. In August 1999 another 180 stores were earmarked for closure. Later that year, 1st Quench launched its Alchemy at Work staff training and motivation programme designed to mould its workforce into a 'formidable force in the market'. It was designed to encourage more than 18,000 shop staff to 'buy into the FQ vision, mission and values'. The company has now settled at around 2,675 outlets. Alchemy was a famous medieval wheeze, you will recall, aiming to persuade people that lead, and other base metals, could be changed into gold. It remains to be seen whether FQ has, in this respect, succeeded where history reports nothing but failure.

Other high peaks were reached. In autumn 1999 seven VW and Thresher employees raised £12,500 for the Meningitis Trust after scaling the three highest mountains in England, Scotland and Wales. More meaningfully for wine buyers, the company dispatched human resources staff to the shop floor. Thirty-eight head-office personnel ended up working in stores to get an idea of the problems faced by shop staff. Indeed, certain senior managers, including managing director Jerry Walton, actually worked in 1st Quench stores on New Year's Eve.

As the millennium celebrations abated, it was reported that a sale of 1st Quench, valued at around £300 million and jointly owned by Whitbread and Punch Taverns, was reportedly 'edging closer'. Possible future owners were conjectured to be the current management team or the Parisa group. Mr Haghighi, who runs the latter retailer, said that the acquisition of FQ was something of a personal quest as he had entered the business as a sales assistant in a Thresher outlet. The *Sunday Telegraph* reported that 1st Quench was 'poised for a buyout'. I bet a professional wine trade watcher that it was all hot air and nothing would come of it. Nothing did (except I became ten quid richer). Finally, a Japanese bank, Nomura, bought 1st Quench.

Earlier this year, 1st Quench was said to be the subject of a BBC2 documentary called *Naked Work* which explored the ethos of management consultants. Other subjects were purported to be Amstrad and Cadbury-Schweppes. 1st Quench kept pretty quiet about this programme, if it ever went on air and I never managed to catch any of this series. About this time the managing director, Jerry Walton, and the finance director, Bob Warne, upped and left, for reasons I know not. Thresher's marvellous senior wine buyer, Kim Tidy, also left some time later to get involved in an e-commerce venture.

But to counter such important defections the company announced that its In-house Wine Sales Advice Certificate had now been awarded to 2,000 members of staff. One reader, whose anonymity I shall respect, to whom I conveyed this information, replied 'so some of them have now learned how to say good morning and good afternoon'. Such cynics, some readers.

More thrilling, an ex-Thresher employee, Set Pavlou, aged twenty-nine, sold his first screenplay to Hollywood and also wrote a novel which is also attracting interest from film companies. His movie, *The 51st State*, is being shot, mainly in Liverpool, and stars Samuel L. Jackson and Robert Carlyle. His sci-fi thriller, called *Decipher*, is due to be published in spring 2001. Mr Pavlou, so my assiduous research assistant informs me, once earned £3.55 an hour at Thresher. My research assistant, I should point out, earns a good deal more than that (but then he's far from full-time).

In May 2000 a third round of store closures was deemed necessary. This third wave will result in a further 100 branches being shut down, bringing the total closures since the 1998 merger to 430. When the merger was first announced, the company said it would result in 300 store closures as an 'absolute maximum'.

Ah well, only another 2,600 or so branches to go. Let's hope the one you visit to unshelve any of the wines which follow is 1) still open, 2) run by a manager who is the proud possessor of a In-house Wine Sales Advice Certificate, and 3) has the wines you're interested in.

The fact that I can guarantee none of those three things irritates me. I can feel Disgusted of Tonbridge already picking up his pen. If you could remember to enclose a stamped addressed envelope, by the way, Mr Disgusted, it would mean I'd reply all the quicker.

Thresher/Bottoms Up/Wine Rack/Victoria Wine
Enjoyment Hall
Bessemer Road
Welwyn Garden City
Herts
AL7 1BL

Tel 01707 385000 (1st Quench)
Fax 01707 385004
www.enjoyment.co.uk

## ARGENTINIAN RED

Anubis Malbec 1999 — 16 — £5–7

Argento Malbec 1999 — 16.5 — −£5.00

Corazon Bonarda 1999 — 16 — −£5.00

Corazon Tempranillo 1999 — 16.5 — −£5.00

Libertad Malbec Bonarda 1999 — 15 — −£5.00

Libertad Malbec Sangiovese 1998 — 15 — −£5.00

| Martins Andino Malbec Bonarda 1998 | 14 | –£5.00 |
| Norton Privada 1998 | 16.5 | £7–10 |
| Q Tempranillo 1998 | 16.5 | £7–10 |
| Santa Julia Pinot Noir 1999 | 15.5 | –£5.00 |
| Villa Atuel Syrah 1999 | 15.5 | –£5.00 |

## ARGENTINIAN WHITE

| Corazon Pinot Gris 1999 | 15 | –£5.00 |
| Correas Torrontes Chardonnay 1999 | 14 | –£5.00 |
| Norton Semillon Chardonnay 1999 | 16 | –£5.00 |
| Norton Torrontes, Mendoza 1999 | 15.5 | –£5.00 |
| Santa Julia Viognier 1999 | 17 | –£5.00 |

## AUSTRALIAN RED

| Hardys Nottage Hill Cabernet Sauvignon Shiraz 1998 | 15.5 | £5–7 |
| Leasingham Domaine Cabernet/Malbec 1997 | 10 | £7–10 |
| Lindemans Padthaway Shiraz 1997 | 15.5 | £7–10 |
| Nanya Estate Malbec/ Ruby Cabernet 1998 | 10 | –£5.00 |
| Oxford Landing Cabernet Sauvignon Shiraz 1999 | 15.5 | £5–7 |
| Oxford Landing Merlot 1999 | 14 | £5–7 |
| St Hallett Barossa Shiraz 1997 | 13 | £7–10 |

| Tatachilla Grenache Shiraz 1998 | 16 | £5–7 |
| Tollana Red, S E Australia NV | 13.5 | –£5.00 |
| Yalumba Bush Vine Grenache 1997 | 14 | £7–10 |

## AUSTRALIAN WHITE

| David Traeger Verdelho, Victoria 1998 | 16 | £7–10 |
| Hardys Nottage Hill Riesling 1998 | 15.5 | –£5.00 |
| Oxford Landing Sauvignon Blanc 1999 | 15 | –£5.00 |
| Penfolds Rawsons Retreat Bin 202 Riesling 1999 | 15 | –£5.00 |
| Pewsey Vale Riesling 1997 | 16 | £5–7 |
| Riddoch Coonawarra Chardonnay 1998 | 15 | £5–7 |
| Samuels Bay Riesling, Eden Valley 1997 | 16 | £5–7 |
| Tollana Unoaked Chardonnay 1999 | 15.5 | –£5.00 |

## BULGARIAN RED

| Copper Crossing Red NV | 14 | –£3.50 |
| Domaine Boyar Premium Oaked Cabernet Shumen 1997 | 13.5 | –£5.00 |
| Domaine Boyar Premium Reserve Cabernet Sauvignon 1996 | 14 | –£5.00 |
| Domaine Boyar Premium Reserve Merlot 1996 | 14.5 | –£5.00 |

## BULGARIAN WHITE

| | | |
|---|---|---|
| Boyar Muskat & Ugni Blanc NV | 11 | –£3.50 |
| Copper Crossing Dry White NV | 10 | –£3.50 |
| Copper Crossing Medium White NV | 12 | –£3.50 |

## CHILEAN RED

| | | |
|---|---|---|
| Caliterra Cabernet Sauvignon 1998 | 15.5 | –£5.00 |
| Casa Lapostolle Cuvée Alexandre Cabernet Sauvignon 1997 | 16.5 | £7–10 |
| Casa Lapostolle Cuvée Alexandre Merlot 1997 | 17.5 | £10–13 |
| Casa Lapostolle Merlot 1998 | 16.5 | £5–7 |
| Concha y Toro Casillero del Diablo Cabernet Sauvignon 1998 | 16.5 | –£5.00 |
| Cono Sur Cabernet Sauvignon, Rapel 1998 | 16.5 | –£5.00 |
| Errazuriz Cabernet Sauvignon 1998 | 17.5 | £5–7 |
| Errazuriz Reserva Cabernet Sauvignon 1997 | 16 | £7–10 |
| Isla Negra Cabernet Sauvignon 1998 | 15.5 | £5–7 |
| La Palmeria Cabernet/ Merlot 1998 | 16 | –£5.00 |
| Las Colinas Cabernet Merlot 1999 | 15 | –£5.00 |
| Las Colinas Chilean Red NV | 13.5 | –£3.50 |

| | | |
|---|---|---|
| Las Colinas Merlot 1999 | 15 | –£5.00 |
| Martins Don Rui Cabernet Sauvignon 1997 | 13.5 | £5–7 |
| Santa Ines Legado de Armida Cabernet Sauvignon Reserve 1997 | 16.5 | £5–7 |
| Santa Ines Legardo de Armida Reserve Malbec 1997 | 16 | £5–7 |
| Valdivieso Malbec 1998 | 16 | –£5.00 |
| Valdivieso Merlot 1999 | 15.5 | –£5.00 |
| Valdivieso Reserve Pinot Noir 1996 | 14.5 | £7–10 |
| Veramonte Cabernet Sauvignon 1997 | 16 | £5–7 |
| Veramonte Merlot 1997 | 14 | £5–7 |

## CHILEAN WHITE

| | | |
|---|---|---|
| Casa Lapostolle Sauvignon Blanc 1999 | 17 | £5–7 |
| Concha y Toro Casillero del Diablo Chardonnay 1997 | 17 | –£5.00 |
| La Palmeria Chardonnay 1998 | 16 | –£5.00 |
| Las Colinas Chardonnay 1999 | 15 | –£5.00 |
| Las Colinas Riesling 1997 | 15.5 | –£5.00 |
| Santa Ines Legardo de Armida Reserve Chardonnay 1998 | 16.5 | £5–7 |
| Veramonte Chardonnay 1998 | 13.5 | £5–7 |

## FRENCH RED

| | | |
|---|---|---|
| Abbotts Cumulus Minervois 1998 | 16.5 | £5–7 |
| Beaujolais AC Regional Classics 1997 | 13.5 | –£5.00 |
| Beaujolais Villages Duboeuf 1997 | 13 | £5–7 |
| Château Sauvage Premier Côtes de Bordeaux 1997 | 13 | £5–7 |
| Château Suau, 1er Côtes de Bordeaux 1997 (unoaked) | 13.5 | £5–7 |
| Claret Regional Classic, Sichel NV | 14 | –£5.00 |
| Côtes de Beaune Villages 1996 | 12 | £7–10 |
| Côtes du Rhône Villages Les Faisans 1998 | 14 | –£5.00 |
| Dark Horse Cahors 1998 | 14 | –£5.00 |
| Domaine Peyrat Cabernet Sauvignon 1997 | 15 | £5–7 |
| Fitou Terroir de Tuchan 1998 | 17 | £7–10 |
| Fleurie Georges Duboeuf 1998 | 11 | £7–10 |
| Fleurie Regional Classics 1998 | 13.5 | £5–7 |
| French Revolution Le Rouge 1999 | 16 | –£5.00 |
| La Ramillade Côtes du Rhône Rasteau 1997 | 16 | £7–10 |
| Morgon Domaine des Côtes de Douby 1998 | 13.5 | £5–7 |
| Old Bush Vines Carignan 1998 | 13.5 | –£5.00 |
| Pinot Noir, Louis Jadot 1998 | 12.5 | £7–10 |
| Sirius Red 1997 | 13.5 | £5–7 |

## FRENCH WHITE

| | | |
|---|---|---|
| Chablis Domaine de Bieville 1998 | 14 | £7–10 |
| Chablis Regional Classics 1997 | 13.5 | £7–10 |
| Chablis Vieilles Vignes, Defaix 1996 | 11 | £10–13 |
| Chablis Vieilles Vignes, La Cuvée Exceptionelle, Defaix 1997 | 12.5 | £13–20 |
| Château Filhot Sauternes 1990 | 15 | £20+ |
| Château Petit Moulin Blanc, Bordeaux 1998 | 12.5 | £5–7 |
| Domaine Pré Baron Sauvignon de Touraine 1998 | 14.5 | £5–7 |
| Domaine Tariquert Sauvignon Blanc 1999 | 14 | £5–7 |
| French Revolution Le Blanc 1999 | 13 | –£5.00 |
| Le Vieux Mas Marsanne Viognier VdP d'Oc 1998 | 15 | –£5.00 |
| Les Pierres Blanches Sancerre 1998 | 12 | £7–10 |
| Old Bush Vines Grenache Blanc 1999 | 14 | –£5.00 |
| Orchid Vale Medium Chardonnay 1999 | 10 | –£5.00 |
| Petit Chablis de Maligny 1996 | 13.5 | £7–10 |

| | | |
|---|---|---|
| Riesling Wintzenheim Zind Humbrecht 1997 | 14 | £7–10 |
| Riesling Zind Humbrecht Clos Hauserer 1997 | 14 | £13–20 |
| Tequirat Côtes de Gascogne 1998 | 14 | –£5.00 |
| Tokay Pinot Gris, Turckheim 1998 | 15.5 | £5–7 |
| Turckheim Alsace Blanc 1998 | 13 | –£5.00 |
| Turckheim Gewürztraminer 1998 | 16 | £5–7 |
| Turckheim Pinot Blanc 1998 | 14.5 | –£5.00 |
| Zind Humbrecht Pinot d'Alsace 1997 | 16 | £7–10 |

## GERMAN WHITE

| | | |
|---|---|---|
| Piesporter Michelsberg QbA 1997 | 10 | –£3.50 |
| Tokay Pinot Gris Herrenweg, Zind Humbrecht 1997 | 16.5 | £13–20 |

## HUNGARIAN WHITE

| | | |
|---|---|---|
| AK 28 Sauvignon Blanc 1998 | 14.5 | –£5.00 |
| Hilltop Gewürztraminer 1997 | 15.5 | –£5.00 |
| The Unpronounceable Grape 1997 | 12 | –£3.50 |

## ITALIAN RED

| | | |
|---|---|---|
| Amarone della Valpolicella Via Nova 1997 | 18 | £7–10 |
| Amarone della Valpolicella Zenato 1995 | 17 | £13–20 |
| Barbera Bricco del Bosco 1997 | 14 | £5–7 |
| Barolo Terre da Vino 1996 | 13 | £10–13 |
| Brunello di Montalcino, Casanova di Neri 1994 | 15.5 | £20+ |
| Cecchi Sangiovese 1998 | 14.5 | –£5.00 |
| Chianti Classico Riserva Rocca Guicciadia, Ricasoli 1997 | 16.5 | £7–10 |
| Chianti Grati Poggio Galiga, Banda Blu 1997 | 13 | £7–10 |
| Formulae Sangiovese di Toscana, Ricasoli 1998 | 13.5 | £5–7 |
| Graticciaia Puglia 1994 | 17 | £13–20 |
| La Bella Figura Merlot Cabernet 1998 | 15.5 | –£5.00 |
| Merlot Corvina Fiordaliso 1998 | 13.5 | –£5.00 |
| Montepulciano d'Abruzzo Umani Ronchi 1999 | 14 | –£5.00 |
| Montepulciano Selva Torta 1998 | 15.5 | £5–7 |
| Rosso di Montalcino, Casanova di Neri 1998 | 15 | £10–13 |
| Salice Salento Vallone 1997 | 13.5 | £5–7 |
| Trulli Primitivo 1997 | 14 | –£5.00 |

| | | |
|---|---|---|
| Valpolicella Classico Superiore Zenato 1997 | 16 | –£5.00 |
| Valpolicella Classico Zenato 1997 | 16.5 | –£5.00 |
| Valpolicella Ripassa Superiore Zenato 1997 | 17 | £7–10 |
| Vigna Flaminio, Brindisi Rosso 1996 | 15 | £5–7 |

## ITALIAN WHITE

| | | |
|---|---|---|
| Falerio Pilastri Saladini 1999 | 15.5 | –£5.00 |
| La Bella Figura Chardonnay/Pinot Grigio 1999 | 14.5 | –£5.00 |
| Marc Xero Chardonnay NV | 15 | –£5.00 |
| Pinot Grigio Fiordaliso 1999 | 14.5 | –£5.00 |
| Pinot Grigio Terrazze della Luna 1999 | 14 | £5–7 |
| Selva Torta Verdicchio 1999 | 14 | £5–7 |
| Soave Classico Zenato 1999 | 16.5 | –£5.00 |
| Verdicchio dei Castelli di Jesi Verbacco 1999 | 15.5 | –£5.00 |

## NEW ZEALAND RED

| | | |
|---|---|---|
| Awatea Cabernet Sauvignon/Merlot 1997 | 13.5 | £13–20 |
| Church Road Cabernet Sauvignon/Merlot 1998 | 15 | £7–10 |
| Felton Road Pinot Noir, Otago 1998 | 13.5 | £13–20 |
| Martinborough Pinot Noir 1998 | 13.5 | £13–20 |

| | | |
|---|---|---|
| Montana Cabernet Sauvignon Merlot 1999 | 15 | £5–7 |
| Montana Reserve Merlot 1998 | 16.5 | £7–10 |
| Palliser Pinot Noir 1998 | 14 | £10–13 |
| Te Mata Estate Cabernet Merlot 1998 | 16.5 | £7–10 |
| Timara Cabernet/Merlot 1998 | 14 | –£5.00 |

## NEW ZEALAND WHITE

| | | |
|---|---|---|
| Azure Bay Sauvignon/ Semillon 1999 | 13.5 | –£5.00 |
| Babich Pinot Gris, Marlborough 1999 | 16 | £5–7 |
| Church Road Chardonnay 1998 | 16 | £7–10 |
| Church Road Reserve Chardonnay 1998 | 17 | £10–13 |
| Craggy Range Old Renwick Vineyard Sauvignon Blanc 1999 | 15 | £7–10 |
| Dashwood Sauvignon Blanc 1999 | 16 | £5–7 |
| Elston Chardonnay 1998 | 16.5 | £13–20 |
| Framingham Pinot Noir 1998 | 12 | £10–13 |
| In the Black Chardonnay 1998 | 16.5 | £5–7 |
| Montana Chardonnay 1999 | 15.5 | £5–7 |
| Montana 'O' Ormond Estate Chardonnay 1998 | 15.5 | £10–13 |
| Montana Reserve Chardonnay 1999 | 17 | £7–10 |

| | | |
|---|---|---|
| Montana Reserve Gewürztraminer 1999 | 16 | £7–10 |
| Montana Reserve Sauvignon Blanc, Marlborough 1999 | 16 | £7–10 |
| Montana Sauvignon Blanc 1999 | 15.5 | £5–7 |
| Oyster Bay Chardonnay, Marlborough 1999 | 16.5 | £5–7 |
| Oyster Bay Sauvignon Blanc 1999 | 16.5 | £5–7 |
| Oyster Bay Sauvignon Blanc 2000 | 16 | £5–7 |
| Palliser Estate Sauvignon Blanc, Martinborough 1999 | 14 | £7–10 |
| Quartz Reef Pinot Gris 1999 | 13.5 | £10–13 |
| Sacred Hill Basket Press Cabernet Sauvignon 1998 | 16 | £7–10 |
| Te Mata Estate Chardonnay 1999 | 17 | £7–10 |
| Timara Dry White 1999 | 13 | –£5.00 |
| Tohu Sauvignon Blanc, Marlborough 1999 | 16 | £7–10 |
| Villa Maria Lightly Oaked Chardonnay 1999 | 16 | £5–7 |
| Villa Maria Private Bin Riesling 1999 | 16 | £5–7 |
| Villa Maria Private Bin Sauvignon Blanc 1999 | 16 | £5–7 |
| Villa Maria Reserve Sauvignon Blanc, Wairau Valley 1998 | 15.5 | £7–10 |
| Villa Maria Reserve Sauvignon Blanc, Wairau Valley 1999 | 17 | £7–10 |

## PORTUGUESE RED

| | | |
|---|---|---|
| Dom Ferraz Dao 1997 | 15 | –£5.00 |
| Fiuza Cabernet Sauvignon 1997 | 14 | –£5.00 |
| Pedras do Monte 1998 | 16 | –£5.00 |
| Segada Tinto 1998 | 15.5 | –£5.00 |

## ROMANIAN RED

| | | |
|---|---|---|
| River Route Limited Edition Cabernet Sauvignon 1997 | 13.5 | –£5.00 |
| River Route Pinot Noir 1998 | 12 | –£5.00 |

## ROMANIAN WHITE

| | | |
|---|---|---|
| River Route Limited Edition Chardonnay 1997 | 15.5 | –£5.00 |

## SOUTH AFRICAN RED

| | | |
|---|---|---|
| Cape View Cinsault/ Shiraz 1998 | 12 | –£5.00 |
| Capells Court Cabernet 1998 | 14 | £5–7 |
| Oak Village Cabernet Sauvignon 1998 | 15 | –£5.00 |
| The Pinotage Company Pinotage 1999 | 13.5 | £5–7 |
| Villiera Pinot Noir G & G Reserve 1997 | 13 | £7–10 |
| Winelands Cabernet Sauvignon/Franc, Stellenbosch 1997 | 13.5 | £5–7 |

## SOUTH AFRICAN WHITE

African Legend
Sauvignon Blanc 1998 · 13 · £5–7

Capells Court
Chardonnay 1998 · 14 · £5–7

Carisbrook Chenin/
Chardonnay 1999 · 14 · –£5.00

Hartenberg 'Occasional'
Auxerrois 1997 · 16 · £5–7

Hartenberg 'Occasional'
Bush Vine Chenin Blanc
1997 · 15.5 · £5–7

Hartenberg 'Occasional'
Pinot Blanc 1997 · 15 · £5–7

Hartenberg Weisser
Riesling, Stellenbosch
1997 · 13 · £5–7

Oak Village Chardonnay
1999 · 13.5 · –£5.00

Villiera Chenin Blanc
1997 · 15 · –£5.00

## SPANISH RED

Abadia Retuerta Rivola,
Duero 1996 · 16.5 · £5–7

Alvaro Palacios Finca
Dofi Priorat 1996 · 18 · £20+

Alvaro Palacios 'Les
Terrasses' DO Priorat
1997 · 13.5 · £13–20

Baron de Ley Rioja
Reserva 1996 · 13 · £7–10

Casa Rural Tinto NV · 14.5 · –£3.50

Castillo Ygay Rioja Gran
Reserva 1989 · 10 · £13–20

Chivite Reserva, Gran
Feudo, Navarra 1995 · 13.5 · £5–7

Conde de Valdemar Rioja
Crianza 1997 · 13.5 · £5–7

Conde de Valdemar Rioja
Reserva 1995 · 14 · £7–10

Contino Rioja Reserva
1995 · 15 · £20+

Cune Reserva 1995 · 13.5 · £7–10

Dominio di Montalvo
Rioja 1998 · 13 · £5–7

El Meson Rioja NV · 15 · £5–7

Finca Valpiedra Rioja
1995 · 12 · £13–20

Jumilla Senorio de Robles
1998 · 16 · –£3.50

Marques de Aragon
Garnacha 1998 · 15 · –£5.00

Marques de Grinon Rioja
1998 · 15.5 · £5–7

Marques de Grinon Rioja
Reserva 1996 · 14 · £7–10

Marques de Grinon
Valdepusa Cabernet
Sauvignon 1997 · 16.5 · £7–10

Marques de Grinon
Valdepusa Syrah 1997 · 17 · £10–13

Marques de Murrieta
Rioja Reserva Especial
1995 · 13 · £13–20

Marques de Riscal
Reserva 1996 · 14 · £7–10

Navajas Rioja Crianza
1997 · 13.5 · £5–7

Ochoa Gran Reserva,
Navarra 1992 · 14 · £10–13

Raimat Cabernet Sauvignon 1996 — 15 — £7–10

Raimat Merlot 1996 — 15.5 — £7–10

Remonte Cabernet Sauvignon 1996 — 15.5 — −£5.00

Torres Gran Coronas 1996 — 17 — £7–10

Torres Gran Sangre de Toro 1996 — 16 — £5–7

Vina Real Gran Reserva 1988 — 13 — £13–20

Vina Real Gran Reserva 1991 — 13.5 — £13–20

## SPANISH WHITE

Albarino Condes de Alberei 1999 — 14.5 — £5–7

Albarino Enexebre 1997 — 15.5 — £7–10

Campo Viejo Barrel Fermented Viura 1998 — 13 — £5–7

Casa Rural White NV — 15.5 — −£3.50

Castillo de Liria Rosé NV — 15 — −£3.50

Conde de Valdemar Barrique Fermented Rioja 1996 — 16 — £7–10

Conde de Valdemar Barrique Fermented Rioja 1998 — 12 — £7–10

Conde de Valdemar Rosado 1999 — 14 — −£5.00

Dominio di Montalvo White Rioja 1998 — 15.5 — £5–7

Enexbre Albarino Condes de Albarei 1997 — 15 — £5–7

Torres Vina Esmeralda 1999 — 14 — £5–7

Torres Vina Sol 1999 — 14 — −£5.00

## USA RED

Clos du Bois Merlot 1996 — 14.5 — £13–20

E & J Gallo Ruby Cabernet 1999 — 14 — −£5.00

Eagle Peak Merlot, Fetzer Vineyards 1998 — 15.5 — £5–7

Fetzer Valley Oaks Cabernet Sauvignon 1997 — 15.5 — £5–7

Redwood Trail Pinot Noir 1997 — 13.5 — £5–7

Robert Mondavi North Coast Cellars Zinfandel 1995 — 15 — £7–10

Talus Zinfandel 1997 — 13 — £5–7

Turning Leaf Cabernet Sauvignon 1997 — 12 — £5–7

Turning Leaf Zinfandel 1996 — 12.5 — £5–7

Vendange Californian Red 1998 — 14 — −£5.00

Woodbridge Mondavi Zinfandel 1996 — 14 — £5–7

## USA WHITE

Columbia Crest Chardonnay 1997 — 15.5 — £5–7

Dunnewood Chardonnay 1998 — 16 — £7–10

Fetzer Barrel Select Viognier 1997 — 17 — £7–10

| | | |
|---|---|---|
| Fetzer Sundial Chardonnay, 1998 | 16 | £5–7 |
| Fetzer Syrah Rosé 1999 | 13 | £5–7 |
| Fetzer Viognier 1999 | 15 | £7–10 |
| Jekel Chardonnay, Gravelstone Vineyards 1996 | 15.5 | £7–10 |
| St Supery Sauvignon Blanc 1997 | 15.5 | £7–10 |
| Vendange Californian Dry White 1998 | 11 | –£5.00 |
| Vendanges White Zinfandel 1998 | 9 | –£5.00 |
| Wente Riva Ranch Chardonnay 1996 | 16 | £7–10 |
| Woodbridge Californian Sauvignon Blanc, Robert Mondavi 1996 | 13 | £5–7 |

## SPARKLING WINES

| | | |
|---|---|---|
| Bollinger RD 1985 | 13 | £20+ |
| Bollinger Special Cuvée NV | 14 | £20+ |
| Canard Duchene Charles VII NV | 14.5 | £20+ |
| Charles Heidsieck 'Mis en Caves 1995' NV | 13 | £20+ |
| Cool Ridge Sparkling Chardonnay Pinot Noir Brut NV (Hungary) | 12 | –£5.00 |
| Deutz NV (New Zealand) | 15 | £10–13 |

| | | |
|---|---|---|
| Gosset Grande Millesime 1989 | 15 | £20+ |
| Gosset Grande Reserve NV | 14 | £20+ |
| Green Point Brut 1996 | 15 | £10–13 |
| Krug Grande Cuvée NV | 13 | £20+ |
| Krug Vintage 1989 | 13.5 | £20+ |
| La Corunna Cava NV | 15 | –£5.00 |
| Lanson Vintage Gold Label 1993 | 13.5 | £20+ |
| Lindauer Brut NV (New Zealand) | 14 | £7–10 |
| Lindauer Brut Rosé NV (New Zealand) | 15 | £7–10 |
| Lindauer Special Reserve NV (New Zealand) | 16 | £7–10 |
| Louis Roederer Brut Vintage 1993 (magnum) | 13 | £20+ |
| Mumm Cuvee Napa Brut (California) | 16 | £7–10 |
| Out of the Blue Lightly Sparkling (Italy) (4%) | 10 | –£3.50 |
| Perrier-Jouet Brut Vintage 1992 | 12 | £20+ |
| Pinot Grigio Frizzante NV (Italy) | 15 | –£5.00 |
| Piper Heidsieck Rare 1985 | 17 | £20+ |
| Pol Roger Sir Winston Churchill Cuvée 1988 | 16 | £20+ |
| Pommery Vintage 1991 | 12 | £20+ |
| Veuve Clicquot La Grande Dame 1990 | 16 | £20+ |

**SEE STOP PRESS SECTION AT END OF BOOK FOR LAST-MINUTE ADDITIONS OR UPDATES TO THIS RETAILER'S RANGE.**

# UNWINS

I've been saying for years that this is a sleepy dog with an appetite and fangs to match and so events proved. Who would have believed that this is the retailer which snapped up Fullers, busily spending August 2000 painting every one of the shops in its corporate bee-sting yellow. Every branch. That's right. No 'rationalisation', no closures, no streamlining.

Unwins is in a bullish mood. (It even sells Pelorus 1995, 18 points, one of the greatest bubblies on the planet, for £12.49, cheaper than anyone else.)

In 1999 it experimented with two forecourt formats in Rochester and Witney, Oxfordshire, teaming up with Elf Oil. It rapidly won a retail award for one of them, snatching the prize for Best Site With a Licence to Sell Alcohol in the Forecourt Trader of the Year. No, madam, I did not make that up. It's absolutely true.

The company also announced its intention to look at Internet selling possibilities and has launched a website which can now take orders when previously the site only pushed in-store promotions. Harder to win a Best Site award in this category, I would have said, but we shall see.

Late in 1999 Unwins opened a pilot store which offered freshly baked bread and a cheese counter in addition to the booze. The store was in Tunbridge Wells and was originally part of the Davisons chain (which small chain Unwins snapped up a few years ago). The company is, so it was said, not planning to diversify by setting up new specialist formats but is keen to give its stores 'individual characteristics to suit certain locations'. It was said the Tunbridge Wells outlet was a 'one-off'. I recommend Booze, Bread & Cheese as the brand name: BBC – you've got to admit it has a ring.

Unwins continued to haul in the awards when David Hitchens of the Unwins branch in Wootton Bassett won the 1999 Off-Licence of the Year Award. Wootton Bassett? Shame on you. Historical place, Wootton Bassett, in Wiltshire. Known as Wodeton in the Domesday Book (no Unwins branch recorded) and the early-English-style church is worth a visit if you're passing (as, presumably, is Mr Hitchens' branch).

But of course the big event for Unwins was that acquisition of Fuller Smith & Turner's 61 wine shops for a wholly reasonable, not to say cheap, £7.5 million. Slightly above-average footballers change clubs for sums like that, and so Unwins knew they had a bargain on their hands. There was some *sotto voce* mutterings by wine gossips at this news. Unwins is seen, by some wine commentators, as a vulgarian from the outer suburbs, while Fullers was judged to be more up-market. Unwins reacted by dismissing the suggestion that it will 'dumb down' the wine range at Fullers, though it failed to hold on to one of the brightest wine buyers around, Roger Higgs, who had transformed the wine range in a few short years. Mr Higgs eschewed offers from Unwins and elsewhere in the trade to go and work for a dynamic British wine importer, saying to me, after a few months in the job, 'how wonderful it is not to have to worry about wearing a suit to work'.

Unwins said a new list combining some of the current ranges from both Fullers and Unwins would be unveiled in the spring, but when I tasted the range it struck me that Unwins' wines firmly predominated. Debate raged at this point about whether the Fullers shops would stay as they were or would be subsumed into the yellow belly of the great bee. Amusingly, the trade magazine *Retail Week*'s Good Shop/Bad Shop features showed at this time the Unwins store in Merton Road, London SW18, as an example of a bad shop contrasting it with, no, not a Fullers outlet but with Galeries Lafayette in Paris. I take no defensive brief from Unwins, but I do think the Good Shop/Bad Shop idea only works if you compare like with like.

At last, the integrated Unwins/Fullers wine list was revealed in late spring 2000. The merged list comprised some 900 wines, 100 more than on the previous Unwins list. Unwins said it had added about 100 wines, keeping some 54% of the Fullers range, from which we can conclude they must have delisted some of their own wines. Roger, old sport, your prowess lives on without you.

Around this time, an Unwins personnel manager, Philip Dudman, who had invented bogus employees in a £100,000 scam, was jailed for a year. There was also, I believe, a *femme fatale* element to this, but it is not my business to track her down. The superbly monikered Mr Dudman apparently conned Unwins out of this large sum over an eighteen-month period, having been with the company for twenty years. Unwins announced that it was resuming the old company practice of circulating memos detailing staff misdemeanours (though one assumes few reach Mr Dudman's level of inventive chutzpah). Though these memos do not, so it was said, necessarily name names, some staff were reported to be less than happy about the revival of this practice.

I look forward to my mole sending me copies of these memos.

Unwins Wine Group Limited
Birchwood House
Victoria Road
Dartford
Kent
DA1 5AJ

Tel 01322 272711
Fax 01322 294469
www.unwins.co.uk (under construction at time of going to press).

## ARGENTINIAN RED

J & F Lurton Bonarda/ Tempranillo 1998   10   −£5.00

Magdalena River Malbec/ Cabernet Sauvignon, Mendoza 1997   13   −£5.00

Magdalena River Sangiovese/Bonarda, Mendoza 1998   12   −£5.00

Norton Cabernet Sauvignon 1999   15   −£5.00

Santa Julia Malbec Oak Reserve 1998   16   £5–7

Santa Julia Tempranillo Oak Reserve 1998   17   £5–7

Terrazas Malbec 1999   15   £5–7

## ARGENTINIAN WHITE

Alamos Ridge Chardonnay 1997   16   £5–7

Catena Agrelo Vineyards Chardonnay 1997   14   £7–10

J & F Lurton Pinot Gris 1998   13   −£5.00

Magdalena River Chardonnay, Mendoza 1997   15   −£5.00

Santa Julia Oak Reserve Chardonnay 1997   16.5   £5–7

## AUSTRALIAN RED

Baileys 1904 Block Shiraz 1994   14   £10–13

Banrock Station Shiraz 1997   11   −£5.00

Clancy's Shiraz/Cabernet Sauvignon/Merlot/ Cabernet Franc 1998   17   £7–10

Hill of Hope Shiraz 1997   14   £5–7

Ironstone Shiraz Grenache 1998   16.5   £5–7

J J McWilliam Merlot 1997   13   £5–7

Leasingham Clare Valley Grenache 1996   14.5   £7–10

Oxford Landing Cabernet Sauvignon Shiraz 1999   15.5   £5–7

Penfolds Koonunga Hill | 15 | £5–7
Shiraz/Cabernet
Sauvignon 1999

Rosemount Estate Shiraz | 15.5 | £5–7
Cabernet 1999

Vine Vale Grenache 1998 | 14.5 | –£5.00

Wakefield Cabernet | 16 | £5–7
Sauvignon, Clare Valley
1998

Woodvale Shiraz 1998 | 13 | –£5.00

## AUSTRALIAN WHITE

Capel Vale C V | 15 | £7–10
Unwooded Chardonnay
1999

David Wynn | 16 | £5–7
Chardonnay, S. Australia
1998

Grant Burge Late Harvest | 16 | –£5.00
Muscat 1997

Grant Burge Old Vine | 14 | £7–10
Semillon, Barossa Valley
1997

Howcroft Bin 6000 | 15.5 | £5–7
Verdelho 1998

Ironstone Semillon | 17 | £5–7
Chardonnay 1999

Lindemans Botrytis | 16 | £5–7
Riesling 1997 (half-bottle)

Oxford Landing | 15 | –£5.00
Sauvignon Blanc 1999

Oxford Landing Viognier | 16 | £5–7
1998

Peter Lehmann The | 16.5 | £5–7
Barossa Semillon 1998

Peter Lehmannn Vine | 15.5 | –£5.00
Vale Chenin Blanc 1998

Rosemount Estate | 16 | £5–7
Diamond Label
Chardonnay 1999

Stanton & Killeen | 16 | £5–7
Rutherglen Muscat NV
(half-bottle)

Stockman's Bridge White | 14 | –£5.00
NV

Tim Gramp Watervale | 16.5 | £7–10
Riesling 1997

Tyrrells Long Flat | 14 | £5–7
Chardonnay 1999

Wakefield Chardonnay, | 13 | £5–7
Clare Valley 1997

Wakefield White Clare | 14 | £5–7
Crouchen/Chardonnay
1997

Woodvale Chardonnay | 15 | –£5.00
1999

Woodvale Semillon/ | 15.5 | –£5.00
Chardonnay 1999

## BULGARIAN RED

Country Wine Merlot/ | 14 | –£3.50
Pinot Noir NV, Sliven

## BULGARIAN WHITE

Country Wine Muskat & | 14 | –£3.50
Ugni Blanc, Shumen NV

## CHILEAN RED

Canepa Cabernet | 16 | –£5.00
Sauvignon/Malbec 1999

| | | |
|---|---|---|
| Canepa Zinfandel 1999 | 14 | −£5.00 |
| Carmen Cabernet Sauvignon 1996 | 16 | −£5.00 |
| Casa Donoso Cabernet Sauvignon Domaine Oriental 1998 | 12.5 | −£5.00 |
| Casa Donoso Reservado Cabernet Sauvignon 1998 | 12 | £5–7 |
| Cono Sur Reserve Pinot Noir 1998 | 16 | £5–7 |
| Donoso Limited Edition 1997 | 13.5 | £13–20 |
| Errazuriz Cabernet Sauvignon 1998 | 17.5 | £5–7 |
| Errazuriz Merlot 1999 | 16.5 | £5–7 |
| Errazuriz Syrah Reserva 1998 | 16 | £7–10 |
| Gracia Merlot Reserve, Aconcagua 1997 | 16.5 | £7–10 |
| La Palmeria Merlot 1999 | 17 | −£5.00 |
| Penta Morande Cabernet Sauvignon/Malbec 1999 | 16.5 | −£5.00 |
| Valdivieso Cabernet Franc Reserve 1997 | 17.5 | £7–10 |
| Vina Porta Cabernet Sauvignon, Maipo 1999 | 16.5 | −£5.00 |
| Vina Porta Limited Edition Merlot 1998 | 15 | −£5.00 |
| Vina Porta Reserve Cabernet Sauvignon 1998 | 16 | −£5.00 |

## CHILEAN WHITE

| | | |
|---|---|---|
| Canepa Semillon, Colchagua Valley 1999 | 16.5 | −£5.00 |
| Casa Donoso Chardonnay Domaine Oriental 1999 | 13 | −£5.00 |
| Casa Donoso Reservado Chardonnay Domaine Oriental 1999 | 12 | £5–7 |
| Casa Lapostolle Chardonnay 1998 | 17 | £5–7 |
| Casa Lapostolle Cuvée Alexandre Chardonnay, Casablanca 1996 | 17.5 | £7–10 |
| Casablanca Chardonnay 1998 | 15.5 | £5–7 |
| Concha y Toro Gewürztraminer 1999 | 16 | −£5.00 |
| Errazuriz Wild Ferment Chardonnay, Casablanca 1998 | 17 | £7–10 |
| Isla Negra Chardonnay 1997 | 16 | £7–10 |
| La Palmeria Chardonnay 2000 | 15.5 | −£5.00 |
| Valdivieso Chardonnay 1999 | 16.5 | −£5.00 |
| Valdivieso Reserve Chardonnay 1997 | 15.5 | £5–7 |

## FRENCH RED

| | | |
|---|---|---|
| Ash Ridge Grenache/ Merlot 1998 | 12 | −£5.00 |
| Ash Ridge Syrah d'Oc 1998 | 13 | −£5.00 |
| Chapelle St Marie Syrah 1998 | 16.5 | −£5.00 |
| Chassagne Montrachet Louis Jadot 1994 | 11 | £13–20 |

| | | |
|---|---|---|
| Château Astruc Minervois 1998 | 14.5 | −£5.00 |
| Château Beychevelle St Julien 4eme Cru 1995 | 12 | £20+ |
| Château de Cazeneuve Le Roc de Mates Pic St Loup 1997 | 15 | £7–10 |
| Château de Cazeneuve Les Terres Rouges Pic St Loup 1997 | 15.5 | £5–7 |
| Château Giscours Margaux 3eme Cru 1995 | 11 | £20+ |
| Château Trignon Côtes du Rhône Villages Sablet Ramillades 1998 | 17.5 | £5–7 |
| Châteauneuf-du-Pape Louis Mousset 1998 | 13.5 | £10–13 |
| Côte Rotie Guigal 1996 | 17 | £20+ |
| Côtes du Rhône Guigal 1998 | 16 | £7–10 |
| Domaine de l'Arneillaud Cairanne Côtes du Rhône Villages 1999 | 18 | £5–7 |
| Domaine de la Grand Bellane, Valreas 1997 | 16 | £5–7 |
| Domaine de la Soleiade, Vacqueyras 1998 | 15 | £5–7 |
| Fitou Château de Segure 1998 | 15.5 | £5–7 |
| Gigondas Domaine des Amandiers 1998 | 14 | £7–10 |
| Hautes Côtes de Beaune 1997 | 10 | £7–10 |
| James Herrick Cuvée Simone VdP d'Oc 1998 | 16.5 | −£5.00 |
| La Cigaliere Côtes du Rhône 1998 | 15 | −£5.00 |
| Les Beaux Sites Domaine de Castan Cabernet Sauvignon 1997 | 15.5 | −£5.00 |
| Madiran Château de Crouseilles 1993 | 14 | £7–10 |
| Mauregard Château La Grave Bordeaux 1999 | 13.5 | −£5.00 |
| Saumur Domaine de la Sicardiere 1997 | 15.5 | −£5.00 |
| St Emilion 1998 | 13 | £5–7 |
| Valreas Domaine de la Grande Bellane 1998 (organic) | 16.5 | £5–7 |
| Wild Pig Barrel Reserve Shiraz 1998 | 14 | −£5.00 |

## FRENCH WHITE

| | | |
|---|---|---|
| Anjou Blanc 1997 | 11 | −£5.00 |
| Ash Ridge Grenache/ Viognier 1999 | 13 | −£5.00 |
| Château Vieux Malveyren Monbazillac Domaine Vilate 1990 | 16.5 | £13–20 |
| Condrieu Guigal 1998 | 15.5 | £13–20 |
| Corbieres Les Producteurs du Mont Tauch | 12 | −£5.00 |
| Côtes du Rhône Guigal 1998 | 14.5 | £7–10 |
| Cuvée Philippe VdP du Comte Tolosan 1999 | 12.5 | −£3.50 |
| Domaine de Saubagnere Côtes de Gascogne 1998 | 14.5 | −£5.00 |
| Domaine des Forges Coteaux du Layon-Chaume 1997 | 16 | £7–10 |

Domaine Valette Pouilly-Vinzelles Vieilles Vignes 1997 `16` `£13–20`

La Chablisienne Chablis Vieilles Vignes 1997 `13` `£7–10`

Les Trois Herault Les Chais Beaucarois NV `13` `–£3.50`

Macon Lugny Les Charmes 1998 `14` `£5–7`

Marquis de Beausoleil NV `15.5` `£5–7`

Marsanne/Roussane Frederic Roger 1999 `14.5` `–£5.00`

Muscadet sur Lie Pierre Brevin 1997 `13.5` `–£5.00`

Petit Chablis Albert Bichot 1999 `12` `£5–7`

Pinot Blanc d'Alsace Cave de Turckheim 1999 `14` `–£5.00`

Pouilly Fume Les Griottines 1998 `10` `£7–10`

Sancerre Harmonie Oak Aged 1997 `12` `£13–20`

Sancerre Les Roches Vacheron 1999 `13.5` `£10–13`

Sancerre Les Romains Vacherons 1999 (rosé) `13.5` `£7–10`

St Veran Domaine des Deux Roches 1999 `15.5` `£7–10`

## GERMAN WHITE

Fitz Riter Durkheimer Hochbenn Riesling Kabinett 1997 `13` `£5–7`

## GREEK WHITE

Samos Vin Doux Naturel NV `15.5` `–£5.00`

## ITALIAN RED

Barocco Rosso del Salento 1999 `13` `–£5.00`

Chianti Classico Reserva Villa Antinori 1997 `14` `£7–10`

Ciro Classico 1998 `14` `–£5.00`

La Mura Rosso Casa Girelli 1999 `14` `–£5.00`

Montepulciano d'Abruzzo, Miglianico 1997 `15.5` `–£5.00`

Primitivo Merum 1998 `13` `–£5.00`

Villa Cafaggio Chianti Classico 1997 `13` `£5–7`

## ITALIAN WHITE

Carato Barrique Chardonnay 1999 `13.5` `£5–7`

Chardonnay Mezzo Mondo 1998 `14` `–£5.00`

Moscato d'Asti Araldica 1998 `10` `–£5.00`

## LEBANESE RED

Château Musar 1994 `10` `£10–13`

## NEW ZEALAND RED

Rippon Pinot Noir 1998 `10` `£13–20`

Sacred Hill Basket Press | 14 | £7–10
Merlot/Cabernet,
Hawkes Bay 1996

## NEW ZEALAND WHITE

De Redcliffe | 15 | £7–10
Mangatawhiri
Chardonnay 1997

Hunter's Sauvignon | 16 | £7–10
Blanc 1999

Kim Crawford Sauvignon | 16 | £7–10
Blanc 1999

Kumeu River | 16 | £10–13
Chardonnay 1998

Marlborough Gold | 14.5 | £5–7
Sauvignon 1999

Oyster Bay Chardonnay, | 16.5 | £5–7
Marlborough 1999

Oyster Bay Sauvignon | 16.5 | £5–7
Blanc 1999

## PORTUGUESE RED

Bela Fonte Jaen 1998 | 16 | –£5.00

Dao Dom Ferraz Reserva | 15.5 | –£5.00
Caves Primavera 1999

Pedras do Monte 1999 | 15 | –£5.00

Portada Vinho Regional | 13.5 | –£5.00
Estremadura 1999

Quinta das Setencostas, | 16.5 | £5–7
Alenquer 1998

Quinta do Crasto Reserva | 17 | £7–10
1997

Segada Red 1998 | 15.5 | –£5.00

## PORTUGUESE WHITE

Bical Bela Fonte 1998 | 15 | –£5.00

Segada White 1998 | 13 | –£5.00

## SOUTH AFRICAN RED

African Legend Pinotage | 14 | –£5.00
1998

Bellingham Pinotage 1998 | 16 | £5–7

Cape Cinsault/Merlot | 13 | –£5.00
1999

Cathedral Cellar | 15 | £7–10
Cabernet Sauvignon 1995

Clos Malverne Cabernet/ | 14.5 | £5–7
Shiraz, Stellenbosch 1997

Clos Malverne Pinotage, | 16 | £5–7
Stellenbosch 1999

Jordan Cabernet | 16 | £7–10
Sauvignon 1997

Leef Op Hoop Cabernet | 14 | £5–7
Sauvignon/Merlot,
Stellenbosch 1998

Millbrook Cinsault 1998 | 14 | –£5.00

Neil Joubert Cabernet | 13 | £5–7
Sauvignon 1998

Spice Route Shiraz 1998 | 16 | £7–10

## SOUTH AFRICAN WHITE

Bellingham Chardonnay | 15 | £5–7
1999

Cape Chardonnay 1999 | 13 | –£5.00

Cape White 1999 | 13.5 | –£5.00

Cathedral Cellar | 15.5 | £7–10
Chardonnay 1997

| Coastline Chenin Blanc 2000 | 13.5 | −£5.00 |
|---|---|---|
| Fairview Chardonnay 1999 | 16.5 | £5–7 |
| Jordan Barrel Fermented Chenin Blanc, Stellenbosch 1999 | 16.5 | £5–7 |
| Jordan Chardonnay, Stellenbosch 1998 | 16.5 | £7–10 |
| L'Avenir Chenin Blanc 1998 | 15.5 | £5–7 |
| Vergelegen Chardonnay 1998 | 16 | £5–7 |

## SPANISH RED

| Castillo Perelada Cabernet Sauvignon 1997 | 13.5 | £7–10 |
|---|---|---|
| Conde de Valdemar Reserva 1995 | 14 | £7–10 |
| Cosme Palacio y Hermanos Rioja 1997 | 16 | £5–7 |
| Gran Vos Reserva 1995 | 15 | £7–10 |
| Marques de Grinon Tempranillo 1998 | 15 | £5–7 |
| Martinez Bujanda Gran Reserva 1993 | 13.5 | £13–20 |
| Nekeas Barrel Fermented Merlot 1997 | 13.5 | £5–7 |
| Ochoa Tempranillo 1997 | 15 | £5–7 |
| Tapon de Oro Garnacha 1998 | 12.5 | £5–7 |
| Valdepusa Cabernet Sauvignon Marques de Grinon 1997 | 16.5 | £7–10 |
| Vina Albali Reserva 1995 | 13 | −£5.00 |

| Vinas del Vero Cabernet Sauvignon 1998 | 16.5 | £5–7 |
|---|---|---|

## SPANISH WHITE

| Nekeas Barrel Fermented Chardonnay 1998 | 15 | £5–7 |
|---|---|---|
| Vinas del Vero Chardonnay 1998 | 14 | −£5.00 |
| Vinas del Vero Clarion, Somontano 1997 | 13 | £7–10 |

## USA RED

| Beaulieu Vineyard Coastal Pinot Noir 1998 | 14 | £5–7 |
|---|---|---|
| Blossom Hill NV | 10 | −£5.00 |
| De Loach Zinfandel Platinum 1996 | 10 | £7–10 |
| Delicato Cabernet Sauvignon 1998 | 14 | £5–7 |
| Delicato Zinfandel 1998 | 13 | £5–7 |
| Fetzer Private Collection Cabernet Sauvignon 1994 | 15 | £13–20 |
| Fetzer Syrah 1997 | 14 | £5–7 |
| Ironstone Vineyards Cabernet Franc 1997 | 15 | £5–7 |
| King Estate Pinot Noir 1995 | 12 | £13–20 |
| R H Phillips Cabernet Sauvignon 1997 | 15 | £5–7 |
| Saintsbury Garnet Carneros Pinot Noir 1998 | 13.5 | £10–13 |
| Schug Pinot Noir 1996 | 11 | £10–13 |
| Seven Peaks Cabernet Sauvignon 1996 | 16.5 | £7–10 |

| | | |
|---|---|---|
| Stonehedge Merlot 1998 | 15 | £5–7 |
| Thornhill Pinot Noir 1996 | 12 | –£5.00 |
| Turning Leaf Cabernet Sauvignon 1997 | 12 | £5–7 |
| Turning Leaf Zinfandel 1996 | 12.5 | £5–7 |
| Wente Cabernet Sauvignon 1996 | 16 | £7–10 |
| Wente Charles Wetmore Reserve Cabernet Sauvignon 1995 | 12.5 | £10–13 |
| Wente Crane Ridge Reserve Merlot 1997 | 13.5 | £10–13 |
| Wente Reliz Creek Reserve Pinot Noir 1996 | 14 | £10–13 |
| Wente Zinfandel 1998 | 11 | £5–7 |

## USA WHITE

| | | |
|---|---|---|
| Blossom Hill NV | 10 | –£5.00 |
| Bonterra Viognier 1998 (organic) | 15 | £7–10 |
| Byron Chardonnay, Santa Barbara 1996 | 13.5 | £13–20 |
| Coastal Chardonnay, Robert Mondavi 1997 | 17 | £10–13 |
| Fetzer Sundial Chardonnay 1997 | 16 | £5–7 |
| Redwood Trail Chardonnay 1998 | 15.5 | £5–7 |
| Seven Oaks Reserve Chardonnay 1997 | 14.5 | £10–13 |
| Seven Peaks Chardonnay 1997 | 15 | £7–10 |
| Sutter Home Chardonnay 1997 | 14 | –£5.00 |

| | | |
|---|---|---|
| Sutter Home White Zinfandel 1998 | 8 | –£5.00 |
| Wente Chardonnay 1998 | 14 | £5–7 |
| Wente Riva Ranch Reserve Chardonnay 1996 | 14 | £7–10 |
| Wente Sauvignon Blanc 1998 | 13 | £5–7 |
| Wente White Zinfandel 1998 | 10 | £5–7 |

## FORTIFIED WINES

| | | |
|---|---|---|
| Calem 10 Year Old Port | 11 | £13–20 |
| Calem Colheita Tawny Port 1987 | 10 | £20+ |
| Calem Late Bottled Vintage Port 1994 | 14 | £7–10 |
| Calem Quinta da Foz Port 1987 | 13 | £13–20 |
| Calem Vintage Port 1983 | 10 | £20+ |
| Cockburns 1991 | 13 | £20+ |
| Croft 1991 | 13 | £20+ |
| Dos Cortados Dry Old Oloroso Sherry | 14 | £7–10 |
| Henriques & Henriques Aged 10 Years Malmsey Madeira | 16 | £13–20 |
| Henriques & Henriques Aged 5 Years Finest Medium Dry Madeira | 15 | £10–13 |
| Lustau Old East India Sherry | 17 | £7–10 |
| Matusalem Sweet Old Oloroso Sherry | 14.5 | £7–10 |

Quinta do Noval 1991   13   £20+

Warres 1991   16   £20+

## SPARKLING WINES

Alain Thienot Brut 1990   10   £20+

Cuvée Princesse de Aimery Blanquette de Limoux 1997   13   £5–7

Duchatel Blanc de Blancs Brut NV   12.5   £13–20

Duchatel Brut Champagne NV   13   £10–13

Duchatel Champagne Brut 1994   13.5   £13–20

Duchatel Rosé Brut Champagne NV   11   £13–20

Freixenet Cava Brut NV   15.5   £5–7

Graham Beck Brut NV (South Africa)   14   £5–7

Jacob's Creek Sparkling Chardonnay/Pinot Noir NV (Australia)   15   £5–7

Lindauer Brut NV (New Zealand)   14.5   £7–10

Pelorus Brut 1995   18   £10–13

SEE STOP PRESS SECTION AT END OF BOOK FOR LAST-MINUTE ADDITIONS OR UPDATES TO THIS RETAILER'S RANGE.

# VICTORIA WINE

See Thresher/Bottoms Up/Wine Rack/Victoria Wine – 1st Quench, page 423.

## ARGENTINIAN RED

| | | |
|---|---|---|
| Anubis Malbec 1999 | 16 | £5–7 |
| Argento Malbec 1999 | 16.5 | –£5.00 |
| Corazon Bonarda 1999 | 16 | –£5.00 |
| Corazon Tempranillo 1999 | 16.5 | –£5.00 |
| Libertad Malbec Bonarda 1999 | 15 | –£5.00 |
| Libertad Malbec Sangiovese 1998 | 15 | –£5.00 |
| Martins Andino Malbec Bonarda 1998 | 14 | –£5.00 |
| Villa Atuel Syrah 1999 | 15.5 | –£5.00 |

## ARGENTINIAN WHITE

| | | |
|---|---|---|
| Corazon Pinot Gris 1999 | 15 | –£5.00 |
| Correas Torrontes Chardonnay 1999 | 14 | –£5.00 |
| Norton Semillon Chardonnay 1999 | 16 | –£5.00 |
| Norton Torrontes, Mendoza 1999 | 15.5 | –£5.00 |

## AUSTRALIAN RED

| | | |
|---|---|---|
| Hardys Nottage Hill Cabernet Sauvignon Shiraz 1998 | 15.5 | £5–7 |
| Leasingham Domaine Cabernet/Malbec 1997 | 10 | £7–10 |
| Leasingham Grenache 1996 | 14.5 | £7–10 |
| Lindemans Padthaway Shiraz 1997 | 15.5 | £7–10 |
| Nanya Estate Malbec/ Ruby Cabernet 1998 | 10 | –£5.00 |
| Tatachilla Grenache Shiraz 1998 | 16 | £5–7 |
| Wynn's Coonawarra Shiraz 1996 | 16.5 | £5–7 |
| Yalumba Bush Vine Grenache 1997 | 14 | £7–10 |

## AUSTRALIAN WHITE

| | | |
|---|---|---|
| David Traeger Verdelho, Victoria 1998 | 16 | £7–10 |
| Hardys Nottage Hill Riesling 1998 | 15.5 | –£5.00 |
| Lindemans Botrytis Riesling 1996 (half-bottle) | 17 | £5–7 |

Mitchelton Chardonnay 1996 — 15 £7–10

Oxford Landing Sauvignon Blanc 1999 — 15 −£5.00

Pewsey Vale Riesling 1997 — 16 £5–7

Tollana Unoaked Chardonnay 1999 — 15.5 −£5.00

Wolf Blass South Australia Barrel Fermented Chardonnay 1999 — 16 £7–10

Wolf Blass South Australia Chardonnay 1999 — 16 £7–10

## BULGARIAN RED

Domaine Boyar Premium Oaked Cabernet Shumen 1997 — 13.5 −£5.00

Domaine Boyar Premium Reserve Cabernet Sauvignon 1996 — 14 −£5.00

Domaine Boyar Premium Reserve Merlot 1996 — 14.5 −£5.00

## BULGARIAN WHITE

Boyar Muskat & Ugni Blanc NV — 11 −£3.50

Copper Crossing Dry White NV — 10 −£3.50

Copper Crossing Medium White NV — 12 −£3.50

Domaine de Boyar Targovischte Chardonnay 1997 — 12 −£3.50

## CHILEAN RED

Casa Lapostolle Cuvée Alexandre Cabernet Sauvignon 1997 — 16.5 £7–10

Casa Lapostolle Cuvée Alexandre Merlot 1997 — 17.5 £10–13

Casa Lapostolle Merlot 1998 — 16.5 £5–7

Cono Sur Cabernet Sauvignon, Rapel 1998 — 16.5 −£5.00

Cono Sur Pinot Noir 1998 — 14.5 −£5.00

Errazuriz Cabernet Sauvignon 1998 — 17.5 £5–7

Errazuriz Reserva Cabernet Sauvignon 1997 — 16 £7–10

Isla Negra Cabernet Sauvignon 1998 — 15.5 £5–7

La Palmeria Cabernet/ Merlot 1998 — 16 £5–7

Las Colinas Cabernet Merlot 1999 — 15 −£5.00

Las Colinas Chilean Red NV — 13.5 −£3.50

Las Colinas Merlot 1999 — 15 −£5.00

Martins Don Rui Cabernet Sauvignon 1997 — 13.5 £5–7

Valdivieso Malbec 1998 — 16 −£5.00

Valdivieso Merlot 1999 — 15.5 −£5.00

Valdivieso Reserve Pinot Noir 1996 — 14.5 £7–10

Veramonte Cabernet Sauvignon 1997 — 16 £5–7

Veramonte Merlot 1997 — 14 £5–7

VICTORIA WINE

## CHILEAN WHITE

| | | |
|---|---|---|
| Casa Lapostolle Sauvignon Blanc 1999 | 17 | £5–7 |
| Concha y Toro Casillero del Diablo Chardonnay 1997 | 17 | –£5.00 |
| Cono Sur Gewürztraminer 1998 | 15.5 | –£5.00 |
| La Palmeria Chardonnay 1998 | 16 | –£5.00 |
| Las Colinas Chardonnay 1999 | 15 | –£5.00 |
| Las Colinas Riesling 1997 | 15.5 | –£5.00 |
| Santa Ines Legardo de Armida Reserve Chardonnay 1998 | 16.5 | £5–7 |
| Veramonte Chardonnay 1998 | 13.5 | £5–7 |

## FRENCH RED

| | | |
|---|---|---|
| Abbotts Cumulus Minervois 1998 | 16.5 | £5–7 |
| Château Sauvage Premier Côtes de Bordeaux 1997 | 13 | £5–7 |
| Château Suau, 1er Côtes de Bordeaux 1997 (unoaked) | 13.5 | £5–7 |
| Cornas Les Nobles Rives, Côtes de Tain 1994 | 14 | £10–13 |
| Côte Rotie, Domaine de Bonserine 1996 | 10 | £20+ |
| Côtes de Beaune Villages 1996 | 12 | £7–10 |
| Côtes du Rhône Villages Les Faisans 1998 | 14 | –£5.00 |
| Dark Horse Cahors 1998 | 14 | –£5.00 |

| | | |
|---|---|---|
| Domaine Peyrat Cabernet Sauvignon 1997 | 15 | £5–7 |
| Fitou Special Reserve 1997 | 14.5 | –£5.00 |
| Fitou Terroir de Tuchan 1998 | 17 | £7–10 |
| Fleurie Georges Duboeuf 1998 | 11 | £7–10 |
| Fleurie Regional Classics 1998 | 13.5 | £5–7 |
| French Revolution Le Rouge 1999 | 16 | –£5.00 |
| Grenache VdP des Coteaux de l'Ardeche 1997 | 14.5 | –£3.50 |
| Mont Tauch Old Bush Vines Carignan 1998 | 13 | –£5.00 |
| Morgon Domaine des Côtes de Douby 1998 | 13.5 | £5–7 |
| Old Bush Vines Carignan 1998 | 13.5 | –£5.00 |
| Pinot Noir, Louis Jadot 1998 | 12.5 | £7–10 |
| Red Burgundy Vergy 1997 | 12 | –£5.00 |
| Sirius Red 1997 | 13.5 | £5–7 |

## FRENCH WHITE

| | | |
|---|---|---|
| Bordeaux Sauvignon Calvet 1997 | 12 | –£5.00 |
| Chablis Domaine de Bieville 1998 | 14 | £7–10 |
| Chablis Regional Classics 1997 | 13.5 | £7–10 |
| Chablis Vieilles Vignes, Defaix 1996 | 11 | £10–13 |

Chablis Vieilles Vignes, La Cuvée Exceptionelle, Defaix 1997 — 12.5 £13–20

Château Filhot Sauternes 1990 — 15 £20+

Château Petit Moulin Blanc, Bordeaux 1998 — 12.5 £5–7

Domaine Pré Baron Sauvignon de Touraine 1998 — 14.5 £5–7

French Revolution Le Blanc 1999 — 13 −£5.00

Le Vieux Mas Marsanne Viognier VdP d'Oc 1998 — 15 −£5.00

Les Pierres Blanches Sancerre 1998 — 12 £7–10

Meursault, Les Chevaliers, Domaine Rene Monnier 1996 — 12 £13–20

Montagny Premier Cru Oak Aged Chardonnay 1997 — 13.5 £5–7

Old Bush Vines Grenache Blanc 1999 — 14 −£5.00

Rivers Meet White Bordeaux 1997 — 11 −£5.00

Teuqirat Côtes de Gascogne 1998 — 14.5 −£5.00

Turckheim Alsace Blanc 1998 — 13 −£5.00

Turckheim Gewürztraminer 1998 — 16 £5–7

Turckheim Pinot Blanc 1998 — 14.5 −£5.00

## GERMAN WHITE

Kendermann Dry Riesling 1998 — 13.5 −£5.00

## HUNGARIAN WHITE

AK 28 Sauvignon Blanc 1998 — 14.5 −£5.00

Hilltop Gewürztraminer 1997 — 15.5 −£5.00

The Unpronounceable Grape 1997 — 12 −£3.50

## ITALIAN RED

Amarone della Valpolicella Via Nova 1997 — 18 £7–10

Barolo Terre da Vino 1996 — 13 £10–13

Brunello di Montalcino, Casanova di Neri 1994 — 15.5 £20+

Cecchi Sangiovese 1998 — 14.5 −£5.00

Formulae Sangiovese di Toscana, Ricasoli 1998 — 13.5 £5–7

La Bella Figura Merlot Cabernet 1998 — 15.5 −£5.00

Merlot Corvina Fiordaliso 1998 — 13.5 −£5.00

Montepulciano d'Abruzzo Umani Ronchi 1999 — 14 −£5.00

Montepulciano Selva Torta 1998 — 15.5 £5–7

Rosso di Montalcino, Casanova di Neri 1998 — 15 £10–13

Salice Salento Vallone 1997 — 13.5 £5–7

Trulli Primitivo 1997 — 14 −£5.00

Valpolicella Classico Superiore Zenato 1997 — 16 −£5.00

Valpolicella Classico Zenato 1997 — **16.5 −£5.00**

449

## ITALIAN WHITE

Falerio Pilastri Saladini 1998 — 13.5 — −£5.00

Pinot Grigio Fiordaliso 1998 — 13.5 — −£5.00

Verdicchio dei Castelli di Jesi Verbacco 1999 — 15.5 — −£5.00

## NEW ZEALAND RED

Awatea Cabernet Sauvignon/Merlot 1997 — 13.5 — £13–20

Awatea Cabernet Sauvignon/Merlot 1997 — 13.5 — £13–20

Church Road Cabernet Sauvignon/Merlot 1998 — 15 — £7–10

Montana Cabernet Sauvignon Merlot 1999 — 15 — £5–7

Montana Reserve Merlot 1998 — 16.5 — £7–10

Timara Cabernet/Merlot 1998 — 14 — −£5.00

## NEW ZEALAND WHITE

Church Road Chardonnay 1998 — 16 — £7–10

Montana Reserve Chardonnay 1998 — 16.5 — £7–10

Timara Dry White 1998 — 13.5 — −£5.00

Villa Maria Lightly Oaked Chardonnay 1999 — 16 — £5–7

Villa Maria Private Bin Riesling 1999 — 16 — £5–7

## PORTUGUESE RED

Dom Ferraz Dao 1997 — 15 — −£5.00

Fiuza Cabernet Sauvignon 1997 — 14 — −£5.00

Pedras do Monte 1998 — 16 — −£5.00

Segada Tinto 1998 — 15.5 — −£5.00

## ROMANIAN RED

River Route Limited Edition Cabernet Sauvignon 1997 — 13.5 — −£5.00

River Route Pinot Noir 1998 — 12 — −£5.00

## ROMANIAN WHITE

River Route Limited Edition Chardonnay 1997 — 15.5 — −£5.00

## SOUTH AFRICAN RED

Cape View Cinsault/Shiraz 1998 — 12 — −£5.00

Oak Village Cabernet Sauvignon 1998 — 15 — −£5.00

The Pinotage Company Pinotage 1999 — 13.5 — £5–7

## SOUTH AFRICAN WHITE

African Legend Sauvignon Blanc 1998 — 13 — £5–7

Capells Court Chardonnay 1998 — 16 — £5–7

Oak Village Chardonnay 1999 — 13.5 — −£5.00

## SPANISH RED

Abadia Retuerta Rivola, 16.5 £5–7
Duero 1996

Baron de Ley Rioja 13 £7–10
Reserva 1996

Casa Rural Tinto NV 14.5 –£3.50

Chivite Navarra Vina 13 –£5.00
Marcos 1997

Chivite Reserva, Gran 13.5 £5–7
Feudo, Navarra 1995

Conde de Valdemar Rioja 13.5 £5–7
Crianza 1997

Conde de Valdemar Rioja 14 £7–10
Reserva 1995

Dominio di Montalvo 13 £5–7
Rioja 1998

El Meson Rioja NV 15 £5–7

Jumilla Senorio de Robles 16 –£3.50
1998

Marques de Aragon 15 –£5.00
Garnacha 1998

Marques de Riscal 14 £7–10
Reserva 1996

Navajas Rioja Crianza 13.5 £5–7
1997

Remonte Cabernet 15.5 –£5.00
Sauvignon 1996

## SPANISH WHITE

Albarino Condes de 14.5 £5–7
Alberei 1999

Campo Viejo Barrel 13 £5–7
Fermented Viura 1998

Casa Rural White NV 15.5 –£3.50

Castillo de Liria Rosé NV 15 –£3.50

Conde de Valdemar 14 –£5.00
Rosado 1999

Dominio di Montalvo 15.5 £5–7
White Rioja 1998

Moscatel de Valencia NV 16 –£5.00

Torres Vina Esmeralda 14 £5–7
1999

Torres Vina Sol 1999 14 –£5.00

## USA RED

Blossom Hill Californian 10 –£5.00
Red NV

E & J Gallo Ruby 14 –£5.00
Cabernet 1999

Eagle Peak Merlot, Fetzer 15.5 £5–7
Vineyards 1998

Fetzer Valley Oaks 15.5 £5–7
Cabernet Sauvignon 1997

Redwood Trail Pinot 13.5 £5–7
Noir 1997

Talus Zinfandel 1996 13.5 £5–7

Talus Zinfandel 1997 13 £5–7

Turning Leaf Cabernet 12 £5–7
Sauvignon 1997

Turning Leaf Zinfandel 12.5 £5–7
1996

Vendange Californian 14 –£5.00
Red 1998

Woodbridge Mondavi 14 £5–7
Zinfandel 1996

## USA WHITE

Columbia Crest 15.5 £5–7
Chardonnay 1997

451

| | | | | | |
|---|---|---|---|---|---|
| Fetzer Sundial Chardonnay, 1998 | 16 | £5–7 | Cuvée Napa Brut, Mumm NV | 16 | £7–10 |
| Fetzer Syrah Rosé 1999 | 13 | £5–7 | Deutz Marlborough Cuvée NV | 13.5 | £10–13 |
| Vendange Californian Dry White 1998 | 11 | –£5.00 | Gosset Grande Millesime 1989 | 15 | £20+ |
| Vendanges White Zinfandel 1998 | 9 | –£5.00 | Gosset Grande Reserve NV | 14 | £20+ |
| Wente Riva Ranch Chardonnay 1996 | 16 | £7–10 | Green Point Brut 1996 | 15 | £10–13 |
| | | | Krug Grande Cuvée NV | 13 | £20+ |

## FORTIFIED WINES

| | | | Krug Vintage 1989 | 13.5 | £20+ |
|---|---|---|---|---|---|
| Dows LBV 1992 | 13.5 | £10–13 | La Corunna Cava NV | 15 | –£5.00 |
| Quinta de Vargellas Vintage Port 1986 | 15 | £13–20 | Lanson Vintage Gold Label 1993 | 13.5 | £20+ |
| Taylors Quinta de Terra Feita 1986 | 17 | £13–20 | Louis Roederer Brut Vintage 1993 (magnum) | 13 | £20+ |
| | | | Marquis de la Tour Demi Sec NV (France) | 8 | –£5.00 |

## SPARKLING WINES

| | | | Marquis de la Tour Rose NV (France) | 14 | –£5.00 |
|---|---|---|---|---|---|
| Blossom Hill Sparkling NV (USA) | 13 | £5–7 | Piper Heidsieck Rare 1985 | 17 | £20+ |
| Bollinger RD 1985 | 13 | £20+ | Pol Roger Sir Winston Churchill Cuvée 1988 | 16 | £20+ |
| Bollinger Special Cuvée NV | 14 | £20+ | Pommery Vintage 1991 | 12 | £20+ |
| Canard Duchene Charles VII NV | 14.5 | £20+ | Seaview Brut Rosé | 14 | £5–7 |
| Charles Heidsieck Mis en Caves 1995 | 13 | £20+ | Veuve Clicquot La Grande Dame 1990 | 16 | £20+ |
| Cool Ridge Sparkling Chardonnay Pinot Noir Brut NV (Hungary) | 12 | –£5.00 | | | |

**SEE STOP PRESS SECTION AT END OF BOOK FOR LAST-MINUTE ADDITIONS OR UPDATES TO THIS RETAILER'S RANGE.**

# WAITROSE

I have a strong suspicion that Waitrose's wine sales have not increased much for some years. Indeed, its share of the overall market will have slightly fallen, whereas its most significant competitors are doing burgeoning business and increasing market share. Yet *Supermarketing* magazine reported late in 1999 that Waitrose was putting pressure on Sainsbury's by ending the year with like-for-like sales growth of 6%. Total sales in the chain's 121 stores were reported to be up by 9%. Waitrose also set itself the target of becoming the leader in the on-line food retailing market by 2001, going head to head with Tesco.

It announced ambitious expansion plans, claiming it will increase its trading space by 18% in 2000, with the opening of six new stores, the acquisition of eleven sites from Somerfield and the expansion of existing stores. By January 2001, Waitrose expects to boast some 2.5 million square feet of trading space.

A statistic which leaves me utterly cold.

I don't think Waitrose and statistics go together. Waitrose doesn't trade in numbers. It trades, as far as I am concerned, in bottles. Bottles with personality.

Waitrose remains a marvellous place to buy wine, even if its wine sales aren't as dynamic or growing as fast as the rest of its business. A certain competitor may have said to me that the 'atmosphere in a Waitrose is like an old-fashioned chemist's shop', but I see elegance, not clinical stuffiness. If Waitrose is not significantly expanding its share of the wine market, then the problem could be, as I see it, that there are not enough exciting New World wines and not sufficient numbers, if at all, of wine ranges created by the wine department's own initiatives. Wine is something purchased at Waitrose. It is not something conceived or caused to be made 'in the style our customers prefer' – though, that said, there is no doubt that its Good Ordinary Claret, the most honestly labelled wine in the world, owes its softness and seductive structure to overtures by the wine department to Bordeaux to make less austerely tannic Cabernet and Merlot.

Waitrose is an institution and Mr Julian Brind, the most civilised of heads of wine-buying departments, is an institution also. His buyers are also mini-institutions, and I sometimes feel that, apart from Ms Susan McCraith and Ms Dee Blackstock (who manages to winkle out of Rheims some sublime Champagnes), some of them wear a tie to bed along with pinstriped pyjamas. Is this a long-winded way of saying that Waitrose is a splendid example of the British stiff upper lip? Perhaps. But wine buyers who wear pinstriped pyjamas also exhibit respect, patience and good manners – and not just at bedtime. No supermarket wine buyers are more respected or possess better manners than Waitrose's. Even Mr Joe Wadsack, the youngest member of the department and a man who sleeps, I am sure, iconoclastically (and against company policy) in the nude, has acquired a courtly aspect to his demeanour over the past year, and this can only be because of his proximity to gentlemen like Julian, Simon Thorpe, Nick Room, and Waitrose Direct's fine-wine specialist, James Snoxell.

They're all MWs. The lot of them. (Mr Wadsack is the one exception, but he is devotedly studying for the qualification.) You could say this is Waitrose's wine-buying strength, but it can also be seen to be its competitive weakness. MWs, I have heard it said, care more about wine than about people (i.e. customers) and a supermarket wine buyer's finest qualification is a superb nose for what customers will go for – something no MW is taught or can academically acquire.

However, whatever anyone else says, I think we need Waitrose to stay the way it is. I don't want Waitrose to turn into a Tesco or an Asda, and its customers don't either. Keep it up, Julian, boys and gels. You're doing a great job (and a lot of your competitors are just plain jealous).

Waitrose Limited
Customer Service Department
Southern Industrial Area
Bracknell
Berks
RG12 8YA

Tel 0800 188884 Customer service
Tel 0800 188881 Waitrose Direct mail order
www.waitrose.com

## ARGENTINIAN RED

| | | |
|---|---|---|
| Familia Zuccardi Q Merlot 1998 | 16.5 | £7–10 |
| Finca el Retiro Malbec, Mendoza 1999 | 15.5 | £5–7 |
| Finca el Retiro Tempranillo, Mendoza 1999 | 15 | £5–7 |
| Sierra Alta Cabernet Sauvignon/Malbec, Mendoza 1999 | 14 | −£5.00 |
| Sierra Alta Shiraz, Mendoza 1999 | 16.5 | −£5.00 |
| Trivento Sangiovese, Mendoza 1999 | 15 | −£5.00 |

## ARGENTINIAN WHITE

| | | |
|---|---|---|
| Bodega Lurton Pinot Gris, Mendoza 1999 | 14.5 | −£5.00 |
| Santa Julia Viognier Reserve 1999 | 16.5 | £5–7 |

## AUSTRALIAN RED

| | | |
|---|---|---|
| Brown Brothers Barbera 1996 | 14 | £5–7 |
| Brown Brothers Nebbiolo 1996 | 13.5 | £7–10 |
| Brown Brothers Tarrango 1999 | 13 | £5–7 |
| Bushmans Crossing Cabernet/Merlot 1999 | 14 | −£5.00 |
| Château Reynella Basket-Pressed Shiraz 1997 | 17 | £10–13 |
| Church Block Cabernet Shiraz Merlot, Wirra Wirra Vineyards 1998 | 17 | £7–10 |
| Clancy's Red 1998 | 15 | £7–10 |
| Deakin Estate Merlot 1999 | 15.5 | £5–7 |
| Eileen Hardy Shiraz 1996 | 14.5 | £20+ |
| Fishermans Bend Cabernet Sauvignon 1998 | 12 | −£5.00 |
| Garry Crittenden Sangiovese 1998 | 13.5 | £10–13 |
| Henschke Keyneton Shiraz/Cabernet Sauvignon/Merlot 1996 | 12 | £13–20 |
| Jindalee Shiraz 1999 | 14 | −£5.00 |
| Kingston Reserve Petit Verdot 1997 | 12 | £13–20 |
| Nanya Vineyard Malbec/Ruby Cabernet 1999 | 12 | −£5.00 |
| Penfolds Organic Merlot/Shiraz/Cabernet 1998 | 15.5 | £7–10 |
| Peter Lehmann The Barossa Shiraz 1998 | 17 | £5–7 |
| Rosemount GSM, McLaren Vale 1996 | 15 | £13–20 |
| Rosemount 'Hill of Gold' Shiraz, Mudgee 1998 | 17.5 | £7–10 |
| Settler's Station Tempranillo 1999 | 13 | £5–7 |
| Stonewell Shiraz, Barossa Valley 1994 | 14 | £13–20 |
| Tatachilla Cabernet Sauvignon/Merlot, McLaren Vale 1998 | 14.5 | £7–10 |
| Tatachilla Foundation Shiraz 1997 | 14 | £13–20 |
| Tatachilla Growers Grenache Mataro 1999 | 10 | −£5.00 |

455

The Angelus Cabernet Sauvignon, Wirra Wirra 1997 — 14 £13–20

Wrattonbully Cabernet Sauvignon, Limestone Coast 1998 — 16 £5–7

## AUSTRALIAN WHITE

Broken Bridge Chardonnay/Colombard 1999 — 13 −£3.50

Broken Bridge Colombard Chardonnay 1999 — 14.5 −£3.50

Brown Brothers Late Harvested Orange Muscat & Flora 1999 (half-bottle) — 16.5 £5–7

Bushmans Crossing Semillon/Chardonnay 1999 — 13.5 −£5.00

Château Tahbilk Unwooded Marsanne, Victoria 1998 — 16 £5–7

Hardys Stamp of Australia Grenache Shiraz Rosé 1999 — 13.5 −£5.00

Houghton Classic Dry White 1998 — 15.5 £5–7

Leasingham Domaine Chardonnay 1997 — 16 £5–7

Nepenthe Vineyards Sauvignon Blanc 1999 — 14 £7–10

Oxford Landing Sauvignon Blanc 2000 — 14 −£5.00

Pendulum Chardonnay 1999 — 15 −£5.00

Penfolds Bin 95a Chardonnay — 13.5 £13–20

Penfolds Clare Valley Organic Chardonnay/ Sauvignon Blanc, 1998 (organic) — 15.5 £7–10

Penfolds Old Vine Semillon, Barossa 1998 — 16 £5–7

Penfolds Rawson's Retreat Bin 202 Riesling 1999 — 15 −£5.00

Petaluma Piccadilly Chardonnay 1998 — 16.5 £13–20

Tatachilla Sauvignon/ Semillon, McLaren Vale 1999 — 15 −£5.00

Voyager Estate Chardonnay 1997 — 17.5 £10–13

Wirra Wirra Oaked Chardonnay 1998 — 17 £7–10

## AUSTRIAN WHITE

Bouvier Beerenauslese Munzenrieder 1996 — 12 £5–7

## BULGARIAN RED

Domaine Boyar Merlot/ Gamza, Iambol 1999 — 15 −£3.50

## CHILEAN RED

Carmen Nativa Cabernet Sauvignon 1998 (organic) — 15 £7–10

Errazuriz Merlot 1999 — 16 £5–7

Gracia Estate Vineyards Cabernet Sauvignon Reserva 1997 — 15 £5–7

| | | |
|---|---|---|
| Mont Gras Carmenere Reserva 1998 | 14 | £5–7 |
| Valdivieso Barrel Selection Cabernet/ Merlot 1997 | 16.5 | £5–7 |
| Valdivieso Pinot Noir Reserve 1997 | 16 | £5–7 |

## CHILEAN WHITE

| | | |
|---|---|---|
| Canepa Semillon, Colchagua Valley 1999 | 16.5 | –£5.00 |
| Carmen Vineyards Insigne Gewürztraminer 1999 | 16 | £5–7 |

## ENGLISH RED

| | | |
|---|---|---|
| Chapel Down Epoch I 1998 | 10 | £5–7 |

## ENGLISH WHITE

| | | |
|---|---|---|
| Chapel Down Flint Dry 1998 | 13.5 | –£5.00 |
| Summerhill Oaked Dry White NV | 12 | –£5.00 |

## FRENCH RED

| | | |
|---|---|---|
| Abbotts Ammonite Côte du Roussillon 1999 | 15 | –£5.00 |
| Beaujolais Villages 1998 | 12 | £5–7 |
| Bistro Rouge VdP d'Oc 1999 | 13.5 | –£5.00 |
| Boulder Creek Red VdP du Vaucluse 1999 | 15 | –£3.50 |
| Cabernet Sauvignon La Cité VdP d'Oc 1998 | 15.5 | –£5.00 |

| | | |
|---|---|---|
| Cahors Côtes d'Olt 1999 | 14 | –£5.00 |
| Château Cazal-Viel, Cuvée des Fees St Chinian 1998 | 16 | £5–7 |
| Château de Caraguilhes Corbieres 1998 (half-bottle) (organic) | 16 | –£5.00 |
| Château de Targe 'Les Tuffes' Saumur Champigny 1997 | 15.5 | £5–7 |
| Château Falfas Côtes de Bourg 1997 | 14 | £7–10 |
| Château Haut d'Allard Côtes de Bourg 1997 | 15 | £5–7 |
| Château Haut Nouchet Pessac-Leognan 1996 (organic) | 13 | £10–13 |
| Château Leoville Las-Cases 2eme Cru Classé, St Julien 1994 | 16 | £20+ |
| Château Les Tuileries Bordeaux Superieur 1998 | 13.5 | –£5.00 |
| Château Meynard Bordeaux 1998 | 14.5 | –£5.00 |
| Château Palmer 3eme Cru Classé Margaux 1990 | 12 | £20+ |
| Château Pech-Latt, Corbieres 1998 | 15 | –£5.00 |
| Château Saint-Maurice Côtes du Rhône 1998 | 15 | –£5.00 |
| Château Tayac Cru Bourgeois, Margaux 1995 | 13 | £13–20 |
| Clos de Tart Grand Cru Mommessin 1993 | 15 | £20+ |
| Cornas Chapoutier 1997 | 13 | £13–20 |
| Côte Rotie Les Jumelles 1997 | 13 | £20+ |

Côtes du Rhône 1999, Waitrose — 13 −£5.00

Côtes du Rhône Villages, Domaine de Cantemerle 1998 — 14 −£5.00

Côtes du Ventoux 1998 — 14 −£5.00

Crozes Hermitage Cave des Clairmonts 1998 — 14 £5–7

Crozes Hermitage Domaine de Thalabert 1997 — 13 £10–13

Cuvée Andre St Estephe 1996 — 14.5 £13–20

Cuvée Eugenie Château Capendu, Corbieres 1998 — 15 £7–10

Domaine de Courtille Corbieres 1998 — 16 £7–10

Domaine de Rose Syrah/Merlot, VdP d'Oc 1998 — 16 −£3.50

Domaine du Moulin "The Cabernets", VdP d'Oc 1998 — 13 −£5.00

Fleurie Montreynaud 1999 — 12 £7–10

Gallerie Tempranillo/Syrah VdP d'Oc 1998 — 15.5 −£5.00

Good Ordinary Claret Bordeaux, Waitrose — 14 −£5.00

Hautes Côtes de Nuits 1998 — 11 £5–7

L'Enclos Domecque Mourvedre/Syrah VdP d'Oc 1998 — 14 −£5.00

La Bernardine Châteauneuf-du-Pape, Chapoutier 1997 — 14 £13–20

La Colombe Côtes du Rhône 1999 (organic) — 14 −£5.00

Les Fontanelles Merlot/Syrah VdP d'Oc 1998 — 15.5 −£5.00

Maury, Les Vignerons du Val d'Orbieu NV — 16 −£5.00

Merchants Bay Merlot/Cabernet Sauvignon 1997 — 13.5 −£5.00

Mercurery Rouge 1er Cru 'Les Puillets', Château Le Hardi 1998 — 13 £10–13

Oaked Merlot VdP d'Oc 1999 — 14 −£5.00

Organic Merlot VdP d'Oc 1999 — 13 −£5.00

Prieurs de Foncaire, Buzet Grande Reserve 1998 — 15.5 −£5.00

Saint Roche VdP du Gard 1999 (organic) — 13.5 −£5.00

Saint-Joseph, Cave de Saint-Desiderat, Cuvée Medaille d'Or 1997 — 15.5 £7–10

Santenay Bouchard Père 1997 — 10 £10–13

Saumur Rouge Les Nivieres 1998 — 14 −£5.00

Savigny les Beaune Bouchard Père 1998 — 11 £10–13

Special Reserve Claret, Cotes de Castillon Limited Edition Millennium Magnum 1996 (magnum) — 16 £10–13

St Emilion Yvon Mau NV — 13 £5–7

Valreas Côtes du Rhône Chapoutier (half-bottle) — 16.5 −£3.50

| | | |
|---|---|---|
| Volnay 1er Cru Les Chevret 1996 | 13 | £20+ |
| Volnay 1er Cry les Caillerets, Clos des 60 Ouvrees, Domaine de la Passe d'Or 1996 | 14 | £20+ |

## FRENCH WHITE

| | | |
|---|---|---|
| Alsace Gewürztraminer 1998, Waitrose | 16.5 | £5–7 |
| Alsace Pinot Blanc, Paul Blanck 1999 | 14 | –£5.00 |
| Anjou Blanc Ackerman 1999 | 13 | –£3.50 |
| Bistro Blanc VdP d'Oc 1999 | 13.5 | –£5.00 |
| Bordeaux Blanc Medium Dry, Yvon Mau NV | 12 | –£3.50 |
| Chablis Gaec des Reugnis 1998 | 14.5 | £7–10 |
| Chablis Grand Cru Les Clos 1996 | 13 | £13–20 |
| Château Carsin Bordeaux Blanc Cuvée Prestige 1997 | 15.5 | £7–10 |
| Château de Caraghuiles Organic Rosé 1999 | 15.5 | £5–7 |
| Château Filhot Grand Cru Classe Sauternes 1989 | 13.5 | £20+ |
| Château Vignal Labrie, Monbazillac 1997 | 17 | £7–10 |
| Clos des Chenoves Blanc 1998 | 14 | £5–7 |
| Domaine de l'Olivette, Corbieres 1999 | 15.5 | –£5.00 |
| Domaine de Planterieu VdP de Gascogne 1999 | 15 | –£5.00 |
| French Connection Viognier VdP d'Oc 1999 | 15.5 | –£5.00 |
| Gewürztraminer Wintzenheim Domaine Zind Humbrecht 1998 | 16.5 | £7–10 |
| Hermitage Le Chevalier de Sterimberg 1997 | 17.5 | £20+ |
| James Herrick Chardonnay VdP d'Oc 1999 | 16 | –£5.00 |
| L'Enclos Domeque Barrel Fermented Marsanne/ Roussanne VdP d'Oc 1999 | 16.5 | –£5.00 |
| La Cité Chardonnay, VdP d'Oc 1999 | 14.5 | –£5.00 |
| 'Les Fleurs' Chardonnay/ Sauvignon VdP des Cotes de Gascogne 1999 | 16 | £5–7 |
| Maury Vin Doux Naturel NV | 14 | –£5.00 |
| Merchants Bay Sauvignon/Semillon 1998 | 14 | –£5.00 |
| Mercurey Blanc Château le Hardi 1998 | 14 | £10–13 |
| Meursault Louis Jadot 1997 | 12 | £13–20 |
| Montagny 1er Cru Bouchard Père 1998 | 13 | £7–10 |
| Muscadet sur Lie 'Fief Guerin' 1999 | 14 | –£5.00 |
| Muscat Sec Domaine de Provenquiere, VdP d'Oc 1999 | 16 | –£5.00 |

WAITROSE

| Muscate de Beaumes de Venise NV (half-bottle) | 16 | −£5.00 |
| Pinot Gris Grand Cru Rangen de Thann Clos St Urbain, Domaine Zind Humbrecht 1996 | 18.5 | £20+ |
| Pouilly Fume Chatelain 1999 | 12.5 | £7–10 |
| Puligny Montrachet 1er Cru Champs Gains 1997 | 13 | £20+ |
| Quincy La Boissiere 1999 | 13 | £5–7 |
| Rosé d'Anjou 1999 | 13 | −£5.00 |
| Saint-Aubin Premier Cru Ropiteau 1998 | 15 | £13–20 |
| Sancerre Blanc Domaine Naudet 1999 | 13 | £7–10 |
| Sancerre Reserve Alfonse Mellot 1998 | 10 | £10–13 |
| Saumur Blanc 'les Andides' Saint Cyr-en-Bourg 1999 | 14 | −£5.00 |
| Sauvignon Blanc 'Les Rochers', VdP des Côtes de Gascogne 1999 | 13.5 | −£5.00 |
| Sauvignon Bordeaux Calvet 1999 | 13.5 | −£5.00 |
| Tokay Pinot Gris Vendanges Tardives, Hugel 1990 | 18 | £20+ |
| Top 40 Chardonnay VdP d'Oc 1999 | 17 | £5–7 |
| Touraine Sauvignon 1999, Waitrose | 13.5 | −£5.00 |
| Vin Blanc Sec VdT Francais NV, Waitrose | 12 | −£3.50 |
| Winter Hill Syrah Rosé, VdP d'Oc 1999 | 14 | −£3.50 |

| Winter Hill VdP d'Oc 1999 | 15 | −£3.50 |

## GERMAN WHITE

| Devil's Rock Masterpiece, St Ursula 1999 | 10.5 | −£5.00 |
| Johannisberger Klaus Riesling Spatlese, Schloss Schonborn 1990 | 16.5 | £5–7 |
| Kendermann Vineyard Selection Dry Riesling 1998 | 13.5 | −£5.00 |
| Liebfraumilch Rheinhessen 1999, Waitrose | 14 | −£3.50 |
| Piesporter Michelsburg Mosel-Saar-Ruwer 1999, Waitrose | 13 | −£3.50 |
| Ruppertsberger Dry Riesling Auslese 1996 | 13 | £5–7 |
| Wehlener Sonnenuhr Riesling Auslese 1990 | 17 | £13–20 |
| Wehlener Sonnenuhr Riesling Spatlese, JJ Prum 1994 | 14 | £13–20 |

## GREEK RED

| Vin de Crete Kourtakis 1998 | 14 | −£3.50 |

## HUNGARIAN WHITE

| Deer Leap Dry White 1999 | 15.5 | −£3.50 |
| Deer Leap Gewürztraminer, Mor 1999 | 15.5 | −£5.00 |

460

| Deer Leap Sauvignon Blanc 1999 | 16 | −£5.00 |
|---|---|---|
| Matra Springs 1999 | 14 | −£3.50 |
| Matra Springs Dry White 1999 | 15 | −£3.50 |

## ITALIAN RED

| Amarone della Valpolicella Classico Riserva 1990 | 13 | £20+ |
|---|---|---|
| Amarone della Valpolicella Classico Vigneti Casterna 1995 (50cl) | 16 | £7–10 |
| Barolo Terre da Vino 1996 | 13 | £10–13 |
| Bonarda Sentito, Oltrepo Pavese 1999 | 15.5 | −£5.00 |
| Brunello di Montalcino Tenuta Nova 1994 | 14 | £13–20 |
| Emporio Barrel Aged Syrah 1998 (Sicilia) | 16.5 | £5–7 |
| Mezzomondo Negroamaro 1999 | 16 | −£5.00 |
| Montepulciano d'Abruzzo, Umani Ronchi 1998 | 16 | −£5.00 |
| Nero d'Avola Syrah, Firriato 1998 | 14 | −£5.00 |
| Pendulum Zinfandel 1999 | 15.5 | −£5.00 |
| Sangiovese Marche, Waitrose | 13 | −£3.50 |
| Summit Sangiovese di Maremma 1997 | 16 | £7–10 |
| Tenute Marchese Antinori Chianti Classico 1996 | 16 | £10–13 |

| Tenute Marchese Antinori Chianti Classico Riserva 1997 | 14.5 | £10–13 |
|---|---|---|
| Tenute Marchese Chianti Classico Riserva 1996 | 16 | £10–13 |
| Teroldego Rotaliano, Ca'Vit 1999 | 14 | −£5.00 |
| Terra Viva Merlot del Veneto 1999 (organic) | 14 | −£5.00 |
| Vigna Alta Merlot & Cabernet Basilicata 1998 | 16.5 | −£5.00 |

## ITALIAN WHITE

| Catarratto Chardonnay Firriato 1999 (Sicily) | 16 | −£5.00 |
|---|---|---|
| Frascati Superiore Tenuta delle Marmorelle 1999 | 15.5 | −£5.00 |
| Lugana Villa Flora 1999 | 16.5 | £5–7 |
| Mezzo Mondo Chardonnay 1998 | 14 | −£5.00 |
| Pinot Grigio Alto Adige San Michele-Appiano 1999 | 14.5 | £5–7 |
| Verdicchio dei Castelli Jesi, Moncaro 1999 | 16 | −£5.00 |

## MEXICAN RED

| L A Cetto Petite Syrah 1997 | 16 | −£5.00 |
|---|---|---|

## NEW ZEALAND RED

| Grove Mill Marlborough Pinot Noir 1998 | 11 | £10–13 |
|---|---|---|
| Hamilton Russell Pinot Noir 1997 | 13 | £13–20 |

Jackson Estate Marlborough Pinot Noir 1998 — 15 £10–13

Montana Cabernet Merlot 1999 — 15 £5–7

Unison Selection, Hawkes Bay 1998 — 13.5 £13–20

## NEW ZEALAND WHITE

Craggy Range Winery Chardonnay, Hawkes Bay 1999 — 16 £10–13

Jackson Estate Sauvignon Blanc 1999 — 15 £7–10

Missionvale Chardonnay 1997 — 14 £10–13

Montana Reserve Barrique Fermented Chardonnay 1998 — 16 £7–10

Oyster Bay Marlborough Sauvignon Blanc 1999 — 16.5 £5–7

Tiki Ridge Dry White 1999 — 12.5 −£5.00

Villa Maria Private Bin Chardonnay, Gisborne 1998 — 14 £5–7

Villa Maria Private Bin Riesling 1999 — 16 £5–7

## PORTUGUESE RED

Terra de Lobos, Quinta do Casal Branco 1999 — 14 −£5.00

Trincadeira Joao Portugal Ramos 1999 — 16 £7–10

Vila Santa Alentejo 1998 — 16.5 £7–10

Vinho do Monte, Alentejo 1998 — 13.5 −£5.00

## PORTUGUESE WHITE

Quinta de Simaens Vinho Verde 1998 — 10 −£5.00

Terras do Rio Quinta de Abrigada 1998 — 15 −£3.50

## ROMANIAN WHITE

Willow Ridge Sauvignon/Feteasca 1999 — 15.5 −£3.50

## SOUTH AFRICAN RED

Avontuur Estate Cabernet Sauvignon/ Merlot 1998 — 13 −£5.00

Clos Malverne Basket Pressed Pinotage, Stellenbosch 1999 — 16 £7–10

Goats Do Roam Fairview, Paarl 1999 — 15.5 −£5.00

Hidden Valley Pinotage, Devon Valley 1996 — 15 £13–20

Kumala Reserve Cabernet Sauvignon 1998 — 16.5 £7–10

Spice Route Cabernet Sauvignon/Merlot 1998 — 16.5 £7–10

Spice Route Flagship Merlot 1998 — 17 £13–20

Steenberg Merlot, Constantia 1998 — 15 £7–10

Thelema Mountain Vineyards Cabernet Sauvignon 1996 — 14 £13–20

## SOUTH AFRICAN WHITE

Culemborg Cape Dry White 1999 — 14 — -£3.50

Culemborg Unwooded Chardonnay, Western Cape 1999 — 15 — -£5.00

Fairview Barrel Fermented Chenin Blanc 1999 — 16 — -£5.00

Spice Route Abbotsdale Colombard/Chenin Blanc 1999 — 15 — £7–10

Springfield Sauvignon Blanc Special Cuvée 1999 — 15.5 — £5–7

Steenberg Sauvignon Blanc 1999 — 16 — £7–10

Thelema Mountain Vineyard Sauvignon Blanc 1999 — 17 — £10–13

Warwick Estate Chardonnay, Stellenbosch 1999 — 17.5 — £5–7

## SPANISH RED

Agramont Tempranillo/Cabernet Sauvignon, Navarra 1996 — 14.5 — £5–7

Espiral Oaked Tempranillo 1998 — 15 — £5–7

Espiral Tempranillo/Cabernet Sauvignon 1998 — 16 — -£5.00

La Rioja Alta Gran Reserve 904, 1989 — 13.5 — £13–20

Torres Gran Sangre de Toro Reserva 1996 — 16 — £5–7

Totally Tinto Tempranillo, La Mancha NV — 15 — -£3.50

Totally Two Thousand Tempranillo NV (magnum) — 15.5 — -£3.50

Vina Fuerte Garnacha, Calatayud 1999 — 16 — -£5.00

## SPANISH WHITE

Albarino Pazo de Seoane, Rias Baixas 1999 — 15.5 — £7–10

Espiral Macabeo/Chardonnay 1998 — 15.5 — -£5.00

Lustau Moscatel de Chipiona NV — 15 — -£5.00

Vinas del Vero Chardonnay 1998 — 14 — -£5.00

## URUGUAYAN RED

Pisano Family Reserve Tannat 1998 — 14.5 — £7–10

## USA RED

Bonterra Vineyards Merlot 1997 (organic) — 16.5 — £7–10

Fetzer Valley Oaks Cabernet Sauvignon 1997 — 15.5 — £5–7

Shafer Cabernet Sauvignon 1995 — 13 — £20+

Stags Leap Cabernet Sauvignon 1995 — 16 — £20+

Stonebridge Cellars Zinfandel 1997 — 13 — £5–7

| | | |
|---|---|---|
| Yorkville Cellars Cabernet Franc 1997 (organic) | 14 | £7–10 |
| Yorkville Petit Verdot 1997 | 16 | £7–10 |

## USA WHITE

| | | |
|---|---|---|
| Acacia Chardonnay 1995 | 14.5 | £10–13 |
| Fetzer Unoaked Chardonnay 1999 | 14.5 | £5–7 |
| Fetzer Viognier 1999 | 15 | £7–10 |

## FORTIFIED WINES

| | | |
|---|---|---|
| 10 Year Old Tawny Port, Waitrose | 14 | £10–13 |
| Apostoles Palo Cortado Muy Viejo (half-bottle) | 18.5 | £10–13 |
| Apostoles Palo Cortado Oloroso (half-bottle) | 15.5 | £7–10 |
| Comte de Lafont Pineau des Charentes | 15 | £5–7 |
| Dry Fly Amontillado | 12 | £5–7 |
| Fino Sherry, Waitrose | 15.5 | –£5.00 |
| Fonseca Traditional LBV 1983 | 15 | £13–20 |
| Matusalem Oloroso Dulce Muy Viejo (half-bottle) | 16.5 | £10–13 |
| Oloroso Sherry, Waitrose | 13 | –£5.00 |
| Solera Jerezana Dry Amontillado, Waitrose | 16 | £5–7 |
| Solera Jerezana Dry Oloroso, Waitrose | 16.5 | £5–7 |
| Solera Jerezana Old Oloroso, Waitrose | 16.5 | £5–7 |

| | | |
|---|---|---|
| Vintage Warre Quinta da Cavadinha 1987 | 17.5 | £13–20 |

## SPARKLING WINES

| | | |
|---|---|---|
| Alexandre Bonnet Brut Rosé NV (France) | 12 | £13–20 |
| Banrock Station Sparkling Shiraz NV (Australia) | 17 | £7–10 |
| Brut Vintage 1990, Waitrose | 13 | £13–20 |
| Cava Brut NV, Waitrose | 15.5 | –£5.00 |
| Champagne Blanc de Blancs NV, Waitrose | 15 | £13–20 |
| Champagne Blanc de Noirs NV, Waitrose | 15 | £10–13 |
| Champagne Brut NV, Waitrose | 12.5 | £13–20 |
| Champagne Fleury 1993 | 13 | £20+ |
| Champagne Fleury Brut NV | 18.5 | £13–20 |
| Chandon Argentina Brut NV | 15 | £7–10 |
| Chandon Australia Brut NV | 15.5 | £7–10 |
| Chapel Hill Pinot Noir/ Chardonnay NV | 15 | –£5.00 |
| Charles Heidsieck Champagne Blanc de Blancs 1982 | 20 | £20+ |
| Charles Heidsieck Reserve Mise en Cave en 1993 | 13.5 | £20+ |
| Clairette de Die Tradition (half-bottle) (France) | 14 | £5–7 |

Cremant de Bourgogne Blanc de Noirs, Lugny `14` `£5–7`

Cremant de Bourgogne Rosé NV (France) `14` `£7–10`

Cuvée Royale Blanquette de Limoux NV `13` `£5–7`

Duc de Marre Special Cuvée Champagne Brut Non Vintage `13.5` `£13–20`

Jacob's Creek Sparkling Chardonnay/Pinot Noir NV (Australia) `15` `£5–7`

Le Mesnil Blanc de Blancs Grand Cru Champagne Brut Non Vintage `14` `£13–20`

Lindauer Brut NV (New Zealand) `14` `£7–10`

Saumur Brut NV, Waitrose `14` `£5–7`

Seaview Brut NV `14` `£5–7`

Seaview Brut Rosé NV `13.5` `£5–7`

Sparkling Burgundy NV (France) `13` `£5–7`

Taittinger Comtes de Champagne Blanc de Blancs 1990 `13` `£20+`

**SEE STOP PRESS SECTION AT END OF BOOK FOR LAST-MINUTE ADDITIONS OR UPDATES TO THIS RETAILER'S RANGE.**

# WINE CELLAR

My advice, in order to appreciate the tasty nub of this retailer, is to get your laughing gear around some of Mr David Vaughan's southern French wines. Mr Vaughan is the hero here, battling solo for so many years buying wine, but lately he has acquired, I believe, an assistant, although I've yet to see hide or hair of her/him.

Wine Cellar is a modest set of 70 wine shops spread over the land. It does not innovate by developing its own brands, via own-label wine ranges for example, but relies simply on wines purchased by the estimable Mr Vaughan. The Wine Cellar wine list is dominated by major brands like Penfolds, Gallo, Skalli, KWV, certain Chilean and New Zealand setups (Errázuriz, for example, and Villa Maria), Mondavi, Fetzer and so on. The French wines I admire you'll have to search the list for (because, I would guess, they don't pay a premium to the retailer for receiving star billing).

Wine Cellar is owned by a holding company called Parisa, which is keen to prove itself but strapped for the vast reserves of cash, or leverage potential, to do so on any huge scale. There were suggestions it might bid for part of the 1st Quench estate, but this was pure speculation, more likely fantasy, along the lines of Millwall dreaming of buying David Beckham.

Parisa also operates fourteen Parisa Café Bars and says it wants to open more. These places offer customers the chance to choose from 250 wines at normal off-licence prices or to buy a bottle of wine plus £3 corkage and drink it with food in the café. It also runs Right Choice, a chain of 65 outlets in the north and Midlands offering groceries, drinks, videos and newsprint. There used to be outfits called Cellar 5 and Berkeley Wines but they got the chop. Parisa also removed Night Vision, its off-licence/video store format, from its portfolio of retail fascias.

Booze Buster is still going and it is, like Spar, a franchise. Individuals buy the Booze Buster concept, giving them access to Parisa's central buying powers, and are thus enabled, in the company's own words, to 'compete with supermarkets'. This blueprint sounds grand but since most of the top-selling wines at supermarkets are around £3 – just a little less in some cases, just a touch more in others – and are, most crucially, own-label ranges or ranges that the supermarkets themselves have caused to be created in their various countries of origin, it is difficult to see how anyone running a Booze Buster can even offer the same wines as supermarkets except, of course, the ranges from the big companies like Penfolds, Gallo, Skalli, KWV, certain Chilean and New Zealand setups (Errázuriz, for example, and Villa Maria), Mondavi, Fetzer and so on. Booze Busters do not, on this basis, compete with supermarkets. They simply compete with small off-licences.

The Parisa Group talks proudly. It claims to be 'recognised as the most innovative and successful UK company in its sector'. Questions loom large immediately now. Recognised by whom? Innovative in what way? Successful how? And what in heaven's name is the sector in which it can justifiably claim all these terms of self-congratulation? The answer is that Parisa is the only company, of any size, in its sector, and this sector is the one it has itself termed the 'specialist drinks retailing and leisure' sector. Once you conjure up your own pigeonhole, which no one else fits, then it is no hard job, if you stay solvent, to claim innovation and success in it. As far as this joker is concerned, this single wine guide writer, Parisa is just a booze retailer and as such it has to be stacked up against everyone else, from Oddbins to Unwins, Tesco to Marks & Spencer. On this more sober, realistic basis, Parisa has a lot of catching up to do (though patently not in hype, in which spicy but superficial augmentation it excels).

Well, the Parisa coffee bar/restaurant/wine shop format has been done before, but only by individuals running their own establishments. It has never been used as an idea for a nationwide chain, and it remains to be seen whether it can work on this scale. All we're talking about here is Café Rouge and Nicolas combined, nothing more original than that (though it needs saying here there is very little genuine invention and true innovation in wine and food retailing and the single company which has been most dynamically innovative is McDonald's).

I have not eaten in one of these Parisa cafés but I welcome the idea because I am a great fan of eating out but I don't like paying obscene restaurant mark-ups on my wine. However, I have yet to visit but every time I cycle past the Putney branch, which isn't, admittedly, very often nowadays, I've just seen a few dull-looking young people, far too young to put up with a crusty old bastard like me, puffing away on fags inside what looks like a routinely outfitted, mass-designed bar like the deadly All Bar One setup (which is fearfully po-faced).

Parisa has relaunched its website in a bid to be 'at the forefront' of Internet selling. It will be 'radically different', so I'm told. The site will offer around 700 wines with 48-hour delivery. This is yet to come on-stream at the time of writing, but I wish it well. Wine retailers who operate e-commerce sites have the advantage that duff wines can easily be returned to the branches. How can you send a wine tainted by its cork back via the Internet? Indeed, I posed this question in my *Guardian* column, when ItsWine.com were offering a bargain deal on a Penfolds wine and Rodney Kearns, purchasing director of this e-commerce retailer, was pleased to write to me saying 'YES – we have a money-back policy on duff bottles and we make an instant refund via the customer's credit card. We do not ask for the bottle back (within reason).' Ah, within reason. Yes, of course.

Shall we tiptoe away from this subject, and this retailer, now? Drink the wines I rate highly in the listing which follows. If you don't like them write to me c/o the *Guardian*, 119 Farringdon Road, London EC1R 3ER, and tell me I'm a prat. Just as Mr Haghighi, the company's MD, is in all probability, doing right now.

Wine Cellar
PO Box 476
Loushers Lane
Warrington
Cheshire
WA4 6RR

Tel 01925 454545
Fax 01925 454546
e-mail: cellarman@parisa.com
www.parisa.com

## AUSTRALIAN RED

| | | |
|---|---|---|
| Cleveland Brien Shiraz/ Cabernet 1994 | 11 | £7–10 |
| Cleveland Macedon Pinot Noir 1996 | 10 | £10–13 |
| Jim Barrie McCrae Wood Shiraz 1996 | 14.5 | £13–20 |
| Penfolds Rawsons Retreat Bin 35 Cabernet Sauvignon/Shiraz/Ruby Cabernet 1998 | 14 | £5–7 |
| Rosemount Estate Grenache/Shiraz 1999 | 15 | £5–7 |
| Three Steps Cabernet Sauvignon 1998 | 13.5 | £5–7 |
| Vasse Felix Cabernet Sauvignon 1997 | 16 | £13–20 |

## AUSTRALIAN WHITE

Capel Vale Verdelho 1999 | 16 | £7–10

Hardys Stamp of | 15 | –£5.00
Australia Chardonnay
Semillon 1999

Heggies Chardonnay | 16 | £7–10
1997

Three Steps Chardonnay | 13.5 | £5–7
1998

Wolf Blass President's | 17 | £7–10
Selection McLaren Vale
Chardonnay 1997

## BULGARIAN RED

Domaine Boyar Cabernet | 15.5 | –£3.50
Sauvignon NV

Domaine Boyar | 14 | –£3.50
Cabernet/Merlot 1998

Domaine Boyar Reserve | 14.5 | –£5.00
Merlot/Gamza 1996

## CHILEAN RED

Casa del Bosque Merlot | 12 | £5–7
1998

Cono Sur Merlot 1999 | 15.5 | £5–7

Mapocho Cabernet | 13 | –£5.00
Sauvignon 1998

Mont Gras Cabernet | 14.5 | £5–7
Sauvignon 1998

Mont Gras Quatro 1998 | 15 | £5–7

Valdivieso Barrel Select | 15.5 | £5–7
Merlot 1999

Valdivieso Pinot Noir | 16 | £5–7
Reserve 1997

## CHILEAN WHITE

Casa del Bosque | 10 | £5–7
Sauvignon Blanc 1998

La Palmeria Chardonnay | 16 | –£5.00
1999

## FRENCH RED

Abbotts Cumulus Shiraz | 16.5 | £5–7
Minervois 1998

Big Frank's Cabernet | 14 | £5–7
Frank 1998

Château Agnel Minervois | 16 | –£5.00
1998

Château Bonhomme | 13 | £5–7
Minervois 1997

Château Cotes de | 13.5 | £5–7
Bellevue, Côtes de Bourg
1996

Château Grand Berthaud, | 16 | £5–7
Premieres Côtes de Blaye
1997

Château La Chapelle, | 14 | –£5.00
St Chinian 1998

Château Lamargue | 16 | –£5.00
Costieres de Nimes
Grand Reserve 1998

Château Quinsac | 16 | –£5.00
Bellevue, Bordeaux 1998

Château Saint-Germain | 13.5 | £5–7
Bordeaux Superieur 1997

Château Saint-Gilles, 1er | 14.5 | –£5.00
Cote de Bordeaux 1998

Domaine Coste Blanque, | 17 | £5–7
Montpeyroux, Coteaux
du Languedoc 1998

| | | |
|---|---|---|
| Domaine de Villemajou, Corbieres 1998 | 16 | £5–7 |
| Domaine des Amandiers, Côtes du Roussillon Villages 1998 | 15 | –£5.00 |
| Domaine du Bosquet Merlot VdP d'Oc 1998 | 16 | £5–7 |
| Domaine du Grand Bosc, Fitou 1998 | 15.5 | –£5.00 |
| James Herrick Cuvée Simone VdP d'Oc 1998 | 16.5 | –£5.00 |
| La Chasse du Pape Côtes du Rhône 1998 | 16.5 | –£5.00 |
| Old Git Grenache Syrah 1999 | 15.5 | –£5.00 |
| Rhone Valley Red VdP de Vaucluse NV | 13 | –£5.00 |
| Shiraz Foncalieu 1998 | 16 | –£5.00 |
| Tastevinage Bourgogne Hautes Côtes de Nuits Yves Chaley 1997 | 10 | £7–10 |
| Thierry & Guy Utter Bastard Syrah 1998 | 14.5 | £5–7 |
| Vacqueyras Les Agapes 1998 | 16.5 | £5–7 |
| Wild Pig Barrel Reserve Shiraz 1998 | 14 | –£5.00 |

## FRENCH WHITE

| | | |
|---|---|---|
| Château l'Ermitage Blanc, Costieres de Nimes 1998 | 16 | –£5.00 |
| Château l'Ermitage Rosé, Costieres de Nimes 1998 | 15.5 | –£5.00 |
| Château Lacroix Rosé 1999 | 13 | £5–7 |

| | | |
|---|---|---|
| Château Lacroix Semillon/Sauvignon 1998 | 13.5 | £5–7 |
| Domaine l'Orgeril Reserve Chardonnay, VdP d'Oc 1997 | 12 | £5–7 |
| Orchid Vale Medium Dry Chardonnay 1998 | 13 | –£5.00 |
| Rhone Valley White, VdP de Vaucluse NV | 11 | –£5.00 |
| Sancerre Seduction Vieilles Vignes 1998 | 12 | £10–13 |

## GREEK RED

| | | |
|---|---|---|
| Hatzimichalis Cabernet Sauvignon 1997 | 16 | £7–10 |
| Sillogi Lafazanis Red 1997 | 13 | £5–7 |
| St George Skouras, Nemea 1996 | 15.5 | £5–7 |

## GREEK WHITE

| | | |
|---|---|---|
| Hatzimichalis Chardonnay 1998 | 12 | £7–10 |
| Sillogi Lafazanis White 1998 | 12 | £5–7 |

## ITALIAN RED

| | | |
|---|---|---|
| D'Istinto Sangiovese Merlot 1998 (Sicily) | 14 | –£5.00 |

## ITALIAN WHITE

| | | |
|---|---|---|
| Monte Tenda Soave 1998 | 12 | –£5.00 |

## NEW ZEALAND WHITE

| | | |
|---|---|---|
| Delegat's Reserve Chardonnay, Barrel Fermented 1998 | 14.5 | £7–10 |
| Matua Valley Chardonnay 1999 | 14 | £5–7 |
| Matua Valley Sauvignon Blanc 1999 | 16 | £5–7 |
| Montana Reserve Barrique Fermented Chardonnay 1998 | 16 | £7–10 |
| Oyster Bay Sauvignon Blanc 1999 | 16.5 | £5–7 |

## PORTUGUESE RED

| | | |
|---|---|---|
| Belafonte Baga, Beiras 1998 | 14 | −£5.00 |
| Portada Tinto Estremadura 1995 | 16 | −£5.00 |
| Terra Boa 1997 | 12 | −£5.00 |

## SOUTH AFRICAN RED

| | | |
|---|---|---|
| Jordan Merlot 1998 | 16 | £7–10 |
| L'Avenir Cabernet Sauvignon 1996 | 13 | £7–10 |
| Neil Joubert Cabernet Sauvignon 1998 | 13 | £5–7 |
| Neil Joubert Pinotage 1998 | 16 | £5–7 |
| Paradyskloof Cabernet Sauvignon/Merlot 1997 | 13.5 | £5–7 |
| Simonsig Pinotage 1998 | 16 | £5–7 |

## SOUTH AFRICAN WHITE

| | | |
|---|---|---|
| Jordan Chardonnay 1998 | 16.5 | £7–10 |

## SPANISH RED

| | | |
|---|---|---|
| Montalvo Reserva Rioja 1994 | 14.5 | £7–10 |
| Ondarre Reserva Rioja 1994 | 13 | £7–10 |
| Ondarre 'Rivallana' Crianza Rioja 1996 | 13 | £5–7 |
| Valdetore Calatayud Grenache 1998 | 15 | −£5.00 |
| Vinas del Vero Merlot 1997 | 15.5 | £5–7 |

## SWISS RED

| | | |
|---|---|---|
| Pinot Noir Trilogy 1996 | 12 | £5–7 |

## USA RED

| | | |
|---|---|---|
| Clos du Val Le Clos NV | 14 | £7–10 |
| Fetzer Pinot Noir, Santa Barbara 1996 | 13 | £5–7 |
| Fetzer Valley Oaks Cabernet Sauvignon 1996 | 16.5 | £5–7 |
| Gallo Sonoma Barrelli Creek Cabernet Sauvignon 1994 | 15.5 | £10–13 |
| Gallo Sonoma County Pinot Noir 1995 | 13.5 | £7–10 |
| Gallo Sonoma Frei Ranch Cabernet Sauvignon 1994 | 14 | £10–13 |
| Mondavi Coastal Merlot 1997 | 16 | £7–10 |

WINE CELLAR

## USA WHITE

Gallo Sonoma County      10    £7–10
Chardonnay 1995

Quady Essensia Orange    16    £5–7
Muscat, California 1996
(half-bottle)

Quady Starboard Batch    15    –£5.00
88, California (half-bottle)

## SPARKLING WINES

Jansz Tasmanian NV       12    £7–10

Pelorus NV (New          17    £10–13
Zealand)

# PART 4

# TOP TENS

# THE TOP TEN PRE-COITAL MASTERPIECES

(I.E. APERITIFS, PRE-PRANDIAL TIPPLES, LIBATIONS FOR THE LIBIDO)

SPARKLING WINE **Charles Heidsieck Champagne Blanc de** `20` `£89.99`
**Blancs 1982, Waitrose**
Perfect Champagne. As good as it is possible for Chardonnay to get with
bubbles. It is perfectly mature, rich and complex but finally dry and
delicate. It is so elegant it defines what Champagne is. Only from
Waitrose Direct.

SPARKLING WINE **Pelorus Brut 1995, Unwins** `18` `£12.49`
Better than Krug. It's got beautifully smoky fruit, richness with elegance,
bite with delicacy.

SPARKLING WINE **Pelorus Brut NV (New Zealand), Sainsbury's** `17` `£12.99`
One of the most richly elegant bottles on the planet in this blend (almost
all Chardonnay). It has to be compared with absurdities like Krug to get
some idea of the value here.

CHILEAN RED **Chilean Merlot 1999, Somerfield** `17` `£4.49`
It ignites in the mouth like a leather and spicy cherry/blackcurrant
grenade. Hugely impressive depth and richness here.

FORTIFIED WINES **Lustau Old East India Sherry, Booths,** `17` `£9.99–`
**Unwins** `10.99`
Magnificent name, recalling the excesses of empire, just as the intense
sweet fruit (molasses and butterscotch with crème brûlée overtones) is
redolent of excess around Victorian dinner tables. A taste of history. Quite
marvellous stuff.

FORTIFIED WINES **Manzanilla, Asda** `17` `£4.97`
A staggeringly well-endowed, aromatic, yet subtle sherry of immense
charm and richness. Unusually well textured and soft (uniquely so, I
suggest) and so warm and approachable it must convert those who
previously found the tealeaf and hard edge of this style of wine too
austere.

AUSTRALIAN WHITE Oxford Landing Limited Release Viognier `17` `£5.99`
1999, Majestic
One of the greatest Viogniers in the world in this vintage. The lingering
apricots and gentle spice are remarkable.

NEW ZEALAND WHITE Montana Reserve Chardonnay 1999, `17` `£7.99`
Thresher
Intensely classy and enormously creamy and rich without being too ripe
and obvious. A provocative blend of smoky melon and fine acids. Has
elegance, elongation and ease of effort.

NEW ZEALAND WHITE Te Mata Estate Chardonnay 1999, `17` `£8.49`
Thresher
A lot of money but a lot of wine. It has old-fashioned vegetality of the
Montrachet kind and limpid acids of the Kiwi kind. The marriage is
superb: angular, classy, finely wrought and outstandingly, compactly
balanced. Wine Rack and Bottoms Up only.

SOUTH AFRICAN WHITE Jordan Chardonnay 1998, Booths, `16.5` `£9.99`
Unwins, Waitrose
Melon and lime yoghurt with a hint of walnut. An individual approach to
the Chardonnay riddle and an original solution. Deliciously so.

# THE TOP TEN REFLECTIVE PURSUIT BOTTLES

## (I.E. WINES AS STIMULATING COMPANIONS FOR THE MIND)

ITALIAN RED Aglianico del Vulture 1997, Majestic `18` `£9.99`
A real mineral-tinged treat. The elegance, the concentrated ripeness, the
typical Vulture richness. A beautiful, confident, stunning mouthful.

FRENCH WHITE Bott-Geyl Gewürztraminer Grand Cru `17.5` `£15.99`
Sonnenglanz 1998, Majestic
About as good as young Gewürz gets: pears, peaches, rose petals,
raspberries and honey and intriguing acids. Left for seven to eight years
it'll rate twenty.

CHILEAN RED Valdivieso Cabernet Franc Reserve 1997, `17.5` `£9.99`
Unwins, Tesco, Safeway
Wonderfully expressive of herbs, spice, vegetal fruit and ripe tannins.

CHILEAN RED 35 Sur Cabernet Sauvignon 1999, Asda,    17   £4.49
Sainsbury's
Utter magic. Dark, rich, firm yet supple, wonderfully seriously fruity
(leather, spice, blackcurrants) and hugely lingering. Brilliant for the
money, quite brilliant.

AUSTRALIAN RED Church Block Cabernet Shiraz/Merlot,    17   £8.99
Wirra Wirra Vineyards 1998, Oddbins
Wonderful brisk tannins coat the chocolate and Cassis fruit. Marvellous
stuff. Benchmark blend.

AUSTRALIAN RED Clancy's Shiraz/Cabernet Sauvignon/    17   £7.99
Merlot/Cabernet Franc 1998, Unwins, Safeway
Perfection at its peak – almost. Will it rate higher if cellared and left to
mature? How can it? It has wonderfully integrated generous tannins and
plum/cherry/blackberry fruit.

USA WHITE Coastal Chardonnay, Robert Mondavi 1997,    17   £9.99
Sainsbury's, Unwins
Beautiful biscuity texture, subtle vegetal fruit and very elegant on the
finish. 60 stores.

SPANISH RED Costers del Gravet Celler de Capcanes 1998,    17   £8.99
Majestic
Huge yet delicate, expansive yet lithe, effortless yet eager to delight.
A very concentrated, compelling amalgam of multi-layered fruit, fine
tannins and superb acids, which all work dynamically to produce a
rousing, tenacious finish.

SOUTH AFRICAN RED Fairview Pinotage 1999, Sainsbury's    17   £5.99
One of South Africa's, perhaps the world's, most joyously juicy yet
seriously delicious and multi-layered wines. It has wonderful graduated
texture, a middle wallop of berries and a striking, witty finish.

SOUTH AFRICAN RED Spice Route Flagship Merlot 1998,    17   £11.99
Sainsbury's, Waitrose
A big, rich special-occasion Merlot of massive depth, lingering tannins and
huge food compatibility.

# THE TOP TEN *VINS POUR LES GRANDES BOUFFES*

(I.E. IMPRESSIVE BOTTLES FOR FESTIVE MEALS AND IMPORTANT DINNERS)

ITALIAN RED Amarone Valpolicella Tedeschi 1996, Majestic　18　£12.99
One of the more perfect specimens of this extravagant breed. Lively,
serious, hugely amusing, concentrated and unites the joyous elements of
wine (sugar, acid, tannin) into something original and very fine.
Liquorice, prunes and hedgerows: they're all there.

CHILEAN RED Errázuriz Cabernet Sauvignon, El Ceibo Estate,　17.5　£5.99
Aconcagua 1998, Safeway
Wonderful baked, brown fruit here, full of fleshiness contained by a
delicious shellac of prime tannins. Immense drinkability combined with
sublime, provocative richness. A stunning wine.

FORTIFIED WINE González Byass Matusalem NV (half-bottle),　17.5　£10.23
Sainsbury's
Wonderful! One of the world's great dessert wines. The texture and the
colour of engine oil, it has a butterscotch and crème brûlée sweetness and
a complex smoky honeyed edge. Selected stores.

ITALIAN RED Amarone della Valpolicella Zenato 1995,　17　£17.99
Thresher
Liquorice, figs, ripe cherries and damsons, and marvellous tannins. Even
so, I'd cellar it for five or six years and see it reach, perhaps, perfection at
twenty points. Wine Rack and Bottoms Up only.

SOUTH AFRICAN RED Bellingham Pinotage 1999, Somerfield　17　£5.49
Stunning tannins! Even Lafite doesn't get tannins this exciting, this tasty,
this deep. Limited distribution.

FRENCH WHITE Château Vignal Labrie, Monbazillac 1997,　17　£8.99
Waitrose
Most individual and exotic specimen. Has a gorgeous waxy texture and
very ripe, complex undertones. Real whack of sweet fruit on the finish.

FRENCH RED Châteauneuf-du-Pape Château de la Grande　17　£12.49
Gardiole 1998, Sainsbury's
Expensive but mountainous. Intense richness and herby hauteur. Selected
stores.

FRENCH RED **Chaume Arnaud Domaine Côtes du** 17 £7.49
**Rhône-Villages 1998 (organic), Booths**
It develops on the palate with insidious deliciousness providing herbs, savoury tannins, a hint of rustic orchards, and a deal of characterful texture. Marvellous stuff.

CHILEAN RED **Cono Sur Cabernet Sauvignon Reserve 1998,** 17 £6.49
**Somerfield**
Nothing reserved about the fruit. It pulsates with generosity and tongue-lashing tannic tenacity.

ARGENTINIAN RED **Famiglia Bianchi Cabernet Sauvignon, San** 17 £15.99
**Rafael 1996, Oddbins**
Has such superb multi-layered, faintly lush Cassis and cheroot-tinged fruit that it surprises the palate by its developing richness on the tongue. A very classy red.

# THE TOP TEN SUPER-MODEL WINES

## (I.E. EXCEPTIONALLY ELEGANT WHITE WINES)

CHILEAN WHITE **Casa Lapostolle Cuvee Alexandre Chardonnay** 18.5 £9.99
**1997, Oddbins**
Utterly magical oily texture, huge depth of woodily creamy fruit and a magnificent finish. It is a great wine at any price and hugely drinkable and food-friendly. It has everything great Meursault has and doubles it. Classicists (aka snobs) will say it's OTT and the malolactic influence and the wood are too oppressive. But I think the fruit triumphs.

FRENCH WHITE **Pinot Gris Grand Cru Rangen de Thann Clos** 18.5 £35.00
**St-Urbain, Domaine Zind Humbrecht 1996, Waitrose**
Stunning elegant spiciness and richness here. Extraordinary depths of deliciousness. Only from Waitrose Direct.

FRENCH WHITE **Hermitage Le Chevalier de Sterimberg 1997,** 17.5 £20+
**Waitrose**
The acme of French arrogance. Has little fruit but mighty dry yet oily-textured richness. Only from Waitrose Direct.

CHILEAN WHITE **Montes Alpha Chardonnay 1998, Morrisons** `17.5` `£8.99`
Chile's Montrachet – if that isn't to insult it. It has a creamy vegetality, beautiful smooth texture, subtle complex charms on the tongue, and a lingering smokiness as it descends – and hits the soul.

SOUTH AFRICAN WHITE **Vergelegen Reserve Sauvignon Blanc** `17.5` `£9.99`
**1999, Sainsbury's**
Outpoints Sancerre at the same price by ten to one. It's subtly grassy, very concentrated (melon and soft, spiced gooseberry) and the finish is sublime. 30 stores.

SOUTH AFRICAN WHITE **Warwick Estate Chardonnay,** `17.5` `£6.99`
**Stellenbosch 1999, Waitrose**
The best-value Chardonnay in the world. Lovely creamy woodiness, alert acids underpinning good melon/vegetal fruit and it'll get more like Montrachet as it ages over the next five years.

SOUTH AFRICAN WHITE **Call of the African Eagle Chardonnay** `17` `£6.99`
**1999, Sainsbury's**
Beautifully natural and pure-seeming – as elegant as a nun's wimple. The fruit is quite remarkably refined and rich, complex, seamlessly stitched and elegant. 120 stores.

CHILEAN WHITE **Casa Lapostolle Chardonnay 1998, Oddbins,** `17` `£6.99`
**Unwins**
Breathtakingly elegant, subtle, complex, rich and so quaffable it has undertones of ambrosia and choirs of angels.

CHILEAN WHITE **Concha y Toro Casillero del Diablo** `17` `£4.99`
**Chardonnay 1997, Thresher, Victoria Wine**
Beautifully ornate fruit, oily and rippling with multi-flavoured riches, and the acidity gives the whole structure backbone and precision.

NEW ZEALAND WHITE **Church Road Reserve Chardonnay 1998,** `17` `£11.99`
**Thresher**
Such extreme elegance and controlled fruitiness make the taste buds weep with pleasure. Marvellous texture and big finish. Wine Rack and Bottoms Up only.

# THE TOP TEN TIPPLES TO ENJOY BEFORE FACING A FIRING SQUAD

## (I.E. GORGEOUS REDS TO STIFFEN THE SINEWS AND SUMMON UP THE BLOOD)

SPANISH RED **Alvaro Palacios Finca Dofi Priorat 1996,** | 18 | £59.99
**Thresher**
£60! Sixty quid! Yes, but it may well be one of the most nigh-perfect red wines in Spain. It is hugely elegant and forceful. The tannins are like gold dust and the finish is sublime. A truly exciting world-class wine, the unique product of an obsessed individual. Wine Rack and Bottoms Up only.

ITALIAN RED **Amarone della Valpolicella Via Nova 1997,** | 18 | £9.99
**Thresher, Victoria Wine**
Superb modern Amarone with classic overtones of liquorice, fig, raspberry, blackcurrant, herbs, jam, tannins and rich acids. The texture is thick and balsamic and lingering. Yet, withal, this is not, in spite of 14.5% of alcohol, a bruising experience. It is very elegant and polished.

FRENCH RED **Domaine de l'Arneillaud Cairanne Côtes du** | 18 | £5.99
**Rhône-Villages 1999, Unwins**
Magnificent herby potency and extremely deep elegance here. Has world-class tannins and intense richness.

CHILEAN RED **Casa Lapostolle Cuvee Alexandre Merlot, Rapel** | 17.5 | £13.99
**1998, Oddbins**
An immense construct which as the thoughtful taster gargles with it around the molars is like some game sauce of quite unusual savoury, ripe, then sweet, then dry complexity. A truly marvellous wine.

CHILEAN RED **Errázuriz Cabernet Sauvignon 1998, Unwins,** | 17.5 | £5.99
**Thresher, Victoria Wine**
Stunning lushness yet extruded elegance – superb texture and heart-stoppingly delicious blackcurrant richness.

FRENCH RED **Château Trignon Côtes du Rhône-Villages Sablet** | 17.5 | £6.99
**Ramillades 1998, Unwins**
Absolutely compelling richness and beautifully earthy tannins. The quintessence of elegant rusticity. Marvellous stuff! From nose to throat it's terrific, taut, tenacious.

**FRENCH RED** Château Flauguergues Coteaux du Languedoc `17.5` `£6.99`
**1998**
Very elegant. The tannins and the fruit are deliciously melded and
softened one into the other and the finish is excellent. A very serious yet
fun-to-drink wine.

**USA RED** Bonterra Cabernet Sauvignon 1997 (organic), Asda, `17` `£8.99`
**Sainsbury's**
Superbly California style: warm, rich, pulsating, brilliant tannins, great
ripe yet serious dry–sweet fruit. Absolutely marvellous stuff.

**FRENCH RED** Château de Valcombe, Costières de Nîmes 1998, `17` `£5.49`
**Oddbins**
Cheroots, hedgerows, garrigues, leather, smoke, tannins, hint of old wood
– enough for you?

**FRENCH RED** Château Grand Escalion, Costières de Nîmes `17` `£5.99`
**1998, Oddbins**
A lot like Château de Valcombe except it's more difficult to get your
tongue round the name.

# PART 5

# STOP PRESS

## ASDA

**Temple Bruer Shiraz/** `16.5` `£5–7`
**Malbec 1998, Australian, Red**
A wonderfully adult blend of rich
jammy Shiraz and dry, tannic Malbec.
The marriage is harmonious and
energetic, food-friendly and deliciously
deep.

**Kumala Cabernet** `16` `−£5.00`
**Sauvignon Shiraz 2000, South
African, Red**
Huge juice and tannins. Lovely meaty
edge.

**Kumala Chenin** `15` `−£5.00`
**Chardonnay 2000, South African,
White**
Biting, clean, nicely fruity.

## CO-OP

**Valentin Bianchi** `16` `£5–7`
**Cabernet Sauvignon 1997,
Argentinian, Red**
Very big and rich and soft and gently
spicy with big tannins.

**Valdivieso Cabernet** `17` `£7–10`
**Franc Reserve 1998, Chilean, Red**
Deep savoury riches tantalise the
tongue and tighten the throat as the
tannins ooze down.

## MAJESTIC

**Valdivieso Cabernet** `17` `£7–10`
**Franc Reserve 1998, Chilean, Red**
Deep savoury riches tantalise the
tongue and tighten the throat as the
tannins ooze down.

**Yellowglen Pinot Noir** `16` `£7–10`
**Chardonnay NV (Australia), Sparkling
Wine/Champagne**
A great bargain! Superb class and
subtly rich fruit. This blend is a terrific
improvement on the last (cf the main
Majestic section of this book).

## MORRISONS

**Penfolds Koonunga Hill** `16` `£5–7`
**Chardonnay 1999, Australian, White**
One of its best vintages for years.
Beautifully couth fruit of texture, style
and controlled lushness. Deliciously
succulent.

**Kumala Sauvignon** `15` `−£5.00`
**Blanc/Colombard 2000, South
African, White**
Terrific rich freshness.

## ODDBINS

**Fabre Montmayor** `16.5` `£5–7`
**Cabernet Sauvignon, Lujan de Cuyo
1997, Argentinian, Red**
Vibrant, richly textured fruit, a very
vague hint of Cabernet pepperiness
(just a nod to varietal expression in
this respect) and lashings of chocolate
fruit. Dazzling turn of wit on the
tongue.

**Fabre Montmayor** `17` `£5–7`
**Merlot, Lujan de Cuyo 1997,
Argentinian, Red**
Superb, almost complete in its
harmony of fruit, acids and tannins.
Immediately charming (nay,
seductive).

**Bleasdale 'Bremer View** `16` `£5–7`
**Vineyard' Shiraz 1998, Australian,
Red**
Customary open-hearted Aussie
welcome. Here's savoury tannin too, a
hint of coriander to spice it up, and an
engaging, molar-hugging texture.

Wirra Wirra RSW Shiraz  18  £13–20
1998, Australian, Red
Elegant, huge, potent yet polite.
World class.

Bleasdale 'Bremer View  16.5  £5–7
Vineyard' Verdelho 1999, Australian,
White
Wonderfully subtle riches here - spicy
yet not overt, soft yet not a pushover.

Nepenthe Vineyards  16.5  £7–10
Lenswood Semillon 1998, Australian,
White
Superb texture and purity of tone here.
The Semillon is gloriously vindicated
as a complex, lingering, stand-alone
grape. Very stylish finish of gently
creamy melon, raspberry and lychee.

Preece Chardonnay 1999,  16  £5–7
Australian, White
Very deep and flavoursome and
hugely food-friendly. Quaffable? If you
can take so much excitement
crammed into a glass: melons, nuts,
pears and yoghurt.

Wirra Wirra Sauvignon  16  £7–10
Blanc 2000, Australian, White
Very grassy and concentrated
gooseberry.

Cono Sur Pinot Noir  16  £5–7
Reserve 1999, Chilean, Red
Chewy, ripe, thick, aromatic, tannic,
lingering. Volnay was never like this!

Cono Sur Reserva Merlot  16.5  £5–7
1999, Chilean, Red
Incredibly thickly knitted and chewy.
Great tannins!

Errazuriz Merlot Reserva,  16.5  £7–10
Don Maximiano Estate Aconcagua,
1998, Chilean, Red
Like drinking a soft velvet glove
suffused with essence of cassis.

Isla Negra Cabernet  16.5  £5–7
Sauvignon, Rapel 1999, Chilean, Red
Gorgeous savoury juice with rich
tannins.

Isla Negra Chardonnay  16  £5–7
1999, Chilean, White
Superb texture and ripe, plump fruit.

Château de l'Engarran  17.5  £7–10
Quetton Saint-Georges, Coteaux de
Languedoc 1998, French, Red
Rather exquisitely refined at first smell
and sip and then a hint of a rugged,
misspent youth appears to garnish the
soft plummy fruit with bite, tannin
and longevity of performance.

Corbieres Alain Grignon  15.5  ~£5.00
1999, French, Red
Beautiful sweet hedgerow fruit, a
touch of earth (tannins in this instance)
and a good firm finish.

Domaine de Montpezat  16  £5–7
Les Enclos, VdP d'Oc 1998, French,
Red
Raisiny aroma, and oddly oaky, and
the thick jammy fruit is then sweet but
slightly nutty and full and rich.
Marvellous veggie stew wine.

Minervois Alain Grignon  16  ~£5.00
1999, French, Red
Tremendous vibrancy, almost
cassis-like, here. Has subtle spice and
supple tannins. A bargain.

Saint Chinian Alain  15.5  ~£5.00
Grignon 1999, French, Red
A soft, hugely quaffable wine of
character and style.

Albert Mann Vieilles  16.5  £10–13
Vignes Tokay Pinot Gris 1999,
French, White
Lot of money best spent by someone
with the patience to wait four or five

years for this aromatic, apricot-rich wine to develop some fascinating 20-point charms. However, it's already nutty and complex enough for most palates, perhaps.

**Mirambelo Ileza Creta** `16` `−£5.00`
**Olympias 1998, Greek, Red**
Wow! I swallow my words, chewing on them with pleasure. Crete can turn out terrific red wine - deep, dry, fruity, warmly tannic.

**Xerolithia 1999, Greek,** `15.5` `−£5.00`
**White**
Makes a marvellously rich change from Chardonnay. Great with food (chicken, grilled tuna). Has real style and substance.

**Mezzomondo** `16` `−£5.00`
**Negroamaro 1999, Italian, Red**
Brilliant value food wine with rich, herby fruit and delicious spicy tannins. Has a first-class texture and concentration of flavours.

**Kumala Merlot Reserve** `16.5` `£7–10`
**1999, South African, Red**
Superb!

**Kumala Reserve** `16.5` `£7–10`
**Cabernet Sauvignon 1999, South African, Red**
Compellingly concentrated and classy and generous.

**Vinum Cabernet** `16` `£5–7`
**Sauvignon, Stellenbosch 1999, South African, Red**
Superbly racy and softly spiced. Terrific texture, deep and all-enveloping, and a lingering, plummy richness of great charm. Developing beautifully in bottle since the summer (cf the main Oddbins section of this book).

**Yonder Hill Merlot,** `16` `£7–10`
**Stellenbosch 1998, South African, Red**
What an energetic, richly vivid Merlot! It has damsons, spice, tannins, savoury finishing fruit (blackberries) and a lovely texture.

**Longridge Chardonnay,** `16.5` `£7–10`
**Stellenbosch 1999, South African, White**
Superb texture and creamy-rich fruit - never over-baked. A lovely, vibrant white wine.

**Merryvale Cabernet** `17` `£13–20`
**Sauvignon 1997, USA, Red**
An alcoholic (14.5%) subterfuge. Cab Sauv? Nope. There's Merlot, Cab Franc and Petit Verdot too. No wonder the French prefer to keep grape names off labels (Alsace excepted). All that said, though, this lying blend lies gorgeously on the taste buds with a polish recalling Lafite in a soft year.

## SAFEWAY

**Cono Sur Pinot Noir** `16` `£5–7`
**Reserve 1999, Chilean, Red**
Chewy, ripe, thick, aromatic, tannic, lingering. Volnay was never like this!

**Errazuriz Merlot Reserva,** `16.5` `£7–10`
**Don Maximiano Estate Aconcagua, 1998, Chilean, Red**
Like drinking a soft velvet glove suffused with essence of cassis. Top 129 stores.

**Valdivieso Cabernet** `17` `£7–10`
**Franc Reserve 1998, Chilean, Red**
Deep savoury riches tantalise the tongue and tighten the throat as the tannins ooze down.

## SAINSBURY'S

**Santa Julia Viognier 2000,** `16.5` `−£5.00`
**Argentinian, White**
Beautiful dry apricot fruit with a touch
of crème brûlée on the finish or is it
gunsmoke? Well, it's a delicate beauty
for all that, but a hugely elegant
aperitif. Most stores.

**Petaluma Bridgewater** `16.5` `£7–10`
**Mill Shiraz 1998, Australian, Red**
Very chewy, coal-edged texture, deep
and rich and softly spicy. Lovely rich
plums, blackcurrants and a touch of
leather. Delicious tannins, too, so it
has backbone and bite. Not at all
stores.

**Concha y Toro Casillero** `16.5` `−£5.00`
**del Diablo Cabernet Sauvignon 1999,**
**Chilean, Red**
Develops on the taste buds from ripe
cherries to smoky blackcurrants, a hint
of spice, a suggestion of gravy. A
lovely, textured Cabernet of great
class.

**Errazuriz Merlot 1999,** `16.5` `£5–7`
**Chilean, Red**
One of the world's most immediately
delicious and deeply drinkable Merlots.
Beautiful texture, and leather-soft,
blackberry and cherry-ripe fruit.

**Chateauneuf-du-Pape,** `17` `£10–13`
**Domaine Michel Bernard 1998,**
**French, Red**
An expensive treat for that festive
fowl. A wine of aroma, depth,
complexity and power. Selected stores.

**Louis Bernard Côtes du** `16.5` `−£5.00`
**Rhône Villages 1999, French, Red**
Superb rustic charmer with
sophisticated manners and tannic style.
Lovely herbs, earth and deep plum
fruit which is gloriously unpretentious.

**Wild Pig Shiraz, VdP** `16` `−£5.00`
**d'Oc 1999, French, Red**
Lovely dry herbiness with plummy
fruit with a very slight cassis edge to it.
Has a rugged feel, yet it isn't too deep
or rich so much as rustically elegant
and gently spicy. Most stores.

**Classic Selection Chablis** `16` `£7–10`
**Domaine Sainte Cecil 1999,**
**Sainsbury's, French, White**
Well, well! Indeed it's classic: dry and
minerally, and with that sedate
crispness which good Chablis has.
Most stores.

**Kumala Cabernet** `16` `−£5.00`
**Sauvignon Shiraz 2000, South**
**African, Red**
Huge juice and tannins. Lovely meaty
edge.

**Bellingham Sauvignon** `16.5` `£5–7`
**Blanc 2000, South African, White**
A high class, high-wire act where fine
acids tiptoe along a fine wire of
gooseberry-rich fruit. Delicately poised
yet potent, this is a lovely wine.

**Danie de Wet Call of the** `17` `£5–7`
**African Eagle Chardonnay Reserve**
**2000, South African, White**
Very delicate, subtle, stealthy artefact
which is consummately delicious as a
sum of its component parts rather than
one dominant element. Thus it is dry
yet vaguely melony and nutty (with a
hint of peach and cream), fresh yet
textured and gently rich, and it finishes
with aplomb (yet not with a wallop -
more of a small sigh). A very assured,
understated wine of great class. 120
stores.

**Kumala Chardonnay** `15.5` `−£5.00`
**2000, South African, White**
Big, rich, smoky, musky, fruit. Brilliant

for oriental food. Also available in a three-litre box at the equivalent of £3.49 a bottle.

**Agramont Tempranillo/** `16.5` `£5–7`
**Cabernet Sauvignon, Navarra Crianza 1996, Spanish, Red**
Gorgeous texture of lingering depth and complexity. Has softness yet dryness with its firm tannins buttressing the blackcurrants and plums and cherries. The finish is terrific. A posh dinner party wine. Better than many more expensive Bordeaux.

**Ochoa Gran Reserva,** `16` `£10–13`
**Navarra 1993, Spanish, Red**
A distinguished grandee of a rich treat: tobacco-edged, rich, very dry and subtly figgy (and a touch raisiny), this is an unusually mature wine to find in a supermarket. It's at its peak of drinkability. 80 stores.

## SOMERFIELD

**Argentine Sangiovese** `16.5` `–£5.00`
**2000, Somerfield, Argentinian, Red**
Superb! If only Chianti could be this thrilling for the money.

**Bright Brothers Barrica** `16` `£5–7`
**Shiraz 1999, Argentinian, Red**
Comes across like an Aussie with attitude - thanks to the tannins. Terrific red wine. Classy, bold, full of character and beguiling fruit.

**Normans Old Vines** `16.5` `–£5.00`
**Grenache 1998, Australian, Red**
Possibly the tastiest under-a-fiver Aussie red around. Has great depth and soft pliability but piles of character from the tannins. Old vines live on! Selected stores.

**Domaine Boyar Bulgarian** `16` `–£5.00`
**Premium Cuvee Cabernet Sauvignon 1999, Bulgarian, Red**
Has a lovely chewy edge of lightly smoked fruit, excellent tannins and a rich, rousing finish.

**Bulgarian Chardonnay** `16` `–£3.50`
**1999, Somerfield, Bulgarian, White**
One of the best Chardonnays I've tasted from this country. There are, I assure you, far less appealing and aromatically adventurous burgundies on sale at ten times the price.

**Chilean Sauvignon Blanc,** `16` `–£5.00`
**Canepa 2000, Somerfield, Chilean, White**
Gorgeous melon and nuts here. Touches of class, suggestions of complexity, hints of real style.

**Isla Negra Chardonnay** `16` `£5–7`
**1999, Chilean, White**
Even more energy and richness to the new vintage. Selected stores.

**Beaumes de Venise,** `16` `£5–7`
**Côtes du Rhône Villages 1998, French, Red**
Stunning blend of Grenache, Syrah, Mourvedre and Cinsault which opens demurely, then goes big and rich, then calms itself, then goes warm and deep. Lovely experience.

**Domaine de Courtilles** `16` `£5–7`
**Côte 125 Corbieres 1998, French, Red**
Most unusually stealthy fruit which moves like lava across the taste buds revealing deliciously soft and warm nuances of flavour. Improving nicely in bottle (cf the entry in the main Somerfield section of this book).

La Solitude `17` `£7–10`
Chateauneuf-du-Pape 1998, French, Red
The sheer velvet class of this fruit - characterful and biting in spite of its polish - is a joy. It has immense and lasting charm.

Vacqueyras Domaine de `16.5` `–£5.00`
la Soleiade 1999, French, Red
The essence of what French country red is all about: characterful, soft, gently tannic, beautifully herby, finely textured. Superb stuff and a great bargain.

L A Cetto Petite Syrah `17` `–£5.00`
1997, Mexican, Red
Quite superb. Like an eccentric combination of Barbaresco, Barossa Shiraz and Priorat. In other words, great tannic texture and uppityness. This is a revolutionary red under a fiver.

Kumala Reserve `16.5` `£7–10`
Cabernet Sauvignon 1999, South African, Red
Compellingly concentrated and classy and generous.

South African Cabernet `16.5` `–£5.00`
Sauvignon 2000, Somerfield, South African, Red
Superb woody, dry fruit, with feisty tannins adding loads of character. A bitingly bonny mouthful of liquefied hedgerows.

Spice Route Pinotage `16.5` `£7–10`
1999, South African, Red
Gorgeous tobacco-scented richness which has compelling texture pulling the taste buds in myriad directions. Wonderful life-affirming quaffing. Selected stores.

Spice Route Shiraz 1999, `16.5` `£5–7`
South African, Red
A truly delicious construct with a beefy texture, a meaty aroma, and a savoury finish. Not a wine, then, to argue with - even if you're a vegetarian. Selected stores.

Bellingham Sauvignon `16.5` `£5–7`
Blanc 2000, South African, White
A high class, high-wire act where fine acids tiptoe along a fine wire of gooseberry-rich fruit. Delicately poised yet potent, this is a lovely wine.

Kumala Sauvignon `15` `–£5.00`
Blanc/Colombard 2000, South African, White
Terrific rich freshness. Limited distribution.

Espiral Tempranillo `16` `£5–7`
Barrique 1999, Spanish, Red
Exciting stuff. Has loads of spicy plums with great tannins. Very urgent fruit, keen to please. Selected stores.

## TESCO

Smithbrook Cabernet `16` `£7–10`
Sauvignon/Cabernet Franc/Petit Verdot 1998, Australian, Red
Claret given soul, heart and lots of soft, fleshy fruit with hard, tannic muscles. Claret made on Mars. Selected stores.

Caliterra Reserve Syrah `16.5` `£7–10`
1999, Chilean, Red
Gorgeous! Quite gorgeous spice, hedgerow fruits, plums, and savoury tannins. A richly serious wine of consummate, well-textured class and style. Selected stores.

STOP PRESS

**Caliterra Syrah 1999,** `16` `£5-7`
**Chilean, Red**
A very leathery, savoury, pliant Syrah
which oozes charm without oozing
OTT fruit. (Yet it is unashamedly
modern.)

**Cono Sur Pinot Noir** `16` `£5-7`
**Reserve 1999, Chilean, Red**
Chewy, ripe, thick, aromatic, tannic,
lingering. Volnay was never like this!

**Errazuriz Don** `16` `£13-20`
**Maximiano 1998, Chilean, Red**
Very deep and delicious, superb
tannins giving the wine personality
and backbone. The overall impression
is of power and concentration. Worth
eighteen quid? When so much
wonderful stuff from Chile costs
around a fiver? Well, it rates 16. The
tannins give it such class.

**Isla Negra Cabernet** `16.5` `£5-7`
**Sauvignon, Rapel 1999, Chilean, Red**
Gorgeous savoury juice with rich
tannins.

**Valdivieso Cabernet** `17` `£7-10`
**Franc Reserve 1998, Chilean, Red**
Deep savoury riches tantalise the
tongue and tighten the throat as the
tannins ooze down.

**Valdivieso Cabernet** `17` `£5-7`
**Sauvignon Reserve 1998, Chilean,**
**Red**
Coffee, cocoa, herbs, roast meat,
tannins - what a liberal assembly of
great riches here. Most stores.

**Montes Alpha** `17.5` `£7-10`
**Chardonnay 1998, Chilean, White**
A tenner very well spent. For this is a
marvellously couth, Burgundy-style
Chardonnay with added creamy
textured richness of great sexiness.
Selected stores.

**Château Haut-Bourcier** `16` `-£5.00`
**Premieres Côtes de Blaye 1999,**
**French, Red**
Stunning bargain here. A truly
concentrated, superbly tannic claret of
depth and daring. Great class here.
Selected stores.

**Domaine Richeaume** `16.5` `£13-20`
**Organic Syrah Côtes de Provence**
**1999, French, Red**
Impressively dry and deep, herby and
splendidly rustic, but, and it's a
delicious but, it has masses of class and
concentrated charm. Wine Advisor
Stores.

**French Revolution Le** `16` `-£5.00`
**Rouge 1999, French, Red**
Hugely different from its white cousin,
in that there is real character and
effortless fruit here. Great depth,
marvellous tannins, firm, rich texture.
Selected stores.

**Jaboulet Côtes du Rhône** `16.5` `£5-7`
**Villages 1998, French, Red**
Beautiful, evolved tannins and fruit. It
develops wonderfully on the tongue,
showing complex fruits and herby
earth all knitted together perfectly.
Selected stores.

**Jaboulet Gigondas 'Pierre** `16` `£10-13`
**Aiguille' 1998, French, Red**
A terrific well-moulded Gigondas of
superb texture and unusual ripeness.
Complex, compelling, very collected.
Selected stores.

**MV Cabernet Sauvignon** `16` `£7-10`
**VdP d'Oc 1998, French, Red**
Superb double whammy of richness
and rousing depth of fruit. Has tannins
and fruit in brilliant form.

490

**Chablis Premier Cru** `16` `£10–13`
**1998, Tesco, French, White**
An exceptionally rich and complex
Chablis of considerable concentration
and class. One of Tesco's so-called
'Finest' range.

**Guigal Condrieu 1999,** `16` `£13–20`
**French, White**
Open for five to six hours at least, to
appreciate the vegetal, apricot fruit -
very dry but very individual. Selected
stores.

**Camelot 1999 (Sicily),** `16` `£7–10`
**Italian, Red**
Stunning earthy fruit of hedgerow
complexity and great concentration.
Great orchestral tannins. Selected
stores.

**Tre Uve Ultima 1998,** `16` `£5–7`
**Italian, Red**
Superb depth of tannic richness geared
to smoothly run alongside smooth
plum/blackberry fruit. Selected stores.

**'I Portali' Basilicata** `16` `–£5.00`
**Greco 1999, Italian, White**
A splendidly vigorous Chardonnay of
dry, mineral freshness and rich
crispness. Individual approach to this
trendy grape. Selected stores.

**Kumala Reserve** `16.5` `£7–10`
**Cabernet Sauvignon 1999, South**
**African, Red**
Compellingly concentrated and classy
and generous.

**Apostles Falls** `16.5` `£5–7`
**Chardonnay 1999, South African,**
**White**
Intensely perfumed and flavoured.
Exhibits a range of stone fruit overcut
by a soft textured richness. Very high
class stuff.

**Kumala Colombard/** `15` `–£5.00`
**Chardonnay 2000, South African,**
**White**
Very bright and lemonic. Terrific fish
wine.

**Kumala Semillon** `15.5` `–£5.00`
**Chardonnay 2000, South African,**
**White**
Delicious, rich, gooseberry fruit. Ripe
yet balanced.

**South African** `15` `–£5.00`
**Chardonnay 2000, Tesco, South**
**African, White**
A rich, ripe food wine. Has a hint of
spicy smoke to the melony fruit.

**Thandi Elgin** `16` `£5–7`
**Chardonnay 1999, South African,**
**White**
Marvellous dash and richness here:
creamy, gently spicy, textured, very
deep. Wonderful food and
conversation wine. Selected stores.

**Thelema Mountain** `17` `£10–13`
**Vineyard Sauvignon Blanc 1999,**
**South African, White**
Perfect herbaceous undertone to
beautifully multi-layered fruit of
massive charm.

**Spanish Monastrell 1999,** `15` `–£5.00`
**Tesco, Spanish, Red**
Soft, immensely so, good, warm
tannins and a touch of spicy from the
plummy fruit.

**Tempranillo 1999, Tesco,** `15` `–£5.00`
**Spanish, Red**
A tastier performer than scores of
Riojas. Has character and class.

**Con Class Selection** `15` `–£5.00`
**Especial 1999, Spanish, White**
A superbly rich, dry food white wine
of great versatility. Suits anything from

roast chicken to spicy scallops. Most stores.

**Barrelli Creek Cabernet** 17 £10–13
**Sauvignon Gallo Sonoma 1995, USA, Red**
Superb complex attack of plums/
blackcurrants/ripe damsons and
hugely warm and spicy tannins. A real
Christmas treat of wonderful texture
and depth.

**Bonterra Cabernet** 16 £7–10
**Sauvignon 1998 (organic), USA, Red**
Deliciously textured and deep,
blackcurrant richness. A classy
specimen.

## THRESHER

**Rosemount Grenache** 17 £13–20
**Syrah Mourvedre 1997, Australian, Red**
Very big, soft, ripe and rich - the
perfect catch for a hungry mate.
Powerful liquorice and figs, berries and
leather. Wine Rack and Bottoms Up
only.

**Tatachilla Grenache** 16 £5–7
**Shiraz 1999, Australian, Red**
Savoury complexity here: rich,
layered, tangy, ripe.

**Lindemans Bin 65** 16.5 −£5.00
**Chardonnay 2000, Australian, White**
Has acquired a nutty undertone in this
vintage. Still up there as one of
Aussie's best value Chardonnays.

**Mitchelton Blackwood** 16 £5–7
**Park Riesling 1999, Australian, White**
Very elegant and tangy. Deliciously
sophisticated tippling.

**Mitchelton Viognier** 17 £10–13
**Rousanne 1997, Australian, White**
Gorgeous freshness on comparatively
middle-aged legs. Oily, rich, vibrant,
textured concentration. Very fine.
Wine Rack and Bottoms Up only.

**Pewsey Vale Riesling** 16 £5–7
**1999, Australian, White**
Delicious mineral tang (subtle) to the
firm, rich fruit. Always a consistently
charming performer.

**Tatachilla Semillon** 16.5 £5–7
**Chardonnay 1999, Australian, White**
Concentration, class, conviction,
caressing cool fruit. A lovely wine.

**The Willows Vineyard** 17.5 £7–10
**Semillon 1996, Australian, White**
Gorgeously mature, creamy, aromatic,
smoky ripeness and riveting richness.
Lovely texture and concentration.
Wine Rack and Bottoms Up only.

**Isla Negra Cabernet** 16.5 £5–7
**Sauvignon, Rapel 1999, Chilean, Red**
Gorgeous savoury juice with rich
tannins.

**Valdivieso Cabernet** 17 £7–10
**Franc Reserve 1998, Chilean, Red**
Deep savoury riches tantalise the
tongue and tighten the throat as the
tannins ooze down.

**Isla Negra Chardonnay** 16 £5–7
**1999, Chilean, White**
Superb texture and ripe, plump fruit.

**Kumala Semillon** 15.5 −£5.00
**Chardonnay 2000, South African, White**
Delicious rich, gooseberry fruit. Ripe
yet balanced.

## UNWINS

**Katnook Estate** `16.5` `£7–10`
**Coonawarra Sauvignon Blanc 1999,**
**Australian, White**
No, it isn't classic Sauvignon, it's too
rich and svelte for that, and the
mineral edge is very subtle. But the
fruit is gloriously engaging and
fulfilling.

**Valdivieso Cabernet** `17` `£7–10`
**Franc Reserve 1998, Chilean, Red**
Deep savoury riches tantalise the
tongue and tighten the throat as the
tannins ooze down.

**Briccolo Cabernet** `16` `£5–7`
**Sauvignon 1999, Italian, Red**
Very jammy and ripe, spicy, tannic.

**Kumala Merlot Reserve** `16.5` `£7–10`
**1999, South African, Red**
Superb!

## VICTORIA WINE

**Tatachilla Grenache** `16` `£5–7`
**Shiraz 1999, Australian, Red**
Savoury complexity here: rich,
layered, tangy, ripe.

**Lindemans Bin 65** `16.5` `–£5.00`
**Chardonnay 2000, Australian, White**
Has acquired a nutty undertone in this
vintage. Still up there as one of
Aussie's best value Chardonnays.

**Mitchelton Blackwood** `16` `£5–7`
**Park Riesling 1999, Australian, White**
Very elegant and tangy. Deliciously
sophisticated tippling.

**Pewsey Vale Riesling** `16` `£5–7`
**1999, Australian, White**
Delicious mineral tang (subtle) to the
firm rich fruit. Always a consistently
charming performer.

**Tatachilla Semillon** `16.5` `£5–7`
**Chardonnay 1999, Australian, White**
Concentration, class, conviction,
caressing cool fruit. A lovely wine.

**Isla Negra Cabernet** `16.5` `£5–7`
**Sauvignon, Rapel 1999, Chilean, Red**
Gorgeous savoury juice with rich
tannins.

## WAITROSE

**Kumala Reserve** `16.5` `£7–10`
**Cabernet Sauvignon 1999, South**
**African, Red**
Compellingly concentrated and classy
and generous.